The Mystery of Union with God

THOMISTIC RESSOURCEMENT SERIES

Volume 4

SERIES EDITORS

Matthew Levering, *Mundelein Seminary*
Thomas Joseph White, OP, *Dominican House of Studies*

EDITORIAL BOARD

Serge-Thomas Bonino, OP, *Institut Catholique de Toulouse*
Lawrence Dewan, OP, *Dominican College of Ottawa*
Gilles Emery, OP, *University of Fribourg*
Reinhard Hütter, *Duke University*
Bruce Marshall, *Southern Methodist University*
Emmanuel Perrier, OP, *Dominican Studium, Toulouse*
Richard Schenk, OP, *Katholische Universität Eichstätt-Ingolstadt*
Kevin White, *The Catholic University of America*

The Mystery of Union with God

Dionysian Mysticism in Albert the Great and Thomas Aquinas

BERNHARD BLANKENHORN, OP

The Catholic University of America Press
Washington, D.C.

Copyright © 2015
The Catholic University of America Press
All rights reserved
The paper used in this publication meets the minimum
requirements of American National Standards for Information
Science—Permanence of Paper for Printed Library Materials,
ANSI Z39.48-1984.

∞

Library of Congress Cataloging-in-Publication Data
Blankenhorn, Bernhard, 1973–
The mystery of union with God : Dionysian mysticism in Albert
The Great and Thomas Aquinas / Bernhard Blankenhorn, OP.
  pages cm. — (Thomistic ressourcement series ; Volume 4)
  Includes bibliographical references and index.
  ISBN 978-0-8132-2749-8 (cloth : alk. paper)
  ISBN 978-0-8132-2915-7 (paper : alk. paper)
  1. Mystical union—History of doctrines.
2. Pseudo-Dionysius, the Areopagite.   3. Albertus, Magnus,
Saint, 1193?–1280.   4. Thomas, Aquinas, Saint, 1225?–1274.
I. Title.
BT767.7.B56 2015
248.2′20922—dc23   2014038667

Contents

Acknowledgments	vii
Abbreviations	ix
Introduction	xi

PART 1: DIONYSIUS AND HIS EARLY INTERPRETERS ON UNION WITH GOD

1. Dionysius on Union with God	3
2. Key Developments in the Dionysian Tradition up to Albert the Great	30

PART 2: ALBERT ON DIONYSIAN UNION WITH GOD

3. Mystical Union and Its Doctrinal Pillars in the Early Albert	49
4. Albert's Dionysian Commentaries on Union with God	122

PART 3: THOMAS ON DIONYSIAN UNION WITH GOD

5. Thomas's Anthropological Synthesis of Aristotle, Augustine, and Dionysius	215
6. Grace in Thomas	249
7. Divine Naming in Thomas	296
8. Dionysian Union in Thomas	317
General Conclusion	443
Bibliography	469
Index of Names	497
Subject Index	502

Acknowledgments

The present work has benefited from the wisdom of many teachers and scholars, most especially Gilles Emery, OP. He directed the dissertation of which the present book is a modified version. His ability to explain medieval theological texts continues to astound. I thank Henryk Anzulewicz of the Albertus Magnus Institut (Bonn, Germany), whose insights sharpened my reading of Albert. The first chapter greatly benefited from the feedback of Ysabel de Andia of the Centre national de la recherche scientifique (Paris) and Franz Mali of the University of Fribourg (Switzerland). I am grateful to Maria Burger of the Albertus Magnus Institute for her expert advice on many historical details and for allowing me to consult the text and notes of her forthcoming critical edition of Albert the Great's *Sentences Commentary,* book 1. Previous drafts for parts of this book were presented orally in various settings, including at an annual editorial committee meeting of the *Revue Thomiste* near Toulouse, France, and at the Boston Colloquy in Historical Theology at Boston College. I thank Emmanuel Perrier, OP, and Boyd Taylor Coolman for their invitations and encouragement. I am grateful to Édouard Wéber, OP, and Walter Senner, OP, for our illuminating discussions on Albert. This study brings to a certain culmination many years of philosophical and theological formation, most especially through the seminars taught by Mark Delp and Richard Schenk, OP, both of whom having taught at the Dominican School of Philosophy and Theology (Berkeley, California). Fr. Schenk's role as a theological mentor has marked me in countless ways. The proofreading skills of Augustine Hilander, OP, proved to be invaluable. I am indebted to the two provincials who gave me the leisure (in the classic sense) to write this dissertation: Emmerich Vogt, OP, and Mark Padrez, OP. I thank several friends, especially Rose, whose theological curiosity and passion for contemplation have inspired the present work. I owe much to the Dominican friars of the Couvent de saint Hyacinthe in Fribourg, who kindly hosted me during my time as a doctoral student, and to the Dominicans of the Albertinum in Fribourg for their kind assistance in various forms. Finally, I am deeply grateful to my parents, Rainer and Hedi, who transmitted to me the Christian faith. Their lifelong fidelity to one another marvelously images the union of Christ and his church.

Abbreviations

BDT	Thomas Aquinas, *Super Boetium de Trinitate*
CCSL	Corpus Christianorum, Series Latina
CH	Dionysius Areopagita, *De coelesti hierarchia*
DC	Thomas Aquinas, *Quaestio disputata de caritate*
DDN	Thomas Aquinas, *In librum Beati Dionysii De divinis nominibus expositio*
DN	Dionysius Areopagita, *De divinis nominibus*
DP	Thomas Aquinas, *Quaestiones disputatae de potentia*
DS	*Dictionnaire de Spiritualité*
DV	Thomas Aquinas, *Quaestiones disputatae de veritate*
EH	Dionysius Areopagita, *De ecclesiastica hierarchia*
EMT	Thomas Gallus, *Extractio de mystica theologia*
EP	Dionysius Areopagita, *Epistulae*
In Ioan.	Thomas Aquinas, *Super Evangelium Sancti Ioannis lectura*
MT	Dionysius Areopagita, *De mystica theologia*
PDN	*Parisian Scholia* on the *Divine Names* (in *A Thirteenth-Century Textbook*)
PG	Migne: Patrologia Graeca
PMT	*Parisian Scholia* on the *Mystical Theology* (in *A Thirteenth-Century Textbook*)
QDDA	Thomas Aquinas, *Quaestiones disputatae de anima*

Abbreviations

RSPT	*Revue des Sciences philosophiques et théologiques*
RT	*Revue Thomiste*
SCG	Thomas Aquinas, *Summa contra Gentiles*
SCH	Albertus Magnus, *Super Dionysium De caelesti hierarchia*
SDN	Albertus Magnus, *Super Dionysium De divinis nominibus*
SEH	Albertus Magnus, *Super Dionysium De ecclesiastica hierarchia*
Sent.	Albertus Magnus, *Commentarii in libros Sententiarum*
	Thomas Aquinas, *Scriptum super libros Sententiarum* (for bks. I–III)
	Thomas Aquinas, *In quatuor libros Sententiarum* (for bk. IV, d. 49)
	Bonaventure, *Commentaria in quatuor libros Sententiarum*
SEP	Albertus Magnus, *Super Dionysii Epistulas* (followed by letter number)
SLC	Thomas Aquinas, *Super librum de causis expositio*
SMT	Albertus Magnus, *Super Dionysii Mysticam Theologiam*
ST	Thomas Aquinas, *Summa theologiae*

Introduction

> *It would be of prime interest to finish the work started here and there on Albert the Great, commentator of Dionysius.*
> —Marie-Dominique Chenu, *Toward Understanding Saint Thomas*, 232

Over half a century after Chenu's remark, the task of mining the riches of the commentaries on Dionysius by Albert, the "father" of Rhineland mysticism and teacher of Thomas Aquinas, remains far from completion. Work has hardly begun on Albert's exposition of the Areopagite's *Mystical Theology*. In recent years, much research has explored Albert the philosopher and his notion of naming God, but only a few articles on his theory of union with God have emerged. Nor do we have an adequate account of how Aquinas appropriates the Areopagite's vision of union or how Albert mediates Dionysius to his student.

The present study argues that Albert and Thomas develop Dionysian mystical theology in ways that emphasize the following four things: (1) what we can know about God (kataphatism); (2) our constant cognitive dependence on mediations; (3) the mind's active participation when it is joined to God; and (4) the trinitarian structure of union. Yet in the process neither Dominican sacrifices a limited apophatism, the cognitive nature of union and the immediacy of God's unifying action. In short, this study primarily aims to demonstrate how Albert and Thomas understand and transform the Dionysian notion of the peak of union with God in this life. I seek not only to show that they continue and develop key aspects of Dionysian mystical thought, but also to explain the continuity as well as the change in their appropriations. Here an approach that is historical-systematic allows one to demonstrate (1) how they interpret key union passages in the Dionysian corpus and (2) how their own doctrines on related themes (e.g., the soul's structure) account for their ways of reading Dionysius. Scholastic commentators pursue not just an author's historical intention but also the truth of a text.[1]

I use the terms "mystical theology" and "mysticism" to refer to a theological exposition of the highest union with God accessible here below. A mystic is one who enters this reality.[2] I am concerned with a theological account of union with God. Union need not refer to extraordinary phenomena such as visions—that is, mysticism need not consist of a transcript of an individual's unusual experiences of a transcendent reality. Various Greek fathers center their mystical theologies not on immanent experiences but on an allegorical exegesis of Moses in the Book of Exodus, though without excluding experience as a theological source.[3] Albert and Thomas develop their theologies of union as they comment on Dionysius and in their systematic accounts of grace, the theological virtues, the Spirit's seven gifts, and other themes. Their scholastic theologies include mysticism. Mystical theology as understood by Dionysius, Albert, and Thomas has an invisible object that is grasped by faith and largely escapes our explicit consciousness. Hence all three theologians call upon Scripture, the doctrines of faith, and philosophy in order to unfold *theologically* a spiritual reality that is believed and lived.

---

1. Marie-Dominique Chenu, *Toward Understanding Saint Thomas*, trans. A.-M. Landry and D. Hughes (Chicago: Henry Regnery, 1964), 142–54 (the French original [*Introduction à l'étude de saint Thomas d'Aquin*] was published in 1950); Ulrich G. Leinsle, *Introduction to Scholastic Theology*, trans. Michael J. Miller (Washington, D.C.: The Catholic University of America Press, 2010), 39–41; Mauricio Narváez, "Portée herméneutique de la notion d' 'intentio' chez Thomas d'Aquin," *Revue Philosophique de Louvain* 99 (2001): 201–19; Jean-Pierre Torrell, *Saint Thomas Aquinas*, vol. 1, *The Person and his Work*, trans. Robert Royal, 2nd ed. (Washington, D.C.: The Catholic University of America Press, 2005), 129.

2. My definition of mystical theology is close to Vladmir Lossky's in his *The Mystical Theology of the Eastern Church* (Crestwood, N.Y.: St. Vladimir's Seminary Press, 1976), 10–11. For a discussion of various approaches to mysticism, see Bernard McGinn, *The Presence of God: A History of Western Christian Mysticism*, vol. 1, *The Foundations of Mysticism: Origins to the 5th Century* (New York: Crossroad, 1991), 265–343.

3. Henri-Charles Puech, "La ténèbre mystique chez le Pseudo-Denys et dans la tradition patristique," *Études Carmélitaines* 23 (1938): 42–52.

Introduction   xiii

Mystical theology as expounded by these three authors poses at least four essential questions. First, *who is being united*—that is, what is our core ontological structure that makes possible the spiritual reality of union? What is the nature of the soul/body relation that enables or problematizes union? What "part" of us most touches God: the intellect, the will, both in unison, or another faculty such as the "spark of the soul"? Second, *to whom are we joined?* To what extent does God's triune identity affect the nature of union? Third, *what does God do* in order to bring about union or its intensification? Does God act on the mystic anew in the moment or state of union? Does he mostly act on the mind, or the will, or elsewhere? Does Christ's humanity play an essential role in this process? Fourth, *what do mystics do* in union? Do their minds become wholly passive, and necessarily so? Do they learn, or do they simply love? Are concept-bound thoughts part of union or obstacles to it? Do image-bound thoughts become problematic? Does God directly incite mystics' acts of unifying love? These inquiries guide this entire study of mysticism.

I will consider these three theologians' theories of the path toward union, but only insofar as these illumine the structure of union itself. A study of the way to union with God would require multiple monographs. For we find various themes related to the path to union throughout the writings of Dionysius, Albert, and Thomas. One finds union themes in their direct comments on Scripture (the contemplation of which lifts up the soul) but also in their study of God's elevating gifts (especially the liturgy and the sacraments), of Christ as mediator of divine life, in Albert's and Thomas's studies of the virtues, and of other topics.

I devote little time to the themes of prayer and meditation, as these are part of the path to the mystical peak. These practices have taken center stage in modern approaches to mysticism, approaches that tend to focus on the details of meditative technique far more than do premodern mystical writers. The popular notion that a book on mysticism is a manual of meditation would have made little sense to Dionysius, Albert, and Thomas. We should study their mystical thought primarily on their terms, not ours. I also devote little space to other related themes, such as Eucharistic theology. Given the limits of the present study, an adequate treatment of the Eucharist and Christ's presence therein would render impossible an extensive study of this sacrament's fruit, the soul's union with the triune God. I will focus on the latter theme.

WHY DIONYSIAN UNION IN ALBERT AND THOMAS?

But why study Dionysius, and why these two Dominican commentators? Perhaps no single figure has dominated Christian mystical theology in both East and West as much as the elusive Dionysius the Areopagite. Today, long after the author's claim to be a direct disciple of St. Paul has been unmasked, his thought continues to draw much scholarly and popular attention.

But which Dionysius should one study? For history presents us with many Areopagites: Paul's convert in Athens, the third-century martyr and bishop of Paris, the fifth-century pseudo-Dionysius who wrote in Greek, and the Areopagite translated into Latin who seemed to *be* all three of these individuals. In the Renaissance the critical work of Lorenzo Valla and Erasmus sundered this composite figure. They prepared the way for Hugo Koch and Josef Stiglmayr, who identified Dionysius as a fifth-century disciple of Proclus, the master of the Academy in Athens, the school that Plato had founded centuries before.[4] Some nineteenth- and twentieth-century scholars painted the picture of Dionysius as a Neoplatonist wolf in the sheep's clothing of Christian theological language, a corrupter of the pure gospel with a barely modified Proclus. In the middle of the twentieth century, Hans Urs von Balthasar and René Roques challenged this image: Some critical historians operated like battle tanks crushing the lush Dionysian garden of Christian mysticism.[5] Roques and von Balthasar resurrected Dionysius the theologian immersed in the patristic tradition. Since then some scholars have made the Areopagite's relation to non-Christian philoso-

---

4. William Riordan, *Divine Light: The Theology of Denys the Areopagite* (San Francisco: Ignatius Press, 2008), 21–34.

5. Hans Urs von Balthasar, *The Glory of the Lord: A Theological Aesthetics*, vol. 2, *Studies in Theological Style: Clerical Style* (San Francisco: Ignatius Press, 1984), 144–46; René Roques, *L'univers dionysien: Structure hiérarchique du monde selon le Pseudo-Denys*, Théologie 29 (Paris: Aubier, 1954).

Introduction   xv

phy wholly secondary.[6] But in the past few decades historians such as Stephen Gersh and Ysabel de Andia have stayed closer to the insights of von Balthasar and Roques as they opted for a middle path—for Dionysius as an inheritor of the Christian tradition *and* of Proclus's thought.[7] The Areopagite, at once deeply Christian and Neoplatonic, takes center stage in this study. Indeed, the current state of the scholarship enables a certain transcendence of unhelpful polemics so as to better grasp the historical doctrine of the "real" Dionysius, a doctrine at once marked by diverse sources and highly original. Also, the early 1990s witnessed the completion of the critical edition of the Greek Dionysian corpus. This edition subsequently enabled de Andia's monograph on union in Dionysius, the most in-depth exploration of his mysticism to date. All of these developments greatly facilitate a new historical comparison of the Greek father with two of his leading medieval commentators. Relying on the fruits of recent Dionysius scholarship, I will focus on the reception of his mysticism in Albert and Thomas.

Albert clearly took great interest in the Areopagite, for he commented on the entire Dionysian corpus. Of all the texts in his massive opus, Albert's *Commentary on the Mystical Theology* contains his most developed exposition of union with God. Also, the remarks on union in his other commentaries on the Areopagite and on Peter Lombard's *Sentences* bear the Greek father's unmistakable fingerprints. Together these commentaries likely constitute the most sophisticated theological works that Albert achieved.[8] One cannot explain Albert's mysti-

6. E.g., Lossky, *Mystical Theology*; Alexander Golitzin, *Et introibo ad altare Dei: The Mystagogy of Dionysius Areopagita, With Special Reference to Its Predecessors in the Eastern Christian Tradition*, Analecta Vlatadon 59 (Thessaloniki: Patriarchikon Idruma Paterikon Meleton, 1994); Jean-Claude Larchet, *La théologie des énergies divines: Des origines à saint Jean Damascène*, Cogitatio Fidei 272 (Paris: Cerf, 2010), 289–329.

7. Ysabel de Andia, *Henosis: L'union à Dieu chez Denys l'Aréopagite*, Philosophia Antiqua 71 (Leiden: E. J. Brill, 1996); Stephen Gersh, *From Iamblichus to Eriugena: An Investigation of the Pre-History and Evolution of the Pseudo-Dionysian Tradition* (Leiden: E. J. Brill, 1978); René Roques, "Denys l'Aréopagite," in *DS* 3 (1957): cols. 244–86; see also John M. Rist, "Pseudo-Dionysius, Neoplatonism and the Weakness of the Soul," in *From Athens to Chartres: Neoplatonism and Medieval Thought, Studies in Honour of Édouard Jeauneau*, ed. Haijo Jan Westra, 135–61 (Leiden: E. J. Brill, 1992).

8. Henryk Anzulewicz signals that Albert's commentaries on Dionysius stand out for their originality and systematic significance within the German friar's corpus; see Anzulewicz, "Albertus Magnus (1200–1280)," in *Kölner Theologen: Von Rupert von Deutz bis Wilhelm Nyssen*, ed. Sebastian Cüppers, 39 (Cologne: Marzellen, 2004).

cism without Dionysius. Albert deeply influenced German theological thought for centuries, especially that of Meister Eckhart and other Rhineland mystics.

But before Eckhart came Thomas. The young Aquinas sat at Albert's feet in Cologne as he taught Dionysius. The Italian friar recorded his notes of Albert's lectures in a manuscript that we still have.[9] The Areopagite evidently fascinated Thomas, as well. He later composed his own *Commentary on the Divine Names*, a text that discusses union at some length. Also, Aquinas often cited Dionysius in his systematic works.[10] The Greek father proved to be a crucial resource for Aquinas as he developed his theology of divine naming, a theology closely linked to the notion of unifying knowledge of God. Thomas also made Dionysius's two key mystical figures, Moses and Hierotheus, the prime examples of the realization of the Spirit's gifts of understanding and wisdom, two gifts that are crucial for Aquinas's notion of union. Thus the rather sparse, explicit references to the *Mystical Theology* in Thomas's corpus conceal the qualitative presence of Dionysian mysticism in Thomas.[11] Also, two key themes in medieval mystical theology are the summit of cognition and the peak of love attainable in this life. The Areopagite's intellect-centered mysticism could be a major source for Thomas's approach to the noetic element of union, not to mention his presentation of Hierotheus "suffering divine things" by love. Finally, his *Commentary on the Divine Names* and various remarks on Dionysius show few traces of other commentators on the Areopagite except Albert, whose fingerprints are omnipresent. One cannot reconstitute an image of Aquinas's Dionysius without Albert.

---

9. Pierre-Marie Gils, "Le Ms. *Napoli, Biblioteca Nazionale I.B. 54* est-il de la main de S. Thomas?" *RSPT* 49 (1965): 37–59.

10. Walter Senner, "Thomas von Aquin und die Kirchenväter: Eine quantitative Übersicht," in *Kirchenbild und Spiritualität: Dominikanische Beiträge zur Ekklesiologie und zum kirchlichen Leben im Mittelalter*, ed. Thomas Prügl and Marianne Schlosser, 25–42 (Munich: Ferdinand Schöningh, 2007).

11. Thomas cites the *MT* only fifteen times (see chapter 8 of this volume). Compare the case of Bonaventure: He only cites the *MT* sixteen times, but it has significant influence on his mysticism; see Jacques Guy Bougerol, "Saint Bonaventure et le Pseudo-Denys l'Aréopagite," supplement, *Études Franciscaines* 18 (1968): 58–59, 113.

Introduction   xvii

THE STATE OF THE SCHOLARSHIP

Despite the recent revival in the historical study of Albert and Thomas, work on their reception of the Areopagite's mysticism has barely begun. We have no exhaustive study on Dionysian union in Albert. Édouard Wéber has written two magisterial articles on this theme, work complemented by Simon Tugwell's introduction to his translation of Albert's *Commentary on the Mystical Theology*.[12] Their interpretations have been taken up or challenged by Kurt Ruh, William Hoye, Alain de Libera, Bernard McGinn, Giuseppe Allegro, Guglielmo Russino, and Anneliese Meis.[13] Still, no one has analyzed all key union texts in Albert's commentaries on the Areopagite. Nor do we possess a more or less complete study of the Dionysian element in Albert's *Sentences Commentary* doctrine of union. His theory of divine naming has received more attention, but not so much in relation to union.[14]

12. Édouard Wéber, "L'interprétation par Albert le Grand de la *Théologie Mystique* de Denys le ps-Aréopagite," in *Albertus Magnus: Doctor universalis, 1280/1980*, ed. Gerbert Meyer and Albert Zimmermann, 409–39 (Mainz: Matthias-Grünewald, 1980); Wéber, introduction to *Commentaire de la "Théologie mystique" de Denys le pseudo-aréopagite suivi de celui des épîtres I–V*, by Albertus Magnus, ed. and trans. Wéber, 22–46, Sagesses Chrétiennes (Paris: Cerf, 1993); Simon Tugwell, "Albert the Great: Introduction," in *Albertus Magnus and Thomas: Selected Writings*, by Albert and Thomas Aquinas, ed. Tugwell, 39–95, Classics of Western Spirituality (New York: Paulist Press, 1988).

13. Kurt Ruh, *Geschichte der abendländischen Mystik*, vol. 3, *Die Mystik des deutschen Predigerordens und ihre Grundlegung durch die Hochscholastik* (Munich: C. H. Beck, 1996), 110–29; William J. Hoye, "Mystische Theologie nach Albert dem Grossen," in *Albertus Magnus, Zum Gedenken nach 800 Jahren: Neue Zugänge, Aspekte und Perspektiven*, ed. Walter Senner, 594–603, Quellen und Forschungen zur Geschichte des Dominikanerordens 10 (Berlin: Akademie Verlag, 2001); Alain de Libera, *Raison et foi: Archéologie d'une crise d'Albert le Grand à Jean-Paul II*, L'ordre philosophique (Paris: Seuil, 2003), 270–86; Bernard McGinn, *Presence of God*, vol. 4, *The Harvest of Mysticism in Medieval Germany* (New York: Crossroad, 2005), 12–27; Giuseppe Allegro and Guglielmo Russino, introduction to *Tenebra luminosissima: Commento alla "Teologia Mistica" di Dionigi l'Areopagita*, by Albertus Magnus, ed. Allegro and Russino, 3–42, Machina Philosophorum 15 (Palermo: Officina di Studi Medievali, 2007); Anneliese Meis, "El misterio de la alteridad en Alberto Magno: *Super Mysticam Theologiam Dionysii*," *Teología y Vida* 47 (2006): 541–74; Meis, introduction to *Sobre la Teología Mística de Dionisio*, by Albertus Magnus, ed. Meis, 17–35, Anales de la Facultad de Teología 59 (Santiago, Chile: Pontificia Universidad Católica de Chile, 2008).

14. Francis Ruello, *Les "Noms divins" et leurs "raisons" selon saint Albert le Grand commentateur du "De Divinis Nominibus*," Bibliothèque Thomiste 35 (Paris: Vrin, 1963); Édouard Wéber, "Langage et méthode négatifs chez Albert le Grand," *RSPT* 65 (1981):

The labors of Chenu and Jean-Pierre Torrell have renewed the study of Thomas in light of his historical context and patristic sources.[15] Much has been done on Dionysius's place in Aquinas's notion of divine naming and metaphysics.[16] Yet few have pondered his theory of union in darkness or the unitive element of "unknowing" God in light of the sources. We have no extensive analysis of union in Aquinas's *Commentary on the Divine Names* and of his remarks on the *Mystical Theology*. Little has been done on his vision of the gift of understanding and its relation to Dionysius. Many have studied the gift of wisdom, above all the school of Thomistic spirituality formed by Ambroise Gardeil, Réginald Garrigou-Lagrange, and Jacques Maritain, the spiritual sons of John of Saint Thomas.[17] But one can ask whether these commentators sometimes obscure Aquinas's doctrine. We still have no adequate historical comparison of Dionysius's and Thomas's Hierotheus.[18] Nor has anyone thoroughly compared Albert and Thomas on union.

75–99; Wéber, "Négativité et causalité: Leur articulation dans l'apophatisme de l'école d'Albert le Grand," in *Albertus Magnus und der Albertismus: Deutsche philosophische Kultur des Mittelalters*, ed. Maarten J. F. M. Hoenen and Alain de Libera, 51–90 (Leiden: E. J. Brill, 1995); Thierry-Dominique Humbrecht, *Théologie négative et noms divins chez saint Thomas d'Aquin*, Bibliothèque Thomiste 57 (Paris: Vrin, 2005), 321–478; Humbrecht, "Albert le Grand commentateur de la *Théologie mystique* de Denys," *RSPT* 90 (2006): 225–71; Tobias Weismantel, *Ars nominandi Deum: Die Ontosemantik der Gottesprädikate in den Dionysius-kommentaren des Albertus Magnus*, Regensburger Studien zur Theologie 69 (Frankfurt am Main: Peter Lang, 2010).

15. Chenu, *Toward Understanding Saint Thomas*; Jean-Pierre Torrell, *Saint Thomas Aquinas*, vol. 2, *Spiritual Master*, trans. Robert Royal (Washington, D.C.: The Catholic University of America Press, 2003). Chenu's study of Aquinas's Platonism and Platonic sources was made possible in part by the pioneering work of J. Durantel, *Saint Thomas et le Pseudo-Denys* (Paris: Félix Alcan, 1919).

16. See, for example, Fran O'Rourke, *Pseudo-Dionysius and the Metaphysics of Aquinas* (Notre Dame, Ind.: University of Notre Dame Press, 2005); Humbrecht, *Théologie négative*.

17. John of Saint Thomas, *Cursus Theologicus, In Iam-IIae: De donis Spiritus Sancti*, Collectio Lavallensis (Québec: Armand Mathieu and Hervé Gagné, 1958); Ambroise Gardeil, *La structure de l'âme et l'expérience mystique*, vol. 2 (Paris: J. Gabalda, 1927), 161–229; Réginald Garrigou-Lagrange, *Christian Perfection and Contemplation According to St. Thomas Aquinas and St. John of the Cross*, trans. M. Timothea Doyle (St. Louis: Herder, 1937), 271–336; Jacques Maritain, *Distinguish to Unite or the Degrees of Knowledge*, trans. Gerald B. Phelan (London: Geoffrey Bles, 1959), 247–309.

18. Ysabel de Andia, "'Pati divina' chez Denys l'Aréopagite, Thomas d'Aquin et Jacques Maritain," in *Saint Thomas d'Aquin*, ed. Thierry-Dominique Humbrecht, 549–89, Les Cahiers d'Histoire de la Philosophie (Paris: Cerf, 2010) has begun this comparison, but I will argue in chapter 8 that her historical reading of Thomas falls short.

Introduction   xix

In the past thirty years critical editions for all of Albert's commentaries on Dionysius have become available. While we still have no critical text for Thomas's *Commentary on the Divine Names* or his *Summa theologiae*, the Marietti and Ottawa editions (respectively) are reliable. With the advance in Dionysius, Albert, and Thomas scholarship, the time is ripe to explore Albert's reception of Dionysian mysticism and Thomas's appropriation of both.

THE METHODOLOGY

The heart of my methodology consists of close textual analyses of key union passages in Albert and Thomas in light of their doctrinal sources (theological and philosophical) and their own systematic doctrines of God, grace, and the human being. The close focus on texts seems necessary, for (1) this has yet to be done for all key passages on Dionysian union in Albert and Thomas; (2) paraphrases of texts miss subtle shifts in meaning within comments on the Areopagite; (3) paraphrases can too easily overlook evolutions in thought; and (4) textual analyses best manifest which aspects of Dionysius his commentators highlight, modify, or ignore.

My baseline of comparison is a synthesis of the Areopagite's notion of union in the *Mystical Theology* and the *Divine Names* as expounded by contemporary historians (chapter 1 of this volume). Here I abstract from subsequent theological glosses and focus on the Dionysian text and its various sources. My summary of Dionysian mysticism is not original, but a working tool.

Chapter 2 explores the Dionysian tradition before Albert to determine his and Thomas's textual access to Dionysius, some key features of the main Latin translations, and especially the reception of Dionysian mysticism in late patristic and medieval glosses that were transmitted to the two Dominicans. We need to see how these texts affect the two friars' reading of the Areopagite and which key glosses on union the two friars skip or refuse.

Chapter 3 and part of chapter 4 offer a set of doctrinal syntheses of the "Parisian Albert" (1242–48, essentially the *De homine* and the *Sentences Commentary*) and of the "early Cologne Albert," commentator of Dionysius (1248–50). The *De homine* and the *Sentences Commentary* include Albert's most significant treatments of key themes or "background doctrines" directly related to union in the period preceding his commentaries on Dionysius.[19] I will explain these background doctrines shortly. Chapters 3 and 4 trace internal doctrinal evolutions that justify a distinction between the "Parisian" and "early Cologne Albert."

But why only consider his texts up to 1250? First, an adequate comparison of all of Albert's Dionysianism with Thomas's seems impossible in a single study, given the size of their *Opera Omnia*. Second, Aquinas had a strong familiarity with Albert's work up to 1252, especially his lectures on the *Sentences* and the Areopagite. Third, Albert's doctrinal reception of Dionysian mysticism peaked in his works on the Lombard and Dionysius. The German friar's discussions of Dionysian union in his only late theological synthesis, the *Summa theologiae sive de mirabili scientia Dei*, add little to his earlier writings (see chapter 4 of this volume).

I draw from Thomas's whole corpus for three reasons. First, his reception of Albert's Dionysianism begins in his early *Sentences Commentary*. Second, his *Commentary on the Divine Names* dates from the late 1260s. Third, his best study of the gifts of understanding and wisdom was composed in the early 1270s (in the *Summa*). The sparsity of his direct remarks on Dionysian union outside of the *Commentary on the Divine Names* makes this project viable.

An explanation of how Albert and Thomas develop Dionysian mysticism demands a consideration of some background doctrines. Without a consideration of this kind, it would be impossible to find satisfy-

19. Albert's other early works either lack a critical edition (*De IV coaequaevis*, Borgnet Edition 34 [Paris: 1895]) or do not add significant doctrinal content on union to the *De homine* and the *Sentences Commentary*. Thus *De natura boni* (ed. Ephrem Filthaut, Cologne Edition, vol. 25, part 1 [Münster: Aschendorff, 1974]) only mentions Dionysius three times, and only one brief text relates somewhat to union (tr. 2, pars 3, ch. 4, p. 69.63–76). Albertus Magnus, *De bono*, ed. Heinrich Kühle, Carl Feckes, Bernhard Geyer, and Wilhelm Kübel, Cologne Edition 28 (Münster: Aschendorff, 1951) focuses on the cardinal virtues and ignores the *MT*. Albertus Magnus's *De incarnatione*, ed. A. Ohlmeyer, Ignatius Backes and Wilhelm Kübel, Cologne Edition 26 (Münster: Aschendorff, 1958), has a doctrine of Christ's headship that is surpassed by the *Sentences Commentary*. Albertus Magnus's *De resurrectione*, ed. A. Ohlmeyer, Ignatius Backes, and Wilhelm Kübel, Cologne Edition 26 (Münster: Aschendorff, 1958), has one important article on the beatific vision (tr. 4, q. 1, a. 9), yet all of its essential elements return in Albert's *Sent.* study of eschatology. I will thus only signal key parallel passages from these texts in the footnotes.

ing answers to the four questions posed earlier: Who is being united? To whom are we joined? What does God do to join us to himself? And what do mystics do in union?

As a rational, faith-based reflection on union with God, mystical theology both emerges out of a particular theological anthropology and in turn influences that anthropology. If union is a gift that is received, then one must account for the mode of its reception, for that mode follows upon the receiving being's structure. Thus if one posits the soul as a more or less complete substance, then its contact with a purely spiritual divine reality poses few problems. But if the soul and body are closely linked, then it becomes more difficult to account for such contact.

Every theological anthropology calls for a certain kind of epistemology and vice versa. A noetics that closely connects our knowledge of creatures with our knowledge of God matches a more holistic anthropology. Just as Plato's mysticism is closely linked to his vision of the soul as a temporary visitor in the body, so Albert's and Thomas's notions of mystical cognition flow from a particular vision of the soul/body conjunction.[20] The two friars critique certain dualistic tendencies in thirteenth-century neo-Augustinian anthropologies and turn to Aristotle as well as to Dionysius for alternative approaches. Their ways of integrating and developing these sources help to account for their proximity to or distance from Dionysian mysticism. For example, the mind's ontological relation to the corporeal realm sets the stage for a theory on the place of sense-derived cognition in the intellect's operation within union. Since union is with the wholly immaterial God, a closer soul/body connection may limit what the mind can learn through union. Meanwhile, the soul's intrinsic metaphysical structure shapes, among other things, the theory of self-knowledge, a potential steppingstone to a deeper cognition of God, especially in the Augustinian tradition.

One also needs to consider whether the intellect has the capacity to complete a cognitive act without concepts bound to our knowledge of finite beings. If so, then it can literally pass "beyond mind," following Dionysius. But if all cognition of God somehow remains linked to the

---

20. For Plato, see A. J. Festugière, *Contemplation et vie contemplative selon Platon*, 4th ed. (Paris: Vrin, 1975), 214–15.

knowledge of creatures, can we ever enjoy direct noetic contact with him? The answer to this question will shed light on the kind of graced illumination needed to attain noetic union.

These issues become more complex in light of the doctrines of sin and grace. Grace enables a contact with God well beyond nature's capacities. However, since all three of our authors posit a strong continuity between nature and grace (all the while keeping them distinct), natural structures or dynamics of human knowing and loving help to determine the possibility and mode of graced union with God. For example, if natural human cognition always refers back to concepts and images, then one would expect graced cognition to do so, as well. Grace stretches the capacities of nature, but it does not wholly overturn the structures of human nature. If mystical cognition does in fact remain bound to intelligible forms and phantasms, then theology will need to face the challenge of accounting for the possibility of the mind's direct contact with God.

All of these themes bring us to the question of the *imago Dei*. What aspect of our being is most noble? In what way are we most like God? To what extent does the *imago* function not just as a mirror of three divine persons united in one nature but also as a platform to imitate the divine persons by acts of remembering, knowing, and loving God? Does the *imago* as imitation call for our active cooperation in union, since we imitate an infinitely dynamic God? How do Albert and Thomas modify the place of memory in Augustine's *imago*, perhaps in the direction of Dionysian anthropology, where memory plays no decisive role? The answers to these questions will help to direct our attention to particular kinds of graces as the key to contact with God (e.g., faith, charity, a gift of the Spirit). Thus if a hidden "spark of the soul" (whose function is to love) were to constitute the human spirit's summit, then one would need to distinguish even the most advanced knowledge derived out of revelation from the height of union so that the former would only be a steppingstone to the latter. The relation between memory and intellect also becomes crucial for mystical theology. A tripartite anthropology in which memory constitutes a proper, distinct faculty that imitates the Father by its own act tends to go hand in hand with a mysticism of interiority, as in Augustine. Here mediations such as the sacraments tend to remove obstacles to progress along the inner path, obstacles caused by sin. But if memory is not really distinct from the intellect, then interior ascent to the hidden God becomes much more difficult. In that case exterior ascent take center stage and mediations play a greater role in the mind's elevation to God. Let us recall that the theme of the *imago* stands at the heart of twelfth- and thirteenth-century Latin mystical theologies. Thus Bernard of Clairvaux, William of St. Thierry, Hugh of St. Victor, and Bonaventure closely link the *imago* to love's priority over knowledge in union.[21] The latter issue takes on new urgency in thirteenth-century Dionysian mysticism as several theologians (e.g., Thomas Gallus and Bonaventure) propose an ascent into the dark cloud through love passing beyond mind. Albert and Thomas develop direct and/or indirect responses to such readings of the Areopagite as they seek to retain a qualified priority of intellect within mystical ascent. Several of the two friars' foundational arguments for such a priority can be found precisely in their doctrines of the *imago*.

We find echoes of these themes in our three authors' reflections on the trinitarian structure of union and their explanations of the nature of God's unifying operation. In Dionysius it is not evident how the doctrine of the Trinity impacts his understanding of union in darkness. But Albert and Thomas make the invisible coming of the Son and the Spirit into the minds and hearts of believers central to their mystical theologies. The missions concern the invisible sending of the Son with gifts of wisdom (that is, sanctifying knowledge of God) and of the Spirit with the gift of charity. The missions manifest the link between the structure of union and God's Triune identity. Like the doctrine of the *imago*, the theology of the missions bears considerable implications for questions such as the functional relation between the intellect and the will during union. Indeed, the trinitarian element helps to determine the type of divine action that joins the soul to God in a new or more intense way. Neither Albert nor his Italian student ever mentions the doctrine of the missions when they discuss the Areopagite's Moses in darkness or Hierotheus "suffering divine things." Yet their expositions of Dionysian passages on union presuppose the theology of the missions. Hence, to

---

21. Bernard McGinn, *Presence of God*, vol. 2, *The Growth of Mysticism: Gregory the Great through the 12th Century* (New York: Crossroad, 1994), 168–74, 229–58; vol. 3, *The Flowering of Mysticism: Men and Women in the New Mysticism, 1200–1350* (New York: Crossroad, 1998), 106–7.

grasp the doctrinal intent behind their comments on those passages, we need a firm grasp of their understanding of the missions.

The ontology of divine action forms part of the basic background to mystical theology. This ontology includes and goes beyond the doctrine of the missions. The theory of divine action and mystical theology necessarily pose very similar questions. If God acts more intensely, does human action have to diminish in order to make room for his operation? Or are simultaneous human and divine actions possible due to the noncompetitive nature of God's operation? In other words, when God unites us to himself via knowledge or love (or both), must the soul become passive in the face of the divine guest? The same ontology must also deal with issues such as formal and efficient causality. Does God's action always involve the giving of form (such as a more intense *habitus* of charity), or can it remain at the level of efficiency, where God moves us to know and love? If the latter mode of divine operation is possible, then does human freedom still stand?

The theme of God's action takes us to the topic of grace. In any confrontation between Greek and Latin mystical theologies, the issue of created and uncreated grace naturally takes a central place. If union comes by created grace, does God still act directly to join us to himself? If so, can we still have contact with his nature or his energies? If one posits an actual grace that does not involve the infusion of a new (created) form, then does one need created grace at all in order to account for the divinizing encounter with God? Does grace bear ontological traces of Christ's humanity and his historic acts, so that union by its nature conforms us to Christ? These issues are key in any Latin-Greek dialogue on mystical union.

For Albert and Thomas, created grace underlies the theological virtues. Faith and charity bring us to the perfection of union. But how do these virtues unite us to God? Is faith primarily an act of the will in obedience to the gospel, or is it primarily an act of the intellect? The answer to this question helps to determine the part of the soul in which union primarily takes place. For if faith is not primarily a noetic act, then an intellect-centered mysticism (such as the Areopagite's) becomes virtually impossible. Also, what limits of faith require the extra help of the Spirit's gift of understanding? Why does charity call for no further gift of the Spirit? Indeed, charity is even more important than faith in order to attain union with God, at least for our two Dominicans. If charity is modeled after friendship with Christ, can union involve complete human passivity? And what analogies are most appropriate for charity? Is love for God especially a unitive power (Dionysius), a formal flux (Albert), or friendship (Thomas)? Of these three analogies, the second and the third strongly point toward the essential place of human cooperation in union.

Unlike Albert, Thomas develops a psychology of love that is both distinct from yet closely related to his theology of charity. The same psychology unfolds a theory of connaturality, which is an inclination of the heart that conforms the lover to the heart of the beloved. Aquinas's psychology of love thus undergirds his vision of union with God by charity. The theme of connaturality also becomes crucial for Thomas's notion of the Spirit's gift of wisdom, a gift whereby Hierotheus suffers divine things.

Albert's exposition of key union passages in his commentaries on Dionysius never mentions the seven gifts of the Holy Spirit. However, his *Sentences Commentary* exemplifies the gift of wisdom by invoking the Areopagite's Hierotheus and his union with God. Hence one can ask whether a theology of gifted wisdom stands behind at least some of Albert's readings of union texts in the commentaries on the Dionysian corpus. This possibility gains some credence when we consider that the gifts of wisdom and understanding form an integral part of Albert's doctrine of contemplative ascent to God as presented in his *Sentences Commentary*. Thus, in the so-called treatise on the seven gifts, key themes in mystical theology come to the fore. Do the gifts of understanding and wisdom involve a heightened human passivity in mystical ascent and union, one that might account for the Areopagite's silent union? What place does spiritual experience have in the theology of the gifts? The doctrine of the gifts may underlie or perhaps also complement Albert's interpretation of Dionysian union texts. The link between the Spirit's gifts of understanding and wisdom with Dionysian union themes becomes even more explicit in the work of Aquinas. My analysis of the latter's theology of the Spirit's gifts will take us to the heart of Thomas's Dionysian mysticism. Hence a consideration of that theology will require extensive textual analyses of various passages, especially in the *Summa theologiae*.

The theological virtues and the Spirit's gifts reach their fulfillment in final beatitude. Eschatology also bears a close relation to mystical theology. For the vision of God in heaven represents the most intimate kind of union available to human beings. Thus doctrinal principles that are operative in eschatology should also find their way into mystical theology and vice versa. For example, an eschatology that emphasizes the abiding mystery of God's infinite nature (his incomprehensibility) should find its complement in a more or less apophatic mysticism. Or again, an eschatology that insists on the need for a special grace so that human beings may see God goes hand in hand with a mysticism that greatly insists on the gifted nature of union here below. Overall, eschatology helps to define the nature and limits of union's realization in this life. Albert and Thomas integrate the Areopagite's controversial theophanies into their theologies of the light of glory, theologies that highlight the gratuity of union, the human being's fixed place in the cosmological hierarchy as a soul/body composite, and the need for a created light of glory to see God face to face. Thus eschatology can help to pinpoint the extent to which Albert's and Thomas's far-reaching reinterpretations of the Areopagite's mystical theology still retain key pillars of the latter's view on key doctrines such as grace and anthropology.

The theory of divine naming may stand in even closer relation to mystical theology than does eschatology. Such a theory always comes with a theological epistemology, for naming follows knowing. We can name God truly insofar as we can know him. We will see that Albert's *Commentary on the Mystical Theology* makes naming and noetic union two sides of the same coin. Indeed, these themes must be closely intertwined for readers of Dionysus who accept his important claim that union is a form of knowing God. Albert and Thomas fall into this category, in contrast to numerous thirteenth-century readers of Dionysius. Now for our three authors, the pilgrim's knowledge of God is threefold: (1) natural or philosophical; (2) acquired via Scripture and tradition; and (3) directly infused. What is the relation between the first two categories and the third? The doctrine of divine naming helps to answer this question. For example, a theory of divine predication that emphasizes how little God's philosophical or biblical names tell us about him fits well with an apophatic mysticism wherein infused cognition remains utterly beyond concepts and language. Dionysius also taught Albert and Thomas the importance of noetic ascent to God via the divine names. For Dionysius the limits of divine naming help to shape the structure of union, which is beyond naming. How do the two friars describe this structure? Where (if anywhere) along the contemplative path should naming end, and why? Need naming and union be distinct phases? How much of Dionysian apophatism remains in the two friars' theories of naming?

In their commentaries on Dionysius, neither friar develops an adequate account of the doctrinal pillars just surveyed—that is, those commentaries do not fully manifest the systematic motives behind many of their key exegetical moves when they discuss the Areopagite's teaching on union with God. I therefore need to formulate those motives as they emerge in the two friars' other works, respecting the time limitation for Albert already mentioned. My summary treatments of the background themes are not generic in nature in the style of encyclopedia entries. Rather, I hone in on possible Dionysian influences and on the doctrinal elements that most illumine the structure of union. For example, my studies of the *imago* largely ignore the *imago* as a manifestation of the Trinity so as to center on the *imago*'s operations as imitations of the Trinity that join the soul to the divine persons.

We have seen that discussions of union often assume particular notions of God's action and human cognition. For this reason I offer systematic syntheses of Albert's and Thomas's doctrines of the soul's ontology, the soul/body relation, epistemology, the grace/nature relation, the *imago Dei*, the invisible missions, grace, faith, charity, the Spirit's seven gifts, divine naming, the vision of God, and (for Thomas) divine action and the psychology of love. An articulation of these points helps to surface doctrinal similarities and differences between Dionysius, Albert, and Thomas that partly explain their distinct approaches to union. Hence chapter 1 summarizes Dionysian notions of divine naming, divine action, noetics, and anthropology. I also pay special attention to the Dionysian influence on Albert's and Thomas's background doctrines and identify possible evolutions therein. For even Albert's Dionysian commentaries begun right after his work on the *Sentences* manifest some significant shifts in thought. In the study of Aquinas's underlying themes, I give priority to his mature thought, since most of his comments on Dionysian union date from this period.

I consider the *function* of background doctrines in Albert's and Thomas's expositions of Dionysian union. For example, by pondering the significance of the invisible missions in the theological edifices of Albert and Thomas, I consider whether they add a trinitarian element to their account of Dionysian union.

I also show the function of key Dionysian union texts and mystical figures in Albert's and Thomas's doctrines of union. For example, Albert's *Sentences Commentary* mostly ignores the Areopagite's Moses as an example of union, while his *Commentary on the Mystical Theology* seems to give first priority to union by negations as found in chapter 2 of the Areopagite's *Mystical Theology* more than to Moses in chapter 1 of that text. Meanwhile, Aquinas makes Moses exemplary of a maximum cognition of God here below attained via the gift of understanding, but this gift may not represent the summit of divinizing union.

The various background themes already mentioned and especially the direct analysis of Dionysian union in the two friars' works allow for frequent discussions of other significant doctrinal concerns, especially the place of divine revelation, the liturgy, and Scripture within union. Because these topics are in a way omnipresent in the background themes just surveyed and in many union passages in Albert and Thomas, they do not demand distinct treatments. One should keep a close eye on the function of liturgy and Scripture in Albert and Thomas, for these mediations diminish in importance in later medieval appropriations of Dionysian mysticism, even though liturgy and Scripture constitute the primary setting of Dionysian union. I need to ask to what extent this loss of context for mystical theology alreadys occur with our two friars.

THE PLAN OF STUDY

Chapters 1 and 2 (part 1) of this study are strictly preparatory. Chapter 1 surveys the Areopagite's theology of union and its main theoretical foundations. Chapter 2 introduces the Dionysian tradition before Albert—the main translations, commentators, and key developments in the theory of union. My original contribution comes in the chapters on Albert and Thomas.

Chapters 3 and 4 (part 2) are chronologically ordered. Chapter 3 studies Albert's synthesis of union with God and especially its doctrinal foundations before the Dionysian commentaries of 1248–50. I focus on his two longest philosophical and theological works from this period, the *De homine* and *Sentences Commentary*, respectively. Chapter 4 also analyzes these background themes in Albert's Dionysian commentaries. Here I verify to what extent Albert's commentaries on the Areopagite retain or develop his earlier views of the background doctrines. The heart of chapter 4 comes in a textual study of all key union passages in Albert's *Commentary on the Mystical Theology*. Evidently, the chronological division facilitates a diachronic reading of Albert's main theological positions.

My study of Thomas (part 3) has four thematically arranged chapters, each of which distinguishes early and late doctrines. The inclusion of the young and the mature Thomas motivates this arrangement. Chapters 5 through 7 present mystical union's doctrinal pillars. Chapter 8 presents Aquinas's four major appropriations of Dionysian union: (1) union texts in the *Commentary on the Divine Names*; (2) his discussions of the *Mystical Theology*; (3) Moses in darkness as an example of the gift of understanding's realization; and (4) Hierotheus as a model of inspired wisdom. These four categories essentially account for Thomas's direct reception of Dionysian mysticism. The *Divine Names* often previews union, and Aquinas comments on these passages. The *Mystical Theology* is the key Dionysian text on union, so its reception demands special attention. Finally, Aquinas's theology of the Spirit's gifts of understanding and wisdom is the context for his most explicit remarks on ascent to God by grace in relation to Dionysius's two model mystics. As has already been implied, the background themes considered in chapters 3 through 8 unfold doctrinal issues virtually contained in the four questions: who is united? To whom are we united? What does God do so as to join us to him? And what do mystics do in union?

I need to explain the order of expounding the background doctrines in Albert and Thomas. For both Dominicans all is received in the mode of the receiver (even union), and operation follows being. Hence I begin with a study of their notions of the human being's ontological structure, starting with the soul/body relation. That is, I first consider the mystical subject, the human being called to union, a hermeneutical key for other background doctrines. Ontological anthropology precedes epistemology, respecting the medieval order between metaphysics and noetics. The relation of body and spirit also helps to manifest the soul's internal metaphysical structure: we move from the more evident to the less evident. Turning from being to operation, I then take up epistemology. Here Albert and Thomas navigate between the possibilities of direct, interior or indirect, exterior noetic paths to God. Do we have direct access to the eternal forms, which are reflections of God's light? To what extent does the agent intellect mediate God's light or bypass our dependence on sense data? The issue of noetic interiority or exteriority in epistemology prepares the way for a discussion of the *imago*, for Augustine's *imago* is closely linked with interior ascent to God.

Grace modifies the nature of our noetic operations. That is, one needs a grasp of noetics before turning to the grace/nature relation. How does grace elevate nature? Albert's approach to grace/nature emerges in his noetics, his eschatology, and throughout his Dionysian commentaries. This theme becomes even more programmatic in Thomas, which calls for a distinct study.

I offer a separate survey of Thomas's psychology of love in his *Summa* treatise on the passions, for this treatise constitutes an exception in high scholasticism. The study of Thomas's psychology of love precedes the section on the *imago*, since a consideration of the passion of love (nature) illumines a reflection on the loving imitation of God (grace). Albert's psychology of love comes integrated in his notions of the *imago*, charity, and the beatific vision. That psychology helps to manifest the place of the Areopagite's ecstatic love (the Dionysian motor toward union) in his commentators' thought.[22]

I complete the study of anthropological background doctrines with a consideration of the *imago Dei*, for here the theological analysis of the human being's structure reaches its apex. In addition, for these two friars, the *imago*'s mirror doctrine is that of the trinitarian missions. The doctrinal elements of the former influence the latter and vice versa. The

22. The study of Albert's evolving anthropology and epistemology as well as their relation to Augustine and Dionysius build on two recent articles of mine: "How the Early Albertus Magnus Transformed Augustinian Interiority," *Freiburger Zeitschrift für Philosophie und Theologie* 58 (2011): 351–86; and "Aquinas as Interpreter of Augustinian Illumination in Light of Albertus Magnus," *Nova et Vetera* (English ed.) 10 (2012): 689–713.

missions stand at the center of both friars' theologies of union. Given these close thematic links, the theme of the missions is best treated right after that of the *imago*.

The missions, grace, and infused virtues perfect the *imago*. Hence grace and the virtues are also best treated in proximity to a study of the *imago*. Indeed, the theology of the missions intertwines with the doctrine of grace. The two friars even develop theories of created grace under the influence of Dionysius, who has no notion of created grace. But how does grace as form or *habitus* synthesize with a vision of grace as motion toward God, a classic Dionysian category? Can created grace effect unity, or is it a spiritual tool whereby God effects unity? These questions also call for a distinct consideration of the evolution in Aquinas's theory of divine action, a theme covered in Albert's doctrines of the missions and grace.

For both friars grace "overflows" onto the theological virtues. Thus I ponder faith and charity right after considering the former topic. The limits of the knowledge that the virtue of faith can attain set up a doctrine of the Spirit's gift of understanding, for this gift elevates or perfects faith's cognition. Also, the theology of the gift of wisdom partly develops out of an understanding of charity's grandeur. Thus I treat the seven gifts after the theological virtues. The doctrine of the seven gifts in particular naturally builds on the theology of the seven gifts in general. For this reason I treat the seven gifts in general before turning to understanding and wisdom.

The perfect instance of union with God is found not here below but in the eschatological vision of God. This doctrine crowns the theology of ascent to God via the missions, grace, the theological virtues, and seven gifts. Glory comes at the end of the pilgrimage, but direct vision is preceded by the pilgrim's acts of knowing and naming God. The doctrine of divine naming is intertwined with theological epistemology. The theology of the vision of God constitutes part of that epistemology. The theme of naming God also links with the doctrines of the *imago* and of the virtue of faith. Knowing and naming God are acts that perfect the graced *imago*. Indeed, naming God is also an act of faith.

xxxii Introduction

A NOTE ON CITATIONS AND REFERENCES

My use of translations varies by author. For Dionysius and his commentators before Albert, I rely on existing translations, especially as chapters 1 and 2 of this volume are not original. The most literal English translation of the Dionysian corpus as a whole remains that of John Parker.[23] I rely on this version mostly for the Areopagite's *Divine Names*. For the *Mystical Theology* I usually employ John D. Jones's less readable but more faithful translation.[24] My use of recent secondary literature and my discussion of key Greek terms in chapter 1 of this volume make up for the fact that Parker's and Jones's translations predate the critical edition. We still lack a literal English translation based on the critical text of Dionysius. For Albert and Thomas all translations are my own, thus assuring maximum access to the literal sense of the original. For Albert's *Commentary on the Mystical Theology* I have consulted and often follow Tugwell's fine translation.[25]

Citations of Albert's and Aquinas's commentaries on Dionysius respect the various editors' practice of keeping the friars' quotes of the Dionysian text in italics. This avoids interrupting the textual flow with numerous quotation marks. References to Dionysius give the abbreviated title, chapter, and section (e.g., *DN* 1.1), then the critical edition page and line numbers (e.g., p. 80.1–3), as well as the section number in the Migne Patrologia Graeca, volume 3 (e.g., 585B), then the translation used (e.g., Jones, 211).

The critical edition and Migne references enable easy cross-referencing.[26] Book numbers are given using roman numerals, following

---

23. Dionysius Areopagita, *The Works of Dionysius the Areopagite*, trans. John D. Parker (London: James Parker, 1897).

24. Dionysius Areopagita, *The Divine Names and Mystical Theology*, trans. John D. Jones, Medieval Philosophical Texts in Translation 21 (Milwaukee: Marquette University Press, 1980).

25. Tugwell, ed., trans., *Albert and Thomas: Selected Writings*, by Albert and Aquinas, 133–98.

26. Dionysius Areopagita, *Corpus Dionysiacum I: De divinis nominibus*, ed. Beate Regina Suchla, Patristische Texte und Studien 33 (Berlin: Walter de Gruyter, 1990); Dionysius Areopagita, *Corpus Dionysiacum II: De coelesti hierarchia, De ecclesiastica hierarchia, De mystica theologia, Epistulae*, ed. Günther Heil and Adolf Martin Ritter, Patristische Texte und Studien 36 (Berlin: Walter de Gruyter, 1991); see the recent reprint of the Migne text: *Dionysius Areopagita*, PG 3 (Turnhout: Brepols, 2001).

Introduction xxxiii

standard usage in medieval studies. For the critical editions of Albert, Aquinas, and Thomas Gallus, I also give the page and line numbers (e.g., p. 2.1–11). Latin citations of Albert and Aquinas in the footnotes sometimes give an alternate reading from the critical apparatus, which I place within the signs "< >." For the critical Cologne edition of Albert's *De homine* I include the article title, as the Borgnet edition employs a completely different system of article numbers. For Thomas's *Sentences Commentary* I use the edition by Pierre Mandonnet and Maria Fabianus Moos, except for the last part of book 4, where the only twentieth-century Latin edition is the one by Roberto Busa.[27]

27. Thomas Aquinas, *Scriptum super libros Sententiarum*, vols. 1–2, ed. Pierre Mandonnet; vols. 3–4, ed. Maria Fabianus Moos (Paris: P. Lethielleux, 1927–47); Aquinas, *In quatuor libros Sententiarum*, Opera Omnia 1, ed. Roberto Busa (Stuttgart: Frommann-Holzboog, 1980).

PART 1

Dionysius and His Early Interpreters on Union with God

1

Dionysius on Union with God

Saint Paul's sermon on "the unknown God" at the Areopagus in Athens gained only a few converts, among them a certain Dionysius the Areopagite (Acts 17). The Greek philosophers had little patience for Paul's message about bodily resurrection. Four centuries later another Dionysius proposed a creative development and fusion of Greek patristic and pagan Neoplatonic mystical doctrines within a highly systematic corpus that climaxes with Moses meeting "the unknown God" in darkness. Here the resurrected Jesus is the ultimate hierarch through whom divine light descends. I thus begin with the "real" Dionysius, the Christian theologian so deeply marked by Athens. I start with his historical setting, corpus, and teaching. I will only consider his thought insofar as it illumines his vision of being joined to God. Here I propose not an original interpretation of Dionysian thought but a synthesis of historians' research. The present chapter focuses on the Greek Dionysius, not the Latinized one, since I seek to identify and explain both the proximity and the distance between the Areopagite and his most important medieval Dominican commentators. The subsequent chapter takes up the Latin Dionysius that mediates between the Greek Areopagite and the Dominicans.

This chapter comes in six sections. First, I will consider the historical setting for our author and give an overview of his corpus. I will then survey two key background themes for the theology of union: anthropology and divine naming, the chapter's second and third sections. Fourth, I will study union passages in the *Divine Names*. Fifth, I will proceed to the heart of this chapter, a textual commentary on union texts in the *Mystical Theology*. Sixth, I will conclude by considering some unresolved doctrinal tensions and lacunae related to my main theme.

THE HISTORICAL SETTING AND CORPUS OF DIONYSIUS

The historical Areopagite's real name, year of birth, and date of death remain shrouded in mystery. Everything that we know about him comes from his corpus. It contains abundant references to the works of Proclus and clear allusions to a creed first introduced in the Syrian-Antiochene rite in 476. The Areopagite's works are first mentioned by Severus of Antioch between 518 and 528. Dionysius therefore wrote sometime between 476 and 528.[1] He is not a pretender but a literary figure. His long citations of Neoplatonic writers suggest a desire to reveal the pseudonym nature of authorship, even though all of his disciples before the Renaissance failed to pick up on these clues. References to Philo, Clement of Alexandria, Origen, and Plotinus suggest the author's familiarity with the library of Caesarea in Palestine that Origen had founded. We can thus locate him in Syria, perhaps in its capital, Antioch, or in northern Palestine. The Alexandrian theological sources and (bilingual) Western Syrian ecclesial setting help to explain the fusion of Greek Platonic thought and Syrian liturgical culture in the Dionysian corpus.[2] The Areopagite may have studied under Proclus at the Academy in Athens. He may have been a monk, perhaps a priest, or even a layman.[3]

The surviving Dionysian corpus includes four treatises and ten epistles. The treatises come in two pairs. The *Celestial Hierarchy* is followed by the *Ecclesiastical Hierarchy*. Their main theme is how the angels and liturgical rites transmit, reveal, and conceal divine light, a light that is at once cognitive and metaphysical, informative and transformative. The *Divine Names* is followed by the *Mystical Theology*. The *Divine Names*

---

1. Roques, "Denys l'Aréopagite," 248–56; Beate Regina Suchla, *Dionysius Areopagita: Leben, Werk, Wirkung* (Freiburg im Breisgau: Herder, 2008), 20–21.
2. Suchla, *Dionysius*, 18–23.
3. Riordan, *Divine Light*, 26–28.

presents a Neoplatonic interpretation of God's biblical names. The focus is on "intelligible names" such as "wisdom" and "life," not metaphorical names. God's names are also informative and transformative, leading the soul toward the hidden God from whom we remove all names. The *Mystical Theology* reviews the affirmative and negative divine names, yet it focuses on union, which is beyond naming. The textual order of the two pairs of treatises remains unclear. Finally, the ten epistles preview or review many of the major themes found in the rest of the corpus. The place of the epistles within the corpus is uncertain.[4] Dionysius also refers to other works, such as the *Symbolic Theology*, but we do not know if these were actually written and lost or if they are literary constructs.[5]

The entire Dionysian corpus is closely linked to the theme of being joined to God. The *Celestial Hierarchy* and *Ecclesiastical Hierarchy* manifest how the angels and the liturgy mediate divine light that assimilates us to God. The two hierarchical treatises offer a mystagogia, an explanation of the sacred veils or mediations of the Scriptures and the liturgy.[6] These veils guide the disciple on the path of return to the transcendent source of every hierarchy, an ascent made possible by the light that descends through the veils. In the *Ecclesiastical Hierarchy* the baptismal rite imparts a (nonpantheistic) share in divine being whereby spiritual progress can begin. The Eucharistic rite is all about union with God. Hierarchy is necessary for union.[7] The *Divine Names* explains how God's biblical (and Neoplatonic) names manifest his activity in the cosmos and how they fall short of the divine reality, thus concealing the infinite mystery. Initiation into the proper interpretation of affirmative and negative names is an essential preliminary step to union. The final passage of the *Divine Names* arrives at a climax of negations and then union beyond naming, thus leading to the *Mystical Theology*.[8] God's names constitute a mystical ladder, a necessary steppingstone toward union with him.

---

4. Paul P. Rorem, *Pseudo-Dionysius: A Commentary on the Texts and an Introduction to Their Influence* (Oxford: Oxford University Press, 1993), 6.

5. Suchla, *Dionysius*, 55–60.

6. *EH* 2.1, p. 75.3–9, 400B. Assimilation is a condition for union (*EH* 3.9, pp. 91.12–92.7, 441B–C); see de Andia, *Henosis*, 292, 297; Roques, "Denys l'Aréopagite," 283; Rorem, *Pseudo-Dionysius*, 53.

7. *EH* 2, p. 69.4–13, 392B; 3, p. 79.7–11, 424C; Roques, "Denys l'Aréopagite," 276–77.

8. Riordan, *Divine Light*, 43; Rorem, *Pseudo-Dionysius*, 166, 183, 209–10.

The corpus therefore needs to be read as a whole. For Dionysius, hierarchy and direct contact with God, liturgy and noetic ascent, theological doctrine and mysticism go together.[9]

DIONYSIAN ANTHROPOLOGY: MYSTICAL ASCENT THROUGH THE BODY AND BY DIVINE GIFTS

Dionysius inherited a rich pagan Neoplatonic mystical tradition about contemplative ascent to the One. Its ancient source was Plato, its greatest exponent was Plotinus, and its last formidable promoter was Proclus. A brief summary of central Platonic anthropological doctrines will help to identify some key elements of the Areopagite's vision of the human being. His notion of the mystical subject, especially the role of the human body, plays a crucial role in his theology of union. His understanding of the soul also distances his theology of divine gifts from his non-Christian sources.

Five pillars of Plato's anthropology as it was received in the Neoplatonic tradition should be mentioned. First, the soul's true home is in heaven, for it is as if naturally divine. Philosophy and contemplation are fundamentally about our return to this origin. Second, the soul is an uncomfortable visitor in the body and stands in tension with the material realm. Third, moral and intellectual detachment from the material world enables the soul's ascent to a vision of the forms, and ultimately of the One that is their source. Fourth, this ascent is not a movement outward but rather inward, an awakening to lost memory, a recovery of knowledge already possessed but obscured by our bodily existence and vice. Finally, the soul has an intrinsic capacity to attain a vision of the forms, but not to arrive at a glimpse of the ultimate form, the Good or the One. This ultimate contemplation is suddenly received or given.[10]

Plotinus develops Plato's teachings. He systematizes the relation between the One and Mind (*Noūs*), which is the realm of the forms that the One illumines. Plotinus posits a far stricter separation between

---

9. Von Balthasar, *Glory of the Lord*, 2:154, 204; Roques, "Denys l'Aréopagite," 283.

10. Andrew Louth, *The Origins of the Christian Mystical Tradition: From Plato to Denys* (Oxford: Clarendon Press, 1983), 1–13. Plato's historical doctrine of forms is disputed. I focus on the classic interpretation.

the One and the forms than does Plato. All thought is in the realm of duality or the subject-object division. Even *Noūs* is part of this realm. The human soul retains within itself part of *Noūs* or the realm of the forms. The soul ascends to *Noūs* via concept-bound contemplation, a necessary preliminary stage to union with the One. Yet it can only attain such union by leaving behind all thought, for the One is beyond duality. Desire or *erōs* drives the soul to surpass duality and return to pure simplicity, though the soul is never fully fused with the One.[11] Plotinus radicalizes the Platonic alienation of the soul from the world.

One of Proclus's key contributions to the Neoplatonic heritage is his emphasis on hierarchy mediating union with the One, a process that involves philosophy and liturgy. Proclus significantly limits the "interiority" of Plato and Plotinus as he emphasizes our need for symbols in ascent to the One. Liturgy and cosmic hierarchy are intimately connected for Proclus. The soul is only joined to the One through a step-by-step ascent of the hierarchy of hypostases. The visible mediation of liturgical acts and symbols finds its complement in the invisible hierarchy below the One. The gods inspire the theurgist or priest to employ symbols that attract divine powers so that the symbols unite us to gods. The latter in turn establish our union with *Noūs*, the prelude to union with the One. Proclus emphasizes the soul's finitude and posits a positive aspect of material existence largely missing in Plato and Plotinus.[12]

Dionysius refuses the Platonic-Plotinian conviction that the soul is naturally divine. The Christian doctrine of creation *ex nihilo* demands nothing less—a theology that Dionysius seems to imply when he states that the Good is the Source and End of all things that causes and preserves their being.[13] Second, there is virtually no discussion of memory in the Dionysian corpus. The Areopagite cuts off the two main

---

11. Werner Beierwaltes, "Reflexion und Einung: Zur Mystik Plotins," in *Grundfragen der Mystik*, edited by Hans Urs von Balthasar, Werner Beierwaltes, and Alois M. Haas, 10–31 (Einsiedeln: Johannes Verlag, 1974); Dominic O'Meara, *Plotin: Une introduction aux "Ennéades*," 2nd ed., Vestigia 10 (Fribourg, Switzerland: Academic Press, 2004), 43–52.

12. R. M. van den Berg, *Proclus' Hymns: Essays, Translations, Commentary*, Philosophia Antiqua 90 (Leiden: E. J. Brill, 2001), 80–85; Louth, *Origins*, 162–64; Riordan, *Divine Light*, 78–80.

13. *DN* 4.4, p. 148.8–12, 700A–B; 5.4, pp. 182.17–83.11, 817C–D; Riordan, *Divine Light*, 100–2.

sources of interior ascent: divine likeness and the recovery of obscured memory. Nor does he discuss God hidden in the heart, unlike Gregory of Nyssa.[14] Dionysius also goes beyond Gregory and other Greek fathers as he emphasizes the soul's intimate connection with the body.[15] Partly inspired by Proclus, Dionysius proposes an "exterior anthropology," which is a major reason for his long explication of biblical names and liturgical symbols. The soul begins its ascent not by going to the God hidden within or the memory of forms, but by moving outward to the illumination brought by the divine names and liturgical symbols.[16] This revalorization of material mediations pertains to the *beginning* of contemplative ascent and serves the need of the soul's "impassioned" or lower part, which naturally strives after symbols. Having satisfied the lower soul, ascent attains completion in the soul's higher or "passionless" part. Here "simple visions" and unified thoughts are the proper aim as cognition mediated by the senses eventually becomes an obstacle to union.[17] Consequently, progress in sanctifying cognition passes through a highly structured series of symbols and names that reveal their luminous content to those who are properly disposed to learn them and to receive the proportion of divine light that they transmit.[18] In other words, the Areopagite's semi-Proclan anthropology calls for a mysticism of mediations, at least for the initial stages of ascent to God.

A second major trait of the Areopagite's anthropology is his emphasis on divine gifts or the soul's dependence on God's gratuitous illumination. The soul cannot rely on a natural divine similitude for its return to the One. While all of creation bears a certain likeness to

---

14. De Andia, *Henosis*, 18–19.

15. Wiebke-Marie Stock, *Theurgisches Denken: Zur "Kirchlichen Hierarchie" des Dionysius Areopagita*, Transformation der Antike 4 (Berlin: Walter de Gruyter, 2008), 176–86; von Balthasar, *Glory of the Lord*, 2:160–61. Liturgical allusions throughout the Dionysian corpus also emphasize the need for sensible mediations.

16. See von Balthasar, *Glory of the Lord*, 2:160–61, 180; Riordan, *Divine Light*, 85–90; Paul P. Rorem, *Biblical and Liturgical Symbols within the Pseudo-Dionysian Synthesis*, Studies and Texts 71 (Toronto: Pontifical Institute of Medieval Studies, 1984), 56; Edith Stein, "Ways to Know God: The *Symbolic Theology* of Dionysius the Areopagite and Its Factual Presuppositions," *Thomist* 9 (1946): 379–420.

17. *DN* 4.11, p. 156.13–19, 708D; *EP* 9.1, p. 198.1–14, 1108A–B; Roques, *L'univers dionysien*, 202, 235.

18. *DN* 3.3, pp. 142.14–43.2, 684C; Roques, *L'univers dionysien*, 119, 203, 209.

God, this link remains insufficient without the gift of divine assimilation. The Dionysian theology of divine gratuity centers on the doctrine of divinization, which in turn is founded upon the Greek philosophical axiom that "like knows like." The divine gifts assimilate the soul to God.[19] Therefore, mystical cognition of God by "unknowing" is not just the outcome of an intellectual ascent to the hidden Deity, but rather a path opened up by the elevating gift of faith. However, Dionysius does not propose a doctrine of created grace. He emphasizes that the entire ascent to God lies beyond the soul's intrinsic capacity. Hence the soul must go outward to receive mediated divine light. The mind's ecstasy is not its own operation but a gift preceded by activity already illumined by God.[20] Christ himself is the divine ray that elevates the soul to the Father.[21]

DIVINE NAMING AS A MYSTICAL LADDER

For Dionysius the foundation of all intelligible divine naming is creation's similitude to God (Ws 13:1, Rom 1:20). Similitude entails the doctrine of participation. God's creative act is the diffusion of his perfections. Creatures receive or rather are similitudes of divine perfections. The Creator's causal activity leaves divine images and likenesses in all of creation. Still, Dionysius does not have a doctrine of a trinitarian image in the human being.[22]

Similitude enables affirmative and negative discourse about God. Affirmative theology describes the processions from the One or God's manifestation in his creatures. The positive way of descent finds its complement in the negative way of ascent, the return of creatures to their source. The first way is God's ecstasy or his going out of himself, while the second way is our ecstasy, our going beyond creaturely limitations so as to dive into the divine mystery.[23] Affirmation and negation are not separate activities, but rather closely intertwined and inter-

19. DN 7.1, p. 194.13–15, 865D–68A; de Andia, *Henosis*, 429.
20. CH 3.2, p. 19.3–8, 165C; DN 2.7–8, p. 132.1–13, 645B–C; de Andia, *Henosis*, 169–70.
21. CH 1.2, p. 7.9, 121A; Riordan, *Divine Light*, 192.
22. De Andia, *Henosis*, 106–9, 240.
23. MT 2, p. 145, 1025A–B; DN 7.3, p. 197.20–22, 869D; de Andia, *Henosis*, 378, 387–88; Werner Beierwaltes, *Denken des Einen: Studien zur neuplatonischen Philosophie und ihrer Wirkungsgeschichte* (Frankfurt am Main: Klostermann, 1985), 150.

dependent.[24] Negations are meaningless without affirmations, yet by themselves affirmations are so inadequate that they become false.

But what do names name? Do they refer to God himself and his attributes, or to God's activity, power, or energies? Endless doctrinal disputes between East and West, between the supposedly apophatic theologies of the Oriental tradition and the supposedly kataphatic theologies of the Latin scholastics, abound. The question is also central to the debate concerning the Areopagite's relation to non-Christian Neoplatonism. Did Dionysius Christianize the philosophical apophatism of Plotinus and Proclus, or did he stealthily import non-Christian ideas into Christian theology? A brief comparison of the function of divine names in Plato, Plotinus, and Proclus will offer a partial answer to these questions.

In Plato's *Parmenides* negations refer to the first hypostasis or the One and affirmations refer to the second hypostasis below the One.[25] For Plotinus affirmative and negative theologies are linked to distinct hypostases below the One. The latter cannot be named, either positively or negatively. All discourse about the One is really about that which comes from the One.[26] Proclus refers affirmative and negative names to distinct hypostases below the One, but he expands Plotinus's teaching as he grants the possibility of negative names about the One.[27]

The Areopagite's favorite affirmative names are One, Good, Being, Life, and Wisdom. The Platonic tradition before him identifies the One with the Good. Dionysius introduces a radical innovation by eliminating all hypostases between the One and finite beings. Rather, God *as cause* is being, life, and wisdom, for he is the direct creative cause bringing all things into being without intermediary hypostases.[28] For Plotinus a mingling of the One and the divine mind is a monumental error, but that is precisely what Dionysius does.[29] His Christian theology of creation leads to a significant transformation of the Neoplatonic tradition. An adequate account of this development demands a consideration of two other themes: (1) the distinction between God's hidden es-

24. Rorem, *Pseudo-Dionysius*, 203.
25. De Andia, *Henosis*, 389–90.
26. Beierwaltes, "Reflexion," 22; O'Meara, *Plotin*, 64, 75.
27. Rorem, *Pseudo-Dionysius*, 163.
28. Riordan, *Divine Light*, 82–84; Rorem, *Pseudo-Dionysius*, 163.
29. De Andia, *Henosis*, 202.

sence and processions; and (2) the function of transcending negations.

One of the Areopagite's fundamental teachings is that affirmative names such as Being refer to the divine powers that proceed from God's hidden essence. Affirmative names do not directly predicate attributes of God's essence.[30] Divine powers are God's activity in creation. More precisely, our discourse about God's powers ultimately refers to the one infinite power that is God's dynamic activity spreading "beyond itself."[31] The distinction between God's essence and his powers is crucial for the interpretive tradition centered on Gregory of Palamas, which turns the Dionysian powers into the uncreated energies. Yet Ysabel de Andia warns us that both the Palamasian essence-energy distinction and Aquinas's confidence in directly naming the divine essence go beyond the Areopagite.[32] But if the Dionysian powers are not distinct from the divine essence in a Palamasian sense, then we have not yet attained an adequate response to the question concerning the highest object of the divine names.

The Areopagite insists that affirmations and negations do not contradict:

it being our duty both to attribute and affirm all the attributes of things existing to It, as Cause of all, and more properly to deny (*apophaskein*) them all to It, as being above all, and not to consider the negations (*apophaseis*) to be in opposition to the affirmations, but far rather that It, which is above every abstraction (*aphairesin*) and definition, is above the privations (*stereseis*).[33]

Affirmations refer the attributes of creatures to God in his powers, but not to his essence. Thus the wisdom of beings leads to the statement, "God is wise." The first set of negations or *apophaseis* also refers to God as cause, but in view of him "being above all" or above the processions.

---

30. *DN* 2.5, p. 131.7–10, 645A; de Andia, *Henosis*, 109. The unknowability of the divine and even created natures can already be found in Basil of Caesarea and Gregory of Nyssa; see Lewis Ayres, *Nicaea and Its Legacy: An Approach to Fourth-Century Trinitarian Theology* (Oxford: Oxford University Press, 2004), 197, 282.

31. De Andia, *Henosis*, 114–18.

32. De Andia, *Henosis*, 115. Jean-Claude Larchet harmonizes Dionysius and Palamas on this point, but ignores de Andia's proposal; see Larchet, *La théologie des énergies divines*, 289–329. I will return to this point later.

33. *MT* 1.2, p. 143.3–7, 1000B, following Parker's translation (131), as Jones's reading is confusing.

The formality differs for affirmative and negative names: God in his processions and God as *not being* the processions. Both types of names relate to the processions.

However, these negations (*apophaseis*) do not have the last word, for they move on the same plane as affirmations: that of beings. Dionysius also employs a second term for negations: *aphaireseis*. These pertain *more* directly to God as transcending all beings. *Aphaireseis* or transcending negations have four major functions. First, they signal that there is no privation in God. Whereas *apophaseis* focus on the contrast between God and beings, *aphaireseis* limit *apophaseis* to the level of beings. Negating the wisdom of God does not mean that he is not wise at all. Transcending negations are not designed to say nothing about God, but rather imply a positive element in God.[34] Second, Dionysius employs transcending negations in relation to eminent terms such as "God beyond good."[35] He also relates transcending negations to seeing God in darkness by not-seeing. Dionysius thus celebrates the superessential God *through* the negation of all beings.[36] Transcending negations are hymns of praise whereby we recognize all beings (the source of affirmations and their complementary negations) as veils that conceal the hidden God. But transcending negations do not predicate positive eminent names of the divine essence, for Dionysius considers eminence not so much as a way of naming particular attributes of God as a way of designating God's nonprivative, transcendent excellence. Transcending negations both save the possibility of divine discourse and refuse any discourse that pretends to master the divine reality. The celebration of God as "beyond good" moves the mind beyond any perfection encountered in creation. Not even transcending negations qualify God's essence, although the negation of privation excludes the absence of perfections in God.[37] Yet naming and thinking about the divine essence as including such attributes moves the mind back to the level of creation. This paradox or quasi-dialectic of the refusal to affirm eminent names of God's essence and the exclusion of all privation remains

---

34. De Andia, *Henosis*, 378–80; René Roques, "Contemplation, extase et ténèbre chez le Pseudo-Denys," in *DS* 2.2 (1953): col. 1893.

35. *DN* 2.3, p. 125.14–16, 640B.

36. *MT* 2, p. 145.4–5, 1025A–B.

37. De Andia, *Henosis*, 132, 378, 383, 392; de Andia, *Denys l'Aréopagite: Tradition et Métamorphoses* (Paris: Vrin, 2006), 134.

unresolved in Dionysius.[38] Third, he names God as beyond all transcending negations and thus *posits* his absolute transcendence precisely that for which human thought has no adequate category. Fourth, transcending negations only prepare the way for the entry into luminous darkness. Ultimately, all negations must be left behind, for the mystical way is beyond all discourse. In the end we deny even this higher type of negation (or negate negations), because God is beyond all human speech.[39] A doctrine of naming that places firm limits on the reach of divine predicates leads to an apophatic mysticism.

The primary function of the divine names is to prepare for union. However, some names also have a unifying power: Monad, Henad, Eros, Peace, Goodness, One, Love. Dionysius follows Proclus as he teaches that the divine names effect what they signify. The names refer to divine powers that are both the source of all created gifts (*exitus*) and the cause of our return to the One (*reditus*).[40] This has nothing to do with the practice of sacred mantras that automatically or magically produce a mystical experience. For Dionysius the proper reception and understanding of the divine names are mediated by the liturgy and presuppose moral rectitude—that is, the proper purification required for participation in the sacred rites. These mediations and ethical preconditions enable a fruitful application of human reason to the study of God's names.[41] Divine names unify because they are properly understood and sung as sacred hymns of praise.

UNION IN THE *DIVINE NAMES*

Dionysius employs the term "mystical union" (*mystikē henōsis*) only once, in reference to the obscure figure of Hierotheus in chapter 2 of the *Divine Names*. This work offers two major previews of Moses in the *Mystical Theology*: in its exposition of union "beyond mind" (*hyper noūn*) and in its presentation of Hierotheus. Since both themes will

---

38. For the Areopagite's method of naming as a form of dialectic, see Puech, "Ténèbre mystique," 37–38; Roques, "Denys l'Aréopagite," 284.

39. *MT* 1.2, p. 143.7, 1000B; 5, p. 150.5–9, 1048B; de Andia, *Henosis*, 382, 393; Roques, "Contemplation," 1894, 1903.

40. De Andia, *Henosis*, 114–15.

41. De Andia, *Henosis*, 240, 297; von Balthasar, *Glory of the Lord*, 2:154; Golitzin, *Et introibo*, 230.

take center stage in Albert's and Thomas's reception of Dionysian mysticism, they merit particular attention. Finally, I will take up the Areopagite's notion of ecstatic love.

In the *Divine Names* Dionysius mentions three major, necessary, preliminary steps for union with God beyond those already noted. First, God's light enables an accurate explication of the revealed divine names. Here God's gratuitous gifts do not bypass or suppress but rather enable and elevate rational human reflection. Second, the mind must be without the passion or disturbance caused by vice, a spiritual state that is the fruit of moral discipline.[42] Third, the mind's proper activity must ultimately cease—that is, it should stop contemplating God in his created similitudes. We ascend *toward union* by negations that detach the mind from its gaze upon beings, for they are not God. The *Divine Names* is a book of hymns whereby we praise and thus know God in his positive attributes. Negations are also hymns of praise, but these shatter our conceptual idols. The *Divine Names* climaxes in negations and silence, for the act of removing God's names causes the intellect's repose and simplification. The active quieting of the mind's activity *is* its ascent by negations, which leads to a certain noetic silence.[43] Apophatic ascent is structured by contemplative hierarchies. The liturgy, the bishop's preaching, and the Areopagite's counsel to Timothy guide the disciple along a path whereby he or she progressively abandons all forms of contemplation wherein the noetic object remains tied to finite realities.[44] But union is beyond the mind's power, for it only occurs by God's action.[45]

Union beyond mind is itself ineffable or unknowable, for one is joined to the unknowable God. It could only be understood if object and subject were perfectly knowable, which is impossible. Unlike Gregory of Nyssa, Dionysius does not posit the unknowability of the soul.[46] Having surpassed the normal human ways of knowing God, which are not false but limited, the mind attains a more divine understanding, the paradox of knowing in unknowing, which Dionysius connects to

---

42. *DN* 1.4, p. 115.1–3, 592C; de Andia, *Henosis*, 238–40.
43. *DN* 2.7, p. 131.5–11, 645A; 13.3, pp. 229.10–30.5, 981A–B; de Andia, *Henosis*, 375, 383, 394, 402; Golitzin, *Et introibo*, 138; Rorem, *Pseudo-Dionysius*, 165–66.
44. Roques, "Contemplation," 1893.
45. *DN* 1.1, p. 108.1–3, 585B; de Andia, *Henosis*, 233.
46. De Andia, *Henosis*, 280.

Paul's discourse about God's inscrutable wisdom. It is the equivalent of Moses in darkness.[47] Also, the object of union is not the divine essence, but divine light.[48] The question of distinguishing God's power and essence thus returns. The image of a blinding ray for union emphasizes God's immanence and thus the soul's real, nonpantheistic union with God. The hiddenness of God's essence emphasizes his transcendence, so that union never exhausts the divine mystery.

The soul passes beyond all intellectual operations into utter silence because it is being deified in a radical way, utterly drenched in divine light. The gift of union "turns off" the mind. This second type of noetic silence is not a deliberate human act.[49] God's suppression of the mind's operation seems to suggest that the first humanly initiated suspension of operation was either imperfect or too brief, though Dionysius is not clear on this point. In union the mind no longer acts, yet mind itself is not left behind. Like Plotinus, Dionysius has no interest in an irrational or emotional ecstatic union. The Areopagite's ecstasy is a passing beyond human limitations to the passive reception of the highest illuminations. The subject encountering God's light in a perfect way is nothing but the soul with its mind, now radically transformed.

In the *Divine Names* the mystic *par excellence* is the Areopagite's "teacher" Hierotheus. Here mystical ascent has three essential steps: (1) the reception of a tradition via the apostolic writings or Scripture; (2) a rational reflection on this tradition and the liturgy; and (3) a special initiation into divine things. As in Neoplatonic philosophy, tradition is both public and secret. The second step centers upon biblical exegesis under the guidance of a teacher. The third step is the Holy Spirit's work, for he is the ultimate mystagogue.[50]

The fruit of these three stages of ascent is that Hierotheus "learns" (*mathōn*) and "suffers divine things" (*pathōn ta theia*). Dionysius mentions this phrase almost in passing, but it will be crucial for Albert

---

47. *DN* 7.3, p. 198.12–15, 872B; *MT* 1.3, p. 144.5–15, 1000D–1001A; de Andia, *Henosis*, 276–77.

48. *DN* 1.5, pp. 116.14–17.1, 593B–C; 5.1, p. 180.9–13, 816B; de Andia, *Henosis*, 254, 279–80.

49. *DN* 4.11, p. 156.15–19, 708D; de Andia, *Denys l'Aréopagite*, 51; de Andia, *Henosis*, 400.

50. *DN* 2.9, pp. 133.5–34.6, 648A–B; see also 1.1, pp. 107.3–8.5, 585B–88A; *MT* 1.1, p. 142.5–9, 997B; de Andia, *Denys l'Aréopagite*, 23; de Andia, *Henosis*, 239–42.

and Thomas.⁵¹ *Pathōn* can also be translated as "experience."⁵² What does Hierotheus receive or learn? He probably attains a knowledge of Christ's divinity. "Learning by suffering" almost certainly alludes to Christ's experience on the cross as recounted in Hebrews 5:8–9, where Jesus learns by suffering.⁵³ The incarnate Word is the object and model of learning. By his incarnation he has made such experiential knowledge possible for us.⁵⁴ Because of the unity of the three divine persons, union with Christ is simultaneously union with the One. Such learning surpasses the realm of discourse and conceptual knowledge. Hierotheus passes through the order of reflection on the tradition to the third stage, which is marked by passivity before God. The realm of faith is not left behind but perfected.⁵⁵ Dionysius nowhere suggests any intention to offer an alternative path to the Christian faith.

"Suffering divine things" thus appears to refer to an experience, yet Dionysius does not recount his own experience. Rather, the only experience worth discussing is that of a model hierarch. Furthermore, Dionysius is in no position to initiate the reader into a technique whereby one can attain the same experience. Such learning cannot be taught, for it is the fruit of a gratuitous gift. All that the reader can do is imitate Hierotheus's first two steps. The third step is precisely one that no human being can traverse by his or her own volition. Christ himself learned it through suffering. Whenever Dionysius recounts what may be a mystical experience, it is that of a teacher in the tradition: Hierotheus, Paul, or Moses. Even if the figure of Hierotheus were a literary construct, Dionysius would have constructed him precisely to refer his doctrine to a tradition and not to his own interior states.⁵⁶ The last thing Dionysius intends to do is to speak about himself. Even a hermeneutic of suspicion that proposes that Dionysius places his own doctrine in the mouths of real or invented teachers must take into account at least two

---

51. *DN* 2.9, p. 134.2, 648B; de Andia, *Henosis*, 436. Dionysius seems to use this language in an original way. He relates both terms to *sympatheia*, perhaps marked by Iamblichus; de Andia, *Denys l'Aréopagite*, 18–24.

52. Rorem, *Pseudo-Dionysius*, 143.

53. *DN* 2.9, p. 133.4–12, 648A; de Andia, *Denys l'Aréopagite*, 22–25; de Andia, *Henosis*, 239–42.

54. De Andia, *Henosis*, 436.

55. De Andia, *Denys l'Aréopagite*, 23–25; de Andia, *Henosis*, 239–42.

56. Rorem, *Pseudo-Dionysius*, 142–43.

central elements of the Areopagite's mystical theology. First, it is a development of a patristic mystical tradition that centers on Moses in the Book of Exodus.[57] Second, this theology builds on a creative appropriation of Neoplatonic philosophical tools.[58] In these two ways Dionysius passed on a (reinterpreted) tradition whose relation to the Areopagite's experience remains obscure.

There is another clue about the nature of Hierotheus's union. In chapter 3 of the *Divine Names*, following a likely reference to the Dormition of the Blessed Virgin Mary, an event supposedly witnessed by Hierotheus and Dionysius (!), the apostles and Hierotheus praise God for taking Mary's body into heaven. Hierotheus the hierarch or bishop exceeds the apostles in his praise, being so inspired that he experiences communion with the (divine) things praised (*ta humnoumena koinōnian paschōn*).[59] In the *Ecclesiastical Hierarchy* the terms "communion" and "the things praised" refer to the Eucharistic bread and cup.[60] The passage on the Dormition echoes Hierotheus's suffering divine things.[61] His being "caught up" after Mary's assumption refers to ecstasy, an indispensable element of Dionysian union. We thus find three intertwined aspects of Hierotheus's union with God: (1) an illumined instruction; (2) a Eucharistic setting; and (3) ecstasy beyond concepts and discourse. Strikingly, every explicit discussion of union in the Dionysian corpus involves a hierarch celebrating the liturgy. The Areopagite's *Epistle 8* mentions Carpos, who enjoys extraordinary visions before celebrating the Eucharist. We will see that Moses's ascent of Mt. Sinai in the *Mystical Theology* also contains liturgical allusions.[62]

Finally, the *Divine Names* fills an important gap that the *Mystical*

---

57. Puech, "Ténèbre mystique," 46.

58. Werner Beierwaltes rightly emphasizes that such appropriation still allows philosophy to shape or co-determine theology; see his *Platonismus im Christentum*, Philosophische Abhandlungen 73 (Frankfurt am Main: Klostermann, 1998), 12.

59. *DN* 3.2, p. 141.6–12, 681D–84A; Rorem, *Pseudo-Dionysius*, 147. The allusion to Mary remains uncertain. Beate R. Suchla sees a reference to the Eucharist; see her notes to Dionysius Areopagita, *Die Namen Gottes*, trans. Suchla, Bibliothek der Griechischen Literatur 26 (Stuttgart: Anton Hiersemann, 1988), 112–13n73.

60. *EH* 3.1, p. 81.7–8, 425D; 3.10, p. 90.10, 440B; 3.12, pp. 92.17, 93.1, 444A; Rorem, *Pseudo-Dionysius*, 147.

61. Rorem, *Pseudo-Dionysius*, 143, 147.

62. *EP* 8.6, p. 188.11–14, 1097B; Golitzin, *Et introibo*, 171–74; Rorem, *Pseudo-Dionysius*, 191.

Theology leaves open, for the latter text never mentions love in its exposition of union. The *Divine Names* closely connects union with the language of ecstasy (*ekstasis*) or being lifted up beyond mind.[63] Dionysius primarily employs the term "ecstasy" in relation to love, not intellect. The latter is a faculty distinct from the faculty of love. Like most of the Greek fathers, the Areopagite hardly develops an ontology of the will. However, he offers an original doctrine of *agape* and *erōs* in chapter 4 of the *Divine Names*. The Areopagite connects ecstasy with St. Paul's mystical experience. The apostle was so taken over by divine love that he no longer belonged to himself. Being wholly detached from himself, he participated in God's ecstatic power and could say, "It is no longer I but Christ who lives in me" (Gal 2:20).[64] Dionysius alludes to an intense form of union with God, though he draws no explicit connection with union in darkness. Yet the language of the soul's dispossession finds echoes in two other texts: (1) in the opening passage of the *Mystical Theology*, where dispossession of self is directly related to being carried upward; and (2) in chapter 7 of the *Divine Names*, where not belonging to oneself is connected to union beyond mind.[65] The apostle's ecstatic love for God leads to a new share in divine life.

Affective ecstasy is crucial partly because Dionysius develops a Proclan theology of love as a unitive power. Indeed, while the subject of union is *noũs* insofar as it is the site of cognition, the highest knowledge remains inaccessible without love. *Noũs* includes the faculty of love, but affective desire for God functions as an indispensable motor of noetic ascent *toward* union. *Erōs*, which Dionysius identifies with *agape* or charity, moves us back to God, for it comes from him. The Dionysian model for love is not that of two lovers (as in Song of Songs mysticism) but the unifying power received from the One who is also the Beautiful. Knowledge retains priority in Dionysian union, while love has an essential though secondary place.[66]

---

63. *DN* 7.1, p. 194.12–15, 865D–68A; Roques, *L'univers dionysien*, 117, 238.

64. *DN* 4.13, p. 159.3–6, 712A.

65. *MT* 1.1, p. 142.5–11, 1000A; *DN* 7.1, p. 194.12–15, 865D–68A; Riordan, *Divine Light*, 202.

66. *DN* 4.12, p. 158.7–18, 709D; Ysabel de Andia, *La Voie et le Voyageur: Essai d'anthropologie de la vie spirituelle* (Paris: Cerf, 2012), 102; de Andia, *Henosis*, 149, 252–53; Roques, *L'univers dionysien*, 120; Rorem, *Pseudo-Dionysius*, 150–51. For the historical background on *eros* and *agape*, see John M. Rist, *Eros and Psyche: Studies in Plato, Plo-*

Finally, the doctrine of ecstasy means that union does not occur in the soul's hidden spark but "outside" of itself. We encounter and know the unknown God without, not within. Ecstasy and union are simultaneous. Dionysius presents a paradox: the mind is united to divine realities only "outside of itself." This does not involve a metaphysical contradiction but the epistemological condition for union. By God's gift we transcend all things and ourselves so as to possess God alone.[67] That possession comes to the fore in the *Mystical Theology*.

UNION IN THE *MYSTICAL THEOLOGY*

We now come to the heart of this chapter, a textual study of union passages in the *Mystical Theology*. As a preface, I will review the book's content, structure, and genre.

This short treatise contains five chapters. Dionysius discusses divine darkness wherein Moses knows God by unknowing and is united to him (chapter 1), how negations lead toward unknowing or a vision of divine Beauty (chapter 2), the signification of affirmative and negative names, including symbolic or metaphorical names (chapter 3), that the divine Cause transcends all sensible things (chapter 4), and that the divine Cause transcends all intelligible things (chapter 5). The first chapter is the longest. It leads up to the example of Moses by invoking two figures associated with union: Paul's disciple Timothy and the apostle Bartholomew. Dionysius teaches Timothy how to attain union, and Bartholomew instructs the reader on mystical ascent. Moses's journey up Mt. Sinai symbolically demonstrates this process. Chapter 2 treats mystical ascent via negations. Chapters 2 through 5 offer technical clarifications concerning divine names and their relation to God, especially negations. Union is the book's main theme.[68]

The *Mystical Theology* begins with a prayer:

O Trinity, beyond being, beyond divinity, beyond goodness, and guide of Christians in divine wisdom, direct us to the mystical summits (*logiōn*) more than unknown and beyond light. There the simple, absolved und

---

tinus and Origen, Phoenix Supplementary Volumes 6 (Toronto: University of Toronto Press, 1967).
67. De Andia, *Henosis*, 420–21.
68. Ibid., 356.

unchanged mysteries of theology lie hidden in the darkness beyond light of the hidden mystical science.[69]

The author will consider the proper human disposition to receive the Trinity's uplifting power. Elevation enabled by divine gifts leads to noetic contact with the reality that the sacred oracles reveal. In the Dionysian corpus summits or oracles (*logia*) usually refer to the revelation transmitted in sacred Scripture, but they can also refer to the words passed on in the liturgy.[70] The "unchanged mysteries of theology" or divine realities are the object of revelation and union. In the patristic tradition the term "mystical" often refers to the hidden, allegorical meaning of Scripture. For Origen allegory constitutes a path to union with the divine spouse. In Philo and Gregory of Nyssa the patriarch on Mt. Sinai takes center stage in a broad Judeo-Christian tradition of mystical theology. Dionysius also engages in allegorical interpretation in his commentary on Moses as he integrates and develops Philo's and Gregory's exegesis.[71] While we cannot exclude the Areopagite's personal experience as a source for his writing, the close link to a tradition of patristic exegesis and the extensive use of technical philosophical terminology show that the *Mystical Theology* is primarily a doctrinal treatise about the ontological reality of the mind's union with God. Dionysius does not offer a transcript of special inner psychological states but rather explains the preconditions and constitutive elements of being joined to God. The focus on doctrine and metaphysics is typical of patristic mystical writers.[72]

Dionysius therefore does not primarily invoke his own spiritual experience to inspire the reader's imitation. Rather, he seeks to dispose the reader to receive the power of the "oracles" passed on in Scripture and the liturgy. The text manifests the summit of a spiritual path that passes through ritual mediations as well as the proper combination of affirmative and negative names. Dionysius the hierarch guides the disciple through the right interpretation of liturgical and biblical veils, symbols, and names, leading to a climax where all interpretation

---

69. *MT* 1.1, pp. 141.1–42.2, 997A–B, Jones, 211.

70. *DN* 1.1, pp. 107.5–8.9, 587–88A; 1.4, p. 114.1–3, 592B; de Andia, *Henosis*, 1–3, 240; Rorem, *Pseudo-Dionysius*, 190–92.

71. Gregory of Nyssa, *La vie de Moïse*, ed. and trans. Jean Daniélou, 3rd ed., Sources Chrétiennes 1 bis (Paris: Cerf, 2007); de Andia, *Henosis*, 355–70; Louth, *Origins*, 64.

72. Puech, "Ténèbre mystique," 42–49.

runs into a wall, where the mind falls silent in the presence of God. The *Mystical Theology* is anything but an individualistic treatise, for by it a teacher initiates his student into a tradition.[73] It is an authoritative, quasi-apostolic interpretation of a mystical tradition.

Dionysius completes his prayer to the Trinity with a preview of Moses on Mt. Sinai as he begs God to lead believers into "super-luminous darkness." He exhorts Timothy to follow this path and so presents mystical ascent a second time:

And you, dear Timothy, in the earnest exercise of mystical contemplation (*theamata*), abandon all sensation and intellectual activities, all that is sensed and intelligible, all non-being and all beings; thus you will unknowingly be elevated (*anatathēti*), as far as possible, to the unity of that beyond being and knowledge ... you will be purely raised up (*anachthēsē*) to the rays of divine darkness beyond being.[74]

The intense exercise of gazing upon oracles probably refers to the anagogical interpretation of Scripture and liturgical symbols, which occurs in the soul's passionless part. Such contemplation constitutes the last active step in noetic ascent and apparently directly disposes the soul for passive elevation.[75] Then a single, divinely given movement begins with the abandonment of noetic activity and ends in union. "Be elevated" is a passive imperative, an exhortation to strain upward, beyond oneself. Dionysius promises even more divine aid to complete ascent ("you will be purely raised up"), which is the very gift that brings Moses into darkness. Only divine light can unite Timothy to God, but his mind must be silent to receive this ultimate gift.[76]

Dionysius then proceeds to summarize the function of affirmations and negations. He recalls that God is above naming. He invokes an oral tradition that supposedly comes from Bartholomew. The apostle teaches that God is above every concept and word. Hence we should pass beyond all divine lights, sounds, and words so as to enter into gloom.[77]

---

73. Rorem, *Pseudo-Dionysius*, 192, 207.
74. *MT* 1.1, p. 142.5–9, 997B–1000A, Jones, 211–12.
75. Rorem, *Pseudo-Dionysius*, 186; de Andia, *Henosis*, 240, 431. The anagogical interpretation matches the highest contemplation for each liturgical rite (the sections entitled *theoria*) expounded in the *EH*; de Andia, *Denys l'Aréopagite*, 57.
76. De Andia, *Henosis*, 3–4, 355, 375.
77. *MT* 1.2–3, pp. 142.12–43.17, 1000A–C.

Dionysius then introduces Moses by referring to Exodus 19, 24, and 33:

It is not to be taken lightly that the divine Moses was ordered first to purify himself (*apokatharthēnai*), and again to be separated (*aphoristhēnai*) from those who were not pure; after every purification (*apokatharsin*) he hears the many sounded trumpets, he sees the many pure lights that flash forth and the greatly flowing rays. Then he is separated (*aphorizetai*) from the many and, with those who are sacred (*hiereōn*) and select, he overtakes the summits of the divine ascents (*tēn akrotēta tōn theiōn anabaseōn*). Yet with these he does not come to be with God himself; he does not see God—for God is unseen—but the place (*topon*) where God is.[78]

Philo and Gregory of Nyssa had already interpreted Moses as a high priest or priestly mediator between God and human beings.[79] Partly under their influence, Dionysius proposes a subtle parallel between Moses in the *Mystical Theology* and the bishop in the *Ecclesiastical Hierarchy*. Before ascending the mountain, the patriarch is purified (*apokatharthēnai*), just as the hierarch and the priests (*hiereōn*) undergo a ritual washing (*apokatharsin*) during the transition from the liturgy of the word to the celebration of the Eucharist that unites the bishop to divine things.[80] In the liturgy the multitude stands outside the closed doors of the sanctuary, though the lay faithful also enjoy divine communion through the Eucharist. The bishop alone is led by the divine Spirit to intelligible visions in the sanctuary.[81] Likewise, Moses and the priests are separated (*aphorizetai*) from the crowd, yet Moses alone proceeds all the way to the summit, which is higher than God's "place." In his mystagogia of the Eucharist Dionysius explains that the beautifully depicted images at the entrance of the sanctuary propose a contemplation that befits the multitude, while the priests should seek intellectual visions and unconcealed light within the sanctuary. Similarly, Moses and the priests transcend sounds and lights so as to proceed to the contemplation of God's "place" (*topon*).[82] Finally, priestly ordination enables the contemplation of sacred realities and the transmission of this knowledge received in the

---

78. *MT* 1.3, pp. 143.17–44.5, 1000C, Jones, 213–14.
79. De Andia, *Henosis*, 309–11, 320–23; Rorem, *Pseudo-Dionysius*, 190.
80. *EH* 3, p. 81.3, 425D; 3.3.10, p. 89.21, 440A; Rorem, *Pseudo-Dionysius*, 102.
81. *EH* 3, pp. 80.16–81.13, 425C–28A.
82. *EH* 3.3.2, p. 82.5–12, 428C.

sanctuary, a level of illumination below the highest unitive knowledge that cannot be transmitted.[83] The *Mystical Theology* does not show Moses turning to illumine others about what he has learned. Yet by the Dionysian text, Moses becomes a teacher who initiates the reader into the proper order of mystical ascent.

We thus see why Dionysius never distinguishes between a hierarchical or mediated path to God and a mystical or immediate way. The union described in the *Mystical Theology* is a liturgical reality, for Moses is a Syrian-rite bishop celebrating the Eucharist. Dionysius assumes that his readers would pick up on the liturgical allusions. The *Ecclesiastical Hierarchy* presupposes the reader's familiarity with the liturgical rite being described. The sacred veils of liturgical symbols and Scripture mediate a share of divine light, which in turn elevates us toward God. Once the divine ray is received through the mediations, it acts directly in the soul.[84] Hierarchy paradoxically leads to an unmediated encounter with God's light.

Moses and the priests ascend to God's place, which signifies the following:

the most divine and highest of what is seen and intelligible are hypothetical *logoi* (*hypothetikous tinas einai logous*) of what is subordinate to that beyond-having all. Through these is shown forth the presence of that which walks upon the intelligible summits of its most holy places. And then Moses abandons those who see and what is seen and enters into the really mystical darkness of unknowing (*gnophon tēs agnōsias*).[85]

Dionysius mentions three key elements: (1) the place (*topon*) where God "walks" or dwells; (2) darkness (*gnophon*); and (3) unknowing (*agnōsias*). Each element has a subjective and an objective element. Together they reveal the contemplative's spiritual capacities and limits while also expressing the relation between God's immanence and transcendence.[86]

God's place pertains to illumination, the summit of positive hu-

---

83. *EH* 5.2, p. 104.15–22, 501A–B; Rorem, *Pseudo-Dionysius*, 190. Golitzin, *Et introibo*, 171–74, 230, and Roques, "Denys l'Aréopagite," 283, also locate the *MT* at the heart of the *EH*.
84. De Andia, *Henosis*, 437–38.
85. *MT* 1.3, p. 144.5–10, 1000D–1001A, Jones, 214.
86. Puech, "Ténèbre mystique," 36–39.

man knowledge about him. It signifies both God's intelligible presence in the world through the divine powers and the fact that he is greater than this presence. This level stands for the world's intelligible order beyond sensible realities (beyond the sanctuary doors), for God's highest manifestation in creation. Dionysius states that God's place refers to the "hypothetical reason" (*hypothetikoi logoi*). Since this place or the *logoi* pertains to his presence in the cosmos by the divine powers, the *logoi* are the higher sources and objects of affirmative names. These include the names by which God's unifying power is made present to the believer. Thus the level of the *logoi* already enables a partial union with God.[87] God's place is the object of affirmations and their inseparable complementary negations. Since the transcendent God is beyond every human concept and discourse, God's place is below the divine mystery that it manifests.

Moses goes beyond God's place, the realm of God's powers, and penetrates darkness:

And then Moses abandons those who see and what is seen and enters into the really mystical darkness of unknowing; in this he shuts out every knowing apprehension (*kath hon apomuei pasas tas gnōstikas*) and comes to be in the wholly imperceptible and invisible, being entirely of that beyond all—of nothing, neither himself nor another, united most excellently by the completely unknowing inactivity of every knowledge (*tō pantelōs de agnōstō tē pasēs gnōseōs anenergēsia*), and knowing beyond intellect (*hyper noūn ginōskōn*) by knowing nothing.[88]

Darkness signifies the silent state of the ascending intellect and God's absolute transcendence. Earlier, Bartholomew explains that the God hidden in darkness is beyond all affirmations and negations.[89] This means

---

87. De Andia, *Henosis*, 114, 345–47, 357–59; Roques, "Contemplation," 1907. Larchet, in *La théologie des énergies divines*, 326–29, argues that the divine light or darkness that Moses enters is one of the divine powers in the *DN*. He thus conflates the light and darkness of union with the manifestive powers that pertain to God's place. Larchet assigns the light of the *MT* a Palamasian meaning: an uncreated divine energy. His hermeneutic of harmonization cannot account for the gap between God's "place" and darkness. If the Dionysian powers were truly equivalent to Palamas's energies, as Larchet suggests, then the Areopagite's Moses would leave the energies behind in order to meet God in darkness, the darkness that is in fact light and is thus beyond every power.

88. *MT* 1.3, p. 144.9–15, 1001A, Jones, 214.

89. *MT* 1.3, p. 143.9–17, 1000C.

that the negative way in its two senses is below the stage of total silence and a precondition for it. The primacy of silence recalls that affirmations, their complementary negations, and transcending negations all fall short of union. Any type of divine naming remains a discursive mode of understanding, while mystical union is beyond all discourse.[90]

Moses ascends by negations.[91] According to chapter 2 of the *Mystical Theology*, we attain a vision of God's hidden beauty when celebrating him by removing or negating all things of God. Chapter 2 employs various grammatical forms of *aphaireseis* or transcending negations, but not terms related to *apophaseis*. Transcending negations directly precede the divine vision but are not its sufficient cause.[92] Hence they also pertain to God's place. The perfect (liturgical) use and understanding of transcending negations quiets and elevates the mind, imparting the ultimate *disposition* for the reception of the highest gift.[93]

The patriarch then leaves behind all things and goes out of himself so as to attain union. The mind lets go of its own act, for the latter cannot attain the divine mystery sought.[94] This ecstasy recalls the discussion in the *Divine Names* of Paul's saying that Christ lives in him, an ecstatic union caused by divine love.[95] Thus charity makes a quiet appearance in the *Mystical Theology*. In darkness Moses knows God by unknowing. Dionysius excludes a privative reading of darkness. In *Epistle 5* he explains that God's darkness and unapproachable light are identical. Darkness is a paradoxical expression of God's transcendence, of a positive reality.[96] God's light is called darkness because his limitless essence exceeds our grasp. Darkness expresses the immense power of divine light, but from our perspective. Thus Moses enters into blinding light. Because the transcendent God dwells "there" (in a meta-

90. De Andia, *Henosis*, 393; Puech, "Ténèbre mystique," 39–46; Riordan, *Divine Light*, 46.
91. De Andia, *Henosis*, 342; Riordan, *Divine Light*, 187.
92. *MT* 2, p. 145, 1025A–B. The link between *apophasis* and affirmation, the superiority of *aphairesis* over both, and the absence of *apophasis* in *MT* 2 suggest that *apophasis* pertains to God's place, while *aphairesis* and divine gifts constitute the final ladder to the summit. However, this is not clear in the secondary literature, partly because few scholars have distinguished the two types of negations as neatly as de Andia has done.
93. De Andia, *Henosis*, 380, 386.
94. *MT* 1.1, p. 142.9–11, 1000A; Roques, "Contemplation," 1899–1900.
95. *DN* 7.1, p. 194.12–15, 865D–68A; de Andia, *Henosis*, 354–55.
96. *EP* 5, p. 162.1, 1073A; see also *MT* 1.1, p. 142.1, 997B.

phor), the patriarch's encounter with God is not an absolute ignorance, for then God would hardly be above negations. Moses knows "nothing" insofar as unknowing surpasses all previous illuminations. Hence this is a knowing "beyond mind" (*hyper noūn*). Moses knows that God is beyond all things that can be grasped by the intellect or sense perception.[97] He knows in the deepest sense that God is transcendent, a cognition that cannot be contained in human concepts, for it implies God's infinity.[98] At the peak of ascent Dionysius moves toward Gregory of Nyssa, who holds that the truest knowledge of God is the act of not comprehending him.[99] However, the aim of the Areopagite's teaching is not the attainment of an intellectual act whereby one reflectively recognizes God's incomprehensibility in a higher way. Rather, Dionysius exhorts the reader to let go of all noetic activity when divine light invades the soul. God directly teaches the mystic about divine incomprehensibility. This highest knowledge is not the result of a human noetic act, but of spiritual light flooding the mind.[100] The unknowing knowing of the wholly Unknown and union with the Unknown are identical. This may even be the central insight of the *Mystical Theology*.[101]

Union with super-divine light occurs in silence, which is a form of prayer in Neoplatonism. Dionysius invites his readers to imitate the angels in quiet adoration before the divine mystery.[102] He does not refer to a meditative technique. He invokes complete silence only in relation to union beyond mind. The key term is neither silence, nor beyond mind, but union (*henōsis*). Silence without union would only be a ceasing of the human word, not a share in the life of the unknown God. Since union is with the ineffable God, it occurs in silence. Dionysius describes union with God as a kind of cognition. As a good Platonist he was convinced that knowledge is always participatory.[103] Indeed, in the Greek intellectual tradition, cognition is the highest form of on-

---

97. *EP* 5, p. 162.1–10, 1073A; de Andia, *Henosis*, 350–51; Puech, "Ténèbre mystique," 40–41.
98. Rorem, *Pseudo-Dionysius*, 212.
99. Puech, "Ténèbre mystique," 51.
100. *EP* 5, p. 162.1–10, 1073A; de Andia, *Henosis*, 418, 431–32.
101. *MT* 1.1, p. 142.8, 997B; 1.3, p. 144.13–15, 1001A; de Andia, *Henosis*, 352.
102. De Andia, *Henosis*, 394–97.
103. De Andia, *Henosis*, 401, 417–18; see also *DN* 4.11, p. 156.15–19, 708D; 7.3, p. 198.4, 872A.

tological union (short of a conjunction of substances).[104] The mystic moves beyond his or her own words about God so as to be joined to the unutterable Word. Divinization and the highest gifted knowledge are precisely what cause union. Thus Dionysius sees divinization as an operative perfection of the mind. Mystical contemplation is passive, not because the contemplative practices a passive method of meditation, but because the grandeur of the gift cannot but be passively received. Active human knowledge remains stuck within human limitations. Hence mystical union is a sheer gift that cannot be taught.[105] God shuts down the mind's human act so that it can attain a more intense divinized state where it truly shares in divine knowledge, a cognition that cannot be described in human words. God alone fully empties the mind precisely by filling it with light.

LINGERING QUESTIONS

The brevity of the *Mystical Theology* leaves open a few questions concerning union. If Moses is a hierarch, does Dionysius restrict union to the clergy? How long does union last? Are we dealing with a barely Christianized ascent to the Monad wherein the Trinity becomes secondary? What is the function of history in the Dionysian universe, especially the place of the incarnate Word? What about eschatology? I will briefly take up these questions in this order.

The liturgical setting of the *Mystical Theology* resolves one problem while creating another. It excludes a dualistic anthropology but seems to restrict union to ordained ministers. Only Moses turned Syrian-rite bishop penetrates the darkness. All other individual mystics that Dionysius mentions are bishops or priests. The picture is complicated by the Areopagite's theology of monasticism. The monk enjoys a mystical knowledge apparently equaled only by that of bishops. Thus union is not restricted to the clergy. Also, Dionysius seems to limit the laity's ascent to the level of "contemplation" (*theōria*), below the highest cognition, and cognition goes hand in hand with divinization. Thus it is not

---

104. André de Halleux, "Palamisme et Scolastique," in de Halleux, *Patrologie et œcuménisme: Recueil d'études,* Bibliotheca Ephemeridum Theologicarum Lovaniensium 93 (Leuven: Leuven University Press, 1990), 788.
105. De Andia, *Henosis,* 431; Roques, "Contemplation," 1894–95.

clear if the laity can attain the highest union. The Areopagite's mysticism probably suffers from a certain elitism.[106]

The duration of union is more ambiguous. René Roques maintains that it is rare and brief. Ysabel de Andia points out that Dionysius never refers to the Plotinian description of God suddenly ravishing the soul, but otherwise, she remains silent on the question of duration. Alexander Golitzin makes a speculative argument that Dionysius alludes to Christ's or the angels' sudden appearances in the Bible when referring to union, which seems to bring us back to Plotinus.[107] The division of opinion reflects the sparsity of textual evidence.

A trinitarian element is relatively absent from the Areopagite's description of assimilation to God. Dionysius emphasizes the unity of the divine persons in their economic activity, partly to uphold the absolute equality of the three persons. He also has the beginnings of a theology of appropriation.[108] Clearly the Areopagite's God beyond all names *is* the Trinity, for the triune God's power alone enables ascent to the unknown God, as the opening lines of the *Mystical Theology* show. But the Trinity does not clearly structure the mode of mystical ascent.

The Areopagite's theology has often been dismissed as ahistorical. He appears to propose a fixed metaphysical vision of the universe that leaves little place for the contingency of history. On the one hand, this critique overlooks the fact that the celestial and ecclesiastical hierarchies depend on Jesus for their being and illuminating power. Furthermore, the ecclesiastical hierarchy consists of a historically instituted set of rites. Also, the divine names are treated as biblically revealed names, even if their exposition is heavily marked by Platonic metaphysics. None of these mediations are optional for contemplative ascent. On the other hand, the precise role of Jesus in his historical humanity remains vague in the Dionysian corpus.[109] However, the charge of monophysite Christology does not hit the mark.[110]

Finally, the Dionysian corpus suffers from a relative neglect of escha-

---

106. *CH* 3.3, p. 19.9–13, 165D; *EH* 6.3.3–6.3.5, pp. 118.6–19.15, 536A–37A; Roques, "Denys l'Aréopagite," 284; Roques, *L'univers dionysien*, 127, 234–40.

107. De Andia, *Henosis*, 247; Golitzin, *Et introibo*, 225–29; Roques, "Denys l'Aréopagite," 284.

108. De Andia, *Henosis*, 48–49, 240.

109. *CH* 1.2, p. 7.9, 121A; Riordan, *Divine Light*, 192; Roques, "Denys l'Aréopagite," 280.

110. Roques, *L'univers dionysien*, 313–15.

tology. On the one hand, it probably recounts Mary's Dormition and offers a long discussion of the funeral rite.[111] On the other hand, Dionysius only once mentions the saints' vision in glory and offers few details on this theme. The widespread opinion that, in Dionysian eschatology, the beatific vision is always mediated by divine theophanies or energies is not without problems. For while all celestial illuminations pass through the angels, these gifts probably refer to divine decisions, while God's divinizing light reaches human beings without angelic intermediaries.[112] Lights *analogous* to those streaming from the transfigured Christ enable the blessed to reach equality with the angelic vision and to touch God's light directly, though without attaining God's essence. Here rays of light (*aktinōn*) enable participation in God's own light. Whether the hiddenness of God's essence excludes all direct vision of that essence or just comprehensive vision remains uncertain.[113] Consequently it becomes more difficult to evaluate and analyze the Areopagite's understanding of union in this life from the perspective of perfect eschatological union.

CONCLUSION

Dionysius sets out the ontological, epistemological, and ethical preconditions and characteristics of union as he offers a mystical doctrine more than a psychology of extraordinary phenomena.[114] The highest union with God in this life occurs "beyond mind," though it imparts intelligible, ineffable light. The Areopagite's quasi-dialectical method prevents a resolution of the paradox between God's immanence and transcendence, affirmations, and negations. The mystic must pass through the mediations of the Bible and the liturgy, tradition, and creation toward the holy mystery that these veils manifest and conceal. The Dionysian tradition will wrestle with the same challenge of granting the mediations their due without reducing the hidden God to an idol.

111. *DN* 3.2, p. 141.6–17, 681D–84A; *EH* 7, pp. 120.13–32.6, 552D–69A; Golitzin, *Et introibo*, 214–18.

112. *EH* 4.3.2, p. 97.4–18, 476B–C; de Andia, *Henosis*, 234, 254, 438.

113. *DN* 1.4, pp. 114.7–15.5, 592B–C; Christian Trottmann, *La vision béatifique: Des disputes scolastiques à sa définition par Benoît XII*, Bibliothèque des Écoles françaises d'Athènes et de Rome 248 (Rome: École Française de Rome, 1995), 45–50. De Andia attributes to modern Orthodox scholars the restriction of the beatific vision to God's energies; *Henosis*, 254. Her remarks on the Areopagite's position remain inconclusive.

114. Von Balthasar, *Glory of the Lord*, 2:206–7.

2

Key Developments in the Dionysian Tradition up to Albert the Great

Albert and Aquinas appropriated the Areopagite's mystical theology seven hundred years after the first publication of the Dionysian corpus. Their understanding of the Greek father becomes more comprehensible in light of the rich tradition of translation and commentary that bridged these centuries. I will focus on those elements of the late antique and early medieval Dionysian tradition that directly pertain to Albert's and Thomas's interpretations of union. Like chapter 1, this survey of key doctrinal themes and historical developments mostly summarizes the results of contemporary research. The present chapter has a strictly preparatory function for parts 2 and 3 of this study. I will begin with an overview of the translations and commentaries accessible to Albert and Aquinas. I will then proceed to discuss the key mystical doctrines of those texts in chronological order, from sixth-century Syria to thirteenth-century Paris.

AN OVERVIEW OF THE DIONYSIAN TEXTUAL TRADITION AND ITS EARLY COMMENTATORS

The Areopagite's corpus was first transmitted exclusively via two manuscript traditions: the Greek edition by John, bishop of Scythopolis, edited between 536 and 553, and a Syriac version from the same era.[1] Like all later Greek editions, every medieval Latin edition of the corpus depends on John's. His corpus contains the Areopagite's text with variant readings and the bishop's *scholia* in the margins. Maximos the Confessor may have added further *scholia*. Between 867 and 875 the papal librarian Anastasius translated the *scholia* by John (and perhaps Maximos), placing them in the margins of John Scotus Eriugena's Latin translation of Dionysius. He also wrote an interlinear gloss explaining Eriugena's translation. This gloss may include some Greek (Maximian?) *scholia*, as well. Finally, the papal librarian added his own *scholia* and other Greek *scholia*, perhaps authored by Andrew of Crete or Germanus I. He identified the *scholia* attributed to Maximos with a sign of the cross.[2] Most *scholia* probably come from John.[3]

The first major or "old" Latin Dionysian corpus thus included Eriugena's translation, Anastasius's gloss, and the latter's translation of the Greek *scholia*. It was transmitted via Parisian, Italian, and German manuscripts.[4] Before 1240 an unidentified Parisian scholar expanded the Latin translation of Greek *scholia*, adding about one hundred excerpts from Eriugena's *Periphyseon*, including twenty-four for the *Mystical Theology*. The Parisian scholar did not distinguish between the anonymous Eriugena extracts and the *scholia* by John of Scythopolis, Anastasius, and perhaps Maximos. All these extracts and *scholia* were simply

1. István Perczel, "The Earliest Syriac Reception of Dionysius," in *Re-Thinking Dionysius the Areopagite*, edited by Sarah Coakley and Charles M. Stang, 27–28 (London: Wiley-Blackwell, 2009); Suchla, *Dionysius*, 62–69.

2. Suchla, *Dionysius*, 62–66, 79–81; L. Michael Harrington, introduction to *A Thirteenth Century Textbook of Mystical Theology at the University of Paris: The "Mystical Theology" of Dionysius the Areopagite in Eriugena's Latin Translation with the Scholia translated by Anastasius the Librarian and Excerpts from Eriugena's "Periphyseon,"* edited by L. Michael Harrington, Dallas Medieval Texts and Translations 4 (Leuven: Peeters, 2004), 16–18, 26–27, 35–36; Hyacinthe F. Dondaine, *Le Corpus Dionysien de l'Université de Paris au XIIIe siècle* (Rome: Edizioni di Storia e letteratura, 1953), 92–93.

3. For an English translation of John's Greek *scholia*, see John C. Lamoreaux and Paul P. Rorem, eds., *John of Scythopolis and the Dionysian Corpus: Annotating the Areopagite*, Oxford Early Christian Studies (Oxford: Oxford University Press, 1998). Doctrinal comparisons between *scholia* attributed to Maximos and his authentic works remain inconclusive; see Suchla, *Die sogenannten Maximus-Scholien des Corpus Dionysiacum Areopagiticum* (Göttingen: Vandenhoeck and Ruprecht, 1980), 8–9, 29.

4. The old corpus is found in Paris BnF lat. 1618 and Cologne Cathedral Library Codex 30.

attributed to "Maximus."[5] I will call these *scholia,* distinct from the interlinear gloss, the *Parisian Scholia.*

The *Parisian Scholia* were part of a veritable thirteenth-century handbook of Dionysian theology, or "new corpus," that I will call the *Parisian Corpus Dionysiacum.* It survives in several manuscripts and includes: (1) Abbot Hilduin's preface to his ninth-century Latin translation of Dionysius; (2) Anastasius's and Eriugena's letters to Charles the Bald on their corpus; (3) Eriugena's full translation of Dionysius; (4) Anastasius's interlinear gloss mingled with later glosses by anonymous Latin authors; (5) the *Parisian Scholia,* inserted into the body of the work, yet clearly distinct from the Areopagite's text and interlinear gloss; (6) John Sarracenus's full twelfth-century translation of Dionysius, which is less literal but more accessible than Eriugena's; (7) the commentaries on Dionysius's *Celestial Hierarchy* by Eriugena, Hugh of St. Victor, and Sarracenus; and (8) the *Extractio* or paraphrase on the Areopagite by the thirteenth-century Victorine Thomas Gallus, covering all but *Epistles 1–8* and *10–11,* composed around 1238.[6]

Albert and Aquinas resided in Paris in the mid-1240s, just as the *Parisian Corpus Dionysiacum* became available. Albert's Parisian *Sentences Commentary* refers to the translations by Eriugena and Sarracenus and to the *Parisian Scholia,* but not to the *Extractio.*[7]

In the late 1240s Albert commented on the entire Dionysian corpus while in Cologne. His commentaries on the *Celestial Hierarchy* and the

---

5. Dondaine, *Corpus Dionysien,* 69–71, 88–89, 101, 118.

6. Ibid., 15–20, 101. Harrington has published the *Parisian Scholia* and interlinear gloss for the *MT* and part of the *DN* in *Thirteenth Century Textbook* and for the *EH* in *On the Ecclesiastical Hierarchy: The Thirteenth-Century Paris Textbook Edition,* edited by L. Michael Harrington, Dallas Medieval Texts and Translations 12 (Leuven: Peeters, 2011). The spurious *Epistle 11* may have been inserted into the Dionysian corpus before its arrival in the West. Eriugena translated it. However, *Epistle 11* is insignificant for my study.

7. Dondaine, *Corpus Dionysien,* 101–8, 122–28. The surviving Saint Jacques Priory manuscript with the new corpus (Paris BnF lat. 17341) comes from the second half of the thirteenth century. It is a copy of a mid-thirteenth-century text, probably also belonging to Saint Jacques; Dondaine, *Corpus Dionysien,* 15–16. Maria Burger's forthcoming critical edition of bk. I of Albertus Magnus's *Sentences Commentary* identifies one explicit reference to "Maximus" (*Parisian Scholia*) at d. 2, a. 11, objection 1, p. 51.49. Albertus Magnus's *SCH* cites "Maximos" three times. Other references to the *Parisian Scholia* in his Dionysian commentaries simply invoke "the Commentator," as noted in the works' indices.

Ecclesiastical Hierarchy are based on Eriugena's translation, with some references to the Sarracenus version. His other Dionysian commentaries reverse this procedure. Each commentary includes several citations of the Greek *scholia*. While in Cologne Albert employed a German version of the complete "old corpus," a manuscript still available to us, but also had some access to the "new corpus." The German manuscript just mentioned includes, between the lines, a few alternate readings of the Dionysian text written in Aquinas's hand derived from the "new corpus." These alternate readings are reflected in Albert's Cologne commentaries and based partly on *Parisian Scholia* and interlinear glosses (i.e., from the "new corpus") not contained in the "old corpus."[8] This also confirms that Thomas was familiar with the *Parisian Corpus Dionysiacum*. However, Albert may have mediated the references to the *Parisian Scholia* in Aquinas's personal works.[9] Thomas also might have had access to the "old corpus" and its Greek *scholia* in Italy as he wrote his *Commentary on the Divine Names*, but this remains uncertain.[10]

Five doctrinal elements of the Dionysian tradition before Albert deserve consideration. First, John of Scythopolis's *scholia* on the *Mystical Theology* and the *Divine Names* reinsert a human noetic act into union (section 2 of this chapter). Next, some anonymous *Parisian Scholia* tame certain aspects of the Areopagite's apophatism (section 3). Also, the *Parisian Scholia* constitute the most significant transmission of Maximos's mysticism available to theologians in mid-thirteenth-century Paris. I will examine to what extent the Confessor's Dionysian exegesis emerges in the *Parisian Scholia* via *Periphyseon* excerpts (sec-

---

8. Maria Burger, "Thomas Aquinas's Glosses on the Dionysius Commentaries of Albert the Great in Codex 30 of the Cologne Cathedral Library," in *Via Alberti: Texte—Quellen—Interpretationen*, edited by Ludger Honnefelder, Hannes Möhle, and Susana Bullido del Barrio, 565–74, Subsidia Albertina 2 (Münster: Aschendorff, 2009). Albert seems to have gained access to part and perhaps eventually to the entire "new corpus" while commenting on Dionysius in 1248–50. The alternate readings of Codex 30 only make sense if Albert does not have full access to the new corpus early on during his Cologne stay, as he commented on the *CH* and the *EH*. The subsequent *SMT* includes at least one reference to a *scholium* by Eriugena, a passage not found in Codex 30 (*SMT*, ch. 5, p. 474.56–67; *PMT*, ch. 5, p. 100). I am grateful to Maria Burger of the Albertus Magnus Institute in Bonn for her insights on this matter.

9. Dondaine, *Corpus Dionysien*, 102–3, 120–21.

10. Gabriel Théry, "Le manuscrit Vat. grec 370 et saint Thomas d'Aquin," *Archives d'histoire doctrinale et littéraire du moyen âge* 6 (1931): 5–23.

tion 4). Finally, Eriugena's translation opens the door for an "affective" reading of Dionysius. Indeed, the *Parisian Corpus Dionysiacum* witnesses to the birth of "Affective Dionysianism," with key works by Hugh of St. Victor and Thomas Gallus (section 5). I thus proceed to a chronologically ordered analysis of the pre-Albertian Dionysian tradition on key union themes.

THE RETURN OF INTELLECT IN THE *SCHOLIA* BY JOHN OF SCYTHOPOLIS

John of Scythopolis revalorizes the intellect's own activity during union. Two exegetical moves (found in the *Parisian Scholia*) promote this project: the removal of noetic ecstasy and the introduction of multiple definitions for Moses's experience in darkness.

First, John quietly takes the ecstatic element out of Dionysian union. The mind is silent when flooded with divine light, but the contemplative is no longer taken out of himself. John supports this interpretation by a previous identification of the Plotinian cosmic mind with the divine mind. He thus separates Dionysius from the Plotinian doctrine of the One beyond mind and places greater emphasis on union's noetic content than Dionysius seems to have intended. The result is a domestication of the Areopagite's paradoxes.[11]

Second, John's *scholia* on the *Divine Names* distinguish three forms of unknowing. The first kind is a defect: one fails to know what can be known. A second kind of unknowing involves a positive cognition, the realization *that* God is unknowable. As noted in chapter 1 of this volume, for Dionysius this is one of the higher forms of cognition about God, but it remains below unitive cognition. The third type of unknowing surpasses the "motions of reason" wherein one ponders different divine attributes, one after another. The intellect attains simplicity by no longer thinking *about* God, but apparently it does not stop operating. Rather, noetic activity rests in a single inexpressible act of knowing. The Dionysian exhortation to abandon all thought only applies to scattered multiple thoughts, not to thought as such. This high-

---

11. Harrington, introduction to *Thirteenth Century Textbook*, 20; Lamoreaux and Rorem, eds., *John of Scythopolis*, 219–21.

est form of unknowing involves silent union with God, where one becomes "the form of the one who is before all things."[12] The last phrase could suggest that a divine act takes over the human mind, so that all created noetic acts cease, but the first interpretation seems more likely.

One *scholium* by John offers a striking summary of the third kind of unknowing. John explains Moses's separation from the crowd and entry into darkness:

> Moses contemplated the place where God stood, then he was freed from what we look at—that is, everything sensuous—and from what does the looking—that is, everything that reasons. Then he entered the darkness—that is, the unknowing, which concerns God. Here he put aside all aids or supports of knowledge.... He was united through such a mode to unknowing and inactivity or inefficacy—that is, to the one who is altogether unknown to all understanding, and who is the highest of all and supreme. Moses then knew everything by unknowing.[13]

Instead of intellectual ecstasy, union enables the contemplative to know everything (!) in a simple, indescribable way. John seems to imply that the intellect continues its created operations, now supernaturally elevated to the maximum level by the highest noetic object.

Another *scholium* on the *Divine Names* appears to conflate the second and third type of unknowing. Contact with the divine rays, which for Dionysius are received in the mind's ecstasy, comes about through a Plotinian turn inward that leads to the mind's simplification and stabilization, or not being scattered in reasoning. The enjoyment of divine light seems to be accompanied by a knowing that one does not know whatever in the divine mystery remains beyond our reach.[14] This notion of interiority is typical of Plotinus's universal mind, now applied

---

12. *PDN*, ch. 2, 120; see also Lamoreaux and Rorem, eds., *John of Scythopolis*, 195–96; Harrington, introduction, *Thirteenth Century Textbook*, 20–22.

13. *PMT*, ch. 1, 66–67: "quia Moyses, contemplatus locum ubi stabat deus, et dein absolutus ab his quae conspiciebantur—id est sensibilibus omnibus—atque conspicientibus—id est rationabilibus universis—tunc in caliginem introivit—id est in ignorantiam quae est de deo—ubi, omnibus depositis cognoscibilibus auxiliis seu susceptionibus.... Et unitus per talem modum ignorantiae et inoperationi seu inefficaciae—id est ei qui omnino est ignotus ab omni scientia et universorum summus atque supremus—tunc ignorantia omnem cognovit." I retain the odd terminology *dein* and *inoperationi* as given by Harrington's edition; see also Lamoreaux and Rorem, eds., *John of Scythopolis*, 244.

14. *PDN*, ch. 4, 122; see also Lamoreaux and Rorem, eds., *John of Scythopolis*, 206–7.

to the individual contemplative.[15] John inserts a non-Dionysian inward turn between (1) the (scattered) act of knowing God through creation and (2) contemplative ascent to noetic silence.

John's twofold and threefold divisions of "unknowing" as well as the elimination of the mind's ecstasy all suggest a systematic program to bring the human intellect's own act back into union. A kataphatic turn in the Dionysian tradition appears to begin with John of Scythopolis.[16] His *scholia* also operate a shift in theological style away from paradoxical dialectic and toward distinctions, a style that favors doctrinal clarity. Both the kataphatic reading and this new theological method set precedents for the exegesis of Albert and Thomas.

ANONYMOUS LATIN *SCHOLIA* AND GLOSSES: TAMING THE AREOPAGITE

Two key themes in the anonymous *Parisian Scholia* and glosses deserve consideration: (1) a more explicit connection between affirmative, negative, and eminent names than can be found in Dionysius; and (2) the qualification of key apophatic statements in the *Mystical Theology*. First, some *scholia* propose a subtle synthesis of affirmative, negative, and eminent divine names. Eminence includes affirmation and negation. The superlative names allow us to continue the practice of affirming certain characteristics of God, though without adequately expressing the divine attributes. For example, the term *super* in *superessentialis* signifies this inadequacy *and* refers to the (positive) existence of a divine attribute. The prefix functions as the negation of a complete definition of God's being, thus excluding any opposition between eminent, negative, and positive names.[17] Second, a number of the Areopagite's most perplexing negations and images receive significant nuance in the *Parisian Corpus Dionysiacum*. The interlinear gloss twice refers to God's incomprehensibility to explain the darkness on Mt. Sinai.[18] In one *scholium* we learn that God not being in a place or not being seen refers to the impossibility of circumscribing or defining him.[19] This doctrine is in harmony with

15. Harrington, introduction, *Thirteenth Century Textbook*, 21.
16. Lamoreaux and Rorem, eds., *John of Scythopolis*, 243–44.
17. *PMT*, ch. 1, 52; ch. 5, 102.   18. *PMT*, ch. 1, 58, 60.
19. *PMT*, ch. 4, 96.

Dionysius, yet the Greek father places further restrictions on human knowing that the *scholia* do not clearly bring out.

Overall this new approach to superlative names and the interpretation of some highly apophatic Dionysian phrases to signify our inability to define or comprehend God strengthen the place and permanence of affirmative names in mystical ascent. Thus the "new corpus" in Paris also tightens the connection between active human knowledge about God and the gift of unitive light.

THE PARISIAN RECEPTION OF MAXIMOS THE CONFESSOR'S DIONYSIAN EXEGESIS

I will develop two theses concerning Maximos. First, his reception of Dionysian mysticism includes a significant reinterpretation of the Areopagite's negative theology. Second, the martyr's mystical theology penetrated mid-thirteenth century Paris primarily via excerpts from Eriugena in the *Parisian Scholia*, yet these passages were so intermingled with the Irishman's apophatism and the kataphatism of John of Scythopolis that Maximos's doctrine of union became unrecognizable. The first point shows that the Maximian passages in the *Parisian Scholia* are far more than a synthesis of Dionysius. The second point deserves attention following Antoine Lévy's recent proposal that a failed encounter occurred between Maximian theology and mid-thirteenth-century Latin scholasticism, especially Albert and Aquinas.[20]

Maximos reshapes the apophatism of Dionysius partly as a result of the hermeneutics of continuity that he employs in his reading of the Cappadocians and the Areopagite.[21] He introduces a firm distinction between the notion *that God is* and *what God is,* or the divine *ousia.* God's causal activity shows *that* he is, not *what* he is. We know what comes after God, not what he is in himself. Thus, says Maximos, Gregory Nazianzen did not use any affirmation when speaking of God's hid-

---

20. Antoine Lévy, *Le créé et l'incréé: Maxime le Confesseur et Thomas d'Aquin; Aux sources de la querelle palamienne,* Bibliothèque Thomiste 59 (Paris: Vrin, 2006), 106–8, 484–86, develops the thesis of Marie-Dominique Chenu, "Le dernier avatar de la théologie orientale en Occident au XIIIe siècle," *Mélanges Auguste Pelzer* (Louvain: Bibliothèque de l'Université de Louvain), 159–81.

21. For Maximos's harmonizing hermeneutics, see Lévy, *Créé et l'incréé,* 135–36.

den essence. Hence affirmation only pertains to God's activity in the world, while negation pertains to theology or God in himself. For Dionysius, but not for Maximos, affirmations and negations are inseparable. This separation is only possible because the Confessor does not continue the Areopagite's distinction between *apophasis* and *aphairesis*. For Dionysius *apophasis* still concerns the realm of divine causality or processions, while *aphairesis* pertains to God above all beings, but not to the divine essence. *Aphairesis* has a positive element, as it points to God's transcendence. For Maximos, negations clear the way for mystic silence wherein God teaches us directly.[22] He thus employs an interpretive method that John of Scythopolis also uses: he transforms Dionysian paradox and quasi-dialect into clear doctrinal distinctions.

Maximos's new negative theology has direct consequences for his theology of union. He proposes two ways to know God. The first cognition is grounded upon an understanding of God in his energies that begins with our experience of created being. This first union involves the human intellect's act. The second type of union is higher and "true." It involves a direct ineffable "experience" or "sensation" of God, a divinely given cognition that excludes every created word and thought. Uncreated light imparts a real knowledge of God (*theologia*). This cognition penetrates all the way to God's uncreated glory, light, or energies, but not to his hidden essence. In the next life this second type of union will also be the means by which the saints are deified. For Maximos as for Dionysius, union does not exclude all knowledge, since the divinized human being receives the highest cognition.[23]

Finally, Maximos proposes a major Christological development in mystical theology. God's energies elevate the contemplative's created energies to a supernatural level. The human energies retain their integrity, just as Christ's created and uncreated energies remained distinct. Furthermore, our created energies fully depend on God's energies for divinization. Given God's transformation of our created operational capacities, we can truly possess the uncreated energies and thus arrive at *theologia* or the knowledge of the divine *logoi*, even in this life. The divinized soul attains this eminent supernatural cognition with its creat-

---

22. De Andia, *Denys l'Aréopagite*, 156–57, 164–65, 170.
23. Larchet, *La Divinisation de l'homme selon saint Maxime le Confesseur*, Cogitatio Fidei 194 (Paris: Cerf, 1996), 499–518; de Andia, *Denys l'Aréopagite*, 163–64.

ed noetic acts.[24] Maximos therefore only follows Dionysian silence in union insofar as he excludes knowledge acquired from the divine economy from the psychology of the unitive state. Like John of Scythopolis, Maximos inserts active human participation in the event of union, going beyond Dionysian passivity. However, while the doctrinal foundations of John's development may remain somewhat meager, the Confessor's proposal rests on his original doctrine of Christ's two energies, a doctrine officially received at the Third Council of Constantinople (680–681). He connects mystical theology with Christology far more than does the Areopagite.

But to what extent did Maximos's development of Dionysian mystical theology penetrate thirteenth-century Latin scholasticism? Eriugena translated the Confessor's *Ambigua ad Iohannem* and *Quaestiones ad Thalassium*. Yet by the middle of the thirteenth century these texts were only found in monastic libraries. Eriugena's *Periphyseon* includes substantial elements of Maximos's negative theology. But its mingling with quasi-pantheistic theologies by later thinkers led to the work's condemnations in 1210 and in 1225. By 1240 the main access that Parisian scholars had to Maximos came through the *Periphyseon* excerpts included in the *Parisian Scholia*.[25] Did these *scholia* clearly pass on the uniqueness of the Confessor's thought?

Some key Maximian elements of Eriugena's *Periphyseon* do emerge in the *Parisian Scholia*. One *scholium* on the *Mystical Theology* restricts all predication of the divine substance to the realm of metaphor. The divine nature is incomprehensible and ineffable. Here we cannot properly signify any truth.[26] Another *scholium* states that we learn that God is called truth metaphorically because he is the cause of truth. We deny the same name (truth) because of God's excellence or transcendence. Thus negations better signify the Creator beyond all.[27] Eriugena goes

---

24. Lévy, *Créé et l'incréé*, 191–201.
25. Édouard Jeauneau, "Pseudo-Dionysius, Gregory of Nyssa, and Maximos the Confessor in the works of John Scotus Eriugena," in *Études érigéniennes* (Paris: Institut d'Études Augustiniennes, 1987), 179–85; Lévy, *Créé et l'incréé*, 76–81, 88–92, 122.
26. *PMT*, ch. 3, 80 (citing Eriugena, *Periphyseon*, bk. I, pp. 80.20–82.12). I follow Harrington's references to the following edition: John Scotus Eriugena, *Periphyseon*, bks. I–IV, ed. I. P. Sheldon-Williams, Scriptores Latini Hiberniae 7, 9, 11, 13 (Dublin: Dublin Institute for Advanced Studies, 1972–95).
27. *PMT*, ch. 5, 102–4 (citing *Periphyseon*, bk. IV, pp. 36.31–38.20).

beyond Maximos in identifying all affirmations as metaphors, yet he remains faithful to one of the Confessor's main doctrinal intentions as he refuses all affirmative, proper discourse about God's essence. For Eriugena the divine substance is ineffable, so that we can only arrive at an understanding of God's *esse*, not his *quid est*. Rather than seek a definition of the divine substance, we should honor the indescribable Godhead in silence, for he is above intellect. In the same *scholium* the Irish scholar goes beyond Dionysius and Maximos: not even God knows his own *quid est*, for every substance is necessarily finite. Behind Eriugena stands a Platonic understanding of being as essentially limited.[28]

Two other *Parisian scholia* seem to reflect the theology of Maximos. One *scholium* explains that the term "deity" refers not to God's essence, but to his glory. The next *scholium* notes that neither higher powers (angels) nor human souls can know God's essence. What is the context of these *scholia*? They are preceded by the *Periphyseon* exclusion of proper affirmative names and followed by a text according to which God does not know beings as they are.[29]

What could Albert and Thomas make of such daring *scholia*? At least three elements complicate the matter considerably. First, the interlinear gloss consistently interprets the divine darkness on Mt. Sinai as the equivalent of God's incomprehensibility. For thirteenth-century scholastics, *incomprehensibilitas* signifies a lack of total knowledge, not the impossibility of direct cognitive access to an intelligible object and its essence. Second, one Greek *scholium* (probably by John of Scythopolis) calls both affirmative and negative names proper predications of divine greatness, contradicting Eriugena.[30] Third, another Greek *scholi-*

---

28. *PMT*, ch. 5, 108 (citing *Periphyseon*, bk. II, pp. 136.24–38.13, 142.35–44.16): "substantia [dei] per seipsam incognita indiffinibilisque subsistens esse tantum, non autem quid est, manifestatur ... silentio colat tantum ineffabilem et super intellectum omnisque summum scientiae divinae essentiae veritatem.... [Deus] seipsum autem non cognoscit aliquid esse. Nescit igitur quid ipse est.... Omne siquidem quod in aliquo substantialiter intelligitur ita ut proprie de eo praedicetur quid est, neque modum neque mensuram excedit."

29. *PMT*, ch. 5, 104–6. The *scholia* related to Maximos's doctrine cite PG 4:429.1 and PG 4:429.3.

30. *PMT*, ch. 1, 62 (citing PG 4:417.8): "Ipsa enim et positio est et depulsio, nam et proprie utraeque super divina dicuntur magnitudine"; see also ch. 2, 76 (citing PG 4:424.1): "Siquidem positiones sunt quaecumque proprie in deo dicuntur, quia est ut puta on, vita, lux et alia."

um identifies God's name exceeding cognition as "being."[31] These three elements not only oppose the apophatic *scholia* by Eriugena, but also open the door for a reappropriation of eminent names, which in turn opens the way for some cognitive access to God's substance. Consequently, Albert and Aquinas encountered a Maximos mingled with Eriugena's radical apophatism and other, rather kataphatic Greek *scholia* to the point that the Confessor's doctrine became unrecognizable. The Dominicans found *scholia* and glosses filled with internal doctrinal tensions, even an apparent denial of divine omniscience. The *Parisian Scholia* demanded clarification, correction, and development. There simply was no way to disentangle Maximos from John of Scythopolis and Eriugena. A direct encounter between Maximos, Albert, and Aquinas never happened.

Yet the *Parisian Scholia* do far more than obscure the Maximian heritage. They also transmit the Confessor's teaching on the eminent infused knowledge that is inseparable from divinization. In the silence that follows intellectual ecstasy, the contemplative enjoys a higher knowledge of divine truth.[32] Some *Parisian scholia* echo Eriugena's rehabilitation of intellect through the latter's harmonizing synthesis with Augustinian *mens*.[33] But the *Parisian Scholia* do not locate the event of eminent infused knowledge in the soul's contact with divine energies clearly distinct from God's essence, a centerpiece of Maximos's mysticism.[34]

Eriugena's rehabilitation of intellect complements the anthropology of John of Scythopolis. The human being's active participation in divinization does not emerge as clearly in their works as with Maximos, yet Eriugena and John tame the language of ecstasy. They thus lay the doctrinal groundwork that will help Albert and Thomas reinterpret Dionysian passivity. The *Periphyseon* excerpts also remain silent

---

31. *PMT*, ch. 3, 88 (citing PG 4:425.9).
32. *PMT*, ch. 5, 108 (citing *Periphyseon*, bk. II, pp. 136.24–38.13, 142.35–44.16).
33. *PMT*, ch. 1, 56 (citing *Periphyseon*, bk. IV, p. 42.8–26). On Eriugena's harmonizing hermeneutics, see Jeauneau, "Pseudo-Dionysius," 182–84.
34. According to Lévy, Albert and Aquinas failed to appropriate Maximos and sidestepped the *aporias* that the Greek *scholia* and *Periphyseon* presented to a Latin Augustinian world; Lévy, *Créé et l'incréé*, 106–8, 484–86). In fact, the *Parisian Scholia* never adequately transmitted Maximos's uncreated/created antinomy, the antinomy that Lévy thinks Albert and Thomas abandoned. Albert's and Aquinas's Maximos is really a hybrid of John of Scythopolis, Eriugena, the Confessor, and other anonymous commentators.

on Maximos's Christological developments. Thus any accidental medieval scholastic convergence with Maximos will require a *ressourcement* of the early Ecumenical Councils' Christological teachings, one that Aquinas will undertake.

ERIUGENA AND AFFECTIVE DIONYSIANISM

In the twelfth and thirteenth centuries the Dionysian tradition undergoes an "affective turn" in its understanding of divine union. This interpretive school may have received an unintended inspiration from the Areopagite's first reliable Latin translator, Eriugena. In chapter 2 of the *Divine Names* the Irish sholar translates the Greek phrase about Hierotheus's experience of "not only learning but suffering divine things" as "not only learning but also an affection (*affectus*) for divine things."[35] Eriugena's decision to connect the notion of *affectus* with Hierotheus will mark the likes not only of Gallus, but also Albert and Aquinas, as we will see.[36] This element in Eriugena's translation helps to lay the groundwork for a new hermeneutic of Dionysian mysticism. Contemporary studies of the Dionysian corpus locate the heart of its theology of union in the *Mystical Theology*. The *Divine Names* periodically previews this union. Yet things were less clear for the Latin medievals. The affective reading of suffering divine things builds a textual bridge between Hierotheus's experience in chapter 2 and ecstatic love in chapter 4 of the *Divine Names* (the teaching on love is explicitly attributed to Hierotheus). The path is now clear for Hierotheus's affective union to function as the entryway for Dionysian mysticism, especially through an affective reading of union beyond mind in the *Divine Names* and the *Mystical Theology*. Thus the *Divine Names* can displace the priority of the *Mystical Theology*.

The mid-thirteenth-century *Parisian Corpus Dionysiacum* was the fruit of a revival in Dionysian theology that had begun a century earlier. Eriugena's monumental work of translation and commentary had been followed by two hundred years of relative silence on the Areopagite, until Hugh of St. Victor (d. 1141) launched a veritable Dionysian

---

35. Dionysius Areopagita, *Divine Names*, 2.7, in *Dionysiaca*, edited by Philippe Chevallier, 1:104 (Paris: Desclée de Brouwer, 1937).

36. De Andia, *Denys l'Aréopagite*, 32–33.

renaissance. It naturally centered in Paris, the supposed place of the Areopagite's last pastoral activity and martyrdom. Hugh's contribution emerged in the context of the Victorine School. The Victorine and Cistercian masters formed the two most important schools of twelfth-century mystical theology. Significantly, both schools centered their doctrines of divine union on love, not knowledge. Both exerted a deep influence on thirteenth-century scholasticism and medieval monastic piety.[37]

Hugh's key contribution to the Dionysian tradition is his *Commentary on the Celestial Hierarchy*. The bulk of the work consists of a careful exposition of the Areopagite's thought, with few insertions of Hugh's own speculative doctrine, giving the impression that the commentator disappears in order to let "the first bishop of Paris" speak. An exception to this approach comes precisely in the discussion of love's relation to knowledge within contemplative ascent. Hugh offers extensive excursions on the seraphim exceeding the cherubim in the heavenly hierarchy. The seraphim symbolize love penetrating where knowledge (symbolized by the cherubim) cannot go. Also, Hugh proposes Paul's experience of being raptured into the third heaven (2 Cor 12:2) as a source for this doctrine of union, a doctrine that Paul transmitted to Dionysius, his disciple. Thus Hugh attributes his theology of love exceeding knowledge to an oral apostolic tradition, implicitly identifying it as public revelation. For Hugh this revelation came to Paul through the apostle's attainment of the contemplative summit that is the experience of rapture. God himself showed Paul that love is higher than knowledge![38]

None of this can be found in Dionysius. The real source of Hugh's mysticism is the Latin tradition rooted in Augustine and Gregory the Great. Hugh develops this tradition in various works as he consistently argues for love's priority over knowledge in contemplation. However, he does not have the will take over the intellect's functions. Rather, their respective operations enjoy a certain simplification or fusion within which love has priority.[39] With the exception of his *Commentary*

---

37. Rorem, "The Early Latin Dionysius: Eriugena and Hugh of St. Victor," in Coakley and Stang, *Re-Thinking Dionysius*, 74; McGinn, *Presence of God*, vol. 2, *Growth of Mysticism*, 156.
38. Rorem, "Early Latin Dionysius," 75–81.
39. Dominique Poirel, *Hugues de Saint-Victor* (Paris: Cerf, 1998), 120–22.

on the Celestial Hierarchy, all of Hugh's works are thoroughly Augustinian.[40]

Hugh effectively became the founder of affective medieval Dionysianism, inspiring a broad mystical tradition carried forward by the likes of Gallus, Robert Grosseteste, Bonaventure, and the anonymous work *The Cloud of Unknowing.* The movement would eventually impact Teresa of Avila and John of the Cross, thanks to popular vernacular writings by sixteenth-century Franciscan proponents of *recogimiento* spirituality steeped in the works of Gallus and Hugh of Balma.[41]

Still, the primary architect and first systematizer of this "school" was not Hugh, but Thomas Gallus (d. 1246). A contemporary of Albert, Gallus dedicated much of his entire theological career to the Areopagite. He was the first Latin theologian to comment on the entire Dionysian corpus. He has left us the first datable Latin commentary on the *Mystical Theology.* By its inclusion in the *Parisian Corpus Dionysiacum,* Gallus's *Extractio* or paraphrase on the Areopagite was guaranteed a widespread influence.[42] It also ensured Albert's and Thomas's access to the thought of Gallus before their transfer from Paris to Cologne in 1248.

Gallus systematically integrates Hugh's Gregorian-Cistercian notion of love as knowledge into his exegesis of Dionysian union passages. Commenting on Moses's ascent into darkness, the *Extractio* identifies God's "place" as the eternal exemplars of creatures in the eternal Word, which render God cognitively present to us. These intelligibles must be left behind, for the contemplative must surpass all divine lights—that is, even the lights of Scripture that are at the foundation of the *Divine Names.*[43] By grace the soul is united to the incomprehen-

40. McGinn, *Presence of God,* vol. 2, *Growth of Mysticism,* 384–95; Rorem, "Early Latin Dionysius," 78–81.

41. Luis M. Girón-Negrón, "Dionysian Thought in Sixteenth-Century Spanish Mystical Theology," in Coakley and Stang, *Re-Thinking Dionysius,* 164–74; Rorem, *Pseudo-Dionysius,* 219–22.

42. Boyd Taylor Coolman, "The Medieval Affective Dionysian Tradition," in Coakley and Stang, *Re-Thinking Dionysius,* 88–90; James McEvoy, introduction to *Mystical Theology: The Glosses by Thomas Gallus and the Commentary of Robert Grosseteste on "De Mystica Theologia,"* by Thomas Gallus and Robert Grosseteste, ed. James McEvoy, Dallas Medieval Texts in Translation 3 (Leuven: Peeters, 2003), 4; Rorem, *Pseudo-Dionysius,* 218–19.

43. *EMT,* ch. 1, 710a–b.

sible divine mystery that the intellect cannot ponder. This is a union of love, which Gallus elsewhere describes as occurring in the "summit of affection" or the "peak of the soul."[44] Such union causes an infused cognition greater than anything we can attain by our noetic activity, even with the help of grace. By love the patriarch leaves behind all words, propositions, and concepts and passes into ecstasy as he *deliberately* suspends the intellect's operation.[45] Love causes the highest cognition. Gallus sometimes speaks of union as if it could be activated by an intrinsic power of the soul's "peak," but other passages show that he considers this capacity to be the work of grace.[46] Gallus was the first Latin thinker to propose that union by love alone is the teaching of the *Mystical Theology*. His project involves a fusion of the Areopagite with Song of Songs bridal mysticism, a stream of mysticism entirely missing from the thought of Dionysius. Here Augustinian anthropology, Bernard of Clairvaux's biblical exegesis, and Gallus's speculative thought radically reshape the *Mystical Theology*.[47]

Gallus found a ready theological ally for his project of fusing the Areopagite with the Victorine-Augustinian contemplative tradition in his friend Robert Grosseteste, the Oxford master and bishop of Lincoln. Between 1240 and 1246 Robert translated the whole Dionysian corpus. A master of philology, Robert insisted on transmitting the sense of the Greek as much as possible. Robert joined Gallus in promoting an affective reading of the Areopagite's mysticism.[48] Oddly, Robert's translations and commentaries had little influence on the Dominican reception of Dionysius.

---

44. Thomas Gallus, *Extractio de divinis nominibus*, ch. 7, 696a: "summum affectionis"; Gallus, *Explanatio super mystica theologia*, in *Explanatio in libros Dionysii*, edited by Declan Anthony Lawell, Corpus Christianorum Continuatio Mediaeualis 223 (Turnhout: Brepols, 2011), ch. 1, p. 13.246: "per summum apicem synderesis."

45. *EMT*, ch. 1, 710b; McEvoy, introduction, *Mystical Theology*, 8.

46. Coolman shows the necessity of other infused graces before union ("Medieval Affective Dionysian Tradition," 92–94), limiting the "peak's" intrinsic capacity to unite itself to God. In his longest commentary on the *MT*, Gallus presents both grace and the soul's act of love as causes of ascent and union; see Gallus, *Explanatio super mystica theologia*, ch. 1, pp. 15.286, 29.615.

47. Coolman, "Medieval Affective Dionysian Tradition," 90–91; Rorem, *Pseudo-Dionysius*, 218.

48. McEvoy, introduction, *Mystical Theology*, 55–57, 126–27.

CONCLUSION

At least three characteristics of the "old" Dionysian corpus and the *Parisian Corpus Dionysiacum* impacted Albert's and (through him) Thomas's reception of the Areopagite.

First, the "old corpus" and the *Parisian Corpus Dionysiacum* were almost certainly Albert's major access to the Greek *scholia* as he wrote his commentaries on the *Sentences* and on Dionysius. Likewise, Aquinas's knowledge of the Greek reception of the Areopagite most likely came through these two bodies of text, though probably mediated by Albert.

Second, the *Parisian Corpus Dionysiacum* offers conflicting interpretations of Dionysian mysticism. The *Parisian Scholia* present the Greek patristic and Anastasian intellectual reading of divine union that Gallus's paraphrase (included in the same *Parisian Corpus*) rejects. The *Parisian Scholia* reinsert the mind's activity into union. Gallus's interpretation moves in the opposite direction, adding love where the Areopagite remains silent. Thus Albert and Thomas encounter not only a Dionysian primary text in need of clarification, but also a Dionysian tradition in need of the same. Finally, when read alongside the *Parisian Scholia*, Gallus's work on the *Mystical Theology* could be recognized more easily for what it was—namely, a major transformation of the Areopagite rather than an explanation of quasi-apostolic mysticism.

Third, the removal of the Greek authors' names in the *Parisian Scholia* obscured its doctrinal authority. It was no longer clear whether an Eastern Church father or medieval glossator stood behind this or that sentence. Such obscured authorship made it possible for Albert to distance himself from the *Parisian Scholia* when this seemed necessary. For example, in his *Commentary on the Divine Names*, Albert critiques "the Commentator" at least five times for misinterpreting Dionysius.[49] The ambiguous authority of the *Parisian Scholia* and the internal doctrinal conflicts in the *Parisian Corpus Dionysiacum* enabled Albert and Thomas's direct engagement with Dionysius. They thus benefited from an important interpretive tool for the Dionysian corpus and could participate in the *ressourcement* of the Areopagite's thought.

---

49. *SDN*, ch. 3, no. 3, p. 114.39–41; ch. 4, no. 109, p. 207.56–66; no. 143, p. 231.51–53; ch. 5, no. 29, p. 320.11–13; ch. 11, no. 24, p. 423.29–31.

PART 2

Albert on Dionysian Union with God

3

Mystical Union and Its Doctrinal Pillars in the Early Albert

Albert's first extensive treatment of union with God comes in his *Sentences Commentary*. In addition, this and another early work (the *De homine*) contain Albert's longest studies of key anthropological and epistemological themes that undergird any scholastic mystical theology. The present chapter treats these background issues: the soul's structure, its relation to the body, noetics, eschatology, and divine naming. In addition, many of these themes contain elements of a mystical theology, especially the doctrines of the *imago*, the Son's and the Spirit's invisible missions, grace, faith, charity, the Spirit's seven gifts, and glory. Thus many of these doctrines simultaneously serve as theoretical pillars for the theology of union in the Dionysian commentaries. I will offer a synthesis of the background doctrines, not an exhaustive analysis of all relevant passages. This chapter serves as a steppingstone to the next. I begin with a sketch of the historical setting and genre of the *De homine* and the *Sentences Commentary*.

THE SETTING AND GENRE OF ALBERT'S *DE HOMINE* AND *SENTENCES COMMENTARY*

Albert arrived in Paris between 1240 and 1243. Having probably surpassed his fortieth birthday, the German friar had already spent several years as priory lector. At the University of Paris he became bachelor of theology under Guéric of Saint-Quentin. His most important task consisted of lectures on all of Lombard's *Sentences*. Albert incepted as master of theology in 1245. He occupied the foreign chair until 1248 and then moved to Cologne. From 1243 to 1249 he edited his *Sentences Commentary*. Albert apparently published the first book between 1243 and 1245 and the third book between 1243 and 1246. It is certain that he published the second book in 1246 and the fourth in 1249.[1] The date and location for the *De homine* remain uncertain, even after the publication of the critical edition. Because it clearly preceded both the *Sentences Commentary* and the *De bono*, the *De homine* must have been composed before 1246, perhaps around 1242. Its place of origin is either Germany or Paris.[2]

The *De homine* reveals a highly creative, synthetic mind wrestling with newly received and controversial non-Christian philosophies. The text functions as a virtual commentary on Aristotle's *De Anima*, whose thematic order Albert closely follows. Frequent references to Averroes's *Long Commentary on the de Anima* and Avicenna's *Liber VI Nat-*

---

1. Gilles Emery, *La Trinité créatrice: Trinité et création dans les commentaires aux "Sentences" de Thomas d'Aquin et de ses précurseurs Albert le Grand et Bonaventure*, Bibliothèque Thomiste 47 (Paris: Vrin, 1995), 27–29; Senner, *Alberts des Großen Verständnis von Theologie und Philosophie*, Lectio Albertina 9 (Münster: Aschendorff, 2009), 5–6, 14; Tugwell, "Albert the Great," 3–11; James A. Weisheipl, "Albert der Große: Leben und Werke," in *Albertus Magnus: Sein Leben und seine Bedeutung*, edited by Manfred Entrich, 18–26 (Cologne: Styria, 1982). The best text of the *Sentences Commentary* is the non-critical Borgnet edition, which mostly reprints the 1651 Petrus Jammy edition. The latter republishes the first printed edition, from Basel in 1506. The Borgnet edition standardized Albert's biblical citations using the Sixto-Clementina. It follows the Basel edition in transmitting the division of distinctions into articles not found in early manuscripts. The sixteenth- and seventeenth-century editions fail to distinguish between *quaestiones* that exposit the Lombard's text and those that posit topics for further discussion; see Augustin Hiedl, "Zur Basler Ausgabe des Sentenzenkommentars Alberts des Grossen vom Jahre 1506," in *Wege zur Buchwissenschaft*, edited by Otto Wenig, 228–31, Bonner Beiträge zur Bibliotheks- und Bücherkunde 14 (Bonn: 1966). According to Maria Burger, the Basel and Borgnet editions are close to but not based on the texts of three distinct manuscripts that originated near the University of Cologne. The manuscript tradition behind Basel and Borgnet remains somewhat ambiguous.

2. Henryk Anzulewicz, preface, *De homine*, by Albertus Magnus, Cologne Edition, vol. 27, part 2, ed. Anzulewicz and Joachim R. Söder (Münster: Aschendorff, 2008), xv; Anzulewicz, introduction, *Über den Menschen*, by Albertus Magnus, ed. and trans. Anzulewicz and Söder, Philosophische Bibliothek 531 (Hamburg: Felix Meiner, 2004), ix–xlix.

uralium show Albert already engaging the most vexing challenges in Peripatetic anthropology. Also, Albert offers a properly philosophical study of the soul in the first 80 percent of *De homine*.[3] Here he essentially avoids biblical citations and places theological authorities such as Augustine side by side with Greek and Islamic philosophers. Only in the work's last section, where he treats properly theological themes such as the *imago*, does Albert grant Scripture, the fathers, and arguments from faith greater weight than purely philosophical reasoning.[4]

The *Sentences Commentary* has a theological genre and centers on the Lombard's mostly Augustinian theology. However, the first book also shows Albert mining the *Parisian Corpus Dionysiacum*. His study of divine naming synthesizes Dionysius and Augustine. Albert also brings Aristotle and his commentators into conversation with Augustinian anthropology.

The date and location of Albert's commentaries on the *Celestial Hierarchy* and *Ecclesiastical Hierarchy* have long been disputed. But recent research by Maria Burger and Adriano Oliva leaves little doubt that all of Albert's Dionysian commentaries belong to the Cologne period between 1248 and 1250.[5] Therefore, with the exception of the fourth book of the *Sentences Commentary*, one finds strong historical justification to treat the *De homine* and the *Sentences Commentary* as belonging to a doctrinal period that may be distinct from that of the Dionysian commentaries. This is crucial, for Albert was a thinker in motion. Indeed,

---

3. *De homine*, pp. 1–503; Tugwell, "Albert the Great," 10–11.

4. *De homine*, pp. 504–95. Joachim Söder and Georg Wieland thus correctly refuse Loris Sturlese's notion that Albert turned away from theology and to philosophy in 1250 with the commentaries on Aristotle. The early Albert is already highly philosophical; see Joachim R. Söder, "Die Erprobung der Vernunft: Vom Umgang mit Traditionen in *De homine*," in Senner, *Albertus Magnus, Zum Gedenken*, 1–8; Loris Sturlese, *Die Deutsche Philosophie im Mittelalter: Von Bonifatius bis zu Albert dem Großen (748–1280)* (Munich: C. H. Beck, 1993), 332–42; Georg Wieland, *Zwischen Natur und Vernunft: Alberts des Großen Begriff vom Menschen*, Lectio Albertina 2 (Münster: Aschendorff, 1999), 4. Anzulewicz also signals the methodological difference between the philosophical and theological sections of the *De homine*; see Anzulewicz, "Memoria und reminiscentia bei Albertus Magnus," in *La mémoire du temps au Moyen Âge*, edited by Agostino Paravicini Bagliani, 171–73, Micrologus' Library 12 (Florence: Edizioni del Galluzzo, 2005).

5. Burger, "Thomas Aquinas's Glosses," 561–74; Adriano Oliva, *Les débuts de l'enseignement de Thomas d'Aquin et sa conception de la "sacra doctrina," avec l'édition du prologue de son Commentaire des "Sentences,"* Bibliothèque Thomiste 58 (Paris: Vrin, 2006), 218–20.

the interpreter of Albert must be careful not to reconstruct an artificially harmonious system. For while the old image of Albert as an eclectic collector of ideas was quite inaccurate, the immense diversity of traditions that he sought to integrate on key themes, as well as the considerable number of doctrinal shifts in his works, sometimes defy complete systematization.

ALBERT'S ANTHROPOLOGY IN THE *DE HOMINE* AND THE *SENTENCES COMMENTARY*

As noted in this study's general introduction, I begin with a three-part study of Albert's early anthropology: (1) the soul's ontology, (2) epistemology, and (3) the *imago*.

Albert's early metaphysics of the soul emerges out of three major doctrinal streams: (1) the neo-Augustinianism that dominated the Paris theology faculty in the first half of the thirteenth century; (2) Aristotle's works, which gained much influence at the Paris faculty of arts in the 1240s; and (3) the Arab commentators of the Stagirite. One or a combination of these streams consistently drives Albert's anthropological discussions in the *De homine* and in his *Sentences Commentary*. Here, the voice of Dionysius is largely absent, but not for a lack of access to the Dionysian corpus. The various combinations of these three traditions present formidable challenges—especially their tendency to explain the human being as consisting of two distinct substances: soul and body.[6] Such an approach offers a safeguard for the doctrine of personal immortality, but it also fails to provide an adequate explanation for human being as soul-body unity. Albert already confronts this difficulty in the *De homine*.

His opening response to this problem in the *De homine* is subtle

---

6. Édouard Wéber identifies this tendency in the twelfth-century Cistercian compilation *De Spiritu et Anima*, Hugh of St.Victor's *De Sacramentis*, Peter Lombard's *Sentences*, Alexander of Hales's *Glossa in quatuor libros Sententiarum*, William of Auvergne's *De Anima*, and Roger Bacon's *Questions on the Eighth Book of Aristotle's Physics*; see Wéber, *La personne humaine au XIIIe siècle*, Bibliothèque Thomiste 46 (Paris: Vrin, 1991), 18–29, 48–54, 60, 77–80, 133–36. B. Carlos Bazán points to quasi-dualistic anthropologies in Avicenna and numerous Parisian masters of arts in the mid-thirteenth century; see Bazán, "The Human Soul: Form *and* Substance? Thomas Aquinas' Critique of Eclectic Aristotelianism," *Archives d'histoire doctrinale et littéraire du moyen âge* 64 (1997): 103–11.

and vexing. He insists "with all the philosophers" that the soul is a substance *and* the body's form.[7] Thus it is in some way a complete reality in itself, yet its relation to the body is not secondary. Albert fuses the neo-Augustinian language of the soul as a substance with Aristotle's emphasis on the soul as the body's organizing principle.[8] His methodology emerges in the *De homine*. With Avicenna, Albert states that the soul can be considered in one of two ways: by itself or in its relation to the body. By itself, the soul is a substance. Thus, ontologically, the soul does not completely depend on its union with the body, so that the soul can continue to exist after death. Yet the soul is essentially distinct from angelic natures, for it is "inclined" to be a body's act or form.[9] The term *inclinatur* is best understood in the strong sense of "being essentially turned toward," not only as having a certain tendency toward the body. At the core of its being, the soul is wholly ordered to the body. Albert paradoxically posits the soul as a substance with a substantial relation to the body.

Three closely linked doctrines confirm a predominantly holistic tendency in Albert. First, he opposes contemporary hylomorphic theories of the soul. He rejects the notion of spiritual matter central to Franciscan neo-Augustinianism.[10] Rather, the soul's *quo-quod* composition distinguishes it from God's absolute simplicity.[11] By positing the soul as a

7. *De homine*, "De diffinitionibus [animae] sanctorum," a. 3.1.1, p. 10.42–48; Paul Dominikus Hellmeier, *Anima et intellectus: Albertus Magnus und Thomas von Aquin über Seele und Intellekt des Menschen*, Beiträge zur Geschichte der Philosophie und Theologie des Mittelalters, Neue Folge 75 (Münster: Aschendorff, 2011), 58–59.

8. Ibid., pp. 8.26–9.2, cites two Cistercian works: The compilation *De Spiritu et Anima* (attributed to Augustine) and William of Saint-Thierry's *Epistula ad Cartusienses* (attributed to Bernard of Clairvaux).

9. *De homine*, "Quomodo anima sit actus," a. 1.1.1c, p. 31.42–68: "anima inclinatur ad corpus ut actus ... anima, tunc potest considerari duobus modis, scilicet secundum esse quod habet in se, et sic non diffinitur in comparatione ad corpus, vel secundum comparationem ad corpus ... anima dupliciter potest diffiniri, scilicet secundum quod est anima, idest actus corporis et motor, et secundum quod est substantia quaedam contenta secundum seipsam in praedicamento substantiae." The argument for immortality emerges in ad 5, p. 32.25–32. Albert also contrasts the immaterial soul to angels in *De IV coaequaevis*, tr. 4, q. 30, a. 1.

10. Weisheipl, "Albertus Magnus and Universal Hylomorphism: Avicebron, A Note on Thirteenth-Century Augustinianism," in *Albert the Great: Commemorative Essays*, edited by Francis J. Kovach and Robert W. Shahan, 250–58 (Norman: University of Oklahoma Press, 1980).

11. *De homine*, "Utrum humana anima, quae continet in se vegetabile, sensibile et

pure form instead of a form-matter composite, Albert refuses to turn the soul into a complete substance in the proper sense. Second, he insists that the soul is a single substantial form directly actualizing the body. Any theory presenting the soul's vegetative and sensible parts as distinct actualizing principles mediating between body and rational soul contradicts the human being's essential unity and the principle of act/potency.[12] The whole immaterial soul directly informs the body, yet the soul's higher part (essence, intellect, and will) is immaterial. Third, the *Sentences Commentary* does not present the soul as a "this something" (*hoc aliquid*) or spiritual "thing." Such a lacuna qualifies the notion of the soul as a spiritual substance.[13] The consequences of these three doctrines emerge in the discussion on the purpose of the soul-body unity. The soul is joined to the body not only because of an inscrutable divine will for our salvation or to manifest God's miraculous powers (the Lombard's main arguments), but also for the soul's progress in knowledge and virtue.[14] The body is not an obstacle to cognition but the very path to it, though Albert soon qualifies this stance. Overall he presents an ontology of the human being that bears some similarities to the Areopagite's more or less Proclan anthropology, at least in its broad strokes. In other words, Albert's distance from key aspects of thirteenth-century neo-Augustinian anthropologies prepares the way for a broad reception of Dionysian mystical ascent via external mediations such as the divine names of Scripture.

Still, Albert retains some philosophical notions that tend to separate body and soul. He adopts Avicenna's theory that the soul is the body's motor, an analogy that signals the soul's efficient causality on the body.[15] In his *Sentences Commentary* Albert explains this model by referring to Nemesius's image of the navigator and the ship, thus emphasizing the soul's capacity to exist on its own. Here we see part of Al-

---

rationale, sit simplex vel composita," a. 3, p. 92.46–52; "Utrum intellectus agens sit pars animae," a. 2.2.4.1, p. 416.33–41; Albertus Magnus, *I Sent.*, d. 3, a. 33; Léonard Ducharme, "The Individual Human Being in Saint Albert's Earlier Writings," in Kovach and Shahan, *Albert the Great*, 155; Weisheipl, "Albertus Magnus," 239–60.

12. *De homine*, "Quomodo anima sit actus," a. 1.1.1, ad 8, pp. 33.11–34.9.

13. Albertus Magnus, *II Sent.*, d. 17, a. 2, ad 2; Ducharme, "Individual Human Being," 146–48; Hellmeier, *Anima*, 75, 94.

14. Albertus Magnus, *III Sent.*, d. 31, a. 10, sed contra 3.

15. *De homine*, "Per quem modum moveat corpus," a. 3.1.2.1, ad 3, p. 26.12–15.

bert's philosophical style: he seeks to combine multiple philosophical and theological traditions, even at the cost of doctrinal clarity.[16]

Having surveyed Albert's ontological understanding of the soul's relation to the body, I now turn to the relation between the soul's essence and its operative powers. This theme has important consequences for the issues of the agent intellect's self-knowledge and our knowledge of God. In the *De homine* Albert appropriates Avicenna's notion that the soul's higher (immaterial) and lower (corporeal) faculties emanate or "flow" from the soul's substance. Albert aims to prevent the soul's operative powers from becoming distinct substances or essences.[17] The *Sentences Commentary* defines the soul's essence as consisting of its *quo est* and *quod est*.[18] The *De homine* specifies the nature of the soul's internal flow or "flux." The agent intellect emanates from the soul's *quo est*, while the potential intellect flows from its *quod est*.[19] The agent intellect is directly linked to the soul's formal principle, and the potential intellect is linked to its informed principle. We find the same (ontological) anthropology in the *Sentences Commentary*.[20] Since action follows being, the agent intellect's direct emanation from the soul's formal part has noetic consequences. Albert describes *quo est* as the act and *esse* of the rational soul. In receiving an influx of being directly from the source of the human being's substantial actuality, the agent intellect simultaneously receives its noetic actuality. Thus the agent intellect can understand itself as act, independent of the operation of abstracting intelligible species from phantasms.[21] The agent intellect's ontological place in the immaterial soul also lays the groundwork for the soul's immediate self-understanding, as we will see shortly. We should note that Albert's Platonizing exegesis of the agent intellect prepares the way for an interior ascent to God. The connection between

---

16. Albertus Magnus, *I Sent.*, d. 3, a. 33, ad 1; Ducharme, "Individual Human Being," 149–50; see also *De IV coaequaevis*, tr. 4, q. 30, a. 2.

17. *De homine*, "Utrum ista tria in homine sint substantia una vel diversae," a. 1, ad 1, p. 85.28–39.

18. Albertus Magnus, *I Sent.*, d. 3, a. 33c; a. 34, ad 2; Wéber, *Personne humaine*, 205.

19. *De homine*, "Utrum intellectus agens sit pars animae," a. 2.2.4.1c, p. 416.34–42; see also ibid., "Qualiter intelligat, et de modo actionis eius," a. 2.2.6c, p. 421.17–24.

20. Albertus Magnus, *I Sent.*, d. 3, a. 34.

21. *De homine*, "Qualiter intelligat, et de modo actionis eius," a. 2.2.6c, p. 421.17–24; ad 3, p. 421.53–64.

the theory of agent intellect and mysticism will become explicit in the *Commentary on the Divine Names*, as he will see in chapter 4. Finally, this notion of the agent intellect stands in tension with Albert's doctrine of the unicity of substantial form. These competing elements in Albert's anthropology and epistemology have the potential to ground diverse, partly irreconcilable theories of mystical union.

Albert closely links the soul's interior ontological flux centered on the composite structure of *quo-quod* with the question of the essential or substantial status of the soul's faculties, a key concern for the theology of the *imago*, especially since the Lombard. Augustine insists on the substantial status of the soul's knowledge and love, partly to offer an analogy for the consubstantiality of the divine persons.[22] The thirteenth-century arrival of Aristotelian psychology in Latin Christendom created immense problems for standard Augustinian trinitarian theologies, seemingly threatening the entire edifice of the *imago*. Now the question of substantiality became linked to a much more Aristotelian notion of faculties. Albert enters the debate by considering the matter from two angles: (1) in relation to the soul in itself as a spiritual substance; and (2) in relation to the soul's interaction with the body. In the first way the operative faculties are consequent upon or distinct from the soul's (substantial) being or essence (e.g., the agent intellect is distinct from the soul's *quo*). The philosophical distinction that accounts for the soul's composite nature (and differentiates the soul's simplicity from God's) helps to shape Albert's account of the *imago*. But from the second perspective the soul's essence and faculties operate as a single potential (Boethian) whole in relation to the body. Here the faculties have a substantial status, meaning they are necessary for the human being's ontological and operational perfection.[23] The *De homine* specifies that this ontology explains how one soul is essentially present in the *imago*'s triad of memory, intellect, and will, which accounts for the three faculties' mutual indwelling.[24] Albert's complex, perhaps incomplete synthesis of the soul's ontology may be partly driv-

---

22. Augustine, *De trinitate libri XV*, ed. W. J. Mountain and F. Glorie, CCSL, vol. 50, part 2 (Turnout: Brepols, 1968) bk. IX, ch. 4, no. 5; Johannes Brachtendorf, *Die Struktur des Menschlichen Geistes nach Augustinus: Selbstreflexion und Erkenntnis Gottes in "De Trinitate,"* Paradeigmata 19 (Hamburg: Felix Meiner, 2000), 129–31.

23. Albertus Magnus, *I Sent.*, d. 3, a. 34.

24. *De homine*, "De ordine istarum trium potentiarum," a. 6.2.2.2, ad 5, p. 552.48–59.

en by his concern to account for our self-reflective capacities as articulated by Augustine and confirmed by the Stagirite filtered through Peripatetic glosses.[25] Ontology and epistemology exercise a mutual influence on one another. I now turn to the latter.

Albert's noetics in the philosophical part of *De homine* broadly adopts a Platonized (Proclan-Arab) Aristotelianism as an alternative to Augustinian illumination. In the *Sentences Commentary* he partly shifts back toward Augustine. The lectures on the Areopagite will again favor a Platonized Aristotle, though with strong Dionysian influences. I will therefore offer distinct studies of the epistemologies in the *De homine* and in the *Sentences Commentary*.[26]

The *De homine* offers a complete philosophical noetics centered on the agent and possible intellects, leaving little need for Augustinian memory and illumination. Albert rejects the philosopher's need for any interior noetic light beyond that imparted in God's creative causality of the soul. He reinterprets Augustinian illumination with the Proclan model of primary and secondary causality and Aristotle's notion of form as a sufficient operative principle. Albert transforms Augustine partly by introducing a distinction between natural and graced knowing: natural cognition proceeds from a stable, intrinsic, operative capacity.[27] New illuminations of the mind pertain to grace and not to nature. In a single stroke Albert revalorizes the intellect's natural, abiding operative powers and closes off one doctrinal source that could account for philosophical contemplative ascent to God (though without necessarily excluding other sources). Sometimes a theory that extols the grandeur of creation before the coming of grace also thereby plac-

---

25. See Wéber, *Personne humaine*, 219.

26. For a more extensive study of this evolution in Albert's thought, see Blankenhorn, "How the Early Albertus Magnus Transformed," 351–86; see also the remarks on Albert in Blankenhorn, "Aquinas as Interpreter."

27. *De homine*, "Utrum intellectus agens sit intelligentia separata vel non," a. 2.2.3, ad 21, p. 415.25–29: "Ad aliud dicendum quod Augustinus in libro *De Magistro* intendit quod omne lumen nostri intellectus est a causa prima et sine ipso nihil possumus facere; sed naturam illuminandi super intelligibilia intellectus agens habet ab ipso et sub ipso"; ad 22, p. 415.30–36: "quaedam intelligibilia non intelligimus nisi gratia dei illuminante, sicut ea quae sunt supra rationem: quaedam autem rationabilia intelligimus a nobis, sed non quasi ex nobis, sed ex virtute agentis intellectus, quae data est nobis a deo"; see also Markus Führer, "Albertus Magnus' Theory of Divine Illumination," in Senner, *Albertus Magnus, Zum Gedenken*, 144.

es firm limits on the possibility of ungraced creation. The young Albert's implied theory of grace-nature moves toward a doctrine of mystical union by grace alone.

Next Albert insists that we know other beings only by the senses, excepting inspired dreams and prophecies.[28] He reduces the Augustinian notion of intelligibles that are naturally in the soul to the mind's pure potency being actualized by the abstraction of intelligible forms out of phantasms.[29] Albert sidesteps Augustine's insistence that sense experience alone cannot attain certain knowledge of truth. For Augustine we only have access to immutable truth because God's light shines in memory and takes us beyond the material world's noetic instability.[30] Albert's philosophical studies of memory in the *De homine* either focus on sensible memory or reduce memory to Aristotle's potential intellect as a blank slate.[31] Only one passage in the philosophical section of the *De homine* speaks of forms concreated in the soul, but Albert relegates their function to the afterlife.[32] Consciously or not, the *De homine* overcomes Augustine's connection between illumination and certitude about truth by developing Aristotle's doctrine of the agent intellect with the help of the Arab commentators. The agent intellect grants access to the stable, immutable aspect of otherwise mutable beings—namely, their intelligible forms. Albert's theory of the agent intellect goes well beyond the historical Aristotle, though perhaps not Aristotle as Albert understood him. The friar's agent intellect is a constant source of light and actuality for the potential intellect, even when it is not abstracting species from phantasms. At such mo-

---

28. *De homine*, "Quid faciat speciem intelligibilem esse intelligibilem," a. 1, ad 8, p. 446.60–447.5; see "De diffinitionibus [de anima] Senecae et Alexandri in libro De motu cordis," a. 3.1.2.2, ad 3, pp. 27.73–28.3.

29. *De homine*, "An omnia intelligibilia sint in anima, aut abstrahantur a rebus extra," a. 3c, p. 454.33–60.

30. Robert Crouse, "Knowledge," in *Augustine Through the Ages: An Encyclopedia*, edited by Allan D. Fitzgerald and John C. Cavadini, 486–88 (Grand Rapids, Mich.: Eerdmans, 1999).

31. *De homine*, "Quid sit [memoria]," a. 4.1c, pp. 300.41–1.52; "Utrum habitus intellectus speculativi post considerationem manet in ipso," a. 2.4.5c, pp. 441.65–42.30; "An omnia intelligibilia sint in anima," a. 3c, p. 454.33–57.

32. *De homine*, "Qualiter intellectus possibilis intelligit post mortem," a. 2.3.5c, p. 430.51–56, which simply references Albertus Magnus, *De IV coaequaevis*, tr. 4, q. 24, a. 2 (the treatise on the angels).

ments the potential intellect is in a state of "indistinct act." The agent intellect can always understand itself by "converting upon itself," an operation apparently autonomous from the cognition of other beings.[33] The agent intellect's perpetual activity and capacity for self-knowledge through introspection partly mirror Augustine's illumined memory.

The philosophical noetics of the *De homine* presents a human being *mostly* turned to the world, thus matching the dominant element of Albert's metaphysics of the soul. Our nature has a certain integrity in its capacity to know, a capacity almost exclusively actualized via sense experience. I also noted that Albert simultaneously develops a notion of the agent intellect that paves the way for a new illumination theory and points toward a mysticism of interiority.[34] But the theological part of the *De homine* takes a noticeably different approach to Augustinian memory, as we will see shortly.

Albert returns to the intellect's "natural" illumination in the first book of his *Sentences Commentary*.[35] In a complex passage he appears

33. *De homine*, "Qualiter intelligat, et de modo actionis eius," a. 2.2.6, ad 3–8, pp. 421.60–22.31.

34. On Albert's development of Augustinian illumination through the doctrine of agent intellect, see the remarks (largely complementary to my own) by Anzulewicz, "Rezeption und Reinterpretation: Pseudo-Dionysius Areopagita, die Peripatetiker und die Umdeutung der augustinischen Illuminationslehre bei Albertus Magnus," in *Kulturkontakte und Rezeptionsvorgänge in der Theologie des 12. und 13. Jahrhunderts*, edited by Ulrich Köpf and Dieter R. Bauer, 109–17, Archa Verbi: Subsidia 8 (Münster: Aschendorff, 2011).

35. Albertus Magnus, *I Sent.*, d. 2, a. 5c, 59b–60a: "Augustinus dicit, quod mali nihil verum vident: et hoc retractavit, quia mali multa habent a Deo ... dicimus quod in anima ad hoc quod accipiat scientiam veritatis exiguntur quatuor: intellectus possibilis qui paratus sit recipere: et secundo, intellectus agens cujus lumine fiat abstractio specierum ... et tertio, res objecta per imaginem, vel seipsam ... et quarto, principia et dignitates quae sunt quasi quaedam instrumenta proportionantia compositiones et divisiones possibiles et impossibiles et necessarias ex quibus verum accipitur ... quidam Philosophi dixerunt, quod ista sufficerent ad cognitionem veri quod est sub ratione. Sed aliter dicendum, scilicet, quod lux intellectus agentis non sufficit per se, nisi per applicationem lucis intellectus increati ... dupliciter, scilicet, secundum lumen duplicatum tantum, vel etiam triplicatum: duplicatum ut si fiat conjunctio ad lumen intellectus increati, et illud lumen est interior magister. Quandoque autem fit ad conjunctionem intellectus angelici et divini: quia Philosophi quidam animam posuerunt instrumentum intelligentiae, eo quod intelligentia imprimit in eam suas illuminationes. Et hoc vocat Dionysius reductionem nostrae hierarchiae per hierarchiam Angelorum, et Augustinus dicit hoc contingere multis modis. Et hoc vocant quidam Philosophi 'continuationem intellectuum': quia etiam ipsi dixerunt, quod nihil videtur nisi per lucem primam"; ad 1:

to reject his *De homine* position and affirm the necessity of Augustinian illumination for all cognition, both natural and graced, as he insists that the agent intellect's intrinsic operative power is insufficient to attain truth. However, three textual elements demand a more nuanced evaluation. First, Albert does not explain the precise function of illumination. He mentions neither interior access to eternal forms nor the attainment of immutable truth judgments as the fruit of illumination. In fact the agent intellect seems to mediate all noetic light (natural and supernatural). Second, he implicitly affirms the notion that God is the universal agent intellect, though he also posits individual human agent intellects. Third, he displays a clear preference for the technical terminology of the Arab commentators to explain illumination. He unfolds the Augustinian theme of the interior teacher with Avicenna's language of "being conjoined" to the higher agent intellect and Averroes's "conjunction" and "continuation" with the higher intellect.[36] Albert moves in the direction of the Avicennian-Augustinian epistemologies of other Parisian theologians without clearly joining their doctrinal school. Instead, we are left with the supposedly common teaching of a plethora of authorities such as Augustine, Dionysius, and unnamed philosophers who are in fact Averroes and the author of the *Liber de Causis*.[37] Albert's love of harmonizing multiple traditions is unmistakable.

Still, Albert espouses Augustinian noetics in a subsequent *Sentences Commentary* article as he discusses the "higher and lower intellect."[38] One and the same intellect is "higher" when turned to spiritual

---

"si aliquid sciatur in habitu, non fiet conversio ad actum nisi per conversionem ad lucem intellectus increati."

36. Avicenna Latinus, *Liber de Anima seu Sextus de Naturalibus IV-V*, ed. S. Van Riet (Leiden: E. J. Brill, 1968), pars 5, ch. 5, 128–29; Averroes, *Commentarium Magnum in Aristotelis de Anima Libros*, ed. F. Stuart Crawford, Corpus Commentariorum Averrois in Aristotelem, Versionum Latinarum vol. 6, part 1 (Cambridge, Mass.: Medieval Academy of America, 1953), bk. III, no. 36; Alain de Libera, *Métaphysique et noétique: Albert le Grand*, Problèmes et controversies (Paris: Vrin, 2005), 287, 301; L. E. Goodman, *Avicenna* (London: Routledge, 1992), 124–46; Arthur Hyman, "Aristotle's Theory of the Intellect and Its Interpretation by Averroes," in *Studies in Aristotle*, edited by Dominic J. O'Meara, 183–90, Studies in Philosophy and the History of Philosophy 9 (Washington, D.C.: The Catholic University of America Press, 1981).

37. I give Albert's sources following Maria Burger's notes in the forthcoming Cologne Edition of Albertus Magnus's *Sentences Commentary*, bk. I.

38. Albertus Magnus, *I Sent.*, d. 17, a. 4c, 472b: "Si ergo quaeratur, Quomodo intellectus sit potentior ad intelligendum? distinguendum est: quia de natura sui magis se

realities and "lower" when turned to the corporeal world. When it no longer ponders material beings, the mind only receives the agent intellect's light. Here the mind finds a way of cognition more befitting to its immaterial nature, considered in abstraction from the body. Yet our present embodied state makes us more apt to know lower realities. But sense experience also obscures the intellect's vision of spiritual realities, which themselves intensify the mind's capacity to understand them.[39] Albert thus affirms a crucial element of Augustine's epistemology—namely, the heightening of the soul's noetic capacity through the interior presence of an intelligible object. Albert simultaneously uses an Aristotelian approach to cognition of the corporeal world. Again, two competing traditions come together in a certain harmony. Albert prefers an Augustinian understanding of our knowledge of God, with an emphasis on the soul rising above its embodied state to gain direct access to the immaterial realm. He strongly implies that such immediate access is not only possible but preferable to the soul's ascent toward God via created, embodied mediations. Also noteworthy are the Avicennian overtones of Albert's Augustinianism: the agent intellect functions as a conduit of spiritual light that enables interior noetic ascent, a process essentially independent of phantasm-bound cognition.

The doctrine of the higher and lower intellect bears some similarities to the Areopagite's twofold division of the soul. Still, Dionysius calls for ascent to begin with the contemplation of symbols before proceeding to more immaterial cognitive objects, a process that we do not find in Albert's explanation of the knowledge of God. His partial turn toward Augustinian noetics stands in tension with Dionysian anthropology. Hence a generous reception of Dionysian mysticism will require a shift in Albert's thought. I will return to this theme in chapter 4.

For the purpose of his mystical theology, Albert's *Sentences Com-*

---

habet ad superius, de statu autem hujus vitae magis ad inferius ... aliquid enim ita noscitur secundum sui potestatem, quod ipsum est lux et ratio ad alia cognoscenda: et si attendatur potestas notitiae vel intellectus ex parte objecti moventis intellectum, magis erit notum quod noscitur in luce propria et est ratio cognoscendi alia, quam id quod tantum cognoscitur in luce aliena: et hoc modo dicit Philosophus in principio *de Anima*, quod notitia de anima certior est quam notitia de corpore animato.... Alia notitia est secundum potestatem noscentis et intellectus qui movetur ab eo quod noscitur, et secundum illum modum frequenter magis noscuntur quae in natura sunt posteriora."

39. Albertus Magnus, *I Sent.*, d. 17, a. 4, ad 5.

mentary noetics posits two key doctrines: (1) certain knowledge of the material world is best explained through a Peripatetic model that fuses the necessity of sense experience with the agent intellect's constant reception of divine light, one that probably includes so-called Augustinian special illumination; (2) by turning away from the material world and going within to the twofold light of the agent intellect and the indwelling Creator, the mind's capacity to grasp immaterial realities expands. Both doctrines are in partial continuity with the philosophical section of the *De homine*. Albert's noetics somewhat reflects the tensions in his ontological anthropology, between the soul as substance and the soul as the body's form.

Albert's theory of the *imago* completes his epistemology. Here the main source of his theology is Augustine's *On the Trinity*, especially as mediated by the Lombard.[40] I will mostly focus on Albert's *Sentences Commentary* doctrine, which is close to that of the *De homine*.

Albert's first detailed explanation of the *imago*'s essential parts takes up the Lombard's exposition of Augustine's triad of memory, understanding, and will. Memory is

> a power of the rational soul in its superior part, holding within itself the *habitus* of the true and the good that it is by its own nature, and the *habitus* of the true and good which is God. Unless we say what is truer according to Augustine, holding knowledge within itself by presence of the essence, and not the *habitus* of the true and the good that the soul is by nature … nothing is more present to the soul than it is to itself.[41]

The *imago*'s memory belongs to the soul's immaterial part. It seems to be a faculty distinct from the intellect, hence also distinct from the memory in Aristotle's potential intellect. Therefore, it is not exactly a storehouse of forms. Memory's function is to hold the *habitus* of the true and the good within itself. This *habitus* is not an innate intelligible species. Memory's "act" is its direct relation to the soul's essence,

---

40. Albert follows the Lombard's focus on *De trinitate*, bks. IX–X; see Burger's notes on d. 3 in the forthcoming Cologne Edition of Albert's *Sentences Commentary*.

41. Albertus Magnus, *I Sent.*, d. 3, a. 20c, 119b: "Dicendum, quod memoria haec nihil aliud est quam potentia animae rationalis secundum superiorem partem tenens apud se habitum veri et boni quod ipsa est secundum naturam suam, et habitum veri et boni quod Deus est: vel forte quod verius est secundum Augustinum, tenens apud se notitiam per praesentiam essentiae, et non habitum veri et boni quod ipsa anima est secundum naturam. Unde Augustinus dicit, quod nihil praesentius est animae quam ipsa sibi."

which is most present to it. The *habitus* is the soul's direct self-relation, the capacity for immediate noetic access to the soul's essence. Memory primarily refers to the soul's immediate self-presence: "Its act does not consist in acting, but in retaining ... the presence of knowledge in the essence, or by some innate *habitus*."[42] It enables the soul's direct, constant relation to God, the second inner "*habitus* of the true and the good."

Albert's first explication of memory clashes with his philosophy in the *De homine* and with Aristotle. The *Sentences Commentary* faces this challenge as it contrasts Aristotle's potential intellect (a blank slate) to Augustine's intellect, which enjoys perpetual knowledge of the soul via memory. Albert responds by qualifying the term "understanding" in the triad. He holds that this word does not refer to a noetic faculty *as such* or *simpliciter* (i.e., Aristotle's potential intellect), but rather to a faculty insofar as it is informed in relation to a certain intelligible object "such as the soul present to itself, and God who is in it by his essence, presence and power. For the cognition of God is naturally inserted in us."[43] Albert carves out a crucial exception to Aristotelian psychology: the intellect is as if always already informed by its constant relation to the soul and to God. This relation is "natural," meaning it is not acquired by sense experience, for the soul's ontological constitution makes it accessible.

Albert then turns to Augustine's discussion of constant self-memory, self-understanding, and self-love. Through memory's noetic light, which flows out of its direct contact with God's presence and with the soul's essence, *mens* or the immaterial soul has a constant, prereflective self-understanding independently of the noetic light that comes from external objects. Perpetual self-love completes the triad.[44] Albert posits an

---

42. Albertus Magnus, *I Sent.*, d. 3, a. 20c, 119b: "Actus autem ejus non est in agendo, sed tenendo ... praesentiam notitiae in essentia, vel habitu aliquo innato"; see also a. 39.

43. Albertus Magnus, *I Sent.*, d. 3, a. 20, ad qu. 1, 119b–120a: "intelligentia dicitur hic potentia intellectiva formalis non simpliciter, sed respectu intelligibilis cujusdam informata, quod scilicet semper praesens est in anima, sicut anima sibi est praesens, et Deus in ea est essentialiter, praesentialiter et potentialiter: naturaliter enim nobis insita est cognitio Dei"; see also Édouard Wéber, "La relation de la philosophie et de la théologie selon Albert le Grand," *Archives de Philosophie* 43 (1980): 585. Herbert Doms also contrasts this anthropology to Aristotle's; see Doms, *Die Gnadenlehre des seligen Albertus Magnus*, Breslauer Studien zur historischen Theologie 13 (Breslau, 1929), 8.

44. Albertus Magnus, *I Sent.*, d. 3, a. 26; a. 27, ad 3; a. 29; a. 39; Klaus Krämer, *Imago*

innate cognition of God that may refer to the Creator's presence to the soul, or perhaps to an unreflective cognition of eternal truths and moral laws, though this doctrine remains somewhat obscure.[45] He consistently links an indeterminate knowledge of God with the soul's immediate self-knowledge. The latter is the key to our perpetual, indeterminate cognition of God, an important Augustinian theme. Thus some knowledge of God is ontologically prior to our knowledge of other beings.

Albert also uses the tools of Peripatetic anthropology to explain memory. The context is the mutual indwelling of the *imago*'s faculties. Here, Albert's approach centers on the *imago*'s constant acts of remembering, knowing, and loving itself, the so-called "inner *imago*." The agent intellect always shines on the potential intellect, even when the former does not abstract intelligible forms out of phantasms. Such perpetual noetic light allows the potential intellect to "objectify" itself or "be placed before itself."[46] Albert assigns three functions of Augustine's memory to the agent intellect: (1) it is an unending source of noetic light; (2) it imparts an indeterminate cognition of the (active and potential) intellect, without a precise grasp of its properties; and (3) it can operate independently of sense experience. Albert's solution is similar to that of the *Sentences Commentary* article on cognitive illumination, where he implies that the agent intellect mediates all noetic light, both natural and supernatural.[47] In some ways the potential intel-

---

Trinitatis: Die Gottebenbildlichkeit des Menschen in der Theologie des Thomas von Aquin, Freiburger theologische Studien 164 (Freiburg im Breisgau: Herder, 2000), 128–29.

45. Albertus Magnus, *I Sent.*, d. 3, a. 20, ad qu. 1; Michael Schmaus, "Die trinitarische Gottebenbildlichkeit nach dem *Sentenzenkommentar* Alberts des Großen," in *Virtus Politica: Festgabe zum 75. Geburtstag von Alfons Hufnagel*, edited by Joseph Möller and Helmut K. Kohlenberger, 281 (Stuttgart: Frommann, 1974).

46. Albertus Magnus, *I Sent.*, d. 3, a. 29c, 129–130: "quidam Philosophus exponendo Aristotelem ... dicit, quod intellectus ... intelligit se semper: et dicit quod hoc idem est dicere, quod intellectus intelligit se in omni intelligibili ... nullo modo satisfacit dicto Augustini, qui vult, quod sub omni intelligibili alio intellectus semper intelligat se.... Intelligere vero nihil aliud quam notitiae specie vel essentia notitiae se intueri simpliciter sine consideratione sui et discretione suae naturae ... intelligere se non ponat discretionem sui, sed simplicem intuitum sine discretione ... intuitus perficitur duobus, scilicet lumine intelligibili emisso, et objecto: et intueri se nihil aliud est quam in lumine illo sibi objici. Cum igitur lumen intellectus agentis semper splendeat super possibile ... et cum hoc sit intelligere se secundum Augustinum, semper intelligit se."

47. Albertus Magnus, *I Sent.*, d. 2, a. 5c; d. 3, a. 29 (cited earlier in footnotes 35 and 46, respectively, in the present chapter).

lect takes the place of the *imago*'s understanding and the agent intellect takes the place of memory.

While the central ontological pillar of Albert's *imago* is memory, the recreated *imago*'s actualization comes in the exercise of the theological virtues. Faith perfects intellect, hope perfects memory, and love perfects the will. The triad's most perplexing part concerns hope. It involves an expectation of indefectibility whose link with memory comes in that faculty's act of retaining a divine similitude or God's presence.[48] Since memory enables a constant link to the indwelling Creator, it offers a foretaste of God's eternal, indefectible dwelling with the saints in heaven. Similarly, in the *De homine*, Augustine's "external *imago*" (the *imago* as remembering, knowing, and loving God), finds its highest created realization in the graced soul insofar as it actively hopes in unending beatitude, believes in the highest truth, and loves the highest good. The theological virtues enable a "distinct imitation" of the triune life as they cause the faculties' highest actualization, the faculties whose multiplicity in unity mirrors the three Persons.[49]

Still, the *Sentences Commentary* and *De homine* rarely discuss the soul's graced acts as the fulfillment of the *imago*. The *Sentences Commentary* takes up imitation in the sense of the three faculties' acts of remembering, understanding, and loving God, who is naturally present to the soul. Albert contrasts the direct cognition of God to the indirect knowledge of him that comes by reflecting on the soul's faculties, which function like a mirror. He concludes: "the soul can be carried into God directly through intellect, memory and will. And then the soul imitates in act and is formed in act to the Trinity and unity."[50] The foundation of this imitation is the presence of God as Creator. While these acts could be animated by the theological virtues, Albert says nothing in this passage about graced operations. Yet this is his most

48. Albertus Magnus, *I Sent.*, d. 3, a. 21, ad qu. 3, ad 1.
49. *De homine*, "De partibus [imaginis], quas enumerat Augustinus dicens quod est imago creationis et recreationis et similitudinis," a. 6.2.1, ad 12, 546.52–56: "Ad id quod ulterius quaeritur de imagine recreationis, dicendum quod imago dicitur ab imitando distincte; et quia gratia distinctionem in se non habet, propter hoc gratia per se non est imago recreationis, sed intellecta in virtutibus."
50. Albertus Magnus, *I Sent.*, d. 3, a. 22c, 122b: "anima per intellectum, memoriam, et voluntatem potest immediate ferri in Deum: et tunc actu imitatur et formatur ad Trinitatem et unitatem."

extensive *Sentences Commentary* treatment of the dynamic *imago*. The work mostly ignores the recreated *imago* as a dynamic model. Albert even contrasts the graced image with the image of the distinction of persons in one essence—that is, to the natural image of three faculties sharing the soul's single essence, the divine reflection that cannot be lost through sin.[51] His underlying doctrinal concern is to find a created reflection of the divine persons' consubstantiality. The soul's faculties are permanent and substantial (in a qualifies sense, as noted previously), while the graced acts and infused *habitus* that are the theological virtues depend on a contingent divine gift that not every human being has. Albert tends to connect the Trinity more clearly to the natural *imago* than to the graced *imago*, although the *De homine* makes the theological virtues reflections of the trinitarian distinctions.[52] But in the *Sentences Commentary* study of the *imago* the theological virtues have a relatively minor function. Here the doctrine primarily serves to manifest the Trinity rather than the soul's path to perfection, partly since Albert follows the Lombard's thematic structure. By focusing his trinitarian treatise on the three faculties instead of their graced operations, Albert (perhaps unintentionally) loosens the link between the *imago* and grace, a link that his work on the missions and the theological virtues reestablishes.[53] Overall, Albert's *Sentences Commentary* doctrine of the *imago* offers few resources for a trinitarian mysticism.

In light of Albert's doctrine of the *imago*, we now arrive at a fuller synthesis of his theological epistemology in the *Sentences Commentary*. By the *imago* we always know God and the soul's essence, but in an indeterminate, unreflective way. Our reflective knowledge of the soul and God depends on our knowing other beings. Memory, which at times appears to be identical with the agent intellect, has a close ontological proximity to the soul's essence, which enables direct cognition of the soul. The agent intellect has a certain conjunction or continuation

---

51. Albertus Magnus, *I Sent.*, d. 3, a. 25c.

52. Albertus Magnus, *I Sent.*, d. 3, a. 23c; *De homine*, "De partibus [imaginis], quas enumerat Augustinus dicens quod est imago creationis et recreationis et similitudinis," a. 6.2.1, ad 15, p. 546.65–547.5.

53. D. Juvenal Merriell argues that Albertus Magnus's *Sent.* weakens the connection between grace and actual imitation; see Merriell, *To the Image of the Trinity: A Study in the Development of Aquinas' Teaching*, Studies and Texts 96 (Toronto: Pontifical Institute of Medieval Studies, 1990), 73.

with uncreated light in every noetic act, not unlike Averroist and Avicennian notions of illumination by the cosmic agent intellect, now placed in a Christian cosmology wherein each human being has his or her own agent intellect really different from God's intellect. Albert joins the Averroist conversion to the one Agent Intellect with the Augustinian turn inward and the higher intellect's act. This conversion or turn occurs when we distance ourselves from the obscuring influence of the senses that are aids in knowing material beings yet mostly obstacles to our knowledge of the immaterial realm. Hence the *imago*'s noetic faculties are simple, meaning they are made primarily for knowledge of the immaterial realm.[54] From its creation the soul is already turned inward and thus upward. Intellectual progress in knowing the higher realm involves above all an intensification of this inward turn. Albert's early theological epistemology thus finds its natural metaphysical complement in the doctrine of the soul's substantiality. His *imago* seems to leave little room for Aristotle and Dionysius, dominated as it is by a Peripatetic and Augustinian vision of the human soul as having its natural place in the spiritual realm.

Albert's study of the *imago* linked to his Augustinian-Averroist noetics has potential implications for mystical theology. For the more memory grants direct access to the depths of the soul and the natural divine indwelling, the less the soul's ascent seems to depend on sense experience, including the bodily, historical mediations of Scripture and the sacraments. These mediations might thus become entryways to theological knowledge yet then gradually diminish in importance as the soul regains contact with the interior universe hitherto obscured by sin and ignorance.[55] The more intensely the light shines in memory, the more the soul finds its natural place in the eternal realm and the less it needs the noetic lights that shine via corporeal realities. These implications remain latent in the *Sentences Commentary* theology of the *imago* and its doctrine of illumination and lack synthesis with other sections of the same work, such as the study of divine naming, as we will see. Albert's Dionysian commentaries will mostly turn away from the

---

54. Albertus Magnus, *I Sent.*, d. 3, a. 21c; see also Doms, *Gnadenlehre*, 55.
55. Thus, for William of Saint-Thierry, the hermit who relies on the theological virtues only needs the Scriptures to instruct others; see William of Saint-Thierry, *Le Miroir de la foi*, Sources Chrétiennes 301 (Paris: Cerf, 1982), ch. 1, 66.

grand interior universe of Augustine and the Arabs in favor of the Areopagite's mysticism of mediations. Finally, Albert's early theology of the *imago* offers only sparse comments on the intellect's priority over the will in relation to the soul's ascent to God.[56]

THE INVISIBLE MISSIONS IN ALBERT'S SENTENCES COMMENTARY

Albert's most extensive treatment of union with God in the *Sentences Commentary* comes in the so-called treatise on the missions. Since I consider the missions under the formality of their unitive aspect, I take up the following elements of that doctrine: (1) the missions' relation to the eternal processions, which manifests the link between the Trinity's eternal identity and its unifying action; (2) the causal role of created effects in union; (3) the appropriation of the missions' effects; (4) union with the persons sent; (5) the link between the Son's and the Spirit's missions; (6) *habitus* as an effect of the missions; and (7) cognition of the missions. Last, I draw out some of this theology's consequences for the place of cognition and created acts in union.

Albert offers a standard medieval Augustinian definition of the divine mission: "To be sent is to be known as proceeding from another."[57] The missions include the eternal processions of the Son and the Spirit as well as their manifestation. The eternal processions of the Son and the Spirit with their effects in the gift of grace constitute the temporal missions.[58]

Two things are required [for a mission]: first, that something be appropriable to what is proper [to a divine person]; second, that there be an effect of sanctifying grace, to which is always joined the procession of the person, and the person himself. For the very person must be manifested as present in a new way with his effect.[59]

---

56. Albertus Magnus, *I Sent.*, d. 3, a. 38.

57. Albertus Magnus, *I Sent.*, d. 14, a. 3c, 392b: "mitti est cognosci quod ab alio sit"; see Augustine, *De trinitate*, bk. IV, ch. 20, no. 29.

58. Guillermo A. Juárez, *Dios Trinidad en todas las creaturas y en los santos: Estudio histórico-sistemático de la doctrina del "Comentario a las Sentencias" de Santo Tomás de Aquino sobre la omnipresencia y la inhabitación* (Córdoba, Argentina: Ediciones del Copista, 2008), 212–13.

59. Albertus Magnus, *I Sent.*, d. 14, a. 3c, 392b–393a: "duo exiguntur, scilicet appro-

Particular effects of sanctifying grace accomplish the manifestation of the personal property of the Son or the Spirit. This grace is inseparable from the Son's and the Spirit's personal presence. Albert's main addition to Augustine's definition is the created effect. He notes that "cognition of an invisible [reality] only occurs in something that is created."[60] With the *Summa fratris Alexandri* he holds that God's immutability requires that we account for the newness of the divine persons' coming by a change in the creature.[61] Albert adds another reason for such manifestation by a created reality: the properly human mode of cognition. Effects mediate noetic contact with invisible realities. We only know the person sent through an effect such as wisdom, love, grace, or a sanctifying effect.[62] The noetic encounter with God in this life is always mediated, without excluding direct contact with the divine persons. Now for Augustine, in the visible missions, visible signs such as the tongues of fire at Pentecost manifest the persons sent. He also holds that cognition of the persons sent in the invisible missions tends to pass through effects such as wisdom and charity. Yet for him we ultimately know the created through the uncreated.[63] Albert departs somewhat from Augustine's noetics with his rather Dionysian insistence that our cognitive capacities are proportioned to our ontological level.[64]

Exemplarity is key for Albert's notion of mission. The whole Trinity is the efficient cause of created grace, while the effect of grace (e.g., charity) is a divine person's similitude:

But further, there is the procession of the good in the effects of grace sanctifying rational nature, such as charity and the like. And because such ef-

---

priabilitas ad proprium, et quod sit effectus gratiae gratum facientis, cui conjuncta semper sit processio personae, et persona ipsa: oportet enim ipsam personam cum effectu suo praesentem novo modo monstrari"; see also Emery, *Trinité créatrice*, 116–17.

60. Albertus Magnus, *I Sent.*, d. 14, a. 3, ad 1, 393a: "non fit cognitio invisibilis nisi in aliquo quod creatum est."

61. Albertus Magnus, *I Sent.*, d. 14, a. 7; Juárez, *Dios Trinidad*, 169–70.

62. Albertus Magnus, *I Sent.*, d. 14, a. 6c; d. 15, a. 5, ad 1, 4; a. 11, ad sed contra 1.

63. Augustine, *De trinitate*, bk. VIII, ch. 8, no. 12; Juárez, *Dios Trinidad*, 90–91.

64. Albert sometimes clashes with Augustine's notions of the mind's direct access to God in memory and of the soul being at home in the immaterial realm. Yet we saw that both doctrines have a place in Albert's noetics. On Augustine, see Brachtendorf, *Struktur*, 232–33; Olivier Du Roy, *L'intelligence de la foi en la Trinité selon saint Augustin: Genèse de sa théologie trinitaire jusqu'en 391* (Paris: Institut d'Études Augustiniennes, 1966), 72–73, 87.

fects manifest gratuitous love toward us, therefore the giving of the first Gift is manifested in them: and this is the Holy Spirit. Therefore, the procession of the Holy Spirit is manifested in them.[65]

The missions or temporal processions involve a manifestation of the person's eternal procession. Charity is appropriated to the Spirit as to its exemplar. Noetic graces are a similitude of the Son or Wisdom proceeding from the Father. Appropriation is more than a way of speaking, as it is rooted in a likeness between the created gift and the Son's and the Spirit's personal properties.[66]

Albert's preferred terms for the soul's union with the Son and the Spirit are the "giving" and "possession" of the persons.[67] The gift of sanctifying grace always causes a real conjoining of the soul with the person sent.[68] All sanctifying grace already has a mystical element, for a real union with the Trinity occurs by the gifts appropriated to the Son or the Spirit.[69]

The invisible missions find their proximate end in sanctification, which gift includes the person sent and created grace. The missions' ultimate end is the creature's return to God:

the mission's end is sanctification and leading back (*reductio*) [to the triune God]. This does not just come about through the Holy Spirit. For leading back means showing the way, and this belongs to the [mission of the] Son; and it also means obtaining the good, which belongs to the [mis-

---

65. Albertus Magnus, *I Sent.*, d. 14, a. 1, ad 3, 391a: "Sed est iterum processio boni in effectibus gratiae gratum facientis rationalem naturam, sicut est charitas, et hujusmodi: et quia talia manifestant amorem gratuitum ad nos, ideo in his manifestatur collatio doni primi: et hoc est Spiritus sanctus: ergo in his manifestatur processio Spiritus sancti." The term *charitas* is in the Borgnet. Emery points out that procession and mission are only notionally distinct: the first emphasizes an eternal reality, the second the temporal aspect; Emergy, *Trinité créatrice*, 116n5.

66. Albertus Magnus, *I Sent.*, d. 31, a. 2; d. 34, a. 5; Emery, *The Trinitarian Theology of Saint Thomas Aquinas*, trans. Francesca Aran Murphy (Oxford: Oxford University Press, 2007), 320–21.

67. Albertus Magnus, *I Sent.*, d. 14, a. 1, ad 3; d. 15, a. 5; a. 16; d. 17, a. 1, ad 1. He uses *fruibilia* at d. 17, a. 3, ad 1.

68. Here, "gift" refers to wisdom or charity as the effects or gifts of habitual sanctifying grace. This implies a distinction between (1) habitual sanctifying grace itself and (2) the effects of habitual sanctifying grace.

69. Albertus Magnus notes the inseparable link between created grace and the presence of the person sent (*I Sent.*, d. 14, a. 3c; d. 15, a. 7, ad 2; a. 16c; d. 17, a. 1, ad 1), but often takes it for granted (Juárez, *Dios Trinidad*, 215, 230).

sion of the] Spirit. For they are sent simultaneously. Neither [mission] is imperfect or superfluous: for this must be so because of the two parts of our soul, namely, intellect and will (*affectus*).[70]

The Son shows us the way to the Father and the Spirit's gifts enable us to obtain union with the Father. This twofold biblical path of the incarnation as manifestation and Pentecost as the Spirit's coming in power matches the soul's structure: We return to God by the graced elevation of intellect and will. The soul's status as *imago* calls for a double mission, so that history and metaphysics meet. Both point to a balance of knowledge and love in the life of grace.[71]

But must the Son and the Spirit *always* be sent together? Surely they are both sent at the beginning of the spiritual life to enable our return to the Father so that the entire path of return is the fruit of the double mission. Now every new gift of sanctifying knowledge includes a new giving of the Son, while every new gift of charity includes a new giving of the Spirit.[72] Since all sanctification is appropriated to the Spirit, the Son's coming via sanctifying cognition must include the Spirit's coming. Also, the firm link between each mission and sanctifying grace (the common root of sanctifying cognition and love) points to the two missions' inseparability.[73]

Albert usually describes the immediate effect of the missions as sanctification or the effects of grace. Such language also points to a more precise doctrine—namely, that the missions already attain a complete effect in the *habitus* of grace and not just in graced human acts. The formal disposing causality of created charity is the immediate effect of the

---

70. Albertus Magnus, *I Sent.*, d. 15, a. 16, ad 2, 432a: "finis missionis est sanctificatio, et reductio: et hoc non tantum est Spiritus sancti: quia reductio dicit ostensionem viae, et quoad hoc est Filii: et dicit adeptionem boni, et quoad hoc est Spiritus sancti. Simul enim mittuntur: nec tamen alter est imperfectus, vel est superfluus: quia ita oportet propter duplicem partem anima [sic] nostrae, quae est intellectus et affectus."

71. Albertus Magnus, *I Sent.*, d. 15, a. 16c. Albert often notes the link between *reductio* and the missions; see Albert Stohr, *Die Trinitätslehre Ulrichs von Strassburg mit besonderer Berücksichtigung ihres Verhältnisses zu Albert dem Grossen und Thomas von Aquin*, Münsterische Beiträge zur Theologie 13 (Münster: Aschendorff, 1928), 87–88.

72. Albertus Magnus, *I Sent.*, d. 15, a. 19c, 436a: "missio fit in perceptione gratiae et in augmento gratiae."

73. Albertus Magnus, *I Sent.*, d. 14, a. 1, ad 3 (cited earlier, at footnote 65 in this chapter); a. 13, ad 3; d. 17, a. 2c; Juárez, *Dios Trinidad*, 216–17. Albert does not explicitly link the missions' inseparability with the Spirit's procession from the Son.

Spirit's efficient and exemplar causality.[74] The cognition needed for the missions is a habitual knowledge of the persons sent.[75] By implication the *habitus* of sanctifying grace together with the operative *habitus* of sanctifying knowledge and love account for the missions—that is to say, union with God occurs not only in "peak moments" of contemplation. Rather, all those in grace enjoy an ongoing or quasi-permanent kind of spiritual union with the Trinity. This doctrine will be crucial when we read Albert's comments on Moses in the dark cloud.

But precisely which gifts of light and love come from the double mission? "Mission is in the giving of a particular grace to the intellect and the will (*affectus*)."[76] For the Son's mission Albert cites Bernard of Clairvaux on the gift of faith, but perhaps in reference to the Son's visible mission. The *habitus* of faith linked to the mission is animated by charity, for every mission includes sanctification, which is inseparable from charity. The Son's mission presupposes that of the Spirit, at least an already realized mission of the Spirit, and perhaps a new one, as well. Since Albert usually mentions intellectual gifts when he discusses the Son's mission, and since there is no mission of the Son without sanctifying gifts, he implies that all noetic gifts belonging to the Son's mission include sanctifying grace. By implication these include the Spirit's gifts of understanding and wisdom, though as gifts they are appropriated to the Spirit who is Gift and Love.[77] For the Spirit's mission Albert speaks of will (*affectus*), by which he means charity.[78]

Sanctifying grace as a *habitus* accounts for the Son's and the Spirit's abiding presence in all believers, including baptized infants:

The cognition required for the mission ... is threefold, namely, one which is from the part of the [reality] known, namely, that I sense in me the gift in which the person sent can be known as in a sign. Now I call a *sign* that which has the act of sanctifying grace and can be appropriated to the Son

---

74. Albertus Magnus, *I Sent.*, d. 14, a. 13, ad qu. 1, ad 4. Albert focuses on created grace as a formal cause, though it is also a secondary efficient cause (see the section on grace).

75. Albertus Magnus, *I Sent.*, d. 15, a. 17c (cited later at footnote 79 of the present chapter).

76. Albertus Magnus, *I Sent.*, d. 15, a. 16, ad 3, 432a: "missio sit in collatione gratiae particularis ad intellectum vel affectum."

77. Albertus Magnus, *I Sent.*, d. 14, a. 3, ad 3; a. 6c; d. 15, a. 5, ad qu. 1, ad 4.

78. Albertus Magnus, *I Sent.*, d. 14, a. 6c; a. 13, ad qu. 3, ad 2; d. 15, a. 16c & ad 3.

Mystical Union and Its Pillars in Early Albert   73

or to the Holy Spirit. The second [cognition] is habitual cognition. The third one is conjectural [cognition] by signs, as when I see myself able to do easily what those not having grace cannot do, or can only do with great difficulty: [as] when I see my spirit to be free of vain hope, vain love, vain joy, a fallen sadness, worldly fear, and the like. I think that this threefold cognition suffices according to *habitus* for the mission, and I say that it is not necessary that actual cognition be present.[79]

The first type concerns that which accounts for the cognition of the person sent: the mission's created gift in which the person sent is made known—namely, the intellect's and affect's sanctification by the Son and the Spirit respectively. These effects can be appropriated to the Son and the Spirit, especially because of the direct exemplarity of the Son and the Spirit with regard to these effects. The divine persons' sanctifying gifts account for the habitual perception of the divine persons as sent. This is the "objective side" of the mission's manifestation: the person who has been sent is present in us in a new way.

Albert then turns to the "subjective side" of the equation. Habitual cognition means that, given the right circumstances, the person sent *can* be known (because of the created gift) but may not actually be known. Conjectural knowledge may be better translated as probable knowledge by virtue of signs ("conjectural" refers to signs allowing such conjecture). Freedom from particular vices or the effects of certain virtues suggest the presence of divine life. However, those not in grace can, at times and with difficulty, act in ways similar to those in grace, so that one's cognition of the missions remains uncertain.[80] Finally, since growth in grace and growth in union advance at the same rate, Albert indirectly offers a note of caution about confident claims of being the recipient of mystical gifts.

---

79. Albertus Magnus, *I Sent.*, d. 15, a. 17c, 433b: "Cognitio exigitur ad missionem ... triplex, scilicet una quae est ex parte cogniti, scilicet ut sentiam in me donum in quo ut in signo cognoscibilis sit persona missa: *signum* autem voco id quod habet actum gratiae facientis gratum, et appropriabile est Filio vel Spiritui sancto. Secunda est habitualis cognitio. Tertia est conjecturalis ex signis, sicut si videam me posse de facili facere quae non habens gratiam vel non potest, vel cum magna difficultate potest: si videam spiritum meum esse liberum a vana spe, et vano amore, et vano gaudio, et caduca tristitia, et timore mundano, et hujusmodi. Et illam triplicem cognitionem puto sufficere secundum habitum ad missionem, et dico non oportere adesse cognitionem secundum actum."

80. Albertus Magnus, *I Sent.*, d. 17, a. 5c.

Albert's comments on the two missions bear important consequences for his understanding of union: "These missions are not distinguished by their end, but by their proximate acts: for the Son illumines the soul and the Spirit inflames the will (*affectum*)."[81] Any new gift of illumination joined to sanctifying grace is the fruit of the Son's mission, while any new gift of sanctifying love is the fruit of the Spirit's mission. The graced operative *habitus* that enable acts of wisdom and love constitutes the created effects necessary to account for the Son's and the Spirit's missions, and those missions incite new human acts of wisdom and love, for acts are rooted in *habitus*. By implication Gallus's notion of union occurring without the intellect's proper act or in utter noetic passivity may leave behind the Son's mission and center exclusively on the Spirit's mission. But then the Son's mission might only function at a preparatory stage for the summit of the spiritual life, since this mission essentially heightens our capacity for graced acts of wisdom precisely by the giving of *habitus*. Following Augustine, Albert posits a way to union deeply intertwined with the interior life of the Trinity and with the manifestations of the eternal processions of Wisdom and Love in the economy of salvation.[82]

Albert also firmly distinguishes between the fruit of the missions and prophetic gifts or mystical apparitions. With the exception of rapture or visions that necessitate sanctifying grace, supernatural bodily apparitions, images, and the like offer no reliable manifestation of sanctifying union. The key type of experience related to union does not involve extraordinary visions but rather the habitual perception of the persons sent through infused wisdom and charity.[83]

Albert's doctrine of the missions entails a balance of knowledge and love, one called for by salvation history and by the soul's metaphysical structure. He thus offers a subtle corrective of Cistercian and Victorine mystical theologies centered on the will, ironically by developing Augustine's trinitarian mysticism. The cognition-love equilibri-

---

81. Albertus Magnus, *I Sent.*, d. 15, a. 16c, 432a: "in fine istae missiones non distinguuntur, sed in actu proximo: quia Filius illuminat intellectum, et Spiritus accendit affectum."

82. Albert does not separate the Trinity's interior life and the economy of grace, as Franz Courth has pointed out; see Courth, *Handbuch der Dogmengeschichte*, Band 2, Faszikel 1b, *Trinität in der Scholastik* (Freiburg im Breisgau: Herder, 1985), 100.

83. Albertus Magnus, *I Sent.*, d. 15, a. 16, ad 5.

um rooted in the double missions constitutes a crucial background to Albert's *Commentary on the Mystical Theology*, where love seems to be absent. The same equilibrium shows how mystical theology benefits when developed in a systematic theological context. For the relation between knowledge and love in the life of union with the divine persons directly flows from the link between the Trinity's inner life and its saving action, a connection that emerges especially in the treatise on the missions. The scholastic genre offers distinct advantages for the development of a mystical theology.

The missions manifest union from the perspective of trinitarian action. The view "from below" involves sanctifying grace, the theological virtues, and the Spirit's seven gifts, especially understanding and wisdom.

GRACE, FAITH, AND CHARITY IN ALBERT'S
SENTENCES COMMENTARY

Having surveyed the mystical subject's ontology, its way of knowing, its trinitarian likeness, and the coming of the Son and the Spirit, I now turn to the fruit of the divine missions in the believer. Five main elements of Albert's teaching on sanctifying grace and the theological virtues especially lay the groundwork for his approach to union. First, he studies grace in general, abstracting from its concretization in the theological virtues. Here, the grace of the soul's essence stands at the center. Second, he offers a few comments on Adam's grace and knowledge. Third, created grace finds its highest realization in Christ's humanity. As the exemplar of grace, Christ shows its possibilities for believers by an analogous realization of his created gifts. Fourth, grace blossoms in the soul's faculties by the virtues of faith and charity. Faith is an essential noetic path to the union that charity already begins to realize.

Albert's teaching on grace in general develops Alexander of Hales's doctrine of grace as *habitus*. The Dominican expands the Franciscan's distinction between the soul's essence and its operative powers. He synthesizes an Aristotelian structure of the soul with the Dionysian triad of nature—power—operation.[84] For Albert grace is a *habitus* in

---

84. On Albert's development of Alexander's notion of *habitus*, see Juárez, *Dios Trinidad*, 223–27. On the Dionysian triad, see Wéber, *Personne humaine*, 209–10.

relation to the soul's essence and the soul's operational powers. *Habitus* thus signifies a quasi-permanent modification or disposition. In the soul's essence it functions as that by which (*quo*) divine life is given. In the operative faculties it functions as an immediate principle of operation, disposing us toward acts of knowledge and love beyond our natural capacities.[85] By definition grace is an assimilating power (as formal cause) that conforms us to God's goodness.[86] By implication the soul's essence is assimilated to the divine splendor even before grace is concretized in the acts of the theological virtues that reside in the soul's faculties. Here the term "before" primarily signifies ontological priority. Union with God begins in the innermost part of our being. Because Albert posits a real ontological distinction between the soul's essence and operative faculties, he also posits a real distinction between the sanctifying grace of the soul's essence and the theological virtues. Still, he prefers to emphasize the unity of grace, especially by employing dynamic models for grace. His distinction between habitual grace and the theological virtues is neither as explicit nor as developed as in Aquinas.[87]

Second, Albert unenthusiastically repeats the Lombard's teaching that Adam and Eve received grace after the beginning of their existence (and before the fall). Yet Albert holds for the angels' creation in grace, a doctrine that seems to imply a similar gift for the first parents. Also, the primordial couple dwelling in Eden enjoyed an extraordinary knowledge of all things by a special gift (*gratia gratis data*) and saw God through the mirror of creatures.[88] It is not fully clear whether, in this salvific economy, humanity is ordered to graced union with God.

Third, Albert describes grace as a form flowing from the fountain of life, a form that mediates divine life. He again distinguishes between God as the giver of spiritual being (as efficient cause) and created grace understood through the biological model of the heart imparting motion to the body (as intrinsic formal cause). In this way grace is an "in-

---

85. Albertus Magnus, *II Sent.*, d. 26, a. 2c.
86. Albertus Magnus, *II Sent.*, d. 26, a. 1, ad qu. 5, ad 2.
87. Albertus Magnus, *II Sent.*, d. 26, a. 2, ad qu. 1; see also Yves Congar, "Albert le Grand théologien de la grâce sanctifiante," *La vie spirituelle* 34 (1933): 117–18.
88. Albertus Magnus, *II Sent.*, d. 3, a. 12; d. 23, aa. 1–2; d. 24, a. 1; d. 29, a. 1; Albertus Magnus, *De IV coaequaevis*, tr. 4, q. 31, a. 1; Torrell, "Nature et grâce chez Thomas d'Aquin," *RT* 101 (2001): 168.

flux from God to the soul, and it flows continually."[89] The language of flux points to the fusion of a few philosophical streams, beginning with the *Liber de Causis* notion of form as an efflux from the One. Albert's non-Aristotelian model of form (which he considers to be Aristotelian) allows him to emphasize grace as a divine similitude directly caused by God. The image of flux brings Albert's notion of grace closer to the Arab themes of emanation and the giver of forms, notions that the friar attributes to Avicenna, Al-Ghazali, and Plato. Albert also employs this model to explain how God gives charity.[90] In addition, the model of flux shows that Albert uses analogies of God's creative act and human cognition in order to understand grace. He distinguishes between the permanent, continuous outflowing of grace into the soul's essence and the noncontinuous character of graced acts using the model of the agent intellect's constant illumination of the passive intellect, with or without species abstracted from phantasms. In his doctrine of creation Albert presents a similar synthesis of formal flux emanating from the divine agent intellect.[91]

Fourth, Albert invokes the Dionysian axiom of the good as self-diffusive to develop his notion of grace as form within the operating-cooperating grace distinction, a crucial Augustinian theme. Created operating grace refers to a form's action as formal cause. Here Albert seems to refuse created grace as an efficient cause of divine life, though his theology of created charity moves in a different direction, as we will see. Operating grace is nothing other than form's self-diffusion in its subject. Grace does not so much make new life as "give itself." The *Liber de Causis*, Boethian, and Peripatetic theme of flux thus finds its Dionysian complement in the procession of divine gifts. Outside of his treatise on the missions, Albert prefers dynamic metaphors and analogies for created grace to the notion of grace as an accident. Operating

---

89. Albertus Magnus, *II Sent.*, d. 26, a. 5c, 451b–452a: "gratia est vita animae, secundum quod vita formaliter adhaeret vivo, ut forma effluxa a causa et fonte vitae ... vita animae metaphysice loquendo, est Deus dans esse animae, non ut forma, sed sicut portans esse ejus.... Alio modo vivit corpus, secundum quod dicimus, quod spiritus vitalis vehiculum est vitae, quae continue influitur corpori ab animalis speciali organo, sicut cordis.... Et huic metaphysice respondet vita gratiae, quae est influxa animae a Deo, et influitur continue."

90. Albertus Magnus, *I Sent.*, d. 17, a. 1, ad 3.

91. Albertus Magnus, *II Sent.*, d. 26, a. 5, ad sed contra; de Libera, *Métaphysique*, 143, 151–58, 169–77.

grace is the formal causality of created grace, a diffusion of a similitude of God's goodness. Thus operating grace is an elevation of being rather than a direct motion toward act. Operating grace only inclines toward act. Once joined to the human operation of free decision, the same divine gift becomes cooperating grace.[92] Albert will assign an efficient causality to charity at the level of the soul's faculties (i.e., cooperating grace). He implies that the supernatural *habitus* flows from the soul's essence into its faculties, where it becomes cooperating grace. Here its dynamism is joined to properly human operation. The *habitus* of the essence must flow somewhere, and Albert insists that the same grace is in the soul's essence and its inseparable faculties.[93] He does not posit an operating grace that directly elicits a free human act.[94]

Albert's teaching of grace places a strong emphasis on active human cooperation. This doctrine seems hard to synthesize with Moses's passive mind in the dark cloud. The theme of noetic spontaneity or passivity will therefore demand special attention in chapter 4 of this volume. Albert holds that form is an outpouring of God's likeness that reflects the dynamism of its source. Grace as a form diffuses itself in us, and we perpetuate this motion through free human acts, whereby our return to the divine source comes to fulfillment. Grace as a formal flux and a diffusion of goodness fits well with an Augustinian-Aristotelian understanding of *habitus*. Albert's theology of created grace overflows the boundaries of Aristotelian metaphysics.

The German friar's vision of Christ's grace expands upon the theme of flux. He creatively fuses an apparently timeless metaphysics of form with the history of God's saving acts. Christ is the head of the church, efficiently giving grace by his divine nature. In a reference to Christ's headship operating by his two natures, Albert notes that the head

---

92. Albertus Magnus, *II Sent.*, d. 26, a. 7c, 455a: "dicitur operari sicut forma facit esse, non sicut efficiens. Hoc autem facere quod est formae, non est nisi diffusio sui in formato. Et ideo bene concedo, quod forma absolute accepta actu formae non efficientis facit se in format ... quia forma non proprie facit, sed dat, et suum dare est diffusio sui et informatio, ideo forma dat esse quod est actus illius formae, et operatur, et hoc est esse suum in formato."

93. Albertus Magnus, *II Sent.*, d. 26, a. 10, ad 2; a. 12c.

94. Doms holds that Albert's theology of grace is marked more by neo-Platonic than by Aristotelian categories; Doms, *Gnadenlehre*, 275. This seems correct, but grace as an accident remains important for Albert.

Mystical Union and Its Pillars in Early Albert   79

is as an effective principle that also assimilates [us] to himself through something which flows [into souls] as form. Thus, Christ is the head of the blessed and of those existing in grace, into whom he pours (*influit*) a quasi similitude of his own life ... in gifts perfecting intellect and will (*affectum*).[95]

Created grace is not just a divine similitude but also a likeness of the grace concretized in Christ's human life. Formal flux inclines toward the *imitatio Christi*. Albert synthesizes Neoplatonic notions of flux, Dionysian divine similitude, Augustinian headship, and the Bernardian theme of the mysteries of Christ. He turns Neoplatonic metaphysics upside down by inserting the contingency of history into the essence of supernatural being. Thanks to the grace-nature distinction, a certain type of formal flux is open to history. Albert proposes a theology of divine union via conformity to Christ while firmly excluding efficient causality from Christ's activity as man, even on the instrumental plane. Rather, Christ "flows" or pours out grace by merit, by the act of redemption, and by his exemplarity.[96] Albert sketches the beginnings of a doctrine of Christo-forming grace, yet he does not explicitly connect particular mysteries of Christ's life with the nature of sanctifying grace received. Albert outlines an ontology of grace that can closely bind the humanity of Christ with the flourishing of the mystical life. He thus surpasses the theology of Dionysius, who was not able to place Christ at the center of his vision for the spiritual life.

Albert's notion of Christ's graced cognition as man has indirect implications for the possibilities of mystical knowledge in general. His Christology reflects a particular notion of embodied souls' metaphysical and noetic relation to the divine and immaterial realm. Here the

---

95. Albertus Magnus, *III Sent.*, d. 13, a. 2c, 238b: "Si autem consideretur ut principium influens effective tantum, tunc est caput omnino secundum deitatem. Si autem ut est principium effectivum et assimilans sibi per aliquod quod influit quod est ut forma: sic est caput beatorum et existentium in gratia, quibus influit quasi similitudinem suae vitae ... in donis perficientibus intellectum et affectum." The same article restricts the first headship (efficient causality) to Christ in his divinity, a restriction not made for the second headship (formal causality or assimilation).

96. Albertus Magnus, *III Sent.*, d. 13, a. 3c; Theophil Tschipke, *Die Menschheit Christi als Heilsorgan der Gottheit: Unter besonderer Berücksichtigung der Lehre des heiligen Thomas von Aquin*, Freiburger theologische Studien 55 (Freiburg im Breisgau: Herder, 1940), 107–8.

most striking passage concerns Christ's human contemplation of the eternal Word:

> Understanding would not occur without the presence of the thing understood. Now something is more present when it is essentially in the soul than that which is only [present] by similitude ... the Word is more present [to Christ's soul] than any *habitus* can make him present. Moreover, it [the Word] is present to the soul to the extent that it unites [the soul] to itself and penetrates it. Therefore, since this is [in] Christ's soul, his soul knows all things in the Word and not by something else.[97]

We have already encountered such an Augustinian approach to epistemology in the section on noetic illumination. The parallel is important, for we are dealing with the operative conditions of Christ's higher intellect. At this level presence is the key to knowledge, not noetic information. The Word's essential presence refers to the hypostatic union and its consequences for Christ's human cognition. The intensity of hypostatic presence has a direct complement in the realm of cognitive presence. The limitations of a finite soul are essentially overcome through the hypostatic union. Thus the biblical teaching on Christ learning in his humanity refers to the actualization of what he already knew in a habitual way.[98] The embodied status of Christ's soul has minor consequences for the cognitive aspects of his union with the divine essence. By implication, it seems that the intensity of God's dwelling in the hearts of believers can achieve an analogous (though not identical) cognitive union with God. The greater God's presence, the less the character of union is shaped by the soul's identity as the form of the body. Such a mystical epistemology harmonizes well with the *Sentences Commentary* doctrine of memory.

As mediator of grace, Christ gives the virtues of faith and charity. For the early Albert faith opens us to a divine light that joins us to God. I will focus on three key sub-themes: (1) the relation of intellect

---

97. Albertus Magnus, *III Sent.*, d. 14, a. 2, sed contra 2, 257a–b: "Non fieret intellectus sine praesentia rei intellectae: magis autem praesens est quod per essentiam est in anima, quam id quod per similitudinem tantum ... magis praesentatur Verbum, quam aliquis habitus possit praesentare: sed adhuc magis praesentatur animae quam sibi unit et eam penetrat: ergo cum haec sit anima Christi, anima Christi in Verbo et non in aliquo alio cognoscit omnia."

98. Albertus Magnus, *III Sent.*, d. 13, aa. 10, 12.

and will in faith; (2) infused light as an effect of faith; and (3) unitive aspects of faith. The first topic considers faith's "location" in the soul's faculties, which helps to specify the "place" of union by faith. The second topic explicates God's initiative in faith and the noetic effect of being joined to God in faith. I preface the study of these three themes with a historical sketch of the doctrinal context, for it greatly illumines Albert's theological intention.

A significant medieval debate on the nature of faith concerns its relation to intellect and will. Hugh of St. Victor and the Lombard place the act of faith *between* these two faculties. The matter or content of faith consists of creedal propositions, but the substance of faith consists of the will's act of loving trust. Cognition of God and his works is essential to faith, but the will has priority. For Hugh and the Lombard the properly unitive aspect of faith is found above all in the will's graced adherence to God.[99] Faith's cognition comes through Gospel propositions more than by an infused light. These theologies of faith set the stage for a mysticism centered on love.

Albert takes up the question of faith's relation to intellect and will as he distinguishes belief from reason's certain grasp of causes (*scientia*). Belief involves a free human response to revelation, for the noetic object is not so evident that it compels assent:

While faith has knowledge, this arises more from affect (*affectu*) than from reason. Thus Augustine says: "Belief only occurs by willing" ... with respect to some other things, consent is not compelled except [when] one wills it by free will, in that such [objects believed] are not apparent to it [the intellect], and of such things there is faith: and so the masters used to say that in faith, cognition is material and affection (*affectio*) is formal.[100]

The will does not produce knowledge, but rather moves the intellect to accept the gospel message as true. The intellect always mediates cogni-

---

99. Marcia L. Colish, *Peter Lombard*, Brill's Studies in Intellectual History, vol. 41, part 2 (Leiden: E. J. Brill, 1994), 2:496–98.

100. Albertus Magnus, *III Sent.*, d. 23, a. 1c, 405a–b: "Licet enim [fides] habeat cognitionem, tamen illa magis oritur ex affectu, quam ex ratione. Unde Augustinus: 'Caetera potest homo facere nolens, credere autem non nisi volens' ... respectu quorumdam aliorum ad quorum consensum non compellitur nisi ex voluntate libera velit, eo quod talia non sint apparentia sibi, et de talibus est fides: et ideo consueverunt Magistri dicere, quod cognitio in fide est materialis, et affectio formalis"; see also ad 4; a. 4c.

tion, while the will has primacy in the process of adherence to revelation as divine or trustworthy. Albert employs the term *affectus* to refer to the will, which he compares to the intellect or reason. The term *affectio* does not signify an inclination of the intellect to revealed truth, but the will moving the intellect to judge noncompelling cognition to be true. Since affection is formal, the will has primacy.

But Albert soon nuances his position: "as for consent, which is the substance of the faith act ... intellect is about the true for which the principle of consent is the will, and this is the affective understanding."[101] Albert suggests that faith's proper subject is the intellect as moved by affection. The will causes the faith act in its subject, in the *affectivus intellectus*, which is the intellect as moved to assent by the will. He also calls faith a practical science mingled with affect—practical because ordered to beatitude. Albert seeks to safeguard the will as an indispensable cause of faith, for knowledge alone does not suffice.[102] He combines an Augustinian emphasis on the will with a scholastic identification of a virtue's proper faculty.

Albert then integrates a Dionysian notion of faith. The Areopagite refers to a simple truth in us whereby we know what is proposed for belief, but he says nothing about the will. Albert systematizes this cognitive approach to faith by assigning faith cognition to the virtue's effects.

[Faith] places the truth of what is believed in us through the most certain consent. But by the fact that this is not a complex truth, as in a proportion ... or a syllogism's principle, therefore, by faith, those trusting in it [truth] are said to have simple knowledge of truth, that is, a simple light which somehow makes them know the truth of the article of faith.[103]

---

101. Albertus Magnus, *III Sent.*, d. 23, a. 2, ad 4, 408a–b: "quoad consensum, qui est substantia actus fidei ... intellectus veri, cujus consensus principium est voluntas: et ille est affectivus intellectus."

102. Albertus Magnus, *III Sent.*, d. 23, a. 1, ad 1; a. 2, ad 2–3; a. 4c, 413a: "perfectio fidei est a duobus, scilicet intellectu dante actum, et affectu ut informante"; Senner, *Alberts des Großen Verständnis*, 9–12. *III Sent.*, d. 23, a. 4 does not fit Marie-Dominique Chenu's conclusion that Albert makes intellect *and* affect the subject of faith. Chenu incorrectly aligns Albert's theology with Hugh of St. Victor's; see Chenu, "La psychologie de la foi dans la théologie du XIIIe siècle," in *La Parole de Dieu*, vol. 1, *La foi dans l'intelligence,* Cogitatio Fidei 10 (Paris: Cerf, 1964), 94; Chenu, "L'amour dans la foi," in *La Parole de Dieu*, 1:110.

103. Albertus Magnus, *III Sent.*, d. 23, a. 3, ad diffinitionem Dionysii, 410a–b: "diffinitio Dionysii datur de fide secundum proprium effectum ... [fides] locat per consensum

Faith opens us to an infused noetic light that enters the intellect as it consents. This gifted cognition does not consist of a faith proposition to be used in a theological syllogism. Rather, this light elevates one's grasp of the truth of faith statements. The propositional content of the credal articles comes from the gospel that is heard. The simple light seems to deepen our firm adherence to the propositions as true. We are likely dealing with simultaneous parts of a single event. Diverse proximate causes (the act of consent, hearing the gospel and divine light completing adherence) are ordered by ontological priority (i.e., the infused light's efficacy depends on the act of consent). Albert then states that such illumined faith is only "somehow *scientia*," for faith's cognition remains enigmatic. He calls infused light a "similitude of the first truth" included in every faith article.[104] He links his notion of faith with his Dionysian vision of grace as a dynamic similitude of God. He thus also connects faith with the Son's mission, for the latter manifests itself in a noetic effect. The act of consent remains central, as it enables reception of the simple light.

The action of grace follows consent, but grace also precedes it. Faith only sanctifies if it is joined to charity.[105] As Albert defines the nature of an article of belief, he discusses faith's relation to sanctifying grace. He roots the *habitus* of faith and its acts in divine causality:

> the motion of faith begins from the truth of the article, and not from the *habitus*. For the truth of the article makes the *habitus* by its similitude in the soul, and makes that *habitus* tend into the same truth. Thus, the movement of what is moved begins from the first truth, and through the article of the first truth tends into the same [truth], so that the circle of the ray proceeding from the eternal [reality] into the temporal soul of the just may be completed ... as Dionysius says in the first book of the *Celestial Hierarchy:* "Every procession of the manifestation of lights moved by the Father comes into us in the best way and generously ... turning us back to the unity of the gathering Father."[106]

---

certissimum veritatem crediti in nobis: in hoc autem quod non est veritas complexionis, sicut in proportione, quae dignitas vocatur, vel principium syllogismi, ideo dicuntur in ipsa creduli habere simplicem veritatis scientiam, id est, simplum lumen, quod facit aliqualiter scire veritatem credibilis articuli."

104. Albertus Magnus, *III Sent.*, d. 23, a. 3, ad diffinitionem 1, ad 6; see also a. 18, ad qu. 2, ad 1.

105. Albertus Magnus, *III Sent.*, d. 23, a. 5, ad 5.

106. Albertus Magnus, *III Sent.*, d. 24, a. 4, ad diffinitionem 1, ad 3, 451a: "motus fi-

The *habitus* of faith is the turning point between our procession from God (by creation) and our return to him by sanctification. The treatise on the divine missions proposes *habitus* in its intellectual and affective forms as the key to the manifestation and fulfillment of the missions.[107] Albert now traces the dynamism of the faith *habitus* as the principle of a cognitive act back to its divine origin. The truth of the faith proposition is part of the luminous procession whose origin is the Father. The faith *habitus* reflects divine truth. Its effect is to lead us back to our source, to complete the trinitarian cosmic circle of procession and return. The faith *habitus* contains a properly noetic and dynamic unitive power. As a cognitive gift this *habitus* effects a first union with the Father (assuming the presence of charity), thus evoking the Son's mission.[108] Albert places an Augustinian notion of faith centered on consent and enigmatic cognition in a Dionysian framework of procession and return. He offers an Augustinian-Dionysian synthesis on the nature of *habitus*. The Areopagite's theology of illumination enables a fuller valorization of the noetic and unitive aspects of the faith *habitus*, while a thirteenth-century Augustinian notion of created grace helps to explain the human reception of and participation in the gathering motion of God's light. This notion of unitive light harmonizes with the earlier discussion of Dionysian noetic light as an effect of the faith act. The present text discusses the fully formed *habitus* of faith made possible by consent opening the intellect to the light of divine truth communicated in the articles of faith.

Other passages in Albert's "treatise" on faith also point to a balance of knowledge and love in belief's unitive power. He notes that faith working through love by its nature enables us to cling to God. By itself the human act of faith has no unitive power, for it only tends to-

---

dei incipit a veritate articuli, et non ab habitu: veritas enim articuli facit habitum sui similitudine in anima, et facit illum habitum tendere in eamdem veritatem: ut sic sit motus mobilis a prima veritate incipiens, et per articulum primae veritatis in eamdem tendens, ut concludatur circulus egredientis radii ab aeterno in temporalem animam justi, et per veritatem articuli in aeternam veritatem: sicut dicit Dionysius in libro primo de *Caelesti hierarchia*: 'Omnis Patre moto manifestationis luminum processio in nos optime ac large proveniens ... convertit ad congregantis Patris unitatem.'"

107. Albertus Magnus, *I Sent.*, d. 15, a. 17c.

108. Compare *SCH*, ch. 3 (p. 50.33–39) on the Son's mission and the Dionysian divine ray (see chapter 4 of this volume).

ward the object of assent. Adherence to God requires love for him.[109] Albert presupposes charity's presence whenever he refers to unitive faith.[110] This often unspoken premise helps to nuance the intellectual mysticism of his Dionysian commentaries. Yet he clearly refuses to make faith a subset of charity. Rather, the faith *habitus* finds its first completion in an infused light that informs the intellect (moved by the will). Albert's extensive discussion of divine light uniting the intellect to truth has the potential for a doctrine of mystical cognition as the fruit of faith.[111]

Three other passages on the unitive aspect of faith should be mentioned, for they will be of significant help in our reading of Albert's *Commentary on the Mystical Theology*. First, the "adherence" of faith signifies the "union of consent." Second, belief brings about two effects: "it manifests eternal realities" and "convinces the mind of the truth" of the articles of faith. The manifested realities most likely refer to the eternal truths communicated in the Creed. Third, faith enables us to "perceive" God indirectly, while the Spirit's gift of wisdom imparts an experiential taste of God. Perception is a standard metaphor for a noetic act, here in reference to our firm acceptance of things not seen.[112] Albert thus posits the beginning of cognitive union in faith and points to the Spirit's highest gifts as a key site for union with God.

109. Albertus Magnus, *III Sent.*, d. 23, a. 7, ad qu. 1, ad 2, 5.
110. See also Albertus Magnus, *III Sent.*, d. 23, a. 9c, ad 9.
111. Albertus Magnus, *III Sent.*, d. 23, a. 10c, 424b: "fides formatur propria forma ... quod est lumen informans intellectum affectivum secundum tensionem in finem, et illud formale est respectu habitus assentientis Deo ... etiam erit in habitu, quod lumini additum est lumen conjungens intellectum credentis veritati quam credit." Wéber argues that Albertus Magnus has an intellectual definition of faith here, in *III Sent.*, d. 23, a. 4 and a. 18, ad 3, and in the Dionysian commentaries; Wéber, "Relation," 576–79. Tugwell sees an evolution from belief as the will's acceptance of a faith proposition in the *Sentences Commentary* to faith as a reality that directly convinces the mind in the Dionysian commentaries; Tugwell, "Albert the Great," 70–71. But *III Sent.*, d. 23, aa. 10, 18 (and d. 24, a. 4) already include the latter doctrine. Wéber rightly points to the cognitive character of faith in *III Sent.*, but underestimates somewhat the place of affect therein. Albert's *Sent.* doctrine of faith seems to be somewhere between Tugwell and Wéber.
112. Albertus Magnus, *III Sent.*, d. 23, a. 7, ad qu. 1, ad 5, 419a: "adhaerere autem dicit conjunctionem consensus"; a. 18c, 438a: "duo effectus ejus ... unus est, quod res aeternas ostendit ... secundum autem est, quod convincit mentem de veritate illarum rerum"; d. 24, a. 11c, 469b–70a: "Augustinus loquitur de scientia approbationis quae mixta est affectui: sic enim conspicitur mente, dum gustatur per experientiam in donis: et hoc est aliquid ultra fidem et citra visionem."

Like his treatment of faith, Albert's teaching on charity in the *Sentences Commentary* synthesizes multiple doctrinal traditions. One finds the pillars of his doctrine of unitive love in a single article that includes sections on the Lombard, Augustine, Dionysius, Avicenna, and St. Paul.[113] After a brief consideration of charity as a created gift, I will focus on this passage, integrating insights from other articles as I proceed.[114] As a preface let us note that Albert briefly distinguishes charity from Aristotelian friendship. The Stagirite holds that a friend seeks the highest good for his own sake, not for God's, which Albert contrasts to charity for God.[115]

In the treatise on the missions Albert takes up the Lombard's famous thesis that identifies charity with the Holy Spirit. Since created grace is finite, it seems incapable of joining us to God, so that the Lombard's thesis appears to hold. Albert responds:

Created charity as an accident is not as dignified as a substance. But if we consider it from the standpoint of goodness, then charity is more dignified than all created good. For the *ratio* of the good is in it [charity], that it is an effect most similar to the goodness of God, to the point that God himself is never separated from this effect.[116]

If charity is created, then it must be an accident, for it is really distinct from both the uncreated substance of the Spirit and the soul's created substance. As such an accident is metaphysically inferior to substance. But as the created gift that most approximates God's goodness, the splendor of created charity outshines all of creation's glory. Like created grace, created charity is not so much a thing (*quod*) as *that by which* (*quo*) we share God's life.[117] By itself created charity's operative power

---

113. Albertus Magnus, *III Sent.*, d. 27, a. 4.
114. An in-depth study of charity in Albert has yet to be undertaken, but see Johannes Schneider, *Das Gute und die Liebe nach der Lehre von Albert des Grossen*, Veröffentlichungen des Grabmann-Institutes 3 (Munich: Ferdinand Schöningh, 1967); Schneider focuses on forms of love other than charity.
115. Albertus Magnus, *III Sent.*, d. 27, a. 1, ad 1, 3.
116. Albertus Magnus, *I Sent.*, d. 17, a. 1, ad 1, 465a: "Charitas per hoc quod accidens ... indignius aliquid est in genere quam substantia. Si autem attenditur ratio boni, tunc ipsa est dignior omni bono creato: quia ratio boni in ipsa est, quod est effectus simillimus bonitati Dei, ita quod etiam ipse Deus ab effectu hoc numquam separatur, sed semper cum ipso datur ei cui datur charitas ... unde ipse inferiorem in bonitatis ratione naturam potest conjungere naturae superiori"; see also ad 2, 5; d. 14, a. 21c.
117. Gérard Philips holds that created and uncreated grace are two entities in Albert;

is finite. But created charity does not exist by itself. Because of the divine presence, finite charity can and does join us to the infinite God. Albert seems to imply that no similitude of such intensity could even exist without a unique mode of God's dynamic presence.[118] Here one also recalls the doctrine of the Spirit as the efficient cause joining us to the Father through the *habitus* of charity.

The main text from Albert gives the "definition" of charity. Albert harmonizes various doctrinal traditions as he assigns them to distinct parts of charity (e.g., cause, act, effect). The Lombard's definition (love of God and love of neighbor for God's sake) especially relates to the virtue's cause.

> The causes [of charity] are threefold: efficient, formal and final ... charity makes us love and not we [acting] of ourselves. It does so inasmuch as charity is a similitude of the divine goodness. Hence, God's goodness which is God does this. Thanks to its own form and reason: because we do not love accidentally, but for his [God's] sake and as he is. Again, the final cause: for [we do not love] for the sake of something else.[119]

As a created likeness of God's love, charity has a moving force that redirects the heart. Albert employs Aristotelian efficient causality to integrate the Dionysian vision of love as spiritual motion. Charity is a formal cause in that God is the reason of love, which distinguishes this virtue from the love of God for our sake. Earlier in this distinction, Albert employs the analogy of the first cosmic mover to explain the efficient aspect of charity. The first mover within the universe is directly moved by God and moves other agents to desire the ultimate cosmic end. Similarly, charity moves the other virtues to act under the finality of their divine end.[120] By its nature the gift of love does not bring about

---

see Philips, *L'union personnelle avec le Dieu vivant: Essai sur l'origine et le sens de la grâce crée*, Bibliotheca Ephemeridum Theologicarum Lovaniensium 36 (Gembloux: J. Duculot, 1974), 128. But Albert explicilty refuses this model; see his *I Sent.* d. 17, a. 1, ad 6, and Doms, *Gnadenlehre*, 87–90.

118. See Congar, "Albert le Grand," 114–20.

119. Albertus Magnus, *III Sent.*, d. 27, a. 4, ad diffinitionem Magistri, ad 2, 520a: "ibi triplicem causam, scilicet efficientem, formalem, et finalem ... charitas facit nos diligere, non nosipsi nos: et hoc facit in quantum est similitudo bonitatis divinae: et ideo bonitas Dei quae Deus est, hoc facit. Item, gratia formae suae et rationis: quia non per accidens diligimus, sed propter ipsum in quantum ipsum est. Item finalem: quia non propter aliud."

120. Albertus Magnus, *III Sent.*, d. 27, a. 2, ad 2; a. 3, ad 1–2.

a passive clinging to God, but rather engages the whole human being in virtuous operations that constitute the path of return. Like his ontology of grace as formal flux, Albert's notion of charity as a formal cause and moving force prepares the way for a doctrine of union that integrates the free and active cooperation of the human being.

Albert then takes up an Augustinian definition of charity as "the virtue whereby we desire to see and enjoy God."[121] Albert comments, "to enjoy (*frui*) predicates clinging and the taste that follows the beloved, who is seen and possessed. And the fact that he adds the taste of sweetness, has nothing superfluous."[122] Charity aims at knowledge of the beloved that is realized in noetic possession and perfected in the beatific vision. The act of enjoyment involves union with the beloved and a spiritual taste of his sweetness. While all of the virtues cause a certain enjoyment in their actualization, charity possesses a proper form of enjoyment in that it brings about a direct experience of divine sweetness or goodness in the attainment of the divine end.[123] Above all Albert's brief analysis of Augustine provides a list of key terms for beatific union: *frui, inhaesio, visio, habitum,* and *gustus dulcedinis*. The terms *frui* and *gustus* are directly connected to charity. The section on the gift of wisdom below will allow us to trace the analogous application of some of these terms to the summit of grace in this life.

Albert's direct treatment of the Areopagite assigns love (*amor*) and its providential effects (e.g., angels caring for embodied beings) to the genus of love distinct from its species that is charity. Albert's most creative application of the Areopagite's notions of love and the good to the doctrine of charity comes outside of the same article's section on Dionysius in the study of charity according to St. Paul. The latter section serves as a platform for a veritable synthesis of love as being for God's sake. Paul's "definitions" of charity refer to what generates this theological virtue (1 Tm 1:5 mentions faith, a good conscience, and a pure heart) and to its ultimate perfection (Col 3:14 refers to the bond

---

121. Albertus Magnus, *III Sent.*, d. 27, a. 4, 517a: "Charitas est virtus qua Deum videre perfruique desideramus."

122. Albertus Magnus, *III Sent.*, d. 27, a. 4, ad diffinitionem Augustini, ad 2, 520a: "non superfluit 'perfrui': quia 'frui' dicit inhaesionem et gustum consequentem amatum, quod est visum et habitum: et quia addit gustum dulcedinis, ideo non abundat."

123. Albertus Magnus, *III Sent.*, d. 27, a. 4, ad diffinitionem Augustini, ad 3.

of love). Between these two elements Albert inserts the notion of charity as efficient and formal cause: "Charity is ... efficient and [a] form, for it makes flow something of itself and of its form into all meritorious works and virtues."[124] Like created grace, charity has the characteristic of formal flux, which also grounds its efficient causality. Thus created grace as formal flux may well imply efficient causality, after all. Charity as form enjoys a certain metaphysical integrity; it "is something of itself," for it brings about a real modification of the soul. As a flowing form charity pours itself into the soul's entire organism. Charity thus reveals one aspect of its nature as a divine similitude as it diffuses its goodness into the lower powers in imitation of God's goodness. Albert again unites formality and efficiency. Charity naturally overflows onto the other parts of the soul and moves them to meritorious works. Charity pours itself out not as an agent, but as an indwelling, dynamic form. By its very nature charity participates in the motion of divine goodness in the cosmos, guiding the whole human being on the path of return to God. Dionysian similitude and diffusion join the Proclan-Boethian-Arab theme of formal flux, the Peripatetic motion of the first mover, Christianized virtue ethics, and the theology of merit, all squeezed within a Pauline framework. Albert proposes an ambitious synthesis. I should note that the ultimate effect of love as binding us to the beloved is not a strictly Pauline theme. While love as a bond is a favorite Pauline refrain among medieval mystical theologians, Albert began the article by citing the *Divine Names* on love's unitive power. His direct treatment of Paul emphasizes this aspect of charity. This virtue effectively "conjoins us to the ultimate end." The "ultimate conjunction is through love (*amorem*)," the Areopagite's preferred affective term.[125]

Finally, Albert briefly mentions charity's act in the beatific presence of the beloved.

---

124. Albertus Magnus, *III Sent.*, d. 27, a. 4, ad diffinitionem Apostoli, ad 1, 521b: "illa diffinitio data est penes ea quae generant charitatem in nobis. Charitas ... est efficiens et forma: quia aliquid de se et de sua forma influit omnibus operibus et virtutibus meritoriis. Finis autem est consummationis sive perfectionis. Et ideo dicit Apostolus, quod charitas est vinculum perfectionis [Col. 3:14]."

125. Albertus Magnus, *III Sent.*, d. 27, a. 4, ad diffinitionem Apostoli, ad 1, 521b: "Charitas ... effective ... conjungit cum fine ultimo ... est autem ultima conjunctio per amorem."

[Charity] penetrates the intimate things of the beloved by tasting them. Thus, the blessed Dionysius attributes [to love] sharpness, mobility and great fervor. For it penetrates the beloved by the sharp point of affection, is moved into him and goes into great fervor for him according to whatever measure of divine sweetness [is given].[126]

Albert thus alludes to the ecstatic element of love taking us "beyond mind" and makes it concomitant with the beloved's presence. In contrast, the Areopagite considered the ecstasy of love a prelude to union. Also, Albert offers his remarks in the context of eschatology. The treatise on charity does not consider ecstasy in this life. The latter theme is only taken up indirectly in the *Sentences Commentary* study of the divine names, as we will see. Before 1248 Albert mostly ignores or avoids one of the most troubling aspects of Dionysian mysticism—namely, the relative absence of love in union by unknowing. However, he does take up the question in an indirect way as he answers an objection. In heaven, "cognition will be perfect, and so, love will also be perfect." Augustine's principle that nothing can be loved unless it is known applies. Indeed, knowledge becomes a measure of love's realization.[127] Applied to this life, this principle would firmly exclude the possibility of union beyond mind in a strict sense.

Overall, Albert's teaching on the unitive aspect of charity seeks to integrate diverse theological traditions. His originality comes in his application of formal flux to the doctrines of grace and charity and in his manner of synthesizing somewhat heterogeneous traditions. Charity has a conjoining effect, but without leading to a doctrine of union by love beyond mind. Still, we can only fully evaluate the Areopagite's place in Albert's early mystical theology by considering his doctrine of the Spirit's gifts, divine naming, and glory.

---

126. Albertus Magnus, *III Sent.*, d. 31, a. 9c, 588b: "In actu autem modo dilectum absens desiderat, sed tunc praesens diligit, et penetrat gustando intima ipsius. Propter hoc enim attribuitur ei a beato Dionysio acutum et mobile et superfervidum: quia acumine affectus penetrat amatum, et movetur in ipsum, et superfervet ipsum secundum quamlibet rationem dulcedinis divinae."

127. Albertus Magnus, *III Sent.*, d. 31, a. 9, ad 2, 589a: "nihil diligit nisi cognitum aliquo modo ... in patria, non tamen destruetur cognitio, sed erit perfectissima: et ideo perfectissima dilectio."

THE GIFTS OF UNDERSTANDING AND
WISDOM IN ALBERT'S *SENTENCES COMMENTARY*

The early Albert's doctrine of the Spirit's gifts of understanding and wisdom completes the noetic element of his theology of union. The doctrine of the gifts provides the ultimate view of noetic union "from below," while the doctrine of charity does so for affective union. Because Albert directly links only the gifts of understanding and wisdom to contemplation and union, we can pass over his teaching on the other five gifts. Given the crucial function of the gifts in union, I will pay special attention to Albert's sources so as to better discern his proper contribution and doctrinal intention. Given the lack of patristic consensus on the gifts, Albert and other scholastics had the opportunity to make a very original contribution to mystical theology.[128]

The scholastic's first task was to distinguish the seven gifts from the virtues, which also helps to specify their respective functions in the ascent to God. Albert explains that the virtues can be imperfect in relation to their proper acts. As an example, he cites the intellect's order to first truth that the virtue of faith only partially perfects, since the latter grants knowledge of God in an enigma (1 Cor 13:12). The gifts are really distinct infused *habitus* that aid the virtues, enabling a higher or second operative perfection. Albert cites Gregory the Great, though he is also influenced by Philip the Chancellor and Alexander of Hales.[129]

Albert then proceeds to a standard scholastic threefold distinction. Following Philip and Alexander, he divides the virtues, gifts, and beatitudes into a hierarchy of dispositions or *habitus*.

The virtues perfect the soul for its first acts, the gifts for its second acts, the beatitudes for its third acts, and fruits for the end ... faith is not perfected by virtue in view of consent to the first truth, which it does not see, except as in a mirror and in an enigma. But it happens that one sees it [first truth]

---

128. For an overview of Albert's doctrine of the gifts, see M.-H. Lavaud, "Les dons du Saint-Esprit d'après Albert le Grand," *RT* 36 (1931): 162–83. For the medievals' originality on the gifts, see Jacques de Blic, "Pour l'histoire de la théologie des dons avant saint Thomas," *Revue d'Ascétique et de Mystique* 22 (1946): 117–79.

129. Albertus Magnus, *III Sent.*, d. 34, a. 1c; Odon Lottin, *Psychologie et morale aux XIIe et XIIIe siècles*, vol. 3, part 2, sect. 1 (Louvain: Abbaye du Mont César; Gembloux: J. Duculot, 1949), 360–63, 374–75.

better in the light of illumination by the inspiration of grace, and that one tastes [it] through experience in its very *ratio*.... And the gifts perfect in this way. Again, it happens that sight fixes upon it [truth] in a higher way, with maximum certitude, and then there is the act of the beatitude of perfect purity, as is said, "Blessed are the pure of heart, for they shall see God." It also happens that one is refreshed in the taste of this certitude, and so there will be the *habitus* that is called a fruit, and which the Apostle calls faith.[130]

Albert's approach to the function of these *habitus* also has doctrinal precedents. Philip speaks of the gift of wisdom imparting a taste of what we believe and the pure of heart enjoying a vision of God insofar as is possible in this life. Alexander refers to the gifts of understanding and wisdom together granting knowledge of God with a taste of the things believed.[131] Albert's original contribution appears to be his classification of the fruits as *habitus* that impart "refreshment."[132] But here we come upon a perplexing lacuna in his *Sentences Commentary*— namely, the virtual absence of any further discussion of the beatitudes and the Spirit's fruits. The end of the same article acknowledges that the beatitudes deserve their own treatise, one that Albert never wrote.[133] The Dionysian commentaries also barely mention the beatitudes and fruits.[134] Albert's teaching on the perfection of the virtues fully centers on the seven gifts.

The gifts perfect us for acts, like the virtues. The gifts are operative dispositions or *habitus* distinct from the virtues. He calls wisdom a light that enjoys its proper act. He also notes that while the *habitus*

---

130. Albertus Magnus, *III Sent.*, d. 34, a. 2c, 622a: "virtutes perficiunt animam ad actus primos, et dona, ad secundos, et beatitudines ad tertios, et fructus in finem ... quia non perficitur fides virtute ad consensum primae veritatis, quam non videt, nisi in speculo et in aenigmate: hanc autem contingit melius videre in lumine illustrationis per inspirationem gratiae, et contingit sapere per experimentum sui in ratione (alias, in re) ipsa: et sic perficiunt dona. Item, contingit visum defigere in ea altius cum certitudine maxima: et tunc est actus beatitudinis perfectae munditiae, ut dicitur: 'Beati mundo corde, quoniam ipsi Deum videbunt.' Contingit etiam refici in gustu certitudinis illius: et sic erit habitus qui dicitur fructus, et vocatur ab Apostolo fides."

131. Lottin, *Psychologie*, vol. 3, part 2, sect. 1, 360–63, 373–75, 384.

132. Albertus Magnus, *III Sent.*, d. 34, a. 2, ad qu. 4 notes that the fruits in general pertain to a taste of the end.

133. Albertus Magnus, *III Sent.*, d. 34, a. 2, ad qu. 3.

134. *SCH*, Prologue, p. 1.49–50; *SDN*, ch. 2, no. 76, p. 92.20–28; ch. 11, no. 15, p. 418.1–5.

of the virtues and gifts are infused simultaneously (at the moment of justification), the act of the gift of understanding follows the act of faith.[135] Yet Albert does not articulate a clear theory of how the gifts in general (as *habitus*) are actualized.

The gifts do not aid all of the virtues, for charity as such is perfect and cannot be surpassed by any other grace.[136] Hence the gifts complete the intellect's ascent to God, which, though appropriated to the Spirit as a gift, seems to be the work of the Son's mission insofar as the gifts perfect the intellect. Also, Albert classifies the gifts of understanding and wisdom as contemplative graces. The other five gifts pertain to the active life.[137] Understanding and wisdom enable the believer to surpass some of faith's limits, especially its mirrorlike vision. Since these gifts perfect faith and sanctify, they also perfect faith's unitive character. The intrinsically imperfect nature of faith opens the way for a consideration of higher noetic graces.

Understanding pertains more to the true, while wisdom pertains more to the good. Both perfect the intellect, but the former involves the mind's motion toward God, while the latter involves the mind's rest in the divine end, a finality that especially relates to the good. Such noetic motion passes through an understanding of invisible creatures leading to God, while the mind's rest in the good that is "seen" through understanding allows one to "adhere to eternal things by tasting them," following Augustine.[138] The key metaphors of these gifts are thus vision and taste, which may come from *On the Spirit and the Soul*, a twelfth-century Cistercian anthology of Augustine's writings.[139] Vi-

---

135. Albertus Magnus, *III Sent.*, d. 34, a. 1, ad 1–5; d. 35, a. 1, ad diffinitionem 2, ad 1; a. 11c.

136. Albertus Magnus, *III Sent.*, d. 34, a. 2, ad qu. 2.

137. This division is already proposed by William of Auxerre, *Summa Aurea*, Spicilegium Bonaventurianum 18b (Grottaferrata: Editiones Collegii S. Bonaventurae, 1986), bk. III, tomus 2, tr. 34, ch. 1, 648.

138. Albertus Magnus, *III Sent.*, d. 34, a. 3c, 625b–26a: "donum intellectus ... est invisibilium creaturarum per quas movetur in Deum ... donum sapientiae: sicut dicit Augustinus, quod aeternis per gustum rebus inhaerescit ... quoad visum est intellectus, et quoad gustum est sapientia saporans."

139. Alexander of Hales and Philip the Chancellor cite the *De Spiritu et Anima* ("mentis visio est intelligentia, gustus sapientia") in their teaching on understanding and wisdom; see Alexander's *Glossa in quatuor libros Sententiarum Petri Lombardi*, Bibliotheca Franciscana Scholastica Medii Aevi 14 (Quaracchi: Ex Typographia Collegii S.

sion leads to union, while the mode of union consists of the experience of tasting divine things. The latter distinguishes wisdom's act from charity's unitive force, though wisdom presupposes charity. Wisdom at once is higher than understanding and depends on it. One tastes the sweetness of what is seen. Understanding attains a better noetic grasp of the divine end than is possible by the virtue of faith alone, while wisdom signifies the intellect's enjoyment of the end attained. Albert employs experiential language derived from a doctrinal tradition.

Albert insists on the properly noetic character of wisdom. He sidesteps more affective definitions of wisdom proposed by Augustine and Gregory and argues that the heart of wisdom is best understood through Dionysian light and Hierotheus, the Areopagite's teacher:

> wisdom is not the same as faith ... it is another light. Hence, as was said about faith, that it is a certain light under which the articles [of faith] are seen, so ... wisdom is a certain light of divine things under which these are seen and tasted by experience. Hence, properly speaking, the gift of wisdom is the taste of God in his gifts, as Dionysius appears to say about Hierotheus, that he learned divine things by suffering, experiencing and tasting them. Therefore, the light shining and warming to such knowledge of divine things through the taste of God in the gifts without which he [God] is not, is called, in my judgment, the gift of wisdom.[140]

Albert identifies the gift of wisdom with Hierotheus's extraordinary experience, a move that may be original. Neither Gallus's paraphrase of the *Divine Names* nor other contemporary works mention Hierotheus in relation to wisdom.[141] Albert brings to the text the conviction that

---

Bonaventurae, 1954), bk. III, d. 35, no. 3, 437; Philip the Chancellor, *Summa de Bono*, edited by Nicolas Wicki, vol. 2, pars posterior, "De Donis Spiritus Sancti," q. 4, 1117, Corpus Philosophorum medii aevi (Bern: Francke, 1985).

140. Albertus Magnus, *III Sent.*, d. 35, a. 1, ad diffinitionem 1, ad 1, 645a: "sapientia non est idem quod fides ... est enim aliud lumen. Unde sicut dictum est supra de fide, quod est quoddam lumen sub quo videntur articuli: ita ... sapientia est quoddam lumen divinorum sub quo videntur et gustantur divina per experimentum. Unde sapientia donum proprie est gustus Dei in donis suis, sicut videtur dicere Dionysius de Ierotheo, quod patiendo et experiendo et gustando divina, didicit divina. Lumen igitur lucens et calefaciens ad hujusmodi scientiam divinorum per gustum Dei in donis sine quibus ipse non est, dicitur meo judicio sapientia donum."

141. Dionysius and Hierotheus are not mentioned in the treatises on the gifts of understanding and wisdom by Alexander of Hales (*Glossa*), Philip the Chancellor (*Summa de Bono*), William of Auxerre (*Summa Aurea*), or in the *Summa fratris Alexandri*.

wisdom is a noetic gift. His understanding of the virtue of charity essentially demands this position. The *Divine Names* passage on Hierotheus's experience states that it involves "perfect unity and faith." Hence this text seems to refer to a noetic gift completing faith. Dionysius also refers to Hierotheus receiving instruction by a "more divine inspiration," which involves a high point of the spiritual life. Now Hierotheus "suffers divine things" or is taught "by compassion" (Sarracenus), terms that suggest direct contact with God. The plural "divine things" could relate to tasting God in himself or in the created effects by which he is present. Interestingly, Albert ignores Eriugena's translation (*affectus divina*), perhaps because it might weaken Albert's firm distinction of the gifts from charity's perfection. Let us note that Gallus's paraphrase of the *Divine Names* has Hierotheus experience divine things (*divinorum experientiam*), language that Philip the Chancellor and William of Auxerre use in relation to the gift of wisdom.[142]

Albert's discussion of faith and wisdom as distinct lights recalls the Dionysian element of his theology of faith as an outpouring of the divine ray leading us back to the Father. Albert now further appropriates Dionysian light metaphysics. The Areopagite conceives of all divine gifts as diverse forms of light. Albert links the gift of wisdom and the light that causes experiential contact with divine things. The theme of light does not emerge in this part of the *Divine Names*. Albert proposes a synthetic reading of the Areopagite. Light is of divine things and in turn manifests them. The light of faith offers a point of comparison. Faith causes the mind's intrinsic elevation *under which* the articles of faith are received. Similarly, wisdom involves a light *under which* the things of God are experienced. The gift of wisdom is a means to touch God, a new light with a distinct operation that unites us more intensely to the one operating.[143] Faith's object remains indirect (its action is linked to the the articles of faith) so that it grants vision as in a mirror. Wisdom's object is *more* direct, though not without qualification,

---

Lottin's study of John of la Rochelle and Odo Rigaldus never mentions Dionysius; Lottin, *Psychologie*, vol. 3, part 2, sect.1, 375–98).

142. Gallus, *Extractio de divinis nominibus*, ch. 2, 679a; Philip the Chancellor, *Summa de Bono*, vol. 2, pars posterior, "De Donis Spiritus Sancti," q. 4, 1118; William of Auxerre, *Summa Aurea*, bk. III, tomus 2, tr. 30, ch. 2, 593. Neither Eriugena nor Sarracenus translates *pathon* as "experience."

143. See also Albertus Magnus, *III Sent.*, d. 35, a. 1, ad diffinitionem 2, ad 1.

for God himself is tasted *in his gifts*. This is precisely how Alexander of Hales describes wisdom. It also parallels a basic principle of William of Auxerre's mystical theology—namely, that creation always mediates the cognition of God here below.[144] Such language takes us back to Albert's view of the missions: the persons are experienced in the created graces that manifest their presence. Such terminology harmonizes with Albert's Dionysian eschatology, as we will see. He may have taken the image of tasting God's sweetness from William's theology of the gift of wisdom.[145] For Albert the primary effect of wisdom that the *Divine Names* proposes is learning. He places the Areopagite's teacher at the summit of a very Latin theology, that of the Spirit's seven gifts.

Albert's subsequent discussion in the same *Sentences Commentary* article reinforces various themes already considered. In this life wisdom remains a mediated form of knowledge (for we are pilgrims), yet it imparts a higher similitude of divine truth and goodness than does faith. These similitudes illumine and enflame the soul. The language of sweetness seems to demand coupling truth and goodness. The theme of similitude harmonizes well with Dionysian epistemology, while the Latin tradition's terminology of taste and sweetness also makes wisdom an affective gift, though this element is secondary. The experience of taste distinguishes wisdom from faith. This metaphor also implies a distinct ontological-noetic contact with divine light. The object of this experience is "the sweetness of God in his gifts" as we taste "divine things in his most similar gifts."[146] Here Albert comes close to William of Auxerre's teaching that wisdom enjoys a perception of God's greatest effects or gifts poured into the soul. But William, unlike Albert, identifies love as the greatest effect that causes the experience of wisdom. The German Dominican makes divine truth the primary object of wisdom's taste.[147] The Spirit's highest gift enables a new awareness of sanctifying graces.

144. Alexander of Hales, *Glossa*, bk. III, d. 34, 419; Boyd Taylor Coolman, *Knowing God by Experience: The Spiritual Senses in the Theology of William of Auxerre* (Washington D.C.: The Catholic University of America Press, 2004), 184.

145. William of Auxerre, *Summa Aurea*, bk. III, tomus 2, tr. 34, ch. 1, 650–51.

146. Albertus Magnus, *III Sent.*, d. 35, a. 1, ad diffinitionem 1, ad 3, 645b: "non sufficit sapientiae cognitio Dei in similitudine, nisi adsit et gustus"; ad 5, 645b: "cognitio speculativa ... non lumen faciens experimentum dulcedinis Dei in suis donis"; a. 3c, 647b: "gustans divina in donis simillimis illis."

147. Albertus Magnus, *III Sent.*, d. 34, a. 2, ad qu. 2; William of Auxerre, *Summa Aurea*, bk. III, tomus 2, tr. 34, ch. 1, 651; Coolman, *Knowing God*, 214–15.

By implication the actualized gift of wisdom is a fruit of the Son's mission and raises our disposition to know the divine missions.

A brief comparison with the Areopagite's teaching on Hierotheus's experience manifests both similarities and divergences. First, while Albert correctly identifies Hierotheus as a mystic par excellence, he ignores Moses and the *Mystical Theology*. Second, by making Hierotheus the model for the gift of wisdom, Albert more easily avoids the theme of union beyond mind that is so crucial for the Areopagite. This hermeneutic shift facilitates Albert's stance that created noetic acts have a place in union with God, a notion implied by the categorization of the gifts as infused, created *habitus* ordering the believer to higher acts. Third, Albert adds the notion of created divine gifts as mediations whereby we taste and know God. He thus connects his teaching to the missions and takes distance from the Areopagite's emphasis on unmediated contact with the divine powers (in darkness). Ironically, Albert proposes a new function for created grace in Hierotheus's experience that (1) emphasizes the noetic distance between God and creatures and (2) highlights the indirect nature of all theological knowledge in this life. The first project is Dionysian, while the second is close to the Areopagite, *except* when it comes to Moses in darkness or Hierotheus celebrating the Eucharist. Finally, Albert and the Areopagite's translators fail to recognize the Christological allusion in Hierotheus "learning by experience," although this gap could be partly filled by Albert's notion of Christological grace.

Albert's brief, original synthesis on the gift of wisdom finds its complement in his doctrine of the gift of understanding, one that retains a certain ambiguity, as Ulrich Horst points out.[148] Understanding comes about through a light really distinct from faith and wisdom:

> understanding ... is a light given by God for the cognition of God's creature, in which God resounds through grace, and this is spiritual, or in which [God] resounds through grace and glory. Therefore it is a light by which we know in a gratuitous way the dispositions of celestial things, and tend toward God thus disposing.[149]

---

148. Ulrich Horst, *Die Gaben des Heiligen Geistes nach Thomas von Aquin*, Veröffentlichungen des Grabmann-Institutes 46 (Berlin: Akademie Verlag, 2001), 35.

149. Albertus Magnus, *III Sent.*, d. 35, a. 3c, 647b: "intellectus ... est lumen datum a Deo ad cognitionem illius creaturae Dei, in qua resultat Deus per gratiam, et haec est

First, Albert insists that the gift of understanding involves a mediated form of cognition. When actualized this infused *habitus* enables deeper insight into the highest *works* of God. Second, understanding's proper object concerns spiritual creatures. Albert notes that understanding enables a higher gaze upon God's work in the angels and saints in glory, which seems to involve (among other things) a new noetic grasp of the eschatological gifts. Later in the same article Albert confirms this interpretation as he notes that understanding involves "a light elevating to things whereby God resounds in a higher way than in the vestige or image, as in the disposition of rewards in the beatitude of spiritual substances."[150] William of Auxerre also refers this gift of the Spirit to the knowledge of God's beatifying action in the angels and saints.[151] The theological virtues suffice to know the reflection of God in the *imago*, while the gift of understanding presents a graced object such as the supernatural blessings enjoyed by a living saint or a saint in glory. Albert comes close to identifying this gift of the Spirit with mystical visions, though his treatment remains quite brief and somewhat ambiguous.

The same passage also reveals what is probably the most important source for Albert's teaching on the gift of understanding:

Augustine says, "In Isaiah, understanding is that by which hearts are purified from the weakness of carnal pleasure, that a pure intention may be directed to the end." Now carnal pleasure seems to be called carnality because it weighs down the attentive gaze at divine things in which God resounds more clearly than in corporeal creatures. And understanding is about these [divine things], and through them, one is directed toward a vision of the Creator. And therefore, in the *Littera* [of Augustine], it says that understanding is of divine things and spiritual creatures and of all good affections of the soul ... understanding sees him [the Creator] in an interior light.[152]

---

spiritualis: vel in qua habet resultare per gloriam vel per gratiam: et ideo est lumen quo cognoscimus gratuite dispositiones coelestium, et tendimus in Deum sic disponentem."

150. Albertus Magnus, *III Sent.*, d. 35, a. 3, ad 3, 647b: "intellectus ... ut visus tantum tendens in verum per lumen elevans ad ea in quibus Deus resultat altius quam in vestigio et imagine: sicut est dispositio praemiorum in beatitudine spiritualium substantiarum."

151. William of Auxerre, *Summa Aurea*, bk. III, tomus 2, tr. 34, ch. 1, 649.

152. Albertus Magnus, *III Sent.*, d. 35, a. 3, ad 3, 647b–48a: "dicit Augustinus: 'Apud Isaiam intellectus est quo ab infirmitate carnalis voluptatis corda mundantur, ut pura intentio dirigatur in finem.' Carnalis enim voluptas ab eo videtur vocari carnalitas depri-

Albert inserts his doctrine of understanding within Augustine's exegesis of Isaiah 11 and the mysticism of interiority that accompanies it. Following the Latin doctor, spiritual creatures become accessible to the mind's gaze by moral purification and a turn toward the gratuitous light that imparts noetic content from within. God shines forth more clearly in spiritual creatures. By progress in grace the ontological and epistemological hierarchies move toward increasing proportionality. For the fallen creature radically healed by grace, God is best understood through the immaterial realm. The soul thus partially recovers its natural noetic domain. These doctrines harmonize well with Albert's earlier discussion of the higher and lower intellect. Finally, Albert adopts Augustine's list of noetic objects for the gift of understanding: divine things, spiritual creatures, and the soul's good affections.

Albert further integrates Augustine's interiority as he notes that this gift enables us to gaze upon a light that is both simple and really distinct from God. Albert contrasts the complex light or revelation that comes through Scripture to the light or truth that is proper to this gift. An objection cites the Dionysian principle that sacred veils mediate all divine light. Albert's response presumes that these veils are the Scriptures. The understanding that Scripture generates comes through hearing, involves a complex truth (faith propositions), and is received through faith. But such complex knowledge is "below" the gift of understanding. In other words, the truth of Scripture is proportioned to the act of faith, while truth communicated interiorly and directly is proportioned to this gift of the Spirit. Scripture exteriorizes, multiplies, or complexifies divine light, while the light of understanding is simple and interior.[153] Oddly, Albert does not mention Moses in the *Mystical Theology* passing beyond all biblical words (or multiple lights) so as to

---

mens a contuitu divinorum in quibus clarius resultat Deus quam in his quae corporalia sunt: et horum est intellectus, et per ea dirigitur ad visum Creatoris. Et ideo dicitur in Littera, quod intellectus est divinarum et spiritualium creaturarum et omnium bonarum affectionum animae ... quia fides simpliciter assentit credita, sed intellectus videt ipsum in lumine interiori."

153. Albertus Magnus, *III Sent.*, d. 35, a. 9, ad qu. 2, ad 1–2, 655b: "auditus Scripturae subservit actui intellectus doni, sed non generat ipsum lumen: quia hoc infunditur ab ipso Deo cum caeteris gratiis gratum facientibus: unde illa complexio qua est in auditis, sub dono est, et non in ipso, sicut in fide ... intellectus Scripturae ... non generat lumen sub quo videntur spiritualia."

enter the darkness that is light. Albert's exposition seems to move in a predominantly Augustinian universe: the Spirit infuses the light of understanding so that we may know God in various kinds of graces.[154] He suggests an elevation of our created operative capacities in the soul's highest noetic encounters with God in this life, paralleling his doctrine of the gift of created glory. Also, the gift of understanding reinforces the kataphatic side of Albert's mysticism: the believer receives new (interior) signs of divine light that *manifest* God.

However, Albert posits neither a permanent activity of higher noetic vision nor the possibility that the believer can decide to activate the gifts. The *habitus* of the gifts are infused together with the theological virtues, but Albert specifies that the actualization of the gift of understanding occurs by distinct lights, a precision not found in his exposition of wisdom.[155] He implies the utter gratuity and unpredictability of actualized understanding. Yet he barely elaborates on these actuating lights. This lacuna parallels his doctrine of grace centered on form or habitual grace. This point is crucial: the early Albert has no well-developed theology of actual grace, for he only posits the latter as a subset of formal flux. This means that Albert may have difficulty accounting for the Dionysian doctrine that God's light or revelatory operation directly floods Moses's mind without imparting a new *habitus* or form. For while the missions involve God's direct operation in the soul, that act always has a new or more intense *habitus* as its term.

Albert's doctrine of the Spirit's two contemplative gifts consists primarily of an original combination of sources. His creative contribution emerges in his use of Hierotheus and in his classification of wisdom as a properly noetic gift. As a whole the theology appears incomplete. The relation of the gifts to the beatitudes and fruits remains obscure. We find no explicit link to the divine missions, even though both understanding and wisdom would seem to constitute the highpoint of the

---

154. Albertus Magnus, *III Sent.*, d. 35, a. 3c (cited earlier at footnote 149 in this chapter); a. 9, ad qu. 1, ad 2; ad qu. 2, ad 1 (cited earlier at footnote 153 in this chapter).

155. Albertus Magnus, *III Sent.*, d. 35, a. 11c, 656b–657a: "est quidam intellectus intuens in lumine accepto a Deo, quod lumen est gratum faciens, et hoc est donum, et est nobilior perfectio intellectus nostri quam fides vel contemplatio: et ideo secundum viam generationis actus, licet non habitus, sequitur fidem et contemplationem. Dico autem non secundum viam generationis habitus: quia habitus simul infunduntur, sed non actus, sed potius actus consequuntur se."

Son's mission. Nevertheless, these two gifts and the virtue of charity represent the summit of the spiritual life. Overall the early Albert proposes a balance of intellect and will in union, a clear place for mystical experience, a strong emphasis on created grace, and (standing in the background) a constant connection between finite grace and the immediate action of the Son and the Spirit. Union imparts an experience of God in his gifts of light and love. It enables immediate ontological contact with God, but not immediate noetic contact, in the sense that even the higher intellect's interior way still passes through mediating lights. The gift of understanding imparts a vision that is mediated by spiritual creatures, while wisdom's knowledge follows upon an experiential taste of divine sweetness.[156]

THE VISION OF GOD IN ALBERT'S SENTENCES COMMENTARY

Albert's early teaching on the vision of God emerges against the background of the much-discussed 1241 Parisian condemnations of eschatologies marked by a strong apophatism and quasi-Greek patristic doctrines. His occasional references to the "calumny against Dionysius" and certain "heresies" reveal the controversy's freshness and intensity. Albert's response to the 1241 crisis is closely linked to his appropriation of Dionysian mysticism.

On January 13, 1241, the bishop of Paris, William of Auvergne, condemned ten propositions, the first of which most directly pertains to the beatific vision: "The first error is that the divine essence will not be seen [in heaven], neither by the human being nor by the angel."[157] William and his theological commission (which included Alexander of Hales) most likely sought to target certain scholastic opinions that had integrated two doctrinal sources: (1) Eriugena's echoes of certain Greek fathers such as Gregory of Nyssa, Dionysius, and Maximos, who

---

156. Albert briefly treats the Spirit's seven gifts in his *Postilla Super Isaiam*. This work's date remains uncertain, but it was probably composed after 1250 or even in the 1260s, which takes us beyond the limits of this study; see Albertus Magnus, *Postilla Super Isaiam*, ed. Ferdinand Siepmann and Heinrich Ostlender, Cologne Edition 19 (Münster: Aschendorff, 1952), xix–xx; Weisheipl, "Albert der Große," 42.

157. Heinrich Denifle, ed., *Chartularium Universitatis Parisiensis*, vol. 1 (Paris: 1889), no. 128: "Primus (error) quod divina essentia in se nec ab homine nec ab angelo videbitur."

emphasize (to varying degrees) the inaccessibility of God's essence; and (2) Avicennian explications of the beatific vision that invoke mediating intelligible impressions conferred by the agent intellect as essential for eschatological knowledge of God—a Platonic-Aristotelian philosophy that leads to a strictly indirect vision of the Godhead.[158] By targeting scholastic Greek-Eriugenan-Avicennian syntheses, the 1241 condemnations rendered suspect the whole of Greek patristic eschatology and negative theology that had managed to penetrate mid-thirteenth-century Paris in fragmentary form. In 1244 William of Auvergne repeated the condemnations.

Albert's teaching on the vision of God involves a triple project: (1) to rehabilitate Greek apophatism; (2) to synthesize oriental and occidental eschatologies; and (3) to refute exaggerated epistemological claims of some neo-Augustinians with little appreciation for negative theology.[159] His *Sentences Commentary* proposes a doctrine of the beatific vision using four key notions: (1) the infinite disproportion between God and his creatures; (2) the impossibility of comprehending God; (3) the possibility of immediate noetic and ontological contact with God's essence or substance; and (4) theophany as a double gift of uncreated light that is God manifesting himself and a created gift of glory disposing us to the Trinity's self-revelation. The first two elements appropriate the Greek fathers; the third is more Augustinian, while the fourth is Albert's original contribution, which forms the cornerstone of his new synthesis.[160]

The significance of Albert's project emerges more clearly in light of the neo-Augustinianism that stands behind the 1241 condemnations. A keystone of William of Auvergne's personal eschatology is the notion that the glorified soul is a similitude by which it enjoys a direct vision

---

158. Dondaine, "L'objet et le 'medium' de la vision béatifique chez les théologiens du XIIIe siècle," *Recherches de théologie ancienne et médiévale* 19 (1952): 99; Lévy, *Créé et l'incréé*, 117; Trottmann, *Vision béatifique*, 116–17, 144–50, 176.

159. Wéber, "L'apophatisme dionysien chez Albert le Grand et dans son école," in *Denys l'Aréopagite et sa postérité en Orient et en Occident*, edited by Ysabel de Andia (Paris: Institut d'Études Augustiniennes, 1997), 379–80; Wéber, "L'interprétation," 425. For an overview of the beatific vision in Albert, see Jeffrey P. Hergan, *St. Albert the Great's Theory of the Beatific Vision* (New York: Peter Lang, 2002).

160. The *De homine* has no developed eschatology, only scattered comments on philosophies of beatitude.

of God's essence. Paul's teaching in 1 Corinthians 13 on seeing God as in a mirror thus refers to the mirror of the soul. This created similitude does not prevent a direct vision of God, for it is a perfect reflection of the divine Image, of God's word. William never asks the question: how can a created essence be a perfect similitude of God's essence?[161]

Similarly, Alexander of Hales sees no need to insist on the lack of proportion between God's infinite being and our finite minds, for God is powerful enough to elevate us to whatever level of noetic capacity he chooses, opening the possibility of a quasi-infinite created receptivity for divine light. Alexander thus simultaneously (and indirectly) opposes two pillars of Greek patristic eschatology: first (with William of Auvergne), the permanent disproportion between God's essence and created minds; and second, the absolute incapacity of any created intellect to understand all of God. However, Alexander introduces the notion of a special divine similitude that disposes the soul to see God face to face in the next life, an idea that Albert will develop.[162]

Albert's response to the doctrinal crisis begins with the first distinction of the *Sentences Commentary* as he treats the possibility of created beings directly seeing God's essence. He draws the first eight objections from Chrysostom's controversial *Homily 15*, the works of Dionysius, and John Damascene's *On the Orthodox Faith*. Albert's solution offers a glimpse of the charged Parisian theological atmosphere: "it is most certain that the divine substance is seen by all the blessed ... immediately by conjunction, so that God offers himself to our intellect."[163] Albert's position is not simply a grudging submission to local Episcopal authority, but especially the fruit of his own reflection. His occasional sharp critiques of neo-Augustinian eschatologies show that he is not afraid to demonstrate the radical shortcomings of Paris's dominant theological school in the 1240s, the school that produced the 1241 condemnations.[164]

---

161. Trottmann, *Vision béatifique*, 155–58.
162. Dondaine, "L'objet et le 'medium,'" 96; Trottmann, *Vision béatifique*, 173.
163. Albertus Magnus, *I Sent.*, d. 1, a. 15, qla. 1c, 36a: "affirmantes quidem certissime, quod divina substantia videtur a beatis omnibus: qualiter autem ... videtur immediate per conjunctionem: ita quod Deus offert se nostro intellectui per substantiam suam, sicut intellectus sibi ipsi." This teaching is also found in Albertus Magnus, *De resurrectione*, tr. 4, q. 1, a. 9.
164. Wéber, "L'apophatisme," 379.

Albert's challenge is to show that the Greek eschatology that had penetrated thirteenth-century Paris need not exclude the direct vision of God's substance or essence. His solution constitutes a doctrinal thread that connects virtually all of the responses to the objections drawn from the Greek fathers. Chrysostom's *Homily 15* proclaims that "no one knows God's substance and *quid est*, except the one begotten by him." For Albert the Son's divine knowledge of the Father's substance is comprehensive. Hence knowing God's substance or quiddity specifically refers to comprehensive cognition. Albert suggests that Augustine and the Greeks equivocate on terms such as "substance." Augustine employs it to affirm direct knowledge of God's nature in heaven, while Chrysostom sees it as referring to comprehensive cognition of God.[165] Albert quietly critiques Alexander's notion of a quasi-infinite created noetic receptivity for the divine substance. Divine incomprehensibility is nonnegotiable; indeed, it is Augustinian.[166]

Albert thus identifies the hidden character of God's essence in Dionysius with the impossibility of exhaustive human knowledge thereof, an interpretive move strongly suggested by several *Parisian Scholia* on the *Mystical Theology*.[167] In the *Disputed Questions on the Resurrection*, written shortly before his lectures on the *Sentences*, Albert attributes this doctrine to Maximos, citing a *scholium* on the *Ecclesiastical Hierarchy*.[168] Albert does not realize that he is reading Maximos against the Confessor's intention, partly because he mines contradictory, kataphatic-

---

165. Albertus Magnus, *I Sent.*, d. 1, a. 15, ad 1. The same interpretation of Chrysostom can be found in ad 2.

166. Albertus Magnus, *I Sent.*, d. 1, a. 15, qla. 1, ad 2; see also Albertus Magnus, *De resurrectione*, tr. 4, q. 1, a. 9, no. 1, ad 1.

167. See *PMT*, ch. 5, 106, which gives a *scholium* by John of Scythopolis (PG 4:429.3; Lamoreaux and Rorem, eds., *John of Scythopolis*, 247–48): "Neque existentia eam cognoscunt aut ipsa est sive quam ipsa sit, nec ipsa cognoscit existentia an existentia sint. Neque enim cognoscunt trinitatem an ipsa sit—id est nihil est ut ipsa ut cognoscant eam an ipsa sit. Nos cognoscimus quidem quid sit humanitas.... Existentia vero trinitatis nescimus quid sit." God's *quid* remains inaccessible, for we can never know it the way we know a finite *quid*.

168. Albertus Magnus, *De resurrectione*, tr. 4, q. 1, a. 9, no. 2c, pp. 329.77–330.17. The *scholium* mingles a text by John of Scythopolis (PG 4:145.5; Lamoreaux and Rorem, eds., *John of Scythopolis*, 175) with an excerpt from Eriugena's *Periphyseon* (bk. V, lines 2984–98); and see the marginal notes in Harrington's, *On the Ecclesiastical Hierarchy*, 128.

sounding *scholia* from other sources that had been falsely linked to the martyr. What a difference the fading of Anastasius's little crosses in the manuscript makes!

Chrysostom also posits an infinite distance between God's substance and finite minds, which would seem to make direct noetic contact impossible. Consequently, we know God through theophanies. Albert agrees that theophanies or divine illuminations partly bridge this endless distance, though a creature's comprehension of God's being remains metaphysically impossible. Everything comes down to the nature of the theophanies. Albert's response takes us back to the Areopagite's divine powers, which are the object of affirmative names. Albert holds that every theophany is a partial revelation of some divine attribute. He then specifies that God's substance is (partly) seen in any of his attributes. This allows him to rehabilitate Chrysostom, as it provides an acceptable interpretation of the church father's saying that God is seen in the theophanies. God's substance shines forth in every divine illumination. The unspoken premise is that God's substance is inseparable from his attributes.[169]

The theology of *lumen gloriae* becomes explicit later in *Sentences Commentary*. An objection calls the Dionysian theophany heretical, for it seems to exclude the angels' immediate vision of God. Albert refers to "calumnies against the sacred books" of Dionysius that misunderstand the meaning of theophany. In response he distinguishes between theophanies directly given by God and lights passed on from one angel to another, thus limiting the Dionysian hierarchical mediation of light. He then offers an original exposition of theophany:

Theophany predicates two things, namely, the light of glory elevating the intellect and strengthening the fantasy, and this is the created glory, that is united to the angel's intellect. It also predicates the intelligible [object] distinguishing and perfecting the intellect, and this is nothing other than God. For just as in the sense of sight, there is a light perfecting and color determining vision, so also in our intellect, the agent intellect's light elevates and illumines, and the intelligible [object] distinguishes. For the intellect's nature cannot be attached there unless strengthened by the light flowing to it from God. And thus the objection ceases. Because that light

169. Albertus Magnus, *I Sent.*, d. 1, a. 15, qla. 1, ad 2–3.

is a sign, not in which God is seen as in a medium, but under which the strengthened intellect is immediately attached to God.[170]

The angels' beatitude is the main theme at hand, though these principles also apply to human beatitude. The language of elevation and illumination seems to imply that the created light is not just a formal but also an efficient cause, which would parallel created grace and charity. Albert later speaks of this light turning the soul to God, again suggesting efficiency.[171]

Albert's explanation of the light's mode of mediation bears Alexander of Hales's fingerprints. The key distinction is between that *under which* the object is seen and the object itself. Created theophanies enable a finite intellect to enjoy a direct vision of God's substance. The law of infinite disproportion requires a gift from above to enable direct noetic contact with God's essence. The first, created sense of theophany is a direct result of Albert's reformulation of Greek apophatism. The second, uncreated sense of theophany is more Augustinian, but with a constant emphasis on the inscrutable divine mystery that prevents comprehensive knowledge. Albert proposes a new theological category, the created light of glory, the keystone that fuses what he holds to be of lasting value in the Greek and Latin patristic traditions.[172] He saves Greek apopha-

---

170. Albertus Magnus, *II Sent.*, d. 4, a. 1, qla. 2c, 105b: "theophania dicit duo, scilicet lumen gloriae elevans intellectum et phantasiam confortans, et hoc est gloria creata quae unitur intellectui Angeli: dicit etiam intelligibile distinguens et perficiens intellectum, et hoc nihil aliud est quam Deus: sicut etiam in sensu visus est lumen perficiens, et color determinans visum: et in intellectu nostro est lumen intellectus agentis elevans et illuminans, et intelligibile distinguens. Natura enim intellectus ibi figi non potest nisi confortetur lumine sibi a Deo influxo. Et tunc cessat objectio: quia tunc lumen illud est signum, non in quo videtur Deus tamquam in medio, sed sub quo confortante intellectum, intellectus immediate figitur in Deo." The same teaching is found in Albertus Magnus's *Quaestiones*, ed. Albert Fries, Wilhelm Kübel, and Henryk Anzulewicz, Cologne Edition vol. 25, part 2 (Münster: Aschendorff, 1993), "Quaestio de visione dei in patria," pp. 98.32–99.37. The work dates from 1245–48, and is thus contemporaneous to our *Sentences Commentary* text; see Torrell, *Recherches sur la théorie de la prophétie au Moyen Âge, XIIe–XIVe siècles: Études et textes*, Dokimion 13 (Fribourg, Switzerland: Éditions universitaires, 1992), 174, 186–88.

171. Albertus Magnus, *IV Sent.*, d. 49, a. 5c.

172. Trottmann notes that the doctrine of created *lumen gloriae* begins with Albert (*Vision béatifique*, 172–73), though it may have partial precedents in Eriugena. Kurt Flasch sketches a genealogy of two opposing traditions concerning the grace/nature distinction and the *lumen gloriae*. He places Albert, Dietrich von Freiberg, and Meister

tism by proposing a new type of created grace! The double theophany incorporates the Dionysian notion of God's self-communication at the hinge of this Greco-Latin eschatology.[173] The double theophany, which expresses Albert's conviction about the radical distance between God and the soul (even when the latter is no longer bound to the body), also shows the proximity between the German friar's eschatology and Dionysian mysticism. For the Areopagite's theories of noetic silence and the inaccessibility of the divine nature proceed from the same conviction.

Albert thus lays the foundation for the doctrine of beatitude that he expounds in the treatise on the last things in the fourth book of the *Sentences Commentary*. The light of glory fills the soul and immediately turns it toward God, where it becomes "one spirit" with him. As God is substantially present to the blessed, there is no need for any *mediating* intelligible species, against Avicennian-Augustinian eschatologies. The Aristotelian (and Avicennian) principle that all understanding comes by abstraction no longer applies. Rather, Albert takes up the Averroist language of noetic conjunction with the separate agent intellect.[174] He explains that some non-Christian philosophers had a vague notion of beatitude. In other words, their insights could be partly integrated and developed. The separate agent intellect now becomes God's intellect. God unites himself to the saint via the latter's individual agent intellect, in contrast to Averroes, who holds that the human potential intellect is assimilated to a higher universal agent intellect.[175] Still, the Arab phi-

---

Eckhart in opposition to these doctrines and Aquinas in their favor; see Flasch, *Meister Eckhart: Die Geburt der "Deutschen Mystik" aus dem Geist der arabischen Philosophie* (Munich: C. H. Beck, 2006), 69, 84–85 106–11. Flasch's reconstruction focuses on a few philosophical works by Albert, takes his philosophical conclusions as general statements of Albert's doctrine of return to God, and ignores his theological corpus. Flasch later seems to make a quiet retraction of this misreading of the *lumen gloriae* in Albert; see Flasch, *Dietrich von Freiberg: Philosophie, Theologie Naturforschung um 1300* (Frankfurt am Main: Vittorio Klostermann, 2007), 221, 408.

173. Wéber, "L'interprétation," 431–32.

174. Albertus Magnus, *IV Sent.*, d. 49, a. 5c, 670b: "Deus ... in patria est in intellectu lumine gloriae replens totam animam ... secundum quod beatitudinis est objectum ... sub illa claritate anima convertitur immediate in Deum, non accipiendo aliud ab ipso quam ipse sit: sed hoc modo unita ei in uno spiritu intelliget eum: et ideo ad hunc intellectum non est necessaria speciei assimilatio formalis quando substantialiter inest"; Wéber, "Relation," 579.

175. Albertus Magnus, *IV Sent.*, d. 49, a. 5, ad 1–2.

losopher provides key philosophical tools that Albert employs within the Augustinian-Dionysian framework of his eschatology.

Albert also asks whether Aristotle defines beatitude well. He grants that Aristotle has a true, partial understanding of beatitude in this life, while the teachings of Augustine and Bernard of Clairvaux pertain to eternal beatitude. According to the Stagirite, our highest operation is the noetic vision of the higher substances, especially God's being. Albert notes that Aristotle identifies earthly beatitude with a contemplative act whereby the human being is quasi-divine. This beatitude is properly in the genre of act.[176] For the moment, Albert restricts the Aristotelian notion of contemplative acts to the present life, partly because they proceed from natural, finite noetic capacities. Albert's patristic-biblical discussion of beatitude in this article remains unclear on the place of created intellectual acts. His division between grace and nature, between this life and the next, seems too neat. We saw a similar problem in his treatment of higher and lower intellect, where Aristotle was a reliable guide for the cognition of corporeal creatures while Augustine was more reliable for the cognition of invisible realities. Because Albert will soon move away from his doctrine of the higher and lower intellect, I will consider whether the Dionysian commentaries open the door to a more Aristotelian understanding of eternal beatitude.

Albert's discussion of Aristotle in another article also helps us to pinpoint the doctrinal consequences of his notion of the agent intellect's eschatological role: "In heaven ... the light of the Deity that is God himself is united to the agent intellect and thus substantially pours [itself] out onto the whole soul and fills it."[177] For Albert the agent intellect is the direct source of all noetic activity, while all noetic receptivity pertains to the potential intellect. Although the agent intellect no longer abstracts species in heaven, it causes direct contact with God's substance. Albert thus also opens the door to a notion of the beatific vision as including the saints' constant created acts of knowledge. The theme of essential human cooperation in the beatific union comes not so much from Aristotle but from Albert's development of Peripatetic

176. Albertus Magnus, *IV Sent.*, d. 49, a. 6c & ad 4, 9.
177. Albertus Magnus, *IV Sent.*, d. 49, a. 5, ad 1, 670b: "Sed in patria ... lumen deitatis quod est Deus ipse, unitur intellectui agenti, et sic effunditur substantialiter super totam animam."

noetics. He removes Averroes's separate agent intellect, which stands between God and created minds, and assigns the separate intellect's various functions either to God or to individual human minds. Because all noetic light passes through the individual agent intellect, the beatified agent intellect is always active. Furthermore, some of the light being mediated is strictly supernatural, a gift calling forth the response of a potential intellect elevated to cognitive acts surpassing natural limits.[178] Thus I will later consider whether the agent intellect plays a key role in the mysticism of the Dionysian commentaries, for union in this life is nothing but a partial realization of perfect union in the next.

At first sight Albert's doctrine of the beatific vision seems to leave open a burning question. How can the created light of glory, a finite power, enable direct knowledge of the uncreated? Albert's implicit response emerges when we reconnect his comments on the light glory scattered across the *Sentences Commentary* with the "treatise" on the missions. The effect of sanctifying grace is always conjoined to the proceeding persons. Created grace without the presence of the Son and the Spirit is impossible.[179] By itself any finite power such as created grace cannot bridge the infinite Creator-creature distance. Yet as a similitude of the divine goodness in which God immediately acts upon the believer, grace becomes (primarily) a formal cause and (secondarily) an efficient cause by which the Son and the Spirit move us back to the Father, so that God's infinite efficient causality overcomes the created/uncreated disproportion.[180] Albert's explanation of the limits of created grace also applies to the created gift of glory, for it is the highest created grace. He thus accounts for the Dionysian doctrine of God's self-communication in theophanies by developing the Augustinian doctrine of the divine missions. The missions' essential link to created grace and glory constitutes Albert's final word on beatitude, not an Averroist agent intellect. The Arab philosopher enables a better understanding of noetic union with God's intellect, but Albert inserts Averroes into the framework of his discussion on grace and glory, both of which are nonsensical without the missions.[181]

---

178. Albertus Magnus, *I Sent.*, d. 2, a. 5c; d. 3, a. 29.
179. Albertus Magnus, *I Sent.*, d. 14, a. 3c; d. 15, a. 16.
180. Albertus Magnus, *I Sent.*, d. 17, a. 1, ad 2.
181. Lévy sees Albert offering an Averroist-Aristotelian theology to explain the Au-

Finally, Albert briefly discusses the relation of intellect and will in the vision of God. On the one hand, the knowledge of God causes eternal life. On the other hand, he distinguishes between vision as the material element and the delight following upon love as the formal element of eternal life, a reasoning analogous to the doctrine of faith.[182] Albert also posits two degrees of union in relation to celestial joy: intellect attains but does not enter into God, while love enters into the beloved. Albert's eschatology thus inclines toward the priority of the will.[183] Albert's eschatology offers an original doctrinal development of the Areopagite, an alternative to the exegesis of Maximos and Eriugena. The martyr's doctrine had become unrecognizable, buried beneath contradictory *scholia* representing Eriugena's apophatism and John of Scythopolis's kataphatism. Albert's hermeneutic finds a partial foundation in certain *Parisian Scholia* authored by John. The early Albert already works out a new hermeneutic for Dionysian eschatology and epistemology, a task necessitated by the 1241 crisis and Albert's determination to save the best of Greek patristic thought in the face of neo-Augustinian kataphatic exaggerations.

DIVINE NAMING IN ALBERT'S
SENTENCES COMMENTARY

Albert's synthesis of Latin eschatology and Dionysian apophatism articulates theological principles that also undergird his approach to divine naming. Here, too, Dionysius becomes a major interlocutor. For the Greek father the divine names constitute the upper half of the mystical ladder. Indeed, a scholastic mystical theology distinct from "Affec-

---

gustinian doctrine of the direct vision of God as dogmatically defined in the 1241 condemnations; Lévy, *Créé et l'incréé*, 483–86. But Lévy never discusses the place of the missions in Albert's eschatology. He does not show how Albert significantly transforms Averroes, nor does he mention how Albert distanced himself from the proponents of the condemnations.

182. Albertus Magnus, *IV Sent.*, d. 48, aa. 4–5.

183. Albertus Magnus, *I Sent.*, d. 1, a. 12, qla. 1, ad 2. Nikolaus Wicki incorrectly sees the will having full priority over the intellect in Albert's eschatology; see Wicki, *Die Lehre von der himmlischen Seligkeit in der mittelalterlichen Scholastik von Petrus Lombardus bis Thomas von Aquin*, Studia Friburgensia, Neue Folge 9 (Fribourg, Switzerland: Universitätsverlag, 1954), 199–200. Herbert Doms more accurately identifies a vague middle path in Albert; see Doms, "Ewige Verklärung und ewige Verwerfung nach dem hl. Albertus Magnus," *Divus Thomas* 10 (1932): 144–46.

Mystical Union and Its Pillars in Early Albert 111

tive Dionysianism" has the potential to integrate this ladder at the heart of its teaching, for the divine names signal the content of graced cognitive acts. Enabled by the direct operation of the Son and the Spirit acting through the formality of created grace, the theological virtues, and gifts of understanding and wisdom, the scholastic contemplative can ascend to union via the names, guided by a (domesticated) Dionysius as hierarch who unveils the meaning and uplifting power of the sacred names. But does Albert integrate the divine names at the heart of his mysticism in the *Sentences Commentary*? Our response to this question manifests the place of the Areopagite's *Mystical Theology* in Albert's thought during his Parisian period. For it is in his *Sentences Commentary* treatise on divine naming that the early (pre-Cologne) Albert comes closest to an appropriation of the *Mystical Theology*, though that reception is mostly mediated by the *Divine Names*.[184]

Albert begins his study of divine naming by considering the conditions necessary for the contemplation of God and his attributes. He first mentions the will's purification from sin and then lists four types of intellectual purification. In order to "discern" God well, the mind needs to be purged of "the presence of the body which is to sense [power], second, the presence of the corporeal image from the image, third, the intellect's act of receiving from a phantasm, fourth, the intellect's act of progressing from self-evident principles known through philosophy."[185] Such purification leads to a contemplative elevation via the

---

184. Following Maria Burger's notes in the forthcoming critical edition for book I of Albertus Magnus's *Sentences Commentary*, only two articles in the section on the divine names refer to the *MT* (d. 2, aa. 16–17). At d. 2, a. 16, objection 5, Albert cites *MT* 5 as proposing that God cannot be named. The response invokes *DN* 13.3: the name "good" is most worthy of God. By implication, God is not beyond all names. In d. 2, a. 17, sed contra 4, Albert refers to *MT* 1.2: we should affirm all names (*positiones*) of God. Albert here invokes an apparently kataphatic passage of the *MT*. In the solution of a. 17 (see footnote 194 later in this chapter), he explains that, according to *MT* 1.2, God is both life and not life. Overall, Albert treats the *MT* as an extension of the *DN* that enables a better understanding of how affirmative, negative, and eminent names function. The *Sentences Commentary* treatise on divine naming simply skips the theme of union in the *MT*. Distinction 2 never mentions Moses in the dark cloud. Albert's approach to the *MT* in the *Sentences Commentary* may have influenced Aquinas, as we will see. However, Albert also analyzes several *DN* passages that directly or indirectly parallel union texts in the *MT* (e.g., God as beyond all names).

185. Albertus Magnus, *I Sent.*, d. 2, a. 3c, 58a: "purgatio.... Ex parte intellectus autem tollitur praesentia corporis quae est ad sensum, et secundo praesentia imaginis corpora-

light of faith that enables the cognition of God as one and three. Here Albert is concerned about the correct understanding of the Creed—that is, the theological project of faith seeking understanding, not a private experience of the Trinity. The senses, imagination, and discursive activity of the intellect alone can never attain or "discern" the Trinity. Only faith can open this path. The fourfold intellectual purification consists of avoiding the perpetual human temptation to identify God with a finite mode of being. The reality of the triune God surpasses anything we encounter through our sense experience and natural process of reasoning. Albert's "moral preface" to the doctrine of divine naming almost seems to coincide with the Areopagite's treatment of metaphors, the contemplative object of the soul's "impassioned" part.

Albert then explains the meaning of the term "God": "In a name, we direct our attention to two things, namely, the form or *ratio* from which it is imposed, and that to which it is imposed."[186] The form or *ratio* is the intelligible content of a divine name, which is distinct from the reality to which the name refers. Form concerns a divine operation. Albert gives examples such as God containing all things—that is, conserving everything in existence.[187] He identifies a first limitation in our language about God—namely, the distinction between the immediate source of a name and its referent. God's creative sustaining work made known in creation and revelation is a partial manifestation of his being and thus a source of divine naming. These works "only belong to God," meaning that angels do not mediate his work of creation. The names refer directly to God because he is immediately active in his works. "God" is the name of an operative nature. By implication, divine names predicate something of God's substance or being.

Albert makes his stance on substantial predication explicit in a comment on Exodus 3:14:

It is true that our cognition begins with creatures, yet it does not reach its term in them, but rather in God. For we proceed through the effect of a power into the power, and through the power into the essence. And there-

---

lis ab imagine, tertio actus intellectus accipientis ex phantasmate, quarto actus intellectus progredientis ex principiis sibi notis secundum Philosophiam."

186. Albertus Magnus, *I Sent.*, d. 2, a. 11c, 66a: "duo sunt attendenda in nomine, scilicet forma sive ratio a qua imponitur: et illud cui imponitur."

187. Albertus Magnus, *I Sent.*, d. 2, a. 11, dubium.

fore we can name the essence, not through some creature, but from that in which we attain cognitive repose as in the end or term. Otherwise, we could never signify anything about God, except under the aspect of his being the cause of creatures.[188]

Human cognition begins in the senses and then goes beyond the material world to attain in an imperfect way something of God himself. We begin by encountering the Creator's effects, then recognize the powers causing these effects, and finally the essence or nature that underlies these operative powers. To begin with effects seems to refer to sense knowledge. But as we saw in the section on epistemology, the same distinction of the commentary posits the possibility of an infused knowledge (i.e., an effect of God) that presents noetic content about God or another immaterial reality in a way that fully bypasses the senses. The tension between these two doctrines seems to remain unresolved in the *Sentences Commentary*. Also, Albert's mention of mediated cognition does not take him out of a properly theological context. The theologian approaches the traces of God in creation, whether the world spoken of in the Bible or the material beings we encounter each day. The article's key claim is the transition from God's power to his essence. Albert explicitly intends to exclude the notion that our names only describe God in his causal relation to the world and not God himself. The metaphysical principle that effects reflect operative powers and that powers reflect their underlying nature applies to all of reality, including God. Let us note the partly Dionysian root of this triad.[189]

Albert then returns to the theme of divine incomprehensibility:

God cannot be defined, although one can express what God is, such as substance, wisdom, goodness and so on. Nevertheless, it must be recognized that none of these names that speak what God is make for us a determined notion of its signification in God, so that nothing would remain beyond the understanding of the reality being signified.[190]

---

188. Albertus Magnus, *I Sent.*, d. 2, a. 13, ad qu. 1, ad 2, 69a: "quod verum est quod nostra cognitio incipit a creaturis: sed non terminatur in creaturis, sed in Deo: venimus enim per effectum potentiae in potentiam, et per potentiam in essentiam: et ideo essentiam nominare possumus, non per aliquam creaturam, sed ab eo in quo ut in fine stet cognitio nostra: aliter enim numquam possemus aliquid significare de Deo, nisi in ratione causae ad creaturas."
189. Wéber, *Personne humaine*, 209–10.
190. Albertus Magnus, *I Sent.*, d. 2, a. 13, ad qu. 2c, 69b: "quia Deus non diffinibilis

No name offers a fixed notion that exhausts God's being. Yet divine names such as "wisdom" truly signify "what God is." Divine names refer to God in his essence, not just his action. God is not just the cause of wisdom; he *is* wisdom.

Albert's reception of Dionysian analogy also reveals significant transformations of the same, the first of which pertains to the divine name "being." Albert asks whether the revealed name "Who is" should be considered as the first or highest divine name. The medievals understood Exodus 3:14 as a revelation of divine being. Throughout the article Albert treats "Who is" as the equivalent of the name "being."[191] The Jewish philosopher Maimonides, a crucial medieval interlocutor for Albert and Aquinas on this topic, identified "Who is" as the ineffable name. Its utter simplicity makes it the name above all names, as its signification excludes divine complexity. It leaves the mind with an utterly simple notion, without addition or specification. Albert embraces Maimonides's conclusion and attributes the priority of being as a divine name to Dionysius. When considering our own notions about God, "being" is the first name, though when we consider God as first cause, "good" is the better name for God.[192] Albert quietly reinserts a key metaphysical name precisely where Dionysius seeks to go beyond language and thought, a move parallel to Albert's transformation of Dionysian union beyond mind that we will find in his commentaries on the Areopagite. He tames the apophatism of Dionysius, but he can only do so by radically limiting the available intelligible content of the name "being." Albert also admits that God is most truly above or beyond naming, for he is incomprehensible.[193] Silence does not end theological discourse, but rather recognizes its inadequacy. This distinction is important: we will find it again in chapter 4.

---

est, licet possit in ipso dici quid est, sicut substantia, sapientia, bonitas, et caetera hujusmodi. Tamen attendendum est, quod nullum horum nominum quae etiam dicunt quid est, facit nobis determinatam notionem suae significationis in Deo: ita quod nihil sit extra intellectum de re ejusdem significati."

191. This is clear in the first set of objections in Albertus Magnus's *I Sent.*, d. 2, a. 14, which switch between *Qui est* and *ens* or *esse* without explanation. The article's corpus identifies the simplicity of uncreated being with *Qui est*.

192. Albertus Magnus, *I Sent.*, d. 2, a. 14c.

193. Albertus Magnus, *I Sent.*, d. 2, a. 16, ad 6, 72b: "Verissime autem dicitur esse supra nomen, et supra narrationem: quia cum non finiatur intellectu, significatur excedere omnem nomen, et omnem rationem."

Albert then offers what may be his key explanation of divine naming before 1248:

Divine names are formed in two ways, namely either [1] from those which are really prior in God and posterior in creatures, and these names are called *mystical* by the blessed Dionysius, such as being, life, understanding, wisdom, goodness and so on. *Mystis* in Greek is the same as *secretum* in Latin. This is so because, by its very nature, that [type of] name is from an imperfect institution and partially signifies that which is perfection and wholly in God. Sometimes it signifies accidentally that which is substantially in God and the divine substance. And so, the divine reality that one names remains hidden to us. For we know him to be above the name, and that our tongue falls short in its discourse. And therefore, Dionysius explains that [God] is life, and not life and beyond life. For in reality, he is life first, and not life according to what the name says. He is above life, in that he is his very own life, and [above the life] inserted into us. Therefore, Dionysius says that "in God, affirmations are incompact, and negations are true." Because with negations, one says what [God] is not, such as incorruptible, incorporeal and so on, and these [names] are simply true. But affirmation is incompact, because the mode of signifying in the name is repugnant to the divine reality, as was said, and chiefly because of three things, namely, because it signifies (1) what is infinitely simple in a composite way, (2) the most perfect in an imperfect way, and (3) sometimes [it signifies] what is substantial in an accidental way ... [2] but from symbolic names.[194]

---

194. Albertus Magnus, *I Sent.*, d. 2, a. 17c, 73a–b: "dupliciter formantur nomina divina, scilicet, aut ab his quae secundum rem per prius sunt in Deo et per posterius in creaturis, et haec nomina dicuntur *mystica* a beato Dionysio, sicut ens, vita, intellectus, sapientia, bonitas, et hujusmodi: *mustis* enim graece, in latino idem est quod *secretum:* et hoc ideo quia nomen illud secundum proprietatem suam quam habet ab institutione imperfecte et in parte significat id quod in Deo est perfectio et in toto: et significat quandoque accidentaliter id quod substantialiter est in Deo et substantia divina: et ideo res divina quam nominat, remanet nobis occulta: quia scimus ipsam esse super nomen, et deficere linguam a narratione ejus. Et ideo exponit Dionysius quod est vita, et non vita, sed supra vitam: est enim vita in re per prius, et non vita secundum id quod nomen ponit: supra vitam, eo quod ipse est vita sua, et inserta nobis: ideo etiam dicit Dionysius, quod in Deo affirmationes sunt incompactae, et negationes verae: quia negationibus dicitur quid non est, sicut incorruptibilis, incorporeus, et hujusmodi: et haec simpliciter vera sunt. Sed affirmatio incompacta est: quia modus significandi in nomine repugnat rei divinae, sicut dictum est, praecipue propter tria, scilicet, quia significat composite quod infinitae simplicitatis est, et imperfecte quod perfectissimum est, et accidentaliter quandoque quod est substantia.... A symbolicis autem nominibus." The Borgnet edi-

Nonsymbolic names signifying perfections such as being and goodness belong first to God because he truly, substantially, and infinitely possesses them, in contrast to symbolic names such as "body" or "anger" that are ontologically inseparable from finite, imperfect ways of being. Mystical names are secondarily in creatures, for they signify participated perfections caused by God. Each affirmative name is rooted in our cognition of a certain property or perfection found in creation, such as the human being's goodness. That is why names are "imperfect by institution" or in the customary way that we employ them, so that they only partly signify what is perfect in God. What is accidental in creation, like wisdom as an acquired human perfection, is substantial in God, who is wise by his nature. Thus the divine reality named remains hidden to us. Here the term "mystical" has nothing to do with a private vision or ecstatic experience.

Albert explains that, because the reality of divine goodness identified by the name remains beyond our complete grasp, we know God to be above all names. There is no perfect name that adequately manifests God's infinite substance. This, he says, is why Dionysius speaks of God as life, as not life, and as beyond or above life. God is above life in that he is his own life, while our life is received from the Creator. The affirmations are "incompact" because our mode of discourse is intrinsically finite and God is infinite. We do not affirm the reality signified (e.g., goodness) without qualification. Now negations are simply true, though the kind of negations that Albert gives as examples is significant: God is incorruptible and incorporeal. These are negations of imperfections, while the affirmations he mentions all concern perfections. The reality of corporeality is in itself no pure perfection, but intrinsically limited. Corporeality is necessarily bound to a created nature and a created mode of being. Something similar holds true for corruptibility. But being and goodness as such are perfect and are not necessarily limited.

Albert's teaching on affirmations and negations significantly transforms Dionysius. The latter employs names in quasi-dialectical fashion, always manifesting yet concealing the divine mystery, to initiate the reader in a contemplative ascent in which he or she depends on

---

tion twice has *supra vitam*. Maria Burger's forthcoming critical text gives the phrase *super vitam* in both instances.

affirmative names yet learns to go beyond them so as to eventually enter the darkness of God's transcendence. Dionysius seeks to leave his reader with the recognition that his or her knowledge of God is true yet well below the divine reality so as to be adequately detached from all thoughts and words about God in order to be taken up into passive union with God. Albert's scholastic method radically changes the genre of the theology of divine naming in three ways. First, his immediate aim is faith seeking understanding of the Trinity. The context of union is not excluded, yet the present text appears to abstract from it—that is, Albert's most extensive treatment of the limits of divine naming in the *Sentences Commentary* occurs within a critical epistemological preface to the rest of the work.[195] In other words, the theme that functions as *the* entryway to Dionysian mystical theology is taken up by Albert primarily in order to manifest the necessary qualifications and limits of theological discourse. But he does not directly follow up with a consideration of the soul's union with God. The theme of union emerged in the treatises on the divine missions, the theological virtues and gifts of the Spirit. Yet nowhere in these texts does Albert take up the topic of divine naming in any significant way. He thus accidentally (and partly) disconnects the study of the divine names from mystical theology. The closest we come to a Dionysian treatment of union in Albert's *Sentences Commentary* is in the study of divine naming and in the short section on the gift of wisdom. But the latter text has Hierotheus (who tastes divine things) at the center of the discussion. The heart of the Areopagite's *Mystical Theology* has no adequate reception in the *Sentences Commentary*.

Second, Albert employs the distinction between the mode of signification and the reality signified, giving the Areopagite's doctrine a Latin scholastic character. He brings much greater clarity to the relation between the names, explaining with new precision how affirmations are true and how they are limited. We already saw precedents for Albert's methodology in the *scholia* by John of Scythopolis, as well as in the teaching of Maximos. Albert's restriction of negations to the mode of signification and the denial of imperfections (e.g., incorruptibility)

---

195. Wéber calls Albert's doctrine of divine naming the inauguration of a new theological epistemology and the first critical negative theology in the West; see Wéber, "L'apophatisme," 380–81.

constitutes a major shift in meaning. Dionysius seems to avoid such clarity. He aims for true knowledge as the path toward union, while Albert's immediate aim is clarity of theological thought. The genre of the *Sentences Commentary* appears to play a decisive role in redirecting the doctrinal purpose of Dionysian mystical texts.

Third, Albert explains the meaning of eminent names: they signify the absolute identity of God's essence and his attributes. God is beyond life in that he is his own life. God is not a being that happens to have life in addition to being. While Dionysius affirms the doctrine of the divine simplicity with the whole of the patristic tradition, he does not employ it as a central explanation of the eminent names. For the Areopagite, eminent names serve as indicators that God's life is always beyond our understanding—that is, eminent names lead to mystic silence. But Albert explains *how* divine life is beyond our finite mode of having life. He brings greater clarity through eminent names precisely where Dionysius wants to move beyond cognitive activity. For Dionysius affirmations refer to that which is "under God." Albert implies that, by negating the mode of signification, affirmations themselves hit the mark, although a subsequent article adds the qualification that, since affirmative names do not adequately signify the divine reality (as their mode is limited), eminent names should also be employed.[196] Affirmations and negations require the complement of eminent discourse.[197] Albert here develops the tendency of certain *Parisian Scholia* to synthesize affirmative, negative, and eminent names, thus continuing the kataphatic turn of the Dionysian tradition, not unlike the exegesis of John of Scythopolis.

---

196. Albertus Magnus, *I Sent.*, d. 3, a. 10c. Thierry-Dominique Humbrecht argues that Albert here inserts Dionysian negativity into an Augustinian positive theology; see Humbrecht, "Noms divins: Les sources de saint Thomas au XIIIe siècle (II)," *RT* 105 (2005): 589.

197. Albertus Magnus's transformation of Dionysian apophatism again manifests itself in *I Sent.*, d. 3, a. 10, where he connects negations with symbolic names, eminent names with divine perfections that are prior in God, and the way of causality as referring to created perfections insofar as they come from the Creator. Eminent names are necessary because of our limited mode of signification. The restriction of negations to symbolic names is a radical shift away from Dionysius, though the previous articles showed that Albert's approach to negations in the *Sent.* is broader and more nuanced, and thus more Dionysian than this text suggests. For the essential link between negative and affirmative names in the thought of Albert, see Wéber, "Négativité et causalité," 54–55.

Albert's reevaluation of eminent names and their function will demand a reformulation of the troubling Dionysian phrase "union beyond mind," a project he will soon carry out in his *Commentary on the Divine Names*. The treatise on the divine names in the *Sentences Commentary* also contains the seeds for a modified Dionysian mystical theology, but Albert will only develop it in his commentary on the Areopagite's little classic.

CONCLUSION

In this chapter I have sought both a synthetic overview of Albert's key doctrines that underlie his reading of Dionysian mysticism and an evaluation of his theology of union in the years immediately preceding his commentaries on the Areopagite. Here I should highlight the key fruits of this synthesis and some major characteristics of his theory of union.

First, Albert's teachings on sanctifying grace, faith, the beatific vision, and divine naming manifest significant Dionysian influences. Grace as a dynamic return to God, the noetic light linked to the virtue of faith, the infinite Creator-creature distance overcome through the double theophany, and a critical theological epistemology all receive considerable emphasis in Albert's commentary on the Lombard. Albert thereby already takes his distance from various neo-Augustinian mystical theologies of his day, especially as he places the virtue of faith between will and intellect and insists on the considerable limits of noetic contact with God here below. Albert is already moving toward a more apophatic mysticism centered on intellect, though his mystical theology is also more kataphatic than the Areopagite's.

Second, despite the Dionysian influence, Albert barely works out a doctrine of actual grace. The elevating motion of God's light passes through grace as a formal flux or faith as a *habitus*. A vision of grace as an efficacious motion emerges out of these themes, but it remains subordinate to and dependent on grace as formal flux. Also, the study of the gifts of wisdom and understanding has only one brief mention of actuating lights distinct from the gifts as *habitus*. Again, formal causality dominates Albert's approach.

Third, Albert's teachings on the agent intellect, illumination, higher/lower intellect, the *imago*, the divine missions, and the Spirit's seven gifts show important Augustinian traces. Like his Parisian contemporaries, Albert fuses Augustinian noetic light with the agent intellect. He seems to affirm an interior ascent to God via (1) the higher intellect's expanding operative capacities, (2) direct access to God via memory, and (3) the interior effects that come with the gift of understanding. All three themes stand in tension with a Dionysian approach to union so that their place, absence, or critique in the Dionysian commentaries will be of the utmost importance. However, Albert's doctrines of the missions and the Spirit's gifts point toward a balance of knowledge and love in the event of union, thus offering subtle correctives to several Augustinian medieval mystical strands—ironically, via the development of Augustinian doctrines.

Fourth, one cannot help but notice the disjoined nature of the treatises. The theological authorities shift significantly depending on which topic is being discussed. The divine names strongly oppose Alexander of Hales, while the missions build on his thought in an extensive way. The doctrines of memory and illumination seem far from the Areopagite, yet Dionysius is the guiding light for the theological epistemology that is inseparable from divine naming. Here Albert's integration of negative theology seems to stand in tension with Augustine's indwelling God, at least as read by thirteenth-century Augustinians. The shift in authorities also helps to manifest an overall lack of systematic doctrinal integration. For example, the gift of understanding bears few Dionysian traces, while Hierotheus exemplifies the gift of wisdom, but both gifts bears little resemblance to an apophatic mysticism. Albert's theological personality leads him to tackle one topic at a time in relative abstraction from other topics, often with immense creativity, sometimes with surprising deference to the established authorities, yet almost always with a generous reception of newly available texts and ideas. Because various parts of the *Sentences Commentary* are relatively disconnected, we cannot speak of a single theology of union in this work. Rather, we find multiple approaches to union. Still, the same work will prove to be an indispensable guide to understand Albert's commentaries on Dionysius.

Despite the doctrinal tensions in *Sentences Commentary*, Albert consistently promotes a doctrine of active human cooperation in grace, even for the highest realization of grace that is union with God in this life. The centrality of created grace consistently emerges in the treatises on the missions, the theological virtues, and the beatific vision. Created grace is a key doctrinal foundation for active cooperation in union. The teaching on the *imago* moves in the same direction, since it is perfected through the operation of the theological virtues. The teaching on divine naming does not yield explicit connections with union, in contrast to the Dionysian commentaries, yet Albert's revaluation of affirmative names and sidelining of mystic silence sets the stage for the intellect's cooperation in union via the activity of divine naming. With the possible exception of the gifts of understanding and wisdom, passivity has little place in the mystical theology of the *Sentences Commentary*.

Albert's theology of union in his commentary on the Lombard is therefore hardly without consistency. Rather, we find a young theologian standing at a crossroads. The work of this *baccalaureus* began at the time of the 1241 crisis around the Greek patristic apophatic theology that he already admired. Yet Augustine clearly remained a theological giant. Albert was marked by Parisian Augustinian-Peripatetic anthropologies, but he saw the need to distance himself from their quasi-dualistic tendencies. He had already acquired a fascination for Aristotle, essentially dedicating a massive philosophical treatise to the Stagirite and his commentators in the *De homine*, well before he arrived in Cologne. Given these widely diverse approaches to God's uplifting action and the human being's path to perfection, should we be surprised that the first theological synthesis was not completely successful? Perhaps we should marvel at how far he had already come. These multiple intellectual streams will continue to influence his thought in the early Cologne period, but in a new way. For on the banks of the Rhine, the Areopagite will take center stage.

4

Albert's Dionysian Commentaries on Union with God

A HISTORICAL INTRODUCTION TO ALBERT'S COMMENTARIES ON THE AREOPAGITE

Albert arrived in Cologne in the summer of 1248 to found a new Dominican *studium*. He had considerable freedom to determine this doctoral school's curriculum. He made the works of Dionysius and Aristotle the foundational texts for the first *studium* courses. Albert also may have lectured on the Bible and the Lombard, though we have neither historical reports nor manuscript traditions for such projects.[1] As noted in chapter 3, recent research shows that all of his Dionysian commentaries date from the early Cologne period—that is, Albert deliberately chose to place the Greek father's entire corpus at the heart of the formation program for his cadre of elite student-friars, a possible first in the history of Western theological education.

Albert lectured on Dionysius from the fall of 1248 to the spring of

---

1. See M. Michèle Mulchahey, "The *Studium* at Cologne and Its Role Within Early Dominican Education," *Listening* 43 (2008): 124–26. She suggests that Albert dropped the magisterial lectures on the Bible but taught the *Sentences*. She refers to Cologne lectures on the fourth book of the *Sentences* in 1248–49 and new lectures on the rest of the *Sentences* in subsequent years. But in fact, in 1249, Albert finished editing the fourth book of his Parisian *Sentences*, given in 1244–45. He need not have taught Scripture, as the practice of masters outside of Paris was uneven; see Torrell, *Saint Thomas Aquinas*, vol. 1, *The Person and His Work*, 145–46.

1250. The prologues and internal references confirm that he followed the traditional Parisian order for the books: the *Celestial Hierarchy*, the *Ecclesiastical Hierarchy*, the *Divine Names*, the *Mystical Theology*, and the eleven *Epistles*. The spurious *Epistle 11* is inconsequential for our purposes. Albert essentially did not know Greek. His lectures rely on the Eriugena and Sarracenus translations as well as the *scholia* and interlinear gloss.[2] Albert produced Dionysian commentaries longer than anything available in the West before 1250, with the possible exception of the *scholia* translations.[3] The genre of his works combines a running commentary that integrates almost the entirety of the primary text interspersed with disputed questions on doctrinal difficulties. Albert sought to clarify the text and to reflect on it in a systematic way. The disputed questions undoubtedly transmit his personal theology, and the running commentary probably often does so, as well. The bulk of the key union passages come from the disputed questions.

In the prologue of his *Commentary on the Celestial Hierarchy* Albert presents the four long Dionysian treatises as systematically structured by the theme of *exitus-reditus*. The prologue consists of an exposition of Ecclesiastes 1:7: "The rivers return to the place from which they originate, that they may flow again." Following the key themes of the first paragraph in the *Celestial Hierarchy*, Albert interprets the rivers of Ecclesiastes as God's natural and supernatural gifts flowing into creation. The rivers return to the divine sea because God's ray leads us back to the Father's unity.[4] The angelic hierarchy is the first form of God's luminous procession. The *Ecclesiastical Hierarchy* continues this theme, for the church receives divine light from the angels and transmits it in the sacraments. The *Divine Names* treats the outflow of effects from the divine cause, the created participations that manifest God's names. The first three treatises focus on the outflow of God's natural and supernatural gifts. The topic of the *Mystical Theology* is the resolution of all things into the hidden God, the rivers' return to their source. The *Divine Names* teaches the science of God as the cause of all things mani-

---

2. Dondaine, "Saint Albert et le grec," *Recherches de théologie ancienne et médiévale* 17 (1950): 315–19. Albert rarely refers to the translations by Abbot Hilduin and Robert Grosseteste, and not at all in the passages that I will consider.

3. Burger, "Thomas Aquinas's Glosses," 562.

4. *SCH*, prologue, pp. 1–2. For an introduction, see Emery, *Trinité créatrice*, 141–43.

festing himself in his effects, a discipline that favors affirmative names. The *Mystical Theology* seeks to ascend to the obscure divine source of all things via negations. It is also a science of divine names, but now gazing upward.[5] Albert's distinction of these two works via affirmation-negation and procession-return is close to the Areopagite's own description of his corpus in the *Mystical Theology*.[6]

In Albert's Dionysian commentaries the most extensive discussion of union with God comes in the work on the *Mystical Theology*. My study of this commentary calls for a threefold preface: (1) Albert's turn toward a more Dionysian anthropology; (2) his understanding of the missions, grace, the light of glory, and theological virtues as principles or causes of unity, which shapes Albert's interpretation of Dionysian unifying light; and (3) Albert's doctrine of analogy in the *Commentary on the Divine Names*. The first preface manifests developments in Albert's vision of the human being that illumine his partial appropriation of Dionysian apophatism. The second preface mostly uncovers elements of continuity with the *Sentences Commentary*, a continuity we cannot take for granted, for Albert was an evolving thinker. The third preface surfaces Albert's most extensive, most systematic comments on the nature of affirmations and negations. The doctrine of naming stands at the heart of the theology of union in the *Commentary on the Mystical Theology*. This triple preface presents the main doctrinal pillars underlying Albert's teaching on union with God in the lectures on the Areopagite.

ALBERT'S EARLY COLOGNE ANTHROPOLOGY: A TURN FROM AUGUSTINE TO DIONYSIUS

From the first pages of the *Commentary on the Celestial Hierarchy* Albert quietly announces the advent of a new anthropology that moves away from key aspects of his previous Augustinianism and toward an Aristotelian-Dionysian emphasis on the soul-body unity. I will briefly summarize this doctrinal evolution and conclude with a glimpse at an

---

5. *SEH*, ch. 1, p. 1.1–10; *SDN*, ch. 1, no. 3, p. 2.25–49; *SMT*, ch. 1, p. 455.40–48; ch. 2, p. 467.41–52.
6. *MT* 3, pp. 146–47, 1033A–D; Rorem, *Pseudo-Dionysius*, 196, 204.

Albert's Dionysian Commentaries on Union with God   125

Averroist-Augustinian interiority that emerges in an isolated but fascinating passage.[7]

In Albert's *Sentences Commentary* the immaterial realm is the natural metaphysical place of the soul considered in abstraction from the body. The intellect is more or less proportioned to know spiritual realities directly. It primarily employs the mediation of the senses because of its connection to the body and perhaps because of original sin. In contrast, the Dionysian commentaries present a vision of the human intellect naturally at home in the material cosmos. The divine light comes to us through the sensible veils of the liturgy and physical creation because all of our knowledge naturally begins with sense experience. Nowhere in the Dionysian commentaries does Albert invoke our fallen nature to explain the sensible mediation of cognition.[8] Nor does the intellect bear an intrinsic capacity to grasp immaterial realities directly. Instead, "our intellect is in potency only to those things which can be received through sensibles, but it is in potency to spiritual things proportionally through some light superadded to nature, namely, grace or glory."[9] This graced elevation enables us not to bypass the senses, but rather to take full advantage of sensible mediations—namely, to receive God's self-revelation poured out through the liturgical veils (in the *Ecclesiastical Hierarchy*), the Bible, and creation (in the *Divine Names*). Contemplative ascent passes through knowledge of God's action in the material cosmos.[10] Albert seems to realize that Dionysian negative theology is closely intertwined with a vision of human cog-

---

7. For a fuller exposition, see Blankenhorn, "How the Early Albertus Magnus Transformed," 370–84.

8. Contrast Albertus Magnus, *I Sent.*, d. 17, a. 4c to *SCH*, ch. 1, p. 12.28–31 and *SEH*, ch. 4, p. 97.63–68.

9. *SCH*, ch. 6, p. 84.28–32: "intellectus noster est in potentia tantum ad ea quae per sensibilia accipi possunt, sed ad spiritualia proportionaliter per aliquod lumen superadditum naturae, scilicet gratiae vel gloriae"; see also ch. 2, p. 22.67–71.

10. *SDN*, ch. 2, no. 56, p. 81.34–38: "omnis nostra cognitio incipit a sensu, non tamen oportet, quod nihil cognoscamus ultra sensibile, sed ex sensibilibus devenimus in intelligibilia. Similiter ex causato devenimus in causam"; ch. 7, no. 27, p. 358.6–7. For intellect's proportion to material beings and disproportion to God, see *SCH*, ch. 1, p. 12.67–72; *SDN*, ch. 4, no. 24, p. 131.57–62; no. 69, p. 179.61–64; Anzulewicz, "Albertus Magnus über die *ars de symbolica theologia* des Dionysius Areopagita," *Teología y Vida* 51 (2010): 315–18. Other texts may imply that grace partly overcomes the disproportion: *SCH*, ch. 6, p. 84.28–32; ch. 9, p. 157.24–29.

nition as properly mediated through the body. Dionysian apophatism, at least as understood by Albert, presumes that the human intellect is quite disproportioned to the divine realm. Because its operational capacities have strict boundaries in a fixed hierarchy of being, the intellect needs mediations of divine light that paradoxically elevate us and (as mediations) simultaneously limit what we can know about God.[11] Albert's new, holistic anthropology therefore moves toward three key mystical doctrines that we find in Dionysius: a strong emphasis on the gratuity of grace; the human being's utter need for grace so as to be joined to God; and divine incomprehensibility.

The evolution in Albert's anthropology has at least two sources. The first is Aristotle, whom Albert cites for the principle that all cognition begins with the senses.[12] The second source is Dionysius. Albert takes the Greek father at his word when the latter mentions his (lost or fictional) treatise, the *Symbolic Theology*. In *Epistle 9* the Areopagite summarizes his doctrine of symbols. Albert's introduction to the epistles states that this mode of divine communication is fitting, as it is natural for us to receive divine things via sensible realities.[13]

Albert's new theology directly opposes key elements of Augustinian epistemology that he had espoused earlier. In the *Sentences Commentary* the higher intellect knows immaterial realities better than material beings, as spiritual noetic objects stretch the intellect's operational capacity. The higher intellect's act is obscured when we turn our attention to material things.[14] The *Commentary on Epistle 9 of Dionysius* reverses this teaching. Since the soul's connatural mode of knowing passes through phantasms, we often turn to the senses to know better the simple noetic objects (e.g., angels) contemplated with the higher intellect. The lower intellect no longer impedes but rather helps us to understand immaterial realities.[15] The *Commentary on the Mystical The-*

---

11. See Richard Schenk, "From Providence to Grace: Thomas Aquinas and the Platonisms of the Mid-Thirteenth Century," *Nova et Vetera* (English ed.) 3 (2005): 307–20.
12. *SCH*, ch. 6, p. 84.1–6.
13. *SEP 9*, p. 528.1–17, 44–49.
14. Albertus Magnus, *I Sent.*, d. 17, a. 4c (see chapter 3).
15. *SEP 9*, p. 539.3–13: "Aliter potest dici, quod in anima sunt duae partes, quaedam quae accipit ipsa simplicia secundum se, ut intellectus simplex, quaedam vero quae accipit a phantasmatibus, et ista magis est connaturalis animae secundum naturam ipsius, et in actu eius frequentius sumus, quia accipimus scientias ex sensibus; sed secundum

ology seems to suggest that the theme of knowing God in darkness has a direct influence on this reinterpretation of Augustine's higher intellect. Thus, as he comments on the Dionysian phrase "learned silence," Albert explains that, while God is most knowable in himself, our intellect relates to him as the eye of the owl relates to sunlight. The *Sentences Commentary* applied this image only to the lower intellect, while the present text offers no such restriction. Here the intellect as such is like the owl.[16] Albert appeals to Aristotle to explain a Dionysian doctrinal conclusion about the limits of our knowledge about God.

Albert's partial opposition to Augustinian noetics surfaces in one of the most striking passages of his Dionysian commentaries. The context is the Areopagite's paradoxical language of knowing God by unknowing. An objection states that the highest noetic vision is the very opposite of knowing in darkness. Following Augustine, God is the highest of the intellect's objects that are essentially present in the soul. Albert responds that the vision of God

has much of non-vision because of the object's eminence, as the Philosopher says. Yet it must be known that Augustine's saying is false (*dictum Augustini habet calumniam*). For in order that something be known, it does not suffice that it be in the possible intellect, unless it [intellect] be informed by its [the thing's] form and so brought into act, just as matter is brought into act through the form of the agent in it, and not through its essence, even if it [the agent] were present in it. Hence, the Philosopher says that the intellect understands itself as it understands other things.[17]

---

primam partem attingit intelligentias; et ideo quando etiam divina sine symbolis accepta sunt, ut melius ea possimus inspicere, reducimus ad sensibilia consueta nobis et connaturalia cognitioni nostrae." Here, Albert gives an alternative solution to a first response that invokes "all philosophers and Greek saints" as teaching that memory only pertains to the sensitive soul (pp. 538.56–539.2). He does not say which position he favors, but the theme of sensible cognition being connatural emerges in several other passages that were previously mentioned. The alternative solution suggests the possibility of attaining some knowledge without sensible mediation. But Albert only mentions "attaining intelligences"—that is, angels, which likely refer to angelically infused prophetic visions.

16. Albertus Magnus, *I Sent.*, d. 17, a. 4c; *SMT*, ch. 1, p. 456.56–61; see also Tugwell, "Albert the Great," 63.

17. *SMT*, ch. 2, pp. 466.91–67.11: "ex parte obiecti, ut dicatur nobilissimus modus visionis, per quam nobilissimum obiectum videmus, et sic est nobilissimus modus divinae visionis; sed iste propter eminentiam obiecti habet plurimum non-visionis, ut di-

For Augustine, God's presence in memory makes possible our knowledge of him, especially as God is the source of illumination and memory is its site. Illumination and the intellect's turn within overcome nonvision, yet the vision we attain is far below the beatific vision, excepting brief glimpses of God's glory such as those recounted in Augustine's *Confessions* or the vision of God *per speciem* that Paul and Moses enjoyed in rapture.[18] In his *Sentences Commentary* Albert mostly appropriates Augustine's doctrines of illumination, memory, the "stretching" of the mind's operational capacities, and its assimilation to the interior noetic object.[19] But in the *Commentary on the Celestial Hierarchy* he holds that assimilation by participation in an object's qualities does not suffice for cognition, as he expressly accepts assimilation by information via species.[20] In the present text he rejects a key element of Augustine's epistemology—namely, that an object's interior presence can suffice for actual cognition.[21] Albert shifts to an Aristotelian paradigm of information that the *Sentences Commentary* limited to the lower intellect. He insists on the need for intelligible forms for the knowledge of God. By implication, mystical cognition would seem to remain bound to concepts. I will come back to this theme later. Furthermore, if the object's interior presence does not cause cognition, then Albert has

---

cit Philosophus. Sciendum tamen, quod dictum Augustini habet calumniam; non enim sufficit aliquid esse in intellectu possibili ad hoc quod cognoscatur, nisi informetur forma eius et sic fiat actu, sicut materia fit actu per formam agentis in ipsa et non per essentiam ipsius, etiam si in ea esset. Unde dicit Philosophus, quod intellectus intelligit se sicut et alia."

18. Augustine, *Confessionum libri XIII*, ed. Lucas Verheijen, CCSL 27 (Turnhout: Brepols, 1981), bk. VII, ch. 10, no. 16; Augustine, *La Genèse au sens littéral en douze livres*, vol. 2, ed. P. Agaësse and A. Solignac, Bibliothèque augustinienne 49 (Paris: Desclée de Brouwer, 1972), bk. XII, ch. 27, no. 55; du Roy, *L'intelligence*, 99–105; Frederick Van Fleteren, "Mysticism in the *Confessiones*: A Controversy Revisited," in *Augustine: Mystic and Mystagogue*, edited by Frederick van Fleteren, Joseph C. Schnaubelt, and Joseph Reino, 311–24, Collectanea Augustiniana 3 (New York: Peter Lang, 1994). Van Fleteren argues that the teaching on the rapture of Moses in the commentary on Genesis goes beyond but does not contradict the *De trinitate*. On the latter, see Lewis Ayres, *Augustine and the Trinity* (Cambridge: Cambridge University Press, 2010), 161–65.

19. Albertus Magnus, *I Sent.*, d. 2, a. 5; d. 17, a. 4c.

20. See also *SCH*, ch. 2, p. 17.38–42: "cognitio nostra non fit per assimilationem, quae est in participando easdem qualitates, qualis est inter intellectum nostrum et angelos, sed per illam quae consistit in informatione per speciem acceptam a re."

21. Albert already signals his opposition to Augustine on this point at *SCH*, chap. 2, p. 18.39–42; see also Tugwell, "Albert the Great," 79–81.

Albert's Dionysian Commentaries on Union with God 129

also quietly dropped the notion of interior objects stretching our operational powers. He uses unusually strong language as he distinguishes between Augustine and his own Dionysian-Aristotelian stance. Perhaps he realizes that the Latin father's noetics is so far from Dionysius (as Albert understands him) that much of the Areopagite's mysticism would become unintelligible without a new approach to the mystical subject. Albert's strong critique of Augustine also signals that his doctrine does not simply shift with the text being commented, but reflects an evolution in his personal thought. Albert develops a new version of Dionysian mysticism. The Areopagite offers authoritative weight to such a project: one can contradict Augustine with a direct disciple of the apostles.[22]

However, a very different side of Albert's "early Cologne anthropology" emerges in a single long passage from the *Commentary on the Divine Names*. The context is the Dionysian doctrine of the mind's three motions. Dionysius posits a "straight motion" from material beings to their divine cause, an "oblique motion" by discursive reflections on the divine lights mediated through the Bible and the liturgy, and a "circular motion" whereby the angels help the soul turn away from the material world and rest in a quiet gaze upon the Good.[23] Albert explains that the circular motion's first (but not ultimate) contemplative object is the human subject's own agent intellect. By the agent intellect's light, we usually focus on sensible objects. If we withdraw the mind's gaze from material beings and turn inward, we behold only the agent intellect's light. This faculty can illumine, for its light mingles with divine light. As we gaze upon the agent intellect alone, the divine light that descends through it elevates us to behold God's light.[24] Albert's exegesis

---

22. This also confirms that, in Cologne, Albert shifts away from an Augustinian to a more Dionysian *theological* anthropology, contra Sturlese's claim of a turn away from theology to philosophy (Sturlese, *Deutsche Philosophie im Mittelalter*, 332–33); see Blankenhorn, "How the Early Albertus Magnus Transformed," 370–75.

23. *DN*, 4.9, pp. 153.10 54.6, 705A-B; Riordan, *Divine Light*, 201–3.

24. *SDN*, ch. 4, no. 103, pp. 202.60–3.12: "sicut dicit Commentator, motus circularis est essentialis animae et est de motibus eius simplicibus, et ideo oportet quaerere motum circularem animae in eo quod in ipsa simplicius et nobilius est, et hoc est lumen intellectus agentis, quod ... lluminat intellectum possibilem virtute luminis divini micantis in ipso ... anima considerando res exteriores non inspicit lumen intellectus agentis nisi particulatum ad hoc vel illud intelligibile, secundum quod est forma huius vel illius. Unde si debeat ipsum lumen secundum se inspicere, oportet, quod retracta ab omnibus

takes us far from Dionysius. He invokes Averroes's agent intellect, but in reference to the human being's individual agent intellect. He replaces the angels' uplifting activity with the agent intellect's illuminating operation. He also invokes the Augustinian theme of the soul always remembering and knowing itself to explain the turn to the agent intellect's light, but within a primarily Aristotelian-Averroist framework. Here the agent intellect's functions far exceed the abstraction of forms from phantasms. Finally, the agent intellect serves as a contemplative steppingstone. Because it mediates divine light, it enables us to gaze upon that light. Albert does not tell us if the agent intellect mediates graced cognition, but the theological genre of the commentary would seem to imply it.[25] Overall, Albert's fusion of Dionysian contemplation and Augustinian interiority, behind which stands Plotinus, parallels the hermeneutic of certain *Parisian Scholia*, where John of Scythopolis uses Plotinian notions of noetic inwardness and concentration to interpret the same section of the *Divine Names*.[26]

Albert never seems to employ this notion of contemplative ascent via the agent intellect in the rest of his Dionysian commentaries. Rather, his exposition of Dionysian mysticism consistently follows the principle of mediated ascent (through the senses) as we will see. Like the *Sentences Commentary*, the Dionysian commentaries include some disconnected doctrinal exposés. Albert's treatment of the Areopagite's circular motion also manifests an abiding tension within his theology of noetic ascent. His later philosophical works will place considerable emphasis on the agent intellect and Platonic-Averroist interiority, a doctrinal stream that will flow with vigor in late medieval German Dominican epistemology and mysticism.[27]

---

exterioribus infigat oculum mentis in se, sicut etiam dicit Augustinus in IX *De trinitate*, quod anima numquam considerat, quod sui semper meminerit et se semper intelligat et diligat, nisi quando retrahitur ab exterioribus ad seipsam. Et ideo in motu circulari animae primo ponit introitum ipsius ab exterioribus ad seipsam, non tamquam partem circularis motus, sed sicut remotionem impedimenti. Quando autem anima conversa est ad seipsam, lumen proveniens a primo in ipsam secundum esse reflectit in primum secundum intellectum, et sic concluditur circulus in ipso primo, sicut dictum est supra de motu circulari angeli."

25. Albertus Magnus's theology of the beatific vision integrates the agent intellect's activity; *II Sent.*, d. 4, a. 1, qla. 2.

26. *PDN*, ch. 4, 122; see chapter 2 of this volume.

27. For the later Albert's noetics, see Anzulewicz, "Vermögenspsychologische Grund-

THE MISSIONS, GRACE, AND THE THEOLOGICAL VIRTUES IN THE DIONYSIAN COMMENTARIES

Albert's reconstitution of the mystical subject may give the impression that Augustinianism has little place in his Dionysian commentaries. But these works manifest a significant systematic achievement—one that seems more successful than the *Sentences Commentary*. For in Cologne Albert manages to synthesize a heavily Dionysian approach to anthropology, analogy, and negations as a mystical ladder with a predominantly Augustinian theology of grace. The latter often operates beneath the surface of the lectures on Dionysius. It is above all in his *Commentary on the Celestial Hierarchy* that Albert transforms the Dionysian discourse on light into a scholastic doctrine of the divine missions, created grace, and illuminating faith. Here the perils of reading his lectures on Moses encountering God in abstraction from the other Cologne texts come to the fore.

My analysis will follow an order similar to the one employed in the previous chapter: first the missions, then created grace and the light of glory, and finally the virtues of faith and charity. The *imago* emerges briefly at a crucial juncture in the *Commentary on the Mystical Theology* and thus will be treated in the section on union. I will not treat the Spirit's gifts of wisdom and understanding, for Albert's commentaries on Dionysius only mention them once in passing, an important lacuna whose significance I will consider later on. In addition to highlighting some subtle shifts in the doctrine of faith, I will focus on Albert's way of harmonizing Augustinian grace with the Dionysian text.

The *Celestial Hierarchy* begins by citing the Letter of James (1:17): "Every perfect gift descends from the Father of lights." Dionysius tells us that the procession of light from the Father has a unifying power and that Jesus is the paternal light through which we have access to the Father. Albert comments that Jesus is called the Father's light because this analogy signifies wisdom and being from another.[28] He employs Augustine's psychological analogy to explain Christ's work of mediat-

---

lagen Kognitiver Leistung des Intellektes nach Albertus Magnus," *Acta Mediaevalia* 22 (2009): 103–15.

28. *CH* 1.1–2, p. 7.1–11, 120B–21A; *SCH*, ch. 1, p. 6.58–65.

ing paternal light, which work is rooted in his eternal trinitarian identity. The Areopagite invokes Jesus as the mediator of light by his incarnation. Albert traces Christ's act of illuminating back to his personal property as Wisdom proceeding from the Father. Albert's trinitarian theology remains Augustinian. It functions as a hermeneutical key for the Dionysian language of deifying light. Later on the *Celestial Hierarchy* refers to a pure reception of the divine ray. Albert explains that the divine "ray in spiritual things is the divine person proceeding in order to perfect the mind, the Son according to intellect and the Holy Spirit according to will (*affectum*)."[29] The term "divine ray" elicits an explanation of the mode of divine action, while the effect of this ray is the graced perfection of angels and souls. For Albert the doctrinal context seems to require a reference to the divine missions, to the mode of divine action that is proper to the effect of sanctifying grace. He soon notes that without the giving of the divine person that accompanies created sanctifying grace, such finite gifts would never suffice to traverse the infinite Creator-creature distance and join us to God.[30] Here one finds complete continuity with the *Sentences Commentary* teaching on the missions. The *imago* also stands in the background, wherein the Son and the Spirit perfect intellect and will, respectively.

Albert also preserves the Areopagite's broader doctrinal intention: union remains impossible without an immediate divine act. For Dionysius the angels manifest God so as to help us ascend to him. God completes this journey as he unifies the soul with himself. Albert specifies the divine light in ways that Dionysius never imagined. In the Areopagite the Trinity's inner life does not structure its work in the divine economy, for Dionysius has no theology of the Son as proceeding Wisdom and the Spirit as spirated Love, nor does he have a doctrine of the divine missions comparable to that of Augustine and his disciples. Albert's development of Augustine's missions gives him a tool to interpret the action of God's light in the economy of salvation through the Trinity's inner life. For Dionysius divine light comes from the God who is communion and leads us into trinitarian communion. Albert goes fur-

29. *SCH*, ch. 3, p. 50.33–36: "radius igitur in spiritualibus est persona divina procedens ad perficiendam mentem, filium quidem secundum intellectum et spiritus sanctus secundum affectum"; see *CH* 3, p. 18.3–4, 165A.
30. *SCH*, ch. 2, p. 41.24–28.

ther as he posits a trinitarian mode of return to God.[31] His commentaries on the *Divine Names* and the *Mystical Theology* never explicitly mention the missions, for they simply presume this doctrine—that is, we can only recognize Albert's full doctrinal contention behind the language of unifying light when we read him against the background of the *Sentences Commentary*.

Albert's Dionysian commentaries include a few brief references to the nature of grace. In the *Commentary on the Ecclesiastical Hierarchy* he follows Dionysius in identifying the incarnate Word as the source of the ecclesial hierarchy. Christ deifies the soul or consummates its return to God. Because Christ imparts a share in divine things, we can attain perfection and divine unity. Albert also describes deification as divine assimilation. God turns us to himself and initiates our path of return or "motion" to divine things through baptism.[32]

In a second series of comments on grace, Albert moves beyond Dionysius. He notes that the soul is perfected in three ways: by an influx of grace in the soul's essence; by a *habitus* in the soul's operative faculties (invoking Augustine); and by operation. The final category seems to involve an actual grace, but Albert does not elaborate. His guiding doctrinal principle is that grace brings about the soul's perfection in each of its parts. Albert joins the theme of perfection to a threefold structure of essence-power-operation, synthesizing Aristotelian anthropology, Dionysian metaphysics, and an Aristotelian-Augustinian notion of *habitus*.[33] Albert soon connects this anthropology to the missions. Following John 14:23 (Jesus and the Father will come and dwell within whoever keeps his word), Albert explains that union with God causes the imprint of a *habitus* in the soul, a divine similitude that inclines our intention toward God.[34] Here union and the infusion of the *habitus* are simultaneous events ordered according to the metaphysical priority of the divine act. Also, the *Commentary on the Celestial Hierarchy* states that the procession of paternal motion (i.e., the Word invisibly sent to believers) would remain ineffective if it did not repair or heal us and make

---

31. See also *SCH*, ch. 7, p. 103.46–52.
32. *SEH*, ch. 1, pp. 6.69–7.8, 7.23–25, 7.31–36, 20.46–47; ch. 2, pp. 28.36–42, 39.66–68.
33. *SEH*, ch. 1, p. 7.31–36. On Dionysius and the triple structure, see Wéber, *Personne humaine*, 209–10.
34. *SEH*, ch. 2, pp. 23.42–24.2.

us sharers of divine unity, an allusion to the transforming power of intrinsic, created grace, the grace imparted whenever the Son or the Spirit are invisibly sent. God's unifying power grants us a real share in spiritual emanation so that we are gathered back into divine unity by both intellect and affect.[35] Albert reads the doctrine of *reditus* via the Areopagite's unifying divine ray, but in the framework of the doctrine of the missions perfecting the *imago* by created gifts of grace. Finally, the *Commentary on Epistle 2 of Dionysius* states that God is the sole effective (or efficient) cause of deification, while grace and glory participate in God and formally deify us.[36] Albert synthesizes Dionysian deification with created grace. The efficient-formal distinction has clear precedents in the *Sentences Commentary*, but Albert now refuses the notion that created grace and glory are secondary efficient causes of divine life. He insists that only a direct divine act divinizes. This doctrinal evolution moves Albert closer to the Areopagite's understanding of divinization.

Five global observations on grace in Albert's Dionysian commentaries are in order. First, excepting the efficiency of created grace and glory, he remains fully consistent with the *Sentences Commentary* theology of grace. Thus, while he says little on grace as an accident, all of his explanations remain in harmony with this notion or presuppose it.[37] Second, he transforms Dionysius's various dynamic images for return and divinization into an exposition of the missions leading us back to the Father via created gifts of grace. Third, the same reinterpreted dynamic images and the emphasis on *habitus* lead to a theology of active cooperation in union. Fourth, Albert's lectures on Dionysius say little on the Christological nature of grace, probably because Dionysius rarely discusses Christology. In the *Commentary on the Ecclesiastical Hierarchy*, Albert notes that the power of Christ's passion operates in baptism, but he does not distinguish between diverse causalities of Christ's distinct natures. Nor does he elaborate on Christ's human knowledge.[38]

35. *SCH*, ch. 1, p. 7.6–23.
36. *SEP* 2, p. 483.49–54: "Dicendum, quod aliquid est principium deificationis dupliciter, scilicet effective, et sic solus deus est principium deificans; est etiam aliquid deificans formaliter, sicut ipsa participatio deitatis assimilans deo vel per gratiam vel per gloriam, et hoc est aliud quam deus."
37. Grace as an accident is mentioned at *SCH*, ch. 11, p. 170.60–63.
38. *SEH*, ch. 2, p. 35.10–12. Albert does not use the Dionysian reference to the theandric acts of Jesus to develop a doctrine of instrumental causality; see *SEP* 4, p. 491.56–69.

The Dionysian commentaries remain fully compatible with the *Sentences Commentary* doctrine of Christological grace. Fifth, Albert departs from the Lombard, as he now clearly espouses Augustine's teaching (via Anselm) that Adam and Eve were created in grace. The first couple was made so as to be properly ordered to its (beatific) end.[39]

Albert's Dionysian commentaries devote little space to the beatific vision. One senses that he is largely satisfied with his teaching in the *Sentences Commentary*, which he mostly presupposes or repeats. His eschatology remains centered on the double theophany of the finite gift of glory (the created theophany) that grants the intellect the heightened receptive capacity necessary to see God's essence (the divine theophany).[40] Still, the eschatology of the lectures on Dionysius goes beyond the commentary on the Lombard in two ways. First, Albert states that the light of glory strengthens intellects in different degrees, so that a hierarchy of created glory becomes the immediate metaphysical cause of the variety of visions among the saints, even as each of them directly beholds God's nature.[41] One does not find this precision in the *Sentences Commentary*. Second, Albert displays a new approach to Aristotle's teaching on contemplation as it relates to beatitude. Albert notes that the fruits of the beatific vision include joy and delight, for the philosopher teaches that our gaze upon the separate substances overflows the soul with the delight that comes when a faculty's natural operation is no longer impeded. Unlike the *Sentences Commentary*, Albert does not hesitate to employ a key element of Aristotle's theory of philosophical contemplation to describe the vision of God—that is, the mode of cognitive perfection in the knowledge of creatures partly manifests the mode of the beatific perfection—namely, the perfection of operative potencies through action, whose natural outcome is delight in actuality. In the background stands a vision of nature and grace in harmony, even as Albert recognizes the difference between Aristotle's acquired philosophical beatitude in this life and the glorious vision in the next. Consequently, beatitude essentially includes active human participation in the reception of divine light. The saints are not simply acted upon; they also act, for they are perfected in virtue, and virtue is

39. *SDN*, ch. 3, no. 4, p. 103.40–57.
40. *SCH*, ch. 3, pp. 53.76–54.3; ch. 4, p. 71.12–40; *SEH*, ch. 1, p. 14.22.
41. *SDN*, ch. 13, no. 27, p. 448.35–47; see also Ruello, "Noms divins," 97.

achieved in act.[42] The commentary on the Lombard only implied active cooperation in beatitude when it posited the agent intellect as a mediator of all divine light, a doctrine that the Dionysian commentaries do not mention. Such cooperation now finds a more solid foundation in Aristotle's virtue-centered metaphysical anthropology. By implication, the same doctrine also stands behind Albert's understanding of the theological virtues. For if we can attain a partial understanding of the saints' vision and delight in heaven with the Aristotelian principles of virtue and perfection by operation, then the same logic applies to the life of grace here below—that is, the full perfection of operation and virtue via the created gift of glory has a partial parallel in the perfection of operation and virtue via created grace in this life. Union with God involves the pilgrim's perfection in virtue and operation and thus human cooperation in grace. This theme can already be found in Albert's theology of grace as *habitus* and the missions. But his broader appropriation of Aristotle's anthropology leads to a fuller integration of the theme of cooperation in his overall vision of the mystical subject.

Albert's new utilization of Aristotle's virtue-centered anthropology in his eschatology points to the centrality of the theological virtues in his mysticism. Three important elements of Albert's teaching on faith deserve mention: (1) faith as an elevation of our noetic capacity to receive divine light; (2) a greater focus on intellect; and (3) faith's identification with Dionysian ecstasy. These three categories constitute the major doctrinal developments in Albert's theology of faith in his commentaries on the Areopagite.

Shortly after he invokes Jesus as the paternal light in the *Celestial Hierarchy*, Dionysius explains that Christ manifests divine glory by illuminations passed on in the holy sayings (of Scripture) and (liturgical) symbols. The mind's eye receives these mediated lights without trembling so as to return to God. Albert explains that the sun blinds the eye of the bat or "night bird" (Aristotle's owl reformulated by Averroes), just as earthly affections and corporeal images hold back the human mind's natural vision. Yet even as we distance ourselves from such affections and images, we still tremble before God's glory, for by the principles of

---

42. *SCH*, ch. 3, p. 54.53–61; *SDN*, ch. 11, no. 15, pp. 417.79–18.4: "Et quia beatitudo, ut dicit Philosophus, est secundum actum perfectae virtutis ... inquantum est ex actu perfecto perfectae virtutis"; contrast to Albertus Magnus, *IV Sent.*, d. 49, a. 6.

reason we only behold divine things from afar. We need the light of faith to strengthen us so that we no longer tremble.[43] Albert recognizes that the symbols mediate light and so assist in contemplative ascent. But he replaces Dionysius's focus on symbolic liturgical mediations as the central (and extrinsic) means of accessing divine light with a focus on faith as an intrinsic elevation of the intellect's receptive capacities. Dionysius presumes that the liturgical subject has faith, but the technicalities of this virtue hardly seem to have interested him. For Albert faith overcomes the natural distance between human reason and divine wisdom. The trembling of the soul becomes a metaphor of our limited capacity to know God by reason alone. Faith as an elevation of our noetic capacity becomes the key to receive mediated, divinizing light. Albert's shift in emphasis also sets the stage for a doctrine that moves away from the centrality of the liturgy in Dionysian mysticism and toward a theology of the soul's ascent through the intellect's adherence to divine light as mediated by the doctrines of faith expressed in the divine names. The latter mysticism continues to acknowledge the importance of mediations, especially as Albert focuses on revealed divine names mediated by Scripture. But this approach places far less emphasis on distinct modes of mediation at various stages of ascent. A highly structured ascent is crucial for Dionysius, who proportions symbols and divine names to particular stages of contemplation.

Second, one passage in the *Commentary on the Divine Names* may suggest a shift toward intellect in the doctrine of faith. Albert explains that philosophical syllogisms do not produce knowledge of the divine names. He treats the *Divine Names* as a theological text. Cognition of these names comes from "the light of faith, which rather moves us to believe by the mode by which nature inclines ... it illumines [us] to know through art and reason that to which we assent through faith."[44] We attain the content of the divine names through Scripture. We accept this divine communication through the infused virtue of faith that moves us toward its object. The divine names are objects of cog

43. *CH* 1.2, p. 7.9–13, 121A; *SCH*, ch. 1, pp. 7.80–8.5.
44. *SDN*, ch. 1, no. 8, p. 4.77–83: "non facit cognitionem de divinis nominibus syllogismus vel quaecumque ratio, sed lumen fidei, quod potius movet per modum naturae inclinans ad credendum, sicut virtus movet, sicut dicit Tullius, quam per modum artis, ut scilicet illuminet ad cognoscendum per artem et rationem illud cui per fidem assentitur."

nition, so that the inclination that Albert compares to the "mode of nature" must also be intellectual. In the *Sentences Commentary* he makes the same comparison to natural inclination, but in reference to the will moving the intellect to consent.[45] In the *Commentary on the Divine Names* Albert specifies that the light of faith remains properly noetic: it illumines us to know. Here he does not mention the will moving the intellect to accept propositions as true, though he implies the will's operation when he speaks of faith's act of assent—that is, as a cause of noetic assent to revelation. But Albert's doctrine of belief now seems to attain a new equilibrium. More clearly than in the *Sentences Commentary*, faith as an interior noetic light causes belief or the act of assent.[46] Albert seems to place more emphasis on God's self-revelation. At the very least he makes more explicit the noetic side of God's direct causality in the faith act. Albert deepens the continuity between the mode of divine action that elevates the intellect in the first act of belief and the saints' perfect union with God, since both take place at different points on the same trajectory of divine light elevating us to God.[47]

Third, two passages from the *Commentary on the Divine Names* display a transformation of Dionysian ecstasy through the doctrine of faith. In chapter 2 of the *Divine Names* Dionysius notes that his work *The Theological Outlines* treats the multiplicity of the divine persons insofar as such a study is possible for human beings who have received revelation. Still, we know whatever God reveals to us by participations—that is, in highly inadequate ways.[48] But some have been mystically united to God above the intellect's operation. Albert explains:

In philosophy, something is demonstrated by resolving it to the first principles, whose place Sacred Scripture holds in theology. But, *by them* [the revelations of Scripture] they are *united* through faith *as to mystical,* that is, to hidden things, *above intellectual operation,* that is, above the power of our intellect.[49]

45. Albertus Magnus, *III Sent.,* d. 23, a. 2, ad 1.
46. Albertus Magnus, *III Sent.,* d. 23, a. 3; see also *SDN,* ch. 7, no. 35, p. 363.70–74.
47. Tugwell, "Albert the Great," 70, sees Albert moving toward a much more noetic approach to faith in the Dionysian commentaries. Wéber, "Relation," 582, detects a clearer explanation of the relation between faith and the will in the lectures on Dionysius after some ambiguity in the *Sentences Commentary*.
48. *DN* 2.7, pp. 130.14–31.7, 644D–45A.
49. *SDN,* ch. 2, no. 54, p. 80.34–39: "in philosophia demonstratur aliquid resolven-

Dionysius distinguishes between the theological knowledge of God's revelation that remains in a properly human mode—that is, tied to finite manifestations of God—and the mystical knowledge received when God pours his light directly into the passive soul. Albert interprets the phrase "above intellectual operation" to include everything here discussed without distinguishing between human and divinely given modes of cognition—that is, the revelation of Scripture takes us beyond the natural operations of the intellect that proceed from reason alone. The intellect is passive insofar as faith is an unmerited, gratuitous gift. But once graced the intellect hardly needs to be passive. Faith has a properly unifying power. Its object involves a divine reality hidden to reason. This also means that directly infused light need not (by itself) impart new noetic content. Albert now applies Dionysian divine light to the elevating power of the virtue of faith so that the new knowledge attained by union above intellectual operation can still come from Scripture—the very mediation whose limits Dionysius seeks to surpass as a true, yet ultimately inadequate manifestation of God. Faith explains the Areopagite's troubling language of going beyond mind. Hence Albert quietly opens the possibility of active human participation in the event of union above mind, for such participation is precisely one of the fruits of faith's light. He simultaneously implies that the intellect need not let go of all images and thoughts to receive God's light. Later on we will find a fascinating parallel between Albert's rereading of noetic ecstasy and his understanding of Moses in the dark cloud. Let us also note that ecstasy is the normal condition of every believer in grace. Albert universalizes a particular gift that the Areopagite had reserved for a contemplative elite.

Albert employs a similar interpretive strategy when he discusses Paul's ecstasy in chapter 7 of the *Divine Names*. According to the Areopagite, the apostle and teacher of Hierotheus has gone out of himself by ecstatic love so as to belong to God alone, a teaching that Dionysius emphasizes in chapter 4 of the treatise. In chapter 7 he notes that "our leaders" (Paul and Hierotheus) have been purified of all errors by divine faith—that is, the perpetual temptation to confuse the manifesta-

---

do ad prima principia, quorum locum tenent < in > theologia sacrae scripturae; *autem*, idest sed, *quibusdam* eorum *uniti* per fidem *sicut mysticis*, idest occultis, *super operationem intellectualem*, idest super virtutem nostri intellectus."

tions of God with God himself (i.e., cognitive idolatry).[50] Albert comments that Paul "was faithful *to the truth, having suffered ecstasy,* that is, [was] placed beyond himself in divine truth *through true faith* inasmuch as he neither believes his own reason nor others' [reason] contrary to the truth of the faith."[51] For Dionysius the contemplative must overcome erroneous perceptions of God in order to complete ascent to him, a process that occurs by sitting at the feet of the Areopagite as hierarch in order to understand the divine names. Ecstasy follows this initiation. Deliberately or not, Albert takes ecstasy beyond the case of advanced disciples of holy hierarchs, just as he previously set aside (deliberately or not) the proportioning of liturgical symbols and divine names to higher and lower stages of ascent to God. Now a faith that trusts the revealed message makes possible adherence to truth, which adherence in turn enables the soul's ecstasy, though Albert does not say that this is the sole condition for ecstasy. He certainly presumes that the power of charity is at work in Paul. Every believer who adheres to the gospel by faith (animated by charity) can also attain Paul's experience of belonging to Christ alone. In Dionysius the hierarch proportions the mediations and leads the disciple on the path to an ever-more divine faith that gradually purifies the soul of every error through an explanation of the divine names. Albert assigns the hierarch's task to biblical truth and the power of faith, though he will soon also attribute that task to the scholastic theologian.

A consistent doctrine of faith as ecstatic and unitive underlies Albert's reading of Dionysian ecstasy and union. Albert's theology of faith is not foreign to Dionysius insofar as key elements of the former find clear inspiration in the latter's theology of light, especially the themes of the influx of light, light as divine self-revelation, light as a noetic gift, and as an elevation of the mind. But we will see that Albert has a much broader understanding of union than the Eastern father. For Dionysius the believer enjoys the presence of God within, but the *Divine Names* and *Mystical Theology* usually reserve the term "union" for the high point of the spiritual life symbolized by Moses in darkness, a

---

50. *DN* 4.13, p. 159.3–6, 712A; 7.4, p. 199.14–18, 872D–73A; de Andia, *Henosis,* 353–54.
51. *SDN,* ch. 7, no. 36, p. 364.30–33: "'Insanis, Paule'; ipse enim fidelis *extasim passus veritati,* idest positus extra se in divina veritate, *per veram fidem,* inquantum rationi suae nec credit nec aliorum contra fidei veritatem."

union that follows a long, arduous path of moral and intellectual purification. For Albert the virtue of faith (joined to charity) bears an intrinsic power to begin the intellect's union with God. Thus by faith Albert understands the created term of the Son's mission, accompanied by the Spirit's mission whose created term is charity, two virtues whereby the divine persons sent unite the intellect and will to God. The *Commentary on the Celestial Hierarchy* recalls that union requires the missions. Thus Albert's doctrine of the missions stands behind his exegesis of Dionysian ecstasy. Albert never mentions the missions in his *Commentary on the Divine Names*, yet without them we cannot explain his reading of the key union texts in the *Divine Names*. The doctrine of the missions may also be the primary reason for Albert's expansion of Dionysian union to a gift enjoyed by all believers.[52]

The subtle presence of the theology of the missions in Albert's Dionysian commentaries offers an important hermeneutical principle as we approach his doctrine of charity. Here, too, his direct comments are sparse as he presumes his *Sentences Commentary* theology of charity. No significant evolution on this doctrine surfaces. Our main question is how Albert synthesizes his theology of charity with the key Dionysian passages on love. The answer comes in Albert's discussion of (1) charity's essential role in noetic union with God; (2) the place of charity in Hierotheus's experience; and (3) love's ecstatic character.

Albert asks whether knowledge alone can perfect the intellect. The context is a discussion of prayer in chapter 3 of the *Divine Names*. An objection cites Augustine, who seems to teach that prayer perfects the will while knowledge perfects the intellect, so that prayer and the will's ascent to God have no apparent relation to knowledge. Albert responds, "Although knowledge is the intellect's perfection, nevertheless, by the affect's perfection we approach God and participate in his light, and thus our intellect is perfected in the things that cannot be grasped through human reason."[53] He refuses the theory that cognition alone

---

52. Wéber maintains that the missions are central for Albert's interpretation of Dionysius; see Wéber, introduction to Albertus Magnus, *Commentaire de la "Théologie mystique,"* 22–46.

53. *SDN*, ch. 3, no. 6, p. 105.10–14: "quamvis scientia sit perfectio intellectus, tamen ex perfectione affectus appropinquamus ad deum et participamus lumen ipsius, et sic perficitur intellectus noster in his quae secundum rationem humanam accipi non possunt"; see also *SDN*, ch. 1, no. 10, p. 5.52–56; *SCH*, ch. 7, p. 92.51–55; Pablo C. Sicouly, "Gebet als

suffices for noetic perfection. In this passage "affect" refers to the will being perfected by charity, since the response concerns Augustine's teaching on the transformative power of prayer. Growth in charity brings us closer to God and leads us to a greater share in divine light, a light that Albert presumes to be inseparably affective and noetic, for his argument proceeds directly from the will's appropriation of light to the intellect's reception thereof. Progress in charity is essential for progress in theological knowledge—that which is beyond reason. Albert's argumentation is very consistent with his doctrine of the missions: the coming of the Son into the intellect presumes the simultaneous presence of the Spirit in the will, either a conjoined or a previous mission of the Spirit. The present text signals that Albert's discussion of noetic ascent in other passages probably presumes a simultaneous ascent of love. This last point is crucial, for Albert's comments on the *Mystical Theology* will follow the thematic flow of the Dionysian text and not offer a systematic exposition of the kinds of graces that are necessary for union. Last, he affirms that the proper *ratio* or nature of love (*amor*) is to unite the lover with the beloved.[54]

The Areopagite's great teacher of love was Hierotheus. In chapter 2 I mentioned that Eriugena translated this hierarch's experience of learning divine things by suffering (*pathōn*) them as learning "from affection for divine things (*affectus divina*)." This translation stands at the heart of Albert's exegesis. The latter explains that Hierotheus received divine things (i.e., revealed doctrine) from the apostles, assiduously studied the sacred (biblical) books, and learned in an even higher way by "affection for many divine things," which he "knew as if through experience." Albert follows Eriugena as he makes affection a synonym for suffering.[55] Here the experience of divine things appears to be caused by love thereof. The hierarch excelled in the subtle analysis of the sacred texts, posing questions *pro* and *contra*, dividing, ordering, and

---

instrumentum theologiae: Zu einer Aussage Alberts des Großen in seinem Kommentar zu Ps.–Dionysius' *De divinis nominibus*," in Senner, *Albertus Magnus, Zum Gedenken*, 619–31. Sicouly rightly points to the essential place of prayer in Albert's vision of theological contemplation and cognition of God's names.

54. *SDN*, ch. 4, no. 135, p. 225.15–17; no. 140, p. 229.4–9.

55. *SDN*, ch. 2, no. 76, p. 91.66–68: "excellentius, ex affectione circa divina multa sibi divinitus revelata sunt, quae quasi per experientiam cognovit"; p. 92.17: "*etiam patiens divina*, idest affectus circa ea."

resolving into properties and causes. Albert's Hierotheus is the scholastic theologian *par excellence*! Still, subtle distinctions do not complete the theologian's task:

He was perfected for the unity of these things, that is, of divine things, through affect and intellect, *and faith,* that is the certain cognition of spiritual things ... the fruit of the Spirit [in] Galatians 5, according to Ambrose's exposition in the *Gloss, un-teachable,* that is, which cannot be perfectly possessed by human teaching, *and mystical,* that is, hidden. And this mode [of teaching] is called most divine, because divine things are perceived by a certain experience ... just as he who tastes wine better knows its sweetness.[56]

Albert continues to read Dionysius with the help of Eriugena, hence the repeated references to affect.[57] An experiential knowledge of God surpasses the theologian's knowledge of the Scriptures acquired by study. Albert appeals to the Dionysian phrase "perfect unity and faith" to show that union does not leave the intellect behind. Yet he seems to recognize that the faith in question surpasses the limits of the theological virtue's operation and calls for an additional grace, thus appealing to the teaching on the Spirit's fruits. The *Sentences Commentary* identified these fruits as ultimate perfections in this life—graces that surpass the Spirit's seven gifts, but without further explanation. Now we again find a fruit of the Spirit at the summit of perfection, with little elaboration. Albert aims to present a balance of will and intellect in Hierotheus's experience: his affection for divine things enables a higher cognition by the Spirit's fruit of faith. Yet Albert offers no further causal explanation. He does not say whether the will is a strictly disposing or preparatory cause or whether the fruit of faith only follows the will's motion. Nor does he specify what the hierarch perceives.[58] Also, Albert says nothing about

---

56. *SDN*, ch. 2, no. 76, p. 92.20–29: "*Perfectus est ad unitionem ipsorum,* idest divinorum, per affectum et intellectum, *et fidem,* idest certam cognitionem spiritualium, ... fructus spiritus Gal. V secundum expositionem Ambrosii in *Glossa, indocibilem,* idest quae per humanam doctrinam perfecte haberi non potest, *et mysticam,* idest occultam. Et pro tanto hic modus dicitur divinior, quia quodam experimento sic percipiuntur divina, sicut ... ille qui gustat vinum, melius scit dulcedinem eius"; see also *SMT,* ch. 1, p. 458.54–62.

57. The Sarracenus translation employs the term *compassione,* not *affectus; SDN,* ch. 2, no. 68, p. 87.67.

58. Wéber interprets *affectus* in this text to refer not so much to love as to the intellect's desire to know God. But this reading makes the couplet "affect and intellect" fairly

ecstasy by love, even though Eriugena's *affectus* translation lends itself to such an interpretation. Albert does not mention the gift of wisdom, an odd lacuna considering the importance of this doctrine in his earlier theology of union, where Hierotheus suffering divine things exemplifies the gift of wisdom. Furthermore, our passage appears to move Albert's understanding of suffering divine things away from his previous notion of the gift of wisdom. The hierarch now learns by a graced act of the will and the fruit of faith. In the *Sentences Commentary* the gift of wisdom complements the virtue of faith and not charity, since the latter needs no further gift for its perfection, while the fruit of faith involves an ambiguous perfection higher than both wisdom and the beatitude of the pure of heart. Albert's new reading of Hierotheus is disconnected from his previous way of structuring the summit of noetic perfection. He does not bring an all-determining theological structure to the text. Here the Dionysian passage as transmitted by Eriugena's *affectus* translation changes Albert's teaching. Albert's new interpretation of the figure of Hierotheus also cautions against the assumption that the *Sentences Commentary* doctrine on the seven gifts stands in complete harmony with his theology in the Dionysian commentaries, although they might be wholly complementary.

The new approach to Hierotheus shows the importance of charity in Albert's theology of union. Yet this very point seems to be thrown into doubt by Albert's main discussion of ecstatic love. He explains the Areopagite's phrase "Divine love brings about ecstasy."[59] The running commentary explains that this ecstasy is distinct from the mind's elevation to an understanding of heavenly things, mentioned in the *Ordinary Gloss* on 2 Corinthians 5:13. Albert notes that the Greek word *extasis* can be translated into Latin by the term *excessus*. The biblical gloss describes the power of a higher nature taking the mind beyond the contemplation that is possible by the mind's nature as the mind is moved

---

unintelligible; Wéber, "L'interprétation," 436. Also, the only reference to Hierotheus in the *SMT* (ch. 1, p. 458.54–62) states that the affect related to divine suffering can be infected by the love of illicit things. Such affect must refer to the will's inclination. José M. Moraga Esquivel also interprets *patiens divina* to involve affectivity; see Esquivel, "El ocultamiento luminoso de Dios Alberto Magno: *Super Mysticam Theologiam Dionysii*," *Veritas: Revista de filosofía y teología* 19 (2008): 366–69.

59. *SDN*, ch. 2, no. 126, p. 219.64 (the Sarracenus text): "Est autem et extasim faciens divinus amor."

into uncircumscribed light. This type of ecstasy cannot apply to God, as it would posit a power above him. In contrast, the *Divine Names* refers to love (*amor*) that makes ecstasy (*extasim*), placing the lover beyond himself and *diffusing itself* into the beloved[60]—that is, such ecstasy does not come from above, but from self-diffusion, from within. Thus we speak of divine love's ecstasy, where God is moved by his own love.

Albert then begins a disputed question. "Some (*quidam*)" explain the term ecstasy in the first mode—that is, as an elevation *of love* caused by a higher power.[61] But can there be an excess of love incited from above, and not just an excess of intellect? Albert responds:

In love properly speaking excess cannot occur. For excess always comes about when the soul is elevated to that which is not possible to it according to its proper power in this [pilgrim] state of life, by the power of some superior light, and it is not fitting that the soul exceed from itself (*a seipsa*) as to its operations, which are according to its proper power. Now there is not some mode of charity above the faculty of our nature, [not] even insofar as we are in this life, because the same mode of charity is in this [pilgrim] life and in heaven, although it is perfected there. Now in the faculty of our nature according to this life there is not a most perfect mode of knowing or delighting, as there will be in heaven in the known and beloved, and therefore, according to cognition, which precedes love, and according to delight, which follows upon it [cognition] as its effect, there can be excess, but not according to love itself, except just as a disposing cause for this, such as fasting, vigils and all other virtues can be a cause of excess in this way.[62]

60. *SDN*, ch. 2, no. 126, p. 219.45–63.
61. The editor of the *SDN* does not identify the *quidam* in the notes.
62. *SDN*, ch. 4, no. 127, p. 220.50–69: "Dicendum, quod in amore proprie loquendo non potest fieri excessus. Semper enim excessus fit, quando anima elevatur ad id quod non est possibile sibi secundum propriam virtutem quantum ad statum viae, virtute alicuius superioris luminis, et non convenit, quod anima excedat a seipsa quantum ad operationes, quae sunt secundum propriam virtutem; non est autem aliquis modus caritatis supra facultatem nostrae naturae, etiam secundum quod in hac via sumus, quia idem est modus caritatis in via et patria, quamvis ibi perficiatur. Non autem est in facultate nostrae naturae secundum hanc viam perfectissimus modus cognoscendi nec iterum perfectissimus modus delectandi, qui erit in patria in cognito et amato, et ideo secundum cognitionem, quae praecedit amorem, et secundum delectationem, quae consequitur ipsam sicut effectus, potest esse excessus, et non secundum amorem ipsum, nisi sicut secundum causam disponentem ad hoc, sicut et ieiunia et vigiliae et omnes aliae virtutes possunt esse causa hoc modo excessus."

Albert employs the term "proper power" to refer not just to a spiritual faculty's strictly natural operational capacities, but to the whole range of intrinsic operational capacities available to the human being, including those attained with grace. Hence he applies to charity the principles developed in relation to proper and higher power. In other words, charity enables a mode of operation here below that becomes part of the soul's "proper power" in this state of life. The key distinction in this passage is not grace-nature, but proper-higher power within the realm of sanctifying grace. Charity's basic mode of operation, which is to will the good of the beloved for the sake of the beloved, remains the same in the eschaton. It is not clear if Albert alludes to Gallus's doctrine of a higher mode of love (in the *apex affectionis*) enabled by grace that follows the intellect's complete silence. Gallus's paraphrases of the *Mystical Theology* and the present *Divine Names* passage (two works likely known by Albert) do not manifest clear linguistic or doctrinal links to the theology of love that Albert refuses, for Gallus says little on ecstatic love.[63]

Albert then takes up the following objection: if the (cognitive) light of faith can bring about excess, then all the more so charity. The objection argues strictly from the objective nature of the gift received in abstraction from the receiving subject's mode of operation. Albert responds, "It belongs to the perfection of love that it cannot bring about an elevation from itself into something higher. Because of this, elevation is from faith (*a fide*), since it is imperfect cognition."[64] Charity already possesses a certain wholeness in that the will can cling unfailingly to God for his own sake. But faith does not enable a perfect knowledge of faith's object, for it has an obscure mode of knowing. In other words, an imperfect mode of cognition pushes the believer to overcome some

---

63. Thomas Gallus, *Extractio de divinis nominibus*, ch. 4, 685a–b; *EMT*, ch. 1, 709b–10b; but see Gallus, *Explanatio de divinis nominibus*, in *Explanatio in libros Dionysii*, ch. 4, p. 238.1458–63: "*Est autem extasim* etc., quasi dicat: cum omnes iusti Deum diligant, est tamen quidam spiritualis amor Dei et preeminens in uiris spiritualibus et perfectis qui excellentia sua rationem et intelligentiam excedit: Eph. 3g: *supereminentem*, etc. Unde iste amor dicitur extaticus uel extasim faciens quia eleuat apicem affectionis super omnem intellectualem cognitionem." Gallus completed this work in 1242 (see the editor's introduction, vii, xxiv). We do not know if Albert had access to this book.

64. *SDN*, ch. 4, no. 128, p. 220.75–78: "hoc est de perfectione caritatis, quod non potest ab ipsa fieri elevatio in aliquid superius; propter hoc enim fit elevatio a fide, quia est cognitio imperfecta."

noetic obscurity, whereas a perfect mode of charity already allows the believer to repose in love. Albert refuses excess in charity not because he considers it secondary on the path of ascent to God, but because he sees it as already having attained a certain completion. Extrinsically caused excess presupposes weakness in the receiving subject, not strength. Charity already possesses the beloved, while faith only possesses the known in an imperfect way. Albert thus extols the grandeur of charity. In contrast, the virtue of faith is the *terminus a quo* (*a fide*) whence divine light takes us beyond our proper (graced) powers and pours into us a knowledge that is higher than what the virtue of faith alone can grasp. There can be excess "according to cognition," meaning, by the elevation of human cognition, beyond what one already knows by faith through the action of divine noetic light. Therefore, excess could refer to a cognitive ascent that is higher than Paul's ecstasy by faith. Yet Albert offers little detail on the identity of the divine light that brings about excess. The *Sentences Commentary* doctrine would call for an appeal to the gifts of wisdom and understanding or the beatitudes or the Spirit's fruits, but here Albert remains silent on these themes.

Édouard Wéber rightly notes that Albert pushes the Areopagite's text on ecstatic love to the limit.[65] However, Albert's primary dialogue partner no longer seems to be Dionysius, but unidentified medieval thinkers (*quidam*). The notion that charity has no excess mode because of its perfection need not contradict the Areopagite's teaching on ecstatic love, since Albert affirms that love is ecstatic as an intrinsic, self-diffusive principle.[66] Furthermore, Albert may have recognized that the Dionysian language of ecstasy usually focuses on intellect (*noūs*) going beyond itself or its operation. For Dionysius the ultimate cause of such ecstasy is an exterior noetic light. Also, the central *Divine Names* text on ecstasy and union is not the hymn of love in chapter 4, but a passage in chapter 7 that treats divine names such as wisdom and truth.[67] Thus Albert's emphasis on noetic ecstasy moves toward a central theme of Dionysian darkness. For him intellect's excess may be the same event as union, which is precisely the Areopagite's teaching. Albert's solu-

---

65. Wéber, "L'interprétation," 427–28.
66. See *SDN*, ch. 3, no. 14, p. 110.64–67. Wéber also mentions the importance of the will in Albert's mystical contemplation; Wéber, "L'interprétation," 420.
67. De Andia, *Henosis*, 266.

tion neatly distinguishes the operations of intellect and will, yet his doctrine of grace shows that he does not separate charity from noetic union. Finally, Albert does not consider love secondary to the mystical life. Precisely when he seems to opt for a hyperintellectual approach to mysticism, he emphasizes love's perfect mode of (unitive) action.

ANALOGY IN THE *COMMENTARY ON THE DIVINE NAMES*

Albert's doctrine of analogy in the *Commentary on the Divine Names* mostly offers a harmonious development of his previous teaching. Here I will focus on five key aspects of that development: (1) analogy as a *theology* of divine naming; (2) the technical meaning of the divine *quia est* and *quid est*; (3) two distinct approaches to affirmation, negation, and eminence; (4) the relation of God's incomprehensibility to the twin themes of God as unnameable or unknown and the soul's ascent beyond mind; (5) an emphasis on God's exemplar causality that inclines toward univocity. The first point confirms the text's genre. The second point clarifies some key terms. The third and fourth points present one of Albert's most creative developments of the Areopagite on the function and cognitive fruit of divine naming. The last point helps to explain Albert's most apophatic statements as a safeguard against univocity.

First, Albert considers the *Divine Names* as a theological work on God's biblical names. His classification of this text is partly inspired by the Areopagite's (problematic) insistence that this book ponders strictly biblical names.[68] Albert does not deny that philosophy has some knowledge of God, but he considers the way of faith more secure. The nature of philosophical argumentation inclines toward univocal cognition and presupposes a proportionality of cause and effect. Thus philosophers find their strictly natural capacities stretched to the limits when speaking about God, where reasoning about a cause proportionate to its effect cannot apply.[69] Since Albert will closely link no-

68. *SDN*, ch. 1, no. 5, p. 3.39–40; no. 10, p. 5.23–41; no. 11, p. 6.1–5; no. 13, p. 7.16–28; Anzulewicz, "Pseudo–Dionysius Areopagita und das Strukturprinzip des Denkens von Albert dem Grossen," in *Die Dionysius–Rezeption im Mittelalter*, edited by Tzotcho Boiadjiev, Georgi Kapriev and Andreas Speer, Rencontres de Philosophie Médiévale 9 (Turnhout: Brepols, 2000), 294–95.

69. *SDN*, ch. 1, no. 16, p. 8.54–75; Wéber, "Relation," 562–63, 570–74.

etic union and analogous knowledge of God, his present remarks on the nature of philosophy suggest that he sees major difficulties in any purely natural attempt to attain contemplative union with God.

Second, the *Commentary on the Divine Names* specifies the meaning of the key phrases "that God is" (*quia est*) and "what he is" (*quid est*). As in the *Sentences Commentary*, Albert takes up Chrysostom's controversial *Homily 15*. He explains that *quid est* strictly refers to the whole of God's boundless essence. Knowing the divine *quid est* becomes a synonym for total cognition of God. Hence, in knowing the divine *quia est*, the saints do not simply know God's existence, but also behold his attributes, for the divine *quia est* is all that they see. *Quia est* signifies God's substance with its attributes insofar as these can be known by creatures.[70] Albert prepares the epistemological groundwork to transform the Areopagite's distinction between (1) God's hidden nature as always beyond our reach, which calls for the mind's silence, and (2) God's powers signified by affirmations. Albert offers a new distinction between the impossibility of comprehending or knowing God's *quid est*, where negations apply, and partial knowledge of God's *quia est*, where affirmations and negations operate.

Albert's exegesis of these key terms seems to draw inspiration from an Eriugenan passage in the *Parisian Scholia*. In chapter 5 of the *Mystical Theology* God is said to have no name. The Irishman comments that when we ask what God is (*quid est*), we seek to define his substance. For created substances we attain a definition by passing from a thing's accidents to its substance. But the human intellect cannot penetrate to the divine substance in this way. We can know that God is (*esse*), but not his *quid sit*.[71] Eriugena thus posits a link between defining God quasi-perfectly and his *quid est*.

70. *SDN*, ch. 1, no. 21, p. 10.64–72: "Dicimus, quod substantiam dei, 'quia est,' omnes beati videbunt; 'quid' autem sit, nullus intellectus creatus videre potest. Cum enim cognitio 'quid est' sit principalis causarum, oporteret, si cognosceretur 'quid est,' ut circumspicerentur termini essentiae eius. Et sic totum esse eius clauderetur in intellectu creato." Lawrence Moonan inadequately interprets God's *quia est* to signify existence; Moonan, "What Is a Negative Theology? Albert's Answer," in Senner, *Albertus Magnus, Zum Gedenken*, 609. A broader reading of *quia est* is favored by Ruello, "Noms divins," 98–101, and Weismantel, *Ars nominandi Deum*, 99. Tugwell, "Albert the Great," 90–91, holds that the beatific knowledge of God's *quia est* still begins with created effects as cognitive objects; he cites *SEP 1*, pp. 481.88–82.40, a reading that I will critique later.

71. *PMT*, ch. 5, 108, citing *Periphyseon*, bk. II, pp. 136.24–38.13; see also Robert

Third, Albert explains the function of the *triplex via*, starting with affirmations. The prologue of the *Commentary on the Divine Names* specifies the work's subject. As he explains why this book does not treat symbolic names, Albert distinguishes between the reality signified and the mode of signification in a way similar to the *Sentences Commentary*:

[In this book of the *Divine Names*, we consider] those [names] which properly name him [God], insofar as he is cause, and according to the attributes, by which things emanate from him as from a univocal cause, participating in a secondary way that which is truly and absolutely in him, as to the reality signified by the name, although the mode of signifying falls short of a representation of it [the divine reality], insofar as it is in God, leaving that [reality's divine mode] in obscurity, because one signifies according to the mode by which that reality [signified] is in us, from which the name is imposed. Hence, they [the names] are also called mystical, that is, hidden.[72]

Like Dionysius, Albert maintains that the *Divine Names* especially explains the names that manifest God's causal activity. Metaphors are improper names, for the realities they signify do not properly belong to God. God is the cause of rocks, but a rock's material qualities are not proper similitudes of the divine substance. In contrast, proper names traverse a metaphysical and noetic bridge that some attributes (e.g., goodness) provide. Created perfections emanate—that is, they are effects of God's creative causality that reflect his attributes. Albert primarily employs the term "univocal cause" in order to differentiate proper and symbolic names. He continues to refuse exhaustive knowledge of God's nature or a strict notion of univocity,[73] and does not refer to a univocal concept that covers divine and created attributes. Rather, the term "univocal cause" signifies God as cause insofar as his effects

---

Wielockx, "Zur *Summa Theologiae* des Albertus Magnus," *Ephemerides Theologicae Lovanienses* 66 (1990): 94–95.

72. *SDN*, ch. 1, no. 3, p. 2.27–38: "de illis quae proprie nominant ipsum, secundum quod est causa, quantum ad attributa, quibus emanant res ab ipso sicut a causa univoca, participantes per posterius illud ipsum quod in eo est vere et absolute, quantum ad rem significatam per nomen, quamvis modus significandi deficiat a repraesentatione eius, secundum quod est in deo, relinquens illud in occulto propter hoc quod significat secundum modum, quo illa res est in nobis, a quibus est impositum nomen. Unde et mystica dicuntur quasi occulta"; see also Albertus Magnus, *I Sent.*, d. 2, a. 17c.

73. *SDN*, ch. 7, no. 29, p. 358.73–86 (analyzed later in this chapter) also excludes strict univocity; see Ruello, "*Noms divins*," 82–86; Humbrecht, *Théologie négative*, 376, 390.

bear a similitude of the specific features of their divine source. Creatures attain this similitude through their participation in created perfections (a theme linked to divine exemplarity, to be considered shortly). God's names are a direct consequence of the nature of his creative activity: "Those names are considered insofar as they make knowledge of the cause according to those things that [the cause] has left in the effects."[74] The *Divine Names* unfolds a metaphysics of the Creator God rooted in Scripture. The revealed names become unintelligible without knowledge of creation. Their meaning lights up when we connect them to the traces of God's attributes in creation. Created perfections constitute a noetic ladder to God in the light of Scripture. The divine names refer not just to God's activity, but to an abiding divine reality, to God's attributes. The real similitude between participated and uncreated perfections makes substantial divine naming possible. The reality signified truly exists in God, but the mode of signifying remains highly inadequate. Our language essentially reflects the finite mode of creatures' share in perfections.

Albert then explains the difference between the *Divine Names* and the *Mystical Theology*:

Now these names can be considered in two ways: [1] either according to the outflow of caused things from the cause, participating the *ratio* of the name by derivation, and one treats these [names] in this book [the *Divine Names*], or [2] according to the resolution of caused things into the cause, leaving that signified by the name unknown, as it is in the cause, because of the cause's eminent mode, and thus one treats the names in the book *On the Mystical Theology*. Hence, the proper subject of this book is the divine name which brings about knowledge of the cause according to its attributes, insofar as caused things go out from it in participation of the attributes.[75]

---

74. *SDN*, ch. 1, no. 1, p. 1.25–27: "tanguntur ipsa nomina, secundum quod faciunt notitiam de causa secundum ea quae relinquuntur in effectibus."

75. *SDN*, ch. 1, no. 3, p. 2.37–48: "Haec autem nomina possunt dupliciter considerari: aut secundum effluxum causatorum a causa, participantium rationem nominis per posterius, et sic agitur de eis in libro isto, aut secundum quod ex resolutione causatorum in causam relinquitur ignotum significatum nominis, prout est in causa, propter modum eminentem ipsius causae, et sic agitur de ipsis in libro De Mystica Theologia. Unde subiectum proprium istius libri est nomen divinum, quod facit notitiam causae secundum attributa, inquantum exeunt ab eo causata in participatione attributorum."

The *Divine Names* ponders names insofar as they manifest a divine reality. God's creative causal activity reveals his nature via the similitude between his attributes (the *ratio* or intelligible feature) signified and creatures' limited perfections. The signification of God's attributes pertains to the *Divine Names*. The meaning of affirmations is this work's subject. The *Mystical Theology* reverses this noetic path. The divine attributes signified by affirmative names remain true, so that negations do not directly contradict what affirmations signify. "God is not life" does not signify that there is no life in God.[76] But because the *mode* of his attributes remains hidden or unknown, the path of return to God follows the way of negations—that is, negations are true insofar as they deny any proportion between (1) the human mode of knowing and signifying and (2) the divine mode of being. Affirmations are true inasmuch as they point to proper similitudes between divine and human perfections (the reality signified). Eminence refers to God's unique mode of being. With the distinction between the reality signified and the mode of signifying, Albert summarizes a twofold way of naming. Eminence is a mode of being cosignified by negations. Consequently, the *Mystical Theology* becomes unintelligible without God's causal activity studied in the *Divine Names*. The former work is also a science of names, a theology of negative names that guides the contemplative to the hidden God.

The *Sentences Commentary* previewed this doctrine of analogy. But chapter 7 of the *Commentary on the Divine Names* uses a new approach to affirmation, negation, and eminence:

we impose names according to that mode by which the reality signified is found in things, which are under our intellect, [things] from which we receive knowledge, and therefore the mode by which this reality is found in things that are above our intellect is different from the mode by which the name signifies. Therefore, the reality signified by a name can be considered in two ways: [1] either insofar as it exceeds the signification of the name, and this mode is through excess, or [2] according to that which is signified by the name, and this in two ways: [a] either insofar as it is in the effect, and this the mode which is through the cause, or [b] insofar as it [what is signified by the name] is in the cause, which is beyond this mode [of the effect], and thus is the mode through separation of all.[77]

76. See *SDN*, ch. 4, no. 92, p. 195.39–52; Wéber, "Langage et méthode," 78.
77. *SDN*, ch. 7, no. 29, p. 358.73–86: "nos imponimus nomina secundum illum mo-

Realities signified found in things subject to or "under" our intellect are participated perfections encountered in material beings. Realities signified also exist in things above our intellect—namely, God and the angels, though Albert ignores the angels for now. A reality or perfection signified always has a mode of being, though this has nothing to do with the univocity of being. Earlier in the commentary Albert explained that affirmations name the divine reality as a cause that emanates perfections into creatures, while negations deny the adequacy of the mode of signification, so that negations move the intellect back to divine eminence.[78] In the present text affirmations name the reality in creatures as an effect of the divine cause, but they no longer name the reality or perfection as it is in the cause. This is one reason that Albert no longer employs the language of a (quasi-)univocal cause. He introduces the current text by discussing the mode that realities signified have in things. In this context the term *modus* primarily refers to a way of being. Affirmations refer to a reality that has a caused mode of being. The primary function of negations is no longer to deny the mode of signification tied to affirmations. Rather, negations refer to the distance between the cause's and the effect's modes of being. Negations do not primarily qualify affirmative divine names, since affirmations no longer directly refer to a divine attribute as cause. Rather, negations both refer to the reality signified as being truly in the divine cause and point to God's distinct mode of being. Since we have no positive cognitive grasp of the divine mode of being, we refer to that mode by way of "separation." Negations thus include affirmation insofar as they refer to the substantial presence of perfections in God as cause. Such perfections are known through effects.[79] Negative names thus become causal names. Now they complete the task previously attributed to affirma-

---

dum quo invenitur res significata in rebus, quae sunt sub intellectu nostro, ex quibus accipimus scientias, et ideo alius est modus quo huiusmodi res invenitur in his quae sunt supra intellectum nostrum, et alius est modus, quo significat nomen. Unde res significata per nomen potest dupliciter considerari: aut secundum quod excedit significationem nominis, et sic est modus, qui est per excessum, aut secundum quod significatur per nomen, et hoc dupliciter: vel secundum quod est in effectu, et sic est modus, qui est per causam, aut secundum quod est in causa, quae est extra istum modum, et sic est modus per omnium ablationem."

78. *SDN*, ch. 1, no. 3, p. 2.27–48 (cited earlier in the main text in this chapter and at footnotes 72 and 75).

79. See also *SDN*, ch. 4, no. 3, p. 114.61–65; Wéber, "Négativité et causalité," 57.

tions. Negations are not pure privations. They almost seem to function as a combination of affirmative and eminent names, not unlike the Areopagite's transcending negations, though Albert's approach is more kataphatic. We therefore need to look for a similarly kataphatic modification of Dionysian negations in Albert's exposition of Moses's contemplative ascent.

The way of negation remains distinct from the way of eminence. Affirmations and negations refer to the reality or perfection signified as effect or as cause, respectively, among which we distinguish two modes of being. Negations refer to God's unique mode of having perfections, the reality "insofar as it is in the cause." Affirmative and negative names are essentially bound to causality, which is why negations are meaningless without affirmations, as Albert states elsewhere.[80] Negative names still refer to an abiding proper similitude between God and creature—to the perfections that are the reality signified *through* the name. Eminence does not involve the denial of the reality signified or its separation from the divine nature. Rather, eminence points to the reality signified as having a mode of being beyond God's mode of being as cause. This has nothing to do with a hidden Godhead really distinct from the Creator. Instead, eminence involves a third mode of being, the mode of excess. The purpose of eminence is not to deny the truth of affirmations and negations, but to manifest the limits of each in relation to God's mode of being. Even purified discourse about the causal power of God's attributes remains inadequate. The exclusion of strict univocity is unmistakable.

But the way of excess does not exclude substantial divine naming. Two pages after our current passage, Albert notes that we name God by an eminent mode. Here he explicitly invokes eminent naming, not just a way of eminence. We separate (or negate) what is imperfect (the finite mode of being), for divine predication concerns "the very essence or nature of the procession [that] is in God eminently ... that which is found in inferior beings is essentially in superior beings, but by a more noble [mode of] being."[81] The perfections emanating in the causal pro-

80. *SMT*, ch. 5, p. 475.22–23.
81. *SDN*, ch. 7, no. 33, p. 361.14–20: "totum nomen sequitur naturam processionis ex esse, quod habet in materia, et secundum hoc non transfertur in deum, sed ipsa essentia vel natura processionis est in deo eminenter ... id quod est inferiorum, secundum essentiam est in superioribus, tamen secundum nobilius esse."

cessions are essentially present in the divine nature in the maximum mode. Therefore, eminent names are substantial names. But this seems to suggest that the cognitive bridge of created perfections grounds eminent names, for Albert never invokes a form of content illumination that accompanies eminent names or noetic ascent to divine eminence. The way of eminence does not consist of pointing into an utterly unknown dimension beyond God's causal activity, but rather continues to affirm perfections of God that have some similitude to created perfections.[82] But Albert does not explain how the excess mode both passes beyond the naming that remains linked to God's causal activity and includes substantial eminent naming.

In chapter 7 Albert's negations function similarly to the Areopagite's affirmations, for the Greek father relates affirmations to God's causal powers manifest in creation. Albert's way of excess partly parallels Dionysian transcending negations. But his way of eminence suffers from an internal tension. One element thereof points to a divine mode of being beyond God's mode of being as cause, not unlike the Areopagite's hidden divine nature beyond the divine powers. Yet the substantial element of eminent names moves back toward affirmations, against the Areopagite's intention. I will come back to this ambiguity later in this chapter.

Fourth, Albert complements his rather kataphatic approach to eminence by his reading of the unnameable God. He explains that God cannot be perfectly named, nor can we say what he is (*id quod est*), as his mode of being remains unknown—that is, we can name God's eminent mode of being, but we have no direct positive knowledge thereof, for this would require comprehensive knowledge. Thus God cannot be named in that we cannot comprehend him. The perfect name would leave nothing unsaid. Here, too, Albert may have drawn inspiration from Eriugena, who connects God having no name to the absence of a divine definition.[83]

82. See *SDN*, ch. 7, no. 5, p. 340.48–50; no. 28, p. 358.38–42.
83. *SDN*, ch. 1, no. 62, p. 39.37–52: "intentio Dionysii est dicere, quod deus secundum omne nomen est innominabilis a nobis perfecte et secundum id quod est, licet nominemus ipsum per huiusmodi nomina, 'quia est,' et hoc confuse, sicut supra habitum est ... ideo modus essendi eius remanet omnia nobis ignotus, scientes tamen 'quia est' confuse"; see also ch. 5, no. 3, p. 304.52–65; ch. 7, no. 30, p. 359.34–38. For Eriugena, see *PMT*, ch. 5, 108.

The category of incomprehension clearly places limits on Dionysian apophatism, which in turn calls for a different mystical subject. Dionysius often refers to the soul's passage into God's eminence (or beyond affirmations and negations) by invoking ascent beyond mind. Here Albert employs one of two interpretive strategies; either (1) we pass beyond strictly natural reason, elevated by the light of grace or faith,[84] or (2) the intellect falls short of comprehending God or understands him to be above all that we can comprehend.[85] In the second approach *God* is above mind so that no noetic ecstasy occurs. Albert consistently reinserts our intellect's active participation precisely when Dionysius seeks to surpass all thoughts and names. Since eminence includes the act of substantially naming God (with reference to created similitudes), no room is left for full ecstasy beyond intellect. The link between eminent names and cognition derived from created similitudes will be key in our study of uniting negations later in this chapter. Let us note that Albert's transformation of Dionysian noetics has precedents in the *scholia* by John of Scythopolis. John identifies one type of unknowing in darkness as the realization *that* God is unknowable.[86] Albert seems to develop the thought of the first Greek Dionysian commentator with a new doctrine of eminence and divine incomprehensibility.

Fifth, Albert's Dionysian commentaries (and perhaps also his *Sentences Commentary*) emphasize God's exemplar causality rather than his efficient causality as the link between divine and created perfections. Diverse participations in a similitude of the divine exemplars (especially God's perfections) enable an "analogy of imitation."[87] In the background there likely stands the notion of formal flux, one of Albert's preferred models to explain God's creative and saving action. The emphasis on form inclines naming toward univocity rather than to equivocity.

---

84. *SDN*, ch. 1, no. 13, p. 7.16–29; nos. 15–16, p. 8.45–74; ch. 2, no. 55, p. 80.34–40.
85. *SDN*, ch. 1, no. 31, pp. 16.60–17.10; no. 46, p. 28.37–46; ch. 2, no. 57, p. 81.68–72; ch. 7, no. 30, p. 359.42–55.
86. *PDN*, ch. 2, 120; ch. 4, 122; see chapter 2 of this volume.
87. *SMT*, ch. 1, p. 459.26–38: "unde dicimus, quod deus, quamvis non communicet cum creaturis genere vel specie vel analogia, per quam aliquid unum sit in ipso et aliis, communicat tamen quadam analogia imitationis, secundum quod alia imitantur ipsum, quantum possunt.... Quaedam imitantur ipsum ut imago vel similitudo ipsius, quae per prius sunt in ipso, sicut sapientia, bonitas etc., et ista dicuntur de ipso essentialiter et causaliter"; see also *SDN*, ch. 1, no. 57, p. 35.45–68; ch. 2, no. 84, pp. 97.37–98.41; ch. 13, no. 22, p. 445.50–68; *SEP* 2, pp. 483.60–84.6.

The relative primacy of divine exemplar causality may help to explain Albert's most apophatic statements in the Dionysian commentaries as safeguards against univocity.[88]

THE PREFACE OF ALBERT'S COMMENTARY ON THE MYSTICAL THEOLOGY

Having considered the background doctrines for union in the early Albert and in the Dionysian commentaries, I now turn directly to our main theme. The entryway thereto is found in the preface of the *Commentary on the Mystical Theology*, where Albert introduces the work and, more importantly, describes the divine gift that grounds the "mystical science."

Albert begins with a standard scholastic preface. He introduces the work's mode or method, the matter or topic, the audience, and its end or purpose. All of this occurs in the framework of a commentary on Isaiah 45:15: "Truly you are a hidden God, the God of Israel, the Savior." The book's mode is that of Scripture, which is attained by divine inspiration and cannot be subject to error.[89] Albert identifies Dionysius as a quasi-biblical author. The Areopagite's claim that he directly received oral apostolic traditions probably stands in the background. Also, John Damascene and numerous medieval writers describe the church fathers as "inspired" by the Holy Spirit: the term was multivalent.[90] As the *Divine Names* claims to limit itself to biblical names, Albert can argue that the Areopagite's teaching remains subject to Scripture. Dionysius does not impart a new revelation, but rather teaches pure truth. Second, the matter or subject of the *Mystical Theology* is "the hidden God" to whom we ascend by "separation (*ablationem*)" or negation. Third, the hearer of this doctrine is "Israel" or the righteous person who has attained clarity of understanding and righteous works. In other words, one must first learn the *Divine Names* that purify the intellect of idolatrous conceptions and practice the moral virtues. The

---

88. Victor Salas, "Albertus Magnus and Thomas Aquinas on the Analogy Between God and Creatures," *Medieval Studies* 72 (2010): 293–98, 312; Humbrecht, *Théologie négative*, 346, 390–93, 417–18.

89. *SMT*, ch. 1, p. 453.9–13; see also *SCH*, ch. 6, p. 84.52–65.

90. Congar, *Tradition and Traditions* (San Diego: Basilica Press, 1966), 125–26.

ultimate purpose of this teaching is salvation or access to the unveiled vision of the divine reality still veiled by negations.[91] The *Mystical Theology* is a steppingstone to eternal beatitude.

Albert then moves to the commentary's first disputed question: on whether a theological science can be called mystical. Negative theologies "remove everything from God and leave our intellect in something confused."[92] This hardly sounds like an adequate foundation for a theological science with certain knowledge. Albert's answer distinguishes the beginning of the mystical science from its deifying end point. The natural disciplines proceed from the principles of reason, while mystical theology proceeds from

> some divine light, which is not an enunciation by which something is affirmed, but a certain reality convincing the intellect, that one adhere to it above all else. And so, it [this reality or light] elevates the intellect to that which exceeds the intellect, because of which the intellect remains in something that is not known in a determined way. And this light is compared to the light by which corporeal sight is strengthened to see, but which does not produce determined cognition of something visible, since there is no proper species.[93]

The mystical science leads to truth not because it argues syllogistically from first principles of reason but because it proceeds from the intellect's absolute attachment to the divine reality. Its foundational principle is not self-evident propositions but God's light.

The precise nature of the reception of this uncreated noetic light may be the most disputed part of Albert's commentary. For Édouard Wéber, we receive the divine light via infused faith, a properly intellectual gift that raises us above our natural noetic capacities. He points to similarities between the present passage and Albert's *Sentences Commen-*

---

91. *SMT*, ch. 1, pp. 453.20–41, 454.3–12.

92. *SMT*, ch. 1, p. 454.78–82: "negativae theologiae ... procedentes removendo omnia ab ipso relinquunt intellectum nostrum in quodam confuso."

93. *SMT*, ch. 1, p. 455.14–24: "Huiusmodi autem doctrina non procedit ex talibus principiis, sed potius ex quodam lumine divino, quod non est enuntiatio, per quam aliquid affirmetur, sed res quaedam convincens intellectum, ut sibi super omnia adhaereatur. Et ideo elevat intellectum ad id quod excedit ipsum, propter quod remanet intellectus in quodam non determinate noto. Et hoc lumen proportionatur lumini, quo corporalis visus confortatur ad videndum, quod tamen non facit alicuius visibilis determinatam cognitionem, cum nullius species propria sit."

tary teaching on faith: the light of belief convinces the intellect about truth beyond reason's limits. The triune God reveals himself through faith because its infusion is the fruit of the Son's mission, the Dionysian divine ray that brings us back to the Father. Thus mystical theology pertains to all believers, not just to a spiritual elite.[94] Simon Tugwell arrives at a similar conclusion. He detects an essentially cognitive doctrine of faith in the Dionysian commentaries, in contrast to the *Sentences Commentary*. The knowledge of faith firmly establishes the mind, analogous to the natural grasp of a thing's cause or *scientia*. Faith convinces the intellect directly, as does the light in the present passage. Tugwell appeals to Albert's transformation of Dionysian union beyond mind as going beyond the principles of reason by grace—an ascent by faith.[95] But William Hoye rejects Wéber's thesis and thus also Tugwell's. The absence of explicit discussions of faith in the disputed passage strikes Hoye as decisive: one cannot go beyond Albert's ambiguous reference to divine light. Rather, the mystical science proceeds by negations and an unidentifiable grace.[96] Alain de Libera argues that the light of the mystical science should be understood with the help of two other doctrines: (1) the *Sentences Commentary* exposition of natural knowledge as a gratuitous gift of the Spirit (*gratis datum*) joining the agent intellect to divine light; and (2) Averroes's *intellectus adeptus* or assimilation to God by "Information," the cognition of all intelligible forms.[97] Finally, José Antonio Pachas suggests an identification of the light with the Spirit's gift of wisdom and an experience of God.[98]

One finds numerous linguistic and doctrinal parallels between the light that grounds the mystical science and faith's light in the early Albert. In the *Sentences Commentary* he explains that Dionysius signals faith's effect, which is "not a complex truth ... or the principle of a syl-

---

94. Wéber, introduction to Albertus Magnus, *Commentaire de la Théologie mystique*, 34–36, 73, citing Albertus Magnus, *III Sent.*, d. 23, a. 17.

95. Tugwell, "Albert the Great," 64–66, 70–72.

96. Hoye, "Mystische Theologie," 594–603.

97. De Libera, *Métaphysique*, 182–83; he refers to Albertus Magnus, *I Sent.*, d. 2, a. 5, ad 1. Yet his other study of Albert espouses much of Wéber's reading centered on the light of faith; see de Libera, *Raison et foi*, 274–76, 468.

98. José Antonio Pachas, "La alteridad a la luz del misterio de Dios en el *Super Dionysii Mysticam Theologiam* de san Alberto Magno," *Archa Verbi: Yearbook for the Study of Medieval Theology* 6 (2009): 145.

logism, but rather ... a simple light that in some way causes us to know the truth of the article of faith."[99] By definition God's light is simple. In the preface of the *Commentary on the Mystical Theology*, the divine light is a *that by which* (*quo*), not a *that which* (*quod*), meaning that it is a principle of cognition, not a noetic object. Similarly, mystical light is compared to corporeal light, for it enables us to see other cognitive objects. Albert's contrast between the light of faith and propositional truth parallels the contrast between the light of the mystical science and an enunciation. In the *Sentences Commentary* faith causes "an adherence to the end."[100] Belief's act is assent to the first truth that is above all. The *habitus* of faith that is the direct cause of this act is perfected by a light that joins the intellect to the truth believed.[101] Clinging to God above all else and the infusion of a gratuitous light by God alone also parallel Albert's description of mystical light. Consequently, faith "manifests eternal things and, by consent, deposes them in the faithful. Second, it convinces the mind about the truth of the things [believed]."[102] One of the main characteristics of the mystical light is that it convinces the intellect.

Albert's analyses of faith in the Dionysian commentaries also resemble his description of mystical light. Faith is a "light that is known *per se*, which does not overflow [come from] the relationship of terms as in the first principles of reason, but is influxed by the first truth, a similitude of it."[103] The principles of reason suffice to communicate certain truth, to pour out (analogously) noetic light, while the light of belief comes not from faith propositions, but directly from the first truth. Like the light of mystical science, the light of faith (as a *quo*) is nonpropositional. Albert refers to faith taking us beyond the intellect's nat-

99. Albertus Magnus, *III Sent.*, d. 23, a. 3, qla. 1c, 410a–b: "non est veritas complexionis ... vel principium syllogismi, ideo ... simplum lumen, quod facit aliqualiter scire veritatem credibilis articuli."
100. Albertus Magnus, *III Sent.*, d. 23, a. 7, qla. 2, ad 2, 419a: "Ex parte vero conjunctionis cum fine est adhaerere."
101. Albertus Magnus, *III Sent.*, d. 23, a. 10c.
102. Albertus Magnus, *III Sent.*, d. 23, a. 18c, 438a: "res aeternas ostendit, et ita per aliquem consensum ponit eas in fideli. Secundus autem est, quod convincit mentem de veritate illarum rerum."
103. *SDN*, ch. 7, no. 35, p. 363.70–75: "fides per se suo lumine nota est; illud tamen lumen non redundat ex habitudine terminorum sicut in primis principiis rationis, sed est influxum a prima veritate, quod est similitudo ipsius."

ural operations to hidden things, a theme often linked to union in the *Commentary on the Mystical Theology*. With the Scriptures, faith unites us to hidden realities above our natural capacities. The Scriptures parallel the function of reason's first principles in philosophy, for they provide faith with a noetic content (*quod*). The light of faith heightens the intellect's operative capacity (*quo*). Thus, by itself, the light of faith does not bring propositional knowledge.[104] Elsewhere, Albert notes that the theological science does not attain biblical truth by reason alone. Rather, this truth is manifested by "a certain simple divine light, which is a certain reality informing the conscience, that one might consent to it."[105] The light in question must be the interior illumination that accompanies the proclaimed Word and elicits the faith act, as faith is the doorway to receiving biblical revelation. The themes of divine light, a dynamic reality, and direct noetic influx come close to the light of the mystical science.

Albert's doctrinal intention in the preface also emerges in a parallel passage to his discussion of the light of the mystical science. In chapter 2 of the *Commentary on the Mystical Theology* Albert states that "our mind receives a certain divine light, which is above its nature, and elevates it above all modes of natural vision, and through that [light] comes to the vision of God, yet knowing 'that' [God is] in a confused and indeterminate way."[106] As in the preface, God's light takes us beyond merely natural capacities (or principles of reason) and elevates us to a confused understanding. A few lines later Albert identifies this light as a habitual gift—in other words, a stable, noetic light.[107] An infused, habitual light of the intellect that elevates us above nature is a precise description of faith. No key terms related to other noetic gifts such as the Spirit's seven gifts emerge in this context. Hence the light

104. *SDN*, ch. 2, no. 54, p. 80.34–39 (cited at footnote 49 in the present chapter; see also ch. 1, no. 9, p. 4.71–83).

105. *SEP* 7, pp. 502.83–503.1: "Sed veritas sacrae scripturae est supra principia rationis, unde non deducitur ex illis per aliquas conexiones argumentorum, sed manifestatur quodam simplici lumine divino, quod est quaedam res informans conscientiam, ut sibi consentiatur"; see also *SDN*, ch. 1, no. 10, p. 5.12–41.

106. *SMT*, ch. 2, p. 466.63–68: "Sed mens nostra suscipit quoddam lumen divinum, quod est supra naturam suam, quod elevat eam super omnes modos visionis naturales, et per illud venit ad visionem dei, confuse tamen et non determinate cognoscens 'quia.'"

107. *SMT*, ch. 2, p. 466.76–77: "receptio cuiusdam habitualis luminis, per quod venit in actum divinae visionis."

of the mystical science is a habitual light, a stable, noetic grace that perfects the mind. Indeed, the disputed text contains no allusions to the gifts of wisdom and understanding.[108] The linguistic and doctrinal links between the theology of faith and the mystical light are too strong to justify their separation. Virtually every element of mystical light has parallels in Albert's descriptions of faith.[109]

De Libera's first proposal does not adequately distinguish between natural and sanctifying light. He cites a *Sentences Commentary* text on universal illumination that enables all operations of the agent intellect. Among other things, such illumination makes possible our philosophical knowledge of sensible beings.[110] The function of this noetic light is far broader than the elevation to an obscure cognition of the hidden God, and the assimilation of the nonsanctifying light of the *Sentences Commentary* (a *gratis data*) to the light of the mystical science cannot account for the *Commentary on the Mystical Theology* doctrine that sanctifying grace is necessary for the realization of the mystical science, a doctrine we will encounter later.[111] Also, Albert's doctrine of illumination evolves significantly between Paris and Cologne, as I argued previously. De Libera's interpretation seems to presume a very systematic Albert. In fact, a certain version of Augustinian-Averroist noetics continues in the *Commentary on the Divine Names*, but much of Albert's early Cologne epistemology moves in a different direction. The anthropology of Albert's lectures on Dionysius may not be fully consistent.

---

108. See *SDN*, ch. 1, no. 51, p. 32.12–22. Wéber points to the *Parisian Scholia* (*PMT*, ch. 1, 54) as a source for Albert's notion that the activity of mystical theology is essentially that of faith; Wéber, "L'interprétation," 434. But the text he mentions does not clearly connect faith with divine light. Albert may be the first to identify mystical light and faith. Weismantel maintains that the light of the mystical science, whose nature he does not specify, is mediated by the angels, since they mediate all illuminations; Weismantel, *Ars nominandi*, 86, referencing *SCH*, ch. 4, p. 69.64–68. But the angelic illuminations that Weismantel cites could refer to noetic content. Also, faith is given with sanctifying grace, for which Albert excludes angelic mediating causality; *SCH*, ch. 1, p. 11.20–24.

109. Hoye exaggerates the ambiguity in Albert and fails to offer an alternative explanation. Anneliese Meis mediates between Wéber and Hoye by refocusing the discussion on divine-human alterity. She does not identify the light of the mystical science; see Meis, "Misterio," 541–74; Meis, introduction to Albertus Magnus, *Sobre la Teología Mística*, 24–25.

110. De Libera, *Métaphysique*, 183, citing Albertus Magnus, *I Sent.*, d. 2, a. 5 (analyzed in chapter 3 of this volume).

111. De Libera's other study avoids this problem; de Libera, *Raison et foi*, 275, 468.

De Libera's second proposal, which compares the light of the mystical science to Albert's appropriation of Averroes's *intellectus adeptus* in the Dominican's philosophical corpus, holds some promise. For the Arab philosopher the separate agent intellect emanates first principles of reason into the potential intellect. Once the potential intellect acquires all forms (by the separate agent intellect's light), it is most fully united to the agent intellect. Then the human being becomes like God, for by analogy to the divine intellect, he or she knows all things.[112]

The light of the mystical science has similarities to Averroes's noetics. Albert compares the function of first principles in philosophy to the function of God's light in the mystical science. This light enables the proper reception of negations, somewhat as Averroes's agent intellect causes the reception of first principles. The divine light makes the student adhere to it above all else, somewhat as Averroes's agent intellect unites itself to us.[113] Albert's notion of God's light leading the intellect to an indeterminate cognition parallels his *De homine* discussion of the potential intellect attaining indistinct act when the light of the (conjoined) agent intellect alone shines upon it without imparting intelligible species. Here the negations of the mystical science, which remove affirmations (in their mode of signifying), may parallel the absence of intelligible forms when the agent intellect alone is active in the potential intellect.[114] Later in the *Commentary on the Mystical Theology* Albert draws an analogy between the light on Mt. Sinai and the agent intellect's light. Here divine light functions differently from the light that grounds the mystical science. God's light on Mt. Sinai mingles with angelic lights to produce the "mirror of eternity," divine visions whereby prophets enjoy extraordinary knowledge, a theme for which Albert cites Aristotle. Averroes also links union with the (separate) agent intellect to prophecy. The divine light on Mt. Sinai imparts a *quod* or noetic content, unlike the light that undergirds the mystical

---

112. Averroes, *Commentarium Magnum*, bk. III, 437, 496–501; de Libera, notes to *L'intelligence et la pensée: Sur le "De Anima,"* by Averroes, 2nd ed. (Paris: Flammarion, 1998), 386–89; de Libera, *Métaphysique*, 325–26.

113. Wéber argues that Albertus Magnus's *Commentary on Aristotle's De Anima*, composed shortly after the *SMT*, synthesizes Aristotle's and Averroes's agent intellect with Dionysian illumination; Wéber, *Personne humaine*, 309–15.

114. *De homine*, "Qualiter intelligat, et de modo actionis eius," a. 2.2.6, ad 3, p. 421.51–70; see also Tugwell, "Albert the Great," 62–63.

science. The latter functions as a *quo,* and its mark is obscurity, not prophetic insight.[115] Finally, for Averroes, conjunction with agent intellect and natural divinization occur by the acquisition of all forms, which in turn leads to the clearest noetic vision. But Albert distinguishes the light of the mystical science by the obscure vision that it causes.

Overall, even the similarity between the light that grounds Albert's mystical science and Averroes's noetics remains fragile. The elements of divine light that may be marked by Averroes can all be explained by Albert's theology of faith. Faith as a unitive, infused, gratuitous, luminous *quo* whereby the Son's mission unites us to God explains the text more clearly, consistently, and exhaustively than does Averroes's epistemology. The main framework for Albert's notion of the mystical science's light is a semi-Dionysian theology of faith, a cadre within which one finds probable traces of Averroes.

The context of Albert's exposition on the light of the mystical science also creates difficulties for de Libera's thesis. Albert's appropriation of *intellectus adeptus* in his philosophical works refers to a natural, presanctifying perfection of the human being. The *Commentary on the Mystical Theology* contrasts the union that it teaches to any strictly philosophical ascent to God.[116] Overall, de Libera does not analyze the light of the mystical science within the Dionysian commentaries, but rather with Albert's diverse references to noetic light in his vast corpus, a method that may not adequately account for different genres.

Albert completes his preface to the *Mystical Theology* by dividing the text. He employs Aristotle's distinction between the mode of investigation and the reality being investigated. He assigns the doctrine's mode to the first three chapters and the doctrine itself to chapters 4 and 5. The doctrine's mode includes its manner of transmission and learning, which show how this teaching is known. The doctrine is taught by prayer, the interior principal divine teacher, and the exterior instrumental human teacher (*MT,* chap. 1). The next chapter shows how intellect attains union with God: "Through the reception of this

---

115. *SMT,* ch. 1, p. 464.38–61 (cited later at footnote 143 in the present chapter). The revealed divine names (also studied in the *SDN*) provide the mystical science its *quod.* These names are to be partly negated; see the present chapter's introduction.

116. Two main examples are *SMT,* ch. 1, pp. 457.52–61, and 462.20–38 (analyzed later in the present chapter).

doctrine, one comes to the union by which we are united to divine things."[117] *Mystical Theology* effects what it signifies; it has a sacramental character. Chapter 3 studies how negations function in relation to affirmations and ends with a hierarchy of negations. Chapters 4 and 5 ponder the doctrine itself: they apply negations to God. Here, Albert enacts the doctrine. The text seems to reach its climax in the last two chapters.[118]

For Dionysius the *Mystical Theology* teaches how to attain union beyond all names. The heart of the work is found in the allegorical exegesis of Moses in chapter 1. Chapter 2 comments on this passage, while chapters 3 through 5 offer clarifications on affirmations and negations. The final three chapters summarize the *Divine Names* and explain how one moves beyond all names. Albert changes the work's structure, since negations function differently in his thought: union occurs by negations, not beyond them. Albert's textual division turns out to be somewhat artificial, even for his own purposes. His commentary on chapters 4 and 5 constitutes less than a third of the work—less than four pages in the critical edition. Albert seems much more interested in how God is known, a theme that dominates the commentary's longest (first) chapter. Also, the *Commentary on the Divine Names* has already offered extensive reflections on negative names. Albert recognizes a distinct purpose for the *Mystical Theology* (union via knowledge gained through negations), yet because he collapses union beyond mind and negative naming, he struggles to distinguish this work from the *Divine Names*.

Albert's preface announces an exegesis opposed to so-called Affective Dionysianism, for the text is all about knowing by names, not about love surpassing knowledge. Albert also insists on the properly supernatural character of this theology. Grace stands at the center of this work.[119]

---

117. *SMT*, ch. 2, p. 465.5–6: "ex perceptione huius doctrinae pervenitur ad unitionem, qua unimur divinis."
118. *SMT*, ch. 1, pp. 455.65–56.5.
119. For the supernatural character of union in the *SMT*, see McGinn, *Presence of God*, vol. 4, *Harvest of Mysticism*, 18–21; Sicouly, "Gebet als *instrumentum theologiae*," 625–28; Trottmann, *Vision béatifique*, 292–302.

UNION WITH GOD ACCORDING TO ALBERT'S COMMENTARY ON THE MYSTICAL THEOLOGY

Albert's primary purpose in his *Commentary on the Mystical Theology* is to show that, how, and why negations unite us to God. I will analyze the central passages of the commentary that implement this project, mostly following the order of the text. I will focus on six key subthemes: (1) Albert's demonstration that negations are the primary topic of the *Mystical Theology*; (2) divine darkness and intellectual ecstasy as not comprehending God; (3) mystical ascent as the perfection of the *imago*; (4) Moses's contemplation of God's place; (5) Moses knowing God in darkness by unknowing; and (6) how the mind is united to God through negations. These six subthemes surface Albert's central doctrines on union, darkness, and negations.

"O super-substantial Trinity and super-God and super-good inspector of divine wisdom of Christians, direct us to the super-unknown, the super-shining and highest peak of mystical sayings."[120] So begins the Sarracenus translation of the *Mystical Theology*. Albert notes that this wisdom is a divine science that surpasses many philosophical errors. God perfectly knows himself, so that he best teaches us by revelation.[121] However, Albert later praises philosophy for its capacity to acquire some knowledge of God's perfection and to recognize its inability to comprehend God.[122] His comments on the first lines of the *Mystical Theology* identify the entire work's main subject: "*Direct us to the highest peak of mystical sayings,* insofar as in negations of all things we come into him [God] as into something hidden."[123] The phrase "mystical sayings" translates the *logia* or oracles—that is, the Bible and the liturgy. The *Parisian Scholia* interpret these sayings as "the arcane words of Sa-

---

120. *SMT*, ch. 1, p. 456.80–81: "Trinitas supersubstantialis et superdea et superbona inspectrix divinae sapientiae Christianorum, dirige nos ad mysticorum eloquiorum superignotum et supersplendentem et summum verticem."

121. Albert's 1251–52 commentary on Aristotle's ethics firmly distinguishes philosophical and theological contemplation; see Albertus Magnus, *Super Ethica: Commentum et Quaestiones, Libros VI–X*, ed. Wilhelm Kübel, Cologne Edition vol. 14, part 2 (Münster: Aschendorff, 1987), bk. X, lect. 16, q. 6c; see Trottmann, *Vision béatifique*, 252–58.

122. *SEP* 7, p. 505.25–42.

123. *SMT*, ch. 1, p. 457.12–14: "*dirige nos ad summum verticem mysticorum eloquiorum,* secundum quod in negationibus omnium in ipsum quasi in quoddam occultum venimus."

cred Scripture."[124] Albert seems to draw inspiration from the *scholia* as he identifies the mystical sayings with the negation of biblical divine names. The Dionysian text itself leads Albert to posit negations as the achievement of mystical theology, since the Areopagite discusses negative names at length in this work.

Following the Sarracenus translation, the highest peak "makes the most luminous shine forth in the most obscure way."[125] For Dionysius the peak where God's light shines is beyond all names. For Albert, this light is obscure, for it involves God's eminence,

> because although through the obscurity that is left in us from the eminence of splendor we fall short of comprehending the divine eminence, still, because we somehow attain it by leaving all behind, the mind is deified and illumined.[126]

Following the Areopagite's *Epistle 5*, Albert identifies divine light and obscurity as two descriptions of the same reality: light is darkness from our perspective. The obscurity is "in us," since the darkness on Mt. Sinai is an allegory for Moses's mind. Obscurity symbolizes a lack of comprehension, the absence of total knowledge about God. Divine light signifies the intelligibility of God's being whose fullness is only proportionate to his mind, while obscurity signifies the same intelligible divine reality insofar as it can be partly grasped by creatures. A few lines earlier Albert refers the expression "silent teaching" to the fact that we cannot speak God's *quid est*, only his *quia est*.[127] The analysis of these terms in the last section confirmed that knowledge of God's *quid est* is synonymous with comprehensive knowledge. Albert therefore announces a major hermeneutical strategy for the *Mystical Theology* that he already employed for the *Divine Names*—namely, the partial reduction of apophatic language to the fact that limited minds cannot fully grasp God's infinite nature. Finally, Albert notes that we touch di-

---

124. *PMT*, ch. 1, 50: "arcanorum verborum sacrae scripturae"; see also de Andia, *Henosis*, 3.
125. *SMT*, ch. 1, p. 456.82–83: "in obscurissimo superclarissimum supersplendere facientem."
126. *SMT*, ch. 1, p. 457.26–30: "quia quamvis per obscuritatem relictam in nobis ex eminentia splendoris deficiamus a comprehensione divinae eminentiae, tamen ex hoc quod attingimus aliqualiter ipsam relictis omnibus, mens deificatur et illuminatur"; see also *SDN*, ch. 7, no. 30, p. 359.42–55; ch. 13, no. 30, p. 449.40–51.
127. *SMT*, ch. 1, p. 456.72–74.

vine eminence in some way because we have left everything behind. But what is left behind? Albert does not say.

He then explains how one learns the mystical science:

Now the mode which he teaches Timothy, to whom he writes ... is that *concerning mystical* understandings he *should leave behind sense* [operations] *and intellectual operations by strong contrition* (*contritione*), as if crushing them under divine light, and that he should abandon *all sensibles and intelligibles*, because nothing of them is God, and here intelligibles mean that which can be comprehended by the intellect.[128]

Contritione literally means "to destroy" or "to grind away." Albert notes that intelligibles are the things that we can comprehend—that is, finite beings. The Areopagite here refers to the intellect abandoning the contemplation of finite objects so as to gaze only upon the hidden God, an event simultaneous with the reception of divine light. Albert explains that we should leave behind existing and nonexisting things insofar as God cannot be compared to anything that exists in a genre. We should recognize their inability to function as adequate manifestations of the divine nature. He sidesteps the radical implications of the term *contritione*. Rather than empty the mind (by an act of grace), we recognize the limits of our cognition, which involves yet another human act of knowing—namely, the judgment that our knowledge is limited. As in the *Commentary on the Divine Names*, noetic silence means noncomprehension.

Albert's paraphrase then gives the alternative translation: "rise up to the imitation of God, who is above every substance and cognition." The origin of the phrase "the imitation of God" is obscure.[129] Sarracenus refers to "union with God," while Eriugena mentions "unity." The shift in meaning is radical, for Albert comments, "*rise up to the imitation of God* ... insofar as the mind, in which the image is reformed through the *habitus* of glory or grace, imitates God in act."[130] This could be the

---

128. *SMT*, ch. 1, p. 457.42–49: "Modus autem, quem docet *Timotheum*, cui scribit ... est, ut *circa* intellectus *mysticos relinquat sensus et intellectuales operationes forti contritione*, quasi conterendo sub lumine divino, et quod derelinquat *omnia sensibilia et intelligibilia*, quia nihil horum est deus, et intelligibilia hic dicuntur, quae intellectu comprehendi possunt."

129. None of the known translations use the term *imitatio*; see *Dionysiaca*, 1:568.

130. *SMT*, ch. 1, p. 457.52–55: "debet *consurgere ad imitationem dei, qui est super om-*

most significant passage of the entire commentary, as Albert reveals a central pillar of his theological project. The term "imitation" opens the door to a discussion of the *imago*. Its subject is the mind, meaning the immaterial soul with its faculties of intellect and will. Yet the *imago* has changed, as memory no longer has any evident doctrinal function in the Dionysian commentaries. The *habitus* of grace or glory elevates the *imago*. The present passage refers to the experience of the beatific vision by the saints, those who possess the *lumen gloriae*, and it refers to those in grace but not yet in glory. The *imago* "in act" concerns the actual operative imitation of God, not just the possession of the immaterial faculties. The acts of the *imago* are nothing other than the created operations of knowing and loving God made possible by the *habitus* of created grace (or glory) joined to the missions of the Son and the Spirit, as we saw in chapter 3 of this volume. My previous studies of these themes thus help to surface the considerable doctrinal implications of Albert's brief remark concerning the *imago*. Timothy's elevation beyond intellect reaches its term in these higher acts of the soul. Having left behind the attempt to *comprehend* God, the graced intellect actively cooperates in grace, being joined to God by knowing and loving him.

In contrast, the present Dionysian passage highlights the passive nature of mystical ascent. Timothy's (active) anagogical interpretation of Scripture and liturgical symbols directly prepares him for gifted elevation, where he truly abandons noetic acts.[131] Albert reads the Areopagite's passive imperative to move beyond *all* finite acts of the soul as an exhortation to a higher type of human activity. His paraphrase ignores the term *sursum agatur*, which translates the phrase "you will be raised up."[132] For Dionysius only the willingness to let go of finite noetic objects allows us to receive the highest knowledge about God. Albert changes this exhortation to a call for active participation in grace. The *imago* is the explicit reason for Albert's refusal of Dionysian passivity in union.

---

nem substantiam et cognitionem, secundum quod mens, in qua est imago reformata per habitum gloriae vel gratiae, actu deum imitatur—*alia littera: unitionem*"; see also *SDN*, ch. 1, no. 46, p. 28.1–30; ch. 7, no. 30, p. 359.42–55.

131. *MT* 1.1, p. 142.5–9, 997B; Rorem, *Pseudo-Dionysius*, 186; de Andia, *Henosis*, 4.

132. *SMT*, ch. 1, p. 457.58. An alternative translation by Sarracenus is *sursum ageris* (p. 458.69–70). Eriugena also gives the term an active sense: *ascendes* (*PMT*, ch. 1, 58).

In fact, Albert transforms Dionysius with Augustine and Augustine with Dionysius. Rather than force one father's thought into the categories of the other, Albert proposes a new synthesis. A semi-Augustinian structure of the soul provides the anthropological foundation—namely, the *imago*'s active operative faculties elevated by grace. The structure is only semi-Augustinian, for the entire mystical doctrine expounded in the Dionysian commentaries stands with a single unessential reference to memory's operation.[133] A scholastic Dionysius manifests the *imago*'s path to perfection here below—the path of obscure cognition attained by negations. For Albert situates the whole discussion of the *imago* within an exposition of how one learns the mystical science, a science whose content is the knowledge of God attained by negations. The doctrine of the *imago* manifests the human mode of employing the mystical science, the subjective side of the act whose cognitive object is the hidden God attained by negations.[134]

This creative fusion of Latin and Greek patrologies may have found inspiration in the *Parisian Scholia* in a citation of the *Periphyseon* that explains the exhortation to Timothy. Eriugena notes that Dionysius here affirms the possibility of the mind's immediate relation to God—that is, a relation not mediated by the angels. Eriugena cites Augustine's axiom that no creature mediates between the soul and God. He continues, "Although human nature, while wound up in this mortal life, cannot cling to God in his very reality, nevertheless, it is said to cling [to God] in his image, since it is also possible and natural for it to cling to its founder by grace."[135] The soul enjoys direct contact with God, especially in that grace comes directly from him. Yet the soul also finds itself limited to indirect cognition, to knowing God in his image. Albert focuses on another aspect of the *imago* in commenting on the same Dionysian text as he describes how finite human acts become a path to

---

133. *SDN*, ch. 7, no. 11, pp. 345.69–346.9 mentions the ever-present obscure *habitus* of God in us.

134. *SMT*, ch. 1, p. 457.37–39; see also p. 455.6–9: "ista doctrina considerat huiusmodi remotionum quae est per negationes, aliae autem considerant affirmationes de deo, ista magis debet dici mystica quam aliae."

135. *PMT*, ch. 1, 58–59, citing *Periphyseon*, bk. IV, p. 42.8–26: "Et quamvis humana natura, dum in hac vita mortali versatur, adhaerere deo re ipsa non possit, verumtamen, quoniam possibile est ei et naturale conditori suo adhaerere eius gratia cui adhaeret, adhaerere in imagine dicitur."

union. Yet Eriugena's discussion presupposes active human cooperation via the graced *imago* in our clinging to God. He assumes a basic compatibility of Augustinian and Dionysian anthropologies, a hermeneutic that Albert partly adopts.

Coming back to our *imago* passage in the *Commentary on the Mystical Theology*, Albert concludes the paragraph by explaining the phrase "going out of oneself unrestrainably ... to the super-substantial ray of divine darkness." He notes that such ecstatic language refers to "not restraining oneself within the principles of reason."[136] The topic at hand remains the imitative activity of the graced *imago*. Noetic ecstasy means surpassing the limits of natural reason or philosophical knowledge about God not by suppressing or crushing reason, but by passing into the additional perfection of graced cognition that comes through the revealed divine names as interpreted by the inspired teacher, the Areopagite. Significantly, Albert does not here mention a special grace such as the Spirit's gifts of understanding or wisdom. Rather, he seems to suggest that the *imago*'s elevating act in question involves its operation of knowing and loving God enabled by the theological virtues. This revisionist reading of Dionysian ecstasy harmonizes well with Albert's teaching on the mind's ecstasy by faith that I considered earlier in this chapter. Now, for Albert, we learn mystical theology through a sanctifying noetic gift, for the *imago* demands sanctifying grace, and the elevating act in question belongs to the intellect. Furthermore, since the primary topic at hand is the imitation of God through revealed knowledge, the primary grace of the *imago* being discussed is most likely the supernatural virtue of faith, for this grace suffices to elevate the soul beyond the principles of reason. This further confirms my interpretation of the light of the mystical science as the gift of faith.

Albert then explains Moses's ascent of Mt. Sinai (I will momentarily skip the section on Bartholomew). Moses enjoys the most divine visions and understandings but realizes that these are not God. They are certain *rationes* subject to God (the Areopagite's *logoi*), meaning that God is present to his noblest creatures and shines forth through them. He is present to all things, yet "in a special way through the effects of

---

136. *SMT*, ch. 1, p. 457.58–61: "*sursum agatur ad radium divinarum tenebrarum, cuncta auferens*, idest deserens, *excedendo* seipsum *irretentibiliter*, quasi non retinendo se intra principia rationis"; see also *SDN*, ch. 4, no. 123, p. 217.30–36.

grace and glory."¹³⁷ Given our previous analyses of the divine missions, we can see that the grace-glory couplet implies the unique presence of the divine persons sent into the hearts of believers by sanctifying grace and sent to the angels by the gift of glory. Albert then proceeds to the Areopagite's explanation of God's place or the intelligible summits. For Dionysius God's place, the *logoi*, and the intelligible summits refer to the same reality—namely, God's operative powers, the highest objects of affirmative names.¹³⁸ Albert interprets the "holy places of intelligible summits" as a reference to "the angels who receive in their highest powers the presence of God coming upon them through the effects of glory, in whose light our soul sees divine things."¹³⁹ The angels are among the noble creatures previously mentioned. Albert treats the angels (symbolized by "holy places") as a species within the genus of the noble creatures manifesting God's presence (at the level of the *rationes*). He inserts a distinction where Dionysius employs synonyms. The interlinear gloss of the *Parisian Corpus Dionysiacum* also identifies the "holy summits" as angels, but it does not connect this passage with the angels' illumination of human souls.¹⁴⁰ Albert develops this exegesis as he inserts the Dionysian angelic mediation of light into the *Mystical Theology*, a connection that the Areopagite does not make. But what do Albert's angels mediate? It cannot be sanctifying grace, since Albert's *Commentary on the Celestial Hierarchy* insists that God alone pours out this gift.¹⁴¹ Rather, we see *divine things* in angelic light. The divine things are the *quod* or object known, while the angels assist in the process of knowing, perhaps by imparting a *quo* or higher operative

---

137. *SMT*, ch. 1, pp. 461.72–462.6: "*divinissima visorum et intellectorum ... esse* non deum, sed *quasdam rationes,* idest species, *subiectorum,* idest rerum, quae subiciuntur deo *excedenti omnia, subiectas,* idest inferiores deo, inquantum in nobilissimis creaturis et effectibus suis est, *per quae divinissima praesentia eius,* scilicet dei, *quae est super omnem cogitationem, monstratur*—est enim praesens omnibus suis effectibus et aliquo speciali modo effectibus gratiae vel gloriae—praesentia, dico."

138. See de Andia, *Henosis,* 345.

139. *SMT*, ch. 1, p. 462.5–11: "*praesentia,* dico, *superveniens intelligibilibus summitatibus sanctissimorum locorum eius,* scilicet dei, et dicuntur loca dei angeli, qui secundum sui supremas virtutes recipiunt dei praesentiam in se supervenientem per suos effectus gloriae, in quorum lumine anima nostra divina videt, secundum quod ab ipsis de divinis illuminatur."

140. *PMT*, ch. 1, 64, 68.

141. *SCH*, ch. 1, p. 11.20–24.

capacity, or perhaps by showing forth divine similitudes in their beatific gifts, though Albert remains vague on this point.[142] The latter category would come close to Albert's earlier theology of the Spirit's gift of understanding, a gift he never explicitly mentions in his *Commentary on the Mystical Theology*.

The third disputed question that follows this running commentary clarifies the place of the angels in Moses's contemplation. Responding to an objection, Albert states that since the agent intellect's natural light does not suffice to know divine things that are beyond the limits of reason, "the light of the angelic intellect ... multiplies species in our souls, in which divine things are seen." He gives the example of prophetic dreams. He adds that the soul is "strengthened" even more when the divine light also descends into soul, though he does not specify the function of God's light. Finally, when divine and angelic light join together, they constitute the "mirror of eternity" in which the prophets see "not what God is, but [what is] from God." Albert compares this prophetic vision with the soul's assimilation to the agent intellect's light. He then identifies all three lights (angelic, divine, and their combination) with the *rationes* or "divine visions" that are "the most noble contemplations in which God himself is not seen."[143] Albert remains consistent with Dionysius insofar as the latter defines the *logoi* (or the

142. *SCH*, ch. 4, p. 68.28–34 posits angelic light as necessary to judge rightly that for which the light of the agent intellect is not proportioned. *SCH*, ch. 8, p. 125.8–11 refers to the angels strengthening us by mode of persuasion, though without explaining the mode of persuasion.

143. *SMT*, ch. 1, p. 464.40–61: "divina non possint accipi per connexiones probabiles vel necessarias ex principiis primis, in quae sola potest lumen intellectus agentis ... ad huiusmodi cognoscenda adveniat sibi lumen intellectus angelici, quod multiplicat in animas nostras species quasdam in quibus videntur divina ... dicit Philosophus *de Divinationibus Somniorum*, quod quia ex principiis primis per modum scientiae speculativae concludi non possunt, unitur ad ea accipienda intellectus noster motoribus superioribus; et multo magis roboratur anima ad videnda divina, secundum quod ipsum divinum lumen descendit in ipsam; et forte coniungitur uterque modus. Et istud lumen vocatur speculum aeternitatis, in quo viderunt prophetae, quod non est deus, sed a deo, et assimilatur illustrationi intellectus agentis super naturaliter cognita. Et istae sunt *rationes*, de quibus hic loquitur Dionysius, quae dicit esse *divina visa*. Et sic patet, qualiter non videtur ipse deus etiam in nobilissimis contemplationibus." Albert's disputed question on prophecy notes that the mirror of eternity allows prophets to know future events. For this text and prophecy as a nonsanctifying grace, see Albertus Magnus's *Quaestiones*, "quaestio de prophetia," q. 1, a. 2. On angels mediating visions to human souls, see also Albertus Magnus, *De IV coaequaevis*, tr. 4, q. 34, a. 2.

rationes) as manifestations of God that are not God himself. But Albert shifts the Areopagite's meaning as he overlooks the connection between the *logoi* and the affirmative names in Dionysius. Instead, Albert's most detailed explanation of the *rationes* focuses on the gift of prophecy and infused intelligible species. He proposes a creative fusion of Arab noetics and a partly Augustinian doctrine of prophecy to explain what Dionysius considers to be an intermediary step in Moses's ascent. Following the interlinear gloss of the *Parisian Corpus Dionysiacum*, Albert partly reifies the *rationes* so that they signify not just God's self-manifestation in his causal activity, but also angelic and prophetic visions. Now the running commentary identifies the *rationes* with gifts of grace and glory, created graces that constitute a *partial* parallel to the Areopagite's divine processions. But Albert shows no sign that he intends to posit an intermediary contemplative stage that one could transcend. Rather, he treats the *rationes* as manifestations of God that make possible *and accompany* union, an interpretation I will confirm shortly. Thus even nonsanctifying graces such as prophecy have a place at the peak of Mt. Sinai, which Moses already attains at the level of the *rationes*.[144] Let us note the heterogeneous nature of Albert's exposition. The running commentary only mentions effects of (sanctifying) grace and glory with a focus on the latter, lights distinct from the angels' transmission of prophetic insight.

I return to the running commentary, where Moses is about to enter darkness. He goes beyond the divine places or angels, "the rays seen that are not the object of contemplation."[145] Albert says little on the transition from the *rationes* or holy places to darkness except that these rays or visions of divine things are no longer the object of the mind's gaze. The intellect must ponder God in a more direct way. "Moses *enters darkness of ignorance … in which he shuts down all cognitive re-*

---

144. *SMT*, ch. 1, p. 464.40–61 is the only *SMT* text that refers to philosophical contemplation as union with separate substances and as prophetic insight. Some of Albert's later philosophical works present this contemplation as a kind of natural mysticism; de Libera, *Métaphysique*, 265–328. In the *SMT*, contemplation via divine light is higher than the philosopher's prophetic cognition: Moses surpasses Aristotle. De Libera (*Métaphysique*, 334–35) presents philosophical mysticism as *the* fundamental doctrine that Albert transmitted to his contemporaries, an interpretation that cannot make sense of this doctrine's marginalization in the *SMT*.

145. *SMT*, ch. 1, p. 462.12–14: "divinissima videt Moyses, *absolvitur ab ipsis visis* radiis, quia non sunt obiectum contemplationis."

ceptions, that is, all natural powers of the soul that know by *reception*, which, being removed from other things, are filled by divine darkness alone."[146] The natural knowledge of God via the senses does not suffice to reach the highest cognition. Recognizing this limit, the intellect no longer looks to created beings as adequate manifestations of God, nor to grace, nor to the angels' glory. The intellect looks to God alone, attaining a more concentrated intentionality, a traditional doctrine that Albert soon confirms.[147] Moses now finds a better union, greater than union by natural or angelic light:

[Moses was united] *to the absolutely unknown*, namely to God, by the *cessation of all* natural *cognition*, because not being turned to other things naturally known, but to God alone, who is known by no natural cognition, and thus natural cognitions cease, *and insofar as he ... knows nothing* by natural cognition, [he is] *knowing above mind*, that is, above his own mind's nature, by the divine light infused from above, by which the mind is elevated above itself.[148]

The *Parisian Scholia* says that "we are united to the unknown by the idleness of all science."[149] Thus Albert was aware of a teaching that matches the historical Areopagite's doctrinal intention in this passage—namely, that the intellect's inactivity constitutes an essential condition for union. Albert deliberately argues against the doctrine of union with the unknown God via noetic silence. For this purpose he uses two hermeneutical tools: (1) the insertion of a grace-nature distinction and (2) the theme of intentionality or gazing upon God alone.

The first tool is the most important. Philosophical cognition of God, which is always mediated by our knowledge of sensible creatures, falls short and thus ceases. Albert does not intend to reject all philosophical knowledge of God, but rather points to its inability to bring

---

146. *SMT*, ch. 1, p. 462.17–22: "*intrat ad caliginem ignorantiae ... in qua claudit* Moyses *omnes cognitivas susceptiones,* idest omnes virtutes naturales animae per susceptionem cognoscentes, quae ab aliis remotae sola divina caligine implentur."

147. Wéber, "L'interprétation," 417.

148. *SMT*, ch. 1, p. 462.30–38: "*unitus ... omnino ignoto*, scilicet deo, *vacatione omnis cognitionis* naturalis, quia ad alia non convertitur naturaliter cognita, sed ad solum deum, qui nulla naturali cognitione cognoscitur, et sic vacant naturales cognitiones, *et eo quod ... nihil cognoscit* connaturali cognitione, *super mentem cognoscens*, idest supra naturam suae mentis, lumine divino desuper infuso, quo mens supra se elevatur."

149. *PMT*, ch. 1, 70: "omnis scientiae otio ignoto unimur."

about deifying union. The highest cognition of God requires a gratuitous, elevating light. Albert's interpretation may have been inspired by Eriugena, who in his *Commentary on the Celestial Hierarchy* employs an Augustinian distinction between nature and grace to distinguish Dionysian procession and return, respectively.[150] The theme of the present passage in the *Mystical Theology* is precisely return to God. For Albert noetic ecstasy that goes *above mind* does not silence its operations, but rather refuses to remain within the limits of strictly natural operations. Instead of going above mind, mind itself goes above its nature: "above mind" becomes "mind above nature." Ecstasy is no longer *out of* the mind but *in* the mind elevated above itself. Elevation above nature is precisely the effect of sanctifying grace. Neither here nor anywhere else in the Dionysian commentaries does Albert ever explicitly posit a higher grace (e.g., the gift of wisdom) that takes us beyond the theological virtues. Rather, he consistently refers ecstasy to grace surpassing nature. Nothing about Moses's ascent into darkness and reception of an unspecified divine light can be clearly distinguished from the actualization of the *imago* by the theological virtues. My interpretation finds support in Albert's approach to earlier passages of the *Mystical Theology* that parallel the peak of Moses's ascent. For example, Dionysius exhorts Timothy to seek the mind's ecstasy and to enter into darkness, which Albert reads through the *imago*. He also consistently links the virtue of faith to the mind's ecstasy.[151] Finally, given Albert's *Sentences Commentary* doctrine of cooperating grace, we should expect him to bypass the Dionysian notion of the mystic's inactivity, for his direct comments on grace mention neither God acting in our place nor God stimulating us by an actual grace.

Albert realizes that the Areopagite's exegesis of Moses's ascent (in Ex 20–24) has reached a climax. The primary text provokes three disputed questions: (1) whether Moses was raptured; (2) the nature of union by unknowing the highest reality; and (3) whether Moses sees God himself. "Rapture" refers to an Augustinian interpretation

---

150. Rorem, *Eriugena's Commentary on the Dionysian "Celestial Hierarchy,"* Studies and Texts 150 (Toronto: Pontifical Institute of Medieval Studies, 2005), 102–4.

151. *SMT*, ch. 1, p. 457.42–56; *SCH*, ch. 1, pp. 7.78–8.3; *SDN*, ch. 2, no. 54, p. 80.34–39. Pachas considers mystical silence an important theme in the *SMT*, but he does not account for Albert's reductive reading of Dionysius on this point; Pachas, "Alteridad," 139, 147.

of Paul's celestial vision in 2 Corinthians 12 as an out-of-body experience enabling a direct gaze upon God's essence.[152] Albert distinguishes Moses in darkness from rapture. The latter constitutes "the better part of contemplation," but this is not the theme that Dionysius intends to discuss. Albert refuses to make Dionysian union in darkness a gift reserved to the privileged few, an extraordinary grace that he explicitly attributes only to Paul (abstracting from Christ's beatific vision). Rather, "the things that are said here about contemplation all pertain to contemplation and not to rapture."[153] Those who have learned the teaching of the *Divine Names* can proceed to the peak of Mt. Sinai, presuming that they are in grace. This explains why the running commentary does not make prophetic gifts necessary for the ascent of Mt. Sinai, for these are only one type of *ratio* that may be seen at "God's place." Another *ratio* would be sanctifying grace or angelic glory. Albert insists that Moses's ascent represents a contemplation accessible to any believer *who learns the mystical science*. Such an interpretation is mostly consistent with Albert's universalizing of ecstasy in the *Commentary on the Divine Names*.

Albert then further differentiates between rapture and Moses's contemplation as he considers the theme of noetic attentiveness in darkness. In answer to the first objection of the same disputed question, Albert notes that someone in rapture cannot employ his or her lower faculties, such as the sense powers. However, for divine contemplation "in general," the soul retains the ability to use such powers, yet it no longer pays attention to their operations, a notion confirmed by Aristotle's explanation of philosophical contemplation.[154] In response to the fourth objection, Albert describes the concentration of the intellect's operation as a separation from its natural powers, again citing the Stagirite.[155] The intellect gazes upon its object so intensely that the contemplative can easily endure physical hardships related to fasting. In answer to the third

---

152. Albertus Magnus, *Quaestiones*, "quaestio de raptu," a. 3, pars 2, 95. He attributes rapture to Paul but not to Moses; see Marianne Schlosser, *Lucerna in caliginoso loco: Aspekte des Prophetie-Begriffes in der scholastischen Theologie*, Veröffentlichungen des Grabmann-Institutes 43 (Munich: Ferdinand Schöningh, 2000), 116–17.

153. *SMT*, ch. 1, p. 462.82–84: "ea quae hic de contemplatione dicuntur, conveniunt omni contemplationi et non raptui, qui est melior pars contemplationis."

154. *SMT*, ch. 1, pp. 462.85–63.3.

155. *SMT*, ch. 1, p. 463.15–24.

objection, Albert takes up the Dionysian language of divine light shutting down all of Moses's cognitive powers. He explains that this pertains to "some cognitive powers as such, namely intellective powers which extend themselves into unbounded light."[156] Here Albert seems to come as close as he ever does to positing a mystical light of contemplation distinct from the light of faith, a higher grace that enables the intellect's steady gaze upon the hidden God. However, it is unlikely that Albert intends to introduce a special contemplative grace. First, the early Albert does not identify a particular grace that causes such intellectual concentration and abstraction from sense data. Even the *Sentences Commentary* does not connect the Spirit's seven gifts to such effects. Second, in the Dionysian commentaries, every other discussion of a light that shuts down the intellect's operations or a light that allows us to transcend certain cognitive operations by moving into darkness consistently refers to surpassing strictly natural operations. This is precisely how the running commentary interprets the divine light that silences Moses's noetic activities, as we saw previously. Another good example comes later in the *Commentary on the Mystical Theology:* "a certain light is received in the soul, which causes non-vision according to natural modes, and that light provides a way into a confused cognition of God."[157] The light that moves us to surpass any strictly philosophical consideration of the hidden divine nature also effectively moves us to attain an obscure knowledge of God. But that is precisely how the preface describes the light of the mystical science. Therefore, the divine light that enables the intellect's steady gaze upon the concealed Godhead is almost certainly the light of faith. The teaching of the mystical science comes to full fruition when the contemplative allows both the light of faith and this science's teaching about the hidden God (attained by negations) to focus the intellect's gaze upon God alone. It seems that the light of faith virtually contains the potential to simplify the mind's act.[158]

156. *SMT*, ch. 1, p. 463.9–11: "incircumscriptum lumen claudit quasdam cognitivas virtutes secundum se, scilicet intellectivas, quae in ipsum se extendunt."
157. *SMT*, ch. 2, p. 466.70–74: "in anima suscipitur quoddam lumen, quod causat non-visionem secundum modos naturales, et illud lumen habet viam in confusam dei cognitionem"; see also ch. 1, p. 458.16–18; *SEP* 5, pp. 493.61–65, 495.33–43.
158. Albert's explication of contemplative repose may have some affinities to the simplification of the intellect's act during unknowing according to John of Scythopolis; see *PDN*, ch. 2, 120.

The disputed question on rapture concludes by specifying the mode of Moses's gaze in darkness. Albert offers a crucial nuance. He distinguishes pilgrims' contemplation from that of the saints in glory: "In heaven, God is seen through himself, but in the contemplation here below, he is seen in the effects of grace and of light descending ... in heaven, the vision will be through the *habitus* of glory, here through the *habitus* of grace."[159] Albert mentions the direct object of cognition and the intellect's operative elevation. He makes no exception for Moses in darkness, as the third disputed question confirms: "[In Exodus 33] Moses did not see God in himself, but in his most noble effects, namely of grace and theophanies."[160] The latter term probably refers to the prophetic visions mentioned later in the same question (analyzed previously). Now, abiding mediating effects are usually graces or lights in the plural, while the soul's elevating light is usually in the singular. Created contemplative *objects* in darkness are in the plural, while divine light in the singular refers to a *principle* of contemplation strengthening operative capacities.[161] The grace of Moses includes a *quo* (*habitus*) as well as objects *quod* ("effects ... of grace and theophanies"). Albert contrasts the latter to the vision of God himself in glory, another object *quod* seen through a distinct *habitus* (of glory). The patriarch in darkness has not surpassed the pilgrim state. Both passages just quoted place great emphasis on the indirect nature of Moses's cognition of God in darkness, where he knows or sees *through* effects. In this life Moses always needs the *rationes*, the site of prophetic dreams and visions and, more importantly, created graces in order to contemplate God, while realizing that they are not God. Albert sees no other possible explanation of Moses's knowledge, especially after having distinguished the patriarch's understanding in darkness from rapture.

---

159. *SMT*, ch. 1, p. 463.28–34: "in patria videtur deus per se, in contemplatione autem viae videtur in effectibus gratiae et luminis descendentis ... ibi erit per habitum gloriae, hic autem per habitum gratiae."

160. *SMT*, ch. 1, p. 464.26–28: "Moyses non vidit ipsum deum in se, sed in nobilissimis suis effectibus, scilicet gratiae et theophaniarum." Contrast this text to *SDN*, ch. 4, no. 103, pp. 202.60–203.12.

161. For light or grace as a cognitive principle in the singular, see *SMT*, ch. 1, pp. 455.15, 462.38, 463.10; ch. 2, p. 468.64–80; *SEP 1*, p. 480.29; *SEP 5*, p. 493.52. For graces, lights, or divine effects in the plural referring to created contemplative objects, see *SMT*, ch. 1, pp. 460.68 (analyzed later in this chapter), 461.15; ch. 3, p. 469.17.

Having rehabilitated created cognitive *acts* as essential for Moses's experience, Albert now draws the doctrinal consequence as he places created cognitive *objects* at the height of the encounter with God (short of rapture). The patriarch sees God, but only in his effects. Albert implies that Moses gazes only upon God as the ultimate *intended* contemplative object, but he immediately beholds the soul's graces and prophetic visions *as* divine manifestations. He defines knowing God by unknowing through two elements that Dionysius assigns below unknowing: the soul's proper operation and created gifts as intelligible objects manifesting divine light. Because Albert primarily defines knowing by unknowing as being beyond nature, he can posit sanctifying graces and other finite gifts as mediating noetic objects in darkness. These objects are precisely the divine similitudes that make affirmative naming possible and thus enable such naming within union in darkness. We thus find a striking synthesis of (1) the doctrine of analogy in the *Commentary on the Divine Names*, (2) the emphasis on the mystic's active cooperation in darkness, and (3) the cognitive function of created similitudes in the dark cloud. This doctrinal harmony further confirms my interpretation of Albert's exposition of the holy patriarch.

Coming back to the running commentary, we can now see Albert's intention behind his ambiguous transition from the contemplation of the *rationes* to entry into darkness. The disputed questions just studied state that Moses still contemplates God through gifts of grace and glory. The running commentary explicitly identifies these gifts with the *rationes*.[162] Also, Moses in darkness leaves behind the soul's natural powers, yet these have already been left behind in the gaze upon the divine gifts of grace and glory at the level of the *rationes*. For Albert darkness does not empty the intellect of finite noetic objects. Albert's transition from the holy place where Moses contemplates the gifts of grace to his contemplation of God alone involves a shift in intentionality, a gaze upon God as inadequately revealed in the gifts, for they are not God, yet he always gazes upon God in the gifts. Other than an intensification of the mind's intentionality, Albert essentially collapses the holy place and the summit of Mt. Sinai into one contemplative "state," an unthinkable move for Dionysius. I will soon show that the transition in inten-

---

162. *SMT*, ch. 1, pp. 461.76–62.5, 463.27–30, 464.26–29, 464.38–61.

tionality that moves Moses into darkness is above all the outcome of knowledge by negations.[163]

I will confirm the claim that Albert collapses God's place and darkness by considering his reading of the Areopagite's sacred veils, the liturgical context that frames Moses's ascent. The *Mystical Theology* discussion of Bartholomew parallels Moses's ascent. The apostle teaches us to pass beyond all creatures, including angels, so as to enter into darkness. Albert asks whether this doctrine refers to a gaze upon the unveiled Godhead. He answers:

The contemplation of God can be considered in two ways: [1] either as that in which God is contemplated, or [in other words], as to the principle of contemplation, and thus Dionysius says in the *Celestial Hierarchy* that we cannot see the divine ray in this life without the veil of signs and effects, because *now we see through a mirror and in an enigma* [1 Corinthians 13:12] ... or [2] as that which we seek through contemplation, and thus it is God himself unveiled, to which [vision] we attain in our final [state], in which we attain the intellectual natures; for investigation by reasoning would be in vain, unless one were to attain intellective union.[164]

We "attain" the intellectual natures or angels by becoming like them in our contemplation—that is, by gazing directly upon the unveiled divine nature in glory. Much of this disputed question compares angels' and human souls' natural and graced contemplative capacities. The angels see God without a veil, a mode of knowing we can only attain by the gift of glory.[165] The final state of contemplation mentioned above is

---

163. De Libera places the *rationes* below union; *Raison et foi*, 272. The running commentary first seems to embrace this doctrine, but Albert later collapses the two realms. This shift in the text has received little attention among Albert's commentators. Wéber explains the mediating effects in darkness via the missions (Wéber, introduction to Albertus Magnus, *Commentaire de la "Théologie mystique,"* 46–54), a reading that needs to be nuanced, as I will argue later.

164. *SMT*, ch. 1, 460.62–74: "contemplatio dei dupliciter potest considerari: vel quantum ad id in quo contemplamur deum, sive quantum ad principium contemplationis, et sic loquitur Dionysius in *Caelesti hierarchia*, quod non possumus videre divinum radium in hac vita sine velamine signorum et effectuum, quia 'videmus nunc per speculum et in aenigmate' [1 Cor. 13:12] ... sive quantum ad id quod per contemplationem quaerimus, et sic est ipse deus non-velatus, ad quod in ultimo nostri pervenimus, in quo intellectuales naturas attingimus; frustra enim esset ratiocinativa inquisitio, nisi perveniret ad intellectivam unitionem."

165. *SMT*, ch. 1, p. 460.35–39, 76–80.

the beatific vision. The natural desire to know God would be in vain if its fulfillment through intellectual union with him were impossible. Albert equates the beatific vision with the term "unveiled." He therefore implies that Bartholomew's description of God appearing unveiled to those who have passed beyond all sounds, words, and understanding does not refer to the pilgrim's union with God. Where Albert refers to the beatific vision, Dionysius speaks of an unveiled vision here below that transcends all finite mediations. Albert may not realize that Dionysius posits a noetic contact with God completely beyond all finite manifestations yet short of the eschaton.

Concerning the pilgrim's contemplation, Albert appropriates the Areopagite's teaching on the necessary conditions to *begin* the contemplative ascent and elevates it to a universal rule for all contemplation here below. Eriugena's translation of the passage from the *Celestial Hierarchy* cited earlier reads as follows: "It is not possible for the divine ray to shine in us except [as] anagogically veiled by a variety of sacred veils."[166] Dionysius reminds the reader that the liturgy constitutes an essential step on the path of return. The hierarch transmits divine light by celebrating the sacred mysteries and offers an anagogical interpretation of those sacred signs, which together enable contemplative progress. In the *Mystical Theology* the exhortation to leave behind sounds and lights in the discussions of Bartholomew and Moses refers to the need to pass through and then leave behind the liturgical symbols as well as the liturgically proclaimed and preached Scriptures. Such transcendence occurs when unmediated light breaks into the soul. But the liturgical allusions behind terms such as "sacred veils," "sounds," and "lights" were no longer visible to Albert. Nor did the Dionysian tradition identify these liturgical references in the glosses available to thirteenth-century scholastics. The *Parisian Scholia* on the *Mystical Theology* says virtually nothing about the liturgy. Albert did not possess the historical and linguistic tools needed to recognize the thematic connections between the *Mystical Theology* and the *Ecclesiastical Hierarchy*. This cultural distance made it possible for Albert to reinsert mediated light at the summit of the contemplative ladder.[167]

---

166. *SCH*, ch. 1, p. 12.77–78: "neque possibile est aliter lucere nobis divinum radium, nisi varietate sacrorum velaminum anagogice circumvelatum."

167. The oversight of the *MT*'s liturigcal setting need not entail the actual separa-

Albert's Dionysian Commentaries on Union with God   183

The veils now become "signs and effects," which Albert links to obscure faith cognition, as he invokes a standard biblical text on faith: "now we see in a mirror and through an enigma." What are these signs and effects? The same disputed question on Bartholomew refers to signs sent by God that elicit inexplicable joy in the will. Albert acknowledges the need to transcend these gifts because they remain distinct from God, who is the proper object of our (highest) contemplation.[168] In another part of this disputed question, Albert insists that we adhere to the "divine lights" sent by God as that under which he is seen.[169] Albert does not specify which lights he has in mind, though these are clearly created manifestations of God. Albert's reading of the Dionysian veils matches his interpretation of Moses: the contemplative continues to ponder finite manifestations of God, but *as* manifestations really distinct from God. We never fully leave behind the conditions for the start of contemplation.[170]

Albert thus expands the function of signs and veils as he broadens these categories to include spiritual, nonsensible effects (e.g., those eliciting spiritual joy). He partly interiorizes the veils. He transforms the Areopagite's insistence on the need for sensible mediations as platforms of noetic ascent into the principle that the pilgrim always needs material *or* finite spiritual mediations. All mystical knowledge in this life remains mediated by some type of created effect. That is why all such knowledge remains a type of faith cognition. Precisely because

---

tion of liturgy and mystical theology. First, Albert commented the whole Dionysian corpus, so that he could treat union in multiple settings, including the *EH* (e.g., *SEH*, ch. 3, pp. 54.55–56.70). He does not treat the *MT* as a stand-alone treatise on contemplation. Second, he notes the necessity of prayer to attain perfect cognition of God and union: *SDN*, ch. 1, no. 10, p. 5.52–56; ch. 3, no. 6, pp. 104.37–5.14; *SMT*, ch. 1, pp. 455.88–56.39; Sicouly, "Gebet als *instrumentum theologiae*," 622–28. Third, Albert's Dominican life combined study and liturgical prayer in an intense way.

168. *SMT*, ch. 1, p. 461.12–30.

169. *SMT*, ch. 1, p. 461.7–11: "divinis luminibus, idest a deo nobis immissis, debemus inhaerere non sicut obiecto, sed sicut his sub quibus videtur obiectum, confortantibus intellectum nostrum."

170. Albert's way of contrasting veiled and unveiled visions shows that Tugwell's description of Albert's eschatology as semi-Eriugenist needs to be qualified. Tugwell argues that, in Albert's Dionysian commentaries, the saints still see God through his effects, yet they also see him directly because the effects are transparent; Tugwell, "Albert the Great," 91–92. But for Albert, the light of created glory is a *quo*, not a *quod*, and the vision of God that he excludes from eternal beatitude is one of a comprehensive nature.

Albert's mystic always continues to gaze upon God through his effects, the obscurity on Mt. Sinai remains limited, since finite lights shine therein. The created lights make it impossible for God to be completely unknown. Albert does not adopt anything like the Dionysian paradox of unmediated knowledge of God's light in darkness that constitutes a middle way between knowing God via finite realities and the beatific vision. Perhaps Albert could have found hints of such a middle way in scattered comments contained in the *Parisian Scholia,* yet the *scholia* lack a clear teaching on this point.[171]

I have considered Albert's threefold explanation in the running commentary on Moses in darkness: the unknown God is beyond natural understanding, beyond comprehension and the sole object of contemplation. I also analyzed the disputed questions on rapture and prophetic lights. I now turn to Albert's final comment on ascent to God and union in the disputed questions of chapter 1 of the *Commentary on the Mystical Theology,* as well as parallel passages in the commentary on the Dionysian epistles.

In the second disputed question concerning Moses, Albert asks whether the highest kind of union is with the unknown. The solution states that union with God must be the height of contemplation. The answer to the second objection specifies that God is unknown not in himself, but in relation to us. Therefore, by union we "acquire more and more knowledge of him."[172] Neither passage explains how we attain such knowledge of God or what its content might be. The answer to the third objection excludes philosophical, univocal knowledge of divine attributes and instead proposes "supernatural cognition under a certain confusion."[173] Overall this disputed question primarily explains the term "unknowing" in relation to natural cognition. Similarly, in the running commentary, divine light as surpassing nature is the

---

171. Gilles M. Meersseman has also emphasized that, in the *SMT,* the nonbeatific vision of God is always mediated by concepts, veils, and effects of grace; see Meersseman, "La contemplation mystique d'après le bienheureux Albert est-elle immédiate?" *RT* 36 (1931): 189–90. Albert's doctrine is consistent, despite certain linguistic inconsistencies; at *SMT,* ch. 3, pp. 468.45–55 and 469.20–23, he notes that the *DN* and *MT* do not treat the manifestation of God in his gifts, but rather "in himself." The terminology shifts, so that "gifts" now signify sacramental graces and signs; thus, knowledge of God *in via* always remains mediated.

172. *SMT,* ch. 1, p. 463.71–84.
173. *SMT,* ch. 1, p. 464.1–3.

sole explanation of the phrase "[Moses was] united to the absolutely unknown."[174]

The Areopagite's *Epistle 1* expounds on the notion of knowing by unknowing. Albert explains: "Similarly, the greater the knowledge we have of God, the more we know his eminence [to be] above us, and the more we find our intellect to fall short of a comprehension of God."[175] He continues to insert a reflective, human noetic act into the encounter with God in darkness: we know that we do not know all of God. Here, too, he may be following John of Scythopolis.[176]

At the end of his *Commentary on Epistle 1 of Dionysius,* Albert interprets the Dionysian language of perfect unknowing to signify the knowledge that one perfectly fails in comprehending God.[177] In the *Commentary on Epistle 5 of Dionysius,* Albert explains the Dionysian paradox of seeing God by not-seeing as the exclusion of univocal or adequate knowledge about God so that "we are joined to him under a certain confusion, as to one exceeding [our cognition]."[178] Albert's interpretations of darkness, unknowing, and not-seeing parallel one of his main approaches to the mind's ecstasy in the *Commentary on the Divine Names,* where it often signifies not comprehending God or understanding that he is beyond all things.[179] The descriptions of knowledge in darkness as the fruit of not comprehending and not knowing in a univocal way take us directly to our final theme: negations as the path to union.

I have analyzed the first five key themes related to union, with a focus on the first chapter of the *Commentary on the Mystical Theology.* This brings us to the sixth and final subtheme of the present section—namely, how negations unite us to God. In chapter 2 Albert demonstrates how cognition attained by negations causes noetic union with God, our sixth and final key theme. I will first consider a twofold ap-

---

174. *SMT,* ch. 1, p. 462.30–38.
175. *SEP 1,* p. 480.34–37: "Similiter quanto maiorem cognitionem habemus de deo, tanto magis cognoscimus eminentiam ipsius super nos, et sic magis invenimus intellectum nostrum deficere a comprehensione dei."
176. *PMT,* ch. 1, 58; *PDN,* ch. 4, 122–23; see also chapter 2 of this volume.
177. *SEP 1,* p. 482.35–37.
178. *SEP 5,* p. 495.33–40.
179. *SDN,* ch. 1, no. 31, pp. 16.60–17.10; no. 46, p. 28.37–46; ch. 2, no. 57, p. 81.68–72; ch. 7, no. 30, p. 359.42–55.

proach to the intellect's union at the beginning of chapter 2. I shall then offer a fourfold consideration of negations' function as proposed in the rest of the commentary, where we find Albert's most extensive comments on negations as the path to union.

Chapter 2 of the *Mystical Theology* begins with the paradox of seeing and not-seeing or knowing and not-knowing God in supersubstantial darkness. Dionysius explains that we praise the hidden God as separate from all existing things. He invokes Plotinus's image of the sculptor uncovering a statue's beauty "hidden" in a block of stone, a process that advances by the negation (*aphaireseōs*) of all beings. Negations are hymns of praise that clear away all that envelops the hidden divine form.[180] In his preface to chapter 2 Albert notes that the reception of the mystical science leads to union with divine things. He adds that the running commentary on the first half of chapter 2 explains the method of such union or how negations unite us to God.[181] Albert then alludes to the example of the statue in two ways: as symbolizing a vision of divine eminence without relation to God's effects and as a representation of negations.

Albert proceeds to his first reading of the Plotinian statue:

We seek a pure vision of God by which he is sought to be seen in himself, without relation to some effect, *and* thus *manifesting only by separation* of others from the very *hidden beauty* of God *in himself,* as if he were to say: by this, as by an express image, the eminence of divine beauty is represented, in that all things are negated from him.[182]

Albert identifies two main functions of negations: they remove all predications from God and they enable a quasi-direct vision that no longer seems to be related to cognition attained from God's effects. Negations

180. *MT* 2, p. 145.4–5, 1025A–B; de Andia, *Henosis*, 383.
181. *SMT*, ch. 2, p. 465.5–6, 12–14: "quia ex perceptione huius doctrinae pervenitur ad unitionem, qua unimur divinis, ideo in isto capitulo determinat modum quantum ad unitionem.... Dividitur autem praesens capitulum in duas partes; in prima ponit modum, quo unimur deo, quia per negationes [p. 465.17–56]; in secunda."
182. *SMT*, ch. 2, p. 465.38–44: "*mundae visioni occulti* dei, qua in se videri quaeritur sine aliquo effectus respectu, *et sic manifestantes sola ablatione* ceterorum ab ipso *occultam* dei *pulchritudinem in seipsa,* quasi dicat: per hoc sicut per quandam expressam imaginem repraesentatur eminentia divinae pulchritudinis, quod omnia ab ipsa negantur." The subsequent lines (p. 465.44–49) refer to a *scholium* that discusses the statue; *PMT*, ch. 2, 74.

now lead directly to eminence, but not the eminence of a cause as such, for that would reintroduce the relation to effects. Albert's gloss on the Plotinian statue is very brief. He essentially paraphrases Dionysius without adding significant doctrinal clarifications. This account of negation matches Moses's *apparent* ascent beyond God's place discussed earlier, an apophatic ascent that the German friar subsequently qualified.

Albert returns to this theme in the running commentary on the second half of chapter 2. He refers to God's unknown eminence being revealed to us without the veil of creatures—that is, without a relation to his effects. How can this manifestation come about? "In all things which are known through their forms, the forms themselves are images of divine beauty. By the negations of these [images], we come into that hidden-ness which is represented in them in a veiled way."[183] Albert seems to take advantage of the link between affirmations and divine processions. Affirmations refer to God through a creaturely veil: "existing" or finite things conceal God. The negations apply to the created forms or images, apparently by removing any proportion between the images and the divine reality. Negations signify that God is higher than any created manifestation of him. Having negated all things, "*we see that super-substantial darkness* of divine eminence *hidden ... from all light*, which is in existing things."[184] Seeing God's eminence apparently means knowing that God's perfections are infinitely beyond created perfections. We seem to attain this cognition by negations alone, for Albert does not mention any new divine light that manifests God. Negations have a superlative signification. We do not deny any perfection of God, but rather identify the imperfect image *as* an imperfect representation of God's perfections, for "by the negations of these [images], we come into that hidden-ness." Perhaps Albert calls such a vision direct because when negations surface the radical limits of all noetic mediations, the intellect's intentionality is wholly directed to the hidden God. Let us note that the phrase "*we see that super-substantial darkness of divine eminence*" almost certainly refers to union. The themes of

---

183. *SMT*, ch. 2, p. 466.11–14: "in omnibus enim rebus quae cognoscuntur per suas formas, ipsae formae sunt imagines divinae pulchritudinis, per quarum negationem venimus in illud occultum quod velate repraesentabatur in eis."
184. *SMT*, ch. 2, p. 466.15–17: "*et videamus supersubstantialem illam caliginem* divinae eminentiae *occultam*, idest occultatam, *ab omni lumine*, quod est *in existentibus*."

darkness and eminence recall Moses on Mt. Sinai. Also, such contemplation is the direct, highest outcome of the negations that the preface of chapter 2 calls "the mode by which we are united to God," while "vision" refers to the maximum knowledge that the mystical science offers, a science whose reception causes unity.[185]

Albert's uniting negations are similar to the way of excess described in chapter 7 of the *Commentary on the Divine Names*. There excess points to a divine mode of being that is higher than our grasp of God's causal mode of being. In the section on analogy I noted an unresolved tension in Albert's approach to eminence, especially in its apparent abiding link to mediated cognition. The intelligibility of eminent names presumes knowledge of perfections only attainable from creatures.[186] The explanation in chapter 2 of the *Commentary on the Mystical Theology* also suffers from this tension: Albert seeks a knowledge of God not veiled by creatures, yet the negation of created images as images apparently leaves standing a created similitude that alone grants some intelligible content to the contemplation of God's eminence. Albert's first explanation of uniting negations remains ambiguous.

I now turn to Albert's second reading of the Plotinian statue. For Dionysius the negations are the sole means of "cutting away." Albert offers an alternative interpretation: "we remove non-living [things] from him [God], and so there remains that he is living, although life, insofar as it is signified by the name, signifies the procession of life, which is not the divine nature, but manifests it just as its similitude."[187] Albert presumes that the affirmations have not been wholly cleared away, but rather qualified. He removes imperfections such as "non-living," not perfections (living). Albert recognizes that affirmations only impart indirect knowledge, as they guide our thought to created similitudes that function as cognitive bridges whereby we attain a partial glimpse of divine perfections. He seems to acknowledge the Dionysian doctrine that affirmations *directly* refer to divine processions and not to the divine nature. But Albert does not draw the doctrinal consequence that Dio-

---

185. *SMT*, ch. 2, p. 465.13–14 (cited earlier at footnote 181 of the present chapter).
186. *SDN*, ch. 7, no. 29, p. 358.73–86 (cited earlier at footnote 77 of this chapter).
187. *SMT*, ch. 2, p. 465.52–56: "removemus ab ipso non-viventia, relinquitur, quod sit vivens, cum tamen vita, secundum quod nomine significatur, significet vitae processionem, quae non est divina natura, sed manifestans ipsam sicut sua similitudo."

Albert's Dionysian Commentaries on Union with God 189

nysius saw therein—namely, that affirmations ultimately prevent union with God. Rather, he implies that qualified affirmations remain as the soul moves into God's hidden beauty. In other words, Moses does not transcend the Areopagite's *logoi* as he enters darkness. Instead, Albert again quietly collapses God's place and divine darkness into a single cognitive sphere. His first explanation of the Plotinian statue proposed that the separation of perfections in "existing things" reveals God's hidden eminence as by "an express image." The second interpretation shows that the negation of imperfections leaves standing an attribute (living) that functions as a similitude manifesting God, like an express image. Albert treats the negation of imperfections as unitive names, for he dedicates this section to union by negations.[188] When we deny that God is "not-living," we recognize more clearly the partial manifestation of God in created life and thus *indirectly* gaze upon eminent divine life in a new way. This second type of uniting negation ends with a created similitude and thus with a type of affirmation! This matches Albert's second, more developed account of Moses's ascent, which collapses God's place (with its divine similitudes) and the dark cloud. It also perfectly fits with the doctrine of the *Commentary on the Divine Names*, where negations include affirmation and a reference to divine causality, as we saw in the last section. Albert's exposition of the Plotinian statue turns the Areopagite's teaching upside down, for Dionysius uses this image to explain that we must transcend all affirmations.

Here I need to pause and take a brief look at one key doctrinal background of Albert's exposition. For Albert, seeing God's eminence means enjoying union with him: "Although through the obscurity that remains in us from the eminence of splendor we fall short of the comprehension of divine eminence, nevertheless, by the fact that we somehow attain it [the eminence], by leaving all [things] behind, the mind is deified and illumined."[189] One "attains divine eminence" by noetic contact or understanding. Hence the reception of the mys-

---

188. *SMT*, ch. 2, p. 465.12–14. I thus disagree with Humbrecht's highly apophatic reading of this part of the *SMT* (p. 465.52–56) as calling for the removal of all effects; Humbrecht, *Théologie négative*, 345.

189. *SMT*, ch. 1, p. 457.26–30: "quamvis per obscuritatem relictam in nobis ex eminentia splendoris deficiamus a comprehensione divinae eminentiae, tamen ex hoc quod attingimus aliqualiter ipsam relictis omnibus, mens deificatur et illuminatur."

tical science brings about union with God. De Andia notes that the Areopagite's central insight in the *Mystical Theology* is the identification of union and unknowing. Albert retains this doctrinal principle, though he modifies the meaning of unknowing. Let us note that his notion of the negation of imperfections as imparting unitive knowledge does not appropriate the Dionysian teaching that certain affirmations such as Monad, Eros, Peace, Goodness, and Love have a unifying power.[190] Albert never comments on this doctrine and probably did not detect its presence in the *Divine Names*. Now, in Albert's corpus up to 1250, the doctrine of unity via negations is proper to his Dionysian commentaries.[191] The *Sentences Commentary* makes no evident connection between naming and union. Instead, Albert's new theology seems to have found its main inspiration in the proximity between negations and union that often emerges in the *Mystical Theology*. After his reinterpretation of divine darkness in chapter 1 and his appropriation of the *imago* as a doctrinal key that joins together the power of divine light and the properly human act of knowing, the stage was set for a fusion of negation and union. Albert's new theology also may have been inspired by the simple dominance of negations in the *Mystical Theology*. He treats this text as an organized whole, for as a scholastic, Albert seeks a single unifying subject in the work. He does not see that the Areopagite's discussion of negations as the path *toward* union in the first two chapters is followed by technical considerations of divine names that largely summarize the doctrine of the *Divine Names*. Albert also would have found confirmation for the principle of cognition as a form of union in Augustine and in the philosophers, including Aristotle. But neither Augustine nor Aristotle seems to have been the major source for the evolution in Albert's thought. Indeed, the early Albert already appropriated the Stagirite's notion of cognitive union before the *Sentences Commentary*.[192] But he did not apply this philosophical principle to the doctrine of knowledge by negations. Albert's doctrine of union

---

190. For Dionysius, see de Andia, *Henosis*, 114–15, 352.

191. For union by negations, see also *SDN*, ch. 1, no. 49, p. 31.11–24; ch. 13, nos. 31–32, pp. 449.63–50.3.

192. See Anzulewicz, *De forma resultante in speculo: Die theologische Relevanz des Bildbegriffs und des Spiegelbildmodells in den Frühwerken des Albertus Magnus*, Beiträge zur Geschichte der Philosophie und Theologie des Mittelalters, Neue Folge vol. 53, part 2 (Münster: Aschendorff, 1999), 2:165.

Albert's Dionysian Commentaries on Union with God 191

by negations constitutes a significant development of his own theology. That development's major catalyst was probably a scholastic misreading of the Areopagite, even as this evolution takes up major Dionysian insights such as the ascending power of negations.

Negations lead to a deeper, more direct knowledge of God and so directly cause a unitive cognition: "in the negations of all things in [or from] him [God], we come, as it were, into a certain hidden-ness," into the cognitive space of union.[193] Negations seem to do this by themselves, though always on the foundation of the light of the mystical science. For Dionysius negations allow God's hidden beauty to shine forth. They *dispose* for the arrival of God's light that causes union.[194] For Albert the negations are a *sufficient* contemplative ladder, yet only because God has already initiated union by the gift of faith, the light of the mystical science. The practice of negations guides the mind to a more perfect understanding, a fuller encounter with God's light or truth. Negations prepare for and efficaciously lead the intellect to a more intense divine light in the sense of knowing God more perfectly. By its nature this higher cognition brings about a better union with God, though this last element often remains implicit.[195]

Albert's running commentary on chapter 2 of the *Mystical Theology* identifies two types of uniting negations: the negation of all created

---

193. *SMT*, ch. 1, p. 457.13–14: "in negationibus omnium in ipsum quasi in quoddam occultum venimus."

194. De Andia, *Henosis*, 432.

195. No one has clearly articulated the unitive function of negations (and their positive noetic content) in Albert. Wéber says little on uniting negations as he focuses on the elevating power of noetic graces; Wéber, introduction to Albertus Magnus, *Commentaire de la "Théologie mystique,"* 24–28; Wéber, "L'interprétation," 416–21. De Libera, *Raison et foi*, 272–77, and McGinn, *Harvest of Mysticism*, 17–24, follow Wéber. Tugwell seems to suggest negations' unitive function, but with some ambiguity; Tugwell, "Albert the Great," 62–63. Humbrecht ignores this part of the *SMT* and appeals to ch. 5, p. 475.21–37 to suggest that one attains union by going beyond negations; Humbrecht, "Albert le Grand," 264. But this text only states that God (not our unity with him) is beyond every negation. Ruh, *Geschichte*, vol. 3, *Mystik*, 120–26, and Allegro and Russino, introduction to Albertus Magnus, *Tenebra luminosissima*, 19–43), essentially ignore uniting negations. Hoye sees the unitive function of negations, but adds that they clear away true (biblical) revelations. Hoye thus overlooks the eminent function of negations; Hoye, "Mystische Theologie," 598. Meis mentions ascent by negations but remains vague on their unitive function; Meis, introduction to Albertus Magnus, *Sobre la Teología Mística*, 30.

manifestations as adequate mediations of God's eminence and the negation of imperfections that points to the real, yet limited power of divine similitudes to unveil God's hidden nature. Both kinds of negations are located between univocity and equivocity, between a divinely created proportion and total dissimilarity. I will confirm this interpretation of negations by considering four other major approaches to negations in chapters 2 through 5 of the *Commentary on the Mystical Theology* and in the *Commentary on Epistle 1 of Dionysius*. In these texts Albert (1) shows that negations manifest the supernatural, nonunivocal character of unitive cognition; (2) implies that negations point the mind's intentionality toward God in abstraction from creatures without producing a new, positive knowledge of the divine nature; (3) offers two possible ways of connecting negation to the reality signified, one of which moves toward the contemplation of God beyond all names; and (4) nuances this third approach by connecting the negation of all things to our inability to comprehend God so that negations ultimately combine affirmation, negation, and eminence.

In the first disputed question after the running commentary on the Plotinian statue, Albert returns to the paradoxical language of vision and nonvision. Here too he links the theme of nonvision to strictly natural ways of knowing. In the solution Albert identifies the latter with knowledge of a thing through its "proportioned effect"—that is, natural cognition essentially involves a quasi-univocal type of knowledge. We leave behind such knowledge by a divine light that elevates us above our nature, a light that causes a confused vision of God's *quia* [*est*].[196] In the response to the third objection, Albert explains:

there is no pure negation, but the mode of natural vision is negated, leaving [us with] the reception of supernatural light, which is nevertheless made known more through negation, in that we do not find something known to us that we properly predicate of God, because of the eminence of his simplicity, since the truth of predication is founded upon some composition.[197]

196. *SMT*, ch. 2, p. 466.59–69.
197. *SMT*, ch. 2, p. 466.78–85: "quia non est pura negatio, sed negatur modus naturalis visionis et relinquitur susceptio supernaturalis luminis, quod tamen magis notificatur per negationem, eo quod non invenimus aliquid notum nobis quod proprie de deo praedicemus, propter eminentiam simplicitatis, cum praedicationis veritas fundetur in aliqua compositione"; see also Wéber, "Langage et méthode," 96.

Albert's Dionysian Commentaries on Union with God   193

Negations manifest the theological nature of union. They signal the need for the elevating power of divine light that is above nature or our natural noetic capacity. Earlier in the same disputed question, Albert notes that this light has a habitual character. My study of the preface to the *Commentary on the Mystical Theology* showed that the divine light mentioned in this passage is the *habitus* of faith. Second, negations are not absolute or "pure," meaning that they do not directly oppose affirmations or deny the presence of perfections in God. The key description of negations involves the opposition between divine simplicity and created complexity. Albert here refers to the complexity of language and its metaphysical foundation. Language necessarily reflects the complex nature of finite perfections, such as the real distinction between an attribute-bearing subject and the attribute. The complex nature of realities signified and the complex mode of predication both call for negation. Here "proper predication" likely refers to univocal naming, not to substantial predication that identifies the presence of perfections in God.[198] We remove such univocity from all affirmative names, both philosophical and theological.

The most ambiguous part of Albert's exposition is his claim that negations better manifest supernatural light. They recall the gratuitous nature of knowing by not-knowing (the topic of the disputed question) as they point to the essentially obscure nature of faith cognition. Belief enables the acceptance of revealed names as true. The knowledge that these names impart elevates us to God. Negations manifest faith's incapacity to grant a clear, adequate understanding of God's nature. Negations recall the obscurity of supernatural light.

In this passage the denial that any manifestation of the divine nature can be adequate appears to be the main function of negations. In the third chapter of the commentary, Albert explains how the soul extends itself into God's eminence: "since our intellect beholds nothing in a determinate way in him, it cannot express [God's eminence] through any affirmations, but only through negations, and so this science is only completed in negations."[199] The mystical science ends *in*

---

198. At *SMT*, ch. 2, p. 467.53–60, Albert employs the term "true predication" to signify univocity.

199. *SMT*, ch. 3, p. 470.66–70: "cum intellectus noster nihil determinate in ipsa aspiciat, non potest exprimere per aliquas affirmationes, sed tantum per negationes, et ideo haec scientia tantum negationibus completur."

negations, not *beyond* them. It remains incomplete with affirmations alone. For Albert "determinate knowledge" consistently refers to an act of knowing that enables the intellect to repose in a stable, noetic object proportioned to the divine reality. The word "determinate" is a synonym for unconfused knowledge, which Albert elsewhere even excludes from the beatific vision.[200] He quietly turns the Areopagite's discussion of going beyond affirmations into an exposition of negations as essential complements of affirmations. In this context the phrase "express God" refers to adequate speech about God. The same sense probably stands behind the conclusion a few lines after the passage cited earlier, where Albert says that the mystical science ends in hiddenness, for, "having removed all, we cannot fittingly (*decenter*) affirm something of him."[201] Negations have a limiting, nonprivate function, just as they do in the *Sentences Commentary* and in the *Commentary on the Divine Names*.

Second, Albert treats the mode of union in the second disputed question of chapter 2 of his lectures on the *Mystical Theology*. Responding to an objection, he notes that affirmations proceed from effect to cause, so that one predicates the effects of the cause. But those who seek the essence of the cause itself proceed by negations, for God is separate from all caused entities. If negations separate our understanding of God from created effects, then they also thereby distance us from the noetic content of affirmations. But Albert does not clearly espouse an *actual* attainment of a negative divine knowledge that *fully* separates itself from the cognition tied to creation. Rather, by negations "the essence of the cause is sought."[202] By negations we move closer to a more

---

200. *SEP* 5, p. 495.33–43. At *SMT*, ch. 1, p. 454.80–84, we know God *in quodam confuso* because we cannot affirm his *quid est*. At ch. 3, p. 466.67–68, we are said to know the *quia* of God *confuse et non determinate*. According to ch. 5, p. 474.86–88, we do not know *determinately* the divine *quid* or *quia*, but rather *confuse tantum*; see also p. 475.14–15. At *SEP* 5, p. 495.38–40, knowing God's *quia* determinately requires an effect proportionate to God's nature. None of these texts offers an adequate foundation to conclude that the confused knowledge in question involves a general concept, as proposed by Humbrecht, *Théologie négative*, 340–41. The last passage from *SEP* 5 confirms the equivalence of univocal knowledge and determinate cognition of God's *quia est*.

201. *SMT*, ch. 3, p. 471.15–18: "haec scientia dicitur mystica prae aliis, quia in occulto terminatur, de quo non possumus omnibus remotis aliquid decenter affirmare."

202. *SMT*, ch. 2, p. 467.46–52: "Sed in via compositionis, quae est de causa separata per essentiam in causata, est modus affirmationis, quia sic manifestatur causa ut causa,

Albert's Dionysian Commentaries on Union with God   195

direct cognitive perception of divine eminence—of God insofar as he is above all created beings. Negations direct the mind's intentionality to God alone in his ever-greater reality. This second characteristic of negations takes us back to the first type of uniting negations, to the quasi-vision of God without relation to his effects.

Third, Albert's *Commentary on the Mystical Theology* employs two approaches to negations and the reality signified. Chapter 5 of the *Mystical Theology* negates all divine names, even the highest affirmations such as "life" and "goodness." In a disputed question Albert offers two ways to understand the denial of the highest perfections. First, following Anselm, he notes that we do not negate the reality signified by affirmative names, since God possesses the perfections signified in a more perfect way than do creatures. Rather, we deny the mode of signification, which remains tied to a creaturely mode of being. By implication the mind's ascent into divine obscurity does not take us beyond the affirmations of the reality signified. Divine naming does not fall silent precisely when Dionysius calls for silence. Albert's response closely parallels the opening disputed question of the *Commentary on the Divine Names*.[203] It also complements Albert's second approach to the Plotinian statue. But then he offers a second solution, without saying which he prefers: "Or it can be said that neither can these [names] be truly predicated of God as to the reality signified. For in any predication, there must be that which is subjected and that to which it is subjected ... [but] in God there is no composition."[204] Affirmations of God's perfections manifested in creation remain bound to a finite way of being, so that the perfection-bearing subject and the perfection predicated of the subject are always distinct. Human language remains complex, as it necessarily reflects creatures' complex way of being: "and

---

quae inquantum huiusmodi recipit praedicationem effectuum, sed per reditum in ipsam quaeritur ipsa essentia causae, et ideo, cum sit separata ab omnibus causatis, oportet, ut per negationes procedatur."

203. *SMT*, ch. 5, p. 473.49–55; *SDN*, ch. 1, no. 3, p. 2.27–48 (cited earlier at footnotes 72 and 75 in this chapter); see also *SEP* 9, p. 536.35–39.

204. *SMT*, ch. 5, p. 474.7–10, 14, 23–25: "Vel potest dici, quod nec etiam quantum ad rem ipsam significatam vere possunt ista dici de deo. In omni enim praedicatione oportet accipere id quod subicitur, et id cui subicitur ... sed in deo nulla est compositio.... Unde patet, quod nihil neque secundum modum nominis neque secundum rem potest proprie praedicari de deo."

because of this, all [things] are more truly removed from him."[205] Insofar as the intelligibility of language about God remains rooted in the creaturely mode of being, or insofar as the realities signified seem inseparable from their mode of being, we negate these realities of God. Here Albert seems to treat the reality signified as having an essentially finite mode, whereas the first response operates on the presumption that the intellect can predicate perfections in abstraction from finite modes of being. On the surface the current passage is similar to the discussion of divine excess in chapter 7 of the *Commentary on the Divine Names*, though the latter text never states that we remove the reality signified.[206] Overall, Albert's second explanation is similar to the first type of uniting negations in chapter 2 of the *Commentary on the Mystical Theology*. But the current passage goes further, especially since the exposition in chapter 2 implied the negation of images as images or of the creaturely mode of being, but not necessarily of the reality signified. In chapter 5 Albert comes closest to espousing an ascent to God that rejects all names, but it remains an atypical text.[207] Not only does it clash with key elements of the early Albert's doctrine of analogy, it is hard to see how this hyperapophatic passage could fit with his anthropology.

The fourth approach to negations nuances the third. Several passag-

205. *SMT*, ch. 5, p. 474.25–26: "et propter hoc omnia ab ipso verius removentur."
206. See *SDN*, ch. 7, no. 29, p. 358.73–86 (cited earlier at footnote 77 in this chapter).
207. For Miguel Lluch-Baixauli, Albert's second, more apophatic solution pertains to philosophical cognition of God, not graced cognition. The text may be open to this reading, but does not give adequate indications in its favor; see Lluch-Baixauli, "Sobre el Comentario Albertino a la *Mystica Theologia* de Dionisio," in *Die Kölner Universität im Mittelalter: Geistige Wurzeln und soziale Wirklichkeit*, edited by Albert Zimmermann, Miscellanea Mediaevalia 20 (Berlin: Walter de Gruyter, 1989), 73–76. Also, Humbrecht questions whether Albert espouses proper affirmative discourse about God in the *SMT*; Humbrecht, "Albert le Grand," 260. But, as I have shown (discussing *SMT*, ch. 2, pp. 466.78–85, 467.53–60), Albert sometimes links proper predication with univocity, which seems to leave the door open for proper, analogous predications. Also, at p. 466.11–17, negations only remove the possibility of adequate divine manifestations, while p. 465.52–56 posits uniting negations that remove imperfections, which leaves standing the affirmation of perfections. Both texts seem to presume the possibility of proper positive predication. My study of analogy in the *SDN* showed that Albert espouses proper affirmative names (ch. 1, no. 3, p. 2.37–48), negations with positive content (ch. 7, no. 29, p. 358.73–86), and eminent names with positive content (ch. 7, no. 5, p. 340.48–50; no. 33, p. 361.14–20). The most apophatic *SMT* texts are best read through the passages just mentioned.

Albert's Dionysian Commentaries on Union with God   197

es seem to evade the Dionysian language of ascent beyond all names. Chapter 1 of the *Commentary on the Mystical Theology* states that we remove all names, since God is above negations and affirmations, for "through neither of these [affirmations or negations] is God's quiddity comprehended."[208] Here God's nameless eminence apparently only applies to the impossibility of a perfect name that adequately signifies the totality of God's nature, an explanation similar to the treatment of God as nameless in the *Commentary on the Divine Names*.[209] Albert does not clearly embrace the transcending of all names because of a firm epistemological conviction. At the end of his *Commentary on Epistle 1 of Dionysius* he notes that God is "not known" in that we do not know him perfectly. Hence we negate "being" from him because of divine eminence—that is, God truly possesses being in an eminent mode that escapes us. Perfect ignorance and perfect knowledge of God overlap, as both consist in perfectly knowing that we do not comprehend God.[210] Thus negations at once (1) manifest God's eminent possession of perfections, implying the affirmation of divine perfections and (2) signify the limits of our understanding and thus point the mind to God's ever-greater perfection. Now negations quietly combine affirmation, negation, and eminence. Thus the last chapter of the *Commentary on the Mystical Theology* invokes the loaded Aristotelian phrase "every negation is founded upon an affirmation."[211] The negation of divine being

208. *SMT*, ch. 1, pp. 458.90–59.2: "oportet causam omnium ponere et super negationes et super affirmationes, quia per neutrum horum comprehenditur quiditas dei"; see also p. 454.78–84; *SDN*, ch. 13, no. 30, p. 449.40–78.

209. *SDN*, ch. 1, no. 62, p. 39.37–52 (cited earlier at footnote 83 in this chapter). Therefore, the *SMT* employs two approaches to God as beyond all names. I can only partly agree with Wéber's thesis that Albert posits a negativity of divine eminence within the limits of given [manifested] perfections and a negativity that rejects every name; Wéber, "Langage et méthode," 81. Wéber identifies the latter approach with *SDN*, ch. 7, no. 29, p. 358.72–86; see the section on analogy. But in this text eminence refers to God's excess mode of being without explicitly negating the reality signified. Here affirmation, negation, and eminence refer to three modes of being (created, God's causal mode, and God's divine mode beyond causality). In this *SDN* passage eminence signifies that God is beyond our names, but it does not reject every name. In fact, Albert's discussion of negating the reality signified in *SMT*, ch. 5, comes closest to implying the denial of every name, yet his other expositions on unitive negations are less apophatic.

210. *SEP 1*, p. 482.27–40 (partly cited later in footnote 212 of the present chapter).

211. *SMT*, ch. 5, p. 475.22–23: "omnis negatio fundatur supra aliquam affirmationem"; see also ch. 3, p. 468.4–7. Wéber notes the simultaneity of affirmation, negation and eminence in Albert; Wéber, "Langage et méthode," 78.

signifies that God is being and that he is not being in the way that we have being, for God's being is ever greater. Such negations occur at the summit of the spiritual life, for here

> someone knows himself to fail in comprehending him [God] perfectly because of his greater perfection, and *perfect ignorance is the cognition of him who is above all that are known*, namely of God. And so, it is clear that he [Dionysius] does not intend that God is not seen in any way, but that he is seen in the very ignorance of himself.[212]

In other words, negations bring about a union with God that does not fully transcend all divine names, but always includes an awareness of their limitations. Albert also implies that the act of judgment that we do not comprehend God can be realized on a hierarchy of stages. Perfect ignorance comes after having learned precisely how to affirm and remove all divine names. We can know more or less perfectly how far the divine reality is above our understanding. Thus not all in grace who know that they do not comprehend God have attained divine union in negations.

Albert's twofold interpretation of uniting negations based on the Plotinian statue confirmed by my fourfold consideration of the function of negations leads to certain conclusions concerning his doctrine of union. The divine light received in the *habitus* of faith precedes and always accompanies the intellect's union with God. Such union is realized through the most perfect knowledge of God possible in this life, a process that unfolds by the faithful reception of divine truth concealed in the Scriptures. Because of its concealed nature, such truth shines through negations and not just through affirmations. The intellect's union with God occurs in negations, not beyond them. Negations unite because they correct the perpetual human tendency to misunderstand God's self-revelation (negations remove the error of univocity) and in their eminent mode better manifest the intelligibility of God's biblical names. The second type of uniting negations mentioned earlier directs the mind to the real similitude between divine and created perfections. Negations simultaneously signify that God's perfections are always infi-

---

212. *SEP 1*, p. 482.35–40: "*Et perfecta ignorantia secundum melius* ignorati, idest in hoc quod aliquis cognoscit se perfecte deficere a comprehensione eius propter sui melioritatem, *est cognitio eius qui est super omnia quae cognoscuntur*, scilicet dei. Et sic patet, quod non vult, quod nullo modo videatur deus, sed quod in ipsa sui ignorantia videtur."

nitely greater than anything we know from his effects. Negative names aid the mind to refuse the futile attempt to represent God adequately via created perfections. Negations offer positive noetic content about God's nature by their implied eminent affirmations, yet also highlight the radical limits of such knowledge. Thus the intellect is left in a certain confusion, though not in absolute obscurity. Unlike Dionysius, Albert's darkness attained by negations does not shut down the contemplation of finite perfections. Rather, Albert reorders the contemplative function of these perfections. His negations have a more kataphatic character than the Areopagite's transcending negations (*aphaireseis*), a parallel to Albert's discussion of created effects mediating Moses's cognition of God on Mt. Sinai. As in Dionysius, Albert's negative knowledge is not the knowledge of nothing. But in contrast to Dionysius, Albert's knowing by unknowing is not received by an overwhelming influx of new divine light at the summit of contemplation. Rather, we attain unitive knowledge by penetrating to the divine light still partly concealed in biblical mediations. We can proceed on this path because of the previous infusion of God's light in the gift of faith as well as the correct understanding of the negations whereby the light of truth transmitted in the Scriptures is grasped as fully as possible. Albert's negations take on the function that Dionysius had assigned to God's light on Mt. Sinai. Albert's hierarch is not a bishop who unveils the hidden meaning of liturgical symbols and liturgically proclaimed Scriptures, but the scholastic theologian who, in faith, has learned the proper distinctions. Albert himself is the hierarch for his Dominican students in Cologne. Because by its nature cognition unites the intellect with the known, and since negations transmit the highest knowledge about God, negations unite. We are witnessing the birth of a theologian's mysticism.[213]

CONCLUSION

According to Albert's *Commentary on the Mystical Theology*, the highest union with God in this life comes through living faith and nega-

---

213. The notion that the acquisition of theological wisdom by study leads to deeper union with Christ has roots in Basil of Caesarea, Augustine, and other early Christian writers; see Basil Studer, *Schola Christiana: Die Theologie zwischen Nizäa und Chalcedon* (Munich: Ferdinand Schöningh, 1998), 15–18.

tions that together lead the mind to the fullness of the pilgrim's divine knowledge. Three final considerations are in order. First, I will compare Albert's new theology to the *Sentences Commentary* teaching on union through charity and the Spirit's seven gifts, especially in light of Édouard Wéber's and Bernard McGinn's readings of Albert. Second, I will point to a few doctrinal consequences of and lingering ambiguities in Albert's early Cologne mysticism. Third, I will return to this study's main thesis and consider in what way the present chapter demonstrates each of its parts.

Wéber argues that the light of faith alluded to in the preface of the *Commentary on the Mystical Theology* begins the mystical science, while unifying knowledge reaches perfection in the Spirit's gift of wisdom. He seems to synthesize Albert's Parisian and early Cologne mystical theologies. Wéber explains that the divine light that leads to union is the eternal Word's gift of himself who, sent to us by the Father through gifts of wisdom, breathes the Spirit into us. He invokes the consequences of the theology of the Spirit's procession from the Father and the Son for the missions and implies that every intensification of the gift of light includes a new gift of the Son, who, as the Word spirating love, always imparts a new gift of the Spirit. Wéber also suggests that, for Albert, knowing by unknowing directly results from inspired wisdom.[214]

Albert's theology of divine light in the *Commentary on the Mystical Theology* is open to Wéber's interpretation. However, Albert does not provide adequate indications that he intends to identify divinizing light with the gift of wisdom. Wéber's judgment seems premature for three reasons. First, while the light of the mystical science as described in the preface of the commentary and elsewhere bears close linguistic and doctrinal parallels to the light of faith as expounded in the Dionysian commentaries and in Albert's previous works, few linguistic or doctrinal affinities emerge between union passages in those commentaries and the gift of wisdom. The discussions of Hierotheus in the *Commentary on the Divine Names* and in a single passage of the *Commentary on the Mystical Theology* do not mention the Spirit's gift of wisdom. Nor do the expositions of union in the latter commentary

---

214. Wéber, introduction to Albertus Magnus, *Commentaire de la "Théologie mystique,"* 36–38, 49; de Libera follows Wéber on this point in *Raison et foi*, 274.

include key wisdom terms such as "tasting God in his gifts," "tasting divine sweetness," or "suffering divine things." Albert only makes one passing reference to the Spirit's gifts in his Dionysian commentaries.[215] Also, when he comments on Moses in darkness, Albert mentions that the patriarch knows God through his gifts—language that might imply the gift of wisdom. But the latter always includes knowledge attained by a newly infused light, whereas it is not clear that Albert's Moses advances by receiving a higher grace.

Second, Albert does not explicitly espouse the notion that, due to the Spirit's eternal procession from the Son, every new mission of the Son brings a new gift of the Spirit (by a more intense *habitus* of charity). Chapter 3 signaled that the *Sentences Commentary* implies an inseparable link between the two missions, but for different reasons. My analysis of the missions in the *Commentary on the Celestial Hierarchy* showed that Albert identifies Dionysian light with the Son's mission in the intellect and the Spirit's mission in the will. Albert does not explicitly unfold an important doctrinal consequence of the Spirit's double procession for the theology of the missions—namely, that mystical ascent consistently involves proportionate progress in both cognition and love. In fact, Wéber's interpretation really applies to Thomas.

Third, returning to my last comment on Moses, Albert consistently explains ascent to God through the infusion of divine light that surpasses nature and the cognition offered by negations. Since the light whereby Moses encounters God in darkness is simply "above nature," it remains indistinguishable from faith. Albert does not clearly refer to a new infusion of divine light, but rather to a single divine light that makes contemplative perfection possible. The only evident difference between Moses and those who have not entered divine darkness consists in the cognition attained by negations. Nothing in the Dionysian commentaries excludes intertwining a gradual intensification of infused wisdom with the methodical application of negations as the way toward union, but it is not clear that this is Albert's intention.

McGinn interprets union in the Dionysian commentaries in a way that is similar to Wéber. While acknowledging that mystical knowledge remains grounded in faith, McGinn identifies a distinct, higher gift of

---

215. On Hierotheus, see *SDN*, ch. 2, no. 76, pp. 91.58–92.36; *SMT*, ch. 1, p. 458.54–62. For the Spirit's seven gifts, see *SCH*, ch. 6, pp. 85.82–86.5.

light as the direct source of such knowledge so that the latter takes on an experiential character. McGinn builds his conclusion on two key texts related to Hierotheus: the passage on suffering divine things in the *Commentary on the Divine Names* and the hierarch's sole appearance in the *Commentary on the Mystical Theology*.[216] McGinn correctly identifies Hierotheus as exemplifying a balance of knowledge and love in mystical *ascent*. In his comments on suffering divine things, Albert twice mentions the term "experience," first as enabling knowledge of divine things, then as granting a perception of divine things.[217] In the *Commentary on the Divine Names* Albert indeed espouses a notion of union through experiential knowledge. But the language of experience barely emerges in the *Commentary on the Mystical Theology*. We only find it in Albert's discussions of spiritual joy and of the requirements for teachers and students of the mystical science. For the first theme Albert mostly focuses on the need to transcend divine signs whereby we experience God.[218] The second theme brings us back to Hierotheus in the *Commentary on the Mystical Theology*. Albert notes that, since the mystical science is not a philosophy based on the principles of reason, it involves the reception of divine things "by a certain experience through *compassion with them*," as in the case of Hierotheus. Therefore, he whose will (*affectus*) has been corrupted by an illicit love cannot really possess this knowledge, for he "fail[s] in the cognition, that is [attained] by experience."[219] Albert here lays out the essential precondi-

---

216. McGinn, *Presence of God*, vol. 4, *Harvest of Mysticism*, 20–21. De Libera also considers "unitive experience" to be central for mystical contemplation and Hierotheus as Albert's model mystic in the *SMT*; de Libera, *Raison et foi*, 272–74, 468. Similar readings are found in Hoye, "Mystische Theologie," 588; Meis, introduction to Albertus Magnus, *Sobre la Teología Mística*, 28; and Wéber, introduction to Albertus Magnus, *Commentaire de la "Théologie mystique,"* 15.

217. *SDN*, ch. 2, no. 76, p. 91.66–68: "ex affectione circa divina multa sibi divinitus revelata sunt, quae quasi per experientiam cognovit"; p. 92.29–30: "quodam experimento sic percipiuntur divina."

218. *SMT*, ch. 1, p. 461.16–30.

219. *SMT*, ch. 1, p. 458.54–62: "divina non accipiuntur per principia rationis, sed quodam experimento per *compassionem ad ipsa*, sicut de Hierotheo dicit Dionysius, quod didicit divina *patiendo divina*. Sed affectus infectus illicito rerum amore non sentit dulcedinem divinae inspirationis, et ideo deficiente cognitione, quae est per experimentum ... realem scientiam non habet, quae est pars beatitudinis." I disagree with Allegro and Russino that this passage signals a negative approach to *affectus* in the *SMT*; Allegro and Russino, introduction to Albertus Magnus, *Tenebra luminosissima*, 21.

tions for the communication of mystical theology and distinguishes this theology from philosophy. Charity must order the heart of teacher and student. A certain experiential knowledge made possible by infused love is crucial *to enter into* the mystical science. However, in this passage Albert says nothing about union, and he never returns to the theme of experiential knowledge in the rest of his commentary. Rather, negations unite the intellect to God. For Albert Moses as the model of negative knowing is the mystic *par excellence* (read through chapter 2 of the *Mystical Theology*). Albert's hermeneutical choice, which partly follows the Areopagite's intention, has significant doctrinal consequences. I thus turn to the second part of my conclusion.

Like Dionysius in the *Mystical Theology*, Albert's lectures on that work leave love in the background. In fact, Albert's emphasis on union through knowledge parallels much of the Greek patristic tradition. He largely ignores the *Sentences Commentary* doctrine of union through charity, the Spirit's seven gifts, and the Spirit's fruits and the beatitudes as he focuses on a theology of hidden union by negative cognition[220]—that is, the wisdom acquired by the careful study of God's names and the Areopagite's inspired writings, always in the context of the life of charity and the practice of the moral virtues and asceticism, directly leads to the highest union with God in this life. Albert offers a mysticism for theologians, though without ever rejecting his previous doctrine centered on charity and the Spirit's seven gifts. Study of God's word sanctifies the soul! Albert reinforces this doctrine by his frequent insistence that *all* negations must be traversed so as to attain union.[221] By essentially ignoring charity in the *Commentary on the Mystical The-*

---

220. Wéber sees a development in Albert's mysticism toward an emphasis on intellect, but his remarks focus on an evolution in the theology of faith; Wéber, "L'interprétation," 435. For Anneliese Meis, the *SMT* grants love an all-important place and integrates Gregory the Great's notion *amor ipse notitia est*, two claims that lack foundation in Albert's Dionysian commentaries; see Meis, "La influencia de Gregorio Magno en Alberto Magno: *Super Dionysii Mysticam Theologiam et Epistulas*," *Teologia y Vida* 51 (2010): 355, 362–63.

221. *SMT*, ch. 1, pp. 454.81–83, 457.13–30, 462.17; ch. 2, pp. 465.44, 467.84–85; ch. 3, p. 471.13–18; ch. 5, p. 474.25–26. Albert's occasionally reductive readings of the Dionysian text on other themes partly confirm that these positive references to the necessity of removing all names from God reflect Albert's personal theology. He could have applied a more reductive reading to Dionysian texts on removing all divine names, but he chose not to do so.

ology, Albert proposes a mystical ascent that becomes almost the exact opposite of Gallus's affective Dionysianism, though without ever mentioning the Victorine canon.[222]

Albert's work on the *Mystical Theology* contains important doctrinal consequences and abiding ambiguities. First, his new theology may bear some elitist traces.[223] For who can possibly understand the obscure teaching of the *Mystical Theology* without sitting at the feet of a scholastic master, a hierarch who no longer preaches liturgical sermons but especially teaches in the *studia* for the most gifted friars? It is not clear that Albert realized this potential consequence of his new mystical doctrine. Might this disadvantage of the evolution in his thought have encouraged Aquinas to propose an infused negative divine knowledge through the Spirit's gift of understanding available to all the faithful, or Eckhart's apophatic preaching to the laity?

However, since the Dionysian commentaries never directly critique the *Sentences Commentary* doctrine of the Spirit's seven gifts, the early Cologne Albert remains open to a mystical theology that sidesteps any spiritual elitism. Indeed, the *Commentary on the Mystical Theology* does not claim that ascent by negations is the only way to perfect union with God. Albert's mysticism for theologians hardly minimizes the need for the sacraments. It is striking that the German friar chose to comment on the *Ecclesiastical Hierarchy*, a decision that was hardly imposed on him. This commentary frequently recalls the human need for sacramentally mediated grace on the path to union with the Father.[224]

Second, Albert's reinsertion of created lights in the darkness of Mt. Sinai may open the door to a doctrine of union through cognition that goes beyond the negation of biblical names. In his explicit statements Albert consistently attributes the summit of noetic union with God to efficacious negations in the context of illumination (or faith). Albert's Moses beholds God through graces and theophanies. This indirect vision always accompanies the intellect in the act of negation.

---

222. Wéber, "L'apophatisme," 384, goes too far in claiming that Albert consciously opposes Gallus. This may be the case, but the textual evidence remains inadequate.

223. Trottmann detects a similar problem in the approach to theological contemplation in Albertus Magnus's *Super Ethica: Commentum et Quaestiones*; Trottmann, *Vision béatifique*, 255.

224. E.g., *SCH*, prologus, p. 2.19–27; *SHE*, ch. 2, pp. 26.59, 28.33–42, 30.58–61, 31.69–32.4, 39.66–68; ch. 3, p. 58.27–30.

In his explanations of Bartholomew and knowledge in darkness, Albert refers to divine lights sent by God under which the divine object is seen (fusing knowledge in darkness and knowledge mediated by the lights of the "holy summits").[225] But if God manifests himself by gifts of grace, then it seems that one could advance toward union not just by negations, but also by the higher knowledge implied in the indirect vision of God that comes through created grace, for graced knowledge causes union. In the context of the theology of grace found in the Dionysian commentaries, such interior divine manifestations almost certainly refer to the knowledge of God in the missions, specifically in the intensification of the *habitus* of faith and charity and perhaps also in the gift of wisdom. Might negations not also be applicable to these interior manifestations, negations that recall that the created signs of the new trinitarian missions are not God, for the Trinity's mode of wisdom and love is eminently greater than anything we perceive? The text is open to an interpretation of biblical negations being complemented by negations qualifying the knowledge communicated through these mediating lights, though Albert does not elaborate on this matter. This ambiguity offers the possibility of a more Augustinian understanding of Albert's Dionysian mysticism. It also enables an interpretation of Albert that moves away from its potentially elitist tendencies, though it also moves away from Scripture as the constant mediating object of knowledge. Wéber's and McGinn's explications of divine light in Albert seem to develop these possibilities of the *Commentary on the Mystical Theology*. Earlier in this chapter we saw that Albert's Dionysian commentaries include a doctrine of ecstatic faith that can ground a mysticism for all believers. His remarks on various graces as mediating lights for Moses harmonize well with that doctrine. At the same time, these lights can enable a theology of noetic ascent that is available to all in grace. This is significant, since a mysticism for all believers tends to emphasize contemplative ascent by love (as in Thomas Gallus and Bonaventure). However, Albert does not clearly make the connection between ecstatic faith, union for all, and graces as mediating lights.

Third, the theology of created grace as concretized in the virtues (especially faith) and the doctrine of the *imago*'s actualization through the active imitation of the triune God emerge as two of the three most

225. *SMT*, ch. 1, pp. 461.7–14, 461.71–462.11, 464.38–61.

important elements of Albert's hermeneutic for Dionysian union (the third being uniting negations). His commentaries on the Areopagite leave no doubt that finite grace must always be thought of in relation to the divine missions. Albert's Augustinian-Aristotelian approach to the soul's operations in turn demands finite objects of contemplation in darkness, which seems to lead to a more kataphatic understanding of Moses's knowledge. But one can also ask if the reinsertion of finite noetic lights in the event of union does not also suggest a new apophatism, since the created lights both reveal and conceal the Son and the Spirit sent therein. Albert's Moses *encounters* God himself in darkness, but only *sees* him in the veil of finite graces. Union *must* involve not just a created gift but also God himself joining us to himself, yet the immediate vision of divine light transcends the pilgrim's state. In some ways Albert emphasizes the distance between our knowledge and God's more than Dionysius. Albert appropriates much of the Dionysian emphasis on the obscure nature of knowing by unknowing in conscious opposition to the dominant, more kataphatic Augustinianism of his day— that is, Albert expounds on the content of the *imago*'s sanctifying acts in a very Dionysian fashion, for here negations and obscure knowledge stand at the center. In this sense the doctrine of created grace (perfecting the *imago*) takes on a somewhat Dionysian character.[226]

Fourth, Albert's Dionysian mysticism has no place whatsoever for Augustinian memory. His astounding rejection of Augustinian knowledge by an object's interior presence in favor of Aristotelian information signals a radically reduced function for memory within his mystical theology. Ascent by divine names essentially replaces the quest for the God hidden within. Memory has virtually disappeared from the anthropology of Albert's Dionysian commentaries. Furthermore, starting in the *Sentences Commentary*, Albert assigns to the agent intellect some of the functions that Augustine attributed to memory. As we saw earlier, the *Commentary on the Divine Names* continues this trajectory with a fusion of Dionysian circular motion, Augustinian interiority,

---

226. Lévy maintains that Albert treats the uncreated in a static manner and conforms Dionysius to Aristotle and Augustine. Lévy does not account for the complexity of Albert's synthesis, especially the non-Augustinian anthropology of the Dionysian commentaries, or the essentially dynamic character of the missions; Lévy, *Créé et l'incréé*, 485.

and an individualized Averroist agent intellect. According to one isolated passage, the soul ascends to God by a simple gaze upon its own agent intellect. But Albert never integrates this text into the theology of union of his *Commentary on the Mystical Theology*. Thus even Albert's Peripatetic version of Augustinian memory remains peripheral to his Dionysian mysticism. Certain unresolved tensions linger in Albert's Dionysian commentaries.

Fifth, Albert's constant emphasis on the grace-nature distinction to explain Dionysian union, the explicitly theological character of his Dionysian commentaries, and the centrality of revealed divine names as the ladder toward union demonstrate the impossibility of reducing Albert's early Cologne mysticism to a philosophical ascent of the mind to God or separate substances in abstraction from the Christian mediations of Scripture and the sacraments.[227] In fact, the most distinctive, major characteristic of Albert's doctrine of union is its astounding emphasis on the power of biblical divine names, which even surpasses the Areopagite's insistence on their importance, since Dionysian negations do not unite. In addition, nothing in the *Commentary on the Mystical Theology* contradicts the clear teaching of Albert's *Commentary on the Ecclesiastical Hierarchy* concerning the unitive power of the Eucharist. In the latter work Albert explains that perfect communion with Christ (in his humanity and his divinity) only comes through the Eucharist, for even the other sacraments cannot effect such perfect union.[228] This Eucharistic doctrine remains a constant presupposition in Albert's theology of ascent via negations, an ascent grounded in the grace-nature

---

227. Flasch contrasts Albert's doctrine of noetic ascent through philosophical learning with a Thomistic doctrine of ascent built upon the grace-nature distinction; Flasch, *Meister Eckhart*, 69, 84–85. Flasch fails to mention that the latter approach is key to noetic ascent in Albert's Dionysian commentaries. Similarly, Loris Sturlese's study of noetic perfection via philosophy in Albert ignores the Dionysian commentaries and other key theological texts (e.g., the *Sentences Commentary* and the late *Summa theologiae*). Sturlese thus fails to place the teaching of *intellectus adeptus* in relation to Albert's doctrine of noetic union with God by grace and theological cognition; see Sturlese, *Vernunft und Glück: Die Lehre vom "intellectus adeptus" und die mentale Glückseligkeit bei Albert dem Großen*, Lectio Albertina 7 (Münster: Aschendorff, 2005).

228. *SEH*, ch. 3, p. 55.40–48. Flasch contrasts Albert's notion of contemplative ascent with that of Aquinas and suggests that Albert's works manifest little interest in the sacraments; Flasch, *Meister Eckhart*, 85. Flasch never mentions the German friar's *Commentary on the Ecclesiastical Hierarchy*.

distinction and the *imago Trinitatis*. The theologian on the path of mystical ascent still needs the hierarch.

Sixth, Albert does not posit a new grace as the cause of Moses's entry into darkness, a lacuna probably related to the relative absence of a theory of actual grace in Albert's thought. In the last chapter we saw the centrality formal flux for his doctrine of grace. Albert has no notion of God directly moving us to acts of faith or charity (without a new or more intense formal influx), nor does his earlier theology of the Spirit's gifts of understanding and wisdom propose that the Spirit moves in *our* noetic operations. On this theme Aquinas will go beyond his teacher. Instead, Albert's mysticism posits negations as the path to allow the luminosity virtually contained in the *habitus* of faith (joined to charity) to shine forth. These cognitive acts of negating actualize the faith *habitus* that begins the mystical science.

The present chapter confirmed each element of my main thesis—namely, that Albert's *Commentary on the Mystical Theology* offers a kataphatic mysticism, emphasizes our enduring need for mediations, insists on the mystic's active cooperation, and proposes a trinitarian structure for union, all the while retaining a limited apophatism, an intellect-centered approach, and the immediacy of God's unifying action. I now turn to the points of this thesis in detail.

First, Albert consistently promotes a kataphatic reading of Dionysius. He posits a plethora of qualifications for the Areopagite's most apophatic sayings: (1) union does not shut down divine naming; (2) negations remove neither the divine reality signified, nor substantial predications of God, nor eminent names whose intelligible content derives from creation and the salvific economy; (3) Albert's mystic can communicate his wisdom, for its realization comes by finite graced acts of naming God, not the inrushing of ineffable light that fills the silent mind. Patient textual analysis of apparently contradictory Albertian texts on affirmations and negations, both in this chapter's section on analogy and in the section on union, enabled the recognition of this kataphatism. I thus challenge the common scholarly assumption that Albert proposes an apophatic vision of perfect contemplation.

Second, the mystic's constant cognitive dependence on mediations emerged in many ways, of which I will mention four. First, we saw that positive names have an unsurpassable function in the practice of negative naming. Indeed, the unitive function of qualified negations shows well the importance of mediations: when the mind removes imperfections from God, it is joined to him in a deeper way, all the while contemplating God through the created perfections that enable positive divine names. Second, the negations essentially qualify the names of God transmitted in Scripture, even though philosophy is not excluded from divine naming. Indeed, the negations allow the full intelligibility of God's names contained in the sacred page to burst forth. Albert offers a mysticism centered on Scripture. Third, the importance of mediations surfaced in Albert's way of inserting created lights of grace at the summit of Mt. Sinai. Fourth, Albert's silence on Augustinian memory in the Dionysian commentaries indirectly revalorizes mediations. This silence gained new significance in light of the epistemology of the *De homine* that was analyzed in chapter 3. In the latter work Albert already heavily modifies the doctrine of memory. At Cologne the Dionysian text seems to inspire the German friar to take an even greater distance from Augustine's conception of the *imago*. The result is a greater need for corporeal mediations such as Scripture and material creation in noetic ascent.

Third, the mind's active participation within union emerged often in the *Commentary on the Mystical Theology*, starting with the prologue discussion on the light that grounds the mystical science. Since this light is the faith *habitus* that joins us to God, noetic silence is not necessary for union. The identity of this light surfaced only with the help of the previous analysis of faith in the *Sentences Commentary*. We saw the profound harmony between cooperation in union and the practice of removing imperfections from God. In the latter case only the intentionality shifts as the mystic contemplates God in his effects. Such a shift essentially replaces noetic silence in darkness. Albert's systematically reductive reading of noetic silence in the *Commentary on the Mystical Theology* thus came into evidence. The background studies of created grace and the theological virtues helped to caution against any hasty acceptance of Wéber's link between the elevating created lights on Mt. Sinai and the gift of wisdom. In other words, the graces of the theological virtues already enable the mind to seek union, to *choose* union, without waiting for God's special help, and this precisely by ascending the ladder of divine negations. Only the clear identification of the mystic's intrinsic though graced ability to climb up Mt. Sinai allowed the full significance of the doctrine of union via negations to shine forth. Having seen the lack of a clear reference to one of the seven gifts of the Spirit assisting the ascent of Mt. Sinai, we saw how crucial the practice of negations is, for the proper use of negations causes union in darkness. Here the background study of analogy also bore fruit: the mystic who continues to name God cannot really pass beyond mind and into complete silence, since the latter excludes the act of naming.

The refusal of mystical passivity surfaced again in the studies of the *imago* and the missions. These helped to illumine Albert's doctrinal intention in his reading of the Areopagite's exhortation for Timothy to rise up beyond all intelligible and sensible things: the mystic imitates God through the graced *imago* that actively knows and loves God. The doctrine of the missions ensured that Moses's active ascent via divine negations primarily draws its spiritual dynamism from the divine persons themselves: the mystic's own cognitive operation does not exclude the primacy of divine action. Here and elsewhere we saw that Albert achieved a highly systematic mysticism in his Dionysian commentaries, though not without some internal tensions. Numerous doctrines fit together so well: a kataphatic theology, the mystic's cooperation, the power of the *imago*.

Fourth, the theology of the missions clarified Albert's intention in his references to God's presence within the created lights of grace and glory that Moses sees at Mt. Sinai: created and uncreated grace are hardly mutually exclusive—indeed, they are deeply complementary. Albert thus includes a strong trinitarian dimension in his teaching on union as he comments on the *Mystical Theology:* the missions are inseparable from the created lights that light up Moses's ascent of the holy mountain. Only the background study in chapter 4 of this volume enabled this identification of a trinitarian theme.

Fifth, despite the rather kataphatic tendency of Albert's doctrine of naming and union, he does not neglect the apophatic side of the Areopagite's mysticism. In his interpretation of the patriarch's journey into darkness, Albert does not clearly posit new graces that manifest God and so bring the illumination necessary for union (e.g., one of the Spirit's seven gifts). Rather, the mystic makes noetic progress when he or she attains an ever sharper grasp of the Creator-creature distance. Here we find no references to the visions of celestial glory as proposed in Albert's theology of the Spirit's gift of understanding in the *Sentences Commentary*. In other words, the possibilities of learning about God through contact with him remain firmly limited. In this sense Albert highlights what we cannot know about God. Finally, the emphasis on God's incomprehensibility is massive in the German friar's commentaries on Dionysius.

Sixth, Albert remains faithful to the Areopagite's intellect-centered approach to mystical ascent. Unlike Thomas Gallus, the German Dominican does not insert an extensive reflection on love's ascent as he comments on the *Mystical Theology*. Charity certainly remains essential for union, but we only find allusions to this, as when, for example, Albert mentions the *imago* to explain the Areopagite's exhortation to Timothy. Now the *Sentences Commentary* presents a relative balance between knowledge and love in union (especially in the "treatises" on the missions and the theological virtues). But one question remains: how much of the silence concerning charity in the *Commentary on the Mystical Theology* results from Albert's practice of following the themes of the Dionysian text? I noted how little the *Mystical Theology* says about love. Now Albert's teaching on the missions and charity in various parts of his other Dionysian commentaries cautions against drawing too great a contrast with the mystical theology of the *Sentences Commentary*. However, the doctrine of union via negations in the *Commentary on the Mystical Theology* is truly new for Albert, and this points to an important development in his thought. This new teaching involves a shift toward a new emphasis on the intellect's primacy in union.

Finally, Albert quietly affirms the need for God's immediate action for the realization of the soul's union with God in this life. The uplifting power of faith remains impossible without the action of the Son in his invisible mission. Such faith elevates only when joined to charity, a gift that demands the sending of the Spirit into our hearts. This theme especially emerged in the *Commentary on the Celestial Hierarchy*. However, the primary effect of the missions is the new or intensified outpouring of a supernatural *habitus*. Acts of faith and charity flow from the infused *habitus*, but Albert does not develop a doctrine of God directly stimulating acts of faith and love. That notion will have to wait for his Italian disciple.

Albert's Dionysian mysticism seems to have reached its zenith in 1250. His only major systematic theological work thereafter, the *Summa theologiae*, repeats some of his earlier appropriations of Dionysius on divine naming and eschatology, but uniting negations disappear. The work's theology of union instead centers on the divine missions and created grace, much like the *Sentences Commentary*.[229] The later Albert's other lengthy study of union is philosophical (in the *De Intellectu et Intelligibili*), but here the Peripatetics dominate.[230]

The influence of Albert's Dionysian commentaries in the so-called "German Albert School" and the Rhineland mystics remains a matter of dispute. The Cologne master's favorite student, Ulrich von Strasbourg, certainly mined that corpus. But Meister Eckhart and others may have been far more influenced by Albert's later philosophical works as they developed their mystical doctrines.[231] Indeed, the first significant reception of Albert's Dionysian mysticism came in the works of Thomas Aquinas.

229. Albertus Magnus, *Summa theologiae sive de mirabili scientia Dei I.1*, ed. Dionysius Siedler, Cologne Edition, vol. 34, part 1 (Münster: Aschendorff, 1978), bk. I, pars 1, tr. 3, q. 13, chs. 1, 4–6; q. 14, ch. 1; q. 16; tr. 7, qq. 32–33.

230. Albertus Magnus, *De Intellectu et Intelligibili*, Borgnet Edition 9 (Paris: 1890), esp. bk. II, chs. 8–11.

231. Ruh argues that Albert's Dionysian commentaries marked Ulrich but not other German Dominicans; Ruh, *Geschichte*, vol. 3, *Mystik*, 121–27. De Libera sees a far broader influence; de Libera, *Raison et foi*, 277–79.

PART 3

Thomas on Dionysian Union with God

5

Thomas's Anthropological Synthesis of Aristotle, Augustine, and Dionysius

Aquinas left Cologne in 1251 or 1252, his notes of Albert's lectures on the Dionysian corpus in hand. Thomas walked to Paris in order to begin his term as *baccalaureus biblicus* before proceeding to comment on the Lombard.[1] One of the first distinctions in Aquinas's work on the *Sentences* already analyzes Moses on Mt. Sinai in very Albertian fashion, as we will see in chapter 8. More importantly, Thomas begins to develop his own vision of union through an intense dialogue with Scripture, Aristotle, Augustine, and Dionysius, not to mention his contemporaries. The synthesis that emerges is unthinkable without these sources, yet it only remains coherent because each of them has been reinterpreted in at times far-reaching ways.

Chapters 5 through 7 treat the background doctrines for Dionysian union in Aquinas, as chapter 3 and part of chapter 4 did for Albert. I give preference to Thomas's mature thought, especially since his most extensive remarks on Dionysian union come from his late period. Doctrinal evolutions will be noted. Unlike in chapter 3, I treat the grace-nature distinction first, for Thomas devotes greater attention to it than does Albert, and the distinction undergirds many of Aquinas's other

---

1. Ruedi Imbach and Adriano Oliva, *La philosophie de Thomas d'Aquin* (Paris: Vrin, 2009), 16.

doctrines. Like chapter 3, the present chapter considers the soul's ontology, epistemology, and *imago*. I also treat the psychology of love in a distinct section, for Thomas was the first scholastic to compose a treatise on the passions. The order of themes mostly follows that of chapters 3 and 4. The few changes in the thematic order essentially mimic the structure of the *Summa*, which maximizes doctrinal clarity. The Spirit's gifts in general are treated in this chapter so as not to interrupt the flow of argumentation in chapter 8. Aquinas also devotes much more attention to the gifts in general than does Albert, which calls for a longer study of Thomas's thought. Besides, this doctrine becomes crucial for a proper reading of Aquinas's Moses and Hierotheus. Finally, my study of Thomas adds an interlocutor not available to Albert before the early 1250s—namely, Bonaventure. Thomas's scholastic thought consistently proceeds in response to various contemporaries, including the Seraphic doctor.[2]

THE GRACE-NATURE DISTINCTION IN THOMAS

Aquinas develops his notions of nature and grace in tandem. He operates a synthesis of the Augustinian and Greek patristic traditions, which respectively emphasize grace as the restoration of our wounded nature and divinization as nature's elevation.[3] Aquinas's doctrines of nature as wounded yet not broken and of grace as both healing and elevating provide much of the framework for his broader anthropology. This framework makes his reception of Aristotle possible and partly guides his transformation of the Stagirite.

The grace-nature distinction is not a scholastic invention, for it quietly runs through much of patristic thought, starting with Irenaeus of Lyon's doctrine of the *imago Dei*. Augustine also uses the distinction, though he usually deals with concrete nature, either fallen or graced.[4]

---

2. Bonaventure finished editing his *Sentences Commentary* in 1253; see Schlosser, *Cognitio et amor: Zum kognitiven und voluntativen Grund der Gotteserfahrung nach Bonaventura*, Veröffentlichungen des Grabmann–Institutes 35 (Munich: Ferdinand Schöningh, 1990), xiii.

3. Bernard Quelquejeu, "'Naturalia manent integra': Contribution à l'étude de la portée, méthodologique et doctrinale, de l'axiome théologique 'Gratia praesupponit naturam,'" *RSPT* 49 (1965): 655; Torrell, "Nature et grâce," 167, 199–200.

4. Adalbert-Gautier Hamman, *L'homme, image de Dieu: Essai d'une anthropologie*

Thomas develops this theme partly under Dionysius's influence. When he appeals to the permanence of human beings' or angels' ontological structure after sin, he often cites the *Divine Names:* "some gifts were given to the demons which never changed, but are integral."[5] Behind the Dionysian doctrine of creation's universal goodness stands his hierarchical vision of the cosmos, wherein each being has a determined place. By implication the nature of all creatures remains stable, even if some (e.g., the demons) do not receive divinizing light. A fallen angel's operative capacities are severely limited, yet his nature abides. This element of Dionysian cosmology was ripe for synthesis with Aristotle's intrinsic, unchanging substantial forms. Both types of Greek metaphysical anthropology helped Thomas work out the grace-nature distinction.

The Dionysius-inspired scholastic dictum "grace presupposes nature" was subject to intense debate in the thirteenth century. Bonaventure mostly restricts its meaning to the fact that created grace as an accident presupposes a substance.[6] Thomas grants the axiom a much broader function. I will briefly mention two of the axiom's applications. First, in response to the objection that we know God's existence by faith and thus cannot demonstrate it by reason, Aquinas maintains that Scripture (Rom 1:20) teaches that we can know God's existence by reason, "for faith presupposes natural cognition, just as grace [presupposes] nature and perfection the perfectible."[7] Faith does not replace reason but rather brings it to completion. Second, unlike a corpse whose matter has no natural potency for a resurrected life, "the soul is naturally capable of grace; for 'because it was made to the image of God, it is capable of God through grace,' as Augustine says."[8] The soul

---

chrétienne dans l'Église des cinq premiers siècles (Paris: Desclée de Brouwer, 1987), 64–68; Bernhard Stoeckle, *"Gratia supponit naturam"*: *Geschichte und Analyse eines theologischen Axioms,* Studia Anselmiana 49 (Rome: Herder, 1962), 37–44, 79–84; Van Fleteren, "Nature," in Fitzgerald and Cavadini, *Augustine Through the Ages,* 585–87.

5. *ST* I, q. 64, a. 1sc (citing *DN* 4.23); Quelquejeu, "'Naturalia manent integra,'" 652n63.

6. Stoeckle, *"Gratia supponit naturam,"* 108–9; Schenk, "From Providence to Grace," 311–20.

7. *ST* I, q. 2, a. 2, ad 1: "enim fides praesupponit cognitionem naturalem, sicut gratia naturam et ut perfectio perfectibile"; see also *BDT,* q. 2, a. 3c.

8. *ST* I-II, q. 113, a. 10c: "naturaliter anima est gratiae capax; 'eo enim ipso quod facta est ad imaginem Dei, capax est Dei per gratiam,' ut Augustinus dicit."

is at once naturally receptive to union with God (by created grace) and unable to attain this union by its natural powers. The axiom need not contradict the gratuity of grace. In the background stands Thomas's wisdom theology—namely, the principle that God harmoniously orders his work of creation and salvation.[9]

Aquinas refuses Bonaventure's application of the axiom to the question of Adam's creation. Like the Lombard and other contemporaries, the Seraphic doctor maintains that Adam was first created only with natural gifts and, in a second moment, received sanctifying grace. In one of his three arguments for this conclusion, Bonaventure maintains that God's justice demands a preparation for grace through the human being's virtuous use of reason, meaning by his or her natural faculties.[10] Thomas engages in an Augustinian *ressourcement* and, especially in his later writings, insists that Adam was created in grace. In paradise Adam's intellect and will were wholly ordered to God, his lower powers (e.g., the passions) were fully ordered to intellect and will, and his body was wholly subject to the soul. Through the fall Adam lost his harmonious relation to God and himself, a loss that manifests the graced source of that harmony, "otherwise, it would have remained after sin, since the natural gifts also remain in the demons after sin, as Dionysius says in chapter 4 of the *On the Divine Names*."[11]

God created Adam and Eve in grace because of humanity's supernatural end of divine communion. Because we are rational beings, our intellect is open to all being and our will desires perfect goodness. Since the intellect cannot rest until it knows the first cause of all being, and since no finite good is perfect, no natural end such as philosophical contemplation can fully satisfy mind and heart. In this sense a state of pure nature cannot suffice for the realization of human finality. The desire for beatitude in general only finds its adequate *specification* in the direct vision of God, the one truly perfect good, whose possibility is revealed by grace. Thus nature desires God insofar as it is naturally in-

---

9. *ST* I, q. 62, a. 6.
10. Bonaventure, *II Sent.*, d. 29, a. 2, q. 2c; Stoeckle, "*Gratia supponit naturam*," 113–14.
11. *ST* I, q. 95, a. 1c: "illa subiectio corporis ad animam, et inferiorum virium ad rationem, non erat naturalis; alioquin post peccatum mansisset, cum etiam in daemonibus data naturalia post peccatum permanserint, ut Dionysius dicit cap. IV *De Div. Nom.*" Thomas's general stance has similarities to Albertus Magnus's *SDN* (see chapter 4 of this volume).

clined to beatitude in general, yet that desire is only specified and fulfilled by grace. Supernatural beatitude is our only ultimate end in this salvific economy. We are ordered both to natural ends proportioned to our natural operative capacities and to the supernatural end. Nature prepares the way for ultimate beatitude that grace alone can attain.[12] Finally, a supernatural end that presupposes a natural desire for God with its natural operative structures and ends presupposes and perfects the metaphysics of the natural desire. Thus philosophical considerations have a greater impact on mystical theology than they would in a theology skeptical of philosophical claims about the structure of human dynamism.

Aquinas develops a rather sober doctrine of God's original creation in critical dialogue with his contemporaries and patristic sources: "Of the things that are above nature, one believes by authority alone; hence, where there is no authority, we ought to follow the condition of nature."[13] In other words, when the biblical witness understood via the lens of tradition remains silent, we should avoid excessive theological speculation and pursue rational reflection about the nature of beings accessible to us. For the Lombard, Adam enjoyed an intuitive, nonbeatific cognition of the indwelling God, even without grace. For Bonaventure, Adam received special theophanies whereby he could see God in a nonenigmatic mirror without infused species or images. Both scholastics minimize the role of the senses in Adam's cognition of God. But for Thomas, Adam in paradise knew God by sensible mediations and a ray of divine truth perceived via natural or graced cognition. In each case Adam had a more lucid understanding than we do in our fallen state, given the perfect harmony of his intellect, will, and senses.[14] Still,

---

12. *DV*, q. 14, a. 10, ad 2; *SCG* III, chs. 25, 39, 48–50; *ST* I, q. 12, a. 1; q. 62, a. 2; I-II, q. 3, a. 8; q. 5, aa. 5, 8; q. 62, a. 1; Georges Cottier, "Désir naturel de voir Dieu," *Gregorianum* 78 (1997): 694–97; Cottier, *Le désir de Dieu: Sur les traces de saint Thomas* (Paris: Parole et Silence, 2002), 224–25; Rupert Johannes Mayer, "Stockwerkphilosophie gegen Stockwerktheologie? Zum 'desiderium naturale' bei Henri de Lubac und Thomas von Aquin," *Freiburger Zeitschrift für Philosophie und Theologie* 56 (2009): 169–92; Torrell, "Nature et grâce," 180–98.

13. *ST* I, q. 101, a. 1c: "de his quae sunt supra naturam, soli auctoritati creditur; unde ubi auctoritas deficit, sequi debemus naturae conditionem"; see also q. 99, a. 1c.

14. *ST* I, q. 94, a. 1; Trottmann, *Vision béatifique*, 111–12, 201–3.

because the soul is accommodated to the governance and perfection of the body according to animal life, the mode of understanding which is by conversion to phantasms belongs to our soul. Hence this mode of understanding also belonged to the first man.[15]

Since being is for the sake of operation, the soul is united to the body so that the soul's faculties may work properly. Thus even special illuminations in paradise could only be understood by a return to the senses. Grace elevates nature's capacities yet respects its operative mode. Thomas's doctrine of grace-nature and his exegesis of Genesis move toward a doctrine of mystical cognition that links infused and sense-bound knowledge. For if the grace of Adam and Eve did not suppress the essential function of phantasms for their most illumined noetic acts, then mystical union after the fall likely will not do so, either.

In relation to Bonaventure, Thomas brings Adam's prelapsarian existence closer to our fallen state, for (1) he places a greater distance between paradise and the eschaton and (2) he has a less pessimistic vision of the fall's consequences. He posits three anthropological structures as he explains the effects of original sin. First, our nature did not change because of the fall, as this would involve a change of species. Here Thomas's reasoning is both Aristotelian (substantial forms do not fluctuate) and Dionysian (nature's integral gifts). Second, the fall diminishes but does not destroy our inclination to virtue. Thus the fallen, ungraced will seeks the good, but in a disordered way. Third, original justice is lost. Concerning the second structure, Aquinas greatly limits the possibility of the will's negative influence upon the speculative intellect (the mind's capacity to grasp truth for its own sake). The fall diminishes our virtuous inclinations, but the intellect's moral virtue (prudence) pertains to the practical realm.[16] Thus the practical intellect is more susceptible to disordered appetites than is the speculative intellect.

Overall, Thomas's Greek-Latin synthesis on the grace-nature relation inclines somewhat toward the Orient, not least because of the cen-

---

15. *ST* I, q. 94, a. 2: "ex hoc quod anima est accommodata ad corporis gubernationem et perfectionem secundum animalem vitam, competit animae nostrae talis modus intelligendi, qui est per conversionem ad phantasmata. Unde et hic modus intelligendi etiam animae primi hominis competebat."

16. *ST* I-II, q. 85, aa. 1, 3; Quelquejeu, "'Naturalia manent integra,'" 651. On original sin in Bonaventure, see Schlosser, *Cognitio et amor*, 84–98.

trality of the Dionysian grace axiom that fits so neatly into a predominantly Aristotelian anthropology. The Stagirite's influence especially emerges in Thomas's metaphysics of the soul and in his epistemology.

THE ONTOLOGY OF THE SOUL IN THOMAS

Two doctrinal pillars in Aquinas's anthropology stand out above the rest: the grace-nature distinction and the unicity of substantial form. Aquinas was not the first scholastic to posit the unicity of form, for Albert had already done so in the *De homine*. But Thomas seems to have been the first to follow through on the unicity of form's major doctrinal consequences. I thus begin with substantial form and then proceed to its major theoretical complements: the human being as a "boundary creature," the purpose of the soul-body union, subsisting form, and the soul's *esse-essentia* and essence-power-operation structures. These topics in Aquinas's anthropology (in addition to the *imago*) especially ground his notion of how we know God.

Aquinas develops his unitary vision of the human being in a context marked by dualistic tendencies. Glossed patristic anthologies such as *On the Spirit and the Soul*, which failed to distinguish between the early Platonic and the later, more biblical Augustine, deeply influenced monastic and university circles. Here we find one-sided Plotinian phrases, such as "the soul is a certain substance sharing in reason and apt to ruling a body," culled from the early Augustine. [17] John Damascene's *On the Orthodox Faith*, the Latin scholastics' main gateway to the Greek fathers, refers to the soul as a living essence using the body. Bonaventure and others synthesized the Latin and Greek patristic tendency to split soul and body with Platonizing notions of form. For the Seraphic doctor and Alexander of Hales, soul and body are in some way two substances. Following Augustine's literal commentary on Genesis, Alexander sees the soul as virtually equal to the angels. For Bonaventure the multiplicity of substantial forms and the soul's "spiritual matter" allow for personal immortality.[18] William of Auvergne in-

---

17. Augustine, *De Spiritu et Anima*, Patrologia Latina 40 (Turnhout: Brepols, n.d.), ch. 1, col. 781 (on *De quantitate animae*, bk. 13, ch. 22): "Animus est substantia quaedam rationis participes, regendo corpori accommodata."

18. Emery, "The Unity of Man, Body and Soul, in St. Thomas Aquinas," in *Trinity,*

tegrates part of Avicenna's anthropology as he identifies the human being with the soul.[19]

Thomas's response to his contemporaries begins with a *ressourcement* of Aristotle's substantial form purified of its Platonizing gloss. He corrects Avicenna's overemphasis on the soul as the body's efficient cause or motor, a favorite Bonaventurian theme. Thomas argues that only if the rational soul directly moves *and* informs the body can we account for the unity of the human being in his or her operations, such as understanding, willing, and sensing. The operating subject's unity leads to a vision of the rational soul as incomplete without the body. The soul's operative link with the body is founded upon their form-matter relationship. As in Albert, the unicity of form excludes spiritual matter, as the latter turns the soul into a complete substance.[20]

Aquinas unfolds his anthropology with the Proclan-Dionysian notion of the "boundary creature," a being on the frontier between the material and immaterial realms.

> By the order of nature, the intellective soul holds the lowest grade among intellectual substances; inasmuch as it does not have the knowledge of truth naturally placed within it, as the angels, but must gather it from divisible things by way of the senses, as Dionysius says in book 7 of *On the Divine Names*.[21]

Thomas retrieves the Areopagite's hierarchical cosmology wherein the soul's providential place in creation is located in its union with and dependence on the body. Thus we advance in knowledge gradually via multiple conceptions that are more numerous and less unified than angelic thoughts. Our need to discover the truth about God and creation

---

Church, and the Human Person: *Thomistic Essays*, trans. Therese Scarpelli (Naples, Fla.: Sapientia Press, 2007), 210–14; Wéber, *Personne humaine*, 18–35, 90–119.

19. Roland Teske, "William of Auvergne's Spiritualist Concept of the Human Being," in *Autour de Guillaume d'Auvergne (d. 1249)*, edited by Franco Morenzoni and Jean-Yves Tilliette, Bibliothèque d'Histoire Culturelle du Moyen Âge 2 (Turnhout: Brepols, 2005), 45–53.

20. *ST* I, q. 76, aa. 1–4; *QDDA*, q. 7c; Bazán, "Human Soul," 105; Emery, "Unity of Man," 214–18; Wéber, *Personne humaine*, 102–6.

21. *ST* I, q. 76, a. 5c: "Anima autem intellectiva, sicut supra habitum est, secundum naturae ordinem, infimum gradum in substantiis intellectualibus tenet; intantum quod non habet naturaliter sibi inditam notitiam veritatis, sicut angeli, sed oportet quod eam colligat ex rebus divisibilibus per viam sensus, ut Dionysius dicit, VII cap. *De Div. Nom.*"

by long, arduous experience mediated through the senses and temporality does not entail a cosmic fallenness from pure unity, but the way of life that God's wisdom assigns to us. The human soul's location at the bottom of the immaterial hierarchy of creatures signifies that its intrinsic operative powers are such that they cannot function properly without sense experience. Hence our bodily and immaterial activities remain distinct yet stand in a necessary continuity.[22]

The soul-body union is primarily for the soul's well-being: "It cannot be said that the intellective soul is united to the body on account of the body, for neither is form on account of matter ... but rather vice versa."[23] If the soul-body union is natural, then the soul's natural operation cannot be impeded thereby, since being is for the sake of operation. But then the Platonic theory of innate forms cannot stand. According to Aristotle, Plato attributes the forgetting of the forms to the soul-body union. Yet if soul and body truly belong together and function in relative harmony, then the intellect must begin with a blank slate wholly dependent on sense experience for learning.[24] Here, too, we find a fusion of Aristotle and Dionysius:

The human intellect, which is last in the order of intellects, and most removed from the divine intellect's perfection, is in potency to intelligibles, and in the beginning is "just as a blank slate on which nothing is written," as the philosopher says in *De Anima* 3.[25]

One of the main objections to the unicity of substantial form centers on its problematic eschatological consequences. How can we account for the soul's survival after death if it is a form whose existence apparently depends on the body? Aquinas subtly transforms the concept of substantial form in order to maintain the doctrinal integrity of his position. He argues that the rational soul is not a substance but a subsisting form, a notion unknown to the Stagirite yet developed with the help of Aristote-

22. *DDN*, ch. 7, lect. 2, no. 713; *QDDA*, q. 1, ad 7; q. 7c; Torrell, *Saint Thomas Aquinas*, vol. 2, *Spiritual Master*, 253–55; Wéber, *Personne humaine*, 323.
23. *ST* I, q. 84, a. 4c: "Non enim potest dici quod anima intellectiva corpori uniatur propter corpus, quia nec forma est propter materiam ... sed potius e converso."
24. *ST* I, q. 84, a. 3; q. 105, a. 5c; *SCG* III, ch. 113, no. 2869.
25. *ST* I, q. 79, a. 2c: "Intellectus autem humanus, qui est infimus in ordine intellectuum, et maxime remotus a perfectione divini intellectus, est in potentia respectu intelligibilium, et in principio est 'sicut tabula rasa in qua nihil est scriptum,' ut Philosophus dicit in III *De Anima*."

lian principles. Aquinas refuses Albert's idea of the rational soul as both the single substantial form of the body and a quasi-substance: "And so it must be that the intellective soul acts *per se*, as having a proper operation without communion of the body. And because anything acts insofar as it is in act, it must be that the intellective soul has *esse per se* absolutely, not depending on the body."[26] Operation reveals being, so that the immaterial operation of abstracting universals from singulars reveals both the rational soul's capacity to subsist alone and the fact that its nature remains incomplete without the body. Thomas invokes the principle that a complete nature is a sufficient principle of a thing's proper operation. As the soul (without the light of glory) needs sense experience for its cognition, it remains ontologically incomplete without the body. Personal immortality stands, yet the separated soul's handicapped ontology means that bodily resurrection takes on much greater significance in the theology of Aquinas than in the eschatology of his opponents.[27]

Thomas's doctrine of substantial form goes hand in hand with his *esse-essentia* or *quo-quod* ontology. Thomas's approach differs from that of Albert, who applies the *quo* and the *quod* to the soul's essence. Aquinas states that "in intellectual substances there is a composition of act and potency, not indeed of matter and form, but of form and participated *esse*."[28] All creatures are composed of act and potency. The rational soul as pure form relates to *esse* as a potential principle to its formal principle, thus safeguarding the Creator-creature difference. The soul's essence constitutes the immediate ontological source of its faculties: the agent intellect, the passive intellect, and the will. For Albert the agent intellect flows from the soul's *quo* and the passive intellect from its *quod*, an ontology that grounds the agent intellect's considerable noetic capacities, even independent of abstraction.[29] His student's *esse-essentia* distinction prepares the way for a more sober evaluation of

26. *QDDA*, q. 1c, p. 8.242–47: "Et sic oportet quod anima intellectiua per se agat, utpote propriam operationem habens absque corporis communione. Et quia unumquodque agit secundum quod est in actu, oportet quod anima intellectiua habeat esse per se absolutum, non dependens a corpore."

27. *QDDA*, q. 1c; Bazán, "Human Soul," 97, 103, 115–25; Emery, "Unity of Man," 228–33; Bryan Kromholtz, *On the Last Day: The Time of the Resurrection of the Dead according to Thomas Aquinas*, Studia Friburgensia 110 (Fribourg, Switzerland: Academic Press, 2010).

28. *ST* I, q. 75, a. 5, ad 4: "In substantiis vero intellectualibus est compositio ex actu et potentia, non quidem ex materia et forma, sed ex forma et esse participato."

29. *ST* I, q. 77, a. 6; *De homine*, "Qualiter intelligat," a. 2.2.6c, p. 421.17–24.

the agent intellect's power. In this way Thomas also begins to close off one of the paths of interior noetic ascent to God's light, a path that we encountered in the Albert's *Commentary on the Divine Names*.

Aquinas adopts the Avicennian notion that the spiritual faculties emanate from the soul's essence, partly to emphasize the soul's unity. He combines this notion with an original ontology of the faculties. Unlike Bonaventure, whose methodology grants the exegesis of Augustine's *On the Trinity* a decisive voice, Aquinas proceeds by a metaphysical analysis of operation: "If the act is not in the genre of substance, the potency which is said in reference to that act cannot be in the genre of substance."[30] Every operative potency or faculty is by nature ordered to operation. Hence its mode of being is proportioned to that of operation. Thomas fills a lacuna left by Aristotle as he proposes the new category of proper accidents, situated between substance and accidents in the usual sense, and assigns this category to the faculties. He refuses the notion that the *imago* requires the consubstantiality of the soul's faculties. He reduces the *On the Trinity* statement that "mind, knowledge and love are substantially in the soul" to the fact that mind knows and loves its very substance.[31] Instead, Thomas traces the faculties' ontology from the nature of their operations, which in turn are known by their respective objects. The unicity of substantial form also helps to identify those objects. The human intellect "is a certain power (*virtus*) of the soul, which is the form of a body.... And so it is proper to it to know form in matter."[32] The unicity of substantial form means that the human intellect is naturally proportioned to know the essences of material beings, not the immaterial soul or God. Aquinas develops the soul's ontology in light of our way of interacting with the material cosmos rather than by an analysis of interior acts of self-knowledge or direct noetic ascent to God.[33]

---

30. *ST* I, q. 77, a. 1c: "si actus non est in genere substantiae, potentia quae dicitur ad illum actum, non potest esse in genere substantiae"; see also Wéber, *Personne humaine*, 202–5, 215–20, 225, 230; Schlosser, *Cognitio et amor*, 46–47.

31. *ST* I, q. 77, a. 1, ad 1, referencing *De trinitate*, bk. IX, ch. 4. For proper accidents, see *QDDA*, q. 9, ad 5. Augustine deliberately opposes an Aristotelian ontology of the soul; see Brachtendorf, *Struktur*, 130–47.

32. *ST* I, q. 85, a. 1c: "Intellectus autem humanus ... est quaedam virtus animae, quae est forma corporis.... Et ideo proprium eius est cognoscere formam in materia quidem corporali individualiter existentem"; see q. 77, a. 3c.

33. *ST* I, q. 86, a. 2; q. 88, a. 1; Wéber, *Personne humaine*, 233, 249.

Aquinas synthesizes his Aristotelian development of accidentality with the Dionysian triad essence-power-operation.[34] By its essence each creature enjoys a fixed place in the cosmos, whence it returns to God by the full actualization of its operative powers. Just as *esse* perfects a thing's essence (first act), so operation perfects its faculty (second act). The Dionysian triad, reinterpreted with Aristotle's act-potency and Thomas's *esse-essentia* distinctions, grounds a cosmology wherein each being comes to its fulfillment by its proper operation. The latter insight includes a Dionysian inspiration insofar as it involves a broad application of the Areopagite's principle that the perfection of the higher creatures in the cosmic hierarchy comes through their active transmission of the divine gifts received to the lower creatures.[35] A partly Dionysian metaphysics of perfection prepares the way for the refusal of sheer passivity in the dark cloud.

EPISTEMOLOGY IN THOMAS

At the center of Thomas's epistemology stands the theory of the sensible mediation of human cognition—my first topic. Sensible beings are a source of knowledge because the agent intellect makes their forms intelligible—my second theme. Third, the fruit of the agent intellect's activity is the potential intellect's formal identity with the object known or cognitive union. These three building blocks of Thomas's noetics entail a reductionist reading of Augustinian memory and illumination—my fourth topic. I will conclude with the soul's self-knowledge.

We have already seen metaphysical arguments for the Aristotelian dictum that all knowledge begins in the senses, which Aquinas cites often. For Thomas the alternative epistemologies imply that the soul-body union is somehow nonsubstantial. With the exception of supernaturally infused intelligible species (e.g., a prophetic gift), the senses are the gateway to all noetic content in this life, although *what* we know can transcend physical beings. The quiddity of material things constitutes the intellect's proper object.[36] But Aquinas goes further:

---

34. Wéber, *Personne humaine*, 227–33, 256–59.
35. *CH* 3.2, p. 18.10–17, 165B; *ST* I, q. 75, prologue; q. 79, a. 1; Wéber, *Personne humaine*, 233–45.
36. *ST* I, q. 84, aa. 2–6; q. 88, a. 3; II-II, q. 173, a. 2; François-Xavier Putallaz, *Le sens*

it is impossible for the intellect according to the present state of life, in which it is joined to a passible body, to understand something in act except by converting itself to phantasms.... For we see that with the act of the imaginative power impeded ... the human being is impeded from understanding in act even that about which he grasped knowledge before [the impediment came about].[37]

The ontological reason for our permanent noetic dependence on phantasms is that our intellect's power is proportioned to know the forms of material beings. Even if the intellect receives pure forms, its natural understanding thereof remains confused until cognition naturally attains completion by a return to corporeal beings. Not even grace, with the exception of the light of glory in heaven, overcomes this confusion. Because of the unicity of substantial form (the intellect "is joined to a passible body") and experience, Aquinas refuses the Areopagite's distinction between passionless and impassioned parts of the intellect, a move that turns Dionysian mysticism upside down.[38]

Albert sometimes comes close to this noetics. In his *Commentary on Epistle Nine of Dionysius* he argues that intelligible species directly infused by revelation are *better* understood with reference to phantasms. But Albert's Aristotelian approach to the beginning of knowledge in the Dionysian commentaries does not clearly find its proper complement in an epistemology wherein the act of understanding always remains dependent on the conversion to phantasms for its proper fulfillment after the initial reception of the species. Albert does not systematically apply the principle that our cognitive power is proportioned to sensible beings.[39]

Thomas partly fuses Dionysian and Aristotelian noetics, a synthe-

---

de la réflexion chez Thomas d'Aquin, Études de Philosophie Médiévale 66 (Paris: Vrin, 1991), 119–21.

37. *ST* I, q. 84, a. 7c: "impossibile est intellectum secundum praesentis vitae statum, quo passibili corpori coniungitur, aliquid intelligere in actu, nisi convertendo se ad phantasmata.... Videmus enim quod impedito actu virtutis imaginativae ... impeditur homo ab intelligendo in actu etiam ea quorum scientiam praeaccepit"; see also q. 85, a. 5, ad 2; q. 86, a. 1c; II-II, q. 15, a. 3; q. 180, a. 5, ad 2; *QDDA*, q. 15c, p. 135.319–29; Thomas Aquinas, *De memoria et reminiscencia*, Leonine Edition, vol. 45, part 2 (Paris: Vrin; Rome: Commissio Leonina, 1985), ch. 2.

38. *ST* I, q. 89, a. 3; *QDDA*, q. 15c, pp. 135.319–29, 136.85–95; *DC*, a. 10, ad 7.

39. *SEP* 9, p. 539.3–18 (cited at footnote 15 in chapter 4 of this volume).

sis whereby he develops an account of the nature of revealed knowledge. Here Thomas's *Commentary on Boethius's "On the Trinity"* offers perhaps the best summary, one fully in harmony with the late Aquinas:

> Indeed, according to the [present] state of life, our intellect cannot be immediately carried into the essence of God and into other separate essences, because it is immediately extended to phantasms ... as is said in *De Anima* 3; and thus the intellect can immediately conceive the quiddity of a sensible thing, but not of some [purely] intelligible thing. Hence, Dionysius says in chapter 2 of the *Celestial Hierarchy* that our analogy cannot be immediately extended into invisible contemplations.[40]

Dionysius here justifies apparently inappropriate biblical metaphors for the angels. Such depictions of celestial beings provide a contemplative starting point that befits our limited noetic capacities. Like Albert, Thomas transforms the Areopagite's platform for the *beginning* of noetic ascent into a universal principle: in this life, *all* cognition comes through the senses—even prophecy in a certain way. The same text adopts Albert's interpretation of the Dionysian veils:

> Although by revelation we are elevated to know something which would otherwise be unknown to us, yet we do not know this in another way than through sensibles; hence Dionysius says in chapter 1 of the *Celestial Hierarchy* that "it is impossible for the divine ray to shine upon us except [as] veiled by a variety of sacred veils."[41]

Thomas's Dionysius thus becomes more Aristotelian, a transformation made possible by the Areopagite's Proclan emphasis on hierarchy and mediations. Aquinas develops his position partly out of his harmonious vision of grace-nature: revelation respects the natural human *mode* of

---

40. *BDT*, q. 6, a. 3c, p. 167.60–67, on *CH* 2.2, p. 10.11–16, 140A: "Immediate quidem intellectus noster ferri non potest secundum statum uie in essentiam Dei et in alias essentias separatas, quia immediate extenditur ad phantasmata ... ut dicitur in III *De anima*; et sic immediate potest concipere intellectus quiditatem rei sensibilis, non autem alicuius rei intelligibilis. Unde dicit Dionisius II c. *Celestis ierarchiae* quod nostra analogia non ualet immediate extendi in inuisibiles contemplationes."

41. *BDT*, q. 6, a. 3c, p. 167.99–106, on *CH* 1.2, p. 8.10–12, 121B: "Unde quamuis per reuelationem eleuemur ad aliquid cognoscendum quod alias esset nobis ignotum, non tamen ad hoc quod alio modo cognoscamus nisi per sensibilia; unde dicit Dionisius in I c. *Celestis ierarchiae* quod 'impossibile est nobis superlucere diuinum radium nisi circumuelatum uarietate sacrorum uelaminum'"; see also *SMT*, ch. 1, p. 460.62–74; *DDN*, ch. 1, lect. 2, no. 69; *ST* I, q. 12, a. 13, ad 2; *QDDA*, q. 16c, p. 145.310–20.

Thomas's Synthesis of Aristotle, Augustine, and Dionysius   229

cognition even as its intelligible *content* transcends the limits of nature.[42] The late Thomas employs the same passage from the *Celestial Hierarchy* to qualify an apparent exception to the rule of sensible mediation for cognition. He maintains that even the noetic content attained by the prophetic gift of infused species cannot be properly understood without recourse to phantasms, an argument similar to yet distinct from Albert's *Commentary on Epistle 9 of Dionysius.*[43] For Thomas our understanding of revelation or of the graced presence of the indwelling God remains incomplete without reference to what we learn by the senses, thus to perceptions rooted in our experience of the cosmos.[44] Such analogies remain imperfect and limit the clarity with which we can understand interior revelations in this life. Thomas thus limits the possibilities of what can be learned via infused cognition more than does Dionysius.

Thomas appeals to the Aristotelian-Dionysian principle of the mediation of the senses to argue that the quiddities of immaterial substances (God and angels) cannot be fully known here below. Natural reasoning from effects to causes or from biblical analogies and metaphors (or a combination thereof) enables a partial, vague understanding of "immaterial forms."[45] Like Albert, but in a more explicit way, Thomas recognizes the close link between a noetics of bodily mediation and analogous knowledge of God. He concludes, "We know of immaterial forms that it is (*an est*), and in place of knowing about them what it is (*quod est*) we have cognition by negation, by causality and by excess; which modes Dionysius also posits."[46]

The human mind can understand material beings and through them the immaterial, for the agent intellect has the power to abstract

---

42. *ST* I, q. 1, a. 9; Serge-Thomas Bonino, "'Les voiles sacrés': À propos d'une citation de Denys." In *Atti del IX Congresso Tomistico Internazionale,* edited by Pontificia Accademia Romana di San Tommaso d'Aquino, Studi Tomistici 45 (Vatican City: Libreria Editrice Vaticana, 1992), 171.

43. *QDDA,* q. 15c, p. 135.330–38; *SEP* 9, p. 539.3–13 (cited at footnote 15 in chapter 4 of this volume).

44. *DV,* q. 12, a. 7, ad sed contra 2; q. 18, a. 5; q. 19, a. 1; *ST* II-II, q. 173, a. 3; Bonino, "Le rôle de l'image dans la connaissance prophétique d'après saint Thomas d'Aquin," *RT* 89 (1989): 547–66. At *III Sent.,* d. 31, q. 2, a. 4, Aquinas also posits the necessity of phantasms for understanding, without making an exception for prophecy.

45. *BDT,* q. 6, a. 3c, p. 167.94–117; see also *ST* I, q. 88, a. 2, ad 1.

46. *BDT,* q. 6, a. 3c, p. 168.177–80: "Ita ergo de formis immaterialibus cognoscimus an est, et habemus de eis loco cognitionis quid est cognitionem per negationem, per causalitatem, et per excessum; quos etiam modos Dionysius ponit."

the forms of physical creatures. Aquinas's notion of the agent intellect continues a trajectory found in Albert's early Cologne works. Thomas follows Albert's Cologne teaching that all knowledge comes through information, a quiet refusal of the Augustinian epistemology of understanding by assimilation to an object's interior presence: "In order to know, it is necessary that there be the similitude of the thing known in the one knowing, as a certain form thereof."[47] But Aquinas also restricts the agent intellect's operations to two functions: the abstraction of forms from phantasms for the possible intellect and the transmission of the power of understanding to the possible intellect. The first function transmits noetic content, while the second transmits an operational capacity. Thomas's agent intellect does not impart intelligible forms directly received from God or angels, for the passive intellect directly receives such gifts that are above the order of nature. These species need not be actualized by the agent intellect, for they are already in act. Aquinas quietly bypasses the Parisian Albert's Augustinian-Averroist ascent to the Creator and Albert's early Cologne notion of turning inward to the agent intellect's light. Thomas disengages Aristotle's noetics from its widely accepted Platonizing gloss, including Albert's.[48] Thomas's agent intellect does not mediate noetic union with God, in contrast to Albert and his later German disciples. Rather, an agent intellect brought back down to earth, with the unicity of substantial form as the guiding thread, sets the stage for a mysticism that centers on historical, corporeal mediations and better emphasizes union as a sheer gift of divine love. An agent intellect with more limited intrinsic, operative capacities entails a greater dependence on God's gratuitous revelation.

Thomas's Aristotelian notion of the abstraction of form involves

47. *ST* I, q. 88, a. 1, ad 2: "Sed requiritur ad cognoscendum ut sit similitudo rei cognitae in cognoscente quasi quaedam forma ipsius." For Albertus Magnus, see *I Sent.*, d. 17, a. 4; *SMT*, ch. 2, pp. 466.87–467.11.

48. *SDN*, ch. 4, no. 103, pp. 202.60–203.12; *ST* I, q. 84, a. 4; q. 85, a. 1; q. 88, a. 2, ad 2; *QDDA*, q. 6, ad 6; q. 15, ad 2, 7; Trottmann, *Vision béatifique*, 302–4; Wéber, *Personne humaine*, 316–37; René-Antoine Gauthier, introduction to *Lectura in librum de anima a quodam discipulo reportata*, by Anonymi Magistri Artium (c. 1245–50), Spicilegium Bonaventurianum 24 (Grottaferrata: Editiones Collegii S. Bonaventurae, 1985), 22*: "La tâche historique de saint Thomas n'a donc pas été de christianiser Aristote. C'était fait, bien fait, trop bien fait même: l'Aristote des Artistes n'était pas seulement un Aristote chrétien, c'était un Aristote platonicien. La tâche historique de saint Thomas a donc été bien plutôt... de rendre à la philosophie d'Aristote sa pureté."

neither an instant grasp of a being's nature nor the mere construction of a nature by reflection on a thing's operations:

> The human intellect does not immediately grasp the perfect cognition of a thing in the first apprehension; but first it apprehends something about it [the object], as the quiddity of the very thing, which is the intellect's first and proper object; and then it understands properties and accidents and the relations surrounding a thing's essence.[49]

Without reliable, partial knowledge of a thing's quiddity, we could not know anything. Hence formal identity with the object known constitutes a foundational pillar for understanding. Through multiple perceptions and reflection on a thing's effects or accidental properties, we refine vague concepts into more precise ones. Yet God alone enjoys an exhaustive understanding of beings. A partial apophatism even marks our relation to the cosmos.[50] The Areopagite's gradual, mediated, analogical ascent to eternal truths stands in the background.[51]

The process of abstraction attains a formal identity of the knower and the known: "the intellect in act is the understood in act because of the similitude of the thing understood, which is the form of the intellect in act."[52] To understand a thing is somehow to become one with it. The similitude's content comes from the object known, while its mode of existence is that of the receiving subject, the immaterial intellect. We do not fully become the thing known. Rather, we enjoy an ontological-intentional union via the similitude of the object known, a likeness that is not constructed but received. The mind's blank slate is the precondition for such noetic union.[53] In chapter 8 we will see how Thomas's

---

49. *ST* I, q. 85, a. 5c: "intellectus humanus non statim in prima apprehensione capit perfectam rei cognitionem; sed primo apprehendit aliquid de ipsa, puta quidditatem ipsius rei, quae est primum et proprium obiectum intellectus; et deinde intelligit proprietates et accidentia et habitudines circumstantes rei essentiam."

50. *BDT*, q. 6, a. 2c, p. 164.81–71; *ST* I, q. 86, a. 6; John P. O'Callaghan, *Thomist Realism and the Linguistic Turn: Toward a More Perfect Form of Existence* (Notre Dame, Ind.: University of Notre Dame Press, 2002), 221, 245–49, 267–73; Josef Pieper, *Philosophia negativa: Zwei Versuche über Thomas von Aquin* (Munich: Kösel, 1953), 11–45; Kurt Pritzl, "The Place of Intellect in Aristotle," *Proceedings of the American Catholic Philosophical Association* 80 (2006): 66–69.

51. *DN* 3.3, pp. 142.14–143.2, 684C; Roques, *L'univers dionysien*, 203.

52. *ST* I, q. 87, a. 1, ad 3: "ita intellectus in actu est intellectum in actu propter similitudinem rei intellectae, quae est forma intellectus in actu."

53. O'Callaghan, *Thomist Realism*, 165, 220, 249; Pritzl, "Place of Intellect," 60–69.

Commentary on the Divine Names links formal noetic conjunction with mystical union in a way that significantly modifies the Areopagite's thought.

The unicity of form, our status as a "boundary creature," and Thomas's recovery of Aristotle's agent intellect lead directly to a reductionist reading of Augustine's memory and its twin doctrine of illumination. Memory stands at the center of Augustine's anthropology. Following the Platonic principle that sense cognition cannot provide noetic certitude, Augustine posits the need for direct contact with the immaterial realm so as to grasp truth, especially necessary truth. Since God dwells in memory, contact with his light becomes possible and we can know him in a metaconceptual way. Augustine's Plotinian contemplative ascent involves a turning away from the senses to the inner self and then to God's light.[54]

In the *Sentences Commentary* Aquinas follows Augustine's notion (transmitted by Albert) that God's natural indwelling and the soul's constant self-presence enable a permanent, preconceptual, indeterminate understanding and love of God and the soul. Thomas distinguishes the intellect's simple act of intuiting realities present to it from Aristotle's act of understanding founded upon information. But the *Sentences Commentary* reduces memory's status as a potency to a "property" of the soul rather than a faculty in the proper sense. The indeterminate knowledge of God plays no clear role in the discovery of truth.[55]

In *On Truth* Aquinas also mentions God's preconceptual presence to the mind, but it remains unclear how he integrates such cognition into his overall noetics. The intellect's non-Aristotelian intuition of interior realities disappears from the discussion, and for good. Aquinas places the accent on memory as the habitual retention of knowledge that the intellect receives and employs: specifically, the potential intellect. One faculty understands in act or habitually.[56]

Thomas further distances himself from Augustinian interiority in

---

54. Augustine, *Retractationum libri II*, ed. Almut Mutzenbecher, CCSL 57 (Turnhout: Brepols, 1984), bk. I, ch. 8, no. 2; Crouse, "Knowledge," 486–88; du Roy, *L'intelligence*, 72–73; Roland H. Nash, *The Light of the Mind: St. Augustine's Theory of Knowledge* (Lima, Ohio: Academic Renewal Press, 2003), 77–92, 105–11, 121.

55. Aquinas, *I Sent.*, d. 3, q. 4, aa. 1, 3–5; Merriell, *To the Image*, 73–77.

56. *DV*, q. 10, a. 2c & ad 5; a. 3c. Putallaz points out that the link between indeterminate cognition of self and God disappears in the *DV*; Putallaz, *Sens*, 93n74.

the *Contra Gentiles* and in the *Summa*. Both works cover memory in the section on epistemology, before the study of the *imago*. Thomas determines memory's ontological status with philosophical arguments independent of Augustine's *imago* triads. The *Summa* articles on memory primarily target the Avicennian refusal of immaterial memory. Secondarily, Thomas correctly attributes the notion of the soul's three "powers" (memory—understanding—will) to the Lombard.[57] As for Augustine, "he takes memory for the soul's habitual retention, understanding for the intellect's act, and will for the act of the will."[58] Thomas grasps Augustine's intention, for the latter has no complete doctrine of the faculties as ontologically distinct. As for the teaching in *On the Trinity*, book 10, that understanding originates in memory, this is true insofar as the intellect's "act [is] from the *habitus*."[59] In other words, understanding proceeds from memory when it employs previously abstracted species preserved in the storehouse of forms. Aquinas ignores memory's key function in Augustine's ascent to God, as all cognitive content now derives from sense experience.

Thomas's reformulation of Augustinian memory goes hand in hand with his treatment of noetic illumination. In the *Sentences Commentary* he argues that even those scholastics who suppose a single, divine agent intellect should admit that, in the realm of natural reason,

> the infusion and emanation of spiritual gifts is not successive, in the way of motion, but rather fixed and permanent. Hence, by one spiritual outpouring, the possible intellect is perfected to know all things proportioned to it. The opinion of others is that the agent intellect is a power of the rational soul. And holding this position, it cannot be rationally maintained that the cognition of truth about which we are speaking would require the infusion of yet another light ... unless perhaps we were to say that the agent intellect were insufficient for this [its operation of making the species intelligible in act]. Thus, human nature would be less perfect than other natures since it would not suffice to carry out its own natural operations. Therefore, it must be said that these truths [proportioned to human nature]

---

57. *ST* I, q. 79, aa. 6–7; Merriell, *To the Image*, 115–16.

58. *ST* I, q. 79, a. 7, ad 1: "ista tria non accipit Augustinus pro illis tribus potentiis; sed memoriam accipit pro habituali animae retentione, intelligentiam autem pro actu intellectus, voluntatem autem pro actu voluntatis."

59. *ST* I, q. 79, a. 7, ad 3: "intelligentia oritur ex memoria, sicut actus ex habitu."

can be known through the natural light of the agent intellect, without any super-added light of grace.[60]

Aquinas reduces Augustine's divine light accessible in memory via moral purification to the intellect's abiding operative capacity. Following John Damascene, each creature possesses an active disposition to carry out its natural operation—in other words, to act according to its substantial form. This Aristotelian anthropology also goes beyond the Stagirite, for Aquinas retains the notion of the cognitive power as a participation in God's light, the first cause of all secondary causes, but within a Proclan-Dionysian cosmology of a stable hierarchy of natures, each with relatively fixed operative powers.[61] Thomas's participation metaphysics allows him to reread Augustine's notions that we know all things in the eternal reasons and that divine truth alone makes possible noetic certitude as references to the intellect's reception of its operative capacity from the Creator. Because in this life the senses mediate all noetic content (with the exception of prophetic illuminations), the ascent to the incorporeal realm involves not a turn away from the material world, but rather a cognition of immaterial realities by analogy to the soul's characteristics.[62] We know the latter via the soul's activity in the world. Also, the graced cognition of the God who is not first-

60. Aquinas, *II Sent.*, d. 28, q. 1, a. 5c, 732: "infusio et emanatio spiritualium donorum non est successiva per modum motus; sed est fixa et permanens; unde secundum unam irradiationem spiritualem, intellectus possibilis ad omnia sibi proportionata cognoscenda perficeretur. Aliorum vero opinio est quod intellectus agens sit quaedam potentia animae rationalis; et hanc sustinendo, non potest rationabiliter poni quod oporteat ad cognitionem veri, talis de quo loquimur, aliquod aliud lumen superinfundi ... nisi forte dicatur quod intellectus agens insufficiens est ad hoc; et ita natura humana aliis imperfectior esset, quae non sibi sufficeret in naturalibus operationibus. Et ideo dicendum est quod haec vera, sine omni lumine gratiae superaddito, per lumen naturale intellectus agentis cognosci possunt."

61. Like Albert, Thomas appeals to God's primary creative causality to reduce Augustine's notion of the divine interior teacher to the human being's abiding capacity to know that which is accessible to reason; see Albertus Magnus, *De homine*, "De Intellectu Agente," a. 2.2.3, ad 21, p. 415.25–29; Aquinas, *II Sent.*, d. 28, q. 1, a. 5, ad 3, which refers back to d. 9, q. 1, a. 2, ad 4. The latter passage employs the *Liber de causis*, proposition 1. For Proclus, see Proclus, *The Elements of Theology*, trans. E. R. Dodds, 2nd ed. (Oxford: Clarendon Press, 1963), propositions 173, 177, 194–95; Lucas Siorvanes, *Proclus: Neo-Platonic Philosophy and Science* (Edinburgh: Edinburgh University Press, 1996), 126, 141. For a more complete study of illumination in Thomas, see Blankenhorn, "Aquinas as Interpreter."

62. *ST* I, q. 84, a. 5c; q. 87, a. 1; q. 88, a. 1, ad 1–2; a. 3, ad 1.

known only becomes intelligible by reference to what we know via the senses, the mediated noetic content made accessible by the agent intellect's "fixed and permanent" share in divine light.

Several of the anthropological doctrines mentioned lay the groundwork for Thomas's non-Augustinian theory of the soul's self-knowledge. Like its studies of memory and illumination, the *Summa* develops a theory of self-knowledge largely in abstraction from the *imago*. After recalling that the intellect is a blank slate, Thomas explains:

> But because it is connatural to our intellect according to the present state of life, that it consider material and sensible things, as was said above; it follows that our intellect understands itself, insofar as it comes into act through the species abstracted from sensibles by the agent intellect's light.... Therefore, our intellect does not know itself through its own essence, but through its own act.[63]

Thomas's language shifts from the soul's self-knowledge to that of the intellect, though the article's introduction implies that the former theme remains the main topic at hand. Aquinas follows Aristotle on the soul's indirect intelligibility. We only come to know the soul through its operations—namely, by its engagement with the world around us. In the background stands the real distinction of the soul's essence and faculties, which makes the latter the necessary means to access the former. This approach contrasts with the full mutual presence of the soul's various elements (not parts) in Augustine. As we have already seen, Thomas holds that the faculties manifest their nature via their activity and activity via their objects. Like the early Cologne Albert, Aquinas refuses Augustine's Plotinian principle that the way to self-knowledge is radically different from the way we know the material cosmos. Augustine's soul is naturally self-transparent, so that the senses mostly constitute an obstacle to self-knowledge, though such knowledge increases or diminishes depending on one's moral state. An objection in the same *Summa* article alludes to this anthropology, with a citation from *On the*

---

63. *ST* I, q. 87, a. 1c: "Sed quia connaturale est intellectui nostro secundum statum praesentis vitae, quod ad materialia et sensibilia respiciat, sicut supra dictum est; consequens est ut sic seipsum intelligat intellectus noster, secundum quod fit actu per species a sensibilibus abstractas per lumen intellectus agentis.... Non ergo per essentiam suam, sed per actum suum se cognoscit intellectus noster."

Trinity: "mind knows itself through itself." Thomas responds that such knowledge presupposes the cognitive act. He does not here mention that intellect passes into act via the abstraction of species.[64]

Thomas discusses two kinds of self-knowledge: perceiving that *I understand* and grasping the soul's nature. The soul's immediate ontological self-presence and any single operation actualize the first or particular kind of cognition, though in contrast to Augustine, that operation involves knowing other beings.[65] The second or universal kind of self-knowledge grasps what the soul's essence and faculties are, a process more demanding than the first:

> we consider the human mind's nature from the intellect's act. But it is true that the judgment and the efficacy of this cognition by which we know the soul's nature belongs to us according to the derivation of our intellect's light from the divine truth, in which the reasons of all things are contained.... Hence Augustine says in *On the Trinity,* book 9: "We intuit the unchanging truth, from which, inasmuch as we can, we perfectly define ... how the human mind ought to be after the eternal reasons."[66]

For Augustine, we discover the soul's nature through a process of study that reaches completion in God's light whereby we see the truth contained in the divine reasons or ideas. Thomas invokes illumination but refers back to a passage that reduces it to our *intrinsic* capacity to make truth judgments. Since Aquinas has also essentially transferred memory's functions to the potential intellect's storehouse of forms and has made the pilgrim soul's noetic self-presence depend on the abstraction of forms, he makes knowledge of the soul's nature depend on its engagement with the world. Thomas also ignores Albert's notion that the agent intellect always understands itself and that its light can keep

---

64. *ST* I, q. 87, a. 1, ad 1; see also a. 3; Putallaz, *Sens,* 29–38, 71–74. For Augustine, see Ayres, *Augustine and the Trinity,* 297–302; Brachtendorf, *Struktur,* 128–50.

65. *ST* I, q. 87, a. 1c; Putallaz, *Sens,* 92–104.

66. *ST* I, q. 87, a. 1c: "naturam humanae mentis ex actu intellectus consideramus. Sed verum est quod iudicium et efficacia huius cognitionis per quam naturam animae cognoscimus, competit nobis secundum derivationem luminis intellectus nostri a veritate divina, in qua rationes omnium rerum continentur, sicut supra dictum est [q. 84, a. 5]. Unde Augustinus dicit in IX *De Trin.*: 'Intuemur inviolabilem veritatem, ex qua perfecte, quantum possumus, definimus non qualis sit uniuscuiusque hominis mens, sed qualis esse sempiternis rationibus debeat.'"

the potential intellect in a state of indistinct act. Aquinas systematically closes off every possible path to immediate interiority.

In a way Thomas's epistemology of the self is a return to Aristotle, but it is also a return to Dionysius. The latter displays little enthusiasm for the interior way. Rather, he holds that true self-knowledge is the fruit of and depends on the encounter with God. This encounter occurs via the created and liturgical mediations. Dionysius helps Thomas to integrate Aristotelian noetics into a mystical ascent that largely bypasses the self, except for a reinterpreted *imago*. The early Cologne Albert already traced a similar path, though his refusal of Augustinian interiority often remains implicit, and his Platonized agent intellect complicates his overall stance on interiority. Thomas develops, systematizes, and explicates key elements of Albert's Cologne anthropology.

THE WILL AND THE PSYCHOLOGY OF LOVE IN THOMAS

The Stagirite's central place in Thomas's epistemology does not prevent Aquinas from developing a metaphysics of the will and a psychology of love that synthesize Aristotelian causality, Augustine's insistence on the will's crucial function in the moral life, and Dionysian love as a unitive power. I will first summarize the key elements of the will's nature, especially its relation to the intellect, and then turn to the psychology of love.

Thomas develops a metaphysics of the will in analogy to physical motion. This ontology builds on Aristotle's and the Areopagite's cosmologies. For Dionysius all things desire and therefore move toward the Good. Aquinas notes, "The will necessarily adheres to the ultimate end, which is beatitude ... every motion proceeds from something immobile."[67] The will's act naturally proceeds to the divine actuality desired under the formality of beatitude in general. Revelation specifies this desire's object as the blessing of face-to-face communion with God. Unlike the intellect, whose action attains completion when the object's likeness is in it, "the will's act is perfected in that the will is in-

---

67. *ST* I, q. 82, a. 1c: "voluntas ex necessitate inhaereat ultimo fini, qui est beatitudo ... omnis motus procedit ab aliquo immobili."

clined to the reality itself as it is in itself," so that, in the present state of life, loving God is a higher act than knowing him, and love can be perfect while cognition is imperfect.[68] Starting in the *Contra Gentiles*, Aquinas treats the intellect as a formal cause and the will as an efficient cause. As the will's formal cause, the intellect always mediates the will's object. The intellect specifies the will's act and the will moves the intellect to act (efficiency).[69] The intellect presents the will its object but the will's activation also requires a free judgment, a decision to love or not to love, as no finite good necessitates the will's adherence.[70]

Thomas's psychology of love, which pertains to the passions and to the will, evolved considerably. His *Sentences Commentary* presents the appetite (including the rational appetite or the will) as a passive power first moved by the good as final cause. The appetite's motion reaches its term in an "information." Here love (*amor*) *is* the form of the beloved in the lover. Once received, this form becomes a *principle* of affective inclinations to act.[71] The *Contra Gentiles* shifts away from this early doctrine centered on form: the lover now possesses the beloved by his or her proportion or inclination to the beloved, not as a form at the end of the appetite's motion.[72] The *Commentary on the Divine Names* continues this teaching, and the *Summa* explicates it most fully. Love includes the lover's connaturality or complacency to the beloved. Aquinas equates connaturality with an inclination or proportion to the good or to the beloved. "Complacency" means being exceedingly pleased with the beloved.[73] It is the means whereby the beloved leaves an imprint in the lover: "All that is ordered to something just as to its own good, has that present to it in some way and is united [to it] according to a certain similitude, at least of proportion."[74] Thus the principle of an affective

68. *ST* I, q. 82, a. 3c: "actus vero voluntatis perficitur ex eo quod voluntas inclinatur ad ipsam rem prout in se est"; see also I-II, q. 27, a. 2, ad 2.
69. *ST* I-II, q. 4, a. 4, ad 2; Michael S. Sherwin, *By Knowledge and By Love: Charity and Knowledge in the Moral Theology of St. Thomas Aquinas* (Washington, D.C.: The Catholic University of America Press, 2005), 79.
70. *ST* I-II, q. 27, a. 1c; Sherwin, *By Knowledge*, 71–74.
71. Aquinas, *III Sent.*, d. 27, q. 1, a. 1; Sherwin, *By Knowledge*, 65–70.
72. *SCG* IV, ch. 19, nos. 3559–60; H.-D. Simonin, "Autour de la solution thomiste du problème de l'amour," *Archives d'histoire doctrinale et littéraire du moyen âge* 6 (1931): 187–88.
73. *ST* I-II, q. 23, a. 4c; q. 27, a. 1c; q. 28, a. 2c.
74. *DDN*, ch. 4, lect. 9, no. 401: "Omne autem quod ordinatur ad aliquid sicut ad

union is established between them. Aquinas integrates the Dionysian phrase that love is a unitive power to explain that two lovers are joined by a harmonious inclination.[75] Affective union involves an inclination or impulse that grounds all affective movements to the beloved. The principle of this impulse is the beloved's attracting power. In the mature Aquinas love (*amor*) becomes primarily a principle of action.[76] As a principle, love or affective union effectively causes "real" union—that is, the beloved's full presence to the lover—for love "moves [the lover] to desiring and seeking the presence of the beloved."[77] The beloved's absence induces desire, while his or her presence brings about joy. Aquinas's psychology of love bears fruit in his doctrines of the *imago*, the virtue of charity, and the Spirit's gift of wisdom.

THE *IMAGO DEI* IN THOMAS

The *imago* forms the capstone of the mature Thomas's doctrine of the mystical subject. His appropriation of this Augustinian theme integrates his ontology of the soul and his epistemology. Aquinas's theology of the *imago* underwent a major evolution. I will summarize this development before turning to Thomas's mature exposition in the *Summa*.

The early Thomas reads Augustine's *On the Trinity* through the Lombard and other scholastics. Following the Lombard, Thomas's *Sentences Commentary* doctrine of the *imago* centers on the three "potencies" of memory, intellect, and will as reflections of the three persons' eternal relative properties. The potencies mirror the Trinity in their proportionate relations and in the "emanation" of one potency from another. Aquinas says little about the *imago*'s acts of knowing and lov-

---

suum bonum, habet quodammodo illud sibi praesens et unitum secundum quamdam similitudinem, saltem proportionis."

75. *DDN*, ch. 4, lect. 9, no. 424; *SCG* IV, ch. 19, no. 3566.

76. *SCG* IV, ch. 19, nos. 3559–60; Sherwin, *By Knowledge*, 77–80. *ST* I–II, q. 26, a. 3c precises that *amor* is a generic term. *Dilectio* signifies *amor* with election, and *caritas* means the perfection of *amor*.

77. *ST* I–II, q. 28, a. 1c: "duplex est unio amantis ad amatum. Una quidem secundum rem, puta cum amatum praesentialiter adest amanti. Alia vero secundum affectum.... Primam ergo unionem amor facit effective quia movet ad desiderandum et quaerendum praesentiam amati."

ing God or the place of grace in the *imago*'s perfection. Like Albert, Thomas's *Sentences Commentary* primarily refers to books 9–10 of *On the Trinity* while virtually ignoring books 14–15. Because the *imago* essentially pertains to our fixed human nature, its relation to the divine missions and indwelling Trinity is not fully developed.[78] Union remains somewhat secondary to the *imago* of the *Sentences Commentary*, partly because of its location at the beginning of the treatise on the distinction of the divine persons.

On Truth displays a more direct familiarity with *On the Trinity*, which helps to explain some important doctrinal shifts. Aquinas now locates the *imago* primarily in the acts of remembering, knowing, and loving rather than in the nature of the faculties. The inner processions of word and love thus also gain a more significant place. The soul's ascent to God now stands at the heart of the *imago*.[79] Furthermore, *On Truth* integrates Bonaventure's notion of intellect and will being conformed to God by directly or indirectly knowing and loving him, a perfection enabled by the varying degrees of God's presence to the soul as its object. Thomas clears the way for a fuller integration of the missions and the divine indwelling with the doctrine of the *imago*.[80]

Starting in the *Contra Gentiles*, Thomas develops his theologies of the Trinity and the *imago* by a creative integration of Augustine's notion of the interior word, but in the framework of an Aristotelian epistemology. Inspired by the Johannine Prologue, Thomas deploys Augustine's analogy for the Son's personal property. The analogy centers on the end-term of the intellect's act of knowing rather than the act of understanding itself, for the latter is common to the three persons. This end-term consists of the "interior word," a similitude of the thing understood, a similitude conceived whenever the intellect's act reaches completion. The interior word's content is either a definition or a complete enunciation. This word is distinct from and metaphysically posterior to the intelligible species and the act of judgment. Like the

---

78. Aquinas, *I Sent.*, d. 3, q. 4, aa. 1, 3–4; Merriell, *To the Image*, 10–11, 51–57, 65–66, 84–91, 148.

79. *DV*, q. 10, aa. 7–8; Merriell, *To the Image*, 110–15, 147–49. Augustine employs his various triads to describe the structure of the soul's acts rather than its faculties; see Ayres, *Augustine and the Trinity*, 304.

80. *DV*, q. 10, a. 7c; Krämer, *Imago Trinitatis*, 250–54; Merriell, *To the Image*, 69, 147.

Son, our interior word proceeds from another (the intellect) and represents another (the object known). As an accident, the human interior word remains distinct from the intellect (as an abiding faculty) and refers to the thing understood.[81] The interior word is linked to intelligible forms, but it is meta- or prelinguistic, for, like the intelligible species, it is common to all peoples.[82] Like the abstracted species, our interior word is not the primary object of knowledge, but rather the means to know an object. The word is not a thing but "that in which" we understand, neither a mirror nor a complete entity that mediates between the intellect's act and the object known, but an "intention." It is that whereby the intellect is directed toward the object of cognition.[83] Thus the word as a similitude of the object known is not an obstacle to full noetic contact with that object but a bridge to it. Indeed, the interior word is the principle of union with the known, a notion that synthesizes Aristotle's knower becoming one with the likeness of the known and Augustine's doctrine of the eternal Word.[84] For Dionysius human concepts are ultimately veils to be surpassed. In the framework of a (Dionysian) metaphysics of unity, the multiplicity of concepts constitutes an obstacle to be overcome. But Aquinas sees concepts as ladders of ascent never to be thrown away. Within a (Thomasian) metaphysics of act, concepts as forms do not so much conceal as manifest. Also, "by

---

81. *SCG* I, ch. 53; IV, ch. 11; *DP*, q. 8, a. 1c; q. 9, a. 5c; Emery, *Trinitarian Theology*, 182–85; Emery, "The Treatise of St. Thomas on the Trinity in the *Summa contra Gentiles*," in *Trinity in Aquinas*, trans. Heather Buttery (Ypsilanti, Mich.: Sapientia Press, 2003), 97–102; Emery, "Trinity and Truth," in *Trinity, Church, and the Human Person*, 79–81; Yves Floucat, "L'intellection et son verbe selon saint Thomas d'Aquin," *RT* 97 (1997): 649–90; Harm Goris, "Theology and Theory of the Word in Aquinas: Understanding Augustine by Innovating Aristotle," in *Aquinas the Augustinian*, edited by Michael Dauphinais, Barry David, and Matthew Levering, 62–78 (Washington, D.C.: The Catholic University of America Press, 2007).

82. Tilman Anselm Ramelow, "Language without Reduction: Aquinas and the Linguistic Turn," *Angelicum* 85 (2008): 497–501, 516. Augustine's *verbum* is also meta-linguistic; see Brachtendorf, *Struktur*, 304.

83. *In Ioan.*, ch. 1, no. 25: "verbum interius ... comparatur ad intellectum, non sicut quo intellectus intelligit, sed sicut in quo intelligit"; *DP*, q. 8, a. 1c: "conceptio intellectus ordinatur ad rem intellectam sicut ad finem: propter hoc enim intellectus conceptionem rei in se format ut rem intellectam cognoscat"; see also O'Callahan, "'Verbum Mentis': Philosophical or Theological Doctrine in Aquinas?" *Proceedings of the American Catholic Philosophical Association* 74 (2000): 103–19.

84. *ST* I, q. 27, a. 1, ad 2; Emery, *Trinitarian Theology*, 59, 184.

understanding the intellect conceives and forms the intention or *ratio* understood, which is the interior word."[85] There is no complete act of understanding without the intellect's active role, which completes its operations of abstracting species, making truth judgments and reasoning. For Aquinas, Aristotle's principles and the *imago* exclude a purely passive mode of understanding. A theology of the Son's eternal procession helps to lay the groundwork for a vision of the intellect's perfection in union via active cooperation. A fully passive intellect would grasp nothing, not even supernaturally infused noetic content, as no interior word would be produced.

Aquinas's new doctrine of the word allows him to take full advantage of Augustine's mature solution for the *imago*, with its focus on the processions of the Son and the Spirit in *On the Trinity*, books 14–15.[86] Albert's influence and that of other scholastics diminishes in the late Aquinas's theology of the *imago*. His brief comments on the *imago* in the *Contra Gentiles* already emphasize the double processions, leaving aside the "static" model of the *Sentences Commentary*, and continue the development of *On Truth*, which emphasizes the *imago*'s acts, even though the latter text struggles to integrate fully the notion of the terms of acts.[87] These doctrinal shifts bear fruit in the *Summa* treatment of the *imago*:

The image of God in the human being can be considered in three ways. In the first mode insofar as the human being has the natural capacity (*aptitudinem*) to understand and love God; and this capacity consists in the very nature of the mind, which is common to all human beings. In another mode, insofar as the human being knows and loves God in act or in *habitus*, though imperfectly; and this is the image through the conformity of grace. In the third mode, insofar as the human being perfectly knows and

---

85. SCG IV, ch. 11, no. 3473: "Intellectus enim intelligendo concipit et format intentionem sive rationem intellectam, quae est interius verbum."

86. Edward Booth sees no significant place for the word's conception in Augustine's triadic images; see Booth, "Saint Thomas Aquinas's Critique of Saint Augustine's Conceptions of the Image of God in the Human Soul," in *Gott und sein Bild: Augustins "De Trinitate" im Spiegel gegenwärtiger Forschung*, edited by Johannes Brachtendorf, 219 (Munich: Ferdinand Schöningh, 2000). But Ayres maintains that bks. IX–X of *De trinitate* center on the notion of the production of the interior word; Ayres, *Augustine and the Trinity*, 302.

87. SCG IV, ch. 26; Merriell, *To the Image*, 10, 147–48, 154, 157.

Thomas's Synthesis of Aristotle, Augustine, and Dionysius   243

loves God in act; and thus the image is taken according to the similitude of glory.[88]

First, Thomas restricts the natural *imago* to the human being's potential to know and love God. He respects the biblical teaching that the human being is created in God's image and places grace at the center of that image. Aquinas can synthesize these two elements because actual imitation has become the new standard of evaluation for the *imago's* existence and perfection. This standard constitutes an original doctrine in Latin scholasticism, though it is inspired by Augustine.[89] Second, in contrast to the *Sentences Commentary* and *On Truth*, Aquinas restricts the *imago's* operative perfection to the realm of grace.[90] By implication, the *imago's* perfect realization demands the missions and the indwelling Trinity, for these are inseparable from sanctifying grace. As a rational being, the human person "is to the image of God in the best way insofar as the intellectual nature can best imitate God. Now the intellectual nature best imitates God in this way that God understands and loves himself."[91] Only grace enables a perfect knowledge and love of God, of a triune God imaged not so much in the faculties' existence as in their acts. However, one could ask whether the late Thomas's thought might also be open to the notion of an imperfect realization of the *imago* by the natural knowledge and love of God. Third, neither the long passage just cited nor the rest of question 93 explains in detail "the conformity of grace," yet this clearly includes the intellect's and the will's operational conformity to God caused by habitual grace, the end-term of the missions. As in Augustine, the graced *imago* enjoys an ongoing, partial perfection via its *habitus* of knowledge and love, not

---

88. *ST* I, q. 93, a. 4c: "Unde imago Dei tripliciter potest considerari in homine. Uno quidem modo, secundum quod homo habet aptitudinem naturalem ad intelligendum et amandum Deum; et haec aptitudo consistit in ipsa natura mentis, quae est communis omnibus hominibus. Alio modo, secundum quod homo actu vel habitu Deum cognoscit et amat, sed tamen imperfecte; et haec est imago per conformitatem gratiae. Tertio modo, secundum quod homo Deum actu cognoscit et amat perfecte; et sic attenditur imago secundum similitudinem gloriae."

89. Krämer, *Imago Trinitatis*, 121.

90. Merriell, *To the Image*, 81–83, 149, 186.

91. *ST* I, q. 93, a. 4c: "est maxime ad imaginem Dei, secundum quod intellectualis natura Deum maxime imitari potest. Imitatur autem intellectualis natura maxime Deum quantum ad hoc quod Deus seipsum intelligit et amat." For Augustine's emphasis on the reformed *imago*, see Ayres, *Augustine and the Trinity*, 300–5.

just its acts. Question 93 later refers to the image as a "representation" of the divine processions, which suggests conformity to God's immanent acts—namely, the speaking of a word and the procession of the love of God.[92] Fourth, God must be the object of knowledge and love, a stance that follows from the new emphasis on the dynamic *imago*, for God is the primary object of his own knowledge and love. Thomas soon adds that the *imago*'s dynamism may follow an indirect path.

In question 93 the only significant discussion of memory refers to its function of retaining habitual knowledge. Aquinas now favors the analogy of the eternal processions of Word and Love, so that he largely ignores the triads of *On the Trinity*, books 9–10.[93]

The divine persons are distinguished according to the procession of the Word from one speaking, and [the procession] of Love connecting each. Now the word in our soul "cannot be without actual cognition," as Augustine says in *On the Trinity*, book 14. And so the image of the Trinity in the mind is first and principally attained according to acts, as namely from the knowledge that we have, by cogitating we form an interior word, and from this we burst forth into love ... secondarily, and as by consequence, the image of the Trinity can be attained in the soul according to [its] potencies, and chiefly according to *habitus*, as the acts virtually exist in them.[94]

The soul's mirror for the Father is no longer memory but one who speaks a word and breathes forth love. The *imago* primarily presents the Father as a source of immaterial processions. The *imago*'s noetic procession now explicitly involves not just an act of cognition but

---

92. *DP*, q. 9, a. 9c; *ST* I, q. 43, a. 5, ad 2; q. 93, a. 8c; Emery, *Trinitarian Theology*, 397–98; Merriell, *To the Image*, 187–88, 221. I will confirm this interpretation of the *imago*'s conformity in the next chapter.

93. *ST* I, q. 93, a. 6, ad 3; Merriell, *To the Image*, 208. Ayres seems to suggest a continuous development of doctrine in bks. IX–XIV; Ayres, *Augustine and the Trinity*, 314. Brachtendorf maintains that Augustine's arguments require this hermeneutic; Brachtendorf, *Struktur*, 163–64, 216.

94. *ST* I, q. 93, a. 7c: "Divinae autem Personae distinguuntur secundum processionem Verbi a dicente, et Amoris connectentis utrumque. Verbum autem in anima nostra 'sine actuali cogitatione esse non potest,' ut Augustinus dicit XIV *De Trin*. Et ideo primo et principaliter attenditur imago Trinitatis in mente secundum actus, prout scilicet ex notitia quam habemus, cogitando interius verbum formamus, et ex hoc in amorem prorumpimus ... secundario, et quasi ex consequenti, imago Trinitatis potest attendi in anima secundum potentias, et praecipue secundum habitus, prout in eis scilicet actus virtualiter existunt."

Thomas's Synthesis of Aristotle, Augustine, and Dionysius 245

the formation of an interior word. The image attains fulfillment in the terms of immanent acts, which implies complete operations of understanding and love. Here we find another reason that Aquinas makes actual imitation the new standard of evaluation: the analogy for what is proper to the Son involves the actual begetting of a *concept* in the broad sense (a definition or proposition). Thomas then works backward to show how the "potency" or natural capacity for such terms of acts, the acts themselves, and their respective *habitus* already realize the *imago* in some way.

Love connects the speaker and the spoken, for it proceeds from both. The will's graced act of love realizes the image insofar as the intellect specifies it.[95] Thomas locates the analogy for the Spirit's procession from the Father and the Son in (1) the will's order to the intellect for the object of love and (2) the rational character of the will's virtuous act. "The divine image is attained in the human being according to the word conceived from the knowledge of God and the love derived from it."[96] Not any love for God, but love flowing out of divine wisdom (knowledge that has God as its object) imitates the Trinity and brings us to perfection. This point is crucial. *The ultimate reason for Aquinas's refusal of mystical ascent by love beyond mind is grounded in the doctrine that the Spirit proceeds from the Father and the Son.* Indeed, love beyond mind would no longer constitute an actual image of the Spirit and thus falls short of union, since the image's perfection cannot be attained without an interior word that elicits love. Love beyond mind does not unite, for only love with knowledge assimilates us to the triune God. The Trinity's inner life shapes Thomas's mystical theology on a crucial point.[97] He shows the analogous correspondence of the Trinity's immanent life, the *imago*, and our spiritual life.

---

95. *ST* I, q. 93, a. 6c: "increata Trinitas distinguatur secundum processionem Verbi a dicente, et Amoris ab utroque"; Michael Dauphinais, "Loving the Lord Your God: The 'Imago Dei' in Saint Thomas Aquinas," *Thomist* 63 (1999): 255.

96. *ST* I, q. 93, a. 8c: "Attenditur igitur divina imago in homine secundum verbum conceptum de Dei notitia, et amorem exinde derivatum."

97. As noted at the end of chapter 4, Wéber sees this link between the *Filioque* and the refusal of union beyond mind in Albert; Wéber, introduction to Albertus Magnus, *Commentaire de la "Théologie mystique,"* 37. That connection is not clearly present in Albert, but it emerges in Aquinas, though no one seems to have pointed this out. Consequently, Karl Rahner's critique of the separation of the "immanent" and "economic Trinity" in scholasticism does not apply to Aquinas; see Rahner, "Remarks on the

Finally, just as understanding is completed in the cognition of a word, so the procession of love attains a term. Love for another leaves an "impression" of the beloved in the lover's affect so that the beloved dwells in the lover, a presence that in turn inclines or moves the lover toward the beloved. The *Summa* "treatise" on the distinction of the persons develops this psychology of love as it distinguishes the Holy Spirit's personal name of Love from the essential name of Love that belongs to each of the persons.[98] Yet the theme of the lover's enduring mark in the beloved remains implicit in the theology of the *imago*.

But precisely which graced acts of knowing and loving God perfect the image? Aquinas notes that God must be the primary object of cognition and love for the image's actualization, but he also allows for an indirect path of ascent. The *imago* mirrors the triune life, so that by the *imago* as realized in the soul's self-knowledge and self-love, the mind or soul "can be carried further into God."[99] Aquinas also speaks of the perfection or "likeness" of the image. For an alternative explanation of the classic phrase "the image and likeness of God," he refers to a long Greek tradition represented by John Damascene. According to John, the image stands for our intellectual nature with its capacity for free decision, but "'by likeness [is signified] the likeness of virtue, insofar as the human being can have it.' In reference to the same reality, similitude is said to pertain to the love of virtue."[100] The love and achievement of virtue bring the image to completion. Significantly, the prologue to the *Secunda Pars*, which introduces the whole moral section of the *Summa*, features the same text by Damascene—that is, the *Secunda Pars* ponders the human being as the image of God, as a free, rational creature on his or her way back to the divine source through the exercise of virtue elevated by grace. In the *Summa* section on the New Law, Thomas equates the "love of virtue" with "life in the Holy Spirit." Thus Aquinas strongly implies that the *imago*'s perfection is attained not just by wor-

---

Dogmatic Treatise *De Trinitate*," in *Theological Investigations*, vol. 4 (Baltimore: Helicon, 1966), 77–102.

98. *ST* I, q. 37, a. 1c; Emery, *Trinitarian Theology*, 227–30.

99. *ST* I, q. 93, a. 8c: "mens ... per hoc ulterius potest ferri in Deum."

100. *ST* I, q. 93, a. 9c: "'secundum similitudinem, virtutis, secundum quod homini possibile est habere similitudinem.' Et ad idem refertur quod similitudo dicitur ad dilectionem virtutis pertinere." On the patristic heritage concerning the *imago*, see Hamman, *L'homme*, esp. 72–76, 229–32.

Thomas's Synthesis of Aristotle, Augustine, and Dionysius   247

ship or deliberate acts of contemplation, but through the whole of the moral life.[101] Similarly, *On Truth* mentions charity for one's neighbor (whose principle object is God) and acts of faith, hope, and wisdom as the means to perfect the image.[102] In other words, the entire Christian life involves a constant intensification or diminishment of the *imago's* perfection, hence of union with God.

The mature Aquinas moves far from the reigning scholastic emphasis on the "static" *imago* but also away from Bonaventure's Victorine accentuation of the will in the dynamic *imago's* perfection.[103] Instead, Thomas lays the groundwork for a theology of union by knowledge *and* by love, never one without the other.

CONCLUSION

Partly under Dionysius's influence, Aquinas develops the grace-nature distinction beyond Albert, although it already stands at the heart of the German friar's mystical doctrine. Unlike his teacher, Thomas clearly posits Adam's and Eve's creation in grace, a notion that grounds humanity's call to union with God. This call was not explicit in Albert's theology. Graced union as a specification of the natural desire for beatitude synthesizes a certain continuity between nature and grace with a firm distinction of the two: nature alone does not yet actively desire graced union but is open to it. Aquinas's notion that Adam's paradisal cognition remained linked to phantasms already sets the stage for a mysticism of mediations.

Thomas's development of Aristotle's and Albert's theory of the unicity of substantial form helps to explain his critique of relatively dualistic anthropologies. Aquinas mines the Dionysian theme of the "boundary creature" (and of sensible veils as mediating divine light) to fuse Aristotle with Christian cosmology. This synthesis leads to a greater emphasis on the place of sense experience in cognition, a synthe-

101. *ST* I-II, q. 107, a. 1, ad 2; Dauphinais, "Loving the Lord," 264–66; A. N. Williams, *The Ground of Union: Deification in Aquinas and Palamas* (Oxford: Oxford University Press, 1999), 71–72.

102. *DV*, q. 10, a. 7, ad 7–8.

103. Bonaventure, *II Sent.*, d. 16, a. 2, q. 3: "Imago reformationis respondet imagini creationis; sed imago reformationis, quae quidem est gratia, principalius est in affectiva quam in cognitiva: ergo et imago creationis."

sis begun by Albert. The soul's *esse-essentia* ontology helps to exclude Albert's notion of interior ascent to divine light via the agent intellect as a viable option. The Dionysian triad of essence-power-operation becomes a pillar for the notion that union includes our active cooperation. Aquinas changes the function of key Dionysian cosmological insights, *perhaps* without realizing it.

Grace perfects nature, so that the soul's ontology and its structures of knowing and loving constitute the providential conditions for union with God. Aquinas's insistence on the mind's return to phantasms further de-Platonizes his teacher's agent intellect, with potentially significant consequences for a theory of mystical knowledge. Thomas manifests the close link between the intellect's proportion to the forms of material beings and the centrality of the *triplex via* for our cognition of God. Like Albert, Aquinas mostly leaves Augustinian noetics behind. Less interiority and a much less Platonic agent intellect increase the mystical subject's need for God's gratuitous manifestations, especially in Scripture. The theory of intelligible form includes an ontology of cognitive union applicable to graced knowledge. The virtual disappearance of Augustinian memory increases the need for mediated types of cognition. Also, self-knowledge becomes a far less important component of noetic ascent than in Augustine. It is striking how many of Thomas's anthropological doctrines points to an "externalized" mystical ascent.

Thomas assigns efficient and formal functions to will and intellect, respectively, thus preparing the way for a balance of knowledge and love in union. His psychology of love, which is considerably marked by Dionysius, adds another key component to Thomas's mysticism of love. Love as an inclination or proportion will return in the discussion of Hierotheus and the gift of wisdom. Finally, Aquinas's mature, original theology of the *imago* excludes total passivity in union: the divinized soul actively imitates the eternal processions of the Son and the Spirit. This brings trinitarian doctrine to the heart of mystical theology, even more so than in Albert. Thomas's approach to the *imago* also contains resources for a mysticism of the active life (by the love of virtue), a theme essentially ignored by the Areopagite. Consequently, Aquinas pursues a Greek patristic line of thought that moves away from the Dionysian position that mystical union is a gift reserved for a contemplative elite.

6

Grace in Thomas

Having considered the structure of Thomas's mystical subject, I now turn to the various modalities of God's gracious gifts that enable union with him. As usual, I will focus only on those elements of key doctrines that illumine Aquinas's understanding of the nature of mystical union. With one exception I treat the same issues that I considered in the study of Albert's "mysticism from above" (chapters 3–4): the divine missions, divine action, grace, the Spirit's seven gifts in general, the virtues of faith and charity, and the vision of God. The exception is the study of divine action. In the 1260s Thomas developed a new theology of God's operation that affected his doctrines of sanctifying grace and the seven gifts. The latter two themes become unintelligible without a preface on divine action. I also devote more space to the Spirit's gifts in general than I did in chapter 3, as Albert offers a somewhat sparse doctrine on this point. Special attention to the nature of the Spirit's motion in his gifts is crucial, for the gifts of wisdom and understanding stand at the heart of Aquinas's mysticism. The order of exposition mostly follows that of chapter 3 and of Thomas's *Summa*, which allows for maximum pedagogical clarity.

THE INVISIBLE MISSIONS IN THOMAS

Thomas's theology of union integrates the Pauline, Johannine, and Augustinian teachings on the sending of the Son and the Spirit into the hearts of believers. I begin with some basic definitions. I then proceed to the descending explanation of the divine persons assimilating us to themselves, the missions' term in habitual grace, and the ascending explanation of knowing and loving God as unitive acts animated by the persons sent. I then turn to the inseparability of the missions and ask if the persons are sent with every new gift of grace. I conclude with the experience of the divine persons. Thomas shifts some emphases in his vision of the missions, yet the key elements of his doctrine remain consistent.[1] Thus I will offer a synthetic reading of his *Sentences Commentary*, the *Summa theologiae*, and the *Commentary on the Gospel of John*.

Because of the missions, the Trinity's inner life structures the salvific economy. The Son's and the Spirit's visible and invisible missions are not separate from their eternal processions: "the temporal procession is not essentially different from the eternal procession, but only adds a reference to a temporal effect."[2] This effect includes the human nature joined to the divine Son (his visible mission), the dove and luminous cloud (the Spirit's visible missions to the Son), the breath and the tongues of fire (the Spirit's visible missions to the apostles), and created gifts of grace for the invisible missions. The Father is not sent, for mission involves procession from another. Since the divine persons are inseparable, the Trinity dwells in us through the Son's and the Spirit's invisible coming. Mission and triune indwelling are distinct but not separate.[3]

God's creative act, whereby he is present in all things as their cause of being, grounds the ontology of the missions. These entail not an absolute beginning of God's presence in us, but a new mode of presence. Any divine indwelling is founded upon operation, and this for two reasons. First, as God is pure actuality, his existence and operation are intertwined. The act of giving being accounts for his natural presence,

---

1. Camille de Belloy, *La visite de Dieu: Essai sur les missions des personnes divines selon saint Thomas d'Aquin* (Geneva: Ad Solem, 2006), 95–97; Emery, *Trinitarian Theology*, 361–62.

2. Aquinas, *I Sent.*, d. 16, q. 1, a. 1c, 371: "Processio temporalis non est alia quam processio aeterna essentialiter, sed addit aliquem respectum ad effectum temporalem"; see also d. 14, q. 1, a. 2; d. 15, q. 1, a. 1; *ST* I, q. 43, a. 2, ad 3. Mission and temporal procession designate the same reality but with different emphases; see Emery, *Trinitarian Theology*, 368–69.

3. *ST* I, q. 43, a. 5c; Aquinas, *I Sent.*, d. 15, q. 2, a. 1, ad 4; Juárez, *Dios Trinidad*, 74.

and the act of giving sanctifying grace accounts for his saving presence.[4] Second, as God is immutable, a creature's new relation to him is based on a creaturely change. The missions cause a supernatural effect that is new for us, not for God:

> God is said to come to us not that he is moved to us, but because we are moved to him. For something is said to come to a place in which it was not before: but this is not fitting for God, since he is everywhere.... A thing is also said to come to something inasmuch as it is there in a new way by which it was not there before, namely, through the effect of grace: and through this effect of grace he makes us come near to him.[5]

The missions continue the eternal processions of the Son as the Word and of the Spirit as Love. While any created effect is the work of the Trinity's single efficient causality, the invisible missions impart gifts whose exemplarity surpasses that of the one divine nature:

> In the rational creature's return to God is understood the procession of the divine person, which is also called mission, inasmuch as the divine person's proper relation is represented in the soul by some received similitude, whose origin and exemplar is the very property of the eternal relation; just as the proper mode by which the Holy Spirit is referred to the Father is love, and the proper mode of referring the Son to the Father is to be his Word manifesting him. Hence, just as the Holy Spirit proceeds invisibly into the mind through the gift of love, so the Son [proceeds] through the gift of wisdom, in which is the Father's manifestation, who is the ultimate to which we return.[6]

---

4. Aquinas, *I Sent.*, d. 37, q. 2, a. 3, ad 3; Juárez, *Dios Trinidad*, 456.

5. *In Ioan.*, ch. 14, lect. 6, no. 1944: "Deus dicitur venire ad nos non quod ipse moveatur ad nos, sed quia nos movemur ad ipsum. Dicitur enim aliquid venire in locum in quem prius non fuit: hoc autem Deo non convenit, cum sit ubique.... Dicitur etiam venire in aliquem, inquantum est ibi novo modo, secundum quem prius non fuerat ibi, scilicet per effectum gratiae: et per hunc effectum gratiae facit nos ad se accedere"; see also Aquinas, *I Sent.*, d. 14, q. 1, a. 1; *ST* I, q. 43, a. 1; a. 2, ad 2; a. 3; Emery, *Trinitarian Theology*, 367, 380.

6. Aquinas, *I Sent.*, d. 15, q. 4, a. 1c, 350: "Ita in reductione rationalis creaturae in Deum intelligitur processio divinae personae, quae et missio dicitur, inquantum propria relatio ipsius personae divinae repraesentatur in anima per similitudinem aliquam receptam, quae est exemplata et originata ab ipsa proprietate relationis aeternae; sicut proprius modus quo Spiritus sanctus refertur ad Patrem, est amor, et proprius modus referendi Filium in Patrem est, quia est verbum ipsius manifestans ipsum. Unde sicut Spiritus sanctus invisibiliter procedit in mentem per donum amoris, ita Filius per donum sapientiae; in quo est manifestatio ipsius Patris, qui est ultimum ad quod recurrimus."

The doctrine of appropriation stands behind this dense passage. Appropriation indicates how the effect of the Trinity's single efficient causality manifests what is proper to a divine person.[7] The appropriation of a created gift to one divine person rests on this person's exemplar causality.[8] We thus appropriate charity to the Spirit and wisdom to the Son. Wisdom includes the cognition of God that comes through living faith, as we will see shortly. We return to God through the habitual possession and actualization of charity and faith. These virtues are created reflections of the Spirit's procession as Love and the Son's procession as the Word, respectively. We participate in the Son's and the Spirit's distinct relations to the Father as we return to him via assimilation to the Son's eternal property (in wisdom) and to the Spirit's eternal property (in love). In the previous passage, the term "similitude" has a thick or realistic meaning. It signifies not so much a faint copy of the original as a likeness whereby the reality being reflected is present to us.[9] By this similitude we are truly assimilated to the person sent, and not just by appropriation.[10] The soul in union becomes a new likeness of the Son and the Spirit.

Aquinas insists that the missions include a manifestation of the persons sent, one that is ontologically grounded in the received similitude of the persons. He links our ability to perceive the missions with a consideration of the grace that is necessary to account for them:

> for the *ratio* of mission, actual cognition of the very person [sent] is not required, but only habitual [cognition], namely inasmuch as in the gift imparted, which is a *habitus*, [what is] proper to the divine person is represented as in its similitude.[11]

If actual cognition of the missions were necessary for the coming of the Son and the Spirit, then Aquinas could no longer account for the effi-

---

7. Juárez, *Dios Trinidad*, 437.

8. See, for example, Aquinas, *I Sent.*, d. 17, q. 1, a. 1c; Emery, *Trinité créatrice*, 314–16, 399–400.

9. De Belloy, *Visite de Dieu*, 38–39; Emery, *Trinitarian Theology*, 376–78.

10. *ST* I, q. 43, a. 5, ad 2–3; Aquinas, *I Sent.*, d. 14, q. 2, a. 1, qla. 1c; Juárez, *Dios Trinidad*, 420.

11. Aquinas, *I Sent.*, d. 15, q. 4, a. 1, ad 1, 351: "ad rationem missionis non requiritur quod sit ibi cognitio actualis personae ipsius, sed tantum habitualis, inquantum scilicet in dono collato, quod est habitus, repraesentatur proprium divinae personae sicut in similitudine"; see also Juárez, *Dios Trinidad*, 442–43.

cacy of infant baptism, since no one becomes a temple of God unless he or she receives the Son and the Spirit. The *habitus* of faith and charity are inclined to operation and thus to the actual manifestation of the missions. By the theological virtues, believers are disposed in a stable way to an actual knowledge of the missions.

From the perspective of the persons' descent, the term of the invisible missions includes the *habitus* of faith, the *habitus* of charity, and the sanctifying grace of the soul's essence. The latter grace imparts a *disposition* needed for union:

Sanctifying grace disposes the soul to have the divine person; and this is signified when it is said that the Holy Spirit is given by the gift of grace. But nevertheless, the very gift of grace is from the Holy Spirit, and this is signified when it is said that "the charity of God is poured into our hearts through the Holy Spirit" [Rom 5:5].[12]

The habitual sanctifying grace of the soul's essence, which is a similitude of the divine nature and inseparable from charity, is the formal cause of union with God.[13] It is God's instrument whereby we attain direct spiritual contact with him. This grace is the intrinsic, formal principle of eternal life. As "formal effects" of habitual sanctifying grace, the gifts of grace (wisdom and charity) are the created principles that account for the persons' *missions*. The Spirit simultaneously gives himself, habitual sanctifying grace, and the charity that disposes us to receive him. The created gift has priority as a disposition (from the side of the receiver), while the person sent has *absolute priority* as the final, efficient, and exemplary cause of his gifts.[14] Aquinas also refers to the divine persons' power being impressed in their gifts or similitude, so that by these created gifts we possess the persons themselves as leading us their our end.[15] Created grace thus seems to function as a secondary efficient cause of union.

---

12. *ST* I, q. 43, a. 3, ad 2: "gratia gratum faciens disponit animam ad habendam divinam Personam; et significatur hoc, cum dicitur quod Spiritus Sanctus datur secundum donum gratiae. Sed tamen ipsum donum gratiae est a Spiritu Sancto, et hoc significatur, cum dicitur quod 'caritas Dei diffunditur in cordibus nostris per Spiritum Sanctum.'"

13. Aquinas often refers to sanctifying grace in the soul's essence as "habitual grace" more than as a *habitus*; see Torrell, notes to *Encyclopédie Jésus le Christ chez saint Thomas d'Aquin*, by Aquinas (Paris: Cerf, 2008), 205–7, 1000.

14. Aquinas, *I Sent.*, d. 14, q. 2, a. 1, qla. 2c; Juárez, *Dios Trinidad*, 380, 475.

15. Aquinas, *I Sent.*, d. 15, q. 4, a. 1c; Emery, *Trinité créatrice*, 410. At *ST* II-II, q. 23, a.

The descending explanation of the missions and their created term finds its essential complement in the ascending explanation, the preferred path of the *Summa:*

> Now above this common mode [of God's presence to creatures], there is one special [mode], which belongs to the rational nature, in which God is said to be as the known in the knower and the beloved in the lover. And because, by knowing and loving, the rational creature attains by his operation to God himself, according to that special mode God is not only said to be in the rational creature, but also to dwell in it as in his temple.[16]

Aquinas alludes to the knower's formal identity with the known and the lover bearing the mark of the beloved (see chapter 5 of this volume). He employs the notion that the object's similitude is intrinsically present to the knowing and loving subject. The psychology of love adds the characteristic of the lover's impulse to the beloved, which is realized in the *habitus* of charity.[17] The passage just cited implies the dynamism of the *habitus* of faith and charity. These are at once (1) the proper effects of habitual sanctifying grace, (2) the principles of our ontological assimilation to the Son's and the Spirit's properties, and (3) the intrinsic operative principles by which (via appropriation) the Son and the Spirit act with us, so that (4) we may be joined to persons sent, and thus to the Father, by acts of knowledge and love.[18] God dwells "radically" in the habitual knower and lover as in his temple by sanctifying grace and the *habitus* of wisdom and charity. He lives in us still more intensely by our cognitive and affective *acts*. Here we rejoin the *imago*'s threefold realization.[19] The missions involve (1) an operative mode of presence, by

---

2, ad 3, Aquinas also links efficient causality with created charity, insofar as the divine agent's power moves through charity as a form.

16. *ST* I, q. 43, a. 3c: "Super istum modum autem communem est unus specialis, qui convenit naturae rationali, in qua Deus dicitur esse sicut cognitum in cognoscente et amatum in amante. Et quia cognoscendo et amando creatura rationalis sua operatione attingit ad ipsum Deum, secundum istum specialem modum Deus non solum dicitur esse in creatura rationali, sed etiam habitare in ea sicut in templo suo."

17. *ST* I, q. 43, a. 3 should be read with a. 5, ad 2: wisdom and charity account for the invisible missions.

18. De Belloy, *Visite de Dieu*, 67–79, 101–3; Emery, *Trinitarian Theology*, 382–83; Emery, "Missions invisibles et missions visibles: Le Christ et son Esprit," *RT* 106 (2006): 54.

19. *ST* I, q. 93, a. 4; Javier Prades, *"Deus specialiter est in sanctis per gratiam"*: *El misterio de la inhabitación de la Trinidad*, *en los escritos de Santo Tomás*, Analecta Gregoriana 261 (Rome: Editrice Pontificia Università Gregoriana, 1993), 395–97.

conformation to the persons sent, and (2) an objective mode of presence, as faith and charity join us to the Trinity as the "object" known and loved (as our beatifying end). Action follows being, so that only the operation of persons in infinite actuality can traverse the endless distance between God and creatures and join us to God. Because of the persons' dynamic presence, created gifts unite us to the Father insofar as they assimilate us to the Son and the Spirit.[20] By our operative assimilation to the persons sent, we are united to the Trinity as the missions' "end" and to the Father as the final "personal term."[21]

The same *Summa* article continues as Aquinas unfolds a prerequisite of the divine persons' operative presence: "We are only said to have that which we can freely use and enjoy. Now to have the power of enjoying a divine person is only by sanctifying grace."[22] This grace is, so to say, the "root" on which the gifts of wisdom and charity can blossom. Here terms such as "use" and "enjoy" refer to the fruit of the acts of knowing and loving, to the beatitude of being joined to divine truth and goodness. We delight in the divine persons themselves.[23]

Aquinas links the inseparability of the divine persons enjoyed with their proper exemplarity: "Now the Son is the Word, not just any word, but the Word spirating Love ... therefore, the Son is not sent according to any perfection of the intellect, but according to such formation or instruction of the intellect by which it bursts forth into the affect of love."[24] Only the illumination that mirrors the Son's spiration of the Spirit accounts for the Son's mission. As continuations of the eternal processions, the missions reflect the Trinity's inner life. Because the divine processions are coeternal, and since the Spirit proceeds from the Son, the missions cannot be separated. Infused knowledge without love and love without cognition both remain imperfect. The term of one mission is always joined to the term of the other, again echoing the

20. Emery, *Trinitarian Theology*, 377–78; Juárez, *Dios Trinidad*, 440, 447.
21. Aquinas, *I Sent.*, d. 37, q. 1, a. 2c; Juárez, *Dios Trinidad*, 387, 413.
22. *ST* I, q. 43, a. 3c: "Similiter illud solum habere dicimur, quo libere possumus uti vel frui. Habere autem potestatem fruendi divina Persona, est solum secundum gratiam gratum facientem."
23. Aquinas, *I Sent.*, d. 14, q. 2, aa. 1–2; Emery, *Trinitarian Theology*, 375–76.
24. *ST* I, q. 43, a. 5, ad 2: "Filius autem est Verbum non qualecumque, sed spirans Amorem.... Non igitur secundum quamlibet perfectionem intellectus mittitur Filius, sed secundum talem institutionem vel instructionem intellectus, qua prorumpat in affectum amoris"; see also Emery, *Trinitarian Theology*, 390–91.

imago. Aquinas explains this doctrine as he comments on Jesus' promise to send the Paraclete. The Spirit's mission manifests and conforms us to the one from whom he eternally proceeds: the Word or Truth. By the charity that conforms us to the Spirit, he moves us to seek the truth in love.[25] Charity as inciting us to the Word inversely parallels the Word breaking forth into love. Since we cannot be joined to God without the missions, a theology rooted in the *Filioque* leads to a balance of cognition and charity in union. Also, as *created* participations in the Son's and the Spirit's personal properties, gifts of wisdom and love find their full realization in *human acts* of knowledge and love. Hence these acts are essential for the height of mystical union. Thomas again moves away from the Dionysian notion that the soul in union remains essentially passive.

The persons are also sent anew to those in grace: "But the invisible mission is chiefly attained by some increase in grace, when someone progresses in some new act, or a new state of grace; as for instance when some advances in the grace of miracles ... [or] undertakes any arduous task."[26] Aquinas alludes to the doctrine that a new infusion of grace (as *habitus*) merited by previous acts pleasing to God occurs when one achieves a difficult act of charity (or an act of charity whose fervor is due to the grace given in the fruitful reception of a sacrament).[27] By implication the persons are sent in any new sanctifying gift. Growth in union does not presuppose a special mystical state, for it occurs whenever one advances in grace.[28] The theology of the missions grounds a mysticism for all believers.

25. *In Ioan.*, ch. 14, lect. 6, nos. 1958–60; ch. 15, lect. 5, nos. 2061–62; ch. 17, lect. 1, no. 2185; Emery, "Trinity and Truth," 95, 102–7; Martin Sabathé, *La Trinité rédemptrice dans le "Commentaire de l'évangile de saint Jean" par Thomas d'Aquin*, Bibliothèque Thomiste 62 (Paris: Vrin, 2011), 494–99, 513, 554.

26. *ST* I, q. 43, a. 6, ad 2: "Sed tamen secundum illud augmentum gratiae praecipue missio invisibilis attenditur, quando aliquis proficit in aliquem novum actum, vel novum statum gratiae; ut puta cum aliquis proficit in gratiam miraculorum aut prophetiae, vel in hoc quod ex fervore caritatis exponit se martyrio, aut abrenuntiat his quae possidet, aut quodcumque opus arduum aggreditur"; see also Aquinas, *I Sent.*, d. 15, q. 5, a. 1, qla. 2.

27. *ST* II-II, q. 24, a. 6. Marie-Michel Labourdette notes that a fervent act of charity sufficiently disposes for the infusion of the *habitus*; see Labourdette, *Cours de théologie morale*, vol. 10, *La charité* (Toulouse: 1960), 72.

28. Emery, *Trinitarian Theology*, 386–87.

Grace in Thomas 257

We can also further specify the term of the Son's mission. Commenting on chapter 17 of John's Gospel, Aquinas explains that Christ asks the Father to sanctify his disciples in the truth "by sending them the Holy Spirit; and this 'in the truth' that is, in the cognition of the truth of faith and of your commandments.... For we are sanctified through faith and cognition of the truth."[29] Thomas refers to the inseparability of the missions. The essential elements of the temporal effect of the Son's invisible coming are sanctification, assimilation to Truth, and faith. The *habitus* of faith linked to charity (inseparable from the Spirit's mission) and thus to habitual sanctifying grace (their root) fulfills these three conditions. An increase in habitual faith accounts for the Son's illumination, which overflows onto love. Thus "gifts of wisdom" can simply refer to the faith *habitus* and are distinct from the Spirit's gift of wisdom.[30]

The themes of the missions' inseparability and our enjoyment of the persons sent, as well as the missions' terms in the *habitus* of faith and charity, come together in Thomas's exposition of the experiential knowledge of the missions. Here he builds on a key Augustinian phrase:

"And then one [divine person] is sent to someone when he [the person sent] is known by him." This should be understood not so much of speculative cognition, but of a cognition that is in a way experiential, which he [Augustine] shows in what follows: "and [the person] is perceived," which properly indicates experience in the gift perceived.[31]

---

29. *In Ioan.*, ch. 17, lect. 4, no. 2229: "'Vel sanctifica eos,' immittendo eis Spiritum sanctum; et hoc *in veritate*, idest in cognitione veritatis fidei et tuorum mandatorum; supra VIII: 'Cognoscetis veritatem, et veritas liberabit vos.' Nam per fidem et cognitionem veritatis sanctificamur"; see also Emery, "Trinity and Truth," 95–97.

30. Torrell, *Saint Thomas Aquinas*, vol. 2, *Spiritual Master*, 93; see also Emery, "'Theologia' and 'Dispensatio': The Centrality of the Divine Missions in St. Thomas's Trinitarian Theology," *Thomist* 74 (2010): 526. If a new mission had to include the Spirit's motion in his gift of wisdom, then any new sanctification would include this operation of the Spirit. Réginald Garrigou-Lagrange and others incorrectly *identify* the wisdom of the Son's mission with the Spirit's gift of wisdom; see Garrigou-Lagrange, "L'habitation de la sainte Trinité et l'expérience mystique," *RT* 33 (1928): 458. The distinction between these two kinds of wisdom has important consequences for our understanding of the place of spiritual experience in Thomas's theology of the seven gifts, as we will see in chapter 8.

31. Aquinas, *I Sent.*, d. 15, expositio, 365: "'Et tunc unicuique mittitur, cum a quo-

Thomas refers to a cognition that is experiential "in a way," not to weaken the meaning of "experience," but to indicate an analogous mode of speech, especially an analogy with sense cognition.[32] He signifies a real spiritual contact with God via the missions. This contact is not as immediate as that of the saints in glory. Pilgrims experience God in the created imprint of knowledge that breaks forth into charity, the graces that speculative cognition recognizes as manifestations of the Son and the Spirit. We experience the persons sent because they act in us through their infused gifts. As experiential cognition is necessary for the missions, the mediating imprint can simply be the *habitus* of faith and charity that account for the missions[33]—that is, the minimum experiential cognition is not explicit consciousness of the persons, but the immediate disposition for actual experience. The latter involves not so much a reflexive awareness of our acts and *habitus* as an ineffable grasp of the missions. Actual experiential cognition goes beyond the precision of concepts and language. Thus Christ invites the apostle Philip:

Mystically he [Jesus] says "Come and see," for the dwelling of God, or glory, or grace, can only be known by experience: for it cannot be explained by words; Apocalypse 2: "[I will give him] a new name on a little stone," etc. And so he says "Come and see." "Come," by believing and operating, "and see" by experiencing and understanding.[34]

Still, we cannot reduce this event to a purely affective experience, for the latter cannot account for the Son's mission.[35] Aquinas posits an experience that transcends concept-bound knowledge without exclud-

---

quam cognoscitur.' Hoc intelligendum est non tantum de cognitione speculativa, sed quae est etiam quodammodo experimentalis; quod ostendit hoc quod sequitur: *atque percipitur,* quod proprie experientiam in dono percepto demonstrat."

32. Aquinas, *I Sent.,* d. 14, q. 2, a. 2, ad 3; Juárez, *Dios Trinidad,* 446; Albert Patfoort, "Cognitio ista est quasi experimentalis," *Angelicum* 63 (1986): 3–13.

33. Aquinas, *I Sent.,* d. 15, q. 2, ad 5; *ST* I, q. 43, a. 5, ad 2; Emery, *Trinitarian Theology,* 394–95.

34. *In Ioan.,* ch. 1, lect. 15, no. 292: "Mystice autem dicit *Venite, et videte* quia habitatio Dei, sive gloriae, sive gratiae, agnosci non potest nisi per experientiam: nam verbis explicari non potest; Apoc. II: *In calculo nomen novum* etc. Et ideo dicit *Venite, et videte. Venite,* credendo et operando, *et videte,* experiendo et intelligendo."

35. Emery, *Trinitarian Theology,* 393–95; Torrell, *Saint Thomas Aquinas,* vol. 2, *Spiritual Master,* 95–98; Patfoort, "Missions divines et expérience des Personnes divines selon s. Thomas," *Angelicum* 63 (1986): 552.

ing it, partly because the act of faith necessarily employs concepts. Thomas's subtle way of including cognition tied to concepts within the deepest spiritual experiences, together with his ability to recognize the definite limits of that which concepts can communicate about God, becomes crucial in Aquinas's exposition of Dionysian mystical ascent, as we will see in chapter 8 of this volume. Speculative and experiential cognition are distinct but not separated, for they are complementary elements in the soul's ascent to God.[36] Because the experience of the persons sent remains ineffable, and because acts of the natural virtues can be difficult to distinguish from acts of infused virtue, we cannot attain absolute certitude of having this experience, barring a personal revelation.[37]

Thomas's theology of the missions bears some similarities to the Areopagite's Moses. Both theologians include in union a more direct divine action, an essential place for cognition, and an ineffable experience. Aquinas's doctrine departs from Dionysian union by its emphasis on created grace, graced human acts, and unitive operations as participations in the properties of the Son and the Spirit. His exposition manifests some Albertian traces, but Thomas develops his teacher's thought by the way he links the Spirit's procession from the Son to the missions.

THE METAPHYSICS OF DIVINE AND HUMAN ACTION IN THOMAS

From the perspective of God's work, Aquinas's doctrine of union centers on the missions with their effects, the Spirit's seven gifts, and ac-

---

36. Ambroise Gardeil seems to reduce the actual experience of the Son's missions to a cognition attained by the Spirit's gift of wisdom. He also *excludes* from this experience all concept-bound knowledge; see Ambroise Gardeil, "L'expérience mystique pure dans le cadre des 'Missions divines' III: La connaissance expérimentale de Dieu," supplement, *La Vie Spirituelle* 32 (September 1932): 67–76, esp. 74. Neither restriction can be found in Aquinas.

37. Aquinas, *I Sent.*, d. 15, q. 4, a. 1, ad 1; *ST* I-II, q. 112, a. 5. Robert A. Delfino incorrectly argues that Aquinas proposes a "mystical science" based on the experience of the divine persons sent, a science more certain than theology rooted in faith. Delfino also presumes that such experience is nonpropositional; see Delfino, "Mystical Theology in Aquinas and Maritain," in *Jacques Maritain and the Many Ways of Knowing*, edited by Douglas A. Ollivant, 257–64 (Washington, D.C.: The Catholic University of America Press, 2002).

tual grace. His teaching on the latter two themes greatly evolves, a shift that becomes intelligible in light of his mature theology of divine action.

The early Aquinas affirms that God immediately operates in every created act. But he explains God's dynamic, universal presence with appeals to the conservation of creatures' *esse* and operative faculties. The young Thomas does not explain that or how God moves agents to particular acts.[38] Beginning in the *Contra Gentiles*, he expands his notion of divine action in three ways. First, he applies more broadly the principle that God is the first cause of all motion, understood in the broad sense of potentiality reduced to act. The first efficient cause imparts to creatures more than just *esse* and form—that is, more than their operative capacity:

Every application of power to operation is principally and first from God. For operative powers are applied to [their] proper operations through some motion, either of the body or of the soul. But God is the first principle of any motion. For he is the first mover.[39]

Finite substantial forms have the inclination toward and capacity for certain types of acts, but as secondary causes. Hence their operative realization depends on the dynamism of the primary cause moving in them; otherwise, the creature would be a quasi first mover.

Second, Aquinas develops a new metaphysics to account for a biblical doctrine of providence wherein God's design extends to every event, even free human acts:

The human being can only employ the will's power given to him inasmuch as he acts in God's power. But that in whose power an agent acts, is cause not only of the power, but also of the act. This is evident in the artisan, in whose power the instrument acts, even if it does not have its proper form from the artisan, but is only applied to act by him.[40]

---

38. Aquinas, *II Sent.*, d. 1, q. 1, a. 4; Bernard Lonergan, *Grace and Freedom: Operative Grace in the Thought of St. Thomas Aquinas*, Collected Works of Bernard Lonergan 1 (Toronto: University of Toronto Press, 2000), 92–93.

39. *SCG* III, ch. 67, no. 2418: "Sed omnis applicatio virtutis ad operationem est principaliter et primo a Deo. Applicantur enim virtutes operativae ad proprias operationes per aliquem motum vel corporis, vel animae. Primum autem principium utriusque motus est Deus. Est enim primum movens"; see also *DP*, q. 3, a. 7.

40. *SCG* III, ch. 89, no. 2648: "Ergo homo non potest virtute voluntatis sibi data uti

Without a metaphysics of "application," God's providence would remain imperfect, limited to the general level and thus incapable of directing all particular events as primary cause.[41]

Third, in the early 1260s, Aquinas discovered an Aristotelian argument that only God's direct action on the human will explains our ability to will anything. According to the Stagirite's *Eudemian Ethics*, the will's free act presupposes deliberation. But one must will to deliberate, and this act of the will cannot always depend on previous deliberation, since that would lead to an infinite regress. Hence God must begin our will's first motion, moving us as free agents.[42]

The artisan using an instrument illustrates the modality of God's causality of every operation. Thomas does not thereby reduce all creaturely acts to instrumental causality in the strict sense. The appeal to the instrumental model has a limited function. First, it manifests the logic of application, a term synonymous with God's primary causality of all acts.[43] Application highlights creatures' dependence on God's act: "An instrument is in some way the cause of the principal cause's effect, not by its proper form or power, but inasmuch as it participates something of the principal cause's power through its motion."[44] The instrument is a real yet insufficient cause of operation by its intrinsic form. Second, the instrumental model emphasizes the operative unity of divine and created agents in a single act: "nature's operation is also the divine power's operation; just as an instrument's operation is through the principal agent's power. Neither nature nor God is impeded from operating the same, because of the order which is between God and nature."[45] A single act has two intertwined causes operating on distinct levels.

---

nisi inquantum agit in virtute Dei. Illud autem in cuius virtute agens agit, est causa non solum virtutis, sed etiam actus. Quod in artifice apparet, in cuius virtute agit instrumentum, etiam quod ab hoc artifice propriam formam non accepit, sed solum ab ipso applicatur ad actum."

41. *ST* I, q. 22, a. 2; q. 105, a. 5c; Lonergan, *Grace and Freedom*, 85–86.

42. *SCG* III, ch. 89, no. 2651; *ST* I, q. 19, a. 8; I-II, q. 9, a. 4c; John F. Wippel, *The Metaphysical Thought of Thomas Aquinas: From Finite Being to Uncreated Being*, Monographs of the Society for Medieval and Renaissance Philosophy 1 (Washington, D.C.: The Catholic University of America Press, 2000), 449–52.

43. *SCG* III, ch. 67, no. 2418; *ST* I, q. 105, a. 5c.

44. *DP*, q. 3, a. 7c: "Instrumentum enim est causa quodammodo effectus principalis causae, non per formam vel virtutem propriam, sed in quantum participat aliquid de virtute principalis causae per motum eius."

45. *DP*, q. 3, a. 7, ad 3: "ipsa naturae operatio est etiam operatio virtutis divinae; si-

Aquinas's mature theology of divine and human action seems to be original in thirteenth-century scholasticism. His creative synthesis of biblical providence and Aristotelian and Proclan-Dionysian causality opens the door for a new understanding of God's unitive action in the soul.[46] Thomas's synthesis will help to show the priority of divine operation in mystical ascent, a theological principle dear to Dionysius. Aquinas's doctrinal evolution also requires a careful distinction between his early and late theologies of actual grace and the Spirit's operation in his seven gifts.

HABITUAL, ACTUAL, AND CHRISTO-FORMING GRACE IN THOMAS

The late Thomas's doctrine of divine action bears fruit in his mature notion of actual grace, which I will consider in relation to habitual grace. For the first category I will focus on the distinction between operative and cooperative grace. I will then consider some of Thomas's favorite analogies for grace. The unitive element of grace will emerge in light of its status as a created and formal cause. I will then consider the cognition of the presence of grace, which relates to mystical awareness. I conclude with Christo-forming grace.

The mature Aquinas develops an original vision of actual grace that has at least two consequences for mystical theology. First, his late doctrine of divine action leads to a theology of actual grace or "divine help" as distinct from habitual grace. Because God is the first cause of every motion (natural or supernatural), the action "of any created being depends on God for two things: in one way, inasmuch as it has from him the perfection or form through which it acts; in another way, inasmuch as it is moved by him to act."[47] The last category, which uses the metaphysics of application, includes actual grace, "the gratuitous help of God interiorly moving the soul."[48] The ontology of operation means that we

---

cut operatio instrumenti est per virtutem agentis principalis. Nec impeditur quin natura et Deus ad idem operentur, propter ordinem qui est inter Deum et naturam."

46. Lonergan, *Grace and Freedom*, 83–89.

47. *ST* I-II, q. 109, a. 1c: "Sic igitur actio intellectus, et cuiuscumque entis creati, dependet a Deo inquantum ad duo: uno modo, inquantum ab ipso habet perfectionem sive formam per quam agit; alio modo, inquantum ab ipso movetur ad agendum."

48. *ST* I-II, q. 109, a. 6c: "auxilium gratuitum Dei interius animam moventis."

can analyze all graced human acts that attain union as proceeding from the infused *habitus* and God's gratuitous, direct motion. Second, Thomas insists that the "divine help" is necessary to remain in communion with God, implying some insufficiency in habitual sanctifying grace. This human need arises from the "infected" passions and the partially skewed vision of the practical intellect. Such human fragility stands behind the petitions of the *Our Father*, wherein we ask God for the gift of perseverance.[49] Aquinas's partly Augustinian understanding of the abiding wounds of sin leads to a greater emphasis on our dependence on grace. Now, if we depend on God's motion simply to remain in communion, then we depend on it all the more to advance in union. Aquinas synthesizes a Greek patristic insistence on the immediacy of God's action with an Augustinian conviction about human fragility.

The late Aquinas accentuates God's initiative even more by his notion of operative grace. "In that effect in which our mind is moved and not moving, but God alone is moving, the operation is attributed to God; and in this sense we speak of operating grace."[50] Actual grace can be operative or cooperative: "There is a twofold act in us. The first indeed is interior to the will. And as to this act, the will relates itself as moved, and God as moving."[51] God's efficient causality reorders the unjustified human being toward the supernatural end. Here our will's motion is neither blind nor forced. God's "aid does not exclude the act of the will from us, but he chiefly does the act in us," as he acts in us according to our mode.[52] Actual operative grace primarily pertains to the will's ontological conversion to the good as the principle of justification. Thomas also treats perseverance in charity as an actual operative grace—that is, God's special help after conversion to avoid grave sin.[53] Aquinas does not discuss operative grace in relation to intensifying union. This omission will be key in our reading of Thomas's theology of the gifts of understanding and wisdom.

49. *ST* I-II, q. 109, a. 9; see also *SCG* III, ch. 155.
50. *ST* I-II, q. 111, a. 2c: "In illo ergo effectu in quo mens nostra est mota et non movens, solus autem Deus movens, operatio Deo attribuitur; et secundum hoc dicitur gratia operans."
51. *ST* I-II, q. 111, a. 2c: "Est autem in nobis duplex actus. Primus quidem interior voluntatis. Et quantum ad istum actum, voluntas se habet ut mota, Deus autem ut movens."
52. *SCG* III, ch. 148, no. 3213: "Eius ergo auxilium non excludit a nobis actum voluntatis, sed ipsum praecipue in nobis facit"; see also *In Ioan.*, ch. 6, lect. 5, no. 935.
53. *ST* I-II, q. 114, a. 9c: "perseverantia ... ependet solum ex motione divina."

He then turns to actual cooperative grace: "But the other [second] act is exterior; it is commanded by the will.... God also helps us for this act, both by interiorly confirming the will, that it may achieve the act, and by outwardly granting the faculty of operating."[54] Practical reasoning proposes means to the end. Will and intellect, which together constitute free decision, choose among the means to the end, and the person passes into "external" operation. This grace is cooperative, for (1) the will is already turned to the supernatural good; (2) God assists our deliberative process preceding an act's execution; and (3) he assists the external act. The second element refers to God strengthening the interior will. The third element refers to his "outwardly granting the faculty" to act.[55] But we should not think of God's motion in actual cooperative grace as essentially different from his motion in actual operative grace. Rather, operative and cooperative grace are distinguished by their effects; God's grace, which first turns us to the supernatural good, continues, but our way of receiving that grace changes.[56] Aquinas applies to the economy of grace the principle that God's motion is the source of all operation. God's motion exceeds his primary, natural causality of created acts. By implication, all of our cooperative acts in grace proceed from the infused *habitus* and God's supernatural help, just as all natural acts proceed from creatures' natural faculties applied to operation by God's motion.[57] At times that motion takes the form of the Spirit's breath in his seven gifts.

Aquinas develops an ontology of grace via his ontology of nature. Both ontologies center on the couplet action-form, motion-*habitus*, or efficient-formal causality. The grace-nature link and the action-form combination help Thomas to synthesize biblical, patristic, and philosophical analogies for grace. God confers the form of grace by recreating us. Just as nature is a principle of operation, so regeneration imparts

---

54. *ST* I-II, q. 111, a. 2c: "Alius autem actus est exterior; qui cum a voluntate imperetur, ut supra habitum est, consequens est ut ad hunc actum operatio attribuatur voluntati. Et quia etiam ad hunc actum Deus nos adiuvat, et interius confirmando voluntatem ut ad actum perveniat, et exterius facultatem operandi praebendo."

55. See *ST* I-II, q. 8, a. 2; q. 18, a. 6; III, q. 85, a. 5; Lonergan, *Grace and Freedom*, 134–40.

56. *ST* I-II, q. 111, a. 2, ad 4.

57. Actual grace even continues in glory; *ST* I-II, q. 109, a. 9, ad 1. For the distinction between God's natural and supernatural motion, see q. 109, a. 6c.

a share in a similitude of God's being whereby we can participate in his operations via the infused virtues. Grace is simultaneously medicinal, as it heals us from the wounds of sin and elevates us to a participation in divine life.[58]

Thomas grounds these doctrines of grace as form and medicine in his notion of grace as created. In the realm of nature God imparts to all creatures motion and intrinsic operative principles that enable and incline to certain kinds of acts. Likewise, in the realm of grace, he imparts to believers his gratuitous motion and infused forms whereby human beings can obtain the eternal good: "just as the faculties flow from the soul's essence, which are the principles of works [acts], so also from grace itself the virtues flow into the soul's faculties, through which the faculties are moved to acts."[59] Created grace divinizes the soul's essence and overflows so as to impart the theological and infused moral virtues, just as the soul's faculties receive their being from the soul's essence. The soul's ontology applied to grace and a virtue-centered ethic lead to the doctrine of created grace. The close link between virtue-ethic and created grace emerges in Aquinas's response to his reading of the Lombard. Thomas sees the latter excluding created charity as a *habitus* in favor of the Spirit's motion in the will. Thomas argues that the latter position makes human charity a passive, involuntary act. The absence of the *habitus* leaves the will without a principle of operation whereby we can freely cooperate with the Spirit. Also, the promptness, ease, and joy of the natural virtues would have no equivalent in charity.[60] Created habitual grace (in the soul's essence) grounds the edifice of the infused virtues (in the faculties).

Thomas explains created grace in terms of *habitus* and formal causality: "grace, insofar as it is a quality [of the soul], is said to act in the soul not by mode of an efficient cause, but by mode of a formal cause."[61] Created habitual grace is (1) that by which we participate in God's na-

---

58. Aquinas, *II Sent.*, d. 26, a. 1, ad 4, a. 3c; *ST* I-II, q. 109, aa. 2, 7; q. 110, a. 3; q. 112, a. 1.

59. *ST* I-II, q. 110, a. 4, ad 1: "sicut ab essentia animae effluunt eius potentiae, quae sunt operum principia; ita etiam ab ipsa gratia effluunt virtutes in potentias animae, per quas potentiae moventur ad actus"; see also a. 2c.

60. *ST* II-II, q. 23, a. 2; *DC*, a. 1.

61. *ST* I-II, q. 110, a. 2, ad 1: "gratia, secundum quod est qualitas, dicitur agere in animam non per modum causae efficientis, sed per modum causae formalis"; see also q. 111, a. 1, ad 1; a. 2, ad 1; *DC*, a. 1, ad 10.

ture and (2) that by which God helps us on the path of return, a disposing cause by which we are able to cooperate with him. Our actualized cooperation depends on God's efficiency moving in the *habitus*. Created grace is not a motion. Rather, it disposes us to cooperate with God's action as secondary causes, not just as instrumental causes. The ontology of divine motion shows why created grace *as a quality of the soul* is not an efficient cause. However, we have already seen that the doctrine of the missions strongly implies such efficiency insofar as created grace bears an imprint of the divine persons' power operative in them.[62]

Like Albert, Thomas seems to take for granted the notion that grace formally unites us to God. He explains the unitive aspect of grace via the Dionysian law of hierarchical illumination:

> The order of things consists in this, that some are brought back to God through others, as Dionysius says in the *Celestial Hierarchy*. Therefore, since grace is ordered to this, that the human being may be brought back to God, this takes place in a certain order, namely, that some are led back to God through others. Accordingly, this grace is twofold. One, by which the human being is conjoined to God, which is called sanctifying grace.[63]

Aquinas picks up on the Dionysian rule that each angelic rank illumines its subordinate ranks and applies it to created grace as a mediation of union. Grace conjoins us to God insofar as it is the formal means of assimilation to him. Since grace enables us to perform Godlike acts via the theological virtues, the latter must be rooted in an elevated nature, just as the natural virtues are grounded in the soul's nature. Grace is a similitude of the divine nature, a share in divine life attained by our regeneration as children of God. Thomas builds a theology of union on his doctrine of created being as a participation in the divine similitude.[64]

---

62. *ST* I-II, q. 111, a. 2, ad 3; *SCG* III, ch. 150, no. 3230. Lévy separates created grace and God's gratuitous help in Aquinas and so wonders how created grace can have the capacity to divinize; Lévy, *Créé et l'incréé*, 395–98. Lévy mostly ignores operative and actual grace. He also gives little attention to Aquinas's theology of the missions.

63. *ST* I-II, q. 111, a. 1c: "In hoc autem ordo rerum consistit, quod quaedam per alia in Deum reducuntur; ut Dionysius dicit, in *De Cael. Hier.* Cum igitur gratia ad hoc ordinetur ut homo reducatur in Deum, ordine quodam hoc agitur, ut scilicet quidam per alios in Deum reducantur. Secundum hoc igitur duplex est gratia. Una quidem per quam ipse homo Deo coniungitur, quae vocatur gratia gratum faciens." He refers to *CH* 4.3, p. 22.14–22, 181A.

64. *ST* I-II, q. 110, a. 3; q. 112, a. 1; III, q. 2, a. 10, ad 1; Luc-Thomas Somme, *Fils adop-*

The inseparable link between God's divinizing action and created grace leads Aquinas to take an apophatic approach to our knowledge of the presence of God's sanctifying gift.

no one can know that he has the science of a conclusion if he ignores the principle. Now the principle and object of grace is God himself, who is unknown to us because of his excellence.... Hence, his presence and absence in us cannot be known with certitude ... hence the human being cannot judge with certitude whether he has grace.[65]

Aquinas agrees with Bonaventure and Albert that, barring a personal revelation, we cannot be certain of having sanctifying grace. But Thomas's argument is original. For Bonaventure the inscrutability of God's judgment of the believer best explains why such certitude escapes us.[66] Albert focuses on the similarity between natural and graced love, an argument that Thomas also uses.[67] In our passage Aquinas argues that reliable cognition (*scientia*) of the presence of grace requires cognition of the cause of grace as active in us. The grandeur of God's light in the soul's essence veils his presence. Elsewhere Thomas explains that God, whose presence escapes certain cognition, is the object and final cause of charity, for an adequate judgment of a *habitus* (here, charity) demands cognition of its object.[68] Like Bonaventure and Albert, Thomas holds that we only have probable knowledge of grace in us by the experience of God's sweetness and various signs of virtue. His explanation befits a mystical theology that remains cautious about the possibility of reliable mystical consciousness. Aquinas's clear stance on this point proceeds from his high estimation of grace.

A study of grace in Aquinas remains incomplete without a consideration of his doctrine of Christo-forming grace, which has no real

---

tifs de Dieu par Jésus Christ: La filiation divine par adoption dans la théologie de saint Thomas d'Aquin, Bibliothèque Thomiste 49 (Paris: Vrin, 1997), 317–63; Williams, *Ground of Union*, 84–87.

65. *ST* I-II, q. 112, a. 5c: "nullus autem posset scire se habere scientiam alicuius conclusionis, si principium ignoraret. Principium autem gratiae, et obiectum eius, est ipse Deus, qui propter sui excellentiam est nobis ignotus.... Et ideo eius praesentia in nobis et absentia per certitudinem cognosci non potest.... Et ideo homo non potest per certitudinem diiudicare utrum ipse habeat gratiam."

66. Bonaventure, *I Sent.*, d. 7, pars 1, a. 1, q. 3.

67. Albertus Magnus, *I Sent.*, d. 15, a. 17; d. 17, a. 5.

68. *DV*, q. 10, a. 10.

equivalent in his time. In the 1260s Thomas benefited from unusual access to ancient Christian literature, especially the texts of the Christological Councils and of St. Cyril of Alexandria. His creative synthesis of these sources with Aristotelian and Neoplatonic metaphysics results in a vision of the Word incarnate as at once the instrumental efficient and exemplary cause of all sanctifying grace for others.[69] We are united to God only through Christ's action in the flesh and in conformity to his grace.

Starting in the *Contra Gentiles,* Aquinas adopts Cyril's and John Damascene's notion that the hypostatic union makes Christ's humanity the living, conjoined, proper instrument of his divinity in analogy to the body's relation to the soul. This analogy manifests the inseparability of the two natures, their operative synergy, and the primacy of the divine nature. Christ's human operations enjoy an elevated ontological mode as they participate in the divine power.[70] An instrument's act *as instrument* transcends the operative capacity of its proper form insofar as it is moved by the principal agent. Christ's saving acts in the flesh depend on his divine nature. His human acts communicate a share in God's life—namely, as operations of an instrument actualized by the divine principal cause. Each cause has a distinct operation, but they realize one action.[71]

An instrumental cause marks the action effected through it. A tool specifies the operation of the principal cause, just as a sharp ax cuts better than a dull one.[72] The operative divine "flux" passes through Christ's acts and suffering in the flesh. Thus the death, resurrection, and ascension of Jesus modify the grace given thereby. The divine power active in these mysteries is not restricted to time, unlike the event of dying or resurrecting. Thus Christ's Passion "has a spiritual power from the divinity united to it. And therefore efficacy is obtained [from it] by a spiritual contact, namely, by faith and the sacraments of faith."[73] The

69. For Aquinas's Christology and his sources, see Blankenhorn, "The Instrumental Causality of the Sacraments: Thomas Aquinas and Louis-Marie Chauvet," *Nova et Vetera* (English ed.) 4 (2006): 275–91.
70. SCG IV, ch. 41, nos. 3796–98; ST III, q. 2, a. 6, ad 4.
71. SCG IV, ch. 36, no. 3748; ST III, q. 19, a. 1c; Torrell, notes to Aquinas, *Encyclopédie,* 370.
72. SCG IV, ch. 41, nos. 3798–3800.
73. ST III, q. 48, a. 6, ad 2: "Dicendum quod passio Christi, licet sit corporalis, ha-

saving acts of God are eternally marked by the history of the incarnate Word, for his two natures cannot be separated.[74]

Christ *effectively* communicates his grace and shares *his* personal grace. Aquinas joins the doctrines of Christ's instrumentality and headship in order to explain the fruitfulness of his saving work as head of the mystical body and the content of the gift imparted to his members. The grace that flows from the head is the same as the created grace that perfects Christ's human nature.[75] The exemplar and (instrumental) efficient cause are one, so that Christ not only models perfect virtue by his deeds but also pours out *his* charity, *his* humility, and so on. Together moral and ontological exemplarity as well as instrumental efficacy make possible the imitation of Christ.[76] Since Jesus is the perfect model and mediator of union, our ascent to union follows the path of assimilation to the Word incarnate, to his grace as manifested in his acts. The heavily Greek Christology of Aquinas allows him to link progress in union with increasing (though analogous) likeness to the grace revealed in the life of Jesus as recounted in the gospels. Here Thomas goes well beyond Dionysius. This difference is key, even though the Italian friar never invokes Christo-forming grace in his direct comments on Dionysius.

The doctrine of sanctifying grace lays the foundation for the theology of the infused, Christo-forming virtues that flow from that grace. But first I will take up the theme of docility to the Spirit by considering the overall modality of the Spirit's action in his seven gifts. Chapter 8 will unfold the gifts of understanding and wisdom that crown the virtue of faith.

---

bet tamen spiritualem virtutem ex divinitate unita. Et ideo per spiritualem contactum efficaciam sortitur, scilicet per fidem et fidei sacramenta"; see also q. 56, a. 1; q. 57, a. 6; Torrell, *Saint Thomas Aquinas*, vol. 2, *Spiritual Master*, 135–40; Blankenhorn, "The Place of Romans 6 in Aquinas's Doctrine of Sacramental Causality: A Balance of History and Metaphysics," in *Ressourcement Thomism: Sacred Doctrine, the Sacraments and the Moral Life*, edited by Reinhard Hütter and Matthew Levering, 139–48 (Washington, D.C.: The Catholic University of America Press, 2010).

74. Emery, "Missions invisibles," 86–99.

75. *ST* III, q. 8, aa. 1, 5.

76. *ST* III, q. 49, a. 3; q. 56, a. 1; Torrell, *Christ and Spirituality in St. Thomas Aquinas*, trans. Bernhard Blankenhorn (Washington, D.C.: The Catholic University of America Press, 2011), 91–100.

THE SPIRIT'S GIFTS IN GENERAL ACCORDING TO THOMAS

Thomas's doctrine of the Spirit's seven gifts constitutes one of his most original contributions to mystical theology. Indeed, this doctrine has stood at the heart of the Thomistic tradition's teaching on union with God. Because Aquinas evolved significantly in his theology of the gifts, I will focus on his only extensive mature treatment of the gifts in general, found in the *Summa theologiae*.[77] I will preface that analysis by looking at some elements of his *Sentences Commentary* teaching. First, I will take up the gifts' status as *habitus*, their functional relation to the virtues, and their relation to the will. I will then proceed to an analysis of the gifts' mode of operation. I will add some complementary considerations on the *Sentences Commentary* before taking up the *Summa*. Overall I will pay special attention to the element of receptivity or docility through the gifts and their relation to the theological virtues. Several fine doctrinal nuances developed here will significantly impact my reading of Aquinas as he explains the figures of Moses and Hierotheus.

Thomas's *Sentences Commentary* treatise on the seven gifts manifests Albert's partial influence. Aquinas refuses several contemporary doctrines on the gifts' ontology and function in the spiritual life. He favors the gifts as *habitus* enabling acts higher than the acts enabled by the virtues. Unlike Albert, Thomas makes the beatitudes the acts of the gifts or "perfect virtues" and the Spirit's fruits the delight that follows upon the beatitudes.[78] The gifts, beatitudes, and fruits are thus more closely linked in Aquinas than in Albert. Thomas drops the notion of the beatitudes and fruits as operative *habitus* at a third and fourth level, respectively, a level surpassing the virtues and gifts. In chapter 3 I noted that Albert never fully explained this upper half of his hierarchy of supernatural *habitus*. The early Aquinas offers a simpler schema wherein

---

77. The three most extensive recent studies on the gifts in Aquinas argue for a major doctrinal evolution; see Cruz González Ayesta, *El don de sabiduría según Santo Tomás: Divinización, filiación y connaturalizad*, Teológica 92 (Navarra: EUNSA, 1998); Ulrich Horst, *Gaben*, 41–69; and James W. Stroud, "Thomas Aquinas' Exposition of the Gifts of the Holy Spirit: Development in His Thought and Rival Interpretations" (Ph.D. diss., The Catholic University of America, 2012).

78. Aquinas, *III Sent.*, d. 34, q. 1, aa. 1, 4–5.

the gifts "assist the virtues," a schema that the late Aquinas essentially retains.[79]

In the *Sentences Commentary* gifts as *habitus* assist all the virtues except charity and hope. The virtues aided by the gifts have an intrinsically imperfect or "human mode" of perfecting our operations.[80] Thus faith sees as in a mirror, but its complementary gift of understanding grants a foretaste of future glory that partly transcends faith's indirect mode of knowing. Like Albert, the young Thomas insists that charity's mode of operation is already complete, for here below we love God by essence, but we do not see him this way.[81] The late Aquinas assigns the gift of fear to hope and the gift of piety to justice, but he still holds that wisdom as a *habitus*, not charity, directly perfects the intellect.[82] Charity's imperfection does not pertain to its mode of operation but to a lack of actuality within its singular mode.

The key dispute in the secondary literature on the theology of the gifts in Aquinas's *Sentences Commentary* centers on their mode of operation. The young Thomas often contrasts the gifts' and virtues' modes of action with the technical phrases "superhuman" and "human mode," respectively. He compares the former to Aristotle's heroic virtue. But the young Aquinas offers no clear explanation of this superhuman mode of operation, in parallel to Albert's relative silence on the gifts' mode of actualization.[83] Thomas seems to invoke a higher form of divine efficiency in his study of the gifts of understanding, wisdom, and fortitude. Yet here he mostly appropriates the causal language of Gregory the Great or Albert without further specifying the mode of causality.[84] The gifts of counsel, knowledge, piety, and fear of the Lord involve a new standard or measure of action, a kind of higher exemplar causality, but the Spirit's mode of efficient causality remains unarticulated.[85]

---

79. Aquinas, *III Sent.*, d. 34, q. 1, a. 4; *ST* I-II, q. 68, aa. 1–3; q. 69, a. 1; q. 70, a. 2.
80. Aquinas, *III Sent.*, d. 34, q. 1, a. 1, ad 5; a. 2, ad 1.
81. Aquinas, *III Sent.*, d. 34, q. 1, a. 1, ad 5.
82. On charity, see *ST* I-II, q. 68, a. 5, ad 1; II-II, q. 45, a. 2; Daria E. Spezzano, "The Grace of the Holy Spirit, the Virtue of Charity and the Gift of Wisdom: Deification in Thomas Aquinas' *Summa Theologiae*" (Ph.D. diss., University of Notre Dame, 2011), 404–17. On hope, see II-II, q. 19, a. 9. On piety, see q. 121, a. 1.
83. Aquinas, *III Sent.*, d. 34, q. 1, a. 1c; Horst, *Gaben*, 48–57.
84. Aquinas, *III Sent.*, d. 34, q. 1, aa. 1–2; q. 3, a. 1; d. 35, q. 2, a. 2, qla. 1c.
85. Aquinas, *III Sent.*, d. 34, q. 1, a. 2; d. 35, q. 2, a. 3, qla. 1c; a. 4, qla. 1c; q. 3, a. 2, qla 1c.

The *Sentences Commentary* does not clearly propose a special kind of divine, efficient causality for each of the seven gifts.

This doctrinal ambiguity fits well with other elements of the commentary's theology of the gifts. First, the technical operational language of "divine instinct" and "divine motion" that dominates the *Summa* analysis of the gifts is virtually missing in the *Sentences Commentary*. Here the term "instinct" emerges only once, without explanation.[86] Second, the commentary does not explicitly state that the *habitus* of the gifts are dispositions for the Spirit's motion, a key notion in Thomas's mature thought. Third, the absence in the *Sentences Commentary* of the divine instinct, divine motion, and the *habitus* disposing for such motion make sense, given that the teaching that God operates in every creaturely act is not clearly developed before the *Contra Gentiles*.[87] Fourth, the early Thomas seems to suggest that we can activate the gifts: "the gifts are only from God.... But the operations of the gifts which are also the beatitudes are also from us."[88] God alone causes the *habitus* of the gifts. The gifts in act are the beatitudes, and these acts come "also from us"—that is, from God and us. This phrase remains a bit ambiguous, but it probably implies that an act of free decision suffices for the gifts' operation. Here the gifts seem to function as elevated cooperative graces, a notion that fits well with the strictly cooperative actual grace of the *Sentences Commentary*.[89] Finally, one passage from

---

86. Aquinas, *III Sent.*, d. 35, q. 2, a. 4, qla. 1c.

87. In his "Le mode suprahumain des dons du Saint-Esprit dans la *Somme Théologique* de S. Thomas," supplement, *La Vie Spirituelle* 7 (March 1923): 126–31, Réginald Garrigou-Lagrange makes the gifts' "superhuman mode" of operation in the *Sent.* equivalent to the *ST* doctrine of the Spirit's motion in the gifts. For him the *Sent.* uses terms such as *mensura* or *regula* to refer to a special efficient causality for the gifts. But these terms probably involve exemplar causality. Horst points to Thomas's mature notion of divine action and the young Aquinas's weak integration of the theological virtues and the gifts to argue for development in the doctrine of the gifts' operation; Horst, *Gaben*, 57, 71–79. Similar arguments are found in González Ayesta, *El don de sabiduría*, 43–52, and in Servais Pinckaers, "Morality and the Movement of the Holy Spirit: Aquinas's Doctrine of 'Instinctus,'" in *The Pinckaers Reader: Renewing Thomistic Moral Theology*, ed. and trans. John Berkman and Craig Steven Titus (Washington, D.C.: The Catholic University of America Press, 2005), 388–89.

88. Aquinas, *III Sent.*, d. 34, q. 1, a. 4, ad 4, 1129: "dona sunt tantum a Deo, et ideo praeordinantur secundum quod sunt perfectiora: sic enim sunt Deo propinquiora. Sed operationes donorum quae sunt etiam beatitudines, sunt etiam a nobis."

89. See Lucien Roy, *Lumière et Sagesse: La grâce mystique dans la théologie de saint*

the commentary affirms that the gifts are necessary for salvation. Yet Thomas does not explain this claim, and the claim does not have an evident function in his overall treatment of the gifts.[90]

The incomplete nature of the *Sentences Commentary* exposition of the gifts in general and the evolution in Aquinas's view means that we need to read the *Summa* without the categories of the earlier text. As I consider the pillars of the *Summa* theology of the gifts, I will focus on human receptivity and the gifts' relation to the theological virtues.

The opening *Summa* article on the gifts distinguishes these from the virtues in a new way. Aquinas appeals to Isaiah 11:2. Seven "spirits" repose on the anointed one, which for Thomas implies a sevenfold inspiration or exterior motion. There is a single twofold moving principle (*duplex principium movens*) or source of operation in us: reason is the interior principle, while God is the exterior principle. Thomas refers to Aristotle's *On Good Fortune*, the book that contains the *Eudemian Ethics*. Aquinas thus recalls his new theology of God as first mover of every human act. But the Spirit's motion in the gifts goes further.[91]

> It is clear that all which is moved must be proportioned to the motor; and this is the perfection of the movable [thing], the disposition by which it is disposed to being moved well by its motor. Therefore, to the extent that a mover is higher, so must the movable be proportioned to it by a more perfect disposition; just as we see that the student must be more perfectly disposed to receive a higher doctrine from the teacher. Now it is clear that the human virtues perfect the human being inasmuch as he is made to be moved by reason in what he does internally or externally. Therefore, there must be present to the human being higher perfections, by which he is disposed to being divinely moved ... the Philosopher also says in the chapter *On Good Fortune* that for those who are moved by the divine instinct, it is not useful to be counseled by human reason ... this is what some say, that the gifts perfect the human being for higher acts than the acts of the virtues.[92]

Thomas d'Aquin, Studia Collegii Maximi Immaculatae Conceptionis 6 (Montreal: L'Immaculée-Conception, 1948), 167.

90. Aquinas, *III Sent.*, d. 36, a. 3, ad 4; González Ayesta, *El don de sabiduría*, 45–46.

91. *ST* I-II, q. 68, a. 1c.

92. *ST* I-II, q. 68, a. 1c: "Manifestum est autem quod omne quod movetur, necesse est proportionatum esse motori; et haec est perfectio mobilis inquantum est mobile, dispositio qua disponitur ad hoc quod bene moveatur a suo motore. Quanto igitur

Human reason and the human will are naturally open to God's primary, natural motion, without further disposing principles. Sanctifying grace and the infused virtues dispose us to cooperate with the dynamism of God's actual grace. In the virtues God moves us via reason's prudential reflection on the means to the end. The acquired and the infused virtues pass into act when we choose to act. Here we are principal, secondary causes actively cooperating with God's motion. The Spirit's motion in the gifts belongs to a higher category. Here our free decision does not trigger an operation, for only the Spirit can initiate this type of act. Since the Spirit moves us in a higher way, we need a higher disposition to receive his action, like the student who receives advanced instruction. We are not blind under the Spirit's action, but rather freely and promptly docile to him. Thomas concludes with Albert's terminology, but that language has new meaning. Thomas now clearly posits a distinct form of divine efficiency for the seven gifts. This development will bring Aquinas closer to Dionysius on a key aspect of mystical union.

The Spirit's motion assists reason's deliberative mode of action, the deliberation proper to "human virtues," including the theological virtues:

> But in the order to the ultimate, supernatural end, to which reason moves insofar as it is somehow and imperfectly formed through the theological virtues, the motion of reason does not suffice, unless there be present from on high the instinct and motion of the Holy Spirit, according to Romans 8: "Those who are acted upon by the Spirit of God, those are sons of God" ... therefore to obtain that end, it is necessary for the human being to have the gift of the Holy Spirit.[93]

---

movens est altior, tanto necesse est quod mobile perfectiori dispositione ei proportionetur; sicut videmus quod perfectius oportet esse discipulum dispositum ad hoc quod altiorem doctrinam capiat a doctore. Manifestum est autem quod virtutes humanae perficiunt hominem secundum quod homo natus est moveri per rationem in his quae interius vel exterius agit. Oportet igitur inesse homini altiores perfectiones, secundum quas sit dispositus ad hoc quod divinitus moveatur.... Philosophus etiam dicit in cap. *De Bona Fortuna*, quod his qui moventur per instinctum divinum non expedit consiliari secundum rationem humanam.... Et hoc est quod quidam dicunt quod dona perficiunt hominem ad altiores actus quam sint actus virtutum."

93. *ST* I-II, q. 68, a. 2c: "Sed in ordine ad finem ultimum supernaturalem, ad quem ratio movet secundum quod est aliqualiter et imperfecte formata per virtutes theologicas, non sufficit ipsa motio rationis, nisi desuper adsit instinctus et motio Spiritus Sancti; secundum illud Rom. VIII: 'Qui Spiritu Dei aguntur, hi filii Dei sunt' ... ideo ad il-

Grace in Thomas 275

This passage offers a new argument for the necessity of the gifts. Earlier in the same article Thomas notes that the perfect possession of a form (e.g., a virtue) means that one can act *per se*, which means that the human agent has a sufficient intrinsic operative capacity to attain the object or end of the form (assuming God's primary motion). Thus we can fully possess the acquired virtues and so be properly ordered to our connatural end. But our imperfect cognition and love of God manifest our incomplete possession of the theological virtues. Such imperfection partly comes from these virtues' abiding link to prudence. Also, the theological virtues cannot by themselves impart a sufficient intrinsic capacity to reach their supernatural end. In the background stands Aquinas's Augustinian doctrine of the grace of perseverance, which insists on our abiding fragility, despite the power of grace. The Spirit's action in the gifts enables reason to suffice in the sense that he carries us beyond our limits.[94] God's impulse does not bypass but rather elevates the act of deliberation, an interpretation I will confirm shortly.[95] Here Thomas probably returns to the theme of a double moving principle, one internal (reason) and the other external (God). The Spirit perfects rather than replaces the acts of the theological virtues, though Thomas does not claim that the Spirit always completes their operation.[96]

---

lum finem consequendum, necessarium est homini habere donum Spiritus Sancti"; see also a. 3, ad 2.

94. Aquinas speaks of the gifts' acts (*ST* I-II, 69, a. 1c; a. 3, ad 1; q. 70, a. 3, ad 4; II-II, q. 139, a. 1, ad 2) and of the gifts disposing the human being (I-II, q. 68, a. 1c) or the faculties (a. 5c) for the Spirit's motion.

95. At *ST* I-II, q. 68, a. 1c (cited in footnote 92 of the present chapter), the paraphrase of Aristotle implies that the Spirit's motion bypasses human deliberation. But when speaking in his own voice, Thomas does not affirm that such motion excludes deliberation, while I-II, q. 68, a. 2 suggests their cooperation. He later calls the gift of *scientia* a participated similitude of God's simple, nondiscursive knowledge, implying a partial simplification of deliberation, not its exclusion; II-II, q. 9, a. 1, ad 1. For the gift of counsel, Thomas notes that the Spirit moves us according to our temporal mode, a mode that involves the inquisition of reason. He implies that the Spirit assists deliberation; II-II, q. 52, a. 1c. Here I disagree with Garrigou-Lagrange, who argues (without textual evidence) that the Spirit's motion by its nature dispenses us from deliberating; Garrigou-Lagrange, *Christian Perfection*, 292–94.

96. I follow Labourdette, "Dons du Saint-Esprit: Saint Thomas et la théologie thomiste," *DS* 3 (1957): col. 1620. He contradicts Ambroise Gardeil, "Les dons du saint Esprit," in *Dictionnaire de théologie catholique*, edited by E. Mangenot, vol. 4, part 2, col. 1742 (Paris: L. Letouzey et Âne, 1920). Like Gardeil, Angela M. McKay argues that the infused virtues always require the Spirit's motion for their operation; see McKay, "The

The gifts are dispositions or *habitus* to receive the Spirit's motion promptly. This motion is an efficient cause and passes into act by God's gratuitous will. The gifts as *habitus* are created, formal causes, for every *habitus* is a form. The gifts are intrinsic perfections of believers' faculties that remain in them as long as they abide in charity. Aquinas compares the relation of the gifts as *habitus* to the Spirit's action with the moral virtues that render the appetitive powers (the will and sensitive appetites) docile to reason's motion.[97] This analogy has two consequences. First, it implies that the gifts enable the faculties to act *with* the "higher reason" of the Spirit's dynamism. The gifts render us more receptive to the Spirit, but this does not exclude the faculties cooperating with the Spirit, especially after having received his motion, just as the moral virtues are more than passive dispositions to reason. The gifts render us docile to the Spirit's action, but this need not imply a passive state of the spiritual life.[98] Aquinas confirms this as he answers an objection that instruments need no *habitus* to be moved by their principal cause. Thomas responds that, unlike inanimate instruments, the human being is not simply acted upon by the Spirit but also acts; therefore he needs a *habitus* that disposes him to the Spirit's motion.[99] By implication, the gifts as *habitus* grant deeper receptivity, enabling a higher subsequent, active spontaneity. Aquinas does not speak of being passive before the Spirit but of "being movable (*mobilis*)."[100] Second, qualitative forms such as

---

Infused and Acquired Virtues in Aquinas' Moral Philosophy" (Ph.D. diss., University of Notre Dame, 2004), 35–50. First, she builds on the notion that each meritorious act includes God's operative grace (45). This overlooks Thomas's limited use of the category of operative grace. McKay seems to identify actual grace after justification with the Spirit's motion in the seven gifts (36, 43–47), an identification not found in the *ST*. Second, McKay's reading leads directly to the stance that the Spirit's motion simply occurs when we decide to act, for the theological virtues (and other infused virtues) can always be actuated by our free decision. Here the Spirit's role seems to be reduced to one of specification. But the late Thomas emphasizes the Spirit's unique efficient causality in the gifts as he builds on his mature doctrine of divine action.

97. *ST* I-II, q. 68, a. 3c.

98. González Ayesta points out that John of Saint Thomas and his disciples harmonize Aquinas's doctrine of the Spirit's gifts with early modern conceptions of stages in the mystical life; González Ayesta, *El don de sabiduría*, 75.

99. *ST* I-II, q. 68, a. 3, ad 2.

100. *ST* I-II, q. 68, a. 1c; a. 8c; II-II, q. 8, a. 5c; q. 19, a. 9; q. 52, a. 1c; q. 121, a. 1c. Garrigou-Lagrange, *Christian Perfection*, 283–94, and Roy, *Lumière et Sagesse*, 168, 196, read the gifts as forms of passivity.

habitus have varying degrees of intensity, as in the case of the moral virtues. The analogy between the gifts and the moral virtues seems to imply that the gifts can grow or diminish in intensity. This means that believers can grow in docility to the Spirit through merit or sacramental grace. Overall the elements of unforeseen outside motion, receptivity, and degrees of receptivity are illustrated well by John of Saint Thomas's classic metaphor of a sailing ship being moved along by the wind.[101]

The gifts cause a greater unity of action between the Spirit and the virtues.[102] This point emerges with some ambiguity in an article on the priority of the virtues over the gifts:

The theological virtues are that by which the human mind is joined to God; now the intellectual virtues are that by which reason is perfected; but the moral virtues are that by which the appetitive powers are perfected to obey reason. Now the Holy Spirit's gifts are that by which all the soul's powers are disposed to receive divine motion. Hence, it appears that the same comparison can be made of the gifts to the theological virtues, by which the human being is united to the Holy Spirit moving, as the moral virtues to the intellectual virtues, by which reason is perfected, which moves the moral virtues. Hence, just as the intellectual virtues have precedence over the moral virtues and govern them; so the theological virtues have precedence over the Holy Spirit's gifts, and govern them.[103]

Rational deliberation perfected by prudence governs and (with an act of free decision) moves the appetitive powers. Here virtuous reason exercises a formal or specifying causality, which enables the will to exer-

101. John of Saint Thomas, *De donis*, no. 174. Olivier Bonnewijn signals the metaphor's limits: the Spirit's wind in the sails seems to act parallel to the virtues, represented by the ship's oars; see Bonnewijn, *La béatitude et les béatitudes: Une approche thomiste de l'éthique* (Rome: Pontifica Università Lateranense, 2001), 365.

102. Pinckaers, "Morality," 389; Dalmazio Mongillo, "Les béatitudes et la béatitude: Le dynamisme de la *Somme de théologie* de Thomas d'Aquin, une lecture de la Ia-IIae q. 69," *RSPT* 78 (1994): 378, 386.

103. *ST* I-II, q. 68, a. 8c: "Virtutes quidem theologicae sunt quibus mens humana Deo coniungitur; virtutes autem intellectuales sunt quibus ratio ipsa perficitur; virtutes autem morales sunt quibus vires appetitivae perficiuntur ad obediendum rationi. Dona autem Spiritus Sancti sunt quibus omnes vires animae disponuntur ad hoc quod subdantur motioni divinae. Sic ergo eadem videtur esse comparatio donorum ad virtutes theologicas, per quas homo unitur Spiritui Sancto moventi, sicut virtutum moralium ad virtutes intellectuales, per quas perficitur ratio, quae est virtutum moralium motiva. Unde sicut virtutes intellectuales praeferuntur virtutibus moralibus, et regulant eas; ita virtutes theologicae praeferuntur donis Spiritus Sancti, et regulant ea."

cise its proper causality. The moral virtues render the appetitive powers receptive to the specification and motion of reason. As we saw, the Spirit's motion in the gifts is analogous to reason moving in the appetitive powers perfected by the moral virtues. The Spirit's motion presupposes sanctifying grace and thus the theological virtues. Aquinas now shifts the analogy. In the *Summa* article just cited, the theological virtues are like the intellectual virtues, not as immediate principles of action, but as perfections of reason, of the faculty that moves the moral virtues. As Marie-Michel Labourdette explains, the virtues are active when the Spirit moves in us, but he pushes our virtuous acts beyond the capacities of the virtues.[104] The light of faith and the affective inclinations of charity and hope "govern" the gifts as (1) links to the Spirit's motion and (2) cooperation with the Spirit in specifying the operation, though the Spirit "stretches" that specification. Aquinas is not clear on the last point, but without the theological virtues' cooperation in the act of specification, the analogy with the intellectual virtues seems to break down. This further confirms that the Spirit's motion does not exclude but rather elevates the human deliberative act.

Thomas affirms an operational link between the theological virtues and the Spirit in his discussion of the beatitudes. He describes the beatitudes as acts of the virtues and the gifts or as acts of perfect virtue.[105] Such language implies that the gifts' operations do not leave the *habitus* of the virtues idle. Also, "all the gifts are ordered to the perfection of the theological virtues as to their end."[106] The gifts open us to a more virtuous act that the Spirit directly incites. Aquinas also signals that the gifts' operations further the perfection of the theological virtues as *habitus*. For if the Spirit moves us to higher *acts* of virtue, then the *habitus* of the virtues are strengthened.[107] This helps to explain why

104. Labourdette, "Dons du Saint-Esprit," col. 1624; see also Pinckaers, *La vie selon l'Esprit: Essai de théologie spirituelle selon saint Paul et saint Thomas d'Aquin*, Amateca, vol. 17, part 2 (Luxembourg: Éditions Saint-Paul, 1996), 207; Spezzano, *Grace of the Holy Spirit*, 360–63.

105. *ST* I-II, q. 69, a. 1c: "Ad finem autem beatitudinis movetur aliquis et appropinquat per operationes virtutum; et praecipue per operationes donorum ... beatitudines distinguuntur quidem a virtutibus et donis, non sicut habitus ab eis distincti, sed sicut actus distinguuntur ab habitibus"; Q. 69, a. 2c; II-II, q. 19, a. 12, ad 1.

106. *ST* II-II, q. 9, a. 1, ad 3: "omnia dona ad perfectionem theologicarum virtutum ordinantur sicut ad finem."

107. Pinckaers, *Plaidoyer pour la vertu* (Paris: Parole et Silence, 2007), 321.

Thomas assigns the gifts not just to particular faculties, but also to specific virtues. Thus progress in the gifts heightens docility to the Spirit *and* the ability to cooperate with his motion. By the gifts we become more receptive to an exterior grace and further our possession of the interior cooperative graces that are the infused virtues as *habitus*. The gifts enable a higher operational integration of the Spirit's action and the virtues. Spiritual progress entails greater docility and spontaneity in moral action, though in different respects. Progress in grace involves a double spiral, a simultaneous growth in the active *habitus* of the infused virtues and in the receptive *habitus* of the gifts. The contrast with Dionysius is striking. Let us also note that we do not find such a double spiral in Albert's theology of the seven gifts or in his commentaries on the Areopagite.

If the operation of the gifts perfects the virtues, then by implication at least one virtue is in act whenever one gift passes into act. Both *habitus* are actualized by a single, Spirit-initiated operation.[108] The *Summa* primarily organizes the gifts according to the faculties and virtues that their acts perfect, instead of the *Sentences Commentary* division centered on the active-contemplative distinction.[109] Understanding and knowledge perfect faith, fear of the Lord perfects hope, counsel perfects prudence, piety perfects justice, and fortitude perfects the virtue of the same name. Wisdom is *sui generis*, for its causes are the Spirit's motion and the *habitus* of charity that bring about a connaturality to divine things and enable an act of judgment.[110]

But Aquinas neither states nor implies that all the theological virtues must be in act when the Spirit moves in us. Nor does he hold that an act of charity accompanies each gift in act. Aquinas draws yet another analogy: charity connects all of the gifts because through it the Spirit dwells in us, ready to move us. Thus, just as prudence connects the moral virtues, so charity links the seven gifts.[111] Labourdette appeals

---

108. Labourdette, "Dons du Saint-Esprit," col. 1625.
109. *ST* I-II, q. 68, a. 4 organizes the gifts by operative faculties; Q. 68, a. 7 employs the active-contemplative distinction to order the gifts by their dignity; *ST* II-II drops the latter division of the gifts as it assigns to wisdom and understanding both contemplative and practical functions (q. 8, a. 3; q. 45, a. 3).
110. *ST* II-II, q. 8, a. 2; q. 9, a. 1; q. 19, a. 9, ad 1; q. 45, aa. 1–2; q. 52, a. 2; q. 121, a. 1; q. 139, a. 1.
111. *ST* I–II, q. 68, a. 5c.

to this doctrine to argue that, just as an act of prudence is necessary to actualize the moral virtues, so charity must be in act whenever the gifts operate.[112] But Thomas assigns two main functions to prudence as the link of the moral virtues. First, the moral virtues incline the appetite to a good end that befits reason, while prudence identifies this end more accurately. Second, the act of the moral virtues presumes that prudence chooses a fitting means to the end.[113] Neither function has a clear parallel in the act of charity. Rather, charity as *habitus* is the necessary condition for the Spirit's motion, the motion that perfects both reason's inclination to the end and the choice of a means to the end. Aquinas uses the analogy between charity and prudence with a limited aim. It is fitting for charity to be in act when the Spirit moves us, but Thomas makes the Spirit's motion, and not that of charity, analogous to perfected reason in act. Thus it seems that charity's act need not always accompany the Spirit's motion. Also, the *Summa* does not justify John of Saint Thomas's extension of the "connaturality to divine things" from the gift of wisdom to the gifts of understanding, knowledge, and counsel. Aquinas only mentions this specific connaturality in relation to the affective union with God that makes wisdom's judgment possible. As we will see in chapter 8 of this volume, Aquinas attributes to the gift of understanding a different type of connaturality, a graced inclination to the beatifying end that disposes the believer to the Spirit's motion.[114]

The necessity of the gifts for salvation and their complementarity to the virtues shows that the Spirit's motion is not reserved to a spiritual elite. Rather, it has an indispensible function in the moral progress of all who are in grace. Also, the *Summa* does not posit a firm hierarchy of motions within the gifts beyond the distinction between the pilgrim state and the state of glory. In other words, the attempt to assign diverse levels of operations within each gift to distinct stages of purification, illumination, and union lacks foundation in the *Summa*.[115] The theology of the gifts in general undergirds a mysticism for all believers.

---

112. Labourdette, "Dons du Saint-Esprit," cols. 1626, 1630–31.

113. *ST* I-II, q. 58, a. 4.

114. *ST* II-II, q. 8, a. 5c; q. 45, a. 2c; John of Saint Thomas, *De donis*, nos. 118, 125–26. González Ayesta points to these problems in John's interpretation; González Ayesta, *El don de sabiduría*, 68–70, 99, 147.

115. On the gifts' action in the pilgrim and the blessed, see *ST* I-II, q. 68, a. 6. Garrigou-Lagrange reads Thomas on the gifts with the lens of charity's three degrees (begin-

FAITH ACCORDING TO THOMAS

Aquinas's originality also extends to his theology of faith, especially in the *Summa*.[116] Under the formality of union, I will focus on faith's object, its interior act, and the *habitus*. These three aspects enable a study of the mediating role of faith propositions for the faith act and belief as an act of intellect and will, as well as the function of belief's twofold infused *habitus*. All of these themes enable (1) an evaluation of faith as noetic ascent to contact with God as first truth, (2) a precision of which faculties are the subjects of ascent, and (3) an explanation of the human contribution to this ascent and of the grace that enables it. All of these themes undergird Thomas's exposition on the gift of understanding, the gift that perfects faith. To conclude, I will take a brief look at the Dionysian element of unitive faith in Thomas, a theme taken up at length in chapter 8.

Aquinas grounds his doctrine of the act and virtue of faith on an analysis of its object, as objects specify acts and operative *habitus*. He identifies the formal object: "the faith about which we are speaking assents to something only because it has been revealed by God; hence, faith rests upon divine truth as a medium."[117] Faith is ordered to God's revelation. Revealed truth gives faith a unified object. We believe something insofar as God manifests it. Faith's material object (or what is believed) includes the triune God in himself and his effects, from creation to eternal life. In itself faith's primary material object (God) is

---

ner, proficient, perfect) that Aquinas mentions at II-II, q. 24, a. 9; Garrigou-Lagrange, *Christian Perfection*, 283. But the *ST* does not apply these degrees to the gifts. For the gifts of understanding (q. 8, a. 4, ad 1–3) and counsel (q. 52, a. 1, ad 2), Thomas mentions a minimal assistance of the Spirit to ensure salvation, but not as a firm category clearly distinct from a "higher" spiritual state. The gift of fear includes a twofold schema (q. 19, a. 8). Q. 45, a. 5c mentions a higher grade of wisdom, but attributes its effects especially to a charism (*gratia gratis data*) at work in some who have sanctifying grace. By itself, a charism does not increase sanctification or union. Similarly, Hans Urs von Balthasar holds that Aquinas makes the stages of purification, illumination, and union central to his mystical theology. He cites the model's application to the cardinal virtues (I-II, q. 61, a. 5); see von Balthasar, "Zur Ortsbestimmung christlicher Mystik," in von Balthasar, Beierwaltes and Haas, *Grundfragen der Mystik*, 54. But the three stages have a minor function in Aquinas's theology of virtue.

116. Sherwin, *By Knowledge*, 130–31.

117. *ST* II-II, q. 1, a. 1c: "non enim fides de qua loquimur assentit alicui nisi quia est a Deo revelatum; unde ipsi veritati divinae fides innititur tanquam medio."

simple, yet we grasp it in a complex way: "the known is in the knower according to the mode of the knower. But that mode proper to the human intellect is to know the truth by composing and dividing."[118] We grasp faith's object by a truth judgment and so through propositions (e.g., "Jesus is Lord"). The faith act reaches its term in the divine reality believed, but due to our composite mode of knowing, the faith act passes *through* propositions. Thus belief essentially presupposes and implies concept-bound cognition. Faith's mode of cognition respects our natural mode of knowing without being restricted to all of nature's limits, a notion to be précised.[119]

Since faith essentially has an enigmatic character, Aquinas locates the assent of belief between the certain knowledge available to reason (e.g., the first principles of reason) and opinion that includes doubt. The will's act moving the intellect to believe distinguishes faith from natural certitude (which has no need of the will to assent) and doubt (where there is no firm assent).[120] Thomas distances himself from his contemporaries' varying emphases on faith's affective element so as to revalorize the noetic character of belief, yet without excluding the will. He can thus more easily account for Augustine's description of belief as "knowing with assent." Thomas explains: "For since the act of faith pertains to the intellect insofar as it is moved by the will to assent, as was said, faith's object can be taken either from the part of the intellect itself, or from the part of the will moving the intellect."[121] The intellect regards God as the material and formal object of faith. The will regards God (first Truth) as our final end. Together these two aspects constitute a single faith act. The analysis of faith's object confirms that the speculative intellect is the proper subject of belief, but as moved by the will. Belief is noetic assent caused by the will's "impulse."[122] Intellect has priority in specifying the object and noetic content believed, while

---

118. *ST* II-II, q. 1, a. 2c: "cognita sunt in cognoscente secundum modum cognoscentis. Est autem modus proprius humani intellectus ut componendo et dividendo veritatem cognoscat."

119. *ST* II-II, q. 1, a. 2, ad 2; a. 5; q. 5, a. 3; Chenu, "Contribution à l'histoire du traité de la foi," in *La Parole de Dieu*, 1:47–48; Sherwin, *By Knowledge*, 131–34.

120. *ST* II-II, q. 1, a. 4c; see also q. 2, a. 1.

121. *ST* II-II, q. 2, a. 2c: "Cum enim credere ad intellectum pertineat prout est a voluntate motus ad assentiendum, ut dictum est, potest obiectum fidei accipi vel ex parte ipsius intellectus, vel ex parte voluntatis intellectum moventis."

122. *ST* II-II, q. 2, a. 2c and ad 1; q. 4, a. 2c and ad 3.

the will has priority in the order of exercise. The late Aquinas builds his theology of faith on his mature psychology of action.[123]

Thomas develops this theology in relation to his late doctrine of grace. The faith act proceeds from two operating principles, each elevated by an infused *habitus*. *On Truth* considers knowledge of eternal rewards as causing the will to move the intellect toward assent. But the *Summa* insists that the will's motion proceeds from habitual and actual grace.[124] The convert responds to the gospel heard only with the help of an interior call, both an interior revelation and an interior instinct impelling the will toward communion with God.[125] Such actual grace finds its complement in habitual grace. Thomas explains that faith's proper subject is the intellect, yet as commanded by the will. Each faculty is elevated by a *habitus*: for "faith which is a gift of grace inclines the human being to believe by an affection for the good, even if it [faith] is not formed"[126] A believer who has lost charity still has an affective (habitual) inclination. Infused faith includes an affective *habitus* distinct from charity. Hence, the faith act proceeds from a noetic *habitus* and an affective *habitus*. Aquinas contrasts this faith with that of the demons.

The noetic *habitus* of belief is the light of faith. The *Sentences Commentary* relates this light to an unspecified vision whereby one recognizes that God is speaking. This vision seems to be a sufficient cause of the intellect's assent. The early Aquinas compares the agent intellect's light manifesting the principles of reason to the light of faith manifesting the articles believed.[127] Such light language becomes more sober in the *Summa*:

by the natural light of the intellect, the human being assents to principles, thus by the habit of virtue the virtuous man has right judgment about the things that belong to this virtue. And in this way also by the light of faith divinely infused in the human being, he assents to those things that belong to faith, but not those that are contrary [to faith].[128]

123. Sherwin, *By Knowledge*, 145. For the psychology of action, see chapter 5 of this volume, in the section on the psychology of love.
124. *DV*, q. 14, a. 1; *ST* I-II, q. 109, a. 6; Sherwin, *By Knowledge*, 137–40.
125. *ST* II-II, q. 6, a. 1; *In Ioan.*, ch. 6, lect. 5, no. 935; Sherwin, *By Knowledge*, 144.
126. *ST* II-II, q. 5, a. 2, ad. 2: "fides quae est donum gratiae inclinat hominem ad credendum secundum aliquem affectum boni, etiam si sit informis." Cf. *DV*, q. 14, a. 4, ad. 7.
127. Aquinas, *III Sent.*, d. 23, q. 2, a. 1, ad 4; q. 3, a. 2, ad 2; Sherwin, *By Knowledge*, 136–39.
128. *ST* II-II, q. 2, a. 3, ad 2: "homo per naturale lumen intellectus assentit principiis,

Faith's light is the "medium under which" one can correctly judge and know the objects of belief.[129] How does this light act upon the intellect? The previous passage focuses on assent to the articles of right faith. When read with another *Summa* text, the passage reveals that the same light enables one to recognize *that* he should believe and *what* he should believe.[130] The latter implies a speculative judgment about truth. A noetic *habitus* inclines the mind to revealed truth, just as virtue inclines to right judgment. This *habitus* inclines to full noetic assent, thus disposing the intellect to obey the will's graced motion.[131] Infused light does not suffice to grant certitude, for otherwise faith would no longer depend on the will. The essential yet insufficient noetic inclination explains why this *habitus* or light is an imperfect participation in beatific cognition. Finally, experience shows that faith does not grant us the certainty of reason's *scientia*.[132] Faith is enigmatic, which partly explains our need for still higher noetic graces like the Spirit's gifts.

The faith act (joined to charity) effects union with God, the fruit of the virtue as formal cause joined to the efficient causality of the Son's mission. Thus union beyond mind is "a certain *unity* to divine things through grace ... *through which* unity, human beings are *conjoined* through faith or whatever cognition, *to those things which are above* the mind's natural power."[133] By understanding the things of God in faith,

---

ita homo virtuosus per habitum virtutis habet rectum iudicium de his quae conveniunt illi virtuti. Et hoc modo etiam per lumen fidei divinitus infusum homini, homo assentit his quae sunt fidei, non autem contrariis"; see also q. 1, a. 4, ad 3. The late Aquinas still employs vision terminology, but his doctrinal intent behind the analogy centers on virtuous inclination.

129. *DV*, q. 18, a. 1, ad 1.

130. *ST* II-II, q. 1, a. 5, ad 1: "Dicendum quod infideles eorum quae sunt fidei ignorantiam habent, quia nec vident nec sciunt ea in seipsis, < nec cognoscunt > ea esse credibilia. Sed per hunc modum fideles habent eorum notitiam, non quasi demonstrative, sed inquantum per lumen fidei videntur esse credenda, ut dictum est."

131. *ST* II-II, q. 4, a. 2, ad 2. In chapter 4 of this volume, we saw that Albertus Magnus's *SDN* (ch. 1, no. 8, p. 4.77–83) presents faith as a noetic inclination and focuses the theology of faith more on intellect than in the *Sent*. The late Aquinas continues and develops this double evolution in Albert, deliberately or without realizing it.

132. *ST* II-II, q. 4, a. 8.

133. *DDN*, ch. 7, lect. 1, no. 705: "mens nostra ... habet quamdam *unitionem* ad res divinas per gratiam ... *per quam* unitionem, *coniunguntur* homines per fidem aut quamcumque cognitionem, *ad ea quae sunt super* naturalem mentis virtutem." *ST* II-II, q. 4, a. 1 refers to faith as the beginning of eternal life, which implies union. Q. 24, a. 12, ad 5 denies that faith unites, but in reference to unformed faith. For the link between

one attains total (though participated) deification. Faith's unitive element is linked to its noetic nature and distinguishes its conjoining function from that of charity, though these virtues operate together.

Faith involves not a direct or simple apprehension but a judgment tied to concepts received through revelation in Scripture, a judgment that leads to a grasp of the truth believed. Faith's noetic light and charity's affective instinct stretch the believer's natural noetic capacity, all the while respecting the intrinsic laws of human cognition, for grace does not destroy nature. If union with God essentially occurs in and by living faith, then it seems that union does not necessarily exclude active human cooperation and concept-bound cognition.

CHARITY IN THOMAS

Thomas's theology of faith indicates the centrality of charity for union with God. The development in his psychology of love calls for a focus on his late texts about charity. First, I will consider charity as friendship, the hermeneutical key to his teaching on this virtue. Second, I will analyze the ontology of charity as a created gift and formal cause of union. This ontology helps to explain charity's relation to cognition, the third topic. Fourth, I will consider the unitive element of charity. I will conclude by relating these themes to the issue of cooperation in union.

Thomas begins his explanation of charity as friendship with two elements of Aristotle's definition of friendship. First, the love of friendship distinguishes itself from the love of concupiscence in that it involves benevolence or willing the good of the other for his or her sake, not for one's own sake. Second, friendship always includes mutuality or an exchange of love. The first element harmonizes well with Augustine's notion of enjoying God for his sake (*frui*).[134] Yet benevolence toward and mutuality with God are only possible on the foundation of a common bond or fellowship, which bond alone can overcome the Stagirite's objection that friendship with God remains beyond our reach. Aquinas notes, "Therefore since there is some communication of the

---

faith, union with God and the missions, see also Aquinas, *I Sent.*, d. 15, q. 4, a. 1c; Emery, *Trinité créatrice*, 410–11.

134. *ST* II-II, q. 23, aa. 1–2; Anthony W. Keaty, "Thomas's Authority for Identifying Charity as Friendship: Aristotle or John 15?" *Thomist* 62 (1998): 590–92.

human being to God insofar as he [God] communicates his own beatitude to us, some friendship must be founded upon this communication."[135] The love founded on this communication is charity: when God pours out sanctifying grace, he simultaneously infuses charity, a share in his self-love (as faith is a share in his self-knowledge). This divine act establishes a relative equality of the friends whereby they can begin a life of mutual exchange.[136]

Aquinas goes beyond the limits of the Stagirite's ethics as he employs the philosopher's categories in new ways. Here a key inspiration is John 15:15, which Aquinas quotes in the first *sed contra* of his "treatise" on charity: "I no longer call you servants but my friends."[137] In Aquinas's *Commentary on the Gospel of John* his explanation of this verse shows the close link between divine friendship, the new covenant or new law whose center is grace, and a theology of revelation. He notes that there are two kinds of servants: those who are moved only by another and those who act by their own will. The first ones are not free, for they are moved by their master as an instrument by its cause. A free act presupposes knowledge. Aquinas continues:

> The Apostles ... were moved by themselves to the good works that should be done, namely, by their proper will inclined through love; and hence the Lord reveals his secrets to them.... For the true sign of friendship is that the friend reveals the secrets of his heart to his friend. For since the heart of friends is one and their soul is one, it appears that the friend does not place what he reveals to his own friend outside of his own heart.[138]

Christ's revelation is an essential condition for the disciples' free participation in the life of grace. Charity needs cognition, for blind love falls

---

135. *ST* II-II, q. 23, a. 1c: "Cum igitur sit aliqua communicatio hominis ad Deum secundum quod nobis suam beatitudinem communicat, super hanc communicationem oportet aliquam amicitiam fundari."

136. H.-D. Noble, notes to *Somme théologique, La charité*, by Thomas Aquinas, vol. 1, 2a–2ae, Questions 23–26 (Paris: Tournai, 1936), 241; Joseph Bobik, "Aquinas on 'Communicatio': The Foundation of Friendship and 'Caritas,'" *Modern Schoolman* 64 (1986): 13–15.

137. Keaty rightfully insists on the importance of John 15 for Thomas's modification of Aristotelian friendship; Keaty, "Thomas's Authority," 586–95.

138. *In Ioan.*, ch. 15, lect. 3, nos. 2015–16: "Apostoli ... a se movebantur ad bona opera facienda, scilicet ex propria voluntate per amorem inclinata; et ideo Dominus secreta sua revelat eis.... Verum enim amicitiae signum est quod amicus amico suo cordis secreta revelet. Cum enim amicorum sit cor unum et anima una, non videtur amicus extra cor suum ponere quod amico revelat."; see also *SCG* IV, ch. 21, no. 3578.

well short of perfect love. The union of hearts that love induces implies that Christ reveals the life of God in the highest degree possible.

The freedom of God's friends also calls for a higher intrinsic operational capacity. Aquinas refuses the Lombard's apparent reduction of charity to the Spirit's motion in the will. Such a doctrine cannot account for believers' dignity as free actors whose charitable acts are truly theirs, truly human. Thomas adds a metaphysical argument for charity's created status:

> Now no act is perfectly produced by some active potency unless it [the act] is connatural to it by some form which is the principle of action ... charity's act exceeds the nature of the will's potency. Therefore, unless some form were superadded to this natural potency by which it would be inclined to the act of love, this [love's] act would be more imperfect than natural acts and the acts of other virtues, and would not be easy and delightful.[139]

The necessity of a formal principle proportioned to the creature, the ontology of act-potency, and the saints' experience of progressively greater ease and joy in the acts of charity by growth in grace call for an infused *habitus* that perfects the will.

In parallel to his theology of grace, Aquinas identifies created charity as a formal cause of union: "charity joins [us] to the infinite good, not effectively, but formally; hence infinite power does not belong to charity, but to the author of charity."[140] The Spirit invisibly sent into our hearts is the primary efficient cause of loving union with the Father. Charity as a formal cause enables the will's efficient causality of virtuous acts. Efficiency is a key function of the will in the psychology of action. By implication the will's graced efficiency is a secondary cause of loving union, yet wholly dependent on the Spirit's immediate, primary causality that (1) infuses charity as a formal cause of action and (2) moves the graced will to its operation. Aquinas's mature doc-

---

139. *ST* II-II, q. 23, a. 2c: "Nullus autem actus perfecte producitur ab aliqua potentia activa nisi sit ei connaturalis per aliquam formam quae sit principium actionis ... actus caritatis excedit naturam potentiae voluntatis. Nisi ergo aliqua forma superadderetur naturali potentiae per quam inclinaretur ad dilectionis actum, esset actus iste imperfectior actibus naturalibus et actibus aliarum virtutum; nec esset facilis et delectabilis."

140. *DC*, a. 1, ad 10: "caritas coniungit bono infinito, non effective, sed formaliter; unde virtus infinita non competit caritati, sed caritatis auctori." The work dates from 1271 to 1272; Torrell, *Saint Thomas Aquinas*, vol. 1, *The Person and his Work*, 203, 336.

trines of divine action and actual grace clarify the will's relation to the Spirit's mission. The will is *a* secondary cause of union, though progress in union also depends on the Spirit's gratuitous motion in his gifts. Finally, each degree of charity enjoys a degree of habitual union, and to that extent we can actualize union with God by loving him in act.

The theme of friendship shows the essential role of knowledge in love. More precisely, the graced will commands virtuous acts while the intellect shows the will its end, a division of labor consistent with Aquinas's mature psychology of love.[141] Charity and graced cognition stand in a relation of mutual dependence. The will needs to be guided to its object, yet faith's cognition remains partial.[142] In this life charity enjoys an excellence that surpasses cognition, as

> the act of an appetitive power is perfected by this, that the appetite is inclined to the reality itself. And therefore it must be that the motion of the appetitive power is toward realities according to their condition. But the act of the cognitive power is according to the mode of the knower.[143]

Pilgrims only attain mediated, partial cognition of God, but they love him directly, in his reality. The will is perfected by its inclination to the thing loved (outside of the will), while the intellect is perfected by the presence of the known in the knower.[144] Hence loving God is greater than knowing him. A modified Aristotelian psychology undergirds this qualified primacy of charity. Faith's cognition serves charity as an essential guide, but charity's perfection goes beyond such cognition, for its only "measure" is God. The will's inclination refers to an operative principle, the perfection of the *habitus* by its intensification, including its *complacentia* in the beloved.[145] Overall the relative primacy of love in union with God distinguishes Aquinas's mysticism from the Areopagite's more intellect-centered approach, even though Thomas remains far from so-called Affective Dionysianism.

---

141. *ST* II-II, q. 23, a. 8; Sherwin, *By Knowledge*, 196–99.

142. *DC*, a. 2, ad 11; Sherwin, *By Knowledge*, 153–54.

143. *ST* II-II, q. 27, a. 4c: "actus autem appetitivae virtutis perficitur per hoc quod appetitus inclinatur ad rem ipsam. Et ideo oportet quod motus appetitivae virtutis sit in re secundum <conditionem> ipsarum rerum; actus autem cognitivae virtutis est secundum modum cognoscentis."

144. See *ST* I, q. 16, a. 1c and the sections on epistemology and the psychology of love in chapter 5 of this volume.

145. *ST* II-II, q. 23, a. 6; q. 27, a. 4, ad 2; Sherwin, *By Knowledge*, 78, 154, 159–61.

Still, charity cannot attain perfection in this life, not because of an intrinsic deficiency of the infused form, but because of the pilgrim's mode of being. As a *habitus* charity's fulfillment comes in operation. Only in heaven can "the whole heart be actually carried into God."[146] The pilgrim cannot always think of God, hence he cannot always love God in act. Bodily necessities require his attention and his "contemplation is not without the imaginative power's action, or that of other corporeal powers, which necessarily become weak by prolonged action."[147] Aquinas links charity's perfection to the possibilities and limits of contemplation, whose seat is the intellect. Contemplation is the best way to love God, for it is the most direct.[148] Aquinas's response should be nuanced by his doctrine of the *imago*'s perfection via the love of virtue, which revalorizes the active life focused on loving God by loving one's neighbor. The active and contemplative lives aim at *acts* of cognition and love whose direct or indirect object is God.

Aquinas posits a distinction between affective and real union. The latter refers to the soul being conjoined to God as to its known and beloved "object," to God in his reality. Chapter 5 of this volume showed that the lover's complacency in the beloved grounds a first affective union. Affective union causes an inclination to the beloved, while charity makes the lover desire what the beloved desires. Charity's act includes benevolence and usually affective union.[149] Real union involves the friends' mutual presence, which is perfected in *conversatio* or shared activities: "to be united to him [God], it is necessary that this be through the operation of intellect and affect, which occurs through charity."[150] Friendship elevates affective union, so that "affection is carried into the reality loved, so that it does not return to itself, because it wills the good of the reality loved ... such love brings about ecstasy."[151] As this affection has its term in God, the lover it taken out of

---

146. ST II-II, q. 24, a. 8c: "totum cor hominis actualiter semper feratur in Deum."

147. DC, a. 10, ad 7: "contemplatio mentis humanae non est sine actione virtutis imaginativae, et aliarum virium corporalium, quas necesse est laxari diuturnitate actionis."

148. ST II-II, q. 182, a. 2c.

149. ST II-II, q. 27, a. 2c; q. 28, a. 1; *DDN*, ch. 4, lect. 9, no. 424; Sherwin, *By Knowledge*, 157.

150. DC, a. 2, ad 7: "requiritur quod uniamur ei per operationem intellectus et affectus, quod fit per caritatem"; see also Bobik, "Aquinas," 17.

151. *DDN*, ch. 4, lect. 10, no. 430: "affectus fertur in rem amatam, quod non recurrit in seipsum, quia ipsi rei amatae vult bonum.... Sic igitur talis amor extasim facit"; see

himself and into God. Such ecstasy primarily refers to the will being carried into the reality loved, not to an interior state. Aquinas found this ontological sense of ecstasy in the Areopagite, for Dionysian ecstasy moves creatures to exercise providential care for lower beings in the cosmic hierarchy. In Thomas Christianized Aristotelian friendship becomes the primary model of love, not the Areopagite's preferred notion of love for the One above us. Thomas also appropriates the Dionysian theme of love as a unitive force. However, for Aquinas love is not a motor *toward* noetic union but one of union's direct causes.[152] Indeed, the *imago* perfected in friendship calls for the will to be the intellect's coprinciple of union. Thomas thus qualifies the Areopagite's intellectual mysticism.

Charity's perfection in real union here below also intensifies through the lover's longing to possess the good for himself, the graced *eros* of hope. Still, such possession presupposes that charity wills God's goodness for his sake.[153] Charity brings joy to the lover, for "the beloved is in the lover by his most noble effect, according to 1 John 4:16: 'Whoever remains in charity, remains in God and God in him.'"[154] Charity in act opens the heart to God's presence, the noble effect of real union. By charity, God is in us and we are in God.[155]

While charity alone does not suffice for union, it constitutes the central measure thereof. Since it is an infused virtue, the *habitus* of charity does not intensify by our acts, but by a new divine gift. This intensification takes place when the fervor of charity's act matches or surpasses the *habitus* already possessed.[156] Because we can merit an increase in charity, growth in habitual union is a gift that can also be merited. Finally, since the two divine missions are inseparable, growth in

---

also Peter A. Kwasniewski, "St. Thomas, Exstasis, and Union with the Beloved," *Thomist* 61 (1997): 593–97.

152. De Andia, *Henosis*, 151–51, 252–53. Like Dionysius, Aquinas says little on bridal mysticism, but his focus on charity as friendship could be synthesized with the Song of Songs.

153. *ST* II-II, q. 17, aa. 2, 6.

154. *ST* II-II, q. 28, a. 1c: "Et ex hoc ipso quod amatur est in amante per nobilissimum suum effectum, secundum illud I Ioann. IV: 'Qui manet in caritate, in Deo manet et Deus in eo.'"

155. *SCG* IV, ch. 21, no. 3576–77; *ST* I-II, q. 66, a. 6; II-II, q. 28, a. 2.

156. Aquinas, *I Sent.*, d. 17, q. 2, a. 3c; *ST* I-II, q. 52, a. 3; II-II, q. 24, aa. 4, 6; Labourdette, *Cours de théologie morale*, vol. 10, *La Charité*, 70.

habitual charity includes growth in faith. The Spirit's procession from the Son entails an ascent in habitual union that takes the form of a double spiral of wisdom and love.

Finally, a theology of charity centered on (1) friendship fulfilled in mutual exchange and (2) *habitus* as a supernatural principle of acts that is given by the divine persons sent naturally entails a mysticism of cooperation, not one of pure passivity. Growth in habitual union (which includes a new sending of the Son and the Spirit) means a higher capacity to cooperate with God.

Like Albert, Thomas integrates the Dionysian theme of love as a unitive force. But Aquinas bypasses his teacher's favorite notion of charity as formal flux and seems to refuse charity an efficient causality. He places greater emphasis on the ontology of *habitus*-act and the theme of friendship, which helps to explain charity's relative priority over cognition in union. That priority can be found in Albert's eschatology, but not in his exposition of the pilgrim's charity.

THE VISION OF GOD IN THOMAS

Aquinas draws much inspiration from his teacher's original eschatology and offers new arguments for some of Albert's doctrines. My study targets the same subthemes of the beatific vision analyzed in chapter 3—namely, (1) beatitude as an operation; (2) the saints' direct, noncomprehensive vision of God; (3) God's essence likened to the intelligible form of beatified minds; (4) the created light of glory; and (5) the relation of intellect and will. I will focus mostly on the *Sentences Commentary*. Thomas's eschatology remains fairly consistent throughout his career. Indeed, his early texts include detailed arguments that later works take for granted.[157]

The commentary takes up beatitude in general before the vision of God. All things are joined to the ultimate end by assimilation. Creatures become most like divine act by attaining the highest act possible for them. Human beings do so by knowing and loving God. Thomas fuses Aristotelian cosmology and an Augustinian *imago* without assigning any role to memory.

---

157. Torrell, "La vision de Dieu 'per essentiam' selon saint Thomas d'Aquin," in *Recherches thomasiennes*, Bibliothèque Thomiste 52 (Paris: Vrin, 2000), 187–89.

the ultimate perfection of anything will be its perfect operation; hence a thing is said to be in view of its operation. Similarly if we consider the conjunction [to the end] that is proper to the rational creature, the human being's ultimate perfection consists in operation: for a *habitus* is not conjoined to an object except by an act's mediation.[158]

While each creature's substantial *esse* and form constitute its primary act, it attains perfection by second act or operation, according to each being's nature. The human being is inserted in the teleology of the cosmos, but as *imago*. As our end is not just any assimilation to God's goodness but a share in his beatitude, such participation must include our operation. And because perfection involves the creature's assimilation to pure act, the operation must truly belong to the creature.[159] Such an eschatology leads toward a mysticism that includes the human being's own cognitive and affective acts within the height of union.

Aquinas then takes up the issue of the saints' direct vision of God's essence. Like Albert, he refuses an Avicennian notion of beatitude that centers on the impression of nondivine forms. Like his teacher, Thomas considers Chrysostom's and the Areopagite's apparent refusal of a direct vision of God to signal the impossibility of comprehending God. Like Albert, Aquinas turns to Averroes for a key doctrine: the separate agent intellect that informs the (individual) potential intellect becomes the divine essence that joins itself to the created intellect, bringing it into act.[160] All cognition requires form, and only the divine form can adequately manifest God, as any created similitude falls short of the divine original. Arab Aristotelianism offers a cognitive analogy for union: "For just as a natural form, by which something has being, and matter make one being absolutely; so the form, by which the intellect

---

158. Aquinas, *IV Sent.*, d. 49, q. 1, a. 2, qla. 2c, 679: "erit ultima perfectio uniuscujusque rei sua operatio perfecta: unde res esse dicitur propter suam operationem. Similiter si consideremus conjunctionem quae est propria rationalis creaturae, ultima perfectio hominis in operatione consistit: habitus enim non conjungitur objecto nisi mediante actu."

159. Aquinas thus develops Albertus Magnus's brief *SDN* comments on beatitude as involving virtue's operative perfection (ch. 11, no. 15, pp. 417.79–418.4); see chapter 4 of this volume and Wéber, *Personne humaine*, 239–43.

160. Aquinas, *IV Sent.*, d. 49, q. 2, a. 1; *ST* I, q. 12, aa. 1–2; Pierre-Marie de Contenson, "S. Thomas et l'avicennisme latin," *RSPT* 43 (1959) : 26–28; Wéber, "Les emprunts majeurs à Averroès chez Albert le Grand et dans son école," in *Averroismus im Mittelalter und in der Renaissance,* edited by Friedrich Niewöhner and Loris Sturlese, 162–68 (Zürich: Spur, 1994).

understands, and the intellect itself are made one in understanding."[161] Intentional unity is distinct from other, higher types of union such as the incarnation. God's essence modifies the possible intellect at the accidental level, so that God and the saints remain substantially distinct. Yet the saints enjoy an ontological union that elevates them at the level of their supreme dignity: that of the perfect *imago*. Aquinas's distinction between the soul's essence and its faculties finds its eschatological payoff. Also, God's essence is his knowledge, so that his essence can bring another intellect into act without a mediating similitude.[162]

The saints can only receive the divine species via a proper disposition of their own noetic capacity. Aquinas combines the principle of disposition with the Avicennian notion of proper operation: "Now the form which is the divine essence exceeds every natural faculty and capacity. For the power and its proper act are always taken in the same genre."[163] Every nature is ordered to certain kinds of operation. For human beings the latter involve the cognition of material creatures' quiddities and created being, since operation follows upon being, and we exist by one substantial form naturally joined to matter. Aquinas synthesizes Aristotelian anthropology with a Dionysian cosmic hierarchy of agents. He adopts Albert's insight on the need for a created light of glory, but he offers a new argument for this light: an anthropology centered on our cognitive proportion to the material cosmos.[164] The fixed, limited operations assigned to rational beings can be elevated by Dionysian theophanies as read by Albert:

Therefore, since the created intellect's natural power does not suffice for seeing God's essence, as was shown, the [created intellect's] power of understanding must be increased further by divine grace. And we call this augmentation of the intellective power illumination of the intellect.[165]

161. Aquinas, *IV Sent.*, d. 49, q. 2, a. 1c, 684: "Sicut enim ex forma naturali qua aliquid habet esse, et materia, efficitur unum ens simpliciter; ita ex forma qua intellectus intelligit, et ipso intellectu, fit unum in intelligendo."
162. Aquinas, *IV Sent.*, d. 49, q. 2, aa. 1, 6.
163. Aquinas, *IV Sent.*, d. 49, q. 2, a. 6c, 688: "Forma autem quae est divina essentia, omnem facultatem et capacitatem naturalem excedit. Potentia enim et proprius ejus actus semper accipiuntur in eodem genere."
164. Aquinas, *IV Sent.*, d. 49, q. 2, aa. 4, 6; *ST* I, q. 12, aa. 4, 7.
165. *ST* I, q. 12, a. 5c: "Cum igitur virtus naturalis intellectus creati non sufficiat ad Dei essentiam videndam, ut ostensum est, oportet quod ex divina gratia superaccrescat

Albert assigns the agent intellect a function in the vision of God. Aquinas cuts out the agent intellect, since the noetic reception of God's essence requires no actualization. But the created light of glory constitutes a centerpiece of both Dominicans' eschatologies. Thomas appeals to it to explain the diversity of vision in heaven, a hierarchy determined by the charity attained in this life. As in Albert, the theology of the missions stands in the background. The created light of glory is given by the divine persons sent.[166] The light of glory is a formal cause disposing us for the efficient, exemplary and final causality of the Son and the Spirit, who lead us to the Father.[167] Aquinas's Christology parallels this insistence on the need for a graced operative principle. Christ's human nature, as human nature, does not share *per se* in the Trinity's uncreated act of knowledge and love. His created nature, taken according to what defines a human nature, has a proper operation. Thus his human act of enjoying God needs elevating grace.[168]

Finally, the late Aquinas refuses Albert's relative priority of the will over the intellect in beatitude. The will's act involves the desire for an absent good or delight in its presence. But the intellect's act reaches completion by making its object intentionally present: "now we obtain it [the end] by the fact that it is made present to us through the intellect's act; and then the will rests in the end obtained, in which it delights."[169] Perfect delight naturally follows and depends on noetic union. Aquinas refuses Albert's division between an imperfect beatific intellectual union and the will's delight as true union. Affective delight completes this union.[170]

CONCLUSION

The doctrine of the missions presents a deeply trinitarian path to and aim of union. Through our ontological and operational conformity to

---

ei virtus intelligendi. Et hoc augmentum virtutis intellectivae illuminationem intellectus vocamus"; see also Aquinas, *IV Sent.*, d. 49, q. 2, a. 6.

166. *ST* I, q. 12, a. 6; q. 43, a. 6, ad 3; Juárez, *Dios Trinidad*, 380–89.

167. *ST* I, q. 12, a. 5; *SCG* III, ch. 53, nos. 2299, 2302. Aquinas makes the *lumen gloriae* a disposing cause of divinization.

168. *ST* III, q. 7, a. 1, ad 1.

169. *ST* I-II, q. 3, a. 4c: "consequimur autem ipsum per hoc quod fit praesens nobis per actum intellectus; et tunc voluntas delectata conquiescit in fine iam adepto."

170. Albertus Magnus, *I Sent.*, d. 1, a. 12 (see chapter 3 of this volume); *In Ioan.*, ch. 17, lect. 1, no. 2186.

the Son and the Spirit, we are conjoined to them and, through them, to the Father. The missions call for a constant balance of knowledge and love on the path to union: progress in charity and faith occur in tandem. The doctrines of the missions, divine action, and actual grace emphasize God's immediate operation in any event or state of union. Indeed, Aquinas's mature notions of actual grace and the Spirit's gifts shatter any lingering illusions about the possibility of a wholly autonomous creaturely ascent to God, yet without excluding human cooperation. Indeed, active human cooperation in ascent manifests the grandeur of grace. Thomas underlines the graced experience of the divine persons but minimizes the role of an explicit consciousness of God's presence. His focus remains on ontology and progress in virtue, not inner awareness. Indeed, if the certitude of being in grace at all usually escapes us, how much more the certain knowledge or reflexive awareness of enjoying the highest gifts of union. Christo-forming grace grants us a visible model of invisible grace at work within us and ensures mysticism's abiding link to the heart of the salvific economy. The Spirit's motion in his seven gifts and its close link to the theological virtues show that union entails a progressive increase in both docility to the Spirit and the graced capacity to act with the Spirit (spontaneity). The doctrine of faith synthesizes cognition attained through propositions and judgments with invisible contact of the divine reality believed, preparing the way for a mysticism that does not so much overcome our temporal mode of being as clear the way to union through our limited mode of being. The theology of charity as friendship further reinforces the interconnection of knowledge and love as well as the centrality of cooperation in union. Indeed, charity crowns the union possible here below. Aquinas's eschatology unfolds the consequences of his Dionysian-Aristotelian insistence that the human being is proportioned to know embodied beings. Such an anthropology leads to an emphasis on divine gifts—especially on the light of glory as an intrinsic elevation of the intellect whose natural place is not in the heavens. Like the theology of charity, the doctrine of beatitude insists on the necessity of created acts in union. Total passivity before God prevents union. Together the doctrines considered in this chapter set the stage for a new approach to Dionysian mysticism.

7

Divine Naming in Thomas

The Dionysian element of Thomas's theology of union proceeds from and in turn marks Aquinas's creative development of the theory of the divine names. Because naming follows knowing, new insights on the manner of our union with God through knowing affect the doctrine of divine naming and vice versa. Since Thomas's approach to the possibility and limits of naming God differs from the Areopagite's, the significance of Moses in the dark cloud also shifts for Aquinas. Like Dionysius, Thomas carefully integrates the pieces of his theological puzzle into a systematic whole. Also, Aquinas's theology of union grants a significant place to (1) Moses, who knows "what God is not" by the Spirit's gift of understanding, and (2) Hierotheus, who suffers divine things and judges by the Spirit's wisdom. The noetic fruit of these two gifts is distinct from, yet complementary to the acquired knowledge expressed by the divine names. The operation of these gifts is linked to the possibility and limits of acquired cognition about God and the practice of divine naming that follows from it. Thus a consideration of the latter helps to identify the precise function of these two gifts of the Spirit in Aquinas's mystical theology.

The current chapter analyzes Aquinas's key texts on divine naming, building on very fine recent scholarship on this topic. To other scholars' interpretive advances I add a consideration of Thomas's relation to Dionysius and Albert, a comparison that has not been adequately undertak-

Divine Naming in Thomas 297

en in the secondary literature.[1] My study of divine naming in Aquinas thus has the twofold formality I employed earlier—namely, the doctrinal link with union and the historical link with Dionysius and Albert as sources. To my knowledge no one has approached Thomas's doctrine of divine naming under this double formality. The order of my exposition mostly follows the order of the *Prima Pars* and its question 13.

Thomas's most complete, mature treatment of divine naming is found in the *Summa* (*Prima Pars*, question 13). It therefore functions as this chapter's key text. Question 13 stands within a carefully structured plan. In contrast, Albert's Dionysian approach to divine naming in his *Sentences Commentary* lacks systematic integration with the same work's rather Augustinian anthropology. In Albert's Dionysian commentaries, his key remarks on the divine names follow the flow of the Areopagite's text rather than a synthetic plan. Aquinas's *Summa* study of divine naming only makes sense in relation to the preceding questions (1–12). Thus, as an essential preface to my analysis of question 13, I will survey the *Summa*'s genre, the "five ways" to God that launch the practice of naming, and the knowledge of God that underlies the divine names.

Like Albert's commentaries on the Lombard and Dionysius, question 13 of the *Prima Pars* expounds on the theory and practice of naming God in a theological context that presumes the gift of faith and God's revelation culminating in Christ, even as it uses notions common to philosophy and theology. I thus need to consider the *Summa*'s theological genre. The five ways and the divine attributes that follow them (questions 2–11) determine the nature of the object studied, a determination that guides the nature of discourse on the object.[2] The metaphysical side of theology precedes and grounds its epistemology (question 12) and theory of discourse (question 13). Finally, I will complete my pref-

---

1. An exception is Humbrecht, *Théologie négative*, 321–478. My comments will be more systematic in nature. Also, Humbrecht's magisterial study does not dwell at length on how Aquinas transformed Dionysius. Gregory P. Rocca, *Speaking the Incomprehensible God: Thomas Aquinas on the Interplay of Positive and Negative Theology* (Washington, D.C.: The Catholic University of America Press, 2004), devotes little attention to Albert. I will develop some of Rocca's insights on the relation between Aquinas and Dionysius on divine naming.
2. Bonino, "La simplicité de Dieu," in *Studi 1996*, edited by Dietrich Lorenz (Rome: Pontificia Università San Tommaso, 1997), 119.

ace to divine naming by considering the difference between philosophical and faith-based knowledge of God, which helps to specify how theological cognition makes possible and structures the nature of naming.

My analysis of question 13 and some parallel passages from Thomas's contemporaneous works focuses on the following themes, each of which reemerge in chapter 8. First, I will consider the relation of knowledge and naming (article 1). The link between cognition and discourse helps to determine to what extent one might or might not insist upon a breakdown in naming during union, a breakdown that parallels or reflects the intellect's silence or inactivity in union. Second, I will take up the notion of naming as an act of judgment (articles 1, 4, and 5). The place of judgment helps to determine the way in which concepts can function as partial noetic ladders to the divine mystery—that is, judgment helps to determine whether concepts are indispensible mediations or ultimately obstacles to the intellect's union with God. Third, I will consider material creatures as the starting point to name God (article 1). A way of naming (and knowing) that remains somehow bound to sensible creatures sets the stage for a doctrine of union that emphasizes the incomplete, indirect status of noetic union with God here below and valorizes naming despite its limitations. Fourth, I will analyze the centrality of God's formal causality and the Creator-creature similitude (article 2), twin doctrines that lead to the theological refusal of an entirely hidden divine substance beyond God's processions. The latter distinction constitutes a pillar of Dionysian apophatism. The fifth theme is substantial divine naming, which directly follows from the fourth (article 2). Here we come to a crossroads for Thomas's kataphatic rereading of Dionysian apophatism. Aquinas's interpretation valorizes the intellect's own proper act of knowing God in union, an act whose object is not limited to God's processions or activity. Sixth, I will consider the distinction between the reality signified and the mode of signification, perhaps Aquinas's most important hermeneutical tool in his appropriation of the Areopagite (articles 3 and 5). This distinction strikes a new balance between kataphatism and apophatism, setting the stage for a gray cloud surrounding Moses's united intellect, neither too dark nor too bright. Seventh, I will consider Thomas's reinterpretation of eminence, which departs significantly from the Areopagite's primarily negative sense of eminence as a path to noetic silence.

The *Summa* presents itself as an exposition of *sacra doctrina*, a term that designates Scripture and the whole body of Christian teaching founded upon it. This doctrine is a "science" that, by the revelation transmitted in Scripture, derives its first principles from God's own knowledge and the knowledge enjoyed by the blessed.[3] Sacred doctrine gives a foretaste of the vision of God in glory. It situates itself between the knowledge of God attained by reason and that enjoyed in the eschaton. The central element or *ratio* of the beatific vision is the direct vision of God's essence without mediating theophanies. By implication, sacred doctrine's partial share in eschatological knowledge must enable it to make some positive claims about God's substance and not just his activity or processions. Sacred doctrine as restricted to knowing God's activity would imply no more than a participation in the vision of theophanies. Yet sacred doctrine cannot take us beyond faith's indirect knowledge. Thus a cognition derived from beatific knowledge implies (1) the possibility of knowing and thus naming God substantially and (2) the impossibility of knowing God's essence in this life. Sacred doctrine as a dim yet real share in God's self-knowledge also seems to entail the first of these two implications.[4]

Thomas presents his famous five ways to demonstrate God's existence in this theological framework. Here his primary opponents are not atheists, who are few and far between in thirteenth-century Latin Christendom, but rather theologians for whom God is first-known.[5] The opening article of question 2 argues precisely against this school of thought. The five ways constitute, among other things, a manifestation of the difficult, indirect nature of the pilgrim's cognition of God. Each way begins with what we know about the universe (e.g., substantial and accidental change). Thomas then argues for the necessity of a divine *cause* of the created reality known. He shows that such a cause must differ from the effect, a process of *removing* creaturely imperfections or potency. Finally, he attains a judgment that there must exist a purely ac-

---

3. *ST* I, q. 1, a. 2c; q. 2 (a preface for the rest of the *ST*): "ad huius doctrinae expositionem intendentes"; Patfoort, *Thomas d'Aquin, les clefs d'une théologie* (Paris: FAC, 1983), 28–46.

4. No one seems to have pointed out this link between sacred doctrine as an impression of beatific knowledge and substantial divine naming.

5. Torrell, *Saint Thomas Aquinas*, vol. 2, *Spiritual Master*, 26.

tual cause whose perfection we know but cannot grasp (*excess*). An appropriation of the Dionysian *triplex via* already structures the five ways to God's existence.[6] The five ways also inaugurate the study of God's nature. They manifest a God of pure act, without change, with the infinite capacity to act as efficient cause, with necessary existence, possessing in a maximum way perfections found in creatures, a God who is the intelligent, final cause of the universe. The five ways contain Thomas's opening arguments for the existence of God's attributes that subsequent questions unfold. Influenced by, though hardly limited to Aristotle, Thomas's demonstrations recall that the Stagirite has an implied doctrine of divine names that includes affirmation (e.g., "God is pure act") and remotion (e.g., "God is motionless").[7]

Aquinas introduces his formal study of the attributes, human knowledge, and names of God (questions 3–13) with a much-discussed preface: "Because we cannot know about God what he is, but [only] what he is not (*quid non sit*), we cannot consider how God is, but rather how he is not (*quomodo non sit*)."[8] This apophatic formula recalls the intense debates surrounding the 1241 condemnations. The language of *quid non sit* has roots in Damascene and Albert. The phrase *quomodo non sit* has its origins in Augustine, Damascene, and Maimonides.[9] What does knowledge of the divine *quid non sit* signify? It cannot exclude the cognition of all positive divine attributes, since the five ways have already manifested some attributes (e.g., pure actuality). However, knowing something of God's actuality does not imply a quidditative grasp of God, for act pertains to *esse*, while quidditative knowledge pertains to essence. *Quid non sit* excludes all claims at definitional or comprehensive as well as representational or intuitional knowledge.[10] Comprehensive cognition would involve a total knowledge of God that he alone can possess. Representational or intuitional knowledge would imply a direct noetic encounter with God, a face-to-face vision of him. Thomas's doctrine

---

6. *ST* I, q. 2, a. 3; Humbrecht, *Théologie négative*, 581.
7. Humbrecht, *Théologie négative*, 51–52.
8. *ST* I, q. 3, Prologue: "Sed quia de Deo scire non possumus quid sit, sed quid non sit, non possumus considerare de Deo quomodo sit, sed potius quomodo non sit."
9. *DP*, q. 7, a. 5, objection 1; Humbrecht, *Théologie négative*, 71–73, 251, 316, 472.
10. Rocca, *Speaking the Incomprehensible God*, 31–32. This apophatism has precedents in Augustine, and not just the Greek fathers; see Ayres, *Augustine and the Trinity*, 161–65.

Divine Naming in Thomas 301

is close to that of Albert, except that, starting in *On Truth,* he usually distinguishes between knowing God's *quid sit* and knowing him comprehensively. The former blessing is reserved to the angels and saints in glory, while the latter remains impossible for any creature.[11] Overall, *quid non sit* leaves open the possibility of indirect, partial, positive knowledge of God's attributes.

Thomas specifies that the divine attributes on which he will expound (in *Prima Pars,* questions 3–11) consider "what God is not."[12] He begins with God's simplicity (question 3), which removes complexity and unfolds a positive divine attribute.[13] He then shows God's perfection (question 4), goodness (questions 5–6), infinity (question 7), existence in all things (question 8), immutability (question 9), eternity (question 10), and unity (question 11). Each attribute (known by the *triplex via*) unfolds with increasing precision the negative difference between God and creatures, but on the foundation of an essentially affirmative theology.[14]

Question 12 considers three ways to know God: by glory, by grace, and by nature. After discussing the direct, noncomprehensive knowledge of God that we attain in glory, Thomas states that, by reason, we can know God in this life through his sensible effects. Because effects metaphysically depend on their cause, "from them we can be led to this, that we may know about God that he is, and that which necessarily belongs to him insofar as he is the first cause of all, exceeding all of his effects."[15] By reason alone we can know those attributes that

---

11. *DV,* q. 8, a. 1, ad 8; Dondaine, "Cognoscere de Deo 'quid est,'" *Recherches de théologie ancienne et médiévale* 22 (1955): 72–75. The late Aquinas's terminology is not consistent. *DP,* q. 7, a. 5, ad 1, 6 employ the Albertian sense of incomprehensibility for *quid est* in response to John Damascene's apophatism. In chapter 8 of this volume, I will consider a similar ambiguity in Aquinas's *DDN*. *ST* I consistently employs *quid est* to refer to God's nature or essence (see q. 3, a. 4, objection 2; q. 12, a. 13, ad 1; q. 13, a. 2, ad 1; a. 8, ad 2). See also *In Ioan.,* ch. 1, lect. 11, no. 213 on the (Augustinian) distinction between the saints seeing the whole (*tota*) divine essence but it not being wholly seen (*totaliter*).

12. *ST* I, q. 3: "Primo ergo considerandum est quomodo non sit [qq. 3–11]; secundo, quomodo a nobis cognoscatur [q. 12]; tertio, quomodo nominetur [q. 13]."

13. Bonino, "Simplicité de Dieu," 118; Humbrecht, *Théologie négative,* 252–53.

14. Rudi Te Velde, *Aquinas on God: The "Divine Science" of the "Summa Theologiae"* (Aldershot: Ashgate, 2005), 73–84.

15. *ST* I, q. 12, a. 12c: "Sed quia sunt eius effectus a causa dependentes, ex eis in hoc perduci possumus ut cognoscamus de Deo an est; et ut cognoscamus de ipso ea quae

must belong to God as cause of creatures. Thomas invokes the threefold way (*triplex via*) of knowing God as cause and as different from all creatures because he super-exceeds them, an excess that calls for remotion. Divine revelation expands this knowledge insofar as more excellent effects and a greater number of effects are shown to us in the works of the divine economy.[16] Knowledge of God through natural reason and through grace comes with the *triplex via*. Sacred doctrine enjoys a broader field of effects to draw upon and revelations such as God's tri-personality. But all cognition of God in this life remains bound to the *triplex via*.

Question 13 makes explicit and explores the details of a doctrine of divine naming already operative in the first questions of the *Summa*. Thomas does not employ a modern methodology that begins with epistemology before proceeding to a metaphysical-theological study of God's attributes. Rather, in its properly theological context, question 13 shows the possibility and limits of the practice of naming God, a possibility that divine revelation and the Christian faith always presume. By faith, Thomas knows that God can and must be named.[17]

The corpus of question 13, article 1 begins with Aristotle's linguistic triangle:

Words are signs of understandings, and understandings are similitudes of things. And so it is clear that words refer to things we signify by mediation of the intellect's conception. Thus something can be named by us insofar as it can be known by the intellect.[18]

The intellect plays an essential mediating role between the divine names and the divine realities that they signify. Hence Thomas ponders the way to know God in question 12 before he considers the na-

---

necesse est ei convenire secundum quod est prima omnium causa, excedens omnia sua causata."

16. *ST* I, q. 12, a. 13, ad 1 (cited in chapter 8, footnote 114 of this volume).

17. Rocca, *Speaking the Incomprehensible God*, 186–87. Since God creates by his Word, the structure of being enables intelligible discourse about God: the mode of the *exitus* shapes the mode of the *reditus*; Humbrecht, *Théologie négative*, 111. Trinitarian theology partly grounds Aquinas's confidence in naming God.

18. *ST* I, q. 13, a. 1c: "voces sunt signa intellectuum, et intellectus sunt rerum similitudines. Et sic patet quod voces referuntur ad res significandas mediante conceptione intellectus. Secundum igitur quod aliquid a nobis intellectu cognosci potest, sic a nobis potest nominari." For a commentary, see Ramelow, "Language," 497–516.

ture of God's names in question 13. The term *conceptio* has a narrow and a broad meaning in Aquinas. In the strict sense "conception" refers to the intellect's first operation of abstracting quiddities. In the broad sense it refers to a complete intellectual act (first and second operation or judgment), such as "God is good."[19] The present text uses the term in the latter sense, for we do not know realities by the intellect's first operation alone. Rather, we signify or name God insofar as we know him by the intellect's first and second operation.

Aquinas's intention in approaching divine naming as a form of judgment surfaces in his subsequent remarks in the same article. He notes that, in this life, God "is known by us from creatures according to the relation of principle, and by mode of excellence and of remotion. Thus, he can be named by us from creatures."[20] Thomas confirms my broad reading of conception, for the threefold way of naming is mediated not by three kinds of concepts, but by judgments that employ concepts. Since we know God through the *triplex via* whose noetic foundation is divine causality, we name him from his effects. No created effect is proportioned to the divine cause, hence no effect adequately makes him known. Thus all knowledge and all language about God follow the path of intellectual purification that removes finitude and points to God's excellence. The disproportion of cause and effect excludes the formation of univocal concepts for God and creatures. All human concepts remain proportioned to finite realities. The noetic and linguistic acts of *removing* limitation and *referring* to God's excellence do not enable the formation of more adequate concepts about God (e.g., infinite goodness). Rather, removing and referring involve acts of judgment. We know and signify *that* God's goodness is without limitation, but we cannot know or say *what* this infinite goodness is. Analogous judgments point to the divine mystery with the help of creature-bound concepts that only give reliable hints of the mystery: "The truth of the judgment is what makes us realize that the concept, *as used but not as conceived*, has been extended beyond the creaturely realm."[21]

---

19. Rocca, *Speaking the Incomprehensible God*, 168–69.
20. *ST* I, q. 13, a.1c: "[Deus] cognoscitur a nobis ex creaturis secundum habitudinem principii, et per modum excellentiae et remotionis. Sic igitur potest nominari a nobis ex creaturis."
21. Rocca, *Speaking the Incomprehensible God*, 350; see also 194, 328.

Finally, judgments about God's nature enjoy a noetic link with judgments about creatures and thus remain intelligible, for they are united by reference to a single reality—namely, the creaturely instantiation of the perfection known and signified[22]—that is, the primary and essential noetic bridge between truth judgments about God and creatures that avoids equivocity is not a concept but a perfection as realized in a created being. Such a bridge avoids univocity because the created perfection signified is a dim metaphysical reflection of its divine cause. Thomas also avoids univocity because creatures *represent*, while concepts are *similitudes* of creatures and names *signify* God through the creatures conceived.[23] Overall Thomas emphasizes divine naming as judgment much more than Albert. Naming as judgment will be a key doctrine in Thomas's interpretation of union passages in the *Commentary on the Divine Names*.

The manner of signifying follows upon the fact that human knowledge is proportioned to material creatures. Thomas's exposition favors the properly material manifestation of God rather than knowledge about God attained directly through interior effects: "Names that we attribute to God signify in this way, according to [the mode that] belongs to material creatures, whose cognition is connatural to us."[24] Knowledge of God must pass through our understanding of material creatures partly because we also grasp God's immaterial effects in the soul (e.g., the intellect's spiritual nature) in relation to our activity in the world (e.g., how we know material beings). Our grasp of finite immaterial realities such as grace remains indirect. Here we find another reason for Thomas to favor a mysticism of exterior ascent via mediations. Aquinas's epistemology is closely linked to the unicity of substantial form. Following his teacher's Cologne doctrine, Thomas joins Aristotelian psychology to the Areopagite's sacred veils.[25]

---

22. *ST* I, q. 13, a. 5c.

23. *ST* I, q. 13, a. 4c; Humbrecht, *Théologie négative*, 315–16; Rocca, *Speaking the Incomprehensible God*, 137–40, 148–50, 315. The doctrine of *esse* offers a further safeguard against univocity. *Esse* signifies an act more than a concept. Hence the *ens* that first falls into the intellect signifies by way of actuality (*SCG* I, ch. 5). All predication is reduced to this *ens* "analogicum" (*ST* I, q. 13, a. 5, ad 1); see Humbrecht, *Théologie négative*, 179–81.

24. *ST* I, q. 13, a. 1, ad 2: "nomina quae Deo attribuimus, hoc modo significant, secundum quod competit creaturis materialibus, <quarum> cognitio est nobis connaturalis."

25. *ST* I, q. 87, a. 1; I-II, q. 112, a. 5; Bonino, "'Voiles sacrés,'" 164–71.

Finite perfections manifest their divine source because of the nature of God's causality:

It was shown above [in question 4] that God has in himself all perfections of creatures, as simply and universally perfect. Hence, any creature represents and is similar to him insofar as it has some perfection ... [it represents him] as an excelling principle of whose form it falls short.[26]

In questions 3–11 Aquinas unfolds the divine attributes with the guiding thread of the doctrines of God as pure act and subsisting being (which imply the identity of God's *esse* and *essentia*). These metaphysical-theological principles allow Thomas to show that God is a transcendent Creator who has all perfections. Thence Aquinas develops a doctrine of formal creative causality that involves the manifestation of God's perfections and his concealment, for he is infinite. Because of the nature of the Creator's efficient and exemplar causalities, creatures bear imperfect similitudes of the divine "form" or nature. Every formal cause effects a likeness of itself. Aquinas integrates key Aristotelian principles of causality into his doctrine of the Creator God, yet complements them with the Dionysian principle that all creatures bear a similitude to their divine source, a likeness grounded in the doctrine of participation, which Thomas synthesizes with act-potency.[27] The late Aquinas employs exemplar causality, but his theology of creation emphasizes God's efficient causality, a model that safeguards him from univocity better than Albert's theology centered on formal flux.[28] Consequently, Thomas has more freedom than Albert to engage in reductive readings of the Areopagite's most apophatic texts.

Thomas's doctrine of divine creative causality leads directly to a theology of substantial divine naming. In other words, the divine names not only refer to God's activity in the cosmos and in history, but also to his very being or nature, a key point of divergence from Dionysius. The Ar-

---

26. *ST* I, q. 13, a. 2c: "Ostensum est autem supra quod Deus in se praehabet omnes perfectiones creaturarum, quasi simpliciter et universaliter perfectus. Unde quaelibet creatura intantum eum repraesentat, et est ei similis, inquantum perfectionem aliquam habet ... sicut excellens principium, a cuius forma effectus deficiunt."

27. *ST* I, q. 3, a. 4; q. 4, aa. 1–3; q. 7, a. 1; O'Rourke, *Pseudo-Dionysius*, 10–14, 45, 68; Rocca, *Speaking the Incomprehensible God*, 243, 256–62, 272–75, 282–86.

28. Humbrecht, *Théologie négative*, 346, 390; Salas, "Albertus Magnus," 298–312; see chapter 4 of this volume.

eopagite maintains that affirmative names are only predicated of the divine processions. Transcending negations point beyond the processions, yet they do not quite attain the hidden divine essence, which we honor in silence. Like Albert, Thomas never clearly signals that he has attained an awareness of the historical Areopagite's teaching. But Aquinas does mention doctrinal positions that come close to this teaching. In the same article that discusses the created similitudes of God's perfections (question 13, article 2), the second objection states that, for Dionysius, God's names praise his processions but not his essence. Thomas's response does not explicitly mention the Areopagite's intention. Instead, he picks up on Albert's *Sentences Commentary* distinction between "that from which" and "that to which" a name is imposed. For Albert a divine operation is the source of a name, but the divine nature is the referent or object of naming.[29] For Aquinas, too, divine names are imposed "from processions of the deity" in that the divine causality of creatures is the epistemological source of the names. Yet the intention or aim of divine naming is not only to signify what God does, but rather "the very principle of things, just as life preexists in him, though in a more eminent way than is understood or signified."[30] Thomas follows Dionysius as he acknowledges that the divine being is infinitely beyond our understanding and signification. But he departs from the Areopagite as he posits the possibility of partial, imperfect understanding and signification of the divine nature: "In this life, we cannot know God's essence as it is in itself, but we know it (*eam*) insofar as it is represented in the perfections of creatures"[31]—that is, we know the divine essence *indirectly*, unlike the beatific vision, and we know his *essence* (*eam*) in a partial way. This striking passage manifests the relative priority of positive theology in Aquinas.[32] Thus, in chapter 8 of this volume, we need to look for a kataphatic mysticism that complements such a theory of divine naming.

29. Albertus Magnus, *I Sent.*, d. 2, a. 11; see chapter 3 of this volume.
30. *ST* I, q. 13, a. 2, ad 2: "haec nomina non imponit ad significandum ipsos processus, ut cum dicitur: Deus est vivens, sit sensus: ab eo procedit vita; sed ad significandum ipsum rerum principium, prout in eo praeexistit vita, licet eminentiori modo quam intelligatur vel significetur"; see also *DDN*, ch. 2, lect. 1, no. 126.
31. *ST* I, q. 13, a. 2, ad 3: "essentiam Dei in hac vita cognoscere non possumus secundum quod in se est, sed cognoscimus eam secundum quod repraesentatur in perfectionibus creaturarum."
32. Humbrecht, *Théologie négative*, 111, 185, 316, 491, 769; Rocca, *Speaking the Incomprehensible God*, 64–72, 297, 313.

The Albertian distinction between the reality signified and the mode of signification plays a crucial role in Thomas's doctrine of substantial divine names. In question 13, article 3 Aquinas considers whether some names are predicated of God in a proper way—that is, not just metaphorically. The corpus focuses on the distinction between perfections signified and the mode of signifying. Perfections such as goodness more properly belong to God than to creatures. In other words, goodness has its source and perfect instantiation in God. But in their mode of signifying, names such as goodness are not properly said of God.[33]

Question 13, article 5 develops the theme of the mode of signifying. Thomas notes that all perfections exist in creatures in a divided way. For example, the wisdom of a human being is really distinct from his or her essence. We simply have a human essence, but we acquire wisdom over time. But, continues Thomas, "when we predicate this name [wisdom] of God, we do not intend to signify something distinct from [God's] essence ... the reality signified remains as uncomprehended and exceeding the signification of the name."[34] Because our mode of signifying is essentially bound to a finite mode of being and knowing, we cannot help but signify the perfections of beings with complex enunciations. The grammatical subject signifies a metaphysical subject, the predicate signifies an attribute, and the copula signifies that the attribute actually belongs to the subject. We also necessarily employ multiple statements, for one statement cannot adequately express all of a being's perfections. We know by an act of judgment that God's essence and wisdom are identical, but we cannot adequately conceptualize the unity of divine perfections, for such unity has no created instantiation.

In his *On the Power of God* Thomas expands on the second explanation of the mode of signifying: "as to the mode of signifying [affirmations] can be negated of God; for any of these names signify some defined form, and they are not attributed to God in this way."[35] The im-

33. *ST* I, q. 13, a. 3c; compare to *SDN*, ch. 1, no. 3, p. 2.23–49.
34. *ST* I, q. 13, a. 5c: "Sed cum hoc nomen de Deo dicimus, non intendimus significare aliquid distinctum ab essentia ... cum hoc nomen sapiens de homine dicitur, quodammodo <circumscribit> et comprehendit rem significatam; non autem cum dicitur de Deo, sed relinquit rem significatam ut incomprehensam et excedentem nominis significationem"; see also a. 12, ad 3; *DP*, q. 7, a. 5, ad 12.
35. *DP*, q. 7, a. 5, ad 2: "Dionysius ... non asserit affirmationes esse falsas ... sed quantum ad modum quem significant de Deo negari possunt: quodlibet enim istorum

mediate cognitive source of any affirmative divine name is a particular form or created perfection, one that is both distinct from other forms or perfections and subject to definition. The mode of signifying created perfections implies the ability to comprehend the perfection signified. The mode of signification (and knowing) points to a limited reality. Perhaps I can comprehend and fully describe the wisdom of a human being, for it is finite. Our mode of signifying is essentially bound to our cognition of corporeal things. Hence, *in their mode of signifying,* affirmations "can be negated of God absolutely."[36] The removal of a finite mode does not lead to any positive grasp of the divine mode of being, for God enjoys a modeless infinity. Such infinity may be the primary truth communicated by Thomas's negations or "removals," not unlike the Areopagite's transcending negations (*aphaireseis*).[37] Yet for Aquinas such negations leave open the possibility of superlative names with positive meaning.

The full significance of Thomas's doctrine only becomes clear when we compare it to his sources. Aquinas selectively adopts key elements of Albert's distinction between the reality signified and the mode of signifying. Albert's *Sentences Commentary* already connects the Dionysian language of affirmations as "incompact" with the denial of the mode of signification, a kataphatic reinterpretation of the Areopagite. The same passage points to our composite way of signifying the simple divine reality. Thomas also adopts the bulk of Albert's explanation in the preface of the latter's *Commentary on the Divine Names.* There Albert links affirmations with the reality signified and notes that the divine mode remains hidden to us, for we signify according to our mode of being.[38] But Thomas bypasses his teacher's exposition in chapter 7 of the same work, where Albert divides the reality signified in three ways: (1) as exceeding signification; (2) as an effect signified by affirmative names; and (3) as a cause (the reality of God as cause) signified by negative names. Thomas agrees with the first step but not the second

---

nominum significat aliquam formam definitam, et sic Deo non attribuuntur, ut dictum est. Et ideo absolute de Deo possunt negari, quia ei non conveniunt per modum qui significatur"; see also ad 5: "id quod significat nomen, est definitio."

36. *DP,* q. 7, a. 5, ad 2: "Et ideo absolute de Deo possunt negari."

37. Rocca, *Speaking the Incomprehensible God,* 340–42. Aquinas prefers *remotio*; Humbrecht, *Théologie négative,* 252.

38. Albertus Magnus, *I Sent.,* d. 2, a. 17; *SDN,* ch. 1, no. 3, p. 2.23–37.

and the third. He insists that the perfections signified by affirmations primarily belong to God.[39] Also, he never employs negative names to signify the divine reality insofar as it is a cause of perfections. Finally, Thomas simply ignores Albert's ambiguous presentation of two conflicting approaches to the reality signified at the end of the *Commentary on the Mystical Theology*. As we saw in chapter 4 of this volume, Albert here proposes that the reality signified also must be negated, inasmuch as divine names continue to refer to perfections that have a creaturely mode of being. Thomas's implied solution to this problem is straightforward: by an act of judgment, we negate complexity in God, for we intend to signify a simple divine reality even as we refer to that reality through an inadequate mode of signification.[40] Thomas streamlines Albert's doctrine and adds epistemological as well as linguistic considerations that further manifest the distance of the divine reality to our mode of knowing and naming. Yet through such clarifications Thomas firmly and consistently states that our affirmations of perfections truly and directly refer to divine realities. He thereby refuses Albert's most apophatic Dionysian statements on affirmations. This was an easy hermeneutical move, since Aquinas chooses to develop Albert's more typical kataphatic explanations, which stand in tension with his occasional highly apophatic statements.

Thomas makes considerable claims about the Areopagite's intention behind his doctrine of negation. The phrase that seems to have troubled him the most comes not from the *Mystical Theology*, but from the *Celestial Hierarchy*: "In divine things, negations are true but affirmations are incompact."[41] An objection in question 13 refers to this passage. Thomas responds:

Dionysius says that such names [affirmations] are negated of God because that which is signified through the name does not belong to him in the mode by which the name signifies, but in a more excellent mode. Hence Dionysius says in the same place that [God] is "above all substance and life."[42]

39. *SDN*, ch. 7, no. 29, p. 358.73–86 (see chapter 4 of this volume); *ST* I, q. 13, a. 6.
40. *SMT*, ch. 5, p. 474.7–26; *ST* I, q. 13, a. 5c (cited in footnote 34 of the present chapter).
41. *CH* 2.3, pp. 12.20–13.2, 141A.
42. *ST* I, q. 13, a. 3, ad 2: "huiusmodi nomina dicit Dionysius negari a Deo, quia id quod significatur per nomen, non convenit eo modo ei, quo nomen significat, sed excel-

In fact the Areopagite's doctrine is related to (1) the divine processions as the proper object of affirmations and (2) negations (*apophaseis*) as a way to signal the infinite distance between the divine manifestations signified by affirmations and God's hidden nature. Thomas employs negations as quasi-eminent names. His response implies the distinction between the reality signified and the mode of signification. The unspoken principle is that the act of negating has *nothing* to do with the reality signified. Rather, negations refer to the creaturely mode of signification and point to God's eminent mode of being or modelessness. When we negate life from God, we simultaneously imply that "God is above created life," for he infinitely surpasses the limitations of finite modes of life in his perfect mode of living. In some ways Thomas's explanation is not far from a key *Mystical Theology* passage on negations. As God is beyond all, "one must more properly deny (*apophaskein*) all of these [the attributes of beings]," a text that then refuses a contradiction between divine affirmations and negations (*apophaseis*).[43] Thomas thus integrates key Dionysian formulas on negations, yet their meaning changes considerably for at least three reasons: (1) Thomas's doctrine of causality centered on God's pure actuality and the cause-effect similitude (discussed earlier); (2) Aquinas's epistemology of affirmations; and (3) the function of eminent names. I now take up the second and third elements.

Thomas's doctrine of divine names is founded upon an Aristotelian epistemology, as we can see in a passage on the relation between affirmations and God's substance:

> An understanding of negation is always founded in some affirmation, which is thus clear, in that every negative is proven through an affirmative. Hence, unless the human intellect were to know something affirmatively about God, it could not negate anything of him. But it would not know if anything which it says of God could be affirmatively verified of him. Therefore, according to the teaching of Dionysius, it must be said that such [affirmative] names signify the divine substance, although deficiently and imperfectly, which is thus clear. Since every agent acts inasmuch as it is in act, and consequently produces something similar [to itself].[44]

---

lentiori modo. Unde ibidem dicit Dionysius quod est 'super omnem substantiam et vitam'"; see also a. 12, ad 1; *DP*, q. 7, a. 5, ad 2; *SLC*, lect. 6, p. 43.

43. *MT* 1.2, p. 143.4–5, 1000B, Jones, 212 (see chapter 1 of this volume).

44. *DP*, q. 7, a. 5c: "intellectus negationis semper fundatur in aliqua affirmatione:

Divine Naming in Thomas 311

As in *Prima Pars*, question 13, article 2, Aquinas's main sparring partner on substantial divine names is not Dionysius but Maimonides, whom he mentions earlier in the article cited. Thomas heavily qualifies the function of negations with an appeal to Aristotelian psychology and logic in book 1, chapter 8 of *On Interpretation*. Any negative proposition presupposes an affirmative proposition. This also holds true for the negation of any concept or of being (*esse*). We must have some positive, substantial knowledge of a thing before we can intelligibly deny anything of it (e.g., "The horse is not white," "The unicorn is not black").[45] Such logic is rooted in the doctrine of the apprehension of being (*ens*) as primordial for all human cognition. I cannot deny whiteness unless I have some understanding of whiteness, nor can I say "is not" unless I already know something about the "is" of a thing. Likewise, to deny materiality of God requires some positive knowledge of God's nature whereby I recognize its incompatibility with matter. While the name "immaterial" is itself negative, we can only predicate it of God with certitude because of a previous positive understanding of a divine attribute such as pure actuality. Aquinas's epistemology significantly modifies Dionysius, who also considers negations meaningless without affirmations, but for different reasons.

The previous passage alludes to God's causal action as the foundation of Dionysian affirmations but ignores their restriction to the divine processions. Proceeding on the basis of an Aristotelian notion of affirmative propositions, Thomas shows that positive knowledge and discourse about God's being must be possible if Dionysian negations are to remain intelligible. Within his creative synthesis of Dionysius and Aristotle, the only way to retain the Areopagite's negative discourse is to recognize the priority of affirmation. Thomas transforms the Areopagite in order to retain key Dionysian principles.

On the one hand, Thomas's kataphatic reinterpretation of the Areopagite follows partly from his metaphysics of being as act that replac-

---

quod ex hoc patet quia omnis negativa per affirmativam probatur; unde nisi intellectus humanus aliquid de Deo affirmative cognosceret, nihil de Deo posset negare. Non autem cognosceret, si nihil quod de Deo dicit, de eo verificaretur affirmative. Et ideo, secundum sententiam Dionysii, dicendum est, quod huiusmodi nomina significant divinam substantiam, quamvis deficienter et imperfecte: quod sic patet. Cum omne agens agat in quantum actu est, et per consequens agat aliqualiter simile"; see also Rocca, *Speaking the Incomprehensible God*, 67, 303.

45. Humbrecht, *Théologie négative*, 181, 279.

es a Neoplatonic metaphysics of unity. Dionysius accepts the Neoplatonic notion that being always remains limited, hence the Areopagite's primary divine names are the Good and the One, not Being. A metaphysics of unity primarily operates via the negation of all multiplicity in contemplative ascent to the One, which necessarily includes the negation of all being, for being as limited remains in the realm of multiplicity. In Neoplatonic theology human discourse is inescapably bound to the realm of being or multiplicity. An abiding affirmation of being thus becomes an obstacle to the encounter of intellect or *noūs* with the One.[46] For Aquinas, being as known in its created mode is most open to divine predication because it can best signify in an indeterminate way. God revealed his highest name to Moses at the burning bush: *Qui est*.[47] Yet at the heart of this most indeterminate name remains a positive, nonquidditative noetic content: the act of being, which is utterly simple in its perfect instantiation and multiple in creation. In chapter 8 I will take a closer look at the mystical consequences of a metaphysics of act and a metaphysics of unity.

On the other hand, Thomas's metaphysics of being displays considerable Dionysian influences. He integrates the Areopagite's doctrines of being as (1) the first created perfection, (2) the first perfection to be participated, and (3) virtually and intensely containing all perfections. Thomas joins these Dionysian elements to a reinterpretation of Aristotelian act within an original synthesis perhaps best exemplified by the famous expression that *esse* is "the actuality of all acts and thus the perfection of all perfections."[48] As with the doctrine of divine causality and similitude, Thomas does far more than force the Areopagite into Aristotelian categories, for *he reads Aristotelian principles such as act in a partly Dionysian way*. Because of the Dionysian elements in Thomas's understanding of being, he can expand his repertoire of arguments for the possibility of positive, eminent predication of divine being.

Nevertheless, Thomas shifts the meaning and function of Dionysian eminence in significant ways, all the while attributing his own *tri-*

---

46. O'Rourke, *Pseudo-Dionysius*, 69, 77–79; Eric D. Perl, *Theophany: The Neoplatonic Philosophy of Dionysius the Areopagite* (Albany, N.Y.: SUNY Press, 2007), 5–15.

47. *ST* I, q. 13, a. 11.

48. *DP*, q. 7, a. 2, ad 9: "esse est actualitas omnium actuum, et propter hoc est perfectio omnium perfectionum." For O'Rourke, *DN* 5.1 is the main inspiration for this phrase; O'Rourke, *Pseudo-Dionysius*, 134–36, 180–83.

plex via to the Areopagite's intention.[49] For Dionysius, transcending negations (*aphaireseis*) surpass affirmations and their complementary negations (*apophaseis*) so as to emphasize the God-creation difference and to posit God's transcendence. It is here that we find such names as "beyond Good." Thomas was unaware of the distinction between these two types of negations.[50] Consequently, he seems not to have recognized that the Dionysian way of eminence has a primarily negative meaning. Aquinas could thus split eminent names from transcending negations, even as his way of eminence includes part of the Areopagite's doctrinal intention behind transcending negations.

Thomas's doctrine of divine eminence depends on the manner in which he intertwines eminence with the way of causality—two ways that Dionysius keeps neatly distinct. In the first chapter of the *Divine Names*, holy minds, having enjoyed union with God beyond mind, celebrate him most of all through negation (*aphaireseōs*), as Cause of all, as none of them, and as beyond all. In his commentary Thomas goes beyond the Areopagite's text as he explains how the themes of celebration and negation interconnect:

God, since he is *cause of all existing things*, is himself *nothing* of existing things, not as if falling short in being (*essendo*), but super-eminently *segregated from all things*. And therefore, the divine super-substantiality, which is the essence of goodness, by those who *are lovers* of divine *truth, which is* above *every truth*, cannot be praised, *in whatever way as it is*, that is, [praised] comprehensively.[51]

God is metaphysically separate from all created things precisely because he is their cause. The very nature of God's creative causality as the pure act on which all other beings depend for their being excludes God being anything within creation. Furthermore, God's causality reveals some-

---

49. *DP*, q. 7, a. 5, ad 2. For *intentio auctoris*, see Narváez, "Portée herméneutique," 201–19. Thomas seems to present the Areopagite's intention by pursuing the truth of the matter.

50. Sarracenus usually translates *apophaseis* as *negationes* and *aphairesin* as *ablationem*, which is close to *remotio*; see Dionysius Areopagita, *Dionysiaca*, 1:571–72.

51. *DDN*, ch. 1, lect. 3, no. 83: "Deus, cum sit *omnium existentium causa*, ipse *nihil* est existentium, non quasi deficiens ab essendo, sed supereminenter *segregatus ab omnibus*. Et ideo divina supersubstantialitas, quae est bonitatis essentia, ab his qui *sunt* divinae *veritatis amatores, quae est* supra *omnem veritatem*, non potest laudari, *quomodocumque est*, idest comprehensive."

thing of his eminence. We signify the infinitude of his eminence that his creative activity manifests by removing any lack of actuality. Thomas follows the Areopagite's intention as he excludes all privation from God. He goes beyond Dionysius as he names God "the essence of goodness" and not just "beyond goodness." For Dionysius the phrase "in whatever way as it is" qualifies the divine supersubstantiality to further emphasize the breakdown of all affirmations before God's eminence, which leads us "beyond mind" toward silent union. For Thomas only comprehensive or adequate praise breaks down. Praise need not cease altogether, because the noetic bridge established by the principle of causality extends (by an act of judgment) all the way to God's boundless goodness. On the one hand, Aquinas follows Dionysius: positive language depends on the manifestive power of divine activity. On the other hand, he goes beyond Dionysius in his confidence concerning what God's causal action reveals: "If the similitude [of cause and effect] is not according to the same *ratio*, but [exists] super-eminently in the cause, the name is not predicated of each according to one *ratio*, but super-eminently of the cause."[52] The divine similitude that every creature bears to some degree of intensity reflects not only God as cause, but his nature, as well. Eminence completes the causal way of naming God; indeed, these cannot be separated. Because similitude extends to God's being, the note of intelligibility or aspect of similitude between God and creature cannot be the same and so excludes univocity. The way of eminent causality enables and limits divine naming.

Aquinas grounds and partly justifies the firm link between causality and eminence with an appeal to the Dionysian formula that God precontains all things in himself. Divine infinitude makes possible and requires both the full presence of being and each of its intelligible aspects (*rationes*) within the divine nature. God's eminent being grounds his manner of causality. It therefore also grounds the way in which we affirm and deny things of God. "Because all things are in him in some way ... *all things are simultaneously predicated* and removed from him."[53] The

52. *DDN*, ch. 1, lect. 3, no. 89: "Si vero non sit similitudo secundum eamdem rationem, sed sit supereminentius in causa, non dicetur nomen de utroque secundum unam rationem, sed supereminentius de causa."

53. *DDN*, ch. 5, lect. 2, no. 661: "Et quia in Ipso, quodammodo, sunt omnia, quasi in se omnia comprehendente, *simul* de Ipso *omnia praedicantur* et simul ab Ipso omnia removentur"; see also ch. 1, lect. 2, nos. 72–73; ch. 7, lect. 1, nos. 702, 708.

way of causality or affirmation is inseparable from the way of eminence. For Aquinas the preexistence of perfections in God's eminence has three essential elements: (1) universality, in that all perfections preexist in him; (2) fullness, in that the divine perfections are without defect; and (3) unity, in that the diverse perfections of creatures are absolutely one in God.[54] I should note that all three elements draw inspiration from the Areopagite, even as their meanings go beyond Dionysian eminence. The third aspect implies God's simplicity, which for Aquinas presupposes the identity of God's *esse* and *essentia*. The latter in turn implies that God is subsistent being itself. Thus Thomas elsewhere explains, "The first cause is above being (*ens*) insofar as it is infinite *esse* itself."[55] Aquinas identifies divine eminence with God's *esse* or pure actuality of being.

Thomas's way of eminence differs from the Dionysian superlative praise of the hidden God partly because it has different doctrinal and spiritual functions. Question 13 of the *Prima Pars* explains a method of eminent naming that Aquinas applies throughout his treatise on God and later in his Christology. The way of eminence constitutes the height and limit of rational, faith-based discourse about God. Thus, whereas Dionysian superlatives launch the soul's noetic attention into silent adoration, Thomas's superlatives enable the intellect to rest in the highest form of knowledge *about* God that is possible in this life.

Despite the centrality of kataphatically reinterpreted eminence in Aquinas's doctrine of divine naming, a legitimate objection remains. Does Thomas's formula, that the highest knowledge of God consists of not knowing "what he is," imply the priority of the negative way? Does his conclusion that *Qui est* or even the Tetragrammaton are the highest divine names point in the same apophatic direction? In fact, God's "most indeterminate name" (*Qui est*) is not strictly apophatic. First, *Qui est* signifies God's "form," which is the identity of *esse* and essence, so that the name predicates infinite being and absolute simplicity of God. Second, *Qui est* predicates minimal "determination" of God and thus minimizes the determination of a "mode of substance"—that is, the created mode of being. We thus return to the distinction between the reality signified and the created mode of signification-knowing-

---

54. Rocca, *Speaking the Incomprehensible God*, 69.
55. *SLC*, proposition 6, p. 47: "causa prima est supra ens in quantum est ipsum esse infinitum"; see also Rocca, *Speaking the Incomprehensible God*, 66–67, 73.

being.[56] The name *Qui est* turns out to be a careful balance of affirmative and negative theology. Yet Thomas retains an important place for remotions in the noetic ascent to God and even connects them to the intellect's union with God, as we will see in the next chapter.

CONCLUSION

Overall, Aquinas's doctrine of divine naming has considerable consequences for mystical theology. First, it tightly interweaves each element we have considered. His doctrine of naming is highly systematic, more so than Albert's. Also, Aquinas further develops Albert's method of introducing distinctions to clarify ambiguities in Dionysius, such as the function of eminent names. Second, the act of judgment plays an indispensable role in this harmonious structure, especially as it allows human conceptions of perfections to play an essential function, even at the summit of acquired cognition about God. Judgment will again take center stage when we consider the gift of wisdom. Third, Thomas significantly reshapes the Dionysian *triplex via*, often following Albert. Yet Aquinas also drops his teacher's most apophatic pronouncements. Here the function of the eminent way undergoes an important shift. Albert's theology of divine naming and Aristotelian epistemology push Aquinas toward a more kataphatic understanding of the *triplex via*. Yet Thomas's theory of divine naming remains unthinkable without Dionysius. Fourth, the metaphysical framework within which Aquinas receives the Areopagite's doctrine of divine naming is at once Aristotelian, Dionysian, and original. Thomas's new metaphysics of *esse* naturally inclines away from apophatism and undergirds a noetics wherein human concepts and judgments never become superfluous, in contrast to a Platonic ontology centered on unity, wherein multiplicity always seems to remain an obstacle to perfection. Such metaphysical principles become crucial for any mystical theology connected to them. These major characteristics of Thomas's theology of divine naming reemerge in his reading of the key union passages in the *Divine Names*, to which I now turn.

56. *ST* I, q. 13, a. 11c: "[Qui est] non enim significat formam aliquam, sed ipsum esse. Unde, cum esse Dei sit ipsa eius essentia, et hoc nulli alii conveniat, ut supra ostensum est, manifestum est quod inter alia nomina hoc maxime proprie nominat Deum.... Quolibet enim alio nomine determinatur aliquis modus substantiae rei; sed hoc nomen Qui est nullum modum essendi determinat."

8

Dionysian Union in Thomas

We now have an overview of the doctrinal framework for Thomas's reception of the Areopagite's theology of union with God. In the last three chapters I articulated Aquinas's understanding of the mystical subject, the structure of elevating grace, and the path of noetic ascent to God by knowing and naming him. Thomas especially appropriates the Dionysian theology of union in four parts of his corpus: (1) in his discussion of union passages in the *Commentary on the Divine Names*; (2) in a few citations of the *Mystical Theology* scattered throughout Thomas's corpus; (3) in his doctrine of the Spirit's gift of understanding, exemplified by Moses in darkness; and (4) in his doctrine of the Spirit's gift of wisdom, exemplified by Hierotheus suffering divine things. The current chapter treats each of these parts in this order. In chapter 7 we saw that Dionysian union also emerges indirectly in Aquinas's discussion of divine naming. Thomas's most significant discussions of the theology of union in general emerge in his studies of the *imago*, the trinitarian missions, and the theological virtues, treated in chapters 5 and 6. Here the Gospel of John, Augustine, and Aristotle outweigh the influence of Dionysius. Thus I will consider in what way the four sites of Dionysian union in Thomas's corpus become crossroads where multiple doctrinal traditions meet.

My method thus shifts away from synthetic doctrinal exposés to close textual analyses. The previous pages on Aquinas essentially served to prepare for an evaluation of how the Areopagite's doctrine of union developed in Thomas. The present chapter has two main objectives as we pursue the overall thesis of this study. First, I need to show *how* Aquinas received the Dionysian understanding of being joined to God. This requires a comparison between the historical Dionysius and Thomas's Areopagite. In other words, what Dionysian mystic is left standing in Thomas's corpus? I can only answer that question through detailed analyses of union passages in Aquinas that discuss the Areopagite's teaching. The second task involves an application of the results of the previous chapters to explain *why* Thomas changed Dionysius as he did. Here I move from a primarily historical analysis to a historical-systematic approach, from a focus on texts to a synthesis developed in close proximity to the texts. Each of the four sections in this chapter takes up these two objectives. Following our main thesis, the themes of Dionysian union that stand at the center of the subsequent analyses are: (1) Thomas's kataphatic turn; (2) the human dependence on mediations; (3) human cooperation in union; (4) the trinitarian structure of the mystic's contact with God; (5) the abiding importance of a limited apophatism; (6) the intellect-centered nature of union; and (7) the immediacy of God's conjoining action. All but the fourth and seventh themes will emerge in the first two sections of this chapter, though the first three themes will appear most frequently. All seven elements will surface in the analyses of the gifts of understanding and wisdom.

UNION BEYOND MIND IN THOMAS'S *COMMENTARY ON THE DIVINE NAMES*

Aquinas commented on the *Divine Names* between 1266 and 1268 as he directed the new Dominican *studium* in Rome.[1] In the same time period he composed the *Prima Pars* of the *Summa*. His *Commentary on the Divine Names* probably consists not of course lecture notes but of a personal work that helped him with the *Summa* treatise on divine naming, just as his *Commentary on Aristotle's "de Anima"* accompanied the *Prima Pars* treatise on anthropology and the *Commentary on Aristotle's*

---

1. Torrell, *Saint Thomas Aquinas*, vol. 1, *The Person and his Work*, 328, 434, following the work of René Gauthier and Adriano Oliva.

"*Nicomachean Ethics*" accompanied the *Secunda Pars*.² Like his teacher, Aquinas knew little Greek. Like Albert, he employed the Sarracenus translation of Dionysius, though with some reference to Eriugena's text. Since Albert's *Commentary on the Divine Names* does not refer to Eriugena's translation when Thomas mentions it in his commentary, Aquinas may have had a partial or complete copy of the Irishman's text before him in Rome.³ Thomas also had his complete personal notes of Albert's Dionysian lectures before him as he commented the Areopagite. Albert's influence on Thomas's reading of Dionysius will emerge throughout this chapter. As for the genre, Albert combines a running commentary or *expositio* with disputed questions, while Aquinas limits himself to an *expositio*, which has two important consequences. First, Thomas's systematic explanations of obscure Dionysian passages are much shorter than Albert's explanations. Second, Aquinas stays closer to the primary text.⁴

The present section includes brief historical explanations of the *Divine Names* passages that Aquinas comments on, followed by an analysis of Thomas's *expositio*. My study of Dionysian union in Albert did not require this additional step, since the key Albertian passages on union are found in his *Commentary on the Mystical Theology*. My study of the latter built on chapter 1. Since Thomas never wrote a commentary on the *Mystical Theology*, I must rely more heavily on his *Commentary on the Divine Names* to reconstruct his reception of Dionysian union.

---

2. Imbach and Oliva, *Philosophie*, 25; Torrell, *Saint Thomas Aquinas*, vol. 1, *The Person and his Work*, 127–28, 173–74. Mulchahey proposes that, like Albert in Cologne, Aquinas gave a course on the *Divine Names* in Rome; Mulchahey, "*Studium* at Cologne," 128. But Albert's Cologne lectures were designated for the order's brightest young friars. The Roman *studium* under Thomas's direction focused on basic theological formation for all friars, an unlikely setting for lectures on a subject as difficult as Dionysius, as Torrell notes. On the Roman *studium*, see Leonard E. Boyle, *Facing History: A Different Thomas Aquinas*, Textes et Études du Moyen Âge 13 (Louvain-la-Neuve: Fédération Internationale des Instituts d'Études Médiévales, 2000), 71–85.

3. The *DDN* has two *aliae translationes* with Eriugena's version (ch. 7, lect. 2, no. 711; lect. 4, no. 731) not found in the *SDN* (ch. 7, no. 10, p. 344.47–47; no. 30, p. 359.24–25). Théry, "Manuscrit Vat. Grec," 5–23, thinks that Thomas may have had access to the whole "old Dionysian corpus" in Italy—i.e., to all of Eriugena's translations of the Dionysian corpus. Thomas had little direct access to Eriugena's personal works; see Dondaine, "S. Thomas et Scot Érigène," *RSPT* 35 (1951): 31–33.

4. On the scholastic genres, see Leinsle, *Introduction to Scholastic Theology*, 39–40.

My study of union in the *Commentary on the Divine Names* comes in four parts. First, I will consider four aspects in the prologue: (1) its presentation of the genre of the Areopagite's corpus; (2) its division of that corpus; (3) its description of the *Mystical Theology* as a book of remotions; and (4) Aquinas's intriguing comments on the Platonists' relation to Dionysius. This first part identifies the overall hermeneutic that Aquinas applies to the *Divine Names*, which significantly influences his reading of union passages. Second, I will study the theme of union beyond mind. Third, I will analyze a few texts on union "by remotion" or "by ignorance." Fourth, I will consider one synthetic passage on union with God by assimilation to the object known. The texts analyzed in the second through fourth parts of this section essentially cover Aquinas's discussion of union with God in the *Commentary on the Divine Names*. I have omitted ecstatic love, for Thomas's commentary never links it to union beyond mind. He also says little on love as a unitive power.[5] Oddly, Thomas develops both themes in the *Summa* (see chapter 6 of this volume), but hardly in this commentary. Hierotheus suffering divine things emerges in one brief passage of the commentary, a text best studied in my section on the gift of wisdom.

"To understand the books of the blessed Dionysius, one must consider that he arranges in a fourfold division those things about God contained in the Sacred Scriptures."[6] Momentarily leaving aside the Areopagite's inspired study of angelic and ecclesial hierarchies, Aquinas argues that the rest of the Dionysian corpus (with its "lost" works) consists of an exposition of biblical discourse about God. The *Theological Outlines* explains the trinitarian names. The *Divine Names* comments on God's biblical names linked to created similitudes that derive from him. Such names are common to the whole Trinity by its single essence. Thus affirmative causal names constitute the primary theme of the *Divine Names*. The *Symbolic Theology* treats God's metaphorical names, where created similitudes are "translated" into God. The *Mystical Theology* considers remotions, for "whatever is known by us in creatures is removed from God, insofar as it is in creatures."[7] Remotions

5. *DDN*, ch. 4, lect. 9, no. 424; lect. 10, nos. 426–41.
6. *DDN*, Prooemium: "Ad intellectum librorum beati Dionysii considerandum est quod ea quae de Deo in Sacris Scripturis continentur, artificialiter quadrifariam divisit."
7. *DDN*, Prooemium: "quicquid in creaturis a nobis cognoscitur a Deo removetur, secundum quod in creaturis est."

target our understanding of what Scripture says about God. For Thomas most of the Dionysian corpus offers a form of Scripture-centered theology.

Aquinas's hermeneutic has a partial foundation in the Areopagite's text and in the Dionysian tradition. The opening lines of the *Divine Names* identify the theologians' "sacred oracles (*hierōn logiōn*)" as the standard for all discourse about God. For Dionysius the theologians are the human authors of Scripture. The sacred oracles are the revelations that they receive and pass on. The *Divine Names* also distinguishes between "the holy veils of the oracles and the tradition of the hierarchs," so that the term "oracles" at times distinguishes biblical revelation from other means of transmission (e.g., the liturgy). But sometimes Dionysian "oracles" signify what is transmitted via the Bible *and* the liturgy. The opening prayer of the *Mystical Theology* asks that the Trinity would direct the reader toward the highest peak of the "mystical oracles" or the words of Scripture and the holy mysteries. The interlinear gloss of the *Parisian Corpus Dionysiacum* interprets these oracles as a reference to the Scriptures.[8] The gloss may well have inspired Aquinas to apply a stricter reading of a key technical term throughout the Dionysian corpus. In his commentary Thomas consistently proposes a biblical meaning for the oracles.[9] Like Albert, he does not recognize the liturgical references behind such terms. The close linguistic, historically contextualized analysis of the Dionysian corpus that uncovers such allusions in our day remained beyond their reach. Nor did a living tradition exist whereby they could have gained access to the text's cultic *Sitz im Leben*.[10]

Aquinas thus approaches the Dionysian corpus as a work of *sacra doctrina*. God is the subject of sacred doctrine in three ways: in himself, as principle, and as end of all things.[11] Indeed, the four Dionysian books mentioned in the prologue mirror the themes of the *Summa*

---

8. *DN* 1.1, pp. 107.5–8.9, 587–88A (cited below at footnote 25 of this chapter); 1.4, p. 114.1–3, 592B; *MT* 1.1, p. 141.1–3, 997A; *PMT*, ch. 1, 50; de Andia, *Henosis*, 3, 240; Rorem, *Pseudo-Dionysius*, 190–92.

9. *DDN*, ch. 1, lect. 1, nos. 6, 9; lect. 2, nos. 44, 53, 64; ch. 2, lect. 1, nos. 112, 125; lect. 4, nos. 172, 190; ch. 3, lect. 1, nos. 251–52; ch. 4, lect. 9, no. 419; lect. 19, no. 533.

10. I have found no liturgical allusions in the *PMT*, the most likely conduit of such references.

11. *ST* I, q. 1, a. 7c.

section on the one and triune God (*Prima Pars*, questions 2–43). The *Theological Outlines* matches the section on the three persons. The *Divine Names* (except for chapter 2), *Symbolic Theology*, and *Mystical Theology* ponder God's names related to the one divine essence. Thomas states that the subject of these four Dionysian works is God insofar as he reveals himself in Scripture. For Aquinas sacred doctrine contemplates God under the formality of revelation.[12] He does not consider the *Divine Names* as a work of natural theology, although he holds that some of its teaching about God is accessible to reason without faith:

> He [Dionysius] shows from what things [principles] one must proceed in this work, because it does not rely on human reason, but on divine revelation ... in his doctrine, Dionysius relies on the authority of Sacred Scripture.[13]

Aquinas mirrors Albert's approach to the corpus, who refers to the *scientia* of the *Divine Names* wherein faith is the ruling *habitus* and Scripture the guide.[14] Thomas seems to pick up on the hermeneutic behind Albert's decision to place the Dionysian Corpus at the center of the Cologne curriculum—that is, to employ a new handbook of the sacred science. Thomas may have drawn inspiration from the Cologne curriculum's implication about the genre of the Dionysian corpus.

Since Dionysius grounds his teaching in the Scriptures, it must be received by faith: "In the doctrine of faith, some things that are unknown and ineffable to the human being are proposed, [things] to which those having faith adhere."[15] Hence the light (of faith) that grounds Albert's

---

12. *ST* I, q. 1, a. 3c. The Areopagite's thematic division for part of his corpus (specifically, the *Theological Outlines*, *Symbolic Theology*, *DN*, and *MT*) virtually mirrors the *Summa*'s distinct treatment of God as one (I, qq. 3–26) and as three (I, qq. 27–43). Aquinas's distinct treatment of the *de Deo uno* and the *de Deo trino* (which remain one treatise for him) also has precedents in Gregory of Nyssa and John Damascene; Emery, *Trinitarian Theology*, 46–47.

13. *DDN*, ch. 1, lect. 1, no. 6: "ostendit ex quibus sit procedendum in hoc opere, quia non est innitendum rationi humanae, sed revelationi divinae.... Innititur enim, in sua doctrina, Dionysius auctoritate sacrae Scripturae"; see also no. 11. O'Rourke acknowledges the Bible's central place in the commentary. But he sometimes suggests that Aquinas also considers the *Divine Names* as a work of natural theology. Thus, reason responds to revelation yet relies on arguments drawn from human wisdom, in reference to *DDN*, ch. 1, lect. 1, no. 7; O'Rourke, *Pseudo-Dionysius*, 28–30. Yet this passage *contrasts* human wisdom to the wisdom of the *Divine Names*.

14. *SDN*, ch. 1, no. 3, p. 2.66–68.

15. *DDN*, ch. 1, lect. 1, no. 7: "Sed in doctrina fidei proponuntur quaedam homini ignota et indicibilia quibus habentes fidem inhaerent."

Dionysian Union in Thomas 323

mystical science is also the light of the science of the *Divine Names* as read by Aquinas and the light of the *Mystical Theology* as he understood it, for this work also unfolds biblical doctrine about God. Thus for Aquinas the *Mystical Theology* proposes doctrines of faith.

Thomas's division of the Dionysian corpus has three further consequences for the nature of the *Divine Names*. First, the focus moves away from the text's many two-sided ladders of affirmations and negations to the manifestation of God by his similitudes in creation. The apophatic side of the ladder has been *formally* moved to the *Mystical Theology*, even though Aquinas will frequently discuss remotion (and excess) in the *Divine Names*, as many apophatic passages remain in Dionysius's text. The Areopagite's two-sided contemplative ladders point beyond themselves to the light encountered above naming. Aquinas's presentation of the *Divine Names* as a book of causal discourse on God obscures this element. Such a hermeneutic inclines the commentator to consider how even passages on God's obscurity might offer some positive cognition, which is the aim of God manifesting himself. Second, the classification of the *Divine Names* as an exposition of scriptural names further reinforces the kataphatic reading of the work. For Aquinas, Scripture's *raison d'être* is positive knowledge of God that moves toward final beatitude. In sacred doctrine God remains concealed insofar as Scripture only offers a noetic foretaste of the beatific vision. Except for the divine incomprehensibility that remains an unbreakable law for all creatures, the lingering obscurity of God is partial and temporary.[16] Third, the *Divine Names* as an exposition of Scripture opens the path to reading terms such as "elevating light" or "unifying light" to signify the light of faith, the light by which believers cling to and know the God revealed in Scripture, the God who is not just hidden but also partly manifest. In the context of the *Divine Names* as *sacra doctrina*, Thomas's notion of faith as a type of knowledge and union leads to a quiet transformation of Dionysian union passages.

This brings me to the second part of my analysis of the prologue, the implications of classifying the *Mystical Theology* as a book of remotions. Aquinas insists that this text prolongs the study of God's biblical names. The work's center is no longer union beyond naming. In fact, negation takes center stage in chapters 2 through 4 of the *Mystical The-*

16. SCG IV, ch. 1, no. 3343; Humbrecht, *Théologie négative*, 268, 736.

ology. Aquinas's description of the *Mystical Theology* in the prologue never employs any union terms. He maintains that the work primarily treats the limits of human discourse and knowledge about God as revealed in Scripture: "Of such remotions by which God remains unknown and hidden to us [Dionysius] made another book."[17] The *Mystical Theology* manifests the distance between biblical divine names as understood by us and the divine reality that they signify. By implication, the text simply makes up one more chapter in the bigger book of divine naming. That is why the *Mystical Theology* remains a work of *sacra doctrina*, a rational exposition of the revelation of God through Scripture, not a guide to transcend all active cogitations about revelation. Instead of signaling the need to pass beyond all human thought and discourse because of their inherent limits, the work is all about identifying the limits of our thought and discourse, but precisely through a rational reflection that remains bound to those limits.

Thomas's interpretation of the *Mystical Theology* closely parallels Albert's hermeneutic.[18] Nowhere else in Thomas's vast corpus do we find a more detailed description of the *Mystical Theology* as a whole than in the prologue of the *Commentary on the Divine Names*:

Because every similitude of the creature to God is deficient and what God is exceeds all that which is found in creatures, whatever is known by us in creatures is removed from God, insofar as it is in creatures; so that, after all that which our intellect can conceive about God being led by creatures, what God is (*hoc ipsum quod Deus est*) remains hidden and unknown ... nor is [God] such life or essence as can be conceived by our intellect and thus what God is remains unknown to us, since it exceeds all that is apprehended by us. Now of such remotions by which God remains unknown and hidden to us [he] made another book which he entitled "of Mystical" that is hidden "Theology."[19]

---

17. *DDN*, Prooemium: "De huiusmodi autem remotionibus quibus Deus remanet nobis ignotus et occultus fecit alium librum quem intitulavit *de Mystica* idest occulta *Theologia*."

18. *SDN*, ch. 1, p. 455.6–8.

19. *DDN*, Prooemium: "Sed quia omnis similitudo creaturae ad Deum deficiens est et hoc ipsum quod Deus est omne id quod in creaturis invenitur excedit, quicquid in creaturis a nobis cognoscitur a Deo removetur, secundum quod in creaturis est; ut sic, post omne illud quod intellectus noster ex creaturis manuductus de Deo concipere potest, hoc ipsum quod Deus est remaneat occultum et ignotum ... nec est talis vita aut essentia qualis ab intellectu nostro concipi potest et sic hoc ipsum quod Deus est, cum

God's manifestation in creatures, a central theme of the *Divine Names*, cannot reveal his *quod est* or quiddity. God's metaphysical excess requires and grounds epistemological and linguistic remotion. By implication, the *Mystical Theology* includes a study of the way of eminence.

Remotions do not target God's biblical names but rather whatever perfections we discern in creatures and only insofar as they are in creatures. Remotions signal the inadequacy of the similitudes used in the *Divine Names*, the similitudes on which the meaning of affirmations depends. We take away the composite, finite mode of perfections in creatures. Rather than hymn God as "not-good," Aquinas employs remotions to purify our understanding of how God is "good" and "supergood." He mentions two types of finitude that call for noetic purification: the limited mode of being and the intellect's limited mode of conceiving perfections. These render impossible a noetic vision of God's *quid est* through biblical revelation. Thomas greatly limits the function of remotion. The doctrinal motives for such a limitation already emerged in chapter 7. The cloud on Mt. Sinai is no longer as thick as in Dionysius.

The meaning of remotion is closely linked to the statement that God's *quid est* remains hidden and unknown. Two interpretations of *quid est* are possible: (1) it may signify the divine essence insofar as it is immediately known in glory; or (2) it could stand for exhaustive cognition of God's nature, which only he has. In the last chapter I noted that while the late Aquinas favors the first reading of *quid est*, his language can be inconsistent. The *Commentary on the Divine Names* uses both senses, so that we cannot appeal to one consistent doctrine in the rest of the commentary to interpret the prologue.[20] But the prologue seems

---

excedat omne illud quod a nobis apprehenditur, nobis remanet ignotum. De huiusmodi autem remotionibus quibus Deus remanet nobis ignotus et occultus fecit alium librum quem intitulavit *de Mystica* idest occulta *Theologia*."

20. Six blocks of texts in the *DDN* are relevant. (1) Ch. 1, lect. 1, no. 19 states that we do not know God's *quod est* because of his infinitude, as our mind is proportioned to finite things, a passage that tends to the identification of knowing the *quod est* and comprehension. (2) In the same lect., no. 26 seems to distinguish between contemplating an essence so as to know a thing's *quid est* and comprehending the essence, though this is not absolutely clear. No. 27 follows up on this distinction as Thomas explains that, while God is incomprehensible to every intellect, his essence cannot be contemplated while our cognition is bound to created things, as in this state of life. Nos. 26–27 thus seem to employ both senses of *quid est*. (3) Still in lect. 1, no. 32 identifies comprehension with

to prefer the first sense, for it does not explicitly speak of God's incomprehensibility. Instead, God's *quid est* remains unknown because it exceeds whatever we can conceive or apprehend, for whatever we know does not belong to God insofar as it is in creatures. The opposite pole of God's *quid est* is the finite, limited mode of cognition. In heaven, the light of glory mostly overcomes the limits of that mode of knowing.[21] The prologue refers to "remotions by which God remains unknown and hidden." It does not focus on God as unknowable in himself (i.e., incomprehensibility) but rather on creaturely limits, limits signified by remotions, that leave God in obscurity. It is not God who dwells in the dark cloud, but we who dwell therein, surrounded as we are by the veil of the body, of creation, and of our limited noetic operative powers, which still lack the light of glory. Aquinas picks up on the Dionysian sense of light being darkness in relation to us and develops it in a more or less Albertian way. Thomas's kataphatic reading of the *Divine Names* and the *Mystical Theology* sets the stage for union by faith or remotions. But first, a word on Thomas the historian.

Unlike Albert, who identifies neither the Areopagite's language nor his thought with "the Platonists," and unlike the early Thomas's conviction that Dionysius follows Aristotle's doctrine, the prologue of Aquinas's *Commentary on the Divine Names* links the Areopagite's "way of speaking" to that of the Platonists, a possible first in medieval Latin Christendom.[22] Here Thomas calls upon two major Platonic themes: (1) the existence of separate forms for all species, which he rejects as false; and (2) God as the essence of goodness, unity and *esse*, so that all

---

knowing God's *quid est.* (4) In ch. 1, lect. 2, nos. 41, 70–74, Aquinas develops a single, complex exposition that consistently ties the hiddenness of God's *quiddity est* to his incomprehensibility. (5) In ch. 7, lect. 4, no. 731, Thomas mentions our ignorance of God's *quid sit* in the context of a discussion that strongly suggests that the blessed know his *quid sit*, as I will argue later. (6) In ch. 13, lect. 3, no. 996, Aquinas contrasts the intellect's heavenly union with God that makes known his essence to our obscure union with him here below that only enables us to know of God *quid non est*, which may imply that the blessed know God's *quid est* (see the analysis at the end of this section).

21. The contrast between God's *quid est* and creature-bound knowledge is close to *DDN*, ch. 1, lect. 1, nos. 26–27 (the second set of texts in the previous note), a passage that implies that God's essence is known in glory.

22. *SDN*, ch. 11, no. 27, p. 425.80–85 states that Dionysius smashes the Platonists' erroneous notion of the divine processions (e.g., being, life) as gods, the only reference to Platonists in the work. The *SMT* never mentions the Platonists. For the early Thomas's conviction that Dionysius follows Aristotle's teaching, see *II Sent.*, d. 14, q. 1, a. 2.

other things are good, one, and being by derivation, a true teaching that stands in harmony with the Christian faith. The prologue specifies that Dionysius adopts the Platonist way of referring to God as super-good. In the commentary Thomas cuts out the Platonists' mediating hypostases for the procession of perfections into creatures. He correctly argues that Dionysius also clears away these intermediate causes of being and of other perfections.[23] Aquinas's insights on the Platonic setting of the Dionysian corpus directly lead him to relate terms such as "super-good" to a strategy of identifying the one God as the sole cause of finite perfections. Thus the nature of Dionysian mystical ascent, where the term *super* often signifies that God is beyond anything that we know of him (so that the mystic does not think *about* God during union), becomes obscured by the task of purifying Platonic errors on causality. Now *super* mostly becomes an eminent, substantial divine name. Finally, Aquinas's remarks on the Areopagite's Platonic way of speaking may help to explain his hesitancy to adopt the most apophatic Dionysian statements, for these can now be read as stylistic markers rather than as direct doctrinal claims.[24]

Having considered the prologue of Thomas's commentary, I now take up his approach to union beyond mind. Aquinas first mentions union in the opening *lectio*'s presentation of the *Divine Names* as a book on the doctrine of faith grounded in God's revelation. The context is the Areopagite's introduction to his sources and method of teaching. Dionysius explains:

Let the divine law of the writings now determine us from the beginning of our inquiry: we are to make known the truth of what is said about God, "not by trusting the persuasive *logoi* of human wisdom but by bringing forth the power" [1 Cor 2:4] of the Spirit which moves the theologians. Hereby, will you be ineffably and unknowingly joined to what is ineffable and unknowable in a far greater union than we can attain through our rational and intellectual powers and activities. In general, then, one must neither dare to say—nor clearly, to conceive—anything about the hidden

---

23. *DDN*, ch. 1, lect. 3, no. 100; ch. 5, lect. 1, nos. 612, 625, 634; lect. 3, no. 664; ch. 11, lect. 4, nos. 932–33.

24. About 1270 (just after the *DDN*), Thomas Aquinas goes further on Dionysius's Platonism in *Quaestiones disputatae de malo*, ed. Pierre-Marie Gils, Leonine Edition 23 (Paris: Cerf; Rome: Commissio Leonina, 1982), q. 16, a. 1, ad 3: "Dionysius qui in plurimis fuit sectator sententie platonice." This insight may be the fruit of the *DDN*.

divinity beyond being contrary to what has been divinely manifested to us in the sacred writings (*hierōn logiōn*).[25]

Dionysius contrasts the Spirit's illumining, unitive power to the inadequacy of human wisdom in noetic ascent. Such inadequacy leads to a reliance on the sacred writings or the Bible so as to speak correctly about God.[26] He then invokes the Spirit's power to guide his exegesis. Dionysius is a reliable hierarch, for his initiation into the hidden meaning of God's names is rooted in the Scriptures inspired by the Spirit, the text that Dionysius expounds with the same Spirit's guidance. Thus the Spirit has three functions: (1) he moves the human biblical authors to speak wisely about God; (2) he moves the expositor of Scripture in an analogous way; and (3) he unites the recipient of revelation and of the Areopagite's teaching to the unknown God. The *Divine Names* effectively prepares the mind for union. The present passage refers to the written apostolic tradition as *the* way toward union. The contemplative should reflect on this tradition with the help of reason, like Hierotheus, who studied the oracles before being initiated into the mysteries of God by divine inspiration. Dionysius guides the disciple's study through his rational, philosophical insights on God's revealed names. The mode of union is the same as that of its object: it is unknowable, hence beyond adequate description.[27] The direct action of the Spirit unites more than his power mediated through the inspired writings, although Dionysius also has a doctrine of the unitive power of the divine names. The Bible enables a correct conceptual understanding of God that prepares the way for the Spirit's conjoining action.

Aquinas follows Dionysius in identifying the "theologians" with apostles and prophets, the direct recipients of divine revelation. He also identifies the sacred oracles (*hierōn logiōn*) as the Scriptures, for in them the apostles and prophets transmit God's revelation. These men manifest the truth about God not by relying on "human wisdom," for they do not proceed by natural reason—that is, by philosophical arguments. Indeed, "in his own doctrine, Dionysius relies on the authority of Sacred Scripture, which has strength and power insofar as the apos-

---

25. *DN* 1.1, pp. 107.5–108.9, 587–88A, Jones, 107. Here, Parker's reading is confusing.
26. Beate Regina Suchla, notes to Dionysius Areopagita, *Die Namen Gottes*, 104.
27. *DN* 2.9, pp. 133.13–134.6, 648A–B; de Andia, *Henosis*, 233, 240.

tles and prophets were moved to speak by the Holy Spirit revealing to them and speaking in them."[28]

Aquinas focuses his explication of the Spirit's power on (1) the inspiration of apostles and prophets and (2) the fruits of this revelation accessible in Scripture. For Thomas, Dionysius continues the apostles' and prophets' work of manifesting God's truth, for his book expounds on God's biblical names. Unlike Albert, who treats Dionysius as an inspired author, Aquinas says nothing about the Areopagite's direct inspiration. Thomas seems more interested in the latter's Platonic sources. He connects his whole explanation of the Spirit's power to its mediation through biblical *doctrines*—to the *content* of prophetic and apostolic speech. This allows him to reinterpret the ineffable union mentioned in this opening paragraph of the *Divine Names*:

In these [philosophical] doctrines, we can rely on the principles of human wisdom in which are passed on things that are knowable and can be said by human beings ... in the doctrine of faith, some things unknown and ineffable to the human being are proposed, [things] to which those having faith adhere, not by knowing or perfectly explaining by word, although they adhere to them with greater certitude, and such adherence is higher than any natural cognition.[29]

We no longer attain unknowable divine things at a level beyond biblical mediations, for Scripture directly mediates the unknowable. Aquinas reframes the knowable-unknowable contrast within a grace-nature distinction, a very Albertian exegetical move.[30] Like John of Scythopolis and Maximos, he reformulates a Dionysian paradox with clear doctrinal distinctions. Scripture's teaching makes known and puts into words that which remains beyond reason alone:

---

28. *DDN*, ch. 1, lect. 1, no. 6: "Innititur enim, in sua doctrina, Dionysius auctoritate sacrae Scripturae, quae robur habet et virtutem secundum quod Apostoli et Prophetae moti sunt ad loquendum a Spiritu Sancto eis revelante et in eis loquente"; see also lect. 1, no. 11; ch. 2, lect. 4, no. 172.

29. *DDN*, ch. 1, lect. 1, no. 7: "In illis doctrinis, principiis humanae sapientiae inniti possumus in quibus ea traduntur quae hominibus cognoscibilia sunt et dicibilia ... in doctrina fidei proponuntur quaedam homini ignota et indicibilia quibus habentes fidem inhaerent, non cognoscendo aut perfecte verbo explicando, licet certius eis inhaereant et altior sit huiusmodi inhaesio quam aliqua cognitio naturalis"; see also lect. 4, no. 173.

30. *SMT*, ch. 1, p. 462.31–38 (cited in footnote 148 of chapter 4 in this volume).

this is what he [Dionysius] says: *By which,* namely, the power of revelation proceeding from the Holy Spirit in the apostles and prophets, we are *joined by faith to the ineffable and unknown,* that is, to the divine truth which exceeds all human speech and cognition. But faith does not join to them [divine things] so that the believer might know and speak them just as they are, for this would be of an open vision, but [faith] joins *ineffably and unknowingly: For now we see through a mirror,* as 1 Corinthians 13 says.[31]

Union to the unknown takes place between two poles: the knowledge of reason alone and the knowledge of glory. Dionysius offers a threefold schema: (1) inadequate human wisdom; (2) Spirit-moved discourse about God in Scripture and the *Divine Names,* and (3) Spirit-enabled union. Thomas presents a twofold schema: (1) natural knowledge or discourse and (2) revealed knowledge or discourse. Both stages in Aquinas's schema make known the divine reality with the help of concepts and words. Aquinas fuses the last two aspects of the Areopagite's threefold schema into one reality with two complementary, intertwined parts. First, the Spirit's revelatory power moves through Scripture, hence through sacred doctrine's or faith's formal object—that is, the first truth insofar as it is mediated through sacred Scripture.[32] Second, the Spirit imparts the gift of faith whereby the human being can adhere with certitude to the truths revealed in Scripture and thus to divine truth itself, faith's formal object. In light of the analysis on the virtue of faith in chapter 6 of this volume, we can see that Thomas's unifying light has two modes: as a historically mediated "external" gift and as a personal, interior grace. The first mode communicates revealed intelligible content, while the second mode enables the reception of that content and of the divine reality itself, for faith joins us to God.

But God's manifestation remains imperfect. Hence Aquinas contrasts the knowledge of faith to the knowledge of beatitude, which accounts for the abiding ineffability in the Dionysian text. But the focus

---

31. *DDN,* ch. 1, lect. 1, no. 8: "hoc est quod dicit: *Secundum quam,* scilicet virtutem revelationis procedentis a Spiritu Sancto in Apostolos et Prophetas, nos per fidem *coniungimur ineffabilibus et ignotis,* idest veritati divinae quae excedit omnem humanam locutionem et cognitionem. Nec fides sic coniungit eis ut faciat ea ab homine credente cognosci et loqui sicut sunt, hoc enim esset apertae visionis, sed coniungit *ineffabiliter et ignote: Videmus enim nunc per speculum* ut dicitur I Cor. XIII"; see also ch. 7, lect. 1, no. 705.

32. *ST* II-II, q. 5, a. 3c.

remains on what can already be known by the Spirit's aid. The sense of "ineffable" and "unknowable" shifts, for Aquinas mainly contrasts these limits with the eschaton. Dionysius contrasts concept-bound cognition with a meta-conceptual cognition accessible in this life. For him union to the unknown includes directly received cognition, yet the recipient cannot conceptualize or say what he or she has learned. For Aquinas the cognition imparted by living faith's union with the unknown is precisely the doctrine of Scripture—that which God has enfleshed in concepts and language. Beyond that, "being joined unknowingly" involves union with what cannot be known in this life insofar as "knowing union" requires an unmediated gaze upon God's essence. Also, Thomas's present exposition of faith implies its vivification by charity, for he emphasizes faith's power of joining us to truth.

Thomas found the interpretation of Dionysian union as being conjoined through faith in Albert, although Aquinas's doctrine of the missions already leads to this reading. Albert's commentary on the same *Divine Names* passage notes that, by the divine writings, we are united by cognition to God, a union that occurs by the light of faith. Thomas follows, expands on, and modifies Albert's interpretation. The latter connects the language of the "ineffable and unknown" to our inability to comprehend God.[33] For Thomas, faith cannot know and speak divine things "just as they are (*sicut sunt*)," that which becomes possible in heaven.

Aquinas's faith-centered reinterpretation of ineffable union has parallels in his comments on chaste silence and the highest hymn mentioned in the *Divine Names*. Dionysius explains:

with a prudent silence, we elevate ourselves to the glories which illuminate us in the sacred Oracles, and are led by their light to the supremely Divine Hymns, by which we are super-mundanely enlightened and moulded to the sacred Songs of Praise.[34]

He refers to the silence befitting God's transcendence or the presence of ineffable realities. In Proclus's *Platonic Theology*, silence involves the inability to speak the ineffable, communion with the ineffable, and the ineffable's celebration by a hymn. A hymn of negations follows silent

33. *SDN*, ch. 1, no. 8, p. 4.48–54, 78; no. 10, p. 5.12–20.
34. *DN* 1.3, p. 111.5–7, 589B, Parker, 4.

union. Dionysius draws inspiration from Proclus but skips the hymn of negations in favor of a paradoxical hymn of silence. Thus Moses's journey peaks with silence in darkness.[35]

Aquinas focuses his exposition of this text on Scripture and faith:

we extend ourselves to the splendors shining upon us in the holy sayings, that is, to the truths of Sacred Scripture revealed to human beings *and from the* splendors of Sacred Scripture, *we are illumined to thearchical hymns,* that is to the knowledge of divine names, by which God is praised. For through these we know to praise God [as] living, good and the like, which are passed on to us about God in the Sacred Scriptures; inasmuch as we are *illumined by these* hymns, *super-mundane,* that is, above the power of natural reason, and in some way [are] *configured to the holy enunciations of the hymns,* that is, of the divine praises passed on through the divine names in the Scriptures, namely, inasmuch as we are informed by faith in them.[36]

Thomas's commentary often interprets the image of divine lights or "splendors" as a reference to truth.[37] Since the (plural) Dionysian lights (not the light on Mt. Sinai) are God's gifts that impart concept-bound knowledge of God and raise the mind to him, Aquinas's interpretation has a partial foundation in Dionysius. Scripture's primary function as a mediation of God's light is to reveal the truth about God and creation. Aquinas considers the "thearchical hymns" equivalent to the "splendors." Indeed, throughout the *Divine Names* and the *Mystical Theology* Dionysius hymns God with his biblical names, either affirmative or negative. Thomas takes him to intend a single, technical meaning for the term "hymns." He sees neither the Proclan background nor the second sense of "hymns" that the Areopagite here uses. The Dionysian paradox of speechless hymning escapes Aquinas's gaze. But the subtle-

---

35. De Andia, *Henosis,* 394–97.

36. *DDN,* ch. 1, lect. 2, no. 44: "*extendimur ad splendores nobis illucentes in sanctis eloquiis,* idest ad veritates sacrae Scripturae hominibus revelatas *et ab ipsis* sacrae Scripturae splendoribus, *illuminamur ad thearchicos hymnos,* idest ad divina nomina, quibus Deus laudatur, cognoscenda. Per haec enim scimus laudare Deum viventem, bonum et alia huiusmodi, quae hic nobis de Deo in Scripturis sacris traduntur; nos, inquam, *illuminati ab ipsis* hymnis, *supermundane,* idest super virtute naturalis rationis et quodammodo *configurati ad sanctas enuntiationes hymnorum,* idest divinarum laudum quae traduntur in Scripturis per divina nomina, in quantum scilicet eorum fide informamur."

37. *DDN,* ch. 1, lect. 1, nos. 15–16; lect. 2, nos. 44, 70, 72; ch. 4, lect. 4, nos. 325, 327, 329–32.

ty of the Areopagite's doctrine and multiple senses of the term "hymning" clear the way for a fundamental rereading of the Dionysian text on the basis of Dionysius himself. Indeed, the latter's text can appear to imply the sense that Aquinas gives it, for Dionysius adds shortly after that we should praise the divine source "as Itself has taught concerning Itself in the sacred Oracles. For instance, that It is cause and origin and essence and life of all things."[38] God teaches the content of praise in the Scriptures. Thomas seems to pick up on this sense of the divine names as praises. But he goes further, as only praise unenlightened by revelation falls silent. Instead of oracles illumining us "to thearchical hymns" whereby we pass beyond biblical discourse into silent praise, Scripture illumines with inspired words that praise God. Having collapsed the hymns into the biblical lights, the light of the hymns becomes not a gift received beyond discourse but the truth about God concretized in language and received by faith. Hence "being configured to the holy enunciations" becomes being conformed to biblical truth by grace. Thomas's exposition partly depends on reading the meaning of the "thearchical hymns" in light of the Areopagite's discussion of hymns in other passages.

Aquinas's reading of the "super-mundane" as exceeding natural reason directly follows upon this reinterpretation of the hymns. Dionysius here seems to signify the metalinguistic nature of certain hymns, in contrast to other hymns in the *Divine Names*. As in his opening *lectio*, Aquinas shifts the Areopagite's contrast between revealed conceptual knowledge and metaconceptual union to the contrast between natural reason and faith. For Thomas the language of illumination by and configuration to the holy sayings refers to faith. The major fruit of faith is the mind's illumination by revelation and the Son's presence in his mission, gifts that configure us to the Son through the Spirit. The study of the missions in chapter 6 of this work shows that, for Thomas, any mention of unitive faith presupposes the conjoining action of the Son sent to enlighten the mind by grace. Furthermore, Thomas's interpretation of Dionysian lights as the biblical truths, articulated praises, and names about God implies that the mode of receiving the divine lights is active and still linked to concepts, while the information imparted

38. *DN* 1.3, p. 111.9–11, 589B, Parker, 4.

about God becomes less ineffable. The subject's concept-bound noetic mode of reception links up with a certain type of intelligible content.[39] The gift of light is for the sake of manifesting God, not concealing him. Aquinas seems to display greater interest in light's cognitive fruit than in its power to effect ineffable union. Finally, throughout his discussions of light, Aquinas does not display an awareness of the liturgical setting that Dionysius thereby evokes. Thomas does not see the allusions to liturgical symbols as the starting point of the mind's ascent to God.[40] This allows for a greater focus on Scripture as a communication of noetic content. Aquinas shifts from a monastic mysticism to a mysticism for all believers, and perhaps also to a mysticism for theologians and preachers.

Thomas's doctrine of union by faith in revelation seems to find partial confirmation in chapter 4, where Dionysius expounds his contemplative psychology. He explains that the divine name *erōs* should not be judged by its sensual meaning, but by a higher meaning. He illustrates this with a parallel. When the soul

> is moved by the intellectual energies to the things contemplated, the sensible perceptions by aid of sensible objects are superfluous; just as also the intellectual powers, when the soul, having become godlike, throws itself (*epiballei*), through a union beyond knowledge, against the rays of the unapproachable light, by sightless efforts (*epibolais*).[41]

"Throws itself" (*epiballei*) could also be translated as "to grasp." "Blind efforts" (*epibolais*) or intuitions involve a technical term signifying the mode of knowledge proper to union beyond mind. Given the presence of divine light, we let go of all active cognition and allow the divine teacher to speak unutterable words. Such intuition or grasping entails docile, quiet reception.[42]

Thomas explains:

> *The intellectual powers* of our natural reason are also useless *when* our *soul* having been conformed to God *throws itself* (*immittit se*) into divine things ... by the movement (*immissione*) of faith, namely, by this that the

---

39. Compare *DDN*, ch. 1, lect. 1, no. 15.
40. Rorem, *Pseudo-Dionysius*, 135–36.
41. *DN* 4.11, p. 156.15–19, 708D, Parker, 46.
42. De Andia, *Henosis*, 236, 249–50; Rorem, *Pseudo-Dionysius*, 150.

unknown and inaccessible divine light unites and communicates itself to us. For when we consider those [things] which pertain to faith, we do not judge about them through natural reason.[43]

Here too, Thomas reads noetic ecstasy with the faith-reason distinction. The truths attained by natural reason are inadequate to judge the truth or falsity of faith's doctrines. Such knowledge is superfluous insofar as it is inadequate. We recognize the limits of reason without denying its value. The soul "conformed to God" can move toward him in faith, since faith comes from God. Through faith the unknown and inaccessible light unites itself to us. Faith is the *terminus ad quod* of God's illuminating action. Here Thomas could have easily invoked the Son's or the Spirit's mission, but he does not. He now refers the inaccessible, unknown light to God as cause of union. The God who remains inaccessible to strictly human powers reveals part of his mystery in faith. The soul's blindness now becomes the incapacity of ungraced reason to make judgments about the mysteries of faith. Thomas picks up on the context of the Dionysian passage: the divine name *erōs* should be judged through Scripture, not the surface meaning of the word. Thomas approaches the paragraph as a systematic whole, a reading that is not completely foreign to the text. But he goes beyond the text with his conclusion that the correct judgment of the meaning of *erōs* is attained in union. The Areopagite's illustrative parallel becomes a hierarchy of truth judgments. The intellect that knows "as through a mirror" judges without seeing and thus still suffers from partial blindness, for one only sees indirectly, via the mediation of faith. Thomas employs a consistent Albertian hermeneutic in his comments on noetic ecstasy and union in darkness, a hermeneutic wherein the grace-nature and faith-reason distinctions play a central role.[44] The act of faith now takes the place of Dionysian noetic receptivity during union. Noetic silence and passivity have essentially disappeared.

The third set of union texts in the *Commentary on the Divine Names*

---

43. *DDN*, ch. 4, lect. 9, no. 414: "*intellectuales virtutes* nostrae naturalis rationis etiam superfluunt *quando anima* nostra Deo conformata *immittit se* rebus divinis, *non* immissione *oculorum* corporalium, sed immissione fidei, scilicet per hoc quod divinum lumen ignotum et inaccessibile, seipsum nobis unit et communicat. Dum enim consideramus ea quae fidei sunt, non diiudicamus ea per rationem naturalem."

44. *SDN*, ch. 4, no. 123, p. 217.30–36.

focuses on the act of remotion. Chapter 1 of the *Divine Names* asks about the possibility of naming God. For Dionysius, we cannot express what the unknown God's essence is, as it is beyond God's processions. Still, deified minds celebrate him. Those who know ineffably speak the ineffable:

> The god-like minds (men) made one by these unions, through imitation of angels as far as attainable (since it is during cessation of every mental energy that such an union as this of the deified minds towards the super-divine light takes place) celebrate It most appropriately through the abstraction (*aphaireseōs*) of all created things—enlightening in this matter, truly and supernaturally from the most blessed union towards It—that It is Cause indeed of all things existing, but Itself [is] none of them, as being super-essentially elevated above all.[45]

We imitate angelic union with God as we attain a holy silence wherein God alone speaks ineffably. Union's subjective condition is the cessation of all noetic activity. Its objective condition is the celebration of God by transcending negation (*aphaireseōs*).[46] The hymn of negations seems to accompany the event of union. Dionysius now follows Proclus more closely as the hymn of silence becomes a hymn of negations. Dionysius does not explain how such praise can occur during the cessation of noetic activity.

Thomas comments on this text in a *lectio* entitled, "How God can be named." He divides the *lectio* into a discussion of three ways to name God: by remotion, by cause, and by superlative as well as symbolic names.[47] Here the last passage cited becomes a summary of the method of remotion. Aquinas transforms a text whose primary theme is union into a discussion on the technicalities of naming God. The holy minds imitating angels are the prophets and apostles. The mediators of biblical revelation celebrate God through remotion. Aquinas continues:

> because *the unity* of holy *minds* to God, who is above every light, *occurs in this way*, namely through remotion from all existing things, *according to the repose of every intellectual operation*, that is, in the ultimate [point], in which all their intellectual operations rests. For this is the ultimate [point]

---

45. *DN* 1.5, pp. 116.14–17.4, 593B–C, Parker, 8.
46. De Andia, *Henosis*, 237–38; see also *DN* 7.1, pp. 194.16–95.2, 868A.
47. *DDN*, ch. 1, lect. 3, nos. 79, 83, 85, 102.

to which we can attain concerning divine cognition in this life, that God is above all that which can be cogitated by us and therefore the naming of God which is through remotion is most proper.[48]

This section of Thomas's *lectio* does not explicitly identify any particular grace as the cause or precondition of union. But a few lines earlier, he cites the Areopagite's phrase "deiform minds," which Thomas identifies as the minds of the saints. Godlike minds belong not to any prophet, but to holy prophets. This qualification is important, for Aquinas elsewhere distinguishes between a nonsanctifying gift of prophecy and sanctifying grace. Later in the commentary he identifies the deiform gift that God imparts to the soul as the gift of grace.[49] Thus the subject of union mentioned here is both in sanctifying grace and the recipient of supernatural revelation destined for Scripture. Balaam the pagan prophet of Numbers does not have a Godlike mind. Yet the immediate cause of union is not so much grace as the intellect's act of removing all created things from God. Hence, while this union occurs in grace, the central theme is not the unifying power of grace, but the manner in which a more intense cognitive union can be attained, given God's sanctifying action. Thomas seeks to describe the perfection of knowledge, which by its nature involves being joined to the known, since the intellect in act is somehow the understood in act.[50] Aquinas again prefers the term "remotion" to "negation." We do not deny that God has some perfection, but rather signify the distance between God and creatures, a function of naming not far from the function of the Areopagite's transcending negation (*aphaireseōs*). For Aquinas the intellect's repose signifies not the ceasing of its operation, but rather its completion or perfection. The noetic content in question, the fruit of remotions, is the recognition that God is beyond all that we can conceive. Aquinas here probably refers to God's incomprehensibility in the strict

---

48. *DDN*, ch. 1, lect. 3, no. 83: "quia *unitio* sanctarum *mentium* ad Deum, qui est super omne lumen, *fit talis*, scilicet per remotionem a cunctis existentibus, *secundum quietem omnis intellectualis operationis*, idest in ultimo, in quo quiescit omnis eorum intellectualis operatio. Hoc enim est ultimum ad quod pertingere possumus circa cognitionem divinam in hac vita, quod Deus est supra omne id quod a nobis cogitari potest et ideo nominatio Dei quae est per remotionem est maxime propria"; see also ch. 2, lect. 4, no. 180.

49. *DDN*, ch. 4, lect. 1, no. 291; *ST* II-II, q. 172, a. 4.

50. *DDN*, ch. 1, lect. 1, no. 38 (cited below at footnote 85 of this chapter).

sense of the term. A few lines later he explains that God "cannot be praised *in any way as he is,* that is, comprehensively."[51] Praise by remotion does not take away any perfection from God, but recalls the infinite distance between divine and created perfections. By attaining a more accurate understanding of God's nature, the prophets and apostles reached a fuller noetic union with him. The act of remotion fills the cognitive space of silence, a noetic act with a triple content: God's infinitude, creaturely finitude, and their difference. Union occurs through the judgment of the Creator-creature distance. Such judgment is effective in bringing about true cognition and thus union because it is founded upon an accurate understanding of true divine names, true because revealed. Aquinas seems to imply that all believers can imitate this union enjoyed by the holy prophets and apostles. For the faithful receive the same sanctifying grace and acquire graced knowledge of God via Scripture.

The Areopagite's manner of explaining the union of Godlike minds and Thomas's exposition thereof help to explain why Aquinas consistently fills Dionysian noetic silence and ecstasy with human cognitive acts. Dionysius seems to propose that holy souls sing a hymn of negations *as* they enjoy union. Actually, the *Divine Names* passage cited previously does not clearly posit a simultaneity of union and praise, though simultaneity seems to be implied.[52] Aquinas follows through on this implication. First, he refuses to exclude human noetic activity from the state of intellectual repose, a doctrine in perfect harmony with his theology of the *imago*. Second, he has already shifted the meaning of transcending negations in a more kataphatic direction with his overall doctrine of divine naming. Thomas's cognitive act, which finds re-

---

51. *DDN*, ch. 1, lect. 3, no. 83: "non potest laudari, *quomodocumque est*, idest comprehensive."

52. John D. Jones detects an "essentialist reading" of *DN* 1.5 in Aquinas (our present passage), partly due to the Sarracenus's mistranslation. For Jones, Dionysius and "the Byzantine tradition" do not at all name God "in himself"; see Jones, "The *Divine Names* in John Sarracen's Translation: Misconstruing Dionysius's Language About God?" *American Catholic Philosophical Quarterly* 82 (2008): 661–82, esp. 678–79. Jones does not mention the great ambiguity of *DN* 1.5 that makes possible Aquinas's conflation of active praise and noetic silence. Also, Jones's essay says little about Dionysius. He reconstructs "the Byzantine tradition" that includes Dionysius mostly on the foundation of Damascius the Diadochus and Gregory Palamas, which begs the question in a comparison of Dionysius and Aquinas.

pose in union, has more noetic content to ponder than the Areopagite's contemplative. Aquinas's unified mind can still contemplate finite noetic objects—precisely that which Dionysius seeks to minimize within, if not eliminate altogether, from the mind's ecstasy. Third, Aquinas changes the nature of cognitive ascent, as the immediate cause thereof becomes the act of removing "existing things" from God. Divine light, now interpreted not as a special gift reserved to a few contemplatives but as sanctifying grace and the light of revelation received by all who have living faith, shifts to the background, though God's light constitutes an essential foundation for cognitive union. The motor of ascent becomes an act of faith judgment that is at our disposal through proper instruction on the truth of Scripture. Yet in a way, remotions remain at a stage below the summit of cognitive union, since such union is the fruit of the judgment whereby we remove from God finitude in all of its modalities. Union is "through remotions," not "in remotions." While the mind's repose does not exclude the contemplation of finite noetic objects, its intention focuses on God insofar as he is above all created things. Here Thomas comes close to collapsing remotion and eminence, perhaps partly because he develops these two paths out of the single Dionysian path of transcending negations.[53]

The proximity of Thomas's exposition to Albert's *Commentary on the Mystical Theology* is striking, especially to Albert's doctrine of union via negations (though Thomas prefers the term "remotions"). For both Dominicans the act of removing "what is not God" is a cause of union. This notion has a twofold Dionysian inspiration: (1) the Areopagite's discussion of the Plotinian statue whose beauty is revealed through negations and (2) the ladder of negations that leads to union at the end of the *Divine Names*. Albert also connects Dionysian noetic repose with the recognition that God is beyond all.[54] Thomas expands on Albert,

---

53. The considerable transformation of the Dionysian text that Aquinas operates here (no. 83) shows that, contrary to Humbrecht, we need not categorize this passage as an intermingling of Dionysian and Thomasien notions with little possibility of discernment between them. Aquinas articulates his personal doctrine throughout this text. The priority of remotion does not distance this passage from *ST* I, where the language of remotion's priority is absent, and bring it close to *SCG* I, ch. 14, which affirms such priority as Humbrecht claims (*Théologie négative*, 407–8). At no. 83, remotion includes some functions of eminence, and eminence bears a partly positive meaning.

54. *SDN*, ch. 1, no. 49, p. 31.14–24.

but the general interpretive line is similar. Aquinas proposes that, in the realm of grace, the method of remotion leads directly to the summit of cognition, which is a knowledge by eminence. The graced *triplex via* brings us to darkness.

Thomas's most extensive explanation of union by remotion in the *Commentary on the Divine Names* comes in chapter 7 of that text. Here the expositions of Dionysius and Aquinas are very dense. One needs to navigate a jungle of technical terms and subtle shifts in meaning so as to discern the respective authors' doctrinal intention. Dionysius offers a virtual outline of the project of the *Divine Names* and of the *Mystical Theology* as he explains how God is known.

> Never, then, is it true to say that we know God; not from His own nature (*physeōs*) (for that is unknown, and surpasses all reason and mind), but, from the ordering of all existing things, as projected from Himself, and containing a sort of images and similitudes of His Divine exemplars, we ascend, as far as we have power, to that which is beyond all, by method and order in the abstraction (*aphairesei*) and pre-eminence (*hyperochē*) of all, and in the Cause of all. Wherefore, Almighty God is known even in all, and apart from all. And through knowledge, Almighty God is known, and through *agnosia*. And there is, of Him, both conception and expression.... And He is neither conceived, nor expressed nor named.... He is celebrated from all existing things, according to the analogy of all things, of which He is Cause. And there is, further, the most Divine Knowledge of Almighty God, which is known, through not knowing (*agnosia*) during the union above mind; when the mind, having stood apart from all existing things, then having dismissed also itself, has been made one with the super-luminous rays, thence and there being illuminated by the unsearchable depth of wisdom.[55]

Having excluded cognition of God's nature (*physeōs*), Dionysius considers the order of beings as a starting point for knowledge about God. The divine similitudes in creation enable a threefold ascent, a rare instance of the *triplex via* in Dionysius, instead of the usual twofold way of affirmation and either *apophasis* or *aphairesis*. God is known by the negation (*aphairesei*) of all, by going beyond all, and as Cause of all. In other passages transcending negation sometimes forms a triad with affirmation

---

55. *DN* 7.3, pp. 197.18–98.15, 869C–72B, Parker, 91–92.

and its complementary negation (*apophasis*).[56] Here transcending negation is the only type of negation mentioned. Eminence (*hyperochē*) now completes the Areopagite's *triplex via*. The *knowledge* of God beyond all is the outcome of this threefold way. God is known "by analogy" and celebrated or praised in reference to all things. Dionysius then begins an important transitional passage about knowing and unknowing centered around a quasi-dialectical litany of praise. I will come back to this litany shortly. Finally, he turns to a higher knowledge, that of "unknowing." This second half of the citation parallels Moses in the *Mystical Theology*. Unknowing occurs in four steps: (1) being separated from all beings; (2) going out of oneself; (3) being united to rays of light; and (4) being illumined by wisdom.[57] The first two steps pass beyond mind, and the last two steps involve union that is beyond mind. Overall, the Areopagite's approach to the knowledge of God consists of four stages: (1) the impossibility of knowing God's nature; (2) the threefold way that begins with beings; (3) a transition via the litany praising God as known yet unknown; and (4) unknowing beyond mind (with its four steps).

Thomas explains that cognition of God "through his nature" exceeds the natural power of angelic and human minds, for it entails the vision of his essence. The latter is only possible by the light of glory. Here below we know God by the order of the cosmos. Thomas's reading of this passage differs from that of Albert, who uses it as an occasion to distinguish between the (accessible) knowledge of God's *quia est* and the (impossible) knowledge of his *quid est*.[58]

Aquinas then proposes an unusual reading of the *triplex via*. It consists

First and principally *in the separation* (*ablatione*) *of all things*, namely inasmuch as we estimate that nothing of the things which we observe in the order of creatures is God or befits God; and secondly through excess, for we do not take away from God the perfections of creatures such as life, wisdom and the like because of a defect in God, but because he exceeds every perfection of creatures, on account of which we remove (*removemus*) wisdom from him.[59]

---

56. E.g., *MT* 1.1, p. 143.3–7, 1000B; de Andia, *Henosis*, 378.
57. De Andia, *Henosis*, 274–76.
58. *DDN*, ch. 7, lect. 4, no. 729; see also *SDN*, ch. 7, no. 27, p. 358.1–3.
59. *DDN*, ch. 7, lect. 4, no. 729: "primo quidem et principaliter *in omnium ablatione*,

A short exposition of causality follows. In the one instance where Dionysius employs a threefold way of transcending negation, eminence, and causality, Aquinas proposes something close to the more typical Dionysian triad of apophatic negation, transcending negation and causal affirmation. Not knowing the technical meaning of *aphairesei*, Thomas treats its Latin translation (*ablatione*) as a mode of separation, which is closer to the Areopagite's *apophasis*. Meanwhile, Aquinas transfers part of the Dionysian doctrine of *aphairesis* to eminence. The Dionysian way of excess prolongs the way of separation but focuses on the nonprivative sense of divine transcendence.

The phrase "knowing by unknowing" emerges twice in *Divine Names*, chapter 7, section 3. We first find it in the dialectical litany (Dionysius's stage 3): "God is known even in all and apart from all. Through knowledge God is known, and through unknowing." Dionysius here transitions from the *triplex via* (stage 2) to unknowing (stage 4), but an ambiguity lingers. The language of separation and eminence can appear to match the litany's apophatic pole: "God ... apart from all." In that case the language of knowing by unknowing would refer back to transcending negation (*aphairesei*) and eminence. The phrase "knowing by unknowing" thus seems to stand in contrast to affirmative knowledge. "Unknowing" seems to describe a way of negative as well as eminent divine knowing and *naming*, although this is not the Areopagite's intention.

Aquinas approaches this transitional passage from the *triplex via* to union in darkness as a conclusion of the exposition on the threefold way. He picks up on the text's apparent link between unknowing and the negation-excess couplet:[60]

God is known in all, as in his effects, *and without all*, as removed (*remotus*) from all and exceeding all ... hence he is known *through* our *ignorance*, inasmuch as this is to know God, that we know ourselves to ignore what God is (*quid sit*).[61]

---

inquantum scilicet nihil horum quae in creaturarum ordine inspicimus, Deum aestimamus aut Deo conveniens; secundario vero per excessum: non enim creaturarum perfectiones ut vitam, sapientiam et huiusmodi, Deo auferimus propter defectum Dei, sed propter hoc quod omnem perfectionem creaturae excedit, propterea removemus ab Eo sapientiam."

60. See the *divisio textus* at *DDN*, ch. 7, lect. 4, no. 727.

61. *DDN*, ch. 7, lect. 4, no. 731: "*Deus cognoscitur in omnibus*, sicut in effectibus *et sine*

This text shows why the previous exposition of the *triplex via* (at no. 729) presents excess as a way of remotion. The remotion-excess connection allows Thomas to link the Dionysian *triplex via* (in no. 729) to the dialectic of knowing and not-knowing whereby he prolongs the discussion of the *triplex via* (in no. 731). The picture becomes more complicated since Thomas's terminology shifts. In the first exposition of the *triplex via* (no. 729), *removemus* pertains to excess, distinct from the way of separation (*ablatione*). In the second, concluding exposition of the *triplex via* (no. 731), *remotus* parallels the way of separation and is distinct from the way of excess. Since Aquinas considers the litany (stage 3) as a conclusion to the section on the *triplex via* (stage 2), he must locate the Areopagite's threefold way within the litany's twofold dialectic. Thomas considers the act of knowing that we do not know God's quiddity as the direct result of both remotion and excess. In the passage just cited, he attributes (1) the knowledge of God in all things to the way of causality and (2) knowledge of God without all things to remotion and excess, though he does not explain how remotion and excess function within this ignorance. Yet the latter must include a partly positive knowledge, for excess has a nonprivate meaning. Finally, Aquinas refers to a reflective knowledge, the realization that our knowledge falls short, a cognition that posits God's excess by an act of judgment and contrasts God's transcendence to the limited mode of being signified by affirmations. The quidditative knowledge that Thomas excludes probably refers to the immediate cognition of God's essence, a theme discussed earlier in this *lectio*.[62] Aquinas thus transforms the Dionysian theme of God's absolutely inaccessible nature into a doctrine on the limits of the pilgrim's knowledge of God's nature.[63]

Aquinas then comments on the passage that parallels Moses on Mt. Sinai, where Dionysius mentions "knowing by unknowing" a second time (stage 4 of the Areopagite's ascent):

---

omnibus, sicut ab omnibus remotus et omnia excedens; et propter hoc etiam *cognoscitur Deus per cognitionem* nostram, quia quidquid in nostra cognitione cadit, accipimus ut ab Eo adductum; et iterum cognoscitur *per ignorantiam* nostram, inquantum scilicet hoc ipsum est Deum cognoscere, quod nos scimus nos ignorare de Deo quid sit."

62. Humbrecht, *Théologie négative*, 469.

63. Thomas's division of the Dionysian text (at *DDN*, no. 730) shows that he treats the paragraph on God's unknown *quid sit* (no. 731) as a conclusion of the expositions of seeing God's essence by grace and the *triplex via* (no. 729). He soon adds that "in all these things God is somehow known, as cause, yet nevertheless *by none* just as he is (*sicut est*)." The term *sicut est* usually describes beatific cognition.

[God] is known and not known: for he is known from all beings and *praised insofar* as they have *proportion* to him, as he *is their cause*. But *further*, there is another, most perfect *knowledge of God* through remotion, namely, by which we know God *through ignorance*, through a certain *union* to divine things above the nature of mind, namely, *when* our *mind receding from all other things* and *then* also *dismissing itself* is united *to super-shining rays* of the deity, namely, inasmuch as it knows God not only to be above all things that are below it [mind], but also above it and above all that can be comprehended by it. And thus knowing God, in such a state of cognition, it [mind] is illumined by the very profundity of divine Wisdom, which we cannot investigate.[64]

Thomas seeks to confirm the sense of the previous passages in *Divine Names*, chapter 7, section 3. He twice states that Dionysius intends to show how the conclusion about divine ignorance (at no. 731) follows from its premises—that is, from the first exposition of the *triplex via* (no. 729).[65] He reads this part of the *Divine Names* as a unified treatment of the *triplex via*, not as a discussion of distinct stages that lead beyond naming. He partly joins the ways of knowing and unknowing, an interpretive move made possible partly by the unclear meaning of the Areopagite's first use of the phrase "knowing by unknowing." Aquinas again links the way of causality or affirmation with the way of ignorance or not-knowing as he overlooks the transition from the litany (stage 3) to unknowing (stage 4). He again shifts terms as he refers to cognition by ignorance as "knowledge through remotion," a change called for by the Areopagite's transition from analogy to unknowing. Thomas's language is unstable, since he combines distinct stages in the Areopagite's text. First, *removemus* signaled a method employed within the way of excess in Thomas's first *triplex via* (at no. 729); then, *re-*

64. *DDN*, ch. 7, lect. 4, no. 732: "cognoscitur et non cognoscitur: ex omnibus enim entibus cognoscitur et *laudatur secundum* quod habent *proportionem* ad Ipsum, ut *quorum est causa*. *Rursus* autem est alia perfectissima *Dei cognitio*, per remotionem scilicet, qua cognoscimus Deum *per ignorantiam*, per quamdam *unitionem* ad divina supra naturam mentis, *quando* scilicet *mens* nostra *recedens ab omnibus aliis* et *postea* etiam *dimittens seipsam* unitur *supersplendentibus radiis* Deitatis, inquantum scilicet cognoscit Deum esse non solum super omnia quae sunt infra ipsam, sed etiam supra ipsam et supra omnia quae ab ipsa comprehendi possunt. Et sic cognoscens Deum, in tali statu cognitionis, illuminatur ab ipsa profunditate divinae Sapientiae, quam perscrutari non possumus."

65. *DDN*, ch. 7, lect. 4, nos. 727, 732.

motus was linked to separation and formed a couplet with excess, two ways that enable cognition by ignorance (no. 731); finally, *remotionem* alone refers to knowledge by ignorance in contrast to the way of causality (no. 732). To summarize:

Dionysius (*DN* 7.3)	Thomas (*DDN*, ch. 7, *lectio* 4, nos. 729–32)
1. God's nature is absolutely inaccessible.	1. God's essence is not seen by our natural powers (no. 729).
2. *Triplex via*: Ascent by negation (*aphairesei*), eminence (*hyperoche*) and to the cause.	2. *Triplex via*: Ascent by separation, removing (*removemus*) finite perfections due to God's excess and knowing God as cause (no. 729).
3. Transitional litany: We know God (a) in all or by knowing (*triplex via*); (b) without all, by unknowing (beyond the *triplex via*).	3. Conclusion of the *triplex via*: We know God (a) in all effects or through cognition (as cause); (b) without all as removed from (*remotus*) and exceeding all, [or] by ignorance (no. 731).
4. Unknowing beyond naming.	4. Unknowing by remotion (no. 732).

In the last passage cited "remotion" has a broad meaning that implicitly includes excess, and this for two reasons. First, this text confirms conclusions reached in the previous paragraphs (nos. 728–31), where the *triplex via* stands at the center of Aquinas's exposition. Indeed, the only other mention of cognition by ignorance in this *lectio* (at no. 731) states that ignorance results from remotion and excess. Thus, at no. 732, the way of excess links with the remotion that is said to bring knowledge by ignorance. Second, Aquinas seems to imply an abiding presence of a remotion-excess couplet in no. 732. He reads "mind receding from all" as knowing that God is above all material beings, that none of them adequately manifest him. The soul "dismissing itself" does not shut down noetic acts, but rather knows that God is above the soul—that no finite spiritual perfection suffices to manifest God's attributes. Both types of remotion imply the way of eminence. Each part of the *triplex via* only fulfills its task as part of the triad. Mind remains within itself but fixes its intentionality on the God who is above mind and above whatever we can comprehend. Union is in the mind with the God greater than mind. Thomas shifts the meaning of ecstasy from the mind's inactivity to God's metaphysical greatness, an ecstasy that mind knows by a reflective act of judgment. Union with divine lights now seems to follow upon cognition by remotion: "*knowledge of God* through remotion, namely, by which we know God *through ignorance,* through a certain *union.*" Ignorance is the outcome of remotion, and it describes the noetic element of union. The subsequent phrase confirms this reading, where mind receding from all things indicates knowledge by remotion-excess, "and then" mind "dismisses itself" so as to be united to divine lights. Like Dionysius, Thomas places ignorance at the center of union. Since cognition "by ignorance" is the result of knowledge by remotion and excess (explicitly in no. 731, implicitly in no. 732), such knowledge measures and apparently brings about union, for mind is "united ... inasmuch as it knows God ... [to be] above all."

Only Aquinas's last comments on incomprehension and illumination resemble Albert's exposition of *Divine Names,* chapter 7, section 3. But Albert's comments on the knowing–not-knowing litany consistently refer the knowledge of God to his *quia est* and ignorance to not knowing his *quid est* or incomprehensibility. Both friars link union with knowing that we do not comprehend God. It is the act of judgment by which one understands that God is above whatever we comprehend.[66] But Aquinas sees incomprehension as only one element in a series of remotions that pertain to knowledge by ignorance. The inaccessibility of direct knowledge of God's essence frames Thomas's whole *lectio.* Aquinas's mystic stretches toward knowable lights and, by better realizing the distance between God and what we already know, enjoys a deeper union without vision.

The last discussion of union by remotion in the *Commentary on the Divine Names* comes in the work's final chapter. Here Dionysius affirms and negates the name "One" as he guides the reader to the cusp of return. The One constitutes the ultimate step on the ladder of negations that prepares us for union. Dionysius presents four steps on the path to union: (1) affirmation of the One; (2) negation of the One; (3) ascending to the nameless God; and (4) union. He uses a typical quasi-dialectic of affirmation and negation to explain the function of the names "One" or "Unit" and "Trinity" or "Triad." God is "celebrated as

---

66. See *SDN,* ch. 7, no. 30, p. 359.22–49, 57–58, though Albert is not as explicit on the function of judgment.

Unit and Triad, the Deity above all is neither Unit nor Triad, as understood by us or by any other sort of being."[67] We find a contrast between the One as cause of all who can be named as cause and the One as superessential who cannot be named, for he transcends all types of unity that we know by conceptual thought. We ponder two aspects of the One (as cause or as transcending), an approach that calls for distinct methods: affirmation and negation.[68]

As he comments on this Dionysian text, Thomas states that the phrase "any sort of existing thing" or being refers to all intelligent creatures—that is, angels and human beings. God is neither one nor three as we understand unity or a triad, which Aquinas interprets as a reference to natural cognition. But the angels understand God as One and Three in their graced vision of the divine essence. Hence the cognition of divine unity being negated is below beatitude. Aquinas applies the same argument to human cognition. By the gift of grace (which here refers to glory), we can see God's essence, but we cannot comprehend him. Thomas here reduces the negation of the name "One" to the impossibility of the beatific vision without grace.[69]

He employs a similar hermeneutical strategy when he takes up the notion that God is nameless. Dionysius states, "no Unit nor Triad ... nor any other existing thing, or thing known to any existing thing, brings forth the hiddenness, above every expression and every mind, of the Super-Deity.... Nor has It a Name."[70] Thomas explains, "*no monad ... nor* anything *else* naturally known from any of the created beings, *draws out*, that is, manifests and perfectly expresses that *hiddenness* of the superexcellent Deity."[71] In this context the term "naturally known" perhaps refers to the knowledge proper to the pilgrim status—that which falls short of glory, not that which falls short of sanctifying grace in general. The present paragraph still contrasts the hidden God to the capacities of human and angelic minds short of glory. Second, the phrase "perfectly expresses" probably refers to comprehension or

---

67. *DN* 13.3, p. 229.6–7, 980D, Parker, 125.
68. De Andia, *Henosis*, 202.
69. *DDN*, ch. 13, lect. 3, no. 992.
70. *DN* 13.3, p. 229.10–14, 981A, Parker, 125.
71. *DDN*, ch. 13, lect. 3, no. 993: "*nulla monas ... neque* quodcumque *aliud* quod a quocumque entium creatorum naturaliter cognoscatur, *educit*, idest manifestat et perfecte exprimit illud *occultum* superexcellentis Deitatis."

to a manifestation linked to comprehension. Aquinas continues, "And because those things received by reason or the mind are expressed by the voice, therefore ... there cannot be a simple *name* nor *composite speech* expressing God as he is in himself."[72] Reason's reception alludes to the limited cognitive mode that underlies the limited mode of signifying. Even in grace the pilgrim still knows and names God in a mode that remains bound to creaturely mediation. Finitude and mediation render impossible a single divine name that expresses God's essence. God is beyond naming not because his inaccessible essence ends the act of naming, but because there always remains more to be known and said. By implication the nameless God becomes the God who must be named endlessly. An abundance of predication replaces silence!

Dionysius then takes up the theme of union via negations. The theologians

> have given the preference to the ascent through negations (*apophaseōn*), as lifting the soul out of things kindred to itself (*tōn heautē symphylōn*), and conducting it through all the Divine conceptions (*theiōn noēseōn*), above which towers that which is above every name, and every expression and knowledge, and at the furthest extremity attaching it to Him, as far indeed as is possible for us to be attached to that Being.[73]

The negation (*apophasis*) of the name "One" leads the soul out of itself and to union with the superessential One. This ecstasy includes two steps: going out of things "kindred" or "connatural (*symphylōn*)" to us and traversing "Divine conceptions (*theiōn noēseōn*)."[74] The ladder of negations itself causes the first part of ecstasy, going beyond "connatural things," a reference to God's symbolic manifestations in the Bible, the liturgy, and creation. Thus chapters 2 through 5 of the *Mystical Theology* ascend to God by first negating symbolic names and then the less inappropriate names (e.g., goodness). Hence the negation of "kindred" things is followed by "Divine conceptions" or God's higher, nonsymbolic manifestations. There is a parallel between "divine conceptions" and Moses's contemplation of God's *logoi*, the manifestations

---

72. *DDN*, ch. 13, lect. 3, no. 993: "Et quia voce exprimuntur ea quae ratione vel mente capiuntur, ideo subdit quod illius occulti quod est super mentem et rationem, nec potest esse *nomen* simplex *neque sermo* compositus, exprimens Ipsum ut in se est."

73. *DN* 13.3, p. 230.1–5, 981A–B, Parker, 125–26.

74. De Andia, *Henosis*, 205–6.

of God's perfections. At this, the level of the processions, the contemplative can still ponder God actively via finite ideas. Once we leave behind all noetic activity and stop gazing upon God in his processions, we can be united to him. All divine names refer to God's processions, not his essence, so that whoever ceases to contemplate the processions also ceases to name God. After all negations we are conjoined to God who is "above every name." Oddly, naming ends with *apophasis*, while *aphairesis* has gone missing.

Aquinas's comments on this text also consider the mind's ecstasy as a way of negation.

First, our soul wakes up, so to speak, and arises from material things, which are *connatural* to our soul; as, when we understand God not to be something sensible or material and corporeal; and thus, our soul proceeds *through all divine intellects (intellectus)* by negating [them], that is, through every order of angels, *from which* God *is* segregated who is *above every name and reason and cogitation*.[75]

Connatural things are material things, for the soul naturally knows through the senses. The first step in ecstasy is to negate materiality from God by an act of judgment. Here, instead of turning the soul's gaze away from finite beings, we find a theological act of judgment that does not exclude an abiding gaze upon material creatures as manifestations of the hidden God, though one understands that God has no corporality. Then, by negating again, the soul proceeds through immaterial things—that is, the orders of angels. The extreme brevity of the Areopagite's explanation, which leaves "Divine conceptions" undefined, opens the door to an angelic interpretation. The Latin phrase *divinus intellectus* can be read in multiple ways. Instead of "cogitations about God," which is close to the Areopagite's intention, Aquinas reads *divinus intellectus* as referring to immaterial beings above the material creatures first considered. He does not invoke the angels as guides in noetic ascent. Rather, we deny that God is a finite spiritual being. This negation leads to an unspoken affirmation, expressed in the form of emi-

---

75. *DDN*, ch. 13, lect. 3, no. 996: "Primo enim anima nostra quasi exsuscitatur et consurgit a rebus materialibus, quae sunt animae nostrae *connaturalia*; puta, cum intelligimus Deum non esse aliquid sensibile aut materiale aut corporeum; et sic, anima nostra negando pergit *per omnes divinos intellectus*, idest per omnes ordines Angelorum, *a quibus est* segregatus Deus qui est *super omne nomen et rationem et cogitationem*."

nence: "God is *above every name, reason, and cogitation.*" Aquinas does not explain how God exceeds these. Nor does he discuss noetic silence. So far he has limited the ladder of negations to the negation of materiality and creaturely finitude.

Thomas then proceeds to the goal of negations:

And indeed this conjunction of the soul to God occurs *inasmuch as is possible to us* to be conjoined to God now: for in the present [life] our intellect is not conjoined to God that it may see his essence; but that it may know of God what he is not (*quid non est*). Hence, this union of ours to God, which is possible in this life, is perfected when we come to this, that we know him to be above the most excellent creatures.[76]

While union occurs by negations, the rungs on Aquinas's apophatic ladder have much greater noetic content than in Dionysius. Adequately purified causal cognition of God remains a possibility in union, since the Areopagite's "divine conceptions" now refer to angels. Cognition bound to God's causal activity has not been fully left behind. The Dionysian text moves between two main poles: between the One as cause of all and the superessential One, God as we can name him, and God as we cannot name him. Negations are the most adequate bridge, though this bridge does not fully link the two poles, for God's superessence is unknowable by definition, since we cannot even know it through unknowing. Negations move the soul toward the passive learning that comes in darkness via contact with God's light, not his essence. Such intelligible light further extends the noetic bridge between the two poles, though without allowing it to reach the divine nature.

Because Aquinas replaces the Areopagite's pole of God's inaccessible nature with the essence seen (though not comprehended) by the saints, the content of union also changes. In the passage just cited Thomas mentions two modes by which God unites himself to us: (1) he excludes the beatific vision from this life, wherein God joins himself to the mind so

---

76. *DDN*, ch. 13, lect. 3, no. 996: "Ad ultimum autem anima nostra Deo coniungitur, ascendendo per negationes, *in ultimis totorum,* idest in supremis finibus universaliorum et excellentiorum creaturarum. Et quidem coniunctio animae ad Deum fit *inquantum nobis possibile est* nunc Deo *coniungi:* non enim coniungitur in praesenti intellectus noster Deo ut Eius essentiam videat; sed ut cognoscat de Deo quid non est. Unde haec coniunctio nostri ad Deum, quae nobis est in hac vita possibilis, perficitur quando devenimus ad hoc quod cognoscamus Eum esse supra excellentissimas creaturas."

that it "may see his essence," and (2) in this life our intellect is conjoined to God "that it may know of God what he is not." The second union refers to more than the realization that God is not a limited being, for that cognition was already attained when the soul traversed the order of material things and angels. The pilgrim's noetic union with God reaches its pre-eschatological summit when he or she knows something about divine excess. Aquinas alludes to knowing that God is beyond the various created perfections, especially those found in human beings and angels, "the most excellent creatures."[77] This is why he firmly limits the negation of the names such as "One" in the present *lectio*. Negations signal (1) that we cannot know God's unity face to face; (2) that as we name God according to what the mind receives—that is, according to the limited mode of cognition and signification—we need to negate this limit; and (3) that we cannot comprehend his unity.[78] Consequently, the knowledge of God as exceeding the highest creatures implicitly includes some positive knowledge of his perfections. The qualification of such knowledge as pre-eschatological signals that this cognition remains mediated by creatures—that is, by God's causal activity. Thomas negates *the limited mode* of signification, cognition, and being, so that the reference to the reality signified (the divine perfections) abides. All of this is part of the knowledge of "what God is not."

But what is the relation between negations, the highest knowledge, and union? Thomas notes that we attain union "by ascending through negations." He adds that the soul is conjoined "that (*ut*) it may know of God what he is not." Here the term *ut* followed by a subjunctive expresses either the consequence of union, its purpose, or perhaps its limited function ("to the extent that"). If Aquinas intends the first or second meaning, this would imply the following causal chain: negations → union → knowing what God is not. If he intends the third meaning, then a second causal chain may be implied: negations → union *and* knowing "what God is not." In the same passage Thomas then explains that union "is perfected when we come to this, that (*quod*) we know Him to be above the most excellent creatures." Here eminent cognition probably functions as a sign that perfect union has occurred. Also,

77. *DDN*, ch. 1, lect. 2, nos. 50–51; *ST* I, q. 13, a. 3.
78. *DDN*, ch. 13, lect. 3, nos. 992–93.

union and "knowing what God is not" now seem to be simultaneous, conjoined effects of negations, which matches the second causal chain just mentioned. Aquinas implies something similar in chapter 7 of the commentary, where union and knowledge by ignorance (or knowing "what God is not") are both the direct result of remotion and excess.[79] But in chapter 1 of the commentary Thomas states that "according to deiformity, we are united to divine things through cognition, inasmuch as this is possible for us, still, something of divine things remains hidden to us."[80] Here grace and a higher knowledge about God that comes through contemplation grounded in Scripture enable union. The causal chain thus appears to be grace → knowledge → union. On the one hand, this last text remains of limited use, for it mentions neither remotions nor negations. On the other hand, it reminds us that all discourse about union in Thomas's *Commentary on the Divine Names* presupposes the union of faith or grace, just as Albert does in his *Commentary on the Mystical Theology*. The question is therefore, given the unitive power of faith joining us to the divine light transmitted in the Scriptures, how do we attain an even higher noetic union? The more likely response would seem to be that union and ignorance are metaphysically simultaneous. Remotion with an eminent and thus causal sense effects noetic union with God. Union's cognitive content is knowing what God is not, or knowing that he is good or wise in a way that exceeds our grasp. The next section of this chapter will confirm this interpretation.

Albert's exposition of the *Divine Names*, chapter 13, includes potential points of inspiration for Aquinas, but also differences. In a disputed question on the possibility of naming God, Albert explains that God has no name because we cannot comprehend his *quid est*.[81] So far, Thomas's approach differs. But Albert adds that God's incomprehensibility follows from his pure actuality. Also, "the intellect by attaining his substance knows him either in his similitude … or immediately, just as in the fatherland."[82] Here we find two important themes that Aqui-

---

79. *DDN*, ch. 7, lect. 4, no. 731: "est alia perfectissima *Dei cognitio*, per remotionem scilicet, qua cognoscimus Deum *per ignorantiam*, per quamdam *unitionem* ad divina."

80. *DDN*, ch. 1, lect. 2, no. 70: "secundum deiformitatem uniti fuerimus per cognitionem rebus divinis, quantumcumque nobis est possibile, adhuc remanet aliquid de rebus divinis nobis occultum."

81. *SDN*, ch. 13, no. 27, p. 448.7–36.

82. *SDN*, ch. 13, no. 27, p. 448.38–41: "Sed intellectus attingendo ad substantiam ip-

nas takes up: (1) pure divine act that must exceed all that we know; and (2) an eschatological interpretation of chapter 13. Albert's identification of God as pure act in this context implies that the highest divine names include a positive sense by way of excess, which in turn suggests that negation and silence cannot have the last word.[83]

Finally, I turn to Aquinas's discussion of the soul's communion with and assimilation to God. Thomas again proposes an Aristotelian-Dionysian synthesis of union's noetic element. Dionysius states that the Good pours out its abundant light "by illuminations analogous to each several being, and elevates to Its permitted contemplation and communion and likeness, those holy minds, who, as far as is lawful and reverent, strive after it."[84] Each being has a precise proportion of divine light accorded to it so that the divine source of light imparts diverse degrees of contemplation to different souls. Aquinas does not explain the proportioning of divine gifts, even though his doctrine of the Spirit's gifts could account for it. Instead, his commentary focuses on the themes of communion and likeness:

> the fact that illumined inferior minds, by using the light given [them] attain to knowing him [God], this is from him. And this is what he adds, that *holy minds reach to the contemplation of him as is possible* for them, because, as was said above, he can be contemplated in some way by all. And because those who contemplate him are in some way made one with him (insofar as the intellect in act is in some way to be the understood in act), and consequently [because they] are assimilated to him inasmuch as they are informed by him, he adds: *and communion and assimilation*.[85]

---

sius cognoscit ipsum vel in sua similitudine, sicut in via per speculum et in aenigmate, vel immediate, sicut in patria."

83. The theme of knowledge by divine similitudes prepares the way to insert a causal understanding of God into the event of cognitive union, for it "attains his substance." The second theme remains less developed in Albert's comments on chapter 13 of the *Divine Names* than in Aquinas, but he may have helped Thomas to discover a hermeneutical tool that tames Dionysian apophatism.

84. *DN* 1.2, p. 110.13–15, 588D–89A, Parker, 3.

85. *DDN*, ch. 1, lect. l, no. 38: "hoc ipsum quod inferiores mentes illuminatae, utentes dato lumine ad Ipsum cognoscendum accedunt, ab Ipso est. Et hoc est quod subdit quod *extendit sanctas mentes ad contemplationem Ipsius possibilem* eis, quia, sicut supra dictum est aliquo modo est omnibus contemplabilis. Et quia qui contemplantur ipsum quodammodo unum cum Ipso efficiuntur (secundum quod intellectus in actu est quodammodo intellectum esse in actu) et per consequens Ei assimilantur utpote ab Ipso informati, subdit: *et communionem et assimilationem*"; see also *DDN*, ch. 4, lect. 4, no. 332.

God is the source of light enabling "lower minds" or intelligent beings below angels in the cosmic hierarchy to have some knowledge of God. In the present commentary God's light consistently refers to his revelation mediated by Scripture and received in faith.[86] Thus God can be contemplated in some way by all believers in grace. Yet contemplation does not just involve gathering revealed knowledge about God. Rather, it also constitutes a form of communion with the known, following the Stagirite's principle that the knower in some way becomes the known. Hence Aquinas speaks of being "informed" by God. The latter phrase implies that, by the knowledge of grace founded on revelation, cognitive assimilation becomes a communion.

The key element of this passage is the link between union and understanding in act. As we saw in chapter 5, for Aquinas, in any act of cognition, the likeness of the reality known is present to the knower by the mediation of an intelligible form of the reality known, so that the mind is assimilated to the known. This principle of cognitive unity also explains why any believer already enjoys some type of union with God. For Thomas, Aristotle helps to account for Dionysian mystical psychology. This psychology centers on knowledge by participation, a model that applies to all cognition, including that of Moses in darkness. Still, Dionysius considers concept-bound knowledge as necessarily limited to knowing finite objects, so that one must let go of such cognition to receive divine light directly. In light of the eschatology that we studied in chapter 6 of this volume, we can see that Thomas employs a model of cognition by form that is open to knowledge of an infinite object to the point that the divine essence becomes like the beatified soul's intelligible form. Concept-bound cognition via finite forms that are similitudes of finite perfections no longer constitutes an obstacle to noetic union with God. Rather, such forms have the potential to impart a foretaste of the beatific knowledge of God's nature.

Due to the psychology of form, a purely negative or privative knowledge can never comprise the totality of any act of cognition, for such understanding would have no object, no content, hence no actuality. Such negative knowledge would really be the absence of a cognitive act. Becoming one with the known demands the mediation of an intelligible

---

86. See *DDN*, ch. 1, lect. 1, nos. 15–16; lect. 2, nos. 44, 70, 72; ch. 4, lect. 4, nos. 325, 327, 329–32.

form gathered from God's created similitudes as revealed in the Scriptures. Hence Aquinas consistently affirms or at least leaves open the possibility of contemplating particular divine attributes such as wisdom within the act of union by unknowing, for the exclusion of such contemplation would make unknowing a purely privative noetic act. Created perfections function as the forms by which we know and so are united to God. In grace, such union is divinizing. Thus, given an Aristotelian epistemology centered on intelligible form, the Dionysian intention of positing a nonprivative form of knowing by unknowing can only be retained if Thomas inserts some type of positive cognition bound to creatures within the act of knowing by unknowing. *Thomas can only save the intelligibility of the Areopagite's doctrine by making it more kataphatic.* The Stagirite is one reason for Aquinas's kataphatic reformulation of Dionysian union, a transformation that simultaneously reaffirms the metaphysical realism of union. The same psychology explains Aquinas's quiet refusal of the intellect's ecstasy. Because knowledge is perfected *in* the intellect through the form of the known that the knower becomes, noetic ecstasy would signify not-knowing in a fully privative sense, which is precisely what Dionysius does not intend by ecstasy.

Overall, Thomas considerably changes the sense of Dionysian union beyond mind, yet without simply reducing it to Aristotelian or Augustinian doctrines. Aquinas's classification of the *Divine Names* as a study of biblical discourse on God frames his entire approach to union as it revalorizes divinely inspired human speech and cognition. Union beyond mind as being joined to God through faith beyond natural reason emphasizes believers' ontological contact with the hidden God and the uplifting power of revelation, all the while guarding a vivid sense of the divine mystery. Aquinas has a greater appreciation of revelation's divinizing power than does Dionysius. Thomas not only expands the mystical function of mediations in general, he has a higher regard for Scripture's uplifting power than does the Areopagite. On the one hand, both the *Divine Names* as *sacra doctrina* and union by faith break out of a potentially elitist approach to mysticism. On the other hand, union by remotions could suggest a theologian's mysticism, though it remains open to all believers. Hence Aquinas's ascent by remotions remains distinct from the subtle elitism of Albert's early Cologne mysticism. Unlike union by faith, Aquinas's ascent by negations is not a divinizing process, but rather the perfection of knowledge founded upon revelation, within the realm of habitual grace. Aquinas distinguishes noetic ascent from divinization because the former does not necessarily include a new gift of charity, the indispensible principle of any sanctification. We found a similar doctrine in Albert's *Commentary on the Mystical Theology*. Yet Thomas surely intends to speak of believers whose noetic ascent remains closely linked to growth in grace. Thomas's firm restriction of remotion to the limited modes of signification, cognition, and being as well as the inclusion of the way of eminence within the ladder of negations insert both human cognitive operations and creature-bound noetic content within the event of perfect knowledge. Silence in darkness has been greatly diminished. Finally, Albert's fingerprints appear throughout Aquinas's exposition of the Areopagite, though more in the two Dominicans' shared central hermeneutical and doctrinal principles (e.g., union above mind through faith) than in frequent textual similarities. At the same time Thomas takes some distance from his teacher, as he often chooses a somewhat more kataphatic reading of Dionysius, with less emphasis on God's incomprehensibility (which he never denies) and more emphasis on the real, partial, indirect knowledge that we attain by the ways of remotion and excess (a theme also found in Albert).

Aquinas offers two major interpretations of union beyond mind in his *Commentary on the Divine Names:* union by faith that joins us to God as revealed through the Scriptures and union by the act of completing remotions. The first union is essentially sanctifying, for it centers on the power of faith animated by charity. The second union can involve a nonsanctifying perfection of the intellect that still presupposes the first union. All those with living faith enjoy the first union, while theologians may find the second most appropriate, yet union is available to all in living faith. I will look for these two types of union and other expositions of the Areopagite's mysticism in Thomas's comments on the *Mystical Theology* and his theology of the Spirit's gifts.

THE *MYSTICAL THEOLOGY* IN THOMAS'S CORPUS

The second important locus of reception for Dionysian union in Aquinas's corpus is his scattered, infrequent discussion of the *Mystical The-*

ology and the Areopagite's *Epistle* 5 on divine darkness. I will analyze almost all of Aquinas's references to the *Mystical Theology* in chronological order. I skip three secondary references as well as those linked to the gift of understanding (treated later) and those in the prologue of the *Commentary on the Divine Names* (treated previously).[87] The present section exposes Aquinas's full range of interpretations of the Areopagite's central union text. Here I aim to show how Thomas did and did not receive Dionysius's most direct treatment of union with God in parallel to my analysis of Albert's *Commentary on the Mystical Theology*. The present section has an essential function within this overall study, especially since it takes up the majority of Thomas's direct comments on the most apophatic Dionysian passages concerning union. Here we must ask whether the Italian friar modifies this apophatism, and if so, how. We also need to consider his way of interpreting the silence of Moses's mind in darkness. Aquinas's comments on the holy patriarch assume the doctrine of analogy, which I analyzed in chapter 7, not to mention his anthropology. We can thus focus more directly on the nuances of Thomas's remarks about the dark cloud.

Aquinas's occasional discussions of the *Mystical Theology* have stood at the center of a lively debate. A main point of contention has been whether Thomas invokes the figure of Moses in order to describe an infused experience of God, or whether his intention remains essentially metaphysical—that is, to describe the culmination of philosophical or theological reflection—in other words, an active contemplative ascent that bears no essential relation to an extraordinary experience or a special gift of grace.[88] The debate has centered on Aquinas's first reference to the *Mystical Theology* in his theological career. We find it in the *Sentences Commentary* treatise on the Trinity, a text he composed within two years of his departure from Cologne.[89] Thomas asks whether

---

87. I skip the following references: *DDN*, ch. 1, lect. 3, no. 104, which simply refers back to the *DDN* prologue (analyzed at the beginning of this chapter); *ST* I, q. 84, a. 5, ad 1, objection 1, which Thomas does not answer; and I-II, q. 3, a. 8, objection 1, where Aquinas only distinguishes union with God as with the unknown from beatific union.

88. Maritain, *Distinguish to Unite*, 237–39n3, identifies a mystical, experiential sense, while Étienne Gilson, "Propos sur l'être et sa notion," in *San Tommaso e il pensiero moderno*, edited by Antonio Piolanti, Studi Tomistici 3 (Rome: Città Nuova, 1974), 13, and Humbrecht, *Théologie négative*, 513–18, favor a metaphysical, nonmystical, theological sense.

89. Oliva, *Débuts de l'enseignement*, 252–53.

God can be properly named *esse*. The article's corpus mentions the Areopagite's doctrine that we name God *esse* because, as a participation, *esse* includes within itself all other perfections such as goodness. The fourth objection cites John Damascene's teaching that God's *quid est* signifies an incomprehensible ocean of substance. Aquinas responds that all divine names include a "determined *ratio*," while *quid est* is not determined by anything else. He continues:

> Therefore, when we proceed into God by way of remotion, we first negate corporeal things from him; and second [we negate] intellectual things, insofar as they are found in creatures, as goodness and wisdom; and then there only remains in our intellect "that is" (*quia est*), and nothing more: therefore one is just as in a certain confusion. But lastly we also remove from him this *esse* itself, insofar as it is in creatures; and then [our intellect] remains in a certain darkness of ignorance, by which ignorance, inasmuch as it pertains to the pilgrim's state, we are joined in the best way to God, as Dionysius says, and this is a certain darkness, in which God is said to dwell.[90]

Thomas never composed anything as apophatic as this text saturated with the methodology, language, and spirit of Dionysius. Nothing in the *Commentary on the Divine Names* compares. The ladder of cognitive ascent consists of a carefully ordered series of "remotions." Thomas does not mention the ways of causality and eminence. The order of remotions, which are also called "negations," begins with corporeal attributes metaphorically predicated of God, such as "God is a rock," followed by "intellectual things" or perfections such as goodness. The ascent by negations and the order of negations both come from the *Mystical Theology* and the closing lines of the *Divine Names*. The daring removal of even the highest perfections such as being can be found in chapter 5 of the *Mystical Theology*. The climax summarizes the Areopagite's presentation of Moses in chapter 1 of that work, read with the

---

90. Aquinas, *I Sent.*, d. 8, q. 1, a. 1, ad 4, 196–97: "Unde quando in Deum procedimus per viam remotionis, primo negamus ab eo corporalia; et secundo etiam intellectualia, secundum quod inveniuntur in creaturis, ut bonitas et sapientia; et tunc remanet tantum in intellectu nostro, quia est, et nihil amplius: unde est sicut in quadam confusione. Ad ultimum autem etiam hoc ipsum esse, secundum quod est in creaturis, ab ipso removemus; et tunc remanet in quadam tenebra ignorantiae, secundum quam ignorantiam, quantum ad statum viae pertinet, optime Deo conjungimur, ut dicit Dionysius, et haec est quaedam caligo, in qua Deus habitare dicitur."

help of *Epistle 5:* darkness signifies the patriarch's ignorance, the union attained therein is the best, and God dwells in darkness. Aquinas thus offers a summary interpretation of almost the entire *Mystical Theology.*

Three elements parallel Albert's Dionysian exegesis: (1) negations as the path of the highest noetic ascent; (2) knowledge of God's *quia est* as a certain summit of cognition; and (3) the mind's state of confusion. Albert lays out all three elements at the start of his *Commentary on the Mystical Theology.*[91] On the surface Thomas's passage seems to match Albert's more apophatic expressions. But Aquinas speaks of negating corporeal attributes of God without qualification. Indeed, properly speaking, God is not a rock in any way. Then he removes or negates attributes not necessarily bound to corporeal reality, such as goodness, "insofar as they are found in creatures." Remotion and negation appear to function as synonyms in this context. Aquinas refers to negating the created mode of having a perfection, the mode that our concepts and language naturally reflect. Then we are left with nothing but God's *quia est.* For Étienne Gilson, Aquinas here refers to "being led into the presence of pure *est,* without any *quid.*"[92] Yet Thomas has not fully left behind the contemplation of God's wisdom or other divine attributes, but only their creaturely mode. The problem for us is that such knowledge does not bring about greater *conceptual* clarity, since we have no new concept to match infinite wisdom. Ultimately we also remove *esse* "insofar as it is in creatures," where it exists in composition with essence and other perfections. We take away not *esse* as such, but its finite realization. This last step leads directly into the darkness of ignorance. But what does Thomas's patriarch see in darkness? He still knows *that* God has *esse* or is wise, but he has no clear conceptual grasp of *what* infinite *esse* or wisdom is, even though he can identify "what God is not." Knowing that God is wise beyond the creaturely mode of being presumes cognition mediated by God's causal activity. Thomas says nothing about Moses learning directly from God. The creature-bound cognition about God attained via causal reasoning remains the foundation of any noetic content—precisely that which Dionysius seeks to transcend in the dark cloud. Because Aquinas's text is saturated with Dionysian language, he transforms its meaning extensively, with remotion

---

91. *SMT,* ch. 1, pp. 454.78–55.28 (see footnotes 92 and 93 of chapter 4 in this volume).
92. Gilson, "Propos sur l'être," 13.

now centered on the created mode of being. This (Albertian) type of remotion dominates the text.[93]

Thomas thus outlines a metaphysical or theological path of active ascent by acquired knowledge about God. The only term that comes close to experiential language is *coniungimur*. As we saw in the *Commentary on the Divine Names*, Aquinas sometimes employs this word to signify a noetic perfection that does not require a new gift of grace or a directly infused divine teaching, since the *triplex via* employed in grace can suffice to attain a higher noetic union.[94] Yet in contrast to the discussions of union by unknowing in the *Commentary on the Divine Names* analyzed previously, it is not clear whether the present text presupposes habitual grace. The ladder of remotions seems to be accessible to the metaphysician, as well.[95]

Our second text is found in the treatise on the last things in the *Sentences Commentary*, where Aquinas offers an unusual explanation of unknowing in darkness. An objection argues that, since we are best united to God as to one unknown, no one can see his essence, not even in glory. Thomas responds that the Dionysian language of the unknown God refers to the absence of every intelligible form that could adequately rep-

---

93. I see no need to attribute the text's doctrine more to Dionysius and Albert than to Aquinas, as Humbrecht suggests; *Théologie négative*, 518. The restriction of remotion makes Dionysius a virtual Thomist. Also, Laura Westra's Gilsonian reduction of Thomas's noetic ascent to a concept-free gaze upon God's existence goes too far; see Westra, "The Soul's Noetic Ascent to the One in Plotinus and to God in Aquinas," *New Scholasticism* 58 (1984): 118–21.

94. E.g., *DDN*, ch. 13, no. 996. Humbrecht calls union in this article passive; *Théologie négative*, 518. But Aquinas employs standard Dionysian language (e.g., the passive form of the verb *conjungimur*), and gives it a more active meaning. Ascent by remotion involves active judgments. Maritain sees a reference to an experienced doctrine attained via the connaturality of charity. His reading fits well with Thomas's gift of wisdom, but has little foundation in the present article, where classic Thomistic terms related to wisdom (i.e., *inclinatio* and *connaturalitas*) are absent; Maritain, *Distinguish to Unite*, 237–39n3.

95. The surviving fragments of what may be Thomas's second *Sentences Commentary*, from the years 1265–66, takes up the same distinction in a different way. The first article of d. 8 no longer asks "whether God is properly called *esse*," but "whether God is his own *esse*." The author skips the ladder of negations and Moses in darkness, perhaps because he considered the doctrine of the young Aquinas too apophatic in its mode of expression; see Aquinas, *Lectura romana in primum Sententiarum Petri Lombardi*, ed. Leonard E. Boyle and John F. Boyle, Studies and Texts 152 (Toronto: Pontifical Institute of Medieval Studies, 2006), d. 8.1.1. Torrell doubts the work's authenticity; Torrell, "Lire saint Thomas autrement," in Boyle, *Facing History*, xxi–xxiv.

resent God in the pilgrim state. In other words, God's essence only becomes like the form of the human intellect in heaven. Here below we know God most perfectly when we know him to be above all that we can conceive, as every intelligible form accessible to us remains finite. Thomas proposes an Augustinian-Aristotelian reduction of the Areopagite.[96] In the later works we do not encounter this argumentation centered on form, although its logic continues to undergird Aquinas's thought.

In the same time period (1252–56), Thomas the *baccalaureus* gave a sermon on the Feast of the Holy Trinity that has the only homiletic mention of Moses in darkness in Thomas's corpus. The Latin homily *Seraphim stabant* (our third text), probably preached before a congregation that consisted mostly of friars and clerics, was transmitted in the form of a *reportatio* or notes by a friar in attendance, notes that Aquinas subsequently revised.[97] Commenting the first Mass reading, which concerns the prophet Isaiah's vision of the celestial temple (in Is 6), he explains the meaning of the seraphims' hymn:

So they make the mystery of the Trinity manifest to us, when they say: "Holy, holy, holy." Concerning this we must know that, as Dionysius says, no way is as successful for getting to know God as the way of remotion. For then God is perfectly known, when we know that he is above every thing that can be thought of. Hence we read about Moses, who was very familiar with God according to what is granted to a human being in this life, that he had access to God in a cloud and a thick mist, that is, by knowing what God is not, he arrived at knowledge of God. Now, this way of remotion is understood by the name "holiness," for, in general, according to all teachers, "holy" is the same as what is pure, and "pure" is what is separated from other things.[98]

---

96. Aquinas, *IV Sent.*, d. 49, q. 2, a. 1, ad 3, 684: "Dionysius ibi loquitur de cognitione qua Deum in via cognoscimus per aliquam formam creatam, qua intellectus noster formatur ad eum videndum. Sed, sicut dicit Augustinus, Deus omnem formam intellectus nostri subterfugit: quia quamcumque formam intellectus noster concipiat, illa forma non pertingit ad rationem divinae essentiae; et ideo ipse non potest esse pervius intellectui nostro; sed in hoc eum perfectissime cognoscimus in statu viae quod scimus eum esse super omne id quod intellectus noster concipere potest; et sic ei quasi ignoto conjungimur. Sed in patria id ipsum per formam quae est essentia sua, videbimus, et conjungemur ei quasi noto."

97. Torrell, "La pratique pastorale d'un théologien du XIIIe siècle: Thomas d'Aquin prédicateur," *RT* 82 (1982): 221.

98. Aquinas, *The Academic Sermons*, trans. Mark-Robin Hoogland, Fathers of the

Thomas begins with a probable allusion to chapter 2 of the *Mystical Theology*, according to which we truly see and know God through the separation (*ablationem*) of all things. A similar doctrine emerged in Thomas's *Commentary on the Divine Names*, where remotion brings about nonsanctifying, noetic union with God. According to the present passage, remotion causes the perfect cognition of God. Since the Areopagite's Moses attains this cognition in darkness, Thomas reads the patriarch's entry into the cloud as a symbol of noetic perfection via the practice of remotions, just as Albert does in his *Commentary on the Mystical Theology*.

Aquinas establishes a link between the Areopagite's Moses and the seraphims' song as he interprets holiness to signify separation from all things. This notion of holiness is related to an interpretation of Old Testament cultic practices, according to which the temple, certain utensils, and animals are "holy" in that they are set aside for exclusive use in worship.[99] The patriarch's purification during his ascent to God's holy place is also a major theme in Exodus and in the *Mystical Theology*. God is holy inasmuch as he is set apart from or exceeds all things. His triple holiness also signifies that the Trinity is above all that we can understand.

The sermon then proceeds to explain how the three creaturely perfections of essence, knowledge, and affection cannot attain divine purity or holiness. Thomas attributes these "excellent things" to the Father, Son, and Spirit, respectively. In fact, he applies the method of appropriating some divine perfections to certain divine persons. The power, unity, and eternity of God's essence are attributed to the Father. These perfections exclude the defects of creaturely corruptibility, composition, and mutability. The divine *Logos* enjoys a knowledge not limited to material beings, does not fail to penetrate beyond the appearanc-

---

Church, Medieval Continuation 11 (Washington, D.C.: The Catholic University of America Press, 2010), 163. Hoogland's translation uses the provisional Leonine text edited by Louis Bataillon. I have modified the translation following the part of the Leonine text published by Torrell, "La pratique pastorale," 241n41: "Nulla uia est adeo efficax ad cognoscendum Deum sicut est uia que est per remotionem. Tunc enim Deus perfecte cognoscitur quando scitur quod ipse est super omne illud quod cogitari potest. Unde et de Moyse qui familiarissimus fuit Deo, secundum quod homini in uita ista conceditur, legitur quod accessit ad Deum in nube et caligine, id est cognoscendo que (quod) non est Deus peruenit ad cognitionem Dei. Hec autem uia remotionis in nomine sanctitatis intelligitur."

99. *ST* II-II, q. 81, a. 8.

es of things, and does not lack clarity of noetic vision. Finally, Thomas attributes to the Holy Spirit the operation of uniting us to God, the self-diffusion of the Good, and the enjoyment or fruition of God.[100] In these three ways the Trinity is above all creatures. The "way of remotion" separates creaturely defects from our understanding of God. Aquinas applies remotion in his explanation of God's essence, knowledge, and affection. The result of such noetic purification includes cognition of God's positive attributes that comes through the whole *triplex via*. God's holiness signifies his eminent possession of the perfections found in creation. Thomas identifies the knowledge of God's attributes attained by the *triplex via* with the content of Moses's cognition in darkness. Aquinas ignores the Dionysian exhortation to leave behind the contemplation of creatures. Also, he says nothing about the special divine illumination that Dionysian darkness symbolizes.

The patriarch's perfect cognition is trinitarian and thus transcends philosophical wisdom. Thomas not only appropriates various forms of holiness or eminence to the three Persons, he also mentions that the Holy Spirit is the bond of love, taking up what is proper to the Spirit. In the *Sentences Commentary* Thomas explains that the Spirit is the Father's and the Son's bond of love because he proceeds from them as Love. In their mutual love, Father and Son spirate their common bond. Aquinas concludes that an adequate understanding of the three Persons' unity demands that we perceive this element of the Spirit's personal property.[101] Hence, in the sermon, the object of perfect cognition in the present state includes knowing how the trinitarian aspect of unitive love exceeds creaturely love. The contemplative penetrates the dark cloud through the correct understanding of the triune God available in grace.

Our fourth text comes from the *Commentary on Boethius's "On the Trinity,"* composed shortly after the *Sentences Commentary*. Thomas asks how God can be known. An objection invokes the *Mystical Theology* to the effect that our best knowledge of God involves being conjoined to him "as to the unknown (*quasi incognito*)." Aquinas's paraphrase moderates the Areopagite's language of "the completely unknown (*omnino incognito*)" God. He answers, "The mind is found to have progressed

---

100. Aquinas, *Academic Sermons*, 163–68.
101. Aquinas, *I Sent.*, d. 10, q. 1, a. 3c; Emery, *Trinitarian Theology*, 239–40.

the most in cognition when it knows his [God's] essence to be above all that which one can apprehend in this state of life, so that, although 'what he is' remains unknown, nevertheless his 'that is' is known."[102] We are joined to God "as unknown" when we know his eminence or that he exceeds all that we know through material creatures—that is, all that we know—for such creatures mediate all human cognition in this life (as we saw in chapters 5 and 7 of this volume). Thomas's answer partly parallels his exposition of union and knowing "what God is not" in chapter 13 of the *Commentary on the Divine Names,* where unitive cognition involves understanding that God exceeds all creatures.[103] The same passage suggests that such cognition is the fruit of theological reflection enlightened by faith. Our present text seems to continue to approach the *Mystical Theology* as a description of the summit of either metaphysical or acquired theological insight. Thomas does not mention faith, though faith may be implied.

The same article's corpus offers a nuance:

In this progress of cognition the human mind is most helped when its natural light is strengthened by a new illumination, as the light of faith and the gifts of wisdom and understanding, by which the mind is said to be elevated above itself in contemplation, inasmuch as it knows God to be above all that it naturally comprehends.[104]

This passage follows right after a summary of the *triplex via.* The language of maximum intellectual progress and divine excellence parallels the text on God's unknown quiddity that we just considered. The corpus identifies the most efficacious path to the highest knowledge of God in this life with three supernatural lights: faith, the Spirit's gift of wisdom, and his gift of understanding. Yet it would seem that philoso-

---

102. *BDT,* q. 1, a. 2, ad 1, p. 85.132–38: "secundum hoc dicimus in fine nostre cognitionis Deum tamquam ignotum cognoscere, quia tunc maxime mens in cognitione profecisse inuenitur, quando cognoscit eius essentiam esse supra omne quod appreendere potest in statu uie; et sic quamuis maneat ignotum quid est, scitur tamen quia est." For *quasi* as having the sense of *quodammodo,* see Patfoort, "*Cognitio,*" 3–13.

103. *DDN,* ch. 13, lect. 3, no. 996 (cited above at foonotes 75 and 76 of the present chapter).

104. *BDT,* q. 1, a. 2c, p. 85.118–24: "In hoc autem profectu cognitionis maxime iuuatur mens humana cum lumen eius naturale noua illustratione confortatur, sicut est lumen fidei et doni sapientie et intellectus, per quod mens in contemplatione supra se eleuari dicitur, in quantum cognoscit Deum esse supra omne id quod naturaliter compreendit."

phers can also understand that God surpasses whatever we can naturally comprehend, although this rational path alone is less reliable than the way opened up by the triple light. Perhaps Thomas intends something like his contrast in the opening article of the *Summa*, between potentially accurate yet error-prone philosophical knowledge of God and the sure way of revelation. In this sense it is not yet clear if these three lights impart a higher noetic content about divine eminence (beyond knowledge of the mysteries of faith). Yet the corpus continues:

But because it [the mind thrice illumined] does not suffice to penetrate to see his essence, it is said in some way to be turned back to God's essence by this excellent light; and this is what is said about Genesis 32, "I saw God face to face," in Gregory's Gloss: "The soul's vision, when it is stretched into God, is driven back [to God] by the flash of immensity."[105]

Aquinas invokes the same three noetic gifts to clarify that these cannot impart a direct vision of God's essence. He cites Gregory the Great's explanation of Jacob's dream about the ladder to heaven whereby he "saw God." Jacob's vision also did not grant a noetic grasp of God's essence. The three gifts grant a better understanding of God's eminence. It is not clear how God shares his excellent light, which imparts a supernatural vision of his immensity. Perhaps Thomas still refers to the effect of the same three lights (faith, wisdom, and understanding). In any case the soul is turned upside down and toward God so that it can "see" him. Thomas's description of the vision is very brief, and later texts do not return to it. He identifies the highest cognition in this life with the correct grasp of God's eminence and an infused, indirect vision of God's greatness (apparently distinct from rapture). The possible link between the gift of wisdom and vision may parallel a partial connection between wisdom and prophecy in the *Summa*.[106]

Our fifth text comes in a contemporaneous passage from *On Truth* that briefly discusses our inability to know God's quiddity. Thomas employs the latter term to signify the cognition that comes through the definition of a thing—that is, comprehensive knowledge. God's quid-

---

105. *BDT*, q. 1, a. 2c, p. 85.124–31: "Set quia ad eius essentiam uidendam penetrare non sufficit, dicitur in se ipsam quodammodo ab excellenti lumine reflecti; et hoc est quod dicitur, Gen. XXXII, super illud 'Vidi Dominum facie ad faciem,' in Glosa Gregorii 'Visus anime cum in Deum intenditur, immensitatis coruscatione reuerberatur.'"
106. *ST* II-II, q. 45, a. 5 (cited below at footnote 276 of the present chapter).

dity always remains hidden to us, so that the height of cognition in this life is that we know God to be above all that we know of him, as Dionysius shows in the *Mystical Theology*.[107] This passage somewhat parallels the answer to the objection from the *Commentary on Boethius's "On the Trinity"* considered previously, although the object of unknowing in *On Truth* is more specific—namely, God's incomprehensibility. No mention is made of any special gifts of light. Elsewhere Thomas explains that natural reason can also know that God is incomprehensible.[108] Hence *On Truth* need not refer to a faith doctrine or an infused insight.

Another passage that comes close to the commentary on Boethius is found in *On the Power of God* (our sixth text), composed about ten years later. The context is the possibility of substantial divine naming. An objection states that, according to the *Mystical Theology*, we are best united to God by knowing that we know nothing of him. Thomas responds that "what God is" remains hidden or unknown to us in such a way that our ultimate understanding is knowing that we do not know God, insofar as we grasp that "what God is" exceeds all that we know of him[109]—that is, we know much more than nothing about God's substance. Thomas does not explain how we attain this summit. He primarily seeks to show the possibility of substantial divine naming. Also, his answer implies that the mind in darkness engages in some activity (an act of judgment), precisely what the Areopagite's Moses has left behind. *On the Power of God* invokes the end-term of acquired cognition, and *On Truth* most likely does, as well.

107. *DV*, q. 2, a. 1, ad 9, p. 42.321–33: "intellectus dicitur scire de aliquo quid est quando definit ipsum, id est quando concipit aliquam formam de ipsa re quae per omnia ipsi rei respondet; iam autem ex dictis patet quod quicquid intellectus noster de Deo concipit est deficiens a repraesentatione eius; et ideo quid est ipsius Dei semper nobis occultum remanet: et haec est summa cognitio quam de ipso in statu viae habere possumus ut cognoscamus Deum esse supra omne id quod cogitamus de eo, ut patet per Dionysium in I cap. *De mystica theologia*."

108. *ST* I, q. 12, a. 12c and ad 1.

109. *DP*, q. 7, a. 5, objection 14: "Praeterea, Dionysius dicit quod optime homo Deo unitur in cognoscendo quod cognoscens de ipso nihil cognoscit." Ad 14: "ex quo intellectus noster divinam substantiam non adaequat, hoc ipsum quod est Dei substantia remanet, nostrum intellectum excedens, et ita a nobis ignoratur: et propter hoc illud est ultimum cognitionis humanae de Deo quod sciat se Deum nescire, in quantum cognoscit, illud quod Deus est, omne ipsum quod de eo intelligimus, excedere."

Dionysian Union in Thomas 367

One of the most striking discussions of the *Mystical Theology* comes in the *Contra Gentiles* (our seventh text). The context is the angels' natural cognition of God:

We also [like the angels] can somehow attain this kind of cognition of God: for through an effect we know that God is (*quia est*) and that he is somehow the cause of other things, super-eminent to them, and removed from all. And this is our ultimate and most perfect cognition in this life, as Dionysius says in his book *On the Mystical Theology*, when we are "conjoined" with God "as unknown" (*quasi incognito*): which indeed occurs when we know of him *what he is not* (*quid non sit*), but what [he is] remains wholly unknown. Therefore, to demonstrate the ignorance of this most sublime cognition, it is said of Moses in Exodus 20 that "he entered the darkness in which God was."[110]

The angels' natural cognition of God also remains imperfect, in distinction from the knowledge that they attain by the beatific vision. But what is the ultimate cognition in the second sentence: the perfect realization of the threefold way mentioned in the preceding sentences, or just knowing "what God is not," discussed later in our passage? The text remains a bit ambiguous, yet the most coherent response would seem to be that it is both. The end of the *Commentary on the Divine Names* identifies our being perfectly joined to God with knowing "what God is not" *and* knowing that he exceeds all creatures.[111] By implication the completion of the *triplex via* in eminence is perfect union. Earlier in the commentary Thomas quietly identifies the completion of the *triplex via* (or naming by remotion) within the realm of grace as the perfect knowledge of God accessible to us.[112] Likewise, as we saw in chapter 7 of this volume, the *Summa* questions on the divine attributes are

---

110. *SCG* III, ch. 49, no. 2270: "Ad quam etiam cognitionem de Deo nos utcumque pertingere possumus: per effectus enim de Deo cognoscimus quia est et quod causa aliorum est, aliis supereminens, et ab omnibus remotus. Et hoc est ultimum et perfectissimum nostrae cognitionis in hac vita, ut Dionysius dicit, in libro *de Mystica Theologia*, cum Deo quasi 'ignoto coniungimur': quod quidem contingit dum de eo 'quid non sit' cognoscimus, quid vero sit penitus manet ignotum. Unde et ad huius sublimissimae cognitionis ignorantiam demonstrandam, de Moyse dicitur, Exod. XX, quod 'accessit ad caliginem in qua est Deus.'"

111. *DDN*, ch. 13, lect. 3, no. 996 (cited above at foonotes 75 and 76 of the present chapter).

112. *DDN*, ch. 1, lect. 3, no. 83 (cited earlier at footnote 48 of the present chapter).

prefaced by the phrase that we can only know God's *quid non est*, a cognition whose content the subsequent questions unfold and thus show to include a reliable yet imperfect grasp of God's positive attributes. Hence we are conjoined to God when we attain accurate cognition of him by the *triplex via*, wherein the way of remotion excludes any direct or comprehensive knowledge of God's quiddity. But why does Thomas employ two phrases: "as unknown" and "wholly unknown"? The latter expression rarely emerges in his corpus. In the present passage he does not distinguish two moments or stages of knowledge, between "as unknown" and "completely unknown." Rather, knowledge of *God*, but not of his *quiddity*, is possible. The latter remains wholly inaccessible either in the sense that the beatific vision remains impossible in this life or in the sense that we cannot comprehend God. Either interpretation has parallels in the *Commentary on the Divine Names*. Consequently, "the ignorance of this most sublime cognition" probably refers to the whole preceding passage, including the knowledge attained by the threefold way. Moses in darkness symbolizes the pilgrim's perfect grasp of positive noetic content (divine attributes) with its limits signified by remotions (noncomprehensive) and the judgment of eminence, the summit of the *triplex via*. Such cognition would seem to be accessible to the metaphysician, since Aquinas dedicates most of the first three books of the *Contra Gentiles* to a study of God following the light of reason alone. But since Moses represents the completion of the *triplex via*, the question becomes whether theology knows more divine effects that extend our knowledge by the *triplex via*, a higher cognition attained by Scripture and an infused light. Aquinas soon takes up this question.[113]

Several of Thomas's explanations of the *Mystical Theology* have left open the question of whether the metaphysician can penetrate the dark cloud. What if any privileged access to union by ignorance does faith grant? The *Summa* takes up this difficulty (our eighth text). An objection refers to Moses in darkness in order to argue that, since natural reason knows our ignorance of God's *quid est*, grace does not enjoy a higher cognition of God. Thomas answers:

113. Olivier-Thomas Venard maintains that our *SCG* passage translates a mystical experience into metaphysical language; see Venard, *Thomas d'Aquin, poète théologien*, vol. 2, *La langue de l'ineffable: Essai sur le fondement théologique de la métaphysique* (Geneva: Ad Solem, 2004), 85–86. Yet the *SCG* passage does not clearly refer to such experience.

although through the revelation of grace in this life, we do not know of what [God] he is, and thus are joined to him as (*quasi*) to the unknown; nevertheless, we know him more fully, inasmuch as more and his more excellent effects are shown to us; and inasmuch as we attribute some things to him from divine revelation, which natural reason does not reach, as that God is three and one.[114]

Revelation does not grant knowledge of God's quiddity. In this sense it shares a limit imposed on metaphysics. But graced and natural cognition do not have identical boundaries. Grace does more than enable simple minds to understand what philosophers know by reason. Revelation imparts three types of new noetic objects: (1) more divine effects; (2) more excellent effects; and (3) certain divine mysteries that reason cannot reach by itself—for example, the Trinity. When he mentions effects Aquinas implies that grace opens new paths to know God with the *triplex via*. The new plethora of effects refers to manifestations of God's works in the economy of salvation as recounted in Scripture. In the article's corpus Thomas refers to prophetic images and the Spirit's visible mission at Jesus' baptism. These are precisely "more excellent effects," to which one must add above all the Torah, the incarnation, and Pentecost, with all of Jesus' words, deeds, and sufferings that Aquinas explains in the *Tertia Pars* of the *Summa*.[115] In the same article he notes how God forms phantasms directly in the prophet's imaginative power so as to impart effects that surpass natural sense data in their ability to express "divine things." One thinks of Isaiah 6, which recounts the prophet's vision of the heavenly temple that manifests God's glory. Applying Aquinas's principle that the *triplex via* must purify all human understanding of God in this life, the believer begins with knowledge of a divine effect (e.g., Naaman's healing from leprosy in 2 Kgs 5), then ascends to behold its divine cause, then removes all im-

---

114. *ST* I, q 12, a 13, ad 1: "licet per revelationem gratiae in hac vita non cognoscamus de Deo quid est, et sic ei quasi ignoto coniungamur; tamen plenius ipsum cognoscimus, inquantum plures et excellentiores effectus eius nobis demonstrantur; et inquantum ei aliqua attribuimus ex revelatione divina, ad quae ratio naturalis non pertingit, ut Deum esse trinum et unum."

115. Emmanuel Durand, "Du concours des effets de nature et de grâce en 'sacra doctrina': Une clé pour l'équilibre d'une théologie d'inspiration thomasienne," *Nova et Vetera* (French ed.) 80 (2005): 10–18.

perfections and predicates a perfection's superlative realization in God (e.g., infinite mercy).[116]

How does such graced knowledge connect with Moses in darkness? The start of the passage cited previously indicates that union occurs without knowing God's quiddity and in the context of revealed knowledge. But if reason can already recognize that we do not know God's quiddity, then it too can enjoy a certain union with God, as some of the texts already studied strongly suggest. Since knowledge by grace exceeds knowledge by reason, union with the unknown must have varying degrees of realization. Metaphysicians and believers are joined to God by knowing what he is not, but their cognition is not identical, hence their degrees of union also vary. Knowing "what God is not" can involve more than acknowledging that he exceeds whatever we know of him, or that he is incomprehensible, since reason already knows this and grace confirms it. If grace offers more than reason, then knowing God's *quid non est* perfectly in this life means knowing *all* of his attributes attained by reason *and* grace, a cognition that must always be purified through the *triplex via*. The believer's knowledge of God is higher because he or she knows all perfections of the triune God, an understanding that attains its summit in remotion and eminence. Revelation unveils divine perfections that in turn enable us to know God as greater even than our mode of understanding *these* attributes, thus leading the believer further into the knowledge of the God-creation difference. Even trinitarian theology stands or falls with the proper application of the *triplex via*.[117] Also, because knowing God's *quid non est* is the fruit of the *triplex via* whose noetic content is enriched by revelation, we are joined not to the absolutely unknown God but to God "as unknown." A theology of revelation stands behind Thomas's kataphatic reformulation of Dionysius.[118] In addition, the metaphysician's union with the unknown does not sanctify, as is clear in the *Commentary on the Divine Names*. Divinizing union presupposes that the intellect's act is intrinsically moved by grace concretized in the *habitus* of faith, a gift that par-

---

116. *ST* I, q. 13, a. 1c.

117. Humbrecht, *Trinité et création au prisme de la voie négative chez saint Thomas d'Aquin*, Bibliothèque de la Revue Thomiste (Paris: Parole et Silence, 2011), 195–525, 723–31.

118. Humbrecht, *Théologie négative*, 267–68, 778.

ticipates in God's sanctifying light and comes to us through the Son's and the Spirit's missions.[119] In faith we are joined to the truth imparted by the revealed names *as* the names of the saving triune God, the truth that is the divine reality itself articulated in the Scriptures, where truth speaks to us through words and concepts.[120]

The emphasis on the graced cognition of God's *quid non est* in this *Summa* passage finds a complement in the *Mystical Theology*'s lone appearance in Aquinas's *Commentary on the Gospel of John* (our ninth text), which probably dates from the early 1270s.[121] Commenting on John 1:18 ("No one has ever seen God"), Thomas explains why key Old Testament passages do not contradict John. Abraham saw God in three angels (Gn 18), Isaiah saw the heavenly throne room (Is 6), and Jacob saw God "face to face" (Gn 28). In fact, all three seers received sensible, imaginary, or intellectual created light that mediated God's manifestation and so excluded a direct vision of his essence. No finite species can truly "represent" the divine nature. God is always seen through creatures in this life. Thus,

through all these cognitions, God's quiddity (*quid est*) is not known, but [rather] what he is not, or that he is. Hence, as Dionysius says in the book of the *Mystical Theology* the perfect mode by which God is known in this life is through privation of all creatures, and of things understood by us.[122]

Aquinas confirms that the highest infused knowledge of God received by the seers remains subject to the law of remotion—that is, to the *triplex via*. Abraham, Jacob, and Isaiah also attained the perfect cognition in knowing "what God is not," although they enjoyed "more excellent" effects by which he manifested himself. Still, the privation of

---

119. Emery, "Trinity and Truth," 92–110.
120. Charles Journet, *Connaissance et inconnaissance de Dieu* (Paris: Egloff, 1943), 93.
121. Torrell, *Saint Thomas Aquinas*, vol. 1, *The Person and his Work*, 198.
122. *In Ioan.*, ch. 1, lect. 11, no. 211: "per omnes illas cognitiones non scitur de Deo quid est, sed quid non est, vel an est. Unde dicit Dionysius libro *Mysticae Theologiae*, quod perfectus modus quo Deus in vita praesenti cognoscitur, est per privationem omnium creaturarum, et intellectorum a nobis." In the provisional Leonine text established by Fr. Reid, the last sentence reads as follows: "Unde sicut Dionysius dicit in libro *De mistica theologia*, potissimum ad quod homo per species creatas pervenire potest in cognitione Dei est per remotionem." This version uses Aquinas's preferred term *remotio*, signals remotion's abiding link to cognition mediated by creatures, but does not specify what is removed.

"things understood" remains ambiguous in our text. It seems to refer to the immense difference between created species and God's essence. A few lines before, Aquinas explains that God's wisdom and goodness are really one, yet creatures cannot adequately represent God's simplicity. Thus we remove from God the finite mode of goodness or wisdom found in creatures. But the primary lesson of the passage from the Johannine commentary is prophetic cognition's subordination to the law of remotion.

Aquinas's lectures on the Pauline corpus include one mention of Moses in darkness (text 10) in the *Commentary on Paul's First Letter to Timothy*, perhaps composed in the mid-1260s, though this remains uncertain.[123] Aquinas comments on 1 Timothy 6:18, a classic apophatic verse: "God dwells in inaccessible light." He notes that the human intellect's natural object is the quiddity of things—that is, material things. God's quiddity remains inaccessible to our *natural* intellectual capacities. Hence we know God by grace in this life and by glory in the next. Thomas does not mention the natural cognition of God that he affirms elsewhere. He continues:

But then how does God dwell in inaccessible light? In Psalm 96 [it says]: "clouds and darkness surround him" and in Exodus 19: "Moses approached the darkness, in which God was." Dionysius answers: "all darkness is inaccessible light." And hence that which is here [in 1 Tm called] light and there [in Ex and Ps 96 called] darkness is the same; but darkness inasmuch as [God] is not seen, and light inasmuch as he is seen.[124]

Aquinas cites Exodus 19:16–20 and the opening line of the Areopagite's *Epistle 5*. In this epistle Dionysius explains that God dwells in darkness because of the exceeding brightness of his light so that God is darkness relative to us. Divine splendor overwhelms our operative capacities, which are proportioned to finite things. Those considered worthy

---

123. Torrell, *Saint Thomas Aquinas*, vol. 1, *The Person and his Work*, 255.
124. Thomas Aquinas, *Super I Epistolam S. Pauli ad Timotheum lectura*, in *Super Epistolas S. Pauli lectura*, vol. 2, ed. Raphael Cai (Rome and Turin: Marietti, 1953), ch. 6, lect. 3, no. 270: "Sed qualiter ergo Deus habitat lucem inaccessibilem? et in Ps. XCVI: 'Nubes et caligo in circuitu eius'; Exod. IX: 'Moyses accessit ad caliginem, in qua erat Deus.' Respondet Dionysius: 'Omnis caligo est inaccessibile lumen.' Est ergo idem quod hic lumen, et ibi caligo; sed caligo est inquantum non videtur, lumen vero inquantum videtur." The actual Exodus text is ch. 19.

may enter darkness, where they know and see God. Dionysius maintains that, by not-knowing and not-seeing, by letting go of all creature-bound contemplation, we advance beyond all words and concepts so as to know "nothing." Here we only know that God "is after (*meta*) all sensible and intelligible perception." Paul knew God "by having known him as being above all conception and knowledge."[125] The parallel with Moses learning unutterable divine things is evident.

Aquinas follows up on the passage cited with a discussion of God's inaccessibility. God is invisible because of the excess of his light. Not even the angels in glory comprehend his nature. The immaterial God is also invisible to the corporeal eye. Nor can he be seen by the mind's eye as long as the soul remains bound to the body, for such an intellect still depends on the mediation of the senses and lacks the gift of created glory (excepting Christ). Finally, no one but God sees God "through himself"—that is, through his own essence, meaning that no creature can know God's essence as he knows himself.[126] Aquinas's interpretation of God's invisibility centers on two principles: (1) the exclusion of comprehension and (2) the mediation of the senses for all cognition here below that prevents a direct vision of God. We saw a similar hermeneutic in the *Commentary on the Divine Names* treatment of knowledge by ignorance. Like the latter commentary, Thomas's gloss on 1 Timothy misses or ignores the mystic's ineffable learning in darkness. Finally, Aquinas's manner of citing *Epistle 5* shows that he recognizes the link between this text and Moses in the *Mystical Theology*.

At this point it seems advantageous to take a closer look at the narrative of Exodus 19–34 in relation to Thomas's doctrine of revelation, so as to better understand some presuppositions behind his treatment of the Areopagite's Moses, for the complexity of the Exodus narrative

125. *EP* 5, pp. 162.1–63.1, 1073A, Parker, 144; de Andia, *Henosis*, 349–50.
126. Aquinas, *Super I ad Timotheum*, ch. 6, lect. 3, no. 270: "Sed aliquid est invisibile dupliciter. Uno modo propter se … et quaedam propter excedentiam eius; et sic Deus nobis quodammodo inaccessibilis est. 'Quem nullus hominum vidit.' Si intelligatur de comprehensione, sic absolute verum est, etiam de angelis, quia solus Deus comprehendit se. Si autem de visione qua attingitur, sic intelligitur tripliciter. Uno modo, nemo vidit oculo corporali. Alio modo secundum essentiam oculo mentis vivens in carne, nisi Christus. Exod. XXXIII: 'Non videbit me homo et vivet.' Tertio modo nemo vidit quid est Deus per seipsum"; see also Thomas Aquinas, *Super Epistolam ad Colossenses lectura*, in *Super Epistolas S. Pauli Lectura*, vol. 2, ch. 1, lect. 4, no. 30.

helps to explain Aquinas's reinterpretation of Dionysian union. A survey of Exodus 19–34 will also facilitate a consideration of Thomas's theology of prophecy in relation to Dionysius.

Exodus 19–34 has at least three types of references to God and Moses on Mt. Sinai. In chapter 19 God begins to seal his covenant with Israel and reveals his glory. In Exodus 19:16–25 Moses descends the cloud-covered mountain to instruct the people on their conduct and then reascends Sinai. In chapters 20–23 he receives the Decalogue and other moral and liturgical laws. At Exodus 24:3 he returns to the base of the mountain and recounts to Israel all of God's words and ordinances. He then goes up with three future priests (Aaron, Nadab, and Abihu) and seventy-two elders. Together they see a corporeal manifestation of God and eat a meal in his presence (24:9–11). The Lord then calls Moses to leave the others behind. After seven days Moses alone enters the dark cloud, where he remains for forty days and nights. He receives the Decalogue "written" on tablets by God. In Exodus 33:18–23, again on the mountain, God refuses the patriarch's request to see his glory. Instead, God announces that his "hand" will cover Moses dwelling in the cleft of the rock, that God will reveal his "back" and pronounce the sacred name. God also states that Moses cannot see his face. At Exodus 34:6 God fulfills this promise. He passes before Moses and speaks of himself as the God of mercy and fidelity. We thus have Sinai as (1) the place of revelation to be communicated to Israel; (2) a privileged place of access to God for Moses alone; and (3) the place where God utters his name and reveals his "back."[127]

In the *Mystical Theology* Dionysius has little need for Exodus 19, since all the mystical images of this chapter are also found in subsequent chapters of Exodus. Dionysius's allegorical exegesis centers on two texts: (1) chapter 24, where Moses leaves the elders, whom Dionysius calls "hierarchs" (*hiereōn*); and (2) the apophatic elements of chapter 33 (God cannot be seen).[128] Dionysius is primarily concerned with two sets of images: (1) the patriarch's separation from the people and hierarchs and (2) apophatic metaphors for God's transcen-

127. For a historical study of Exodus, see Christoph Dohmen, *Exodus 19–40*, Herders Theologischer Kommentar zum Alten Testament (Freiburg im Breisgau: Herder, 2004).

128. *MT* 1.3, p. 144.3, 1000D.

dence. He *adds* to the text the themes of knowing by unknowing and metaconceptual divine instruction.

I noted that Aquinas's comments on 1 Timothy 6:18 refer to Exodus 19. Only two other texts in Thomas's corpus relate Moses in darkness to a particular passage from Exodus. The *Sentences Commentary* also invokes Exodus 19, and the *Contra Gentiles* cites Exodus 20:21: "Moses entered the darkness in which God was."[129] The *Sentences Commentary* and *Contra Gentiles* analyses of Exodus focus on darkness as a symbol of cognition by remotion, though the former text mentions an infused knowledge attained by the gift of understanding. The Exodus reference in the commentary on 1 Timothy centers on darkness as a symbol of God's inaccessibility. In all three texts Thomas offers an apophatic exegesis, like Dionysius. Yet throughout this chapter we have stumbled upon Aquinas's quiet insistence that the summit of our cognition of God remains communicable and bound to concepts, for the *triplex via* is not a noetic ladder to be surpassed. This kataphatic reformulation of Dionysian apophatism finds partial confirmation in Exodus 19–34, especially when we read Exodus in light of Thomas's theology of prophecy.[130]

Beginning in Exodus 19 Moses passes on virtually everything he hears and sees in the dark cloud, apparently word for word. He receives public revelation that he repeats orally to Israel and then (according to Jewish, patristic, and medieval exegesis) sets it down in writing in the Pentateuch. Moses dialogues with God in darkness, in contrast to the Areopagite's total silence in darkness. These elements of the Exodus narrative and the patriarch's key role as mediator of revelation for all of God's people find expression in Thomas's *Commentary on the Divine Names:* by the outpouring of divine truth or light, enfleshed in the language of the Bible, mediated by Old Testament prophets and New Testament apostles, and received in fidelity to the covenant, we enjoy communion with God. Aquinas is hardly explicit on the matter, but he may have reread Dionysius through the Exodus narrative, stripping it of various Platonic glosses and returning to the biblical emphasis on

---

129. *SCG* III, ch. 49, no. 2270 (cited earlier at footnote 110 of the present chapter); Aquinas, *III Sent.*, d. 35, q. 2, a. 2, qla. 2c (analyzed in the subsequent section of the present chapter).

130. Albert identifies Exodus 19–20, 24 and 33 as sources of *MT* 1.3 (*SMT*, ch. 1, p. 461.33–67).

the accessibility of God's word uttered on Sinai.[131] Indeed, the image of Moses as mediator of God's communicable word neatly parallels the Dominican friar preacher who shares the fruits of contemplation. The mystic as mediator and preacher replaces the dominant Dionysian image of Moses as a hierarch who passes beyond the iconostasis and enters the sanctuary in order to receive ineffable divine secrets in the Eucharistic celebration.[132]

Aquinas's exposition of Moses in the *Summa* treatise on prophecy partly confirms that these exegetical and theological presuppositions stand behind his understanding of the patriarch in darkness. Thomas relates Moses seeing God "face-to-face" in the meeting tent of Exodus 33:11 to an "imaginary vision"—that is, one mediated by phantasms (not in the sense of an illusion). Aquinas invokes the same category in the commentary on John as he explains Isaiah's vision of the heavenly temple—that is, when Exodus does not mention a mediating image for Moses's personal encounter with God (e.g., God's "back"), Aquinas adds a mediating veil. Also, his theology subordinates the category of imaginary vision to the supernatural light whereby the prophet judges the truth of the imaginary vision. The pilgrim's "face-to-face" vision of God only comes to completion in the judgment that "this is not God," for a vision is only a manifestation about God or his works. Aquinas affirms that Moses also enjoyed the gift of rapture, but he relates this experience to the patriarch's nonenigmatic communication with God in Numbers 12:8.[133] Here we find an utterly inexpressible en-

---

131. Puech, "Ténèbre mystique," 35–52, and de Andia, *Henosis*, 303–73, esp. 344–49, have traced the influences of Philo, Gregory of Nyssa, and Platonic philosophy on the Areopagite's reading of Exodus 19–33. Philo and Gregory also transmit a more or less Platonized doctrine to Dionysius.

132. *ST* II-II, q. 188, a. 6c: "maius est contemplata aliis tradere quam solum contemplari." The Moses-preacher parallel hardly calls for a reduction of Aquinas's exegesis of Moses to a lived experience as the driving hermeneutic. Aquinas consistently applies a *theology* of revelation to the Dionysian corpus, starting in *DDN* prologue. The cultural setting helps to explain certain emphases on this or that doctrine, but not the whole doctrine. Thomas focuses more on public revelation and its transmission than on the reception of ineffable secrets, and this fits perfectly with the doctrine of God as pure act.

133. *ST* II-II, q. 174, aa. 3–4; *DV*, q. 12, a. 14c; *In Ioan.*, ch. 1, lect. 11, nos. 210–11; Paul Synave and Pierre Benoit, notes to *Somme Théologique, la prophétie: 2a–2ae, Questions 171–178*, by Thomas Aquinas, ed. Torrell (Paris: Cerf, 2005), 272–74; Schlosser, *Lucerna*, 117–22. According to Pierre-Yves Maillard, *In Ioan.*, ch. 1, lect. 8, no. 183 excludes the possibility that Moses saw God directly, in contrast to the *ST* and the *DV*; see Maillard, *La*

Dionysian Union in Thomas 377

counter with God, yet Aquinas reserves it to Moses and Paul, thus implying that rapture is not a model for our union with God.[134] As for Moses's divine encounters in Exodus, we can apply Thomas's principle that, under the old law, prophetic revelation pertains to faith in God's excellence and is given for all the people.[135] The patriarch receives revelation in Exodus 19–31 via imaginary visions. He hears the sound of God's words and attains an infused light that enables an accurate judgment of those words.[136] The height of revelation in Exodus 19–31 involves the manifestation of divine truth that God pronounces with human words, sounds, and images. When Moses and the Israelites accept this communication in faith (with belief in the future Messiah), they enjoy divinizing communion. For Aquinas all of the patriarch's personal visions of God recounted in Exodus and the public revelation of God's nature (the divine names) communicated with words on Mt. Sinai must undergo the noetic purification of the *triplex via*. Aquinas's theologies of revelation and prophecy, applied to a rather kataphatic Exodus narrative, bring about the subordination of Moses's visions undergirding Dionysian mysticism to the activity of affirmation, remotion, and eminence, excepting rapture. Thomas's explicit comments on Moses's visions at Mt. Sinai and in the meeting tent mention prophetic gifts mediated by the imagination, a stage of contemplation below inspired judgment, hence below noetic purification by remotion and eminence. Also, *our* correct understanding of the words transmitted in the Scriptures in turn requires yet another use of the *triplex via* so that we can correctly judge the meaning of revelation. The summit of Aquinas's unknowing involves noetic content that can be mediated, taught, or preached, just as Moses communicated the revelation he received on the holy mountain. Because God's teaching in the dark cloud can

---

vision de Dieu chez Thomas d'Aquin, Bibliothèque Thomiste 53 (Paris: Vrin, 2001), 149. But Aquinas here refers to Moses seeing the glory of the Word incarnate via enigmas, while the apostles saw Christ's glory in the present or clearly; see also *DV*, q. 12, a. 14, ad 1. Torrell describes Aquinas's position on Moses's and Paul's rapture as constant; see Torrell, notes to *Questions disputées sur la vérité, Question XII: La prophétie (De prophetia)*, by Thomas Aquinas (Paris: Vrin, 2006), 238.

134. I thus disagree with Joseph Maréchal's decision to place rapture at the center of Thomas's mysticism; see Maréchal, *Études sur la psychologie des mystiques*, vol. 2 (Paris: Desclée de Brouwer, 1937), 196–250.

135. *ST* II-II, q. 174, a. 6c.

136. *DV*, q. 12, a. 14c.

be communicated, Moses and those who receive the patriarch's message must apply the *triplex via* to its intelligible content. But for Dionysius the patriarch only learns inexpressible things in darkness, so that the cloud is above all affirmations and negations. Aquinas's theology of revelation includes a category that exceeds what Dionysius considered possible (rapture) and centers on a category (imaginary vision and the light of judgment that elevates the prophet's own faculties) that Dionysius would place below the dark cloud.

Aquinas's last word on the *Mystical Theology* comes in his 1272 *Commentary on the Book of Causes* (our eleventh text). Thomas expounds on the Proclan proposition that "the first cause is above discourse." In the late 1260s, shortly after completing the *Commentary on the Divine Names*, Thomas gained access to a translation of Proclus's *Elements of Theology*. This work helped Aquinas to correct the common medieval misattribution of the *Liber de Causis* or parts thereof to Aristotle and to identify its properly Platonic origins. Thomas also recognized the intellectual proximity between Proclus, the Areopagite, and the *Liber de Causis*.[137] Thomas's exposition on the sixth proposition includes comments on the relation between Proclan and Dionysian apophatism.

For the first cause, the most powerful knowledge we can have is this, that he exceeds all our knowledge and speech; for he knows God most perfectly who holds that whatever can be thought or said of him is less than that which God is (*quod Deus est*). Hence Dionysius says in chapter 1 of the *Mystical Theology* that the human being *according to the better* of his cognition *is united* to God just as *to the absolutely* (*omnino*) *unknown, in that he knows nothing* about him, *knowing* him to be *above every mind*. To show this, he [the author of the *Book of Causes*] introduces this proposition: *the first Cause is above discourse*. Now by *discourse* must be understood "affirmation," because whatever we affirm of God does not belong to him insofar as it is signified by us; for names imposed by us signify through the mode by which we understand, which mode the divine being transcends. Hence Dionysius says in chapter 2 of the *Celestial Hierarchy* that *negations in divine things* are *true, but affirmations are incompact* or *unfitting*.[138]

---

137. Vincent A. Guagliardo, introduction to *Commentary on the Book of Causes*, by Thomas Aquinas, ed. and trans. Vincent. A. Guagliardo, Charles R. Hess, and Richard C. Taylor, ix–xiii, xix–xxi (Washington, D.C.: The Catholic University of America Press, 1996); *SLC*, proposition 4, p. 33.12.

138. *SLC*, proposition 6, p. 43.3–18: "De causa autem prima hoc est quod potissime

Much of Thomas's exposition is familiar to us: divine eminence is the object of the highest knowledge, which in turn brings about a certain union with God. Such cognition is complex. It knows (1) God's boundless perfection and (2) the limits of human noetic activity and speech, as well as (3) their distance from divine perfection.[139] This passage also manifests three of Thomas's methods to interpret the most challenging apophatic expressions related to Dionysian union.

First, Thomas apparently has recourse to Eriugena's translation of the *Mystical Theology* in order to posit noetic activity within union. He cites the last sentence about Moses in the *Mystical Theology*. Thomas gives the translation by Sarracenus but then paraphrases Eriugena's. Their translations read as follows:

Eriugena: "to the absolutely unknown, with all knowledge in repose (*in otio*), according to that which is the better of the understanding (*id quod melius est intellectus*), and there is nothing to know above the soul of those knowing (*cognoscentium*) in this way." Sarracenus: "to the absolutely unknown, being without (*vacatione*) all cognition, according to the better unity (*melius unitus*), and by the fact that the one knowing above mind knows nothing."[140]

Thomas explains the Proclan phrase that the One is "fully unknown (*penitus ignotum*)."[141] He skips the note of noetic idleness that both translators mention, partly because it would contradict his appropri-

---

scire possumus quod omnem scientiam et locutionem nostram excedit; ille enim perfectissime Deum cognoscit qui hoc de ipso tenet quod, quidquid cogitari vel dici de eo potest, minus est eo quod Deus est. Unde Dionysius dicit I° capitulo *Mysticae Theologiae*, quod homo *secundum melius* suae cognitionis *unitur* Deo sicut *omnino ignoto, eo quod nihil de eo cognoscit, cognoscens* ipsum esse *supra* omnem *mentem*. Et ad hoc ostendendum inducitur haec propositio: *Causa prima superior est narratione.* Per *narrationem* autem oportet 'affirmationem' intelligi, quia quidquid de Deo affirmamus non convenit ei secundum quod a nobis significatur; nomina enim a nobis imposita significant per modum quo nos intelligimus, quem quidem modum esse divinum transcendit. Unde Dionysius dicit II° capitulo *Caelestis Hierarchiae* quod *negationes in divinis* sunt *verae, affirmationes vero incompactae* vel *inconvenientes.*"

139. See also *DDN*, ch. 1, lect. 3, no. 83 (cited earlier at footnote 48 of the present chapter).

140. Dionysius Areopagita, *Dionysiaca*, 1:578: Eriugena: "omnino autem ignoto, omni scientia in otio, secundum id quod melius est intellectus, et nihil cognoscendum super animam sic cognoscentium"; Sarracenus: "omnino autem ignoto, vacatione omnis cognitionis, secundum melius unitus, et eo quod nihil cognoscit super mentem cognoscens."

141. *SLC*, proposition 6, p. 43 cites the *Elements of Theology:* "'propter quod solum primum penitus ignotum.'"

ation of Eriugena's mistranslation "the better of the understanding." Dionysius here mentions being united in a higher mode (*to kreitton henoumenos*).[142] This is an unusual passage of the *Mystical Theology*, for Sarracenus translates the Greek more faithfully than does Eriugena. The former says "unity" where the latter says "understanding." Also, Sarracenus retains the paradoxical couplet of knowing nothing and knowing above mind. On the one hand, Thomas's paraphrase inserts Eriugena's shift to intellect. Now the cause or measure of union is our better act of cognition, not a divine gift passively received in silence. Thomas identifies the former with our understanding of God's eminence.

On the other hand, and this brings me to my second point, Thomas follows the Areopagite's paradoxical expression that Sarracenus transmits, but then, in typical fashion, reformulates it with the help of a scholastic distinction. The challenge is to make sense of the apparent contradiction between "knowing nothing about God" and "knowing above mind." Thomas assumes that the latter does not signify the intellect's ecstasy or the cessation of its operations. In reading the proposition on the first cause above discourse, Aquinas limits the term "discourse" to affirmations—that is, to causal predication of God's attributes *before* its purification by remotion and eminence. God is above our affirmations in the sense that these necessarily reflect finite modes of understanding. Aquinas invokes the *Celestial Hierarchy* on the unfittingness of affirmations. He again uses translations by Sarracenus (*inconvenientes*) and Eriugena (*incompactae*).[143] As in the *Summa*, Aquinas significantly transforms the meaning of the *Celestial Hierarchy*. The absolute priority of the negative way in Dionysius becomes a qualification of the affirmative way that leaves the door open for eminent, substantial divine naming.[144] Thomas's explanation of the limits of affirmation unfolds his interpretation of the *Mystical Theology*. By union with God, one knows "nothing"—that is, nothing of the divine mode of being that escapes the pilgrim's perception. We know God to be above mind—that is, above the creaturely mode of being intertwined with all affirmations. The achievement of the *triplex via* causes union, since it is

---

142. *MT* 1.3, p. 144.14, 1001A; de Andia, *Henosis*, 352.
143. See the editor's note at *SLC*, proposition 6, p. 43.
144. *ST* I, q. 13, a. 3, ad 2 (see footnote 42 in chapter 7 of the present volume).

the path to know that God is above our affirmations, above all that we can think and say of him. God is absolutely unknown only in the sense that his mode of being escapes our mind's grasp. Perhaps because of Eriugena's mistranslation, and certainly because of a rereading of a key *Celestial Hierarchy* passage, Thomas can invoke a more kataphatic Dionysius in opposition to Proclan noetic silence in union. Aquinas's Areopagite corrects a Proclan mystical doctrine that the historical Areopagite had largely appropriated.

Third, Thomas interprets the apophatism of the *Mystical Theology* by contrasting "Platonic" and Thomistic-Aristotelian-Dionysian metaphysics. The *Elements of Theology* left no doubt in Thomas's mind that "the Platonists" considered God to be above being in the proper sense, for they thought of all being as necessarily finite. Consequently, the One is also beyond intelligibility. But Aquinas explains that

according to the truth of the matter, the first cause is above being (*ens*) inasmuch as it is infinite *esse* itself, while being (*ens*) is predicated of that which finitely participates *esse*, and this is proportioned to our intellect, whose object is the quiddity, as is said in *De Anima* [book] 3, hence that alone can be seized (*capabile*) by our intellect which has a quiddity participating *esse*; but God's quiddity is *esse* itself, hence it is above intellect. And by this mode Dionysius introduces this reason in chapter 1 of the *Divine Names* ... [the divine *esse*] who is above every substance is separate from every cognition.[145]

Thomas holds that, while the pagan Platonists reserved being to the realm of finitude, Dionysius refused to exclude *esse* as a proper divine name and proposed a theology in harmony with the doctrines of infinite divine act and the identity of God's *esse* and *essentia*. While Aquinas unconsciously exaggerates the difference between Proclus and the Areopagite, he correctly refuses to identify their negative theologies. For the historical Dionysius goes beyond Proclus when he employs

---

145. *SLC*, proposition 6, p. 47.11–22: "Sed secundum rei veritatem causa prima est supra ens in quantum est ipsum esse infinitum, ens autem dicitur id quod finite participat esse, et hoc est proportionatum intellectui nostro cuius obiectum est quod quid est ut dicitur in III° *De anima*, unde illud solum est capabile ab intellectu nostro quod habet quidditatem participantem esse; sed Dei quidditas est ipsum esse, unde est supra intellectum. Et per hunc modum inducit hanc rationem Dionysius I° capitulo *De divinis nominibus* ... esse, qui est supra omnem substantiam ab omni cognitione est segregatus."

nonprivative, transcending negations. For Thomas, God is above mind in that his simplicity remains radically disproportioned to our intellect. In this life we can only directly grasp beings with finite being (*esse*), hence entities with finite quiddities really distinct from their intrinsic being (*esse*), the *esse* that is a participation in a similitude of God's *esse*. Here the mystical consequences of Thomas's creative Aristotelian-Dionysian anthropological synthesis that we studied in chapter 6 come to the fore. The metaphysics of act opens up a broad path toward indirect knowledge of God via created actualities, via the participations that reflect their divine source. In a metaphysics of act that stretches all the way to God's infinite *esse*, there is no reason to exclude from the summit of knowledge that which one learns by the contemplation of creatures. Since *esse* is no longer restricted to finitude, the passage from lights to darkness on Mt. Sinai need not shut down the mind's activity whose proper object is beings with finite *esse*. A rupture in the mode of knowledge is no longer necessary. Rather, darkness comes to signify the indirect, confused status of our divine cognition, since the mind's proper object is finite *ens*, not endless *esse*. The originality of Thomas's response consists in this, that the nature of God's *esse* (especially simplicity and infinity) renders him both intelligible and relatively inaccessible. For all of these reasons Aquinas inserts mediated cognition into Moses's dark mind.[146] The historical Areopagite's eminence involves the experience of divine grandeur by a pure gift, while Aquinas's eminence is known and named via the rational, active contemplation of created actualities.

During his career Aquinas uses diverse though complementary approaches to Moses in darkness. The earliest, most apophatic reading of the *Mystical Theology* leaves standing the noetic content linked to the reality signified by the divine names, an obscure gaze toward God wherein content derived from causal knowledge abides. Aquinas always qualifies the formula of union to "the absolutely unknown." He either introduces the term "as unknown" or insists that only God's mode of being remains fully unknown. The bulk of his expositions of Moses in darkness seems to invoke a progression of acquired knowledge about God, a process for which metaphysical wisdom apparent-

---

146. Humbrecht, *Théologie négative*, 717, 779; O'Rourke, *Pseudo-Dionysius*, 56.

ly suffices at times. However, Aquinas also constructs a hierarchy of modes of unknowing wherein graced cognition surpasses philosophical insight. This hierarchy only makes sense if knowing *quod Deus non est* includes a positive understanding of divine attributes. The same hierarchy makes possible diverse grades of unknowing within grace, thus opening the way for a progression in infused understanding that either complements or surpasses acquired theological cognition. If the metaphysician can penetrate the dark cloud, he remains on the periphery while the theologian and saint proceed further toward the center. As in his *Commentary on the Divine Names*, Thomas quietly and systematically eliminates Dionysian noetic silence from the dark cloud. However, Thomas changes Dionysius because of a metaphysics of *esse* and especially a theology of revelation rooted in a doctrine of prophecy whose kataphatic tendencies match well the biblical image of Moses as mediator of revelation. Moses in darkness symbolizes the achievement of divine naming in the sense of full actualization, not as overcoming word and thought. In other words, the *Divine Names* and its *triplex via* already account for the bulk of the *Mystical Theology*'s doctrine.[147]

We have already encountered brief references to another important piece of Thomas's exegesis of Moses: learning about God directly from him. Aquinas pursues this theme in his theology of the Spirit's gift of understanding.

THE GIFT OF UNDERSTANDING IN THOMAS

Aquinas's most original appropriation of the *Mystical Theology* occurs in his theology of the gift of understanding. Here he goes beyond both his comments on union passages in the *Divine Names* and his explanations of Moses that we just studied. The present section focuses on the *Summa*, which builds on Aquinas's mature theology of the Spirit's action in his seven gifts. I begin with the *Sentences Commentary* teaching on the gift of understanding. It already develops some key ideas later taken up in the *Summa* and signals Thomas's relation to Albert and Bonaventure. Aquinas regularly consulted their commentaries on the Lombard as he composed his own.[148]

147. Humbrecht, *Théologie négative*, 354, 370.
148. Ludwig Jeßberger, *Das Abhängigkeitsverhältnis des hl. Thomas von Aquin von Al-*

The main *Sentences Commentary* study of the gift of understanding comes in one article with three sections or "little questions" (*quaestiunculae*). The first section accounts for this gift's place among the Spirit's seven gifts. Thomas notes that *intellectus* refers to knowing a thing's essence, not the accidents surrounding the essence. By reason's discourse, human cognition proceeds from a being's effects to its essence. In contrast, understanding (*intellectus*) involves immediate apprehension, as in the knowledge of first principles.[149]

Bonaventure holds that the gift of understanding involves a gaze upon the eternal forms and a higher type of reasoning.[150] For Aquinas the latter aspect ignores what is proper to *intellectus*. If he had access to Albert's *Commentary on Isaiah*, then Thomas may be developing his teacher's doctrine. Albert also explains the gift of understanding by analogy to the grasp of first principles.[151] The theme of *intellectus* surpassing discourse also harmonizes with a key aspect of the Areopagite's teaching on knowledge in darkness. Aquinas continues:

But just as the human mind only enters into a thing's essence through accidents, so also it only enters into spiritual realities through corporeal things and the similitudes of sensible things, as Dionysius says. Hence, faith which makes one cling to spiritual realities as veiled in a mirror and an enigma, perfects the mind in a human mode; and so it [faith] is a virtue. But if by a supernatural light the human mind is elevated so far that it is led to behold spiritual realities themselves, [then] this is above the human mode. And the gift of understanding that illumines the mind on what is heard does this [elevation], so that as soon as this is heard it is proven to be true, as in the mode of first principles.[152]

---

bertus Magnus und Bonaventura im dritten Buche des Sentenzenkommentars (Würzburg: Richard Mayr, 1936), 171–83. I skip the sparse remarks on this gift in the young Thomas Aquinas's *Expositio super Isaiam ad litteram*, Leonine Edition 28 (Rome: Editori di san Tommaso, 1974), ch. 11, p. 80.158–63, which add nothing to the *Sent.* or the *ST*.

149. For an overview of Thomas's doctrine, see Georges Cottier, "Intellectus et ratio," *RT* 88 (1988): 215–28.

150. Bonaventure, *III Sent.*, d. 35, a. 1, q. 3; Schlosser, *Cognitio*, 181–83.

151. Albertus Magnus, *Postilla Super Isaiam*, ch. 11, p. 170.16–29. This work may have been composed after Aquinas's *Sent.*; see the editor's preface, xx. Its influence on Thomas remains uncertain.

152. Aquinas, *III Sent.*, d. 35, q. 2, a. 2, qla. 1c, 1198–99: "Sicut autem mens humana in essentiam rei non ingreditur nisi per accidentia, ita etiam in spiritualia non ingreditur nisi per corporalia et sensibilium similitudines, ut dicit Dionysius. Unde fides quae

Thomas does not cite a specific Dionysian text, but the editor sees a reference to the *Celestial Hierarchy* and *Ecclesiastical Hierarchy* doctrine that divine light only shines through sensible veils.[153] Given that the article's context pertains to faith cognition, Aquinas probably invokes the Dionysian similitudes so as to refer to creation and revelation. Both types of manifestation grant indirect knowledge of God, as they present analogies and metaphors whose intelligibility (*quoad nos*) depends on created realities. Aquinas then evokes his obscure, early terminology of the "human" and "super-human" modes to distinguish the operative modes of the virtues and the gifts, respectively. The human mode of knowing applies to faith. It causes one to grasp spiritual realities in a veiled manner, which somewhat parallels the Dionysian sensible similitudes, though faith does not simply remain on the level of accidents. But the gift of understanding somehow enables one to gaze into the invisible realities themselves, for it operates above the human mode. A previous article briefly speaks of this gift receiving spiritual things "quasi naked" or illuminating us on what is heard by faith.[154] Thomas suggests a mode of cognition that penetrates more effectively the Dionysian veils so as to better grasp a hidden essence.

The article's second section takes up the gift's act in this life. The objections conclude that this gift's mode of cognition belongs to heaven. Aquinas answers that this gift proceeds to spiritual things in two ways: by remotion and by fixing the mind's gaze upon spiritual realities:

Therefore, in the state of pilgrimage the intellect enters spiritual things, most of all divine things, in the first mode [remotion]; because in the state of pilgrimage human cognition is perfected in this, that we understand God to be separated from all, to be above all, as Dionysius says in the book *On the Mystical Theology*. And Moses came to this, who is said to have entered the darkness in which God was, [at] Exodus 20. And because of this also,

---

spiritualia in speculo et aenigmate quasi involuta tenere facit, humano modo mentem perficit; et ideo virtus est. Sed si supernaturali lumine mens intantum elevetur ut ad ipsa spiritualia aspicienda introducatur, hoc supra humanum modum est. Et hoc facit intellectus donum quod de auditis mentem illustrat, ut ad modum primorum principiorum statim audita probentur."

153. *CH* 1.2, p. 8.10–12, 121B; *EH* 1.4, pp. 66.20–67.15, 376B–C.
154. Aquinas, *III Sent.*, d. 34, q. 1, a. 2c, 1117: "Quod autem spiritualia quasi nuda veritate capiantur, supra humanum modum est; et hoc facit donum intellectus, qui 'de auditis per fidem mentem illustrat,' ut dicit Gregorius."

concerning the state of pilgrimage, purity is posed in the sixth beatitude, which pertains to the intellect's purification from all corporeal things. But we cannot reach the second mode [fixing the mind's gaze upon spiritual realities] in the state of pilgrimage, most of all as to God; but this will be in heaven.[155]

We have two modes of apprehension: negative and positive. Here below we cannot directly apprehend or fix our gaze upon God's essence or the essences of spiritual creatures. Thomas neither affirms nor rejects Albert's and William of Auxerre's doctrine that this gift grants new insight on the angels' blessings in beatitude, but he refuses to follow them in an explicit way. He also passes over in silence Albert's Augustinian claim that this gift fixes the mind's gaze upon the soul's good affections.[156] In chapter 3 I noted that the latter doctrine harmonizes well with the Augustinian interiority of Albert's *Sentences Commentary*, in contrast to the anthropology of Albert's Dionysian commentaries. The early Albert suggests that the gift of understanding makes possible a partial, positive grasp of immaterial realities (e.g., angelic blessings). Bonaventure also offers a relatively kataphatic reading of this gift: it grants a vision of the eternal reasons of things.[157] Aquinas's more "exterior" anthropology helps to explain his apophatic approach to this gift: he highlights the distance between God and his manifestations. Rather than propose new (internal) manifestations of hidden realities, he favors some type of gifted noetic remotion. Albert makes the gift's cognition of angelic beatitude a steppingstone to a deeper knowledge of God, whereas Thomas's solution posits a more direct path to the divine mystery.

With Dionysius, Thomas holds that Mt. Sinai's summit signifies the highest knowledge possible here below. He again adopts the Dionysian

155. Aquinas, *III Sent.*, d. 35, q. 2, a. 2, qla. 2c, 1199: "In statu ergo viae intellectus ingreditur ad spiritualia *primo modo,* maxime ad divina: quia in hoc perficitur cognitio humana secundum statum viae, ut intelligamus Deum ab omnibus separatum, super omnia esse, ut dicit Dionysius in lib. *De mystica theologia.* Et ad hoc pervenit Moyses, qui dicitur intrasse ad caliginem in qua Deus erat, Exod. XX. Et propter hoc etiam quantum ad statum viae munditia ponitur in *sexta* beatitudine quae pertinet ad depurationem intellectus ab omnibus corporalibus. Sed *ad secundum modum* pertingere non possumus in statu viae, maxime quantum ad Deum; sed hoc erit in patria."

156. Albertus Magnus, *III Sent.*, d. 35, a. 3; William of Auxerre, *Summa Aurea,* tomus 2, tr. 34, ch. 1 (see chapter 3 of this volume).

157. Bonaventure, *III Sent.*, d. 35, a. 1, q. 3.

link between remotion and perfection. Knowing God as "separated from all" and "above all" likely alludes to the *Mystical Theology*'s closing line, but Aquinas immediately switches to Moses in chapter 1 of that work.[158] He seems to be the first scholastic to connect the dark cloud with the gift of understanding. Albert had introduced a Dionysian element into the theology of the gifts by linking wisdom to Hierotheus, a connection that Thomas takes up. Yet it is not clear to what extent the early Aquinas follows the Dionysian doctrine that God directly acts in Moses's mind. He uses illumination language to explain the actualized gift of understanding, which seems to suggest God's direct intervention. But like Albert, Aquinas repeats standard scholastic terms for the gift without explaining them. His ontology of the gifts' operation only becomes clear in the *Summa*.

The link between the gift of understanding and Moses may signal Aquinas's deliberate refusal of Bonaventure's theology. The Franciscan's *Sentences Commentary* states, "the gift of wisdom consists in taste, but the gift of understanding consists in the light of reason; and affection ascends further than reason, and union than cognition, according to Dionysius."[159] Here Bonaventure may be appropriating a trademark of Gallus's Dionysian exegesis—namely, that union occurs in darkness via the ascending power of love and with noetic inactivity.[160] This doctrine also fits well with the priority of will over intellect in Bonaventure's thought. Aquinas integrates love into his theology of union, but he gives the dark cloud an essentially noetic meaning, though the cloud linked to the gift of understanding presupposes habitual charity.

Thomas does somewhat clarify the function of illumination: it does not infuse intelligible species, but rather removes God from all created things. A previous article refers to this process as it explains the beati-

---

158. *MT* 5, p. 150.8–9, 1048B; Dionysius Areopagita, *Dionysiaca*, 1:601–2: Eriugena: "et super omnem ablationem excellentia omnium simpliciter perfectione et summitas omnium"; Sarracenus: "et super omnem ablationem est excessus ab omnibus simpliciter absoluti et super tota."

159. Bonaventure, *III Sent.*, d. 35, a. 1, q. 3, ad 5, 779b: "donum *sapientiae* consistit in gustu, donum vero *intellectus* consistit in lumine rationis; et amplius ascendit affectio quam ratio, et unio quam cognitio, secundum quod vult Dionysius"; see also Schlosser, *Lucerna*, 188; Schlosser, *Cognitio*, 200–1.

160. On Bonaventure as a disciple of Gallus, see Bougerol, "Saint Bonaventure," 39–40; McGinn, *Presence of God*, vol. 3, *Flowering of Mysticism*, 94, 106–10; see also the end of the next section in the present chapter.

tude of the pure of heart, the act of this gift's *habitus*. One needs purity "from errors and phantasms and spiritual forms, from all of which Dionysius, in the book *On the Mystical Theology*, teaches those stretching into divine contemplation to withdraw."[161] The gift of understanding keeps one from falling into the trap of erroneous judgments in matters of faith about God. Again, Albert's *Commentary on Isaiah* could be a source for Aquinas. Albert explains that, in the gift of understanding, divine lights function like first principles or rules that exclude heretical error.[162] But Thomas is more precise, for he distinguishes the gift of understanding from the gift of wisdom by the operations of simple apprehension and judgment, respectively. It seems that the gift of understanding enables a subsequent act of true judgment by somehow manifesting the difference between God and creatures, as I will argue later on. Aquinas draws an analogy between grasping the first principles and the operation of understanding.[163] But the young Thomas does not explain how this analogous grasp occurs.

Aquinas mentions that the pure of heart recede from phantasms and spiritual forms, following the Areopagite's counsel to Timothy in the *Mystical Theology*. This purification does not directly pertain to the passions.[164] Aquinas makes a similar comment in his discussion of Moses: the intellect is cleansed of all corporeal things.[165] He takes up the Dionysian theme of the mind transcending visible veils, but he does not explain whether the mystic stops gazing on images or whether his manner of understanding the intelligible content communicated by images improves. As we saw in chapter 5, for Thomas, no cognitive act of the pilgrim reaches completion without returning to phantasms. This principle prevents a full exclusion of image-bound noetic operations and so excludes a key part of Dionysian contemplative psychology. In other words, the analysis of Thomas's epistemology in chapter 5 helps to ex-

---

161. Aquinas, *III Sent.*, d. 34, q. 1, a. 4c, 1127: "ab erroribus et phantasmatibus et spiritualibus formis a quibus omnibus docet abscedere Dionysius in lib. *De mystica theologia*, tendentes in divinam contemplationem."

162. Albertus Magnus, *Postilla Super Isaiam*, ch. 11, p. 170.24–41.

163. Aquinas, *III Sent.*, d. 35, q. 2, a. 2, qla. 1c (cited earlier in footnote 152 of the present chapter); qla. 3c.

164. Aquinas, *III Sent.*, d. 34, q. 1, a. 4c.

165. Aquinas, *III Sent.*, d. 35, q. 2, a. 2, qla. 2c. (cited earlier in footnote 155 of the present chapter).

plain the young Thomas's ambiguity concerning Moses's mode of consciousness.

The *Summa* retains much of Aquinas's early thought on the gift of understanding and develops it within his late theology of the Spirit's action in the seven gifts. Question 8, article 1 of the *Secunda Secundae* returns to the theme of *intellectus* penetrating to the essence of things:

For, under the accidents lies hidden the nature of a substantial thing, under words lie hidden those [which are] signified by the words; under likenesses and figures lies hidden the truth figured (*figurata*); intelligible things are also somehow interior with respect to sensible things that are sensed externally, and effects lie hidden in their causes, and vice versa. Hence one may speak of understanding with regard to all these things.[166]

Aquinas then recalls that our cognition begins with the senses. He contrasts the limited power of the intellect's natural light to reach the heart (*intima*) of things to the power of the gift of understanding. This article does not explicitly invoke Dionysian veils, but the anthropological argument is close to the one used in the *Sentences Commentary*. Since human cognition begins with the senses, we need a noetic light beyond that of our natural capacity and (by implication) above faith so as to know adequately the things of God. As in Dionysius, divine light aids the contemplative in understanding what lies beneath symbols. Aquinas unfolds what he intends by understanding penetrating to a thing's essence: not just grasping the quiddity of material or immaterial realities, but also the meaning of words and the truth of similitudes and figures.

He also specifies the gift of understanding's function by taking up the *Sentences Commentary* contrast between *intellectus* and *ratio*. Natural cognition proceeds from something already known and then, by reasoning, attains new knowledge, which entails noetic repose. But this gift's "superadded light relates to what is made known to us supernaturally just as the natural light to that which we know primordially."[167] The gift of understanding does not form new theological conclusions

---

166. *ST* II-II, q. 8, a. 1c: "Nam sub accidentibus latet natura rei substantialis, sub verbis latent significata verborum, sub similitudinibus et figuris latet veritas figurata; res <etiam> intelligibiles sunt quodammodo interiores respectu rerum sensibilium quae exterius sentiuntur, et in causis latent effectus et e converso. Unde respectu horum omnium potest dici intellectus."

167. *ST* II-II, q. 8, a. 1, ad 2: "ita se habet lumen superadditum ad ea quae nobis su-

about revelation, nor does it directly assist the mind's motion toward such conclusions. Rather, it "concerns first principles of gratuitous cognition, but otherwise than faith [does]. For assent to them pertains to faith, but it pertains to the gift of understanding to penetrate with the mind the things said."[168] This gift seeks to grasp the still obscure meaning of first principles received by faith (in its act of assent). But what are the first principles of gratuitous cognition? Aquinas notes that when demonstrating the things of faith, the "saints" or Fathers proceed from the principles of faith—that is, the authority of Scripture.[169] Reason does not prove the biblical doctrines believed. Rather, faith clings to these doctrines as natural reason clings to its first principles. Thus one believer can convince another of whatever directly follows from the teaching of Scripture, just as any reasonable person can be convinced of whatever directly follows from first principles (e.g., "Socrates cannot sit and stand at the same time"). The gift of understanding essentially pertains to penetrating the meaning of Scripture.

The subsequent *Summa* article specifies the gift's function in relation to faith's principal and secondary objects.[170] The text builds on Thomas's doctrine that belief is principally about the reality we hope to see in heaven. Some truths essentially (or *per se*) pertain to faith: the Trinity, the incarnation, and so on. The articles of faith contain faith's principal objects. These articles do not exhaust the content of Scripture. Other truths are ordered in some way to what essentially belongs to faith. Everything else in Scripture serves faith's principal objects. For example, the fact that Abraham had two sons is not a central mystery of faith, but it manifests the future incarnation (e.g., Isaac's miraculous conception foreshadows that of Jesus).[171]

Aquinas unfolds the function of the gift of understanding as he combines this twofold distinction on faith's objects with the theme of *intellectus* grasping a thing's essence. Here below we cannot perfectly

---

pernaturaliter innotescunt sicut se habet lumen naturale ad ea quae primordialiter cognoscimus."

168. *ST* II-II, q. 8, a. 6, ad 2: "donum intellectus est circa prima principia cognitionis gratuitae, aliter tamen quam fides. Nam ad fidem pertinet eis assentire: ad donum vero intellectus pertinet mente penetrare ea quae dicuntur."

169. *ST* II-II, q. 1, a. 5, ad 2; a. 7.

170. *ST* II-II, q. 8, a. 2c.

171. *ST* II-II, q. 1, a. 6, ad 1; aa. 7–9.

understand the essence of whatever principally pertains to faith—the truth (of a faith proposition) as it is in itself. Indeed, such cognition would require the beatific vision. How else could we perfectly know the triune God? But we can perfectly understand other things in Scripture—that is, *some* of faith's secondary objects. The gift of understanding greatly illumines us on the things ordered to faith's essential objects.[172] The *Sentences Commentary* does not apply this distinction to the gift of understanding. In fact, the early Aquinas hardly comments on this gift's relation to the mysteries of faith.

The *sed contra* of the same *Summa* article offers a good example of this doctrine. It explains how faith does not exclude further illumination: "Someone having faith can be illumined in his mind about the things heard, hence it is said in the last chapter of Luke that the Lord 'opened the mind of his disciples so that they might understand the Scriptures.'"[173] Thomas refers to the risen Christ's last appearance to the apostles (Lk 24:45). Jesus instructs them on the Messiah's paschal mystery as the fulfillment of Old Testament prophecies. These prophecies are ordered to a central mystery of faith. Aquinas does not confound the Spirit's interior light (in the gift of understanding) with Christ's exterior teaching. Rather, he shows that faith still needs a higher light of some kind. Jesus enables the disciples to grasp the hidden Christological prophecies of the Old Testament. The reality signified yet hidden in the words of Scripture becomes manifest with a higher divine light. Likewise, the gift of understanding penetrates to the deep meaning of Scripture, thus strengthening faith. Since this gift focuses on faith's articles more than on Scripture as a whole, it remains accessible to the unlearned or illiterate believer. Also, penetrating the articles of faith involves more than just gathering information about God, for the virtue of faith pertains to an encounter with first truth itself.

Aquinas then relates this gift to the imperfect cognition of faith's principal objects:

---

172. *ST* II-II, q. 8, a. 2c: "Sed quaedam alia ad fidem ordinata etiam hoc modo [perfecte] intelligi possunt."
173. *ST* II-II, q. 8, a. 2sc: "Sed aliquis habens fidem potest esse illustratus mente circa audita; unde dicitur *Luc.* ult. quod Dominus 'aperuit' discipulis suis 'sensum ut intelligerent Scripturas.'"

In another way, something is understood but imperfectly, namely, when the very essence of a thing or the truth of a proposition is not known in its quiddity (*quid sit*) or how it is (*quomodo sit*), and yet is known insofar as the things that appear externally are not contrary to the truth; namely, inasmuch as the human being understands that he ought not to depart from the realities of faith because of the things that appear externally. In this way, during the state of faith, nothing prevents one from understanding even the realities that *per se* belong to faith.[174]

As we cannot directly grasp the *per se* realities of faith, the gift of understanding ponders "what they are not." Aquinas mentions the contrast between the truth of faith and external appearances to explain the gifted knowledge of faith's principal objects. An example of external appearances would be the present success of the unjust, apparently contradicting God's justice and power.

Aquinas's intention emerges more clearly a few articles later. He explains that the gift of understanding purifies us of errors about God so that we not fall into heresy.[175] We can apply this principle to the theme that *per se* objects of faith are grasped imperfectly. The gift of understanding cuts away false notions easily attached to revealed doctrines. It removes foreign accretions from our grasp of the meaning of the articles of faith.[176] Here remotion follows and depends on a biblical affirmation. The removal of error lets the revealed doctrine's intelligibility shine more brightly. Once again, remotion leads to a higher, positive cognition.

The theme of excluding error harmonizes well with Thomas's expansion of the gift's functions to include practical cognition, which goes beyond the *Sentences Commentary*:

the gift of understanding not only relates to the things that first and principally fall under faith, but also to all the things which are ordained to faith. Now good operations have a certain order to faith ... the gift of understanding also extends itself to certain things that can be done; not as being

---

174. *ST* II-II, q. 8, a. 2c: "Alio modo contingit aliquid intelligi imperfecte, quando scilicet ipsa essentia rei, vel veritas propositionis, non cognoscitur quid sit aut quomodo sit, sed tamen cognoscitur secundum quod ea quae exterius apparent veritati non contrariantur; inquantum scilicet homo intelligit quod propter ea quae exterius apparent non est recedendum ab his quae sunt fidei. Et secundum hoc nihil prohibet, durante statu fidei, intelligere etiam ea quae per se sub fide cadunt."
175. *ST* II-II, q. 8, a. 7c (cited later at footnote 189 of the present chapter).
176. Horst, *Gaben*, 115–16.

principally about them, but inasmuch as we are regulated in our actions "by eternal reasons, to which higher reason adheres by contemplating and consulting them," as Augustine states in *On the Trinity* [book] 12, which [higher reason] is perfected by the gift of understanding.[177]

The right regulation of human actions belongs to the secondary objects of faith, for the revealed law leads to beatitude. The gift of understanding does not directly identify the virtuous act for a particular circumstance (this belongs to the gift of counsel) but rather enters further into the "eternal reasons" for such acts. Even when it assists in the practical realm, this gift primarily focuses on eternal things. The eternal law refers to God's wisdom ordering all things to their end. We participate in this law by reason, by our natural and graced virtuous inclinations, and by faith in the revealed law. Only the saints in glory perfectly know the eternal law.[178] By implication the gift of understanding uses the way of remotion to penetrate Scripture's teaching on God's providential wisdom concerning human acts. For example, this gift can better manifest the place of penance in the economy of salvation.

Having shown the gift of understanding's objects, Aquinas specifies the conditions for its operation. The gifts as *habitus* cause docility to the Spirit's motion. The gift of understanding disposes the intellect for the Spirit's illumination. This *habitus* involves a disposition to be moved toward a right estimation about our beatifying end. Aquinas draws an analogy between this *habitus* and the right estimation of the moral virtues:

Now someone only has a right estimation about the ultimate end if he does not err about the end, but firmly adheres to it as to the greatest good. This is only the case for one who has sanctifying grace, just as also in moral matters, a human being has the right estimation about the end through the habit of virtue. Hence, no one has the gift of understanding without sanctifying grace.[179]

---

177. *ST* II-II, q. 8, a. 3c: "donum intellectus non solum se habet ad ea quae primo et principaliter cadunt sub fide, sed etiam ad omnia quae ad fidem ordinantur. Operationes autem bonae quendam ordinem ad fidem habent ... donum intellectus etiam ad quaedam operabilia se extendit, non quidem ut circa ea principaliter versetur, sed inquantum in agendis regulamur 'rationibus aeternis, quibus conspiciendis et consulendis,' secundum Augustinum, XII *de Trinitate*, 'inhaeret superior ratio,' quae dono intellectus perficitur."

178. *ST* I-II, q. 91, aa. 1, 2, 6.

179. *ST* II-II, q. 8, a. 5c: "Rectam autem aestimationem de ultimo fine non habet nisi

Earlier in the *Summa* Aquinas argues that the moral virtues incline to their end, thus enabling a connatural judgment about the final cause. This inclination facilitates prudential decisions about proper means to the end. In the previous passage Aquinas shows that, in its function of rendering possible a correct estimation of the beatifying end (God and life with him), habitual sanctifying grace is a necessary condition for the gift of understanding as *habitus*, just as the connaturality of the moral virtues (as *habitus*) is a necessary condition for prudential knowledge.[180] Aquinas does not identify the gift of understanding's act as a connatural judgment.[181] Rather, the key comparison involves two types of habitual connaturality: the moral virtues and habitual sanctifying grace. The connaturality of this grace disposes for the Spirit's motion. Such *habitual* connaturality is distinct from the gift of wisdom's act of judgment by connaturality.[182]

The theme of connaturality brings us to the relation between the act of judgment and the gift of understanding. John of Saint Thomas assigns a connatural judgment to this gift and to the gift of wisdom. Now Aquinas proposes the following distinction:

> Thus, about the realities which are proposed to faith for belief, two things are required from us. First, that they [the realities proposed] be penetrated or grasped by the intellect: and this pertains to the gift of understanding. But second, it is necessary that the human being have right judgment of these realities, that he may estimate that he should adhere to them and recede from their opposites. So then, for divine things, this judgment pertains to the gift of wisdom; but for created things, it pertains to the gift of knowledge (*scientia*); but as to the application to particular deeds, it pertains to the gift of counsel.[183]

---

ille qui circa finem non errat, sed ei firmiter inhaeret tanquam optimo. Quod est solum habentis gratiam gratum facientem, sicut etiam in moralibus rectam aestimationem habet homo de fine per habitum virtutis. Unde donum intellectus habet nullus sine gratia gratum faciente." This argument is not found in Thomas's *Sentences Commentary*.

180. *ST* I-II, q. 58, aa. 4–5; González Ayesta, *El don de sabiduría*, 68–71, 147–48.

181. Such an identification is proposed by John of Saint Thomas, *De donis*, nos. 118–26, 425; Ambroise Gardeil, *Structure de l'âme*, 2:174; Maritain, *Distinguish to Unite*, 260; Santiago M. Ramirez, *Los dones del Espíritu Santo*, Biblioteca de teólogos españoles vol. 30, part 7 (Madrid: 1978), 180.

182. See *ST* II-II, q. 45, a. 2 (cited later at footnote 247 of the present chapter); González Ayesta, *El don de sabiduría*, 144, 166.

183. *ST* II-II, q. 8, a. 6c: "Sic ergo circa ea quae fidei proponuntur credenda duo re-

Dionysian Union in Thomas 395

For John this text does not exclude judgment from the gift of understanding. First, he recalls the analogy between the mind's natural grasp of reason's first principles and the gift of understanding's grasp of gratuitous first principles. The former involves apprehension and judgment, so the gift of understanding seems to, as well. Second, John notes that this gift concerns truth, which demands judgment. Third, he argues that understanding makes comparisons (e.g., of faith doctrines and external appearances), which implies a judgment. He concludes that the gift of wisdom judges in relation to divine causes, while understanding exercises a "discerning" judgment of revelation's witness, with a focus on the terms proposed.[184]

But John cannot explain why Thomas never explicitly links judgment with the gift of understanding. This lacuna is striking, for Aquinas carefully distinguishes the modes of judgment proper to the gifts of wisdom, knowledge, and counsel. He even states that "the gift of understanding pertains to each cognition, namely, speculative and practical, not as to judgment, but as to apprehension."[185] He does not make an exception to this rule. Also, John's argument seems to presuppose that the gifts operate without the virtues. He overlooks the fact that faith has already judged the gratuitous first principles. The gift of understanding need not exercise a new act of judgment about these principles, but can instead focus on clarifying the meaning of the revealed terms of the principles that faith already judges to be true. In chapter 6 I argued that the Spirit's gifts operate together with their corresponding virtues. By implication the gift of understanding's deeper penetration of the meaning of terms can allow the virtue of faith to judge

---

quiruntur ex parte nostra. Primo quidem ut intellectu penetrentur vel capiantur, et hoc pertinet ad donum intellectus. Secundo autem oportet ut de eis homo habeat iudicium rectum, ut aestimet his esse inhaerendum et ab eorum oppositis recedendum. Hoc igitur iudicium, quantum ad res divinas, pertinet ad donum sapientiae; quantum vero ad res creatas, pertinet ad donum scientiae; quantum vero ad applicationem ad singularia opera, pertinet ad donum consilii."

184. John of Saint Thomas, *De donis*, nos. 289–99, 304, 320–23. Many commentators follow John of Saint Thomas on this point, including Ramirez, *Dones del Espíritu Santo*, 185; Joseph Ignatius McGuiness, "The Distinctive Nature of the Gift of Understanding," *Thomist* 3 (1941): 271–74.

185. *ST* II-II, q. 8, a. 6, ad 3: "donum intellectus pertinet ad utramque cognitionem, scilicet speculativam et practicam, non quantum ad iudicium, sed quantum ad apprehensionem."

more firmly. Thus it is not clear that one needs to assign a judgment to the gift itself. Finally, John mentions comparing faith doctrines and external appearances. But if my previous reading of this theme is correct, then a greater penetration of the doctrines' meaning can suffice to avoid a conflict between faith and appearances. Yet even if an act of comparison (or judgment) were necessary, the gift could supply the right grasp of the terms by which, for example, the virtue of faith could make a comparative judgment. Aquinas does not fully exclude an act of judgment from this gift, but John's reading struggles to account for Aquinas's explicit teaching.

For our purposes the central text on the gift of understanding concerns its operation—in other words, the beatitude that pertains to this gift. Following Augustine, Aquinas assigns a gospel beatitude to each gift. The beatitudes are acts of perfect virtue or of the virtues joined to the gifts.[186] "Blessed are the pure of heart, for they shall see God" refers to the gift of understanding in act. The *Summa* article on this beatitude (question 8, article 7) includes two crucial allusions to the *Mystical Theology*. More than any other text in Aquinas's vast corpus, this article manifests the place of the Areopagite's Moses in Thomas's doctrine of union.

The article begins by recalling that the beatitudes refer to merit and reward. Aquinas alludes to his study of the beatitudes in general in the *Prima Secundae*, which I need to consider briefly in order to surface the significance of Thomas's exposition of the pure of heart. In the *Prima Secundae* he explains that some elements of the gospel beatitudes refer to dispositions for future beatitude, while other elements pertain to a certain beginning of beatitude here below. The latter is a reward granted to holy men and women. The beatitudes express dispositions by way of merit.[187] The *Prima Secundae* integrates the merit-reward or disposition-reward distinction with a third category, the removal of obstacles, to posit a triple hierarchy of spiritual progress in relation to the beatitudes. The first three beatitudes, corresponding to the gifts of fear, fortitude, and knowledge, clear away obstacles to our true end. The next two beatitudes, corresponding to the gifts of piety and counsel, refer to progress in the active life, which especially concerns our neigh-

186. *ST* I-II, q. 69, a. 1; II-II, q. 19, a. 12, ad 1.
187. *ST* I-II, q. 69, a. 2c.

bor. The actualized virtues and gifts of the active life dispose or move us to our ultimate beatitude. Those who thirst for justice and show mercy merit the fulfillment of their desire and God's mercy. The next two beatitudes are more complex, for Aquinas divides them into two parts. For example, in the biblical verse "blessed are the pure of heart, for they shall see God," the first half of the phrase (purity) indicates the ordering of the passions caused by the virtues and gifts of the active life, not the gift of understanding. Progress in the active life disposes for contemplation. When the last two beatitudes refer to the contemplative life, they only indicate a reward. The second half of the phrase ("they shall see God") describes the reward attained by the gift of understanding in act. This act involves an imperfect vision of God here below and a perfect vision in glory. The *Prima Secundae* still divides the gifts via the active/contemplative distinction. Also, this part of the *Summa* does not connect merit or disposition to the gifts of understanding and wisdom. Thomas has already limited these gifts' rewards to the saints (here below and in glory).[188] The *Prima Secundae* makes the seven gifts necessary for salvation, but it does not explain how the parts of the beatitudes that correspond to understanding and wisdom in act are realized in spiritual beginners.

The *Secunda Secundae* fills this lacuna by shifting the merit-reward distinction:

two things are contained in the sixth beatitude, as in the other beatitudes: one by mode of merit, namely, purity of heart; another by mode of reward, namely, the vision of God, as was said above. And each pertains to the gift of understanding in some way. For purity is twofold. One is a preamble and a disposition for the vision of God, which is the affect's (*affectus*) purification from disordered affections; and this purity of heart occurs through the virtues and gifts that pertain to the appetitive power. But the other purity of heart is as perfective in view of the divine vision; and this is the purity of mind purified of phantasms and errors, namely, that the things which are proposed about God not be taken by the mode of corporeal phantasms, nor according to heretical perversities. And the gift of understanding brings about this purity.[189]

188. *ST* I-II, q. 68, a. 7c; q. 69, a. 3c & ad 1; Mongillo, "Béatitudes," 380–82.
189. *ST* II-II, q. 8, a. 7c: "in sexta beatitudine, sicut et in aliis, duo continentur: unum per modum meriti, scilicet munditia cordis; aliud per modum praemii, scilicet visio Dei, ut supra dictum est. Et utrumque pertinet aliquo modo ad donum intellectus. Est enim

Thomas then explains the reward linked to the gift of understanding, as we will see. The present passage identifies this gift's mode of merit with purity of heart. The latter now includes two aspects: (1) a spiritual fruit caused by the gifts that order the passions and (rational) appetite (i.e., gifts directly pertaining to the active life) and (2) a spiritual fruit caused by the gift of understanding itself. Aquinas applies Avicenna's model of disposing and perfecting causality to purity of heart. Disposing and perfecting causes can operate simultaneously, for this distinction is primarily ontological, not temporal.

Indeed, Aquinas intends to affirm that these causes can operate simultaneously, for he has altered Augustine's teaching on the beatitudes' interrelation. Since the Latin father matches the first seven beatitudes to the Spirit's gifts, Thomas simultaneously develops Augustine's teaching on the relation between the gifts. In Augustine's *Commentary on the Sermon on the Mount*, the first three beatitudes pertain to a person's full conversion to the gospel, while the next four beatitudes (including purity of heart) pertain to the subsequent quest for wisdom. The chain of beatitudes with their corresponding gifts traces a path of spiritual progress. For Augustine the first three beatitudes and corresponding gifts temporally precede the next four beatitudes and gifts.[190] For the late Aquinas the Spirit actuates the seven gifts or realizes the beatitudes in all who have sanctifying grace. An act of the gift of understanding is needed for salvation.[191] The *Secunda Secundae* does not refuse all hierarchical divisions of the gifts and beatitudes, but it excludes the notion that some gifts are only activated at a higher stage of the spiritual life.

Because Thomas minimizes the function of Augustine's hierarchy for the beatitudes, the dispositive-perfective distinction primarily in-

---

duplex munditia. Una quidem praeambula et dispositiva ad Dei visionem, quae est depuratio affectus ab inordinatis affectionibus; et haec quidem munditia cordis fit per virtutes et dona quae pertinent ad vim appetitivam. Alia vero munditia cordis est quae est quasi completiva respectu visionis divinae; et hoc quidem est munditia mentis depuratae a phantasmatibus et erroribus, ut scilicet ea quae de Deo proponuntur non accipiantur per modum corporalium phantasmatum, nec secundum haereticas perversitates. Et hanc munditiam facit donum intellectus."

190. Augustine, *De Sermone domini in monte libros duos*, ed. Almut Mutzenbecher, CCSL 35 (Turnhout: Brepols, 1967), bk. I, chs. 3.10–4.11; Pinckaers, *The Sources of Christian Ethics*, trans. Mary Thomas Noble (Washington, D.C.: The Catholic University of America Press, 1995), 145–54.

191. *ST* II-II, q. 8, a. 4c & ad 1.

dicates not temporal but ontological priority. Thus the previous text cited refers to the Spirit's work in believers at all levels of sanctifying grace. The actualized gift of understanding presupposes that *some* spiritual progress has occurred with the help of other gifts, such as the gift of piety perfecting the virtue of justice. Here the Spirit assists the rectitude of the "appetitive power" or the will. But the gifts that aid the will's operation in turn need the intellectual gifts: the will's order to the good relies on knowledge of the truth. Thomas argues that the will's rectitude needs the gift of understanding to remain in grace.[192] In other words, without some purity of heart attained by the gift of understanding, the will would go astray. This further confirms that our passage on disposing and perfecting causality signals ontological priority, not temporally distinct stages of the spiritual life. The disposing/perfecting couplet indicates a metaphysical hierarchy of the gifts' effects.

The conviction that contemplative ascent requires progress in the moral virtues is omnipresent in ancient philosophy, patristic theology, and medieval thought. In chapter 1 we saw that Dionysian union presumes such progress. Indeed, Dionysius and Augustine stand behind Thomas's doctrine on the purity of heart that *disposes* for contemplation. But the Latin father's place in Thomas's exposition of *perfected* purity of heart is more ambiguous. Augustine's exposition of the Sermon on the Mount only briefly describes the pure of heart: they see what eye has not seen (referring to the eschatological vision in 1 Cor 2:9) and gaze upon eternal realities.[193] The first blessing pertains to heaven, while the second blessing remains somewhat undefined. As noted earlier, the *Sentences Commentary* links the beatitude of the pure of heart with the Areopagite's exhortation to Timothy on ascent via purification "from errors and phantasms and spiritual forms," paraphrasing the *Mystical Theology*.[194] Such language overlaps with our *Summa* text on purity of heart. The latter adds "heretical perversities," which is close to errors. Thus Dionysius is the most likely source for Thomas's explanation of perfected purity of heart. But how Dionysian is Aquinas's Areopagite?

192. *ST* II-II, q. 8, a. 4c.
193. Augustine, *De Sermone domini*, bk. I, ch. 4.11–12.
194. Aquinas, *III Sent.*, d. 34, q. 1, a. 4c (cited earlier at footnote 161 of the present chapter).

Question 8, article 7 probably alludes to the following passage of the *Mystical Theology:* "And you, dear Timothy, in the earnest exercise of mystical contemplation, abandon all sensation and all intellectual activities, all that is sensed and intelligible, all non-beings and beings."[195] Dionysius presumes that Timothy's "impassioned" part of the soul has been satisfied in its inclination to sensible images by contemplating God in creation and liturgical signs. Also, the "passionless" part of the soul, including the *noūs*, seeks knowledge beyond sensible images, for it can operate without them.[196] As we saw in chapter 1, Dionysius exhorts Timothy to focus on the anagogical sense of Scripture and liturgical signs, a contemplation that seems to dispose him to receive divine light that moves him beyond all names, including negations. Thomas's paraphrase could also refer to a passage a few lines later in the *Mystical Theology*, where Dionysius insists that the book's teaching should be concealed from the uninitiated, for they deny God to be "preeminent to their ungodly phantasies and diverse formations of it."[197] Both the *Sentences Commentary* and *Summa* texts on purity of heart selectively paraphrase the first chapter of the *Mystical Theology*. Aquinas's key terms (phantasms, errors, spiritual forms) match neither Eriugena's nor Sarracenus's translations nor Gallus's paraphrase.[198] Albert's discussion of "ungodly phantasies" in his *Commentary on the Mystical Theology* bears some similarities to our *Summa* text. Albert refers to the "purgation of affect and intellect from errors and concupiscences."[199] But here Albert discusses an active noetic purification that

---

195. *MT* 1.1, p. 142.5–8, 997B–1000A, Jones, 211; Dionysius Areopagita, *Dionysiaca*, 1:567–68: Eriugena: "Tu autem, o amice Timothee, circa mysticas speculationes corroborato itinere et sensus desere, et intellectuales operationes, et sensibilia et invisibilia et omne non ens et ens"; Sarracenus: "Tu autem, o amice Timothee, circa mysticas visiones forti contritione et sensus derelinque, et intellectuales operationes, et omnia sensibilia et intelligibilia, et omnia non existentia et existentia."

196. Roques, *L'univers dionysien*, 235.

197. *MT* 1.2, p. 143.2–3, 1000B, Jones, 212; Dionysius Areopagita, *Dionysiaca*, 1:570: Eriugena: "nihil eam superare dicunt ab ipsis fictarum impietatum et multiformium formationum"; Sarracenus: "nihil ipsam habere dicunt super compositas ab ipsis impias et multiformes formationes."

198. Aquinas composed the *Sent.* and *ST* II-II at the Priory of Saint Jacques in Paris, whose library possessed a manuscript with the *Parisian Corpus Dionysiacum*, including Gallus's *EMT*; see chapter 2 of this work.

199. *SMT*, ch. 1, p. 458.65–66. This passage is part of a disputed question that follows Albert's running commentary. The question's corpus notes that Hierotheus suffers

precedes entry into darkness, a process for which he does not mention the Spirit's gifts. In Thomas letting go of all sensible images becomes the more modest purification from phantasms. The avoidance of theological error is the closest that Aquinas comes to abandoning intelligible objects.

The doctrinal intention behind the *Summa*'s implicit allusion to Dionysius emerges more clearly by a consideration of the human subject being discussed. Unlike Dionysius, who addresses himself to a contemplative advanced in learning, instructing him on the proper reaction to the coming of God's light ("abandon all sensation and all intellectual activities"), Aquinas's exposition on purity of heart refers to the Spirit's work available to all in grace. Avoiding heretical error with the Spirit's help precisely describes the act of the gift of understanding that is necessary for salvation. Purification from phantasms applies to all believers, since Aquinas implies no distinction of subjects for freedom from error and freedom from phantasms.

The new subject of purification calls for a new reading of Timothy's noetic object. First, Thomas's discussion of the pure of heart sidesteps the theme of transcending intelligible objects, the objects of divine naming. The gift of understanding prevents error by a process of remotion, as we saw earlier. Remotion could simply be a matter of crushing the worst doctrinal errors, or whatever is necessary for salvation. Second, Aquinas retains part of the biblical background of the Areopagite's divine names: affirmations and negations are ladders of ascent. For Thomas the pure of heart avoid erroneous interpretations of the mysteries of faith contained in Scripture. Yet the biblical doctrine in question is broader than in Dionysius, for it now pertains not just to God's biblical names but to all of Scripture, especially the *per se* mysteries. Third, the removal of errors leaves standing biblical affirmations: remotions improve our grasp of the affirmations' intelligible content. In this sense ascent to God by the gift of understanding does not end the mind's gaze upon God's positive attributes or other mysteries of faith. Timothy's silent mind almost drops out. Contemplation's object and mode of operation go hand in hand. Fourth, the function of phantasms changes. By the gift of understanding the Spirit acts so "that the things

---

divine things. Albert states that this presupposes not being infected by an affect for illicit things.

proposed about God not be taken by the mode of corporeal phantasms, nor according to heretical perversities." Thomas shifts the focus from the direct object of the mind's gaze and its mode of operating to the intended *noetic content* or doctrine *about* God. By the beatitude of the pure of heart the Spirit removes corporeal or finite modes of being from our way of understanding God's nature and action.[200] Thomas's shift away from an image-free mode of noetic operation recalls that he cannot follow the Dionysian doctrine of *noūs* operating without images, a doctrine presumed in the advice to Timothy. Aquinas refuses to make an exception to the Aristotelian principle that the pilgrim's complete act of understanding must return to phantasms. Even the Spirit's direct action does not overcome the natural mode of knowing proper to an embodied rational being with one substantial form, a being whose form and operation are proportioned to sensible things. Here Aquinas goes beyond Albert, who does not clearly embrace the principle of the intellect's return to phantasms.[201] The Spirit's special motion does not overturn but stretches nature's capacities. Yet Thomas does not differ from Dionysius on this point simply because of his view of the grace-nature relation. For Dionysius the highest knowledge of God is a direct gift, but the distinction between the soul's impassioned and passionless parts builds on the Platonic doctrine that *noūs* can naturally operate without images.[202] Because Aquinas and Dionysius construct their theologies upon different *philosophical* anthropologies, they arrive at different *theologies* of mystical ascent.

The corpus of the present *Summa* text then turns to the reward for the pure of heart, the "vision" of God. Following the *Prima Secundae*, a reward here below refers to the blessing that holy persons attain in the contemplative beatitudes, including the activated gifts of understanding and wisdom.[203] We saw that the *Secunda Secundae* expands this teaching, so that "blessed are the pure of heart" also pertains to merit or preparation for eternal life via the actualized gift of understanding,

---

200. My reading of *ST* II-II, q. 8, a. 7 complements and develops that of Carl N. Still, "'Gifted Knowledge': An Exception to Thomistic Epistemology?" *Thomist* 63 (1999): 173–90.

201. See *DV*, q. 18, a. 5c; *ST* II-II, q. 180, a. 5, ad 2; see also chapter 5 of this volume.

202. See Festugière, *Contemplation et vie*, 112, 123–28; Beierwaltes, *Denken des Einen*, 261–62, 271–72.

203. *ST* I-II, q. 69, a. 2c; a. 3c.

not just via the gifts purifying the affect. But Thomas retains the *Prima Secundae* teaching that the gift of understanding's reward belongs to pilgrim saints (and to those in glory):

the vision of God is twofold. One is perfect, through which God's essence is seen. The other is imperfect, through which, although we do not see what God is, we still see what he is not; and in this life the more perfectly we know God, the more we understand him to exceed whatever is comprehended by the intellect. And each vision of God pertains to the gift of understanding, for the first [vision pertains] to the consummated gift of understanding, as it will be in heaven; but the second [vision pertains] to the imperfect gift of understanding, as it is possessed on the way [by the pilgrim].[204]

This passage closely resembles the *Sentences Commentary* text on the same beatitude, which mentions the *Mystical Theology*.[205] The commentary states that Moses knows God as separated from and above all. The *Summa* mentions knowing "what God is not" and that he exceeds our comprehension. In a way Thomas offers a typical reading of divine naming and the *Mystical Theology:* perfect cognition means knowing God's excellence. But the latter doctrine functions differently in this setting than it does in Thomas's usual comments on the *Mystical Theology*.

The present, quiet appropriation of the *Mystical Theology* moves closer to Dionysius's intention in at least three ways. First, given the context of this passage, Aquinas makes preparatory stages of affective and noetic purification essential to attain maximum knowledge of God. Much error and vice have been removed before the cognition of "what God is not." The purification of the heart is the Spirit's work (1) in the gifts pertaining to the passions and the will, and (2) in the gift of understanding cleansing from error. This, the stage of merit, ontologically and (it seems) temporally precedes the stage of reward.[206] Such preliminary

204. *ST* II-II, q. 8, a. 7c: "duplex est Dei visio. Una quidem perfecta, per quam videtur Dei essentia. Alia vero imperfecta, per quam, etsi non videamus de Deo quid est, videmus tamen quid non est; et tanto in hac vita Deum perfectius cognoscimus quanto magis intelligimus eum excedere quidquid intellectu comprehenditur. Et utraque Dei visio pertinet ad donum intellectus, prima quidem ad donum intellectus consummatum, secundum quod erit in patria; secunda vero ad donum intellectus inchoatum, secundum quod habetur in via."
205. Aquinas, *III Sent.*, d. 35, q. 2, a. 2, qla. 2c (cited earlier in footnote 155 of the present chapter).
206. *ST* I-II, q. 69, a. 1c.

steps are not as evident in Aquinas's expositions of acquired theological knowledge of "what God is not." In his discussion of the pure of heart, Thomas is not obligated to keep the Dionysian progression from purification to the summit, for he often undertakes a selective reading of the *Mystical Theology*. For example, the present passage ignores Moses's separation from the elders. But Thomas chooses to retain the purification-perfection link and to give both an apophatic sense.

Second, the present text presents maximum apophatic cognition as a gift, a key doctrine for Dionysius. Aquinas thus goes beyond Albert's exposition of Moses in his *Commentary on the Mystical Theology*. Albert's commentary neither explicitly nor implicitly links a grace beyond the virtue of faith (animated by charity) with Moses's entry into darkness. Albert's study of the Spirit's gifts in the *Sentences Commentary* makes no mention of Moses. For Dionysius and Aquinas, God directly acts in the mystic's intellect in a new way. Indeed, the *Summa* doctrine of the Spirit's motion in the seven gifts emphasizes our dependence on God's immediate motion far more than does the early Thomas. His mature theology of the gifts, a fruit of his original doctrine of divine action (a teaching built upon Aristotelian, Proclan, and Dionysian sources), enables a fuller integration of a crucial element of Dionysian union. Without Aristotle's *Eudemian Ethics* Aquinas may never have arrived at this doctrinal integration. On this point Thomas becomes more Dionysian partly because he becomes more Aristotelian! He also signals that his previous expositions of the *Mystical Theology* (focusing on acquired metaphysical or theological cognition of "what God is not") do not exhaust the doctrinal signification of the Areopagite's Moses.[207]

Third, because each beatitude's reward belongs to holy men and women, Thomas follows Dionysius as he assigns to a spiritual elite the divinely given cognition of "what God is not" (signified by darkness).[208] Yet within this doctrinal similitude a key difference emerges. For Aquinas the Spirit infuses a knowledge of divine excess in all who have pro-

---

207. William J. Hoye incorrectly excludes an infused cognition of God's *quid non est* from Thomas's thought (Hoye, "Die Vereinigung mit dem gänzlich Unerkannten nach Bonaventura, Nikolaus von Kues und Thomas von Aquin," in Boiadjiev, Kapriev, and Speer, *Dionysius-Rezeption*, 498–504). Similarly, Humbrecht holds that Thomistic negation is an acquired cognition, not a mystical or infused gift; Humbrecht, "Noms divins," 579. Both authors ignore *ST* II-II, q. 8, a. 7.

208. See *ST* I-II, q. 69, a. 2, to which Thomas likely refers at II-II, q. 8, a. 7, ad 3.

gressed much in grace. The Areopagite's mystic must learn how to affirm and negate all divine names before penetrating darkness. Thomas sees the need for purification from erroneous notions about God before coming to know "what God is not," but he does not posit the necessity of understanding all divine names before reaching the summit. For Dionysius, the highest union seems to belong mostly (perhaps exclusively) to bishops and monks, a stance that Thomas does not take up. He considers the contemplative and religious life better dispositions for union than lay life, but he does not place perfection in the Spirit's gifts beyond the reach of the laity. They too can attain the summit of Mt. Sinai, which symbolizes knowing "what God is not." The Spirit's motion is not directly linked with theological study. Also, since grace constitutes the mystic, Aquinas goes beyond the early Cologne Albert's mysticism for theologians.

Thomas's exposition of knowing "what God is not" by the gift of understanding also bears similarities to Albert's Dionysianism. First, Thomas holds that knowledge of divine excess via remotion remains bound to positive cognition. As we saw in chapter 7 and earlier in this chapter, Thomas's theology of divine naming presents the *triplex via* as a whole wherein no part stands on its own. The *Summa* treatment of the Spirit's gifts does not alter this stance. Indeed, our *Summa* passage on the sixth beatitude links remotion with divine excess or excellence. The latter category has a consistently kataphatic sense in Aquinas, a sense that the article cited earlier reinforces by referring to a lack of comprehension (rather than "not knowing" or "ignorance"). The gift of understanding elevates our cognition of God's transcendence, a knowledge linked to the positive noetic content received in faith. As we saw, Aquinas centers the operation of this gift on the proper grasp of the mysteries of faith—on the hidden realities signified by revelation. He closely links the theme of remotion with our Spirit-led grasp of *per se* mysteries such as the Trinity and the incarnation.[209] Thomas does not separate the penetration of these mysteries from the pilgrim's beatitude of seeing God imperfectly—that is, the Spirit-induced remotions depend on revealed affirmations (transmitted in Scripture and tradition). Thomas's mystic leaves behind neither revelation's nor philosophy's positive divine names. Rather, the Spirit corrects errone-

209. *ST* II-II, q. 8, a. 2c.

ous ways of understanding such names. In Aquinas's noetics, fully transcending affirmations would literally mean knowing nothing, which Dionysian silence does not signify. Like Albert, Aquinas refuses to link Moses in darkness with rapture, an eschatological vision that Dionysius does not intend for Moses. Thomas also seems to exclude the infusion of intelligible species from the gift of understanding. Such an infusion probably could not account for perfect cognition, as it would in turn require remotions. This may explain why Thomas does not appropriate Albert's notion that the gift of understanding manifests the angels' beatitude via infused similitudes.[210] In his *Sentences Commentary* Albert posits a kataphatic knowledge for the gift of understanding that would still require remotion and would thus precede perfection. This point is crucial: for Aquinas the perfect cognition of God and "what he is not" does not leave behind the contemplation of divine attributes and their corresponding affirmative names partly because Thomas refuses to transcend the Word of God's intelligible content. This does not mean that the mystic's consciousness should never turn away from Scripture's words. Rather, it signifies that the Spirit's light constitutes a refinement of faith cognition whose noetic content depends on Scripture and tradition. The Spirit's motion recalls that no biblically (and otherwise) transmitted revelation exhausts the divine mystery, for God is greater than anything we can comprehend by revelation or by reason. By the Spirit's *instinct*, holy men and women grasp that the divine reality signified radically differs from the human mode of knowing and signifying: the gift of understanding functions like the immediate grasp of first principles. On the one hand, Thomas's approach to the gift of understanding seems more apophatic than Albert's, for no new positive manifestations of invisible realities come by this gift. On the other hand, remotions also strengthen our grasp of revelation's positive doctrine. Thomas's reading of knowing "what God is not" is more kataphatic than the Areopagite's, as Aquinas links mystical cognition more closely to revelation. For Dionysius Scripture provides the ladder toward a perfect cognition received *above* the ladder. *For Thomas, Scripture and tradition are like the enfleshed voice of God without which the mystic cannot hear the highest mysteries at all.* The Spirit's action does not replace Scripture (and tradition) but rather fine-tunes our ears to grasp

210. Albertus Magnus, *III Sent.*, d. 35, a. 3c.

its teaching properly. Overall Thomas also better integrates Scripture into the function of the gift of understanding than does Albert, who focuses on new interior effects. Finally, the close relation between union, Scripture, and the articles of faith tightens the link between the soul's mystical ascent and ecclesial mediations. Thus Aquinas's failure to recognize the liturgical setting of Dionysius's theology of union need not entail the separation of mystical theology and liturgy.

Second, like Albert, Thomas links the act of remotion with perfect cognition. For Albert the habitually graced believer's *own* practice of remotion directly effects entry into darkness. For Thomas the Spirit's *infused* remotions directly cause the cognition that God exceeds our cognitive capacities. He specifies that this concerns apprehension. Several of Albert's and Thomas's comments on Dionysius include the combination of remotion, perfect cognition, and a recognition of the infinite gap between the divine reality and our comprehension thereof. Like his teacher, Aquinas relates the language of *quid non est* to knowing that God is beyond whatever we can comprehend. As noted earlier, perfectly knowing "what God is not" involves correctly grasping any of God's attributes accessible by reason *and* revelation.[211] Such cognition goes beyond the realization that we cannot comprehend God.

Third, like Albert, Thomas quietly includes the act of the virtue of faith in mystical darkness. In chapter 6 I noted that Thomas posits the Spirit's gifts (the *habitus*) as enabling a synergy of the Spirit's motion and the virtues. Hence the beatitude of seeing God entails receptivity to the Spirit in the moment of his coming and subsequent, docile cooperation through the act of faith. Consequently, Thomas's dark cloud does not represent a state of pure passivity. In fact the language of passivity is absent from the *Summa* study of the gift of understanding. Instead the Spirit grants a direct perception of the distance between one aspect of the divine mystery (e.g., God's truth) and our comprehension thereof, though Aquinas barely describes how this perception occurs. To synthesize the implied consequences of his teaching, the Spirit elevates the intellect's first act (apprehension), thus assisting a correct judgment of "what God is not." A Spirit-induced apprehension does not grant a positive vision, but a quasi-intuitive insight about God's grandeur. Since the theological virtues operate with the Spirit's motion

---

211. See my analysis of *ST* I, q. 12, a. 13, ad 1 in this chapter's second section.

in the gifts, we can account for the completion of the act of remotion by the judgment of faith, though Aquinas does not explicitly limit the judgment that follows the gift of understanding's apprehension to the virtue of faith. In chapter 6 we saw that the act of belief is primarily a judgment. By the gift of understanding faith's remotions become ever more certain, yet without exhausting the divine mystery. Like Albert, Aquinas mostly ignores Dionysian silence: the human intellect remains active in darkness, although the Spirit initiates its act of remotion. This reinsertion of human noetic activity into the dark cloud is not a scholastic invention, for it begins with John of Scythopolis.[212]

Fourth, since the actualized gift of understanding grants a cognition whose intelligibility depends on revealed affirmations, and since the Spirit's gifts assist but do not replace the virtues' operations, the gift of understanding does not involve a metaconceptual type of knowledge. The latter doctrine stands in harmony with Albert's *Commentary on the Mystical Theology*. For Aquinas all of revelation transmits noetic content that relies on concepts and images for its human appropriation. Since the gift of understanding does not leave Scripture and tradition behind, it does not transcend the mode of cognition proper to their reception. Rather, the Spirit manifests the limits of the attributes predicated of God insofar as we conceptualize them (e.g., finite wisdom) and corrects errors as we predicate various perfections of God. For Thomas any new knowledge attained in this life demands at least the *use* of concepts or intelligible forms, whether previously acquired, newly acquired, or infused. We have seen that purity of heart involves refining the use of phantasms, not their suppression in the intellect's operation. Indeed, if the Spirit does not cause an image-free noetic mode of operation in the contemplation of God (excepting rapture), then all the more reason for him not to induce a concept-free noetic act. This does not mean that the Spirit must always work *directly* through concepts to teach us (e.g., removing imperfections), as we will see in the next section of this chapter. It does mean that a *human understanding* caused by the Spirit's motion always *involves* finite intelligible forms. The Spirit perfects our use of concepts (and thus of judgments that employ them) as we ponder the divine mystery.[213] This helps to explain why Aquinas considers the

---

212. *PDN*, ch. 2, 120; ch. 4, 122.
213. Like Maritain, *Distinguish to Unite*, 688–93, Journet reads the gift of under-

beatitude of seeing God a complex knowledge: we know more fully that God is beyond our comprehension. This judgment is the fruit of the gift of understanding, either by itself or (more likely) working together with the virtue of faith. The highest vision of God in this life includes knowing (1) something about God's excellence, (2) our limited mode of cognition, and (3) the distance between them. The Areopagite's mystic ponders neither his own limitations nor his distance from God, but God alone. We saw Thomas modify other Dionysian union texts to include such a complex noetic act, but in reference to acquired knowledge.[214] Now he posits the dark cloud (knowing "what God is not") as a symbol of Spirit-actuated mystical ascent, but he refuses or skips the Dionysian rupture between concept-bound cognition and the invasion of God's light.

My reading of the gift of understanding finds confirmation in Aquinas's trinitarian anthropology, which demands nothing less than concept-bound cognition for the pilgrim's highest knowledge of God. The *imago* reaches perfection via *created* operations that imitate the eternal processions of Word and love. In chapter 5 I noted that imaging the Son involves actually producing an interior word (by which one knows God), which word is a definition or a complete enunciation. The latter is the fruit of concepts and judgments. The doctrine of the *imago* makes no exception to this principle. Rather, the central *imago* theme of imitating the triune life shows that the principle of human cooperation applies at all levels of grace. From Thomas's perspective pure passivity in the presence of divine light would entail the absence of the Word's image. Albert's *Commentary on the Mystical Theology* already transforms Dionysian darkness in this direction by invoking the *imago*. Aquinas's original theology of the interior word as the term of a noetic procession adds doctrinal depth to Albert's insight: the Spirit's act in the gift of understanding shows the limitations of concepts, yet this very manifestation involves cognition that uses concepts and in turn enables a firmer judgment, hence the production of an interior word.

---

standing (and wisdom) as causing knowledge that takes away all concepts; Journet, *Connaissance*, 116–18, 138. But Ambroise Gardeil posits concept-bound cognition for the gift of understanding; Gardeil, *Structure de l'âme*, 2:161–64. For a good critique of Maritain on this point, see Charles Morerod, "La mystique dans l'épistémologie de Jacques Maritain," *Nova et Vetera* (French ed.) 83 (2008): 121–50.

214. See *DDN*, ch. 1, lect. 3, no. 83; *SLC*, proposition 6, p. 43.3–16 (on *MT* 1.3).

The Areopagite's transconceptual mysticism continues a longstanding Platonic tradition. Aquinas's reinsertion of intelligible forms at the contemplative summit partly involves an Aristotelian-Augustinian trinitarian modification of Platonic anthropology.

Fifth, like Albert, Aquinas sees a close link between union, Moses in darkness, and the perfection of faith. But Thomas arrives at this triple connection by a different path. The Spirit's motion in the gift of understanding increases union insofar as it causes a higher act of faith. As we saw in chapter 6, faith's operation effects noetic union with God. The actuated gift of understanding constitutes the appropriate crowning of faith, for as we saw in Aquinas's *Commentary on the Divine Names*, union beyond mind occurs through faith. The link between Moses in darkness and union beyond mind is evident in the *Mystical Theology*. Thus the connection between Moses in darkness and the gift of understanding harmonizes perfectly with the *Commentary on the Divine Names'* teaching on cognitive union above mind, on union by faith beyond reason. Now, the *Summa* study of the gift of understanding never uses the phrase "union beyond mind," perhaps because Aquinas feels ill at ease with such language. Still, there remains a doctrinal link between them, for his theology of the gift of understanding and the commentary's discussion of union beyond mind both center on the graced knowledge of revelation.[215] Also, the gift of understanding, which the *Commentary on the Divine Names* never mentions, partly enables Aquinas to read union beyond mind in a way that is closer to Dionysius's intention, for this gift integrates the Spirit's direct illumination as a cause of faith's perfect union. As a *habitus* the gift of understanding directly disposes for the Spirit's motion and thus also disposes for greater noetic union. The Spirit's operation moves the virtue of faith toward a new cognitive union. Faith's operation always presupposes an existing ontological assimilation to the Son (via his visible and invisible missions) and the divine act that moves in every created act as its primary cause. Still, an increase of faith does not sanctify by itself, but only if formed by charity. Hence union through faith requires the gift of charity and thus an invisible sending of the Spirit, whose coming is inseparable from the mission of the Son and his noetic light. Of course, the Spirit's motion in the gift of understanding can be simultaneous with a

---

215. See *DDN*, ch. 1, lect. 1, nos. 6–8; lect. 2, no. 44; ch. 2, lect. 4, no. 173.

new gift of charity and so involve a double mission. But Thomas distinguishes between the Spirit's motion linked to the dark cloud and a new *divinizing* union, two elements that Dionysius joins.

The mature Aquinas's theology of the gift of understanding takes several important steps toward the Dionysian doctrine of union, sometimes well beyond Albert, though without ever renouncing his own doctrinal convictions that stand in tension with the Areopagite. Yet Thomas only completes his appropriation of Dionysian mysticism in his teaching on the gift of wisdom.

THE GIFT OF WISDOM AND HIEROTHEUS IN THOMAS

For Thomas the gift of wisdom offers crucial aid on the path to union. Hierotheus is the prime example of this gift's realization. Aquinas's thought on the gifts in general and on wisdom in particular evolves. The *Summa* offers the most extensive, mature study of wisdom. The *Sentences Commentary* constitutes an important first step in that theology's development. My analysis thus begins with the latter work.[216] I then proceed to Hierotheus in the *Commentary on the Divine Names* and the gift of wisdom in the *Summa*. I conclude by comparing Aquinas's theology of the gift of wisdom to the mysticism of Dionysius, Albert, and Bonaventure.

The *Sentences Commentary* offers some key remarks on Hierotheus and wisdom before its main article on this gift. First, in the section on Christ's psychology, Aquinas notes that the term "passion" can (improperly) apply to the intellective appetite (i.e., the will) more than to the intellect. A thing moves the intellect according to the thing's mode of presence to it, but the will is moved by the good as it exists in the thing. Thus Hierotheus learned divine things by suffering them, for he came to understand divine things by "affect" for them.[217] Aquinas para-

216. Thomas's *Expositio super Isaiam*, ch. 11, pp. 79.103–80.195, adds nothing to the *Sent.* on wisdom.
217. Aquinas, *III Sent.*, d. 15, q. 2, a. 1, qla. 2c, 486: "Unde magis recipit anima a re secundum affectum, et vehementius movetur quam secundum intellectum. Et sic dicit Dionysius, II cap. *De div. nom.* quod 'Hierotheus <patiendo divina didicit divina,' idest ex affectu circa divina eorum> intellectum devenit." The last phrase could also read: "'ex patiendo divina didicit divina,' quod ex affectu in divina in intellectum devenit."

phrases the Sarracenus translation and explains it with the help of Eriugena's "affective" reading, perhaps as mediated by Albert.[218] But a lacuna remains on the precise mode of the will's motion. For, as we saw in chapter 5, the early Thomas considers love as the beloved's form in which the appetite rests: love is the term of a motion.[219] An infused form bringing repose could account for Hierotheus suffering divine things, but our passage remains ambiguous on this point. The hierarch receives an affective gift before or at the end of the heart's motion to the beloved or both. Love causes or disposes for a new cognition. For now Thomas focuses on the soul receiving a reality more by the will's act than by the intellect's, without mentioning wisdom.

Second, charity's mode of operation is already perfect in this life, so that no gift of the Spirit perfects it.[220] Hence the gift of wisdom as *habitus* essentially pertains to the intellect.

Third, Aquinas distinguishes between the gifts of understanding, knowledge (*scientia*) and wisdom. Wisdom judges by contact with the highest causes; understanding penetrates and knowledge judges in knowing created causes.[221] Like philosophical wisdom, the actualized gift of wisdom judges or orders inferior realities via the cognition of higher principles. For Aristotle the wise are subordinate to no one, for they see the order of all things to their final cause (speculative cognition) and can order their actions and those of others to their proper moral end (practical cognition).[222] By knowing the goal one can judge how to attain it. Thomas draws an analogy between natural and infused wisdom that centers on the common element of knowing ultimate causes. By the Spirit's wisdom someone "united to the highest causes is transformed into their similitude, through the mode by which 'the one who adheres to God is one spirit with him,' 1 Corinthians 6."[223] The

---

218. Dionysius Areopagita, *Dionysiaca*, 1:104: Sarracenus: "non solum discens sed et patiens divina"; Eriugena: "non solum discens sed et affectus divina"; *SDN*, ch. 2, no. 76, p. 92.17–18. For Eriugena, see chapter 2 of this work.

219. See chapter 5 of this volume and Sherwin, *By Knowledge*, 66.

220. Aquinas, *III Sent.*, d. 34, q. 1, a. 1, ad 5; a. 2, ad 1.

221. Aquinas, *III Sent.*, d. 34, q. 1, aa. 2c, 4c.

222. Bernard Montagnes, "Les deux fonctions de la sagesse: Ordonner et juger," *RSPT* 53 (1969): 676–78.

223. Aquinas, *III Sent.*, d. 34, q. 1, a. 2c, 1118: "Sed quod homo illis causis altissimis uniatur transformatus in earum similitudinem, per modum quo 'qui adhaeret Deo, unus spiritus est,' I Cor. VI."

language of "being united" and "transformed" seems to suggest an infused gift, but Aquinas remains vague on this point. The absence of a clear *Sentences Commentary* doctrine of the Spirit's motion in his seven gifts prevents us from going further in our interpretation. The same text then explains that union allows one to judge speculative truths and human acts, though without describing the transition from union to judgment.

Fourth, Aquinas recites the contemporary opinion that wisdom involves a "taste of experience," signaling neither approval nor disagreement. This lacuna is striking, for the language of experience is omnipresent in Bonaventure's *Sentences Commentary* teaching on the gift of wisdom, not to mention the writings of Philip the Chancellor, William of Auxerre, and Thomas Gallus, and Albert's *Sentences Commentary*.[224]

Fifth, the sections on the seven virtues, the Spirit's gifts in general, and the fear of the Lord precede the main article on wisdom, following the order of the Lombard's text. But the main wisdom text comes right after four articles on the active and contemplative life that Thomas adds to the Lombard's structure. The articles on contemplation include two preliminary steps to the theology of wisdom. First, Thomas states that the contemplative act essentially occurs in the intellect but presupposes charity for God, unlike philosophical contemplation. This solution allows Thomas to account for Gregory the Great's teaching, which seems to grant love priority over knowledge in contemplation, though Aquinas goes beyond Gregory, as he makes the intellect the proper subject of the contemplative act.[225] Thomas sets the stage for a theology of the gift of wisdom as a noetic *habitus* that depends on charity. In the second step he describes the contemplative act in one of a variety of ways: (1) as a noetic repose or "gaze" (*intuitus*) in distinction from reason's motion (*consideratio, inquisitio*); (2) as a noetic vision of conclusions, the outcome of the simple gaze upon (first) principles and the act of reasoning that follows it; or (3) a simple vision of truth somewhat like angelic cognition, again in distinction from reason's motion.[226] Now the articles on contemplation do not assign specific parts

224. Aquinas, *III Sent.*, d. 34, q. 1, a. 2c; Bonaventure, *III Sent.*, d. 35, a. 1, qq. 1, 3. See chapter 3 of this work for the other scholastics.

225. Aquinas, *III Sent.*, d. 35, q. 1, a. 2, qla. 3c. For Gregory, see McGinn, *Presence of God*, vol. 2, *Growth of Mysticism*, 55–63.

226. Aquinas, *III Sent.*, d. 35, q. 1, a. 2, qla. 2, sed contra 1–2; qla. 3c and ad 1.

of the contemplative act to various gifts of the Spirit. But the *Sentences Commentary* describes the gift of understanding as apprehending spiritual realities, like the intellect's first act. Thomas states that the gift of wisdom judges what the gift of understanding apprehends.[227] We have already seen the analogy between the gift of understanding and the grasp of first principles. Thus the *Sentences Commentary* does not justify the assignation of an *entire* contemplative act (as repose or *intuitus*) to wisdom *alone*, though the commentary does not fully exclude such an interpretation. In Thomas's explicit teaching, wisdom as judgment completes a cognitive act whose noetic content is grasped by other means, such as the gift of understanding.

The *Sentences Commentary* devotes one article with three "little questions" or sections to the gift of wisdom. The first section accounts for wisdom being numbered among the seven gifts. Wisdom designates a high cognitive sufficiency and the certitude to judge all things. The philosopher has this sufficiency by study, while others can receive it

"by a certain affinity (*affinitatem*) to divine things," as Dionysius says of Hierotheus in chapter 2 of *On the Divine Names*, that "by suffering divine things he learned divine things": and of such things the Apostle says [in] 1 Corinthians 2: "The spiritual person judges all things," and 1 John 2: "The [Spirit's] anointing will teach you about all things."[228]

This is the only *Sentences Commentary* text that links Hierotheus to the gift of wisdom. One could also translate *affinitatem* as "union" or "marriage." Being joined to divine things seems to be the equivalent of suffering them. Like study, such union causes an eminent kind of cognition. Thomas cites Paul to confirm the link between infused wisdom and the act of judging and perhaps also the habitual capacity to judge, for the spiritual person excels in virtue. Paul and the First Letter of John confirm the possibility of an infused learning that, like philosophical wisdom, can extend to all things in its application. But the corpus ends here. The mode of affective union remains unclear: is it habitual or actual? Aquinas does not say.

---

227. Aquinas, *III Sent.*, d. 34, q. 1, a. 4c.
228. Aquinas, *III Sent.*, d. 35, q. 2, a. 1, qla. 1c, 1193: "in quibusdam talis sufficientia accidit 'per quamdam affinitatem ad divina,' sicut dicit Dionysius de Hierotheo in II. cap. *De div. nom.*, quod 'patiendo divina, didicit divina': et de talibus dicit Apostolus, I Cor. II: 'Spiritualis judicat omnia;' et I Ioan. II: 'Unctio docebit vos de omnibus.'"

The same little question's answer to an objection expounds on the difference between faith and infused wisdom. Aquinas draws an important comparison: as the *virtue* of wisdom relates to the knowledge of first principles, ordering and reducing all things to them, so the *gift* of wisdom relates to faith taken as the simple knowledge of the articles of faith. "For the gift of wisdom proceeds to a certain deiform and explicit contemplation of the articles that faith possesses under a certain veil according to the human mode."[229] The contrast between explicit and veiled contemplation comes close to the distinction that Thomas draws in the next article between faith possessing spiritual realities in a veiled manner and the gift of understanding's illumined gaze on the same realities. Now the apprehension-judgment distinction accounts for the difference between the gifts of wisdom and understanding. Aquinas grounds wisdom's cognition in belief holding the articles of faith, implying that wisdom grants a deeper grasp of faith's mysteries. Infused wisdom is really distinct from faith, for its mode of cognition is more direct and Godlike, yet the noetic object is the same. Aquinas might imply a new apprehension by wisdom when he refers to "explicit contemplation," but this seems to eliminate wisdom's distinction from the gift of understanding. The nature of deiform contemplation remains vague. The late Thomas does not describe wisdom in this way.

The second section of our main wisdom text focuses on this gift's noetic objects: divine and created realities. Inferior things are judged via superior things, hence the wise person must know the latter. Divine things are wisdom's principle object. By knowing them the wise person judges all else. Aquinas does not further explain how wisdom knows divine realities.

The article's third little question considers wisdom's subject. Thomas recalls the definition of wisdom as an eminent form of cognition. We attain this knowledge

through a certain union to divine things, to which we are only united by love (*amorem*), that the one who adheres to God may be one spirit with him: 1 Corinthians 6. Hence the Lord also says in John 15 that he revealed the Father's secrets to the disciples, inasmuch as they were friends. And so

229. Aquinas, *III Sent.*, d. 35, q. 2, a. 1, qla. 1, ad 1, 1194: "Procedit enim sapientiae donum ad quamdam deiformem contemplationem et quodammodo explicitam articulorum quos fides sub quodam modo involuto tenet secundum humanum modum."

the gift of wisdom presupposes love (*dilectionem*) as its principle, and thus is in affection. But as to the [gift's] essence, it is in cognition.[230]

Love enables a union that somehow causes wisdom. The phrase "only united by love" refers to an indispensable means to union, not a sufficient means to it (e.g., without faith). Aquinas again links 1 Corinthians 6:17 with wisdom's union to divine things. He probably cites this verse because love is appropriated to the Holy Spirit and because love accounts for the revelation of secrets. As a noetic gift, wisdom accompanies friendship with Christ, because friendship is far from blind love. This gift has its seat in the intellect while its "principle" is located in the heart or the will. But Aquinas barely expands on this doctrine. Does the Spirit move the heart to an act of charity? Does the Spirit (also) directly act on the intellect, perhaps simultaneously with an infused act of charity? Because he still lacks a clear theology of divine action and actual grace, the early Thomas does not tell us what activates wisdom, beyond the affect serving as a moving principle of cognition. Also, the language of connaturality that Aquinas later employs to explain how union elevates judgment, and thus cognition, is absent from his early theology of the gift of wisdom. Overall this theology seems incomplete, especially compared to his late thought.

Thomas's approach to this doctrine bears similarities and differences to Albert's. Both friars make the intellect the proper subject of wisdom. But for Thomas wisdom proceeds from love to knowledge. Albert sees the divine good as wisdom's end without discussing love as a principle. He calls wisdom a distinct light, language that we do not find in Aquinas's *Sentences Commentary*. Thomas found the wisdom-Hierotheus link in Albert. Yet Thomas makes judgment wisdom's primary act, a theme not mentioned in Albert's early doctrine of wisdom.[231]

The young Aquinas mentions the gift of wisdom in two other texts of minor importance. The first text, from the *Commentary on Boethius's "On the Trinity,"* was analyzed earlier. It concerns faith and the gifts of

---

230. Aquinas, *III Sent.*, d. 35, q. 2, a. 1, qla. 3c, 1195: "sapientiae donum eminentiam cognitionis habet, per quamdam unionem ad divina, quibus non unimur nisi per amorem, ut qui adhaeret Deo, sit unus spiritus: I Cor. VI. Unde et Dominus, Ioan. XV, secreta Patris se revelasse discipulis dicit, inquantum amici erant. Et ideo sapientiae donum dilectionem quasi principium praesupponit, et sic in affectione est. Sed quantum ad essentiam in cognitione est."

231. Albertus Magnus, *III Sent.*, d. 35, a. 1 (see chapter 3 of this volume).

understanding and wisdom. Thomas connects cognition of divine eminence as well as a vision of God's greatness to faith and the two gifts. His corpus usually refers illumination language and knowing God's excess not to wisdom but to the gift of understanding. I will come back to this text later.[232] Second, *On Truth* once mentions that Hierotheus's passion is an "affection to divine things" whereby the things of God are manifested, but without further explanation. This text comes close to some *Sentences Commentary* passages.[233]

Aquinas's longest discussion of Hierotheus's union comes in the *Commentary on the Divine Names*. Dionysius speaks of his teacher suffering divine things after recalling the mysterious character of the incarnation and before citing Hierotheus's hymn to Christ. As noted in chapter 1, for Dionysius, Hierotheus (1) received the apostolic writings, (2) rationally reflected on these oracles, (3) was then initiated by the Spirit, and finally (4) enjoyed a "sympathy for" or suffered divine things. Aquinas notes that Hierotheus's doctrines come from the apostles, the study of Scripture, and a "special revelation." The hierarch engaged in a wise, loving exposition of Scripture and discovered its hidden sense.[234] Thomas then explains this special revelation:

The third mode of having [these doctrines] is that he was taught what he said "from some more divine inspiration" than is commonly made to many, "not only learning, but also suffering divine things"—that is, not only receiving the knowledge (*scientia*) of divine things in the intellect, but also by loving, [he] was united to them through affect (*per affectum*). For passion appears to pertain more to appetite than to cognition, for realities known are in the knower according to the knower's mode and not according to the mode of the realities known, but the appetite moves to the realities according to the mode by which they are in themselves, and so in a way he is moved (*afficitur*) to the very realities.[235]

---

232. *BDT,* q. 1, a. 2c, p. 85.118–31 (cited earlier at footnotes 104 and 105 of this chapter).

233. *DV,* q. 26, a. 3, ad 18, p. 759.475–83: "passio illa de qua loquitur Dionysius, nihil est aliud quam affectio ad divina, quae habet magis rationem passionis quam simplex apprehensio, ut ex praedictis patet. Ex ipsa enim divinorum affectione provenit manifestatio eorundem, secundum illud Ioh. XIV: 'Si quis diligit me, diligetur a Patre meo, et ego diligam eum et manifestabo ei me ipsum.'"

234. *DDN,* ch. 2, lect. 4, nos. 189–90.

235. *DDN,* ch. 2, lect. 4, no. 191: "Tertius modus habendi est, quod doctus est ista quae dixit 'ex quadam inspiratione diviniore,' quam communiter fit multis, 'non solum discens, sed et patiens divina,' idest non solum divinorum scientiam in intellectu ac-

The hierarch's inspiration surpasses what we commonly find among those in grace. Thomas implies degrees of inspiration, for Dionysius praises the subtlety of Hierotheus's teaching. Aquinas leaves the door open for less luminous forms of divine instruction. Hierotheus accessed knowledge by assiduous study and union caused by *his* love. Thomas's use of the term *affectum* signals Eriugena's influence, perhaps via Albert. As in the *Sentences Commentary,* Aquinas uses the term to signify an appetite—in this case, the will. Since union is "through affect," God's inspiration seems to be at work here, through the will. Thomas then turns to a discussion of appetitive motion. For Aquinas the term "appetite" can have a generic meaning: it includes the intellective, concupiscible, and irascible appetites.[236] In our passage the discussion of appetite helps the reader to grasp that the affect or will "suffers" divine realities, for the will is more receptive to the reality loved than is the intellect to the reality known. God's inspiration explains how the affect is moved to divine realities in an eminent way. Thomas changes the Dionysian couplet learns-suffers (*mathon-pathon*) to learns-affects (*discens-affectus*). He appeals to Aristotelian anthropology in order to explain the will's priority over the intellect for the immediacy of union. Aquinas changes Dionysian doctrine as he shifts the primary site of union from the intellect to the will, yet without excluding the former. But he does not say if the will's passion involves an intensification of habitual charity, an infused act of love, or both.[237]

Thomas then further explains the link between the will's passion and knowledge:

---

cipiens, sed etiam diligendo, eis unitus est per affectum. Passio enim magis ad appetitum quam ad cognitionem pertinere videtur, quia cognita sunt in cognoscente secundum modum cognoscentis et non secundum modum rerum cognitarum, sed appetitus movet ad res, secundum modum quo in seipsis sunt, et sic ad ipsas res, quodammodo afficitur."

236. On *affectus* signifying will, see *DDN*, ch. 1, lect. 2, no. 49; ch. 4, lect. 1, nos. 279, 283. At *ST* I-II, q. 28, a. 2c, Aquinas uses the terms "appetitive power" and *affectus* interchangeably.

237. As noted in chapter 6 of this volume, the *SCG* (composed shortly before the *DDN*) develops a theology of divine action that can account for an infused act in the soul that respects human freedom. As was mentioned in chapter 5 of this work, Aquinas simultaneously developed a psychology of love as inclination whence follows motion. In *ST* I-II, q. 26, a. 2c, Thomas primarily assigns love (*amor*) and passion to the appetite's inclination, not to its motion.

Now just as someone virtuous, from the *habitus* of virtue that he has in the affect (*in affectu*), is perfected to judge rightly about the things which pertain to that virtue, so one who is moved (*afficitur*) to divine things, divinely receives right judgment about divine things. And therefore he adds that *from compassion to* divine things, that is from the fact that by loving (*diligendo*) divine things he is conjoined to them (if however the union of love must be called compassion, that is to say, as being also a passion), Hierotheus *was perfected,* that is instituted, *to union and faith in them* [divine things], that is, that he be united through the union of faith to the things which he said.[238]

Here the term "affect" may have the generic sense of an appetitive power (e.g., temperance in the concupiscible power disposes for prudential judgment). Thomas compares the virtuous person's habitual capacity for right judgment with Hierotheus's judgment, though without necessarily identifying the latter's inspiration as a *habitus*. In chapter 5 we saw that the *Commentary on the Divine Names* and other mature texts especially present love (*amor*) as a proportion or inclination of the lover's appetite to the beloved. The present passage begins with an allusion to this inclination's fruit in the virtuous person: a rightly ordered appetite (such as the will) facilitates the prudential judgment that identifies the virtuous act in a concrete situation.[239] Similarly, Hierotheus better judges divine things because he has been subject to an affection (*afficitur*). Some interior or exterior influence *moves* him to divine things somewhat as an affect's virtue (e.g., temperance) *inclines* to the good of virtue. Aquinas then integrates the themes of proportion and attraction to the good (enabling virtuous judgment), love (*dilectio*, meaning *amor* with election), and union by love. The *Summa* synthesizes these themes more clearly, but Thomas already indicates a connaturality to divine things without using the term. Love causes union: both occur at

---

238. *DDN*, ch. 2, lect. 4, no. 192: "Sicut autem aliquis virtuosus, ex habitu virtutis quam habet in affectu, perficitur ad recte iudicandum de his quae ad virtutem illam pertinent, ita qui afficitur ad divina, accipit divinitus rectum iudicium de rebus divinis. Et ideo subdit quod *ex compassione ad* divina, idest ex hoc quod diligendo divina coniunctus est eis (si tamen dilectionis unio, compassio dicit debet, idest simul passio), *perfectus est* Hierotheus, idest institutus, *ad unionem et fidem ipsorum,* idest ut eis quae dixit, uniretur per fidei unitionem."

239. Antonio Moreno, "The Nature of St. Thomas's Knowledge 'Per Connaturalitatem,'" *Angelicum* 47 (1970): 51–61.

the same time. Aquinas gives two complementary descriptions of the same reality: an influence enables right judgment, and compassion to divine things via love effects a union that perfects faith. To synthesize this and the previous passage, God's motion received in Hierotheus's will causes loving union with God (the heart's passion), which in turn enables correct judgment on the things of God and a deeper (or perfect) faith in them. The will is the primary, direct subject of God's inspiration. Still, it remains unclear if such infused charity is an intensification of the *habitus* or an infused act, though the analogy with motion seems to imply the latter.

Faith and love intensify Hierotheus's union, which is "*un-teachable*, that is, which cannot be taught by human instruction; *and mystical*, that is, hidden, for it exceeds natural cognition."[240] The explanation of hidden things parallels the typical reading of union beyond mind in the *Commentary on the Divine Names:* grace or faith exceeds what natural reason can know. Like Albert, Thomas adopts a standard patristic definition of the term "mystical" as he expands its meaning beyond the Areopagite's intention. He also posits a strong link between Hierotheus's advanced inspiration and faith's doctrines. As a result the hierarch knows and expresses in a few words the teaching of various revelations. Thomas's exposition of Hierotheus does not mention the gift of wisdom, yet it provides several building blocks for that doctrine.

Aquinas does not refer to the liturgical setting that Dionysius likely invokes. Dionysius later refers to Hierotheus's ecstasy following a (likely) allusion to Mary's dormition.[241] Thomas agrees with the Areopagite that the hierarch's mode of learning cannot be taught, for it is a sheer gift. But Dionysius partly extends this note of incommunicability to the content of the hierarch's learning. The Areopagite's Hierotheus knows what cannot be expressed, though he also passes on inspired wisdom in his hymn about Christ. Thomas does not state that part of this inspired instruction cannot be transmitted. Indeed, Aquinas's Hierotheus engages in the act of right judgment whose fruit is his correct, written doctrine. Given Thomas's reading of the term "mystical," such access to the noetic fruit of the hierarch's union makes sense.

---

240. *DDN*, ch. 2, lect. 4, no. 192: "*indocibilem*, idest quae humano magisterio doceri non potest; *et mysticam*, idest occultam, quia excedit naturalem cognitionem."

241. *DN* 3.2, p. 141.6–12, 681D–84A; see chapter 1 of this work.

Aquinas's exposition of Hierotheus bears similarities to Albert's *Commentary on the Divine Names*. Both mention the hierarch's *affectus* and distinguish it from intellect. Thomas adds the anthropology of passion, the analogy with virtuous inclination, and the theme of judgment. Albert considers *affectus* a passion only in the improper sense. Love's status as a cause of higher knowledge emerges more clearly in Aquinas. Finally, Albert reads *affectio* and divine inspiration as referring to an experience, a term that Thomas's commentary does not use.[242]

Thomas's fullest explanation of the gift of wisdom comes in the *Summa*. Before the *Secunda Secundae*, three passages discuss one or another aspect of this gift. The first text is found in the work's opening question (on sacred doctrine). Aquinas's teaching is familiar: this gift enables a judgment like the virtuous person's judgment by inclination. Wisdom judges divine things, like Paul's "spiritual man" in 1 Corinthians 2:15. Thomas distinguishes the gift of wisdom from sacred doctrine's wisdom acquired by the study of revelation.[243] All of these elements return in the main *Summa* question on the gift of wisdom. The *Prima Pars* later refers to a twofold graced knowledge of God: (1) the revelation of God's secrets—that is, the knowledge received by Scripture, by Scripture as received and interpreted in the church (or tradition), and faith, and (2) an "affective cognition" that produces a love that involves the gift of wisdom. The former is only partly accessible to demons, while the latter remains beyond them. Aquinas may be distinguishing the primacy of faith and public revelation in the first graced cognition from the primacy of charity in the second graced cognition. Or perhaps the term "affective cognition" only refers to the fact that this cognition produces love.[244]

---

242. *SDN*, ch. 2, no. 76, pp. 91.66–68, 92.15–33.
243. *ST* I, q. 1, a. 6, ad 3: "Contingit enim aliquem iudicare uno modo per modum inclinationis, sicut qui habet habitum virtutis, recte iudicat de his quae sunt secundum virtutem agenda, inquantum ad illa inclinatur.... Alio modo per modum cognitionis, sicut aliquis instructus in scientia morali posset iudicare de actibus virtutis, etiam si virtutem non haberet. Primus igitur modus iudicandi de rebus divinis pertinet ad sapientiam quae ponitur donum Spiritus Sancti, secundum illud I Cor. II: 'Spiritualis homo iudicat omnia,' etc. et Dionysius dicit, II cap. *De Div. Nom.:* 'Hierotheus doctus est non solum discens, sed et patiens divina.' Secundus autem modus iudicandi pertinet ad hanc doctrinam, secundum quod per studium habetur, licet eius principia ex revelatione habeantur."
244. *ST* I, q. 64, a. 1c: "Et ista [cognitio veritatis] quae habetur per gratiam, est du-

The *Summa* study of the passions includes one remark on Hierotheus suffering divine things: "the passion of divine things is called [1] affection to divine things, and [2] union to them through love, which, however, occurs without corporeal change."[245] Aquinas seems to equate passion both with affection and with union. But the article's main purpose is to show that a certain "passion" occurs in a purely immaterial way. A more precise treatment of these terms comes in the formal study on the gift of wisdom.

Thomas synthesizes his teaching on this gift in one scholastic question near the end of the *Summa* treatise on charity. He continues his mature method of treating each gift in the study of its corresponding virtue. He treats wisdom together with charity because this virtue is one of this gift's causes in a special way. This makes wisdom a unique gift of the Spirit, for Aquinas does not explicitly make wisdom the perfection of a particular virtue.

The question's first article accounts for Scripture's inclusion of wisdom among the seven gifts. Aquinas returns to the analogy between this gift and Aristotle's wise man judging and ordering all things via the highest cause. Cognition of this cause grants certitude. Following 1 Corinthians 2, by the Spirit, one can judge everything by divine rules, for the Spirit scrutinizes the depths of God. We saw these themes in the early Aquinas. Following the Letter of James, he adds that the gift of wisdom descends from above. Wisdom differs from faith because "faith assents to divine truth according to itself, but the judgment that is according to divine truth pertains to the gift of wisdom. And so the gift of wisdom presupposes faith."[246] Faith and wisdom have diverse functions in relation to the same object. The first assents to God's truth, while the second judges by this truth as it builds on faith's assent. Aquinas may imply that faith's cognition suffices for wisdom to attain

---

plex: una quae est speculativa tantum, sicut cum alicui aliqua secreta divinorum revelantur; alia vero quae est affectiva, producens amorem Dei; et haec proprie pertinet ad donum Sapientiae." Aquinas also refers to "affective cognition" (without mentioning the gift of wisdom) in *ST* II-II, q. 162, a. 3, ad 1 and in *In Ioan.*, ch. 17, lect. 6, no. 2265.

245. *ST* I-II, q. 22, a. 3, ad 1: "passio divinorum ibi dicitur affectio ad divina, et coniunctio ad ipsa per amorem; quod tamen fit sine transmutatione corporali."

246. *ST* II-II, q. 45, a. 1, ad 2: "fides assentit veritati divinae secundum seipsam, sed iudicium quod est secundum veritatem divinam pertinet ad donum sapientiae. Et ideo donum sapientiae praesupponit fidem."

its noetic content, a reading that I will nuance later. Overall he excludes the notion that wisdom operates independently of faith's articles.

The most important *Summa* text on the gift of wisdom concerns its subject. The article begins with the only explicit link between connaturality and this gift in Thomas's entire corpus. He explains that wisdom in general involves correct judgment via divine reasons. One can attain such judgment by the perfect use of reason (acquired philosophical or theological wisdom), or

because of a certain connaturality to the things of which one judges. Just as, concerning what pertains to chastity, one who has learned the moral science rightly judges through the inquisition of reason, but it is through a certain connaturality to them [the things that pertain to chastity] that one who has the *habitus* of chastity rightly judges about them.[247]

As noted in chapter 5, Aquinas equates connaturality with the inclination that the good causes in the appetite.[248] The term "connaturality" comes from Aristotle, for whom it signifies that the end being sought is present to the acting subject by the moral virtue. This virtue in turn assists prudential judgment about the end. For Aquinas acquired virtues such as chastity attain connaturality by the repetition of similar acts. By consistent virtuous acts the chaste person's concupiscible appetite is more inclined to the good of temperance. Beyond repeated acts, love can change an appetite's disposition—for example, by infused charity.[249]

Aquinas then fleshes out the distinction between acquired and infused wisdom:

Therefore, it pertains to the wisdom that is an intellectual virtue to have right judgment about divine things from the inquisition of reason; but it pertains to wisdom insofar as it is a gift of the Holy Spirit to have right judgment about them [divine things] according to a certain connaturality to them, as Dionysius says, in chapter 2 of *On the Divine Names*, that Hi-

---

247. *ST* II-II, q. 45, a. 2c: "sapientia importat quandam rectitudinem iudicii ... propter connaturalitatem quandam ad ea de quibus iam est iudicandum. Sicut de his quae ad castitatem pertinent per rationis inquisitionem recte iudicat ille qui didicit scientiam moralem, sed per quandam connaturalitatem ad <ipsa> recte iudicat de eis ille qui habet habitum castitatis."

248. *ST* I-II, q. 23, a. 4c.

249. González Ayesta, *El don de sabiduría*, 164; Moreno, "Nature of St. Thomas's Knowledge," 50–53.

erotheus was perfected in divine things, "not only learning, but also suffering divine things." Now such compassion or connaturality to divine things is brought about through charity, which indeed unites us to God.[250]

Charity leads to connaturality, which is the equivalent of suffering divine things. This suffering enables right judgment about divine things. As noted in chapter 5, the beloved is made present in the lover's appetite in such a way that the lover is carried to the beloved by an inclination, impulse, or connaturality to the beloved.[251] Such language recalls the doctrines of the missions and of the Spirit's personal property.[252] The *habitus* of charity that (as a formal cause) makes God dwell in the soul is a participation in that property. Aquinas accounts for the Spirit's personal property as Love through the similitude of the beloved's imprint in the lover that moves the lover to the beloved. By charity as an inclination believers are led to God and can know him as their proper end, and thus know him as the measure of all things.[253] One must grasp the goal in order to recognize the path that leads to it. Thomas does not say that infused wisdom judges divine things better than does acquired wisdom, though this seems to be implied.[254]

Aquinas contrasts acquired wisdom's motion of reason with the gift of wisdom's connaturality, as each kind of wisdom grounds distinct types of judgment. Thomas concludes: "Hence, the wisdom that is a gift has its cause in the will, namely in charity; but it has its essence in the intellect, whose act is to judge rightly."[255] This judgment is spon-

250. *ST* II-II, q. 45, a. 2c: "Sic ergo circa res divinas ex rationis inquisitione rectum iudicium habere pertinet ad sapientiam quae est virtus intellectualis; sed rectum iudicium habere de eis secundum quandam connaturalitatem ad ipsas pertinet ad sapientiam secundum quod donum est Spiritus Sancti, sicut Dionysius dicit, in II cap. *de Div. Nom.*, quod Hierotheus est perfectus in divinis 'non solum discens, sed et patiens divina.' Huiusmodi autem compassio sive connaturalitas ad res divinas fit per caritatem, quae quidem unit nos Deo."

251. *SCG* IV, ch. 19, nos. 3566–67; *DDN*, ch. 4, lect. 9, no. 401 (cited at footnote 74 in chapter 5 of this work).

252. One source for the doctrine of connaturality is Aquinas's original pneumatology, the context in which he develops the notion of love as an inclination to the beloved; Emery, *Trinitarian Theology*, 62–69, 225–33.

253. *ST* I, q. 37, a. 1; II-II, q. 26, a. 1; González Ayesta, *El don de sabiduría*, 156, 166–67.

254. See Horst, *Gaben*, 137–38.

255. *ST* II-II, q. 45, a. 2c: "Sic ergo sapientia quae est donum causam quidem habet in voluntate, scilicet caritatem; sed essentiam habet in intellectu, cuius actus est recte iudicare."

taneous in that it does not proceed *solely* from deductive or practical reasoning, though the gift need not *exclude* rational reflection on the proper means to the end as a disposition or aid for inspired wise judgment. Charity accounts for connaturality, but one needs the intellect to account for cognition of the end made present by charity.[256] Since the gift of wisdom's operation consists in judgment, the intellect must be its proper seat. Because it is a noetic act, perhaps wisdom perfects the virtue of faith, though Thomas does not say.

Thomas does not here explicate which charity causes right judgment: is it only habitual or also actual? If it includes the latter, need this be an infused act of love? This textual lacuna has made possible an interpretive tradition that posits a twofold action of the Spirit in wisdom: he simultaneously inflames the will and illumines the intellect—that is, he moves both faculties to operate. This argument rests on a hermeneutic that reads Aquinas's theology of wisdom with the lens of some modern mystical authors: one first identifies wisdom as the summit of the spiritual life and then concludes that this gift's operation must include an act of charity.[257] Some scholars in this tradition also apply the model of operating grace to the Spirit's motion in the gifts to argue that wisdom's connaturality primarily pertains to an infused act of charity.[258] This also brings us back to Labourdette's claim that actual charity accompanies all seven gifts' operations.

Aquinas provides clues that point to a different reading. First, his psychology of love consistently presents connaturality as an inclination; hence the term's use in the last passage cited may well suggest a reference to habitual charity. Second, as noted in chapter 6, the gifts' status as aids to the theological virtues implies active human cooperation with the Spirit. This clashes with the model of operative grace for the gifts, a model that Thomas explicitly uses only to explain justification and final perseverance in grace, but not the Spirit's motion in his gifts.[259] Third, also in chapter 6, I argued (against Labourdette) that ac-

---

256. González Ayesta, *El don de sabiduría*, 156, 166; de Andia, "'Pati divina,'" 574.

257. John of Saint Thomas, *De donis*, nos. 197–99; Garrigou-Lagrange, *Christian Perfection*, 308–17.

258. See de Andia, "'Pati divina,'" 571–73, who follows Ambroise Gardeil and Labourdette on this point.

259. Marie-Dominique Chenu makes noetic passivity the key to wisdom's contemplation (by suffering divine things), for he reads the gifts' actualization as an operative

tual charity is not necessary for the Spirit's motion in the other gifts, since charity as *habitus* suffices for union with God and so accounts for presence of the acting Spirit. Now Aquinas assigns charity a unique causality for the gift of wisdom in distinction from the other gifts. But this need not imply that charity must be in act when the Spirit moves us to judge wisely. Rather, charity *as an inclination* to divine things uniquely grounds wisdom as a form of judgment, and inclination primarily means *habitus*. Fourth, the actualized gifts of understanding and wisdom in their eminent form of the beatitudes' rewards are realized in the pilgrim saints, but the gifts still function as aids to the theological virtues. These virtues primarily constitute the summit of the spiritual life, though they operate in maximum harmony with the Spirit. Fifth, the *Summa* makes the following comparison:

> the spiritual person has an inclination from the *habitus* of charity to rightly judge all things according to divine rules, from which [rules] he or she pronounces judgment through the gift of wisdom; just as the just person pronounces judgment from the rules of right (*ius*) through the virtue of prudence.[260]

Wisdom's judgment is analogous to prudential judgment. Each proceeds from distinct rules and is realized by a distinct *habitus* (charity or prudence). Just as the virtue of prudence inclines to sound judgment in human affairs, so the virtue of charity inclines to right judgment on the things of God. The analogy remains limited, yet Aquinas seems to imply that habitual charity suffices for the gift of wisdom in act.[261] No intensification of charity as a *habitus* is implied with the Spirit's motion. One should not exclude the possibility or deny the fittingness of an act of charity accompanying wisdom's operation. Also, char-

---

grace; see Carmelo Giuseppe Conticello, "*De Contemplatione* (Angelicum, 1920): La thèse inédite de doctorat du P. M.-D. Chenu," *RSPT* 75 (1991): 380, 414–16.

260. *ST* II-II, q. 60, a. 1, ad 2: "homo spiritualis ex habitu caritatis habet inclinationem ad recte iudicandum de omnibus secundum regulas divinas, ex quibus iudicium per donum sapientiae pronuntiat; sicut iustus per virtutem prudentiae pronuntiat iudicium ex regulis iuris."

261. This helps to explain why recent commentators do not mention actual charity as an essential component of the gift of wisdom's operation; see González Ayesta, *El don de sabiduría*, 159–67, and Horst, *Gaben*, 131–38. *ST* II-II, q. 45, a. 4c and ad 3 state that the gift of wisdom presupposes charity, but without referring to actual charity or to an augmentation of the *habitus*.

ity needs no extra *habitus* to render it docile to the motion of the Spirit, who can infuse an act of love that we freely accept. But since Aquinas identifies the intellect as the subject of wisdom's *habitus*, and since he only explicitly refers to a motion of the Spirit as moving the intellect's operation, habitual charity probably constitutes the sufficient affective cause for wisdom's act.

The passage on wisdom and prudence allows us to return to a question previously left open: does this gift's noetic content or "divine rules" only consist of the articles of faith?[262] What are the "divine rules" by which wisdom judges? In the passage just cited, habitual charity facilitates judgment according to these rules, but charity does not present the intellect with new rules. Now, the *Summa* question on the gift of wisdom uses the terms "divine reasons" and "divine things" as synonyms for "divine rules"[263]—that is, charity unites the believer to the divine realities by which he or she judges. Affective union's object is the divine truth presented in the articles of faith, but as loved. Charity's unitive inclination to divine things guides the intellect, but this inclination does not inform the mind as do intelligible forms. Nor does Aquinas state that wisdom takes over the operation of receiving intelligible content (i.e., apprehension). Rather, its act involves a judgment.[264] Thus love's inclination facilitates the wise judgment of the realities that faith receives via revelation, the same realities that the gift of understanding apprehends more fully. Charity effects a nonnoetic mode of access to the divine rules or realities that faith already knows. Wisdom actually judges by the Spirit directly moving the intellect. If the Spirit were to enact wisdom only through charity, then the intellect would not need a special *habitus* to dispose it for the Spirit's motion. Now Aquinas does not describe charity as directly grasping or "sensing" God without the intellect or concepts. Rather, wisdom judges according to the articles of faith, which include the principles of right human action. But, to take an example, these articles do not explicate

262. Horst replies in the affirmative; Horst, *Gaben*, 130.
263. *ST* II-II, q. 45, a. 1c: "dicitur sapiens simpliciter, inquantum per regulas divinas omnia potest iudicare"; a. 2c: "sapientia importat quandam rectitudinem iudicii secundum rationes divinas ... circa res divinas ex rationis inquisitione rectum iudicium habere pertinet ad sapientiam quae est virtus intellectualis; sed rectum iudicium habere de eis secundum quandam connaturalitatem"; see also a. 4c.
264. See *ST* II-II, q. 45, a. 2, ad 3.

the virtuous act for every situation. Charity's habitual contact with divine things inclines to what is pleasing to God in concrete situations. The human act inclined by charity is perfected and made certain by the Spirit. His impulse and our connaturality manifest more concretely the things of God revealed in Christ. Infused judgment and (habitual) affective inclination move the intellect to divine things by mode of instinct, always in harmony with faith. Thus the divine rules are the things of God as known (1) by faith and the gift of understanding and (2) by wisdom's judgment as inclined by charity and as moved by the Spirit.

The previous textual analyses facilitate a consideration of the relation between the gift of wisdom and the divine missions. I argued in chapter 6 that living faith (faith joined to charity) accounts for the Son's mission, thus precluding the reduction of this mission's (plural) "gifts of wisdom" to the Spirit's (singular) gift of the same name. Now the Spirit's motion in the gift of wisdom occurs on the foundation of a completed double mission previously realized with the *habitus* of faith and charity. Aquinas uses very similar language for the missions and the Spirit's gift of wisdom.[265] A new double mission (by an intensification of habitual faith and charity) occurring simultaneously with the Spirit's motion in the gift of wisdom would be most fitting. This gift's act need not, but can, accompany a new sending of the Son and the Spirit. Also, the actualized gift of wisdom likely constitutes an eminent fruit of the Son's mission.

Having argued that habitual charity probably accounts for wisdom's connaturality and that Aquinas posits two inseparable modes of access to the divine rules, I can now consider a common interpretation of wisdom's judgment as a metaconceptual experience of God. For one interpretive school this gift's mode of operating either proceeds without distinct concepts or excludes all concepts.[266] This highly affective

265. González Ayesta, *El don de sabiduría*, 124–25.
266. Garrigou-Lagrange, *Christian Perfection*, 316, and Maritain, *Distinguish to Unite*, 259–65, exclude the use of distinct concepts from connatural knowledge. Ambroise Gardeil, "L'expérience mystique: La connaissance expérimentale," 68–73, excludes the use of all concepts. Jean-Hervé Nicolas contrasts "mystical theology" or wisdom's connatural cognition to "notional" or concept-bound theology; see Nicolas, *Dieu connu comme inconnu*, Bibliothèque française de philosophie (Paris: Desclée de Brouwer, 1966), 374–90. But Louis Roy points to the close link between conceptual knowledge

reading of Thomas is closely linked to the stance that wisdom's connaturality necessarily involves an infused act of charity, a claim that goes beyond Aquinas's explicit remarks. Also, one finds the phrase "affective experience" neither in the *Sentences Commentary* study of wisdom nor in the *Summa*'s main question on this gift, nor in the *Commentary on the Divine Names* discussion of suffering divine things. The *Summa* only uses this phrase once, in an article that mentions Hierotheus but not wisdom. Thus it seems that experience is a secondary category for the doctrine of wisdom.[267] Some interpreters equate "suffering divine things" with "experiencing divine things" and elaborate a rich vocabulary of mystical phenomena to explain Aquinas's teaching.[268] But the distinction between the divine missions and the Spirit's gift of wisdom prevents us from easily using the experiential language of the former to explicate the latter. While there are grounds to posit a strong link between Hierotheus and experience in Dionysius, that is not the case for Thomas, whose language about wisdom remains strikingly sober. Perhaps this sobriety follows from his (likely) stance that habitual charity suffices for wisdom's operation. It is probably this habitual charity that causes Hierotheus to suffer divine things.[269] In Aquinas's theology of the missions, habitual charity involves a *disposition for* experiencing the divine persons sent while actual experience is available through acts of love "spirated" or produced by wisdom. The affective reading of Thomas is partly correct insofar as wisdom's judgment attains the divine rules through charity's connaturality that assists judgment not by producing

---

and mystical experience in Aquinas; see Roy, "Wainwright, Maritain, and Aquinas on Transcendent Experiences," *Thomist* 54 (1990): 671.

267. *ST* II-II, q. 97, a. 2, ad 2: "Alia autem est cognitio divinae voluntatis sive bonitatis affectiva sive experimentalis, dum quis experitur in seipso gustum divinae dulcedinis et complacentiam divinae voluntatis; sicut de Hierotheo dicit Dionysius, II cap. *De Div. Nom.*, quod 'didicit divina ex compassione ad ipsa.'" This is also the only text that connects "tasting divine sweetness" to Hierotheus. Aquinas twice acknowledges that charity (as wisdom's cause) involves a certain "taste" of an unspecified object, following the Latin etymology and Augustine (*III Sent.*, d. 35, q. 2, a. 1, qla. 3, ad 1; *ST* II-II, q. 45, a. 2, ad 1). He also notes that wisdom makes human acts "sweet" (II-II, q. 45, a. 3, ad 3). He never explicitly links the gift of wisdom to tasting God's sweetness.

268. De Andia, "'Pati divina,'" 566–70; McGinn, *Presence of God*, vol. 4, *Harvest of Mysticism*, 34.

269. *ST* II-II, q. 45, a. 2c: "'et patiens divina.' Huiusmodi autem compassio sive connaturalitas ad res divinas fit per caritatem, quae quidem unit nos Deo."

new concepts but by an affective inclination to divine things. Yet Aquinas insists on the inseparability of the articles of faith from wisdom's operation.[270] We only grasp these articles with the help of concepts.[271] Also, as we saw in chapter 5 of this volume, Thomas consistently holds that any properly human noetic act in this life involves intelligible species. The Spirit's motion does not replace but rather incites *our* act of judgment: grace does not destroy nature. To make explicit what Aquinas leaves implicit, the Spirit moves us to employ simultaneously the concept-bound knowledge attained by faith and to judge with the aid of charity's inclination. It seems that only such a reading can account for Thomas's insistence that the gift of wisdom's operation is grounded in the articles of faith. This would explain why Aquinas says nothing about a deliberate or infused silencing of concept-bound noetic activity when the Spirit actualizes judgment. Thus even distinct concepts have a place in wisdom's operation, but wise judgment is not *limited to* deductions from faith premises that we grasp with concepts. This distinction is important, for it shows how Aquinas can account for mystics' frequent inability to express adequately what they have learned via contact with God (an apophatic theme), even as Thomas greatly revalorizes the mystic's cooperation in union and the role of mediations therein. Finally, Thomas's study of wisdom never excludes the use of images from wisdom's operation, as he remains consistent with his anthropology of the unicity of substantial form and the principle of the intellect's return to phantasms to complete its act.[272] Here, too, we find Thomas avoiding noetic passivity and promoting the function of corporeal mediations in contemplative ascent.

As previously noted, wisdom's judgment pertains to theoretical and practical matters:

---

270. Aquinas, *III Sent.*, d. 35, q. 2, a. 1, qla. 1, ad 1 (cited earlier at footnote 229 of this chapter); *ST* II-II, q. 45, a. 1, ad 2 (cited at footnote 246 in this chapter).

271. Maritain, *Distinguish to Unite*, 264–65, holds that wisdom's act does not leave behind faith's conceptual *formulas*, only the *use* of distinct conceptual formulas, a distinction not found in Aquinas; see Morerod, "Mystique," 121–50.

272. Garrigou-Lagrange, *Christian Perfection*, 314–21, excludes the use of sensible images or phantasms from wisdom's act, a reading taken up by Heather McAdam Erb, "'Pati divina': Mystical Union in Aquinas," in *Faith, Scholarship and Culture in the 21st Century*, edited by Alice Ramos and Marie I. George, 88 (Washington, D.C.: The Catholic University of America Press, 2002).

as Augustine says in *On the Trinity* [book] 12, the superior part of reason is assigned to wisdom, but the inferior [part] to science (*scientiae*). Now, as he says in the same book, superior reason directs the mind to "superior reasons," namely the divine [reasons], "both by perceiving and consulting [them]"; indeed, perceiving insofar as divine things are contemplated in themselves; but consulting insofar as one judges about human acts through divine things, by directing human acts through divine rules.²⁷³

Thomas weakens Aristotle's rather firm distinction between speculative and practical judgment with the help of Augustine. Thomas agrees with the Latin father that eternal reasons must guide our actions. But he sidesteps Augustine's more interior, direct ascent to eternal truths, the proper objects of superior reason. Nor does the Latin father limit wisdom's function to judgment: his superior reason attains or receives the higher rules, thanks to God's light. For Augustine, wisdom concerns eternal things, while *scientia* concerns temporal things.²⁷⁴ But Aquinas gives the term "wisdom" a specific sense. The gift of wisdom disposes for a complete cognitive act (as the intellect's second act completes its first act) whose intelligible content especially derives from lower reason or mediated knowledge. Also, Thomas does not posit a temporal hiatus between contemplation and practical judgment.²⁷⁵ This further confirms the inclusion of concept- and image-bound modes of cognition in gifted wisdom's operation.

Aquinas also draws a connection between the gift of wisdom and the charism of wise speech as he argues that the former is given to all in grace:

some obtain wisdom from union to divine things according to diverse grades. For some only obtain right judgment, as much in the contemplation of divine things as also in the ordering of human things accord-

---

273. *ST* II-II, q. 45, a. 3c: "sicut Augustinus dicit in XII *De Trin.*, superior pars rationis sapientiae deputatur, inferior autem scientiae. Superior autem ratio, ut ipse in eodem libro dicit, intendit 'rationibus supernis,' scilicet divinis, 'et conspiciendis et consulendis'; conspiciendis quidem, secundum quod divina in seipsis contemplatur; consulendis autem, secundum quod per divina iudicat de humanis actibus per divinas regulas dirigens actus humanos."

274. Ronald H. Nash, "Wisdom," in Fitzgerald and Cavadini, *Augustine Through the Ages*, 885–87; Basil Studer, *Augustinus "De Trinitate": Eine Einführung* (Munich: Ferdinand Schöningh, 2005), 99.

275. González Ayesta, *El don de sabiduría*, 161; Montagnes, "Deux fonctions," 686.

ing to divine rules, to the extent that this is necessary for salvation. And this [gift] is not lacking to anyone existing without mortal sin by sanctifying grace.... But some receive the gift of wisdom at a higher grade, both as to the contemplation of divine things, inasmuch as they know certain higher mysteries and can manifest them to others; and also as to the direction of human things by divine rules, inasmuch as they can not only order themselves by them [the rules] but also [direct] others. And this grade of wisdom is not common to all having sanctifying grace, but more pertains to charisms, which the Holy Spirit "distributes as he wills," according to 1 Corinthians 12: "To others is given through the Spirit the speech of wisdom," etc.[276]

Aquinas seems to posit two degrees within the gift of wisdom: the first includes whatever is needed for salvation, while the second includes the gift and a charism. Now the *Summa* formally distinguishes between the gift and the charism.[277] The present passage does not claim that only the charism completes the gift of wisdom—that is, the gift's first degree can include all noetic perfections pertaining to wisdom as one of the Spirit's seven gifts, the gifts that perfect the believer.[278] But in building up the church (teaching and directing others), this gift is either (at least in some cases) the necessary though not sufficient condition to grasp and communicate certain great mysteries, or it is the sufficient condition to grasp those mysteries that are fruitfully shared by the charism of wise speech. As such, charisms do not require sanctifying grace, but they function better with that grace. Concerning the

276. *ST* II-II, q. 45, a. 5c: "ex unione ad divina secundum diversos gradus aliqui sapientiam sortiuntur. Quidam enim tantum sortiuntur de recto iudicio, tam in contemplatione divinorum, quam etiam in ordinatione rerum humanarum secundum divinas regulas, quantum est necessarium ad salutem. Et hoc nulli deest sine peccato mortali existenti per gratiam gratum facientem.... Quidam autem altiori gradu <percipiunt> sapientiae donum, et quantum ad contemplationem divinorum, inquantum scilicet altiora quaedam mysteria et cognoscunt et aliis manifestare possunt; et etiam quantum ad directionem humanorum secundum regulas divinas, inquantum possunt secundum eas non solum seipsos, sed etiam alios ordinare. Et iste gradus sapientiae non est communis omnibus habentibus gratiam gratum facientem, sed magis pertinet ad gratias gratis datas, quas Spiritus Sanctus 'distribuit prout vult,' secundum illud I Cor. XII: 'Alii datur per Spiritum sermo sapientiae,' etc." At *III Sent.*, d. 36, a. 3, ad 1, Aquinas notes that wise discourse "completes" the gifts of wisdom and knowledge. But this text remains brief. Indeed, Thomas only develops a complete doctrine of prophecy starting in the *DV*.
277. *ST* I-II, q. 68, a. 5, ad 1.
278. González Ayesta, *El don de sabiduría*, 184–86.

link between wise speech and the knowledge of mysteries, the preface to the *Summa* "treatise" on the charisms states that prophetic revelation for "the perfect" extends to divine things, including higher mysteries, and that this pertains to wisdom. The charism of wise speech generally enables one to share prophetic knowledge.[279] Wise discourse presupposes either a reception of prophetic cognition (direct or indirect) or the gift of wisdom's insight or both. Like the seven gifts, the charisms' operations depend on the Spirit's gratuitous motion. In the previous passage, Aquinas may be referring to knowledge of great mysteries attained jointly by the gift of wisdom and a prophetic charism.[280] The knowledge of hidden mysteries is precisely for the sake of building up the church. In the very moment that Aquinas sketches the summit of infused wisdom granted to individuals, he reintroduces a communal element.[281] Also, if Thomas here alludes to the presence of prophetic cognition assisting wise speech, he invokes a type of knowledge that can include infused intelligible species, phantasms, or an inspired judgment on the intelligible content communicated thereby. Judgment remains the gift of wisdom's proper act. Finally, this gift's link with charismatic speech points to a connection between the gift's summit and special manifestations of God that some commentators relate to mystical phenomena.[282]

Aquinas completes his study of this gift by pondering its corresponding beatitude: "Blessed are the peacemakers, they shall be called sons of God." Peacemaking pertains to wisdom, for peace is the "tranquility of order," and ordering is a proper act of wisdom (as judgment). Peacemakers are sons of God, for wisdom's reward is a share in the similitude of the Son.[283] We appropriate charity and God's motion in the gifts to the Spirit, who is personal Love, an affective impulse or principle of motion to the beloved. We appropriate the content of wisdom's

279. *ST* II-II, q. 171, prologue; Torrell, *Recherches*, 210.
280. *SCG* III, ch. 154, nos. 3258–59, link wisdom (understood as the knowledge of God, without explicit reference to the Spirit's gift) to prophetic revelation, while no. 3276 seems to link the charism of wise speech to both wisdom and revelation; see also *BDT*, q. 1, a. 2c (cited at footnote 105 of the present chapter).
281. Joachim de Fiore may well have been in Thomas's mind; Horst, *Gaben*, 142.
282. González Ayesta, *El don de sabiduría*, 186–88 refers to Garrigou-Lagrange and Maritain.
283. *ST* II-II, q. 45, a. 6c.

operation (the inspired human act of judging well) to the Son as the exemplar cause.

My analysis of the gift of wisdom entails a key doctrinal consequence. Since Thomas probably makes habitual charity the affective co-cause of wisdom's operation, the latter likely does not require a new or greater affective, actual union with God. In wisdom the Spirit heightens noetic union, but not necessarily the union of love. Wisdom's new cognition can in turn move the believer to a new or more intense act of charity, as wisdom presents the will with an "object." Wisdom powerfully disposes for perfect union, but Aquinas insists that the latter comes by actual charity.[284] Now the gift's operation becomes more efficacious with growth in charity (and union), since this intensifies love's habitual inclination, which is the co-cause of gifted wisdom's act. The doctrine of the *imago* recalls that perfect love proceeds from the inner word formed about God (the object known), so that charity grows together with faith cognition. Since charity bursts forth from graced knowledge, the gift of wisdom becomes a crucial help on the path to perfection. But if habitual charity suffices for wisdom's operation, then in and of itself this operation does not constitute the summit of the spiritual life. Aquinas's preferred mystic is neither Hierotheus nor Moses in darkness, but the apostle John, who exemplifies friendship with Christ as he rests his head on Jesus' bosom.[285] Only when an act of charity accompanies the Spirit's motion in wisdom can the latter realize the perfect term of the missions here below. This is crucial: the theological virtues' acts and especially that of charity take full precedence in Thomas's mysticism.

Aquinas's theology of wisdom and his interpretation of Hierotheus appropriate and transform the Areopagite's mystical doctrine. First, Thomas takes part in the "affective hermeneutic" of suffering divine things that begins with Eriugena's translation. Dionysius does not mention love in his discussion of suffering divine things, though ecstatic love always stands in the background of Dionysian mystical ascent as its essential motor. Second, despite the earlier emphasis on the will and passion, the *Summa* agrees with Dionysius that knowledge is the main

---

284. *ST* II-II, q. 184, a. 2c.
285. *In Ioan.*, ch. 13, lect. 4, no. 1804. The gift of understanding (represented by Moses in darkness) directly perfects faith, not charity.

fruit of Hierotheus's divine encounter. Both theologians posit a direct divine illumination for Hierotheus. Third, Thomas does not recognize the liturgical allusions in the passages on Hierotheus. The Areopagite's Hierotheus attains union by presiding at the Eucharist, like Moses on Mt. Sinai. Instead, Aquinas sees him as the model of a gift available to all believers. As in his exposition of the Areopagite's Moses, Thomas universalizes gifts that Dionysius seems to restrict to the clergy or a learned spiritual elite. All who are in grace possess the gift of wisdom (as *habitus*) and sooner or later enjoy the Spirit's motion to which this gift disposes. Fourth, Thomas grants God's motion absolute priority in the gift of wisdom, an act that must be received with docility, a *partial* parallel to Dionysian passivity in union. But the Spirit's motion enacts *our* operation of judgment, which reintroduces active human cooperation. Thomas's theology of the gifts implies that mystical ascent is a double spiral of greater docility and active spontaneity: the gift's actualization elevates the virtues as *habitus* and their acts. Fifth, as in his treatment of union beyond mind in the *Divine Names* and his teaching on the gift of understanding, Aquinas quietly makes Hierotheus's illumined wisdom a concept-bound cognition. This is precisely what we would expect given Thomas's theology of the *imago* and his overall anthropology. A complete act of cognition imitating the Word's eternal generation *must* produce a created word, the term of a finite noetic act whose intelligible content depends on abstracted intelligible species (though intelligible species do not suffice to account for the formation of the inner word). Sixth, Aquinas does not grant Hierotheus a purely infused cognition wholly autonomous from (concept-bound) knowledge derived from the physical cosmos, Scripture, and the articles of faith, perhaps partly because the gifted knowledge that pertains to apprehension does not belong to wisdom but to the gift of understanding. The operation of the latter gift attains a remotive cognition, hence the gifts of understanding and wisdom continue to depend on abstracted knowledge in their respective operations, for negation is meaningless without affirmation or positive noetic content, content transmitted by creation, Scripture, and ecclesial mediations. Aquinas's reworking of Dionysian remotion helps to explain his refusal of purely metaconceptual cognition for Hierotheus. Indeed, without cognitive content linked to concepts, Thomas's Hierotheus would have nothing to judge.

Thomas's theology of the gift of wisdom has some similarities to his teacher's. First, Albert's *Sentences Commentary* implies that wisdom's act involves some direct divine operation in the intellect, though he barely precises this mode of operation. On this point both friars stay close to the Dionysian insistence on God's direct action in Hierotheus's intellect. Second, Thomas and Albert primarily locate wisdom in the intellect. Both rule out a gift of the Spirit directly assisting charity because of its grandeur. For Albert the gift of wisdom causes noetic repose in the sweetness of God's truth and goodness, while the gift of understanding causes noetic motion toward these divine objects, a distinction not found in Aquinas. Also, Albert says nothing on connaturality or judgment, two key themes for Thomas. Third, Albert presents wisdom's cognition as mediated by newly infused similitudes of divine truth and goodness, yet without adding further precision. In Aquinas the *habitus* of wisdom as a disposition to the Spirit's motion, habitual charity's inclination, and the Spirit's stimulation of an act of judgment seem to replace these similitudes. Albert's infused similitudes likely function as contemplative objects that one beholds interiorly. Thomas links wisdom's act with a divine noetic motion that facilitates judgment on divine realities that revelation makes known (especially the articles of faith it contains and that are accessible to all believers) and to which charity's connaturality inclines. As in his theology of the gift of understanding, Aquinas revalorizes the place of revelation and downplays the function of infused noetic content, in contrast to Albert.

Finally, Thomas does not mention Gallus's doctrine, but we can compare Aquinas to the Victorine's disciple, Bonaventure. The latter's *Sentences Commentary* locates the gift of wisdom's operation at the height of mystical ascent. For the friar minor, wisdom is a *habitus* that directly assists charity. Its act starts in cognition and attains perfection in love. Wisdom's disposing cognitive act comes by separation and negation more than by affirmation, a stance for which Bonaventure invokes the *Mystical Theology*. The act of charity includes tasting God's sweetness, which the Franciscan calls an experiential cognition of God: tasting *is* knowing. At its peak wisdom also accounts for the saints' experience of ecstasy and rapture.[286] The gift of understanding

---

286. Bonaventure, *III Sent.*, d. 35, a. 1, q. 1, conclusio; Schlosser, *Cognitio*, 187–90, 205.

Dionysian Union in Thomas   437

prepares for wisdom's act. The friar minor posits a hierarchy for the Spirit's gifts. As noted in the last section, Bonaventure invokes Dionysius to argue that affective wisdom passes beyond cognition.[287] In his later *Collations on the Six Days of Creation*, he states that Moses's mind in darkness becomes utterly passive but not empty, for loving union includes an infused noetic light. The condition for its reception is abandoning all cognition derived from the senses, though newly infused knowledge abides.[288]

Aquinas's theology of wisdom contrasts sharply with Bonaventure's. They differ on the gift's function in mystical ascent (an aid on the way vs. the summit), its subject (intellect vs. will), the charity that the gift's operation requires (habitual vs. actual), the use of experiential language (rare vs. frequent), the function of acquired cognition (essential vs. absent), and the intellect's state (cooperating with the Spirit vs. wholly passive in wisdom's consummation). The friar minor closely links Dionysian darkness with wisdom, while Thomas connects this image with the gift of understanding. The Franciscan attributes unitive cognition to directly infused light, though such cognition remains bound to the mediation of interior effects of love and grace.[289] Aquinas holds that charity's inclination linked to wisdom helps guide us to knowledge, but the primary divine effects mediating wisdom's cognition remain those contained in Scripture, tradition, and the cosmos— that is, exterior (and not only interior) effects of grace and nature.

CONCLUSION

Thomas reclassifies the *Divine Names* and the *Mystical Theology* as works of *sacra doctrina* that explain God's biblical names. This change finds

287. Bonaventure, *III Sent.*, d. 35, a. 1, q. 3, ad 5 (cited at footnote 159 earlier in this chapter). Bonaventure links love going beyond reason with the gift of wisdom surpassing the gift of understanding, a link already found in Gallus, *Explanatio super Mystica Theologia*, in *Explanatio in libros Dionysii*, ch. 1, pp. 29.610–30.613.

288. Bonaventure, *Collationes in Hexaëmeron*, in *Opera Omnia*, vol. 5 (Quaracchi: Ex Typographia Collegii S. Bonaventurae, 1891), collatio 2, nos. 29, 31; collatio 20, no. 11; Schlosser, *Cognitio*, 200–1. Bonaventure's notion of unitive cognition parallels key aspects of Gallus's thought; see *EMT*, ch. 1, 710; Coolman, "Medieval Affective Dionysian Tradition," 91–99.

289. Schlosser, *Cognitio*, 194–97.

echoes throughout Thomas's expositions of the Areopagite's union passages, Moses, and Hierotheus.

Aquinas performs a reductive reading of Dionysian noetic silence for several reasons. First, the noetic presence of the Word as revealed in the economy of salvation and received by believers should not cease. A certain (trinitarian) doctrine of revelation entails the mystic's spontaneity. Second, like his teacher, Thomas considers eminent naming an inseparable element of the *triplex via*. God's eminence becomes a way of knowing and naming. Knowing that God is above all no longer impedes union, for as we saw in chapter 5, the *imago* finds its proper perfection in an elevated created imitative act. The unbreakable nature of the *triplex via* thus harmonizes well with a trinitarian anthropology that undergirds the structure of mystical union. The content of the *imago*'s noetic operation seems more Dionysian than (medieval) Augustinian: veiled cognition of God becomes the pilgrim's perfect knowledge. Aquinas has not rejected all elements of apophatism. Thomas also follows Albert as he makes remotions a ladder of ascent to noetic union, a path that assumes the presence of sanctifying grace. But as we saw in the analysis of Thomas's approach to the *Mystical Theology*, Aquinas places less emphasis on the traversal of all negations than does his teacher. Thomas more clearly posits a hierarchy of degrees for the knowledge of "what God is not," a hierarchy structured more by the proper grasp of faith's mysteries surpassing natural reason than by scholastic instruction on the chain of negations. This hierarchy includes Moses's prophetic cognition attained on Mt. Sinai that, due to the mediation of revelation by images and sounds, must be purified with the *triplex via* applied in prophetic judgment. The outer reaches of the dark cloud can be accessed by the philosopher, who enjoys nonsanctifying noetic union with God in knowing "what he is not," an odd Thomasian (partial) parallel to the late Albert's philosophical mysticism. The range of perfections in dark knowledge partly rests on the metaphysics of act: created multiplicity no longer poses an obstacle to union, for finite actualities manifest divine actuality. Yet Thomas's original notion of divine *esse* is partly Dionysian. He changes Dionysius with the Areopagite. Aquinas's kataphatism is partly rooted in Dionysian metaphysics.

The originality of Thomas's Dionysian mysticism emerges most of all in his theology of the Spirit's "intellectual" gifts. Aquinas's Aristotelian (and Dionysian) anthropology reinforces a moderately apophatic approach to the gift of understanding, as he emphasizes remotions and not new interior divine manifestations, in contrast to the Parisian Albert's Augustinian theology of the Spirit's gifts. For the late Aquinas the correct Spirit-guided grasp of faith's mysteries becomes crucial for ascent toward sanctifying noetic union with God. Darkness now symbolizes penetrating the heart of revelation. Dark knowledge involves not just God's timeless light (as in Dionysius) or his essence, but also the incarnation and God's saving acts. Metaphysical theology and the salvific economy together provide the mystic's cognitive object. History has a sure place within dark knowledge. The Spirit's removal of false understandings allows the intelligibility of God's word concretized in human words to shine forth ever more brightly. Infused remotions do not crush affirmations; hence concept-bound cognition retains a place in the dark cloud. Aquinas quietly refuses image-free contemplation as a necessary condition for the summit of union. His teaching on the gift of understanding prolongs and deepens the faith-centered mysticism of his *Commentary on the Divine Names:* the Spirit elevates us by strengthening the virtue of faith. Hence the gift of understanding does not shut down but rather refines our use of concepts concerning God and his works. A virtue-centered theology makes mystical ascent available to all. Thomas assigns the center of the dark cloud to pilgrim saints. Instead of Albert's hierarchy of learning, grace now constitutes the stages of ascent to Mt. Sinai. The unitive state or event no longer pertains primarily to bishops and monks.

Thomas's approach to the gifts of understanding and wisdom rests on the hinge of the apprehension-judgment distinction, which adds considerable precision to the theology of the gifts. After some ambiguity in the *Sentences Commentary,* Aquinas's *Commentary on the Divine Names* shifts the site for God's inspiration of Hierotheus from intellect to affect. Here Thomas builds on his mature Dionysian notion of love. The *Summa* shifts our attention back to intellect: a deliberately chosen or infused act of charity seems unnecessary to account for the act proceeding from the gift of wisdom, which act the Spirit directly incites in the intellect. This act remains closely bound to the truth communicated in the articles of faith. Experience has a secondary function in wisdom. Again, concept-bound cognition remains essential in order to account for the *human* reception of divine illumination. Here the study of the Spirit's gifts in general in chapter 6 bore fruit: as in the theory of the gift of understanding, the theory of gifted wisdom's mode of operation shifts considerably once freed from a necessary link with operative grace, a link that encouraged some commentators to exaggerate the place of mystical passivity in Thomas's thought. Aquinas seamlessly joins (1) the importance of Scripture and tradition as aids for the summit of the pilgrim's divine knowledge with (2) the efficacy of loving union as two necessary yet limited means to unfold the inexhaustible richness contained in revelation. Both means of divine guidance (revelation and charity) joined to the Spirit's direct operation make ascent to the summit possible, even as the gift of wisdom remains an aid toward the summit that is primarily constituted by acts of charity. Finally, the link with wise speech shows that Thomas's theology of the gifts grants a real though restrained place to prophetic charisms.

I close by turning to a key difference in Thomas's, Albert's, and Bonaventure's notions of the Spirit's causal activity in the contemplative gifts, a theme that in turn highlights a crucial element of Aquinas's Dionysianism. As already noted, Albert and the Seraphic doctor present the gifts of understanding and wisdom in terms of formal causality. Albert posits a new knowledge of angelic blessings (for understanding) or similitudes of divine goodness (for wisdom). Bonaventure proposes that the gift of understanding allows for a vision of the eternal reasons or forms of things, while the gift of wisdom grants an experience of God's sweetness through interior effects. Aquinas centers the modality of the gifts' operation on the Spirit's motion or efficient causality, not formal causality. Here the gift of understanding improves the graced act of apprehending faith's mysteries already revealed, while the gift of wisdom better judges according to these mysteries. In Thomas we find neither new infused similitudes, nor interior visions of eternal forms, nor an emphasis on interior graced effects. Because of the focus on the Spirit's motion, Thomas can bring the "external" noetic objects of Scripture and the salvific economy to the center of the gifts' Spirit-induced operation. His original theology of divine action sets up a reformulation of gifted knowledge that emphasizes the immediacy of God's action more than do Albert and Bonaventure, while also recentering mystical ascent on the whole economy, not on an interior world of graces (though neither

Albert nor Bonaventure separates union from the economy). A theology of actual grace that fuses Aristotelian, Proclan, and Dionysian sources helps Aquinas to articulate a mysticism that synthesizes in a fuller way the historic mediations of union and the soul's direct contact with God. Here Thomas seems to articulate a more apophatic vision than Albert and Bonaventure, whose theologies of the gifts add new interior positive manifestations of God. Aquinas's approach to the Spirit's action in the gifts also seems to heighten the soul's intimacy with God at the point of operative contact, whereas Albert's approach to the gifts focuses on new created noetic objects that the intellect can behold. Thomas's minimization of interior effects at the summit of mystical ascent preserves an important side of Dionysian apophatism. His mature theory of divine action brings him even closer to Dionysius, even as Aquinas skips the Dionysian distinction between God's nature and God's light.

General Conclusion

Like John of Scythopolis (with his Plotinian reading of "knowing by unknowing") and Thomas Gallus (with his affective hermeneutic), Albert and Aquinas integrate and extensively transform Dionysian mystical theology. I now consider the major results of the preceding chapters. In particular, I will consider how these chapters confirm my main thesis—namely, that Albert and Thomas interpret Dionysian mysticism in a kataphatic way, emphasize our need for mediations as well as the mystic's active cooperation in union, and posit a trinitarian structure for union, all the while retaining a qualified apophatism, the noetic status of union, and the immediacy of God's conjoining action. Since the end of chapter 4 already reviewed how this thesis applied to Albert, I shall focus more on the chapters that treat Aquinas. In addition, I will briefly compare Thomas's way of developing Dionysius to Albert. I shall also ponder the ways in which past interpretations of Albert's and Thomas's mystical doctrines have been developed or nuanced. I will close by pondering some avenues for future research that may have opened up through the present work.

A SYNTHETIC OVERVIEW

Chapter 1 made no pretensions at originality, but rather summarized the work of patristic scholars. I highlighted the Areopagite's partly Proclan anthropology with its emphasis on the soul's need for the body so as to ascend to the divine, immaterial reality. I noted how such an anthropology connected with a highly structured ascent toward divine light. This ascent traverses liturgical, biblical, and various created mediations.

Dionysius the hierarch guides his disciple up the mystical ladder. The theology of naming was seen to involve (1) affirmations and negations of God's powers or operation in the cosmos and, most of all, (2) transcending negations that point to God's excellence. After passing through all positive and negative names, the mystic transcends all names so as to enter a darkness that is beyond every image and human thought. The mystic can only enter darkness by a divine gift. The setting of union is very liturgical: Moses on Sinai greatly resembles a Syrian-rite bishop celebrating the Eucharist. Moses cannot express what he learns in the dark cloud.

Chapter 2 also mostly integrated existing research. I traced the Dionysian textual tradition and summarized the early expositors' work on union. Various kataphatic interpretive turns were noted, starting with the Areopagite's first Greek commentator. The mingling of translated Greek *scholia* with numerous medieval (especially Eriugenan) Latin glosses produced a rather heterogeneous Parisian textbook on the *Mystical Theology* that required selective appropriation and doctrinal clarification on Albert's and Thomas's part. The two friars' reinsertion of the mind's activity in darkness finds precedents in the Dionysian tradition. I showed why Albert's and Thomas's supposed refusal of Maximos's created-uncreated antinomy never occurred: neither friar could have discerned Maximos's original teaching on divinization hidden in the *Parisian Corpus Dionysiacum*. I traced the emergence of "Affective Dionysianism," a highly influential tradition that sharply contrasts with the historical Dionysius and Dominican Dionysianism.

Chapter 3 inaugurated the truly original part of this study. It proposed a synthesis of Albert's *De homine* and *Sentences Commentary* anthropologies that integrates the themes of the soul's ontology, noetics, and the *imago*. These doctrines have not been treated together up to now, and little attention has been paid to internal evolutions and theoretical tensions among them. As in chapter 4, I offered multiple reasons to read Albert one work at a time, even one treatise at a time, yet without reducing him to an eclectic thinker. Albert's pre-1248 anthropology creatively synthesizes Aristotelian, Peripatetic, and Augustinian sources, but not without tension. Sense experience and the soul's unity with the body (as its single substantial form) are important. However, a notion of the soul as a semi-complete substance that can ascend directly to God following an interior path remains. The latter anthropology tends to deemphasize the need for mediations in contemplative ascent, in contrast to the former anthropology. The doctrine of the *imago* complicates the picture, as several of memory's functions are transferred to the agent intellect. The reduction in memory's function has the potential of limiting the possibilities of interior ascent to the God hidden within, though this depends on how much the agent intellect can do without sense data. The dynamic *imago* that imitates God by its operations is almost absent in Albert's work on the Lombard. I noted the strong Aristotelian tendencies of the *De homine* anthropology, in partial contrast to the *Sentences Commentary*, but in proximity to the Dionysian commentaries.

Chapter 3 located the heart of the Parisian Albert's theology of union in his treatment of the missions, the theological virtues, and the Spirit's seven gifts, but not in his doctrines of the *imago* and divine naming. The theology of the missions emphasizes the mediated status of our *experience* of the divine persons sent. The doctrine of the missions highlights the necessity of God's direct efficient causality for the realization of mystical union. This doctrine underlies all of Albert's subsequent thought on graced union. The study of the theology of the missions in the *Sentences Commentary* thus becomes crucial for a proper evaluation of Albert's Dionysian mysticism. Chapter 3 also showed how Albert's theologies of the missions, grace, and the theological virtues grant a strong priority to human cooperation within union: the Son and the Spirit only come to us with (and in) their created gifts, the very gifts that enable us to make acts of saving knowledge and charity. The invisible coming of the Son and the Spirit also incite us toward those acts. The theme of grace as flux further undergirds the mystic's activity during union: grace flows into the faculties, where it becomes cooperating grace. Albert's approach to sanctifying grace focuses on the dynamic analogy of formal flux, a partly Dionysian notion.

I then worked out a synthetic analysis of the virtue of faith in the *Sentences Commentary* that follows up on the studies by Chenu, Tugwell, and Wéber. Here I offered new precision concerning the relation of intellect, will, and divine causality in the virtue of faith. Albert's account locates this virtue in the intellect, though here the will's role seems almost as important. His description of faith as a simple light bringing us back to the Father sets the stage for a crucial debate on Albert's *Commentary on the Mystical Theology*. The light imagery recalls the partial integration of the Areopagite's theology of unifying light in Albert's doctrine of faith. The German friar also explicates charity via the notion of formal flux. Partly as a result, he makes charity both a formal and secondary efficient cause of union.

I proposed a systematic overview of Albert's notion of the seven gifts in general and of understanding and wisdom in particular. The latter two gifts elevate the theological virtues' perfection. Here I noted Albert's original integration of Hierotheus, his dependence on other scholastics for various categories and doctrinal formulations, and his focus on formal causality to explain the effects of the seven gifts. The gifts of wisdom and understanding bring us to deeper union via interior signs of angelic beatitude and divine sweetness (formality). Here immaterial mediations enable a higher noetic union with God. We thus find an interior path to God, yet one that attains God through created lights. Still, the ontology of the Spirit's action in these higher gifts remains ambiguous: Albert does not clearly posit a mode of divine efficient causality distinct from God's action in sanctifying grace and the virtues. This lacuna prevents him from emphasizing the priority of God's action in union as much as Dionysius does. The same lacuna sets up a strong contrast with Aquinas's mature doctrine of the Spirit's gifts and some elements of Thomas's Dionysianism.

The final sections of chapter 3 treated topics that have received extensive attention in the scholarly literature. Chapter 3 showed how the strong Dionysian mark on Albert's early eschatology and theory of divine naming contains elements for a second, complementary approach to mysticism—that is, an approach somewhat distinct from Albert's mysticism that emerged in the studies on the missions, the virtues, and the Spirit's seven gifts. Albert's eschatology synthesizes Augustinian immediacy and Dionysian theophanies: we see God's essence, but only through the created light of glory. The latter doctrine highlights the radical disproportion between our minds and God's being: this is a subtle form of qualified apophatism. The study of the beatific vision responded to Kurt Flasch on the importance of the grace-nature distinction for Albert: his doctrine of theophanies as the created light of glory will greatly influence Aquinas. In response to Antoine Lévy, I noted Albert's original, far-reaching integration of both Augustinian and Greek eschatologies. The study of divine naming in Albert's *Sentences Commentary* highlighted the kataphatic nature of the *triplex via* (affirmations are never left behind), the lack of connection between naming and union (a sharp contrast to the *Commentary on the Mystical Theology*), and the replacement of Dionysian dialectic by clear distinctions. The insertion of distinctions partly mimics the Greek *scholia*. It reduces the paradoxical nature of the Dionysian text. It shifts the genre of discourse in a way that favors a more transparent, accessible, and thus potentially more kataphatic doctrine. I noted Albert's creative synthesis of proper divine predications and Greek apophatism: we truly can name God's substance (kataphatism), yet some neo-Augustinian theologians fail to emphasize that the same substance exceeds our comprehension (limited apophatism). Overall, Albert's constant drive to integrate multiple, even competing doctrinal traditions became more evident.

Chapter 4 signaled a major, partly Dionysian turn in Albert's Cologne anthropology, but also strong continuity in his understanding of the missions, grace, the theological virtues, and eschatology. The evolution in anthropology revalorizes the importance of material mediations for noetic ascent to God: in this life we only know him with the help of intelligible forms derived from sense experience. The Augustinian theology of memory has gone missing in Albert's Dionysian commentary, as the German friar adopts a more Dionysian notion of "externalized" contemplative ascent. I showed how the Cologne Albert likely shifts away from his earlier doctrine—that of created grace and glory as secondary efficient causes of union. This theological evolution further emphasizes the mystic's need for God's motion. We again find the priority of God's action for union. I noted that Albert's eschatology increasingly emphasizes the soul's operative cooperation in the vision of God as he more fully integrates Aristotle's virtue ethics. His eschatology thus supports a mysticism of active cooperation in union. I signaled the German friar's deemphasis on the Areopagite's structured ascent through distinct stages of contemplation in favor of faith as an elevating noetic light. Faith becomes the main element of ecstasy. This doctrine matches well the implied teaching of Albert that the mystical science begins with the light of faith. The interpretive shift away from a structured contemplative ascent reintegrates Scripture-based knowledge into union. The same shift potentially expands union's accessibility beyond Dionysius's mystical elite, though Albert may set up a different kind of elite. I then nuanced Wéber's arguments on charity and the divine missions as essential background themes for Albert's explication of union passages.

Albert's *Sentences Commentary* theology of naming naturally, yet harmoniously progresses in his Dionysian commentaries. This should not surprise us, given that his earlier doctrine already draws heavily on Dionysius. In the chapter 4 study of analogy we saw a range of highly technical explanations for the *triplex via*, including a few highly apophatic expressions. Several far-reaching modifications to Dionysius stood out, especially on the function of naming and the intelligible content left standing by negations: for Albert, remotions always presume the knowledge of created perfections that affirmations indicate.

The same chapter offered extensive new textual evidence and systematic arguments for Édouard Wéber's and Simon Tugwell's thesis that the mystical science begins by faith and not another special grace. Then an extensive study of union passages in the *Commentary on the Mystical Theology* showed (1) the centrality of the grace-nature distinction in Albert's effort to make sense of union beyond mind, (2) the function of divine similitudes in mystical darkness, and (3) the abiding activity of Moses's mind due to the doctrine of the *imago*. Regarding the second point, Albert's doctrine of created grace (worked out especially in chapter 3) has direct implications for the function of mediations in mystical ascent: we touch God through his created gifts. Regarding the third point, Albert consistently reinserts human noetic activity into the dark cloud, a major reversal of Dionysian doctrine. The cooperative role of the mystic's mind is precisely what one needs in order to posit the simultaneity of naming and union (as Albert does). In the study of Albert's exposition on Moses, little-mentioned teachings such as the *imago* became decisive to make sense of the German friar's claims. Indeed, because the *imago* plays such a capital role in Albert's interpretation of the ascent to Mt. Sinai, his Dionysian doctrine of union integrates a trinitarian structure at its center. I demonstrated how Albert collapses God's place (and its divine similitudes) with Mt. Sinai's summit. I did so by pointing to the German friar's claims about the presence of reflexive thought in darkness and to the close link between similitude-grounded contemplation and Albert's kataphatic way of reading negations. Furthermore, I argued that Albert's reinterpretation of the dark cloud proceeds from several other doctrines considered in earlier sections, such as the divine missions, created grace, and ecstasy by faith. I signaled partial precedents for Albert's exegesis in John of Scythopolis, a link hitherto ignored.

Chapter 4 presented a sustained textual and systematic argument that, for the early Cologne Albert, negations directly effect union. Indeed, negations applied in the life of grace are the immediate cause of mystical ascent. Both the underdeveloped nature of a theology of actual grace in the *Sentences Commentary* and that theology's restrained presence in the Dionysian commentaries help to explain why negations become so crucial. Chapter 4 noted that the primacy of learned negations matches the absence of new noetic graces in Albert's account of the journey up Mt. Sinai. Albert neither affirms nor denies the need for a new, direct divine act in every instance of noetic or affective contact with God. However, given his explicit comments, it is highly likely that, for Albert, the only grace that union in darkness requires is the sanctifying gifts (habitual grace, faith, and charity) linked to the coming of the Son and the Spirit into the minds and hearts of the faithful. This too reinforces the mystic's spontaneity, yet without excluding his essential dependence on God's divinizing action to attain union.

Chapter 4 confirmed and somewhat developed the notion that Albert's Dionysian commentaries propose an "intellectual mysticism." His silence on the gift of wisdom (with its affective dimension) and Hierotheus's insignificant presence in the *Commentary on the Mystical Theology* reinforce the importance of the act of negating, an act whose unitive power presumes the presence of the theological virtues. Love and the already-realized divine missions were seen to undergird Moses's graced ascent to unknowing—that is, Albert hardly excludes love from union or considers love secondary, yet his focus is on the intellect as the subject of union. Just as in Dionysius, love truly remains in the background. According to the early Cologne Albert, deeper union with God comes through acts of negating—that is, through noetic acts.

We found a certain tension between Albert's mysticism of negations and his earlier theology of the Spirit's seven gifts, a tension that has not been noticed before. Albert shifts from a notion of mystical ascent via the Spirit's gifts perfecting the virtues, a grace available for all, to a notion of ascent via a ladder of remotions perfecting the knowledge of faith, a ladder taught by a scholastic science, although without clearly overturning the first notion. The *Sentences Commentary* theory of union by the Spirit's seven gifts remains underdeveloped, for Albert barely explicates the Spirit's mode of operation therein, though the theory partly reposes on a rich theology of union via the invisible coming of the Son and the Spirit.

The surprisingly kataphatic character of Albert's *Commentary on the Mystical Theology* emerged in chapter 4. Albert systematically limits the function of negations. In his most typical and elaborate explanations of the Dionysian text, negations do not clear away created similitudes, but only remove imperfections from God or exclude the possibility of adequate divine manifestations and comprehensive divine names. Albert's espousal of proper affirmative names for God's nature goes well beyond Dionysius. Even negative and eminent names often take on an affirmative role. Albert's exposition alternates between brief glosses that sometimes seem to adopt Dionysius's apophatism and other comments, especially in disputed questions, that tame this apophatism. The German friar once espouses the removal of the reality signified (and not just the mode of signifying) from God, a text that is unrepresentative of his thought. He generally qualifies the discourse of the nameless God. Here close textual analyses proved indispensable. Yet the immense focus on naming God gives Albert's mysticism a potentially elitist tendency: the mystical science's foundation on the light of faith does not suffice to make this science available to all believers. Albert's early Cologne approach to union with God seems especially suited for scholastic theologians, unlike the universalizing orientation of his *Sentences Commentary*.

In the *Commentary on the Mystical Theology*, the importance of negations and the absence of new interior noetic lights within ascent surfaces the importance of Scripture for unitive knowledge. Since the mystical theology is a sacred science, *Scripture*'s divine names are (partly) negated so as to reach union. The key function of Scripture within unifying knowledge and naming has received little attention in Albert studies. The centrality of Scripture in Albert's early Cologne mysticism further emerges in light of his essentially kataphatic approach to union with God, for we never fully leave behind God's revealed names and the intelligible content that they communicate. This role of Scripture also involves a mediation-centered vision of contemplation. Scripture's indispensable role partly makes up for Albert's failure to discern the liturgical allusions in Dionysian union passages: the link between union and ecclesial mediations abides. The doctrinal function of Scripture and other themes confirmed a strict distinction between the philosopher's ascent to knowledge of God and Albert's teaching in the *Commentary on the Mystical Theology*.

The category of experience was shown to be quite secondary in Albert's *Commentary on the Mystical Theology*. Such language is more evident in his Parisian account of the Spirit's seven gifts. Still, as an essential component of the missions, the experience of the divine persons already (or newly) sent remains a possibility for the early Cologne Albert's mystic.

Chapter 4 showed that Albert's theology of union in the Dionysian commentaries displays a higher degree of doctrinal cohesion than does his theology in the *Sentences Commentary*. The earlier tensions between an Augustinian-Peripatetic vision of the human being and a Dionysian approach to divine naming greatly diminish. The most apophatic passages that clash with the majority of the texts on naming can be explained through the limits imposed by the Areopagite's work itself: Albert can only bend Dionysius's words so far. The large majority of Albert's explanations about the *triplex via* display a very high degree of theoretical consistency. Albert's early Cologne anthropology of mediations harmonizes well with the mysticism of the same period: just as Albert insists in a new way on human cognition's need for the senses and ignores the function of Augustinian memory, external mediations such as Scripture gain in importance. As part of his rather synthetic theology in the Dionysian commentaries, Albert's anthropology shifts toward the Areopagite in important ways. The virtual absence of Augustinian memory and the critique of the Latin father's noetics lead the German friar to a reformulated version of Dionysian ascent. The early Albert's anthropology moves on a trajectory that leads to Aquinas (the reductive reading of Augustine's epistemology, the unicity of substantial form), a link hardly acknowledged by scholars. Overall the *Commentary on the Mystical Theology* constitutes a significant evolution in Albert's mystical doctrine, now centered on a ladder of remotions that leads straight into a grey cloud. Here the mystic continues to be active, for he or she continues to name God and to behold him through his gifts of grace and glory.

In chapter 5 we saw how Aquinas develops his anthropology partly by reworking a set of Albertian themes: the creative fusion of Aristotelian and Dionysian noetics and the centrality of a clear grace-nature distinction, as well as the importance of the *imago*. Here Albert's influence on Thomas has hardly been noticed. I signaled the significant function of certain Dionysian formulas in Aquinas's grace-nature distinction. Thomas attains new doctrinal clarity about grace-nature distinction as he builds upon and beyond Albert's thought. Here Aquinas operates a *ressourcement* of Augustine's creation theology: since humanity has the supernatural end of union in glory, God created Adam and Eve in grace. Thomas's doctrine of creation already points to mysticism. For this and other reasons his anthropology becomes a veritable hermeneutical key for his mystical theology. Chapter 5 demonstrated how Aquinas fuses Aristotelian as well as Dionysian and Augustinian anthropologies into a systematic whole wherein each source is modified. The consequences of those modifications emerged in various parts of chapter 8—for example, in the doctrine of communing with the known through an intelligible form, or in Aquinas's teaching that the mystic still needs knowledge derived from the senses in order to know anything in the dark cloud. Thomas develops Aristotle's anthropology and strips it of Platonizing Peripatetic glosses, but in conversation with Dionysius. Aquinas's critical reading of historical texts helps to explain the difference between his anthropology and that of Albert. In Thomas's epistemology Aristotle and Dionysius ultimately trump Augustine as the Italian friar builds on Albert's critique of Augustinian illumination. As in Albert, such a noetics makes a mysticism of interiority less likely. I also noted how Aquinas's *esse-essentia* metaphysics helps to account for his refusal of Albert's theory of contemplative ascent via the agent intellect's light. I signaled Thomas's Albertian synthesis of Aristotelian noetics and the Areopagite's sacred veils on the theme of the senses mediating all knowledge here below. This synthesis advances in tandem with (1) a harmonious vision of grace and nature and (2) the insistence that noetic ascent passes through causal, analogous knowledge of God. Regarding the first point, grace does not suppress but perfects our embodied form of cognition. So Aquinas's understanding of the grace-nature distinction entails a high view of (1) cognitive mediations such as creation (which is a similitude of God) and (2) the image-bound modes of cognitive operation that are required to take advantage of the truth communicated by those mediations (e.g., one needs phantasms to grasp the message of a gospel story). I showed that Thomas's holistic anthropology goes further than Albert, as he insists on the mind's return to phantasms for the pilgrim's cognition. This stance had capital importance for the themes studied in chapter 8— especially the gift of understanding. I demonstrated how Thomas closes off the paths of Augustinian interior ascent via memory, illumination, and the turn away from the senses and direct self-knowledge. As a result the mystical subject depends on sensible and historical mediations to know God far more than in Dionysius or Augustine. Consequently, the possibility of knowing God here below remains limited, while our dependence on revelation and grace increases. The former theme seems to entail a limited type of apophatism.

I also noted that diverse ontologies undergird distinct mystical epistemologies: a metaphysics of act (Aquinas) and a metaphysics of unity (Dionysius). Aquinas's metaphysics matches a kataphatic mysticism, since created actualities that imitate pure divine act now take precedence over unified thoughts that imitate divine unity. Created actualities manifest God, while the theme of unified thoughts amplifies the unknowability of God and his distance from creation (the realm of multiplicity).

A partly Aristotelian *imago* brings back a key aspect of Augustinian mysticism, especially the place of love in spiritual perfection. Here the theme of imitating the divine processions through human acts of knowing (expressing a word, especially to know God) and loving (being carried to the beloved) come to the fore. Here, too, we see the centrality of human acts for contact with God, including the acts of the mystic. Thomas's interior word functions as a noetic bridge to God and not as a Dionysian conceptual veil that conceals God. Aquinas's trinitarian mysticism entails a revalorization of concept-bound cognition within union! Trinitarian doctrine thus indirectly leads to a higher estimation for the sources of concept-bound knowledge—namely, various kinds of embodied mediations. Also, because the eternal Word spirates Love, we image the Trinity perfectly when acts of love burst forth from acts of wisdom. Because of the Spirit's procession from the Son, union beyond mind by love alone becomes impossible. Thomas's ultimate answer to the Affective Dionysianism of Bonaventure is not Aristotelian but trinitarian. Finally, I suggested that the *imago*'s realization by the love of virtue opens the way for a spirituality of the active life of charity leading to perfection: the apex of union is not reserved to those who are privileged to pursue frequent contemplation.

Chapter 6 emphasized that union comes by the combination of the Son's and the Spirit's immediate efficient and exemplar causalities as well as by the formal causality of created grace. As in Albert, the doctrine of the missions ensures the necessity and primacy of divine action in union. Because of exemplarity tied to efficiency, the missions constitute an unbreakable link between the Trinity's inner life and our ascent to God: the coming of the Son and the Spirit elevate our operative capacities (efficiency) so that we may imitate the divine processions (exemplarity). The experience of the divine persons invisibly sent involves a type of knowledge that includes concepts without being limited to their intelligible content: direct contact with God necessarily has an inexpressible element. This theme helps to demonstrate that Aquinas remains open to a qualified apophatism, since apophatic knowledge tends to transcend concepts, but that he continues to insist on the importance of mediations for the entire mystical ladder. Finally, we saw that habitual faith and charity dispose us for an experience of the divine persons sent.

I then argued that Thomas's mature approach to divine action and actual grace (partly marked by Proclan and Dionysian metaphysics) prepares the way for greater emphasis both on God's direct unifying action in the soul and on the human capacity to cooperate with him, even at the dark summit. God acts in every human act, most of all in the acts of knowledge and charity that enable contact with God. Yet because divine operation is so different from ours, God's acts hardly exclude ours. Aquinas combines modes of causality that Dionysius neatly separates.

The study of habitual grace signaled that Thomas's high estimation thereof entails a cautious, apophatic approach to the certainty of having attained mystical consciousness. The Christological form of grace guarantees its ontological link to the events of Christ's life. Thomas's mysticism is hardly ahistorical. However, this theme does not come up in Thomas's direct treatment of Dionysian union. One can find it in his doctrine of Christ's headship and his discussion of union with Christ by the sacraments.

Chapter 6 undertook a thorough reinterpretation of Thomas's theology of the Spirit's seven gifts in general, building on the work of Pinckaers and González Ayesta. Close textual analyses proved crucial to tease out some of Thomas's assumptions in comparison with modern glosses that harmonize Aquinas on the seven gifts with other mystical traditions. I signaled the evolution in Aquinas's thought toward a new conception of divine motion closely linked with a virtue-centered theology. New arguments were given to show that the Spirit's gifts function as platforms for our cooperation with divine inspiration. This approach to the seven gifts was summarized by the image of an ascending double spiral that signifies increasing operative spontaneity and docility to the Spirit, but not passivity. I noted the virtual absence of the model of the three ages of the spiritual life from Thomas's mysticism.

Aquinas's notion of faith grants the intellect a certain priority over the will. This doctrine helps to ensure an intellect-centered exposition of Dionysian union, as union comes via faith that surpasses reason. Thomas's theology of faith also balances the cognition of faith propositions and direct noetic contact with First Truth. This balance strengthens the mediating role of the articles of faith in mystical ascent: revealed propositions function as mystical ladders.

In chapter 6 the study of charity pointed to Aquinas's synthesis of Johannine and Aristotelian friendship. More specifically we saw a link between the theology of revelation as the manifestation of the secrets in Christ's heart and the imperfect status of blind love: the friend of Christ knows him most of all, unlike the slave who obeys blindly. I noted charity's priority over cognition as a means and measure of union. Such a theology signals that Thomas can only follow the Areopagite's intellect-centered mysticism so far. Furthermore, the believer has the capacity to actualize loving union with God: believers in grace can choose to love God in act at any moment. This theology flows not from a theory of auto-actuated mysticism but from a series of doctrines that bring out the priority of God's gratuitous conjoining action, including the invisible sending of the Spirit and God's primary motion in every created act. The graced will is a secondary efficient cause of union.

Aquinas's eschatology bears Albertian traces, from the created light of glory to beatitude's status as an operation and not just a reception. The key principle "being is for the sake of operation" emerged in chapters 5 and 6. It implies a mysticism of active human cooperation. But Aquinas's agent intellect is more Aristotelian than Albert's Platonized version: it only abstracts forms out of phantasms and thus has no eschatological function. Aquinas goes further than Albert in taking distance from a mysticism of interiority. Hence Thomas never follows his teacher's unusual yet fascinating remark on ascending to divine light via the illumination of the agent intellect, as found in Albert's *Commentary on the Divine Names*.

Chapter 7 pointed to the link between *sacra doctrina* as a participation in the saints' beatific knowledge and substantial divine names. The mature Thomas acknowledges the eschatological cognition of God's *quid sit* (or essence), a shift away from Albert that obscures their shared kataphatism, since they often do not use the term *quid sit* in the same way. In Thomas we saw a new emphasis on naming as judgment, an utterly central theme for the subjects covered in chapter 8. We also found a link between the *triplex via* and Aristotelian anthropology: every negation presumes an affirmation that we have grasped with our minds (kataphatism); remotions purify our understanding bound to phantasms (cognition bound to mediations); and all knowledge of God remains indirect. I noted Thomas's avoidance of his teacher's most apophatic statements, which clash with Albert's more kataphatic expressions. A creative synthesis of Aristotelian pure act and Dionysian *esse* in Aquinas's theology of the Creator God sets up a positive doctrine of naming, for God's first name is Being, which signifies the actuality of all acts. The same synthesis simultaneously leads to an insistence on God's transcendence and incomprehensibility: *Qui est* is the most indeterminate name. Apophatism has not gone entirely missing.

Chapters 5 through 8 presented a wide range of arguments that the pilgrim's deepest union calls for properly human acts of knowledge and love as well as mediating noetic objects: (1) the dynamic presence of the divine persons sent; (2) the *imago* that imitates the eternal processions; (3) the formation of the interior word; (4) intelligible form as means of communion with the known; (5) God's primary efficient causality of all created acts as enabling human cooperation in union; (6) the possibility of naming God's substance; (7) the indispensability of Scripture for all unifying cognition of God; (8) the mutuality implied in charity as friendship; (9) grace's elevation of nature that respects its structure; and (10) the intellect's return to phantasms that befits an ontology of a single substantial form and our status as a "boundary creature." No one seems to have assembled all of these doctrines and drawn their consequences for Thomas's mystical subject. We can now recognize more clearly that a rich mingling of multiple philosophical and theological traditions with Thomas's original insights stands behind his reductive reading of Dionysian passivity. Also, the extent of Thomas's distance from mystical passivity better comes to light with a *ressourcement* of his theology of the Spirit's seven gifts. Inversely, the list of arguments against mystical passivity given above confirms my somewhat Pinckaersian reading of the Spirit's gifts. The indispensible function of concept-bound and image-bound acts of knowledge in union emerges as a pillar of Thomas's mysticism, a pillar partly constructed with the help of Albert.

Chapter 8 analyzed the four major sites of Thomas's dialogue with Dionysian mysticism. It offered an extensive analysis of union passages in Thomas's *Commentary on the Divine Names* and a complete textual study of Thomas's sporadic comments on the *Mystical Theology* under the formality of union with God. The prologue of the *Commentary on the Divine Names* follows Albert's lead in transforming the *Mystical Theology* into a science of remotions rather than an allegorical commentary on union beyond all names. The *Mystical Theology* thus becomes a work of *sacra doctrina*, of faith-based rational discourse about God, not a guidebook to transcend all discourse. Furthermore, the union passages in the *Divine Names* that preview the *Mystical Theology* take on a similar genre. Aquinas takes advantage of the Areopagite's insistence on the biblical, apostolic foundation for his teaching and rechannels unifying light through the revelation passed on in Scripture. Union beyond mind becomes faith surpassing reason so as to cling to God. The central hermeneutical function of the grace-nature distinction to explain union above mind emerged, a clear Albertian heritage. The Spirit's truth communicated in Scripture and his power active in the virtue of faith together elevate the believer to God. I showed how Aquinas develops various Albertian arguments on the unitive power of faith and revelation so as to shift the Areopagite's discourse on ascent beyond Scripture's divine names to a doctrine wherein union directly occurs by the illumination of faith and the central mysteries of faith. Union beyond mind becomes a gift for all the faithful. Thomas completely sidesteps the theme of noetic silence implied in the Dionysian language of "union beyond mind." Instead, unitive cognition remains bound to concepts and images, for bound to Scripture, for even with Scripture, we know God from creatures. The ambiguity of the Dionysian text facilitates its transformation. Aquinas's Scripture-centered rereading of Dionysian oracles and unitive lights facilitates a new emphasis on the mystical function of mediations. I pointed to Thomas's theology of revelation as a key source for this kataphatic reformulation of Dionysian ecstasy. The *Commentary on the Divine Names* deepens our understanding of faith's mystical element and of Aquinas's revalorization of Scripture in relation to Dionysius.

A comparison of Albert's and Thomas's commentaries on Dionysius showed strong similarities in their explanations of the *triplex via* and of ascent by negations or remotions. Aquinas's *Commentary on the Divine Names* assigns to remotions a twofold, simultaneous fruit: noetic union and perfect cognition (the proper judgment concerning divine eminence). When Aquinas insists that remotions leave standing the affirmation of the reality signified and posits positive noetic content for eminent names, he has firm roots in his teacher's thought. Both doctrines entail a strong turn in a kataphatic direction. The diversity in Albert's expressions on themes such as the function of negations helps to explain the diverse theologies of his disciples, from Thomas to Eckhart. Albert and Thomas both hold that the summit of cognition involves knowledge of God's eminent perfection, not an encounter with the nameless God, except as not-comprehended. Here, too, we find the mystic dwelling in a bright fog rather than in a dark cloud. The Areopagite's transcending negations become eminent names predicating perfections of God in an excess mode. Like Albert, Thomas rereads the Dionysian ladder of negations leading toward darkness as the reflexive recognition that God exceeds whatever we know of him. Such reflexive knowledge points to the abiding activity of the mystic's mind. For Thomas, God's similitudes and the mind's active grasp thereof remain essential to prevent dark knowledge from collapsing into total ignorance. Again as in Albert, the *triplex via* functions as an unbreakable triad, thus ensuring a restrained function for negations. In his *Commentary on the Divine Names* Aquinas follows his teacher as he makes remotions the stairway to the noetic summit. I noted the link between the psychology of form (we become that which we know) and a hierarchy of communion with the known (the more we know of God through his revelation, the more we are joined to him). Both doctrines enable a reconstitution of the Areopagite's nonprivative dark cognition: we hardly know nothing in darkness, especially since all human cognition involves the reception of some intelligible form. Sometimes Thomas can only retain an important Dionysian doctrine by departing from the Areopagite in some way. Finally, even prophetic cognition demands purification by remotion, as God exceeds every self-manifestation. Overall Aquinas's interpretation of Moses fits well with his theology of revelation and an Exodus narrative that primarily presents the patriarch as a mediator of God's word, not a mystic lost in expressible darkness.

The study of Thomas's comments on the *Mystical Theology* showed a consistent hermeneutic. Even the most apophatic readings leave standing the divine reality signified and reflexive cognition of divine excess. Thomas consistently limits the weight of the Dionysian phrase, "being joined to the absolutely unknown [God]." Here and elsewhere Aquinas demonstrates an extremely consistent kataphatic approach to Dionysius. In comparison to his teacher, Aquinas's direct comments on the *Mystical Theology* dwell less on completing a series of learned remotions and more on various ways of entering darkness by knowing "what God is not." Strictly revealed divine attributes and God's saving works become platforms for graced noetic ascent that surpasses philosophy in its knowledge of "what God is not." The believer penetrates the dark cloud further than does the metaphysician. The hierarchy of dark clouds (metaphysical, theological with acquired knowledge, purely gifted with infused remotions) has not been sufficiently acknowledged in the literature. This hierarchy, an implicit feature of Aquinas's thought, emerged as we put his various comments on the *Mystical Theology* side by side.

Thomas thus presents a progression of not-knowing God's quiddity. This also becomes clear in his teaching on the gift of understanding, where the Spirit directly induces an ever more refined grasp of divine excess. The Spirit provokes a refined apprehension of "what God is not." He weeds out errors in the mind so that it may penetrate further into faith's central mysteries. The interior purification of believers' misconceptions allows Scripture's and tradition's positive teaching on God and his saving acts to become more accessible. Remotion stands at the service of affirmation and positive eminence. In Aquinas's theology of the gift of understanding, Moses represents the apprehensive element of noetic perfection, a figure complementary to Hierotheus with his perfectly wise judgment. Thomas creatively joins an Aristotelian analysis of the cognitive act's structure (apprehension and judgment) with Augustine's correspondence of gifts to beatitudes as well as a Dionysian emphasis on not-knowing God perfectly. The originality of Aquinas's link between this gift of the Spirit and the Areopagite's Moses shows that the theme of unknowing is hardly secondary to Thomas's theology of Spirit-guided contemplative ascent. The knowledge imparted by the gift of understanding also pertains to practical revealed truths: the summit of contemplation involves no ivory-tower abstraction from Christian practices. Finally, I presented new arguments to distinguish the gift of understanding's operation from an act of judgment, a distinction often rejected in the scholarly literature.

The analysis of the gift of understanding offered a thorough historical comparison between Dionysius and Aquinas's theology of infused remotions, the element of the Italian friar's thought that comes closest to the doctrine of the *Mystical Theology*. Thomas posits a form of remotive cognition that neither Dionysius nor Albert imagined. The *Summa* offers the most stimulating and clearest synthesis of this doctrine. As in the *Commentary on the Divine Names*, the crucial role of Scripture and especially of the articles of faith as indispensible mediations for the noetic content of the mystic's intellect in union emerged more clearly than in past studies of Thomas. Aquinas's reading of Moses's ascent posits at once a gift granted to all believers (the preservation from fatal errors) and, in its higher form, a gift that makes the saints know ever more perfectly that God exceeds whatever we comprehend. Thomas integrates the Dionysian language of purification from images and thoughts but now refers it not to image-free and concept-free contemplative union but to sound noetic content or a correct understanding about God. Here the mystic's intentionality is purified, while his operative mode of contemplation remains mostly unchanged. Consequently, noetic silence greatly diminishes, but without diminishing the immediacy of divine action in the soul's communion with God. Aquinas's Moses continues to gaze upon God through Scripture, tradition, and creation, not without them. Every pilgrim needs these mediations, even on Mt. Sinai. Aquinas grants a greater role to Scripture at the mystical summit than either Dionysius or the adherents of "Affective Dionysianism." Thomas's mystic applies the *triplex via* with the Spirit's help so as to enjoy deeper cognitive union with God. Since the faith that unites is not an act of blind trust but an operation of the intellect, an act that needs noetic content, and since faith's material and formal objects (the latter being First Truth, as well as the Scriptures and articles of faith that transmit this truth) are inseparable for us, revelation's doctrine is a co-cause of union.

Furthermore, God's action in the economy of salvation, including the incarnation, becomes a legitimate contemplative object in darkness, a position implicit in Albert but more evident in Aquinas. History takes its place at the metaphysical summit of human knowledge. The gap between the event of union and the rest of the economy is closed, yet the limits of the mystical subject's capacity to grasp the richness of revelation are recognized in the theology of the Spirit's seven gifts.

I noted Aquinas's originality in centering the noetic fruit of the gift of understanding on remotions. He moves toward Dionysius by taking distance from Albert's theology of the gift of understanding focused on new interior divine manifestations. For Aquinas all revelation, even prophetic insight, calls for remotion. The insistence on the remotive character of this gift, instead of a reception of infused forms or a higher vision of the divine ideas, throws the mystic back to Scripture and tradition: he or she should seek God's manifestation in public revelation more than within. The "exterior" or revelation-centered mysticism of Thomas's theology of the gift of understanding has hardly been acknowledged by scholars, some of whom construct a psychology of apophatic ascent marked more by modern spiritual authors than by Aquinas's texts.

Thomas somewhat displaces the dark cloud from the summit of union, for the actualized gift of understanding requires neither an operation of charity nor an increase in habitual grace. While Thomas distinguishes naming and perfect union, he also holds that they coexist: correctly naming God is an act of the graced *imago*. Aquinas considers the *triplex via* essential for mystical ascent, but this way does not formally constitute mystical union, since only a participation in the Word spirating Love perfectly imitates the Trinity. The summit of the spiritual life is found in acts of perfect charity, though this charity must be joined to (habitual or also actual) sanctifying wisdom. Aquinas integrates Dionysius into the heart of his mysticism, but he can only follow the Areopagite's intellect-centered approach so far.

The interconnection between (1) revelation-centered mysticism, (2) Thomas's relatively harmonious vision of grace-nature, (3) his Aristotelian anthropology, (4) an almost memoryless *imago*, and (5) the doctrine of pure divine act surfaced. The beginning of Thomas's *Commentary on the Divine Names* and his teaching on the gift of understanding highlighted the unitive power of God's public revelation as transmitted in Scripture and tradition, with a special focus on the articles of faith. This revelation comes through sacred texts, such as the creed, that employ a multiplicity of concepts and images. Now, the more divine unitive light comes through Scripture and tradition, the more that light befits a mode of cognition that always begins with and somehow depends on sense experience. That mode of human cognition (operation) precisely fits with the anthropology of a single substantial form: operation follows being. The human being who is a soul-body unity receives Scripture's unifying light: the mode of union stands in harmony with the mode of the receiver. Because grace does not destroy nature, supernatural cognition essentially respects the fundamental law of the mediation of the senses in human knowledge. Furthermore, since Thomas essentially makes memory the storehouse of forms abstracted out of sense experience, the interior path of ascent to God has been radically limited. This in turn forces the contemplative to look for external mediations of divine truth and light—in other words, Scripture, tradition, and creation. A virtually memoryless *imago* fits well with the ontology of a single substantial form. Now the contemplative's turn "outward" brings a great multiplicity of thoughts and images about God. Yet these need not be obstacles to union, since each divine perfection that revelation and creation manifest comes to us through created actualities that imitate

General Conclusion 463

the divine act. The interconnection among these five themes emerged thanks largely to the combination of background studies in chapters 5 through 7 and the textual analyses in chapter 8.

I then traced an evolution in Aquinas's teaching on the gift of wisdom. I noted the lingering ambiguities of Hierotheus suffering divine things in the *Sentences Commentary* and the *Commentary on the Divine Names*, especially the unclear relation of gifted wisdom to habitual and actual charity. The mature *Summa* exposition of Hierotheus combines direct divine inspiration with an act of judgment and a communicable doctrine. The latter two themes point to a kataphatic mysticism and insert mediated cognition into union, for the mystic can share what he or she learns. Also, the *Summa* more clearly presents the properly noetic character of Hierotheus's grace.

Several new insights emerged pertaining to the Spirit's gifts of understanding and wisdom. The focus on God's efficient causality directly and freely moving the human intellect to remove error and to judge wisely (the fruit of Thomas's mature theory of divine action) overcomes the focus on formal causality in Albert's and Bonaventure's theologies of the Spirit's gifts. As in the theology of the gift of understanding, Thomas's doctrine of the gift of wisdom offers a new synthesis among God's immediate action in the mystic, the mystic's active mind, and a new learning that remains bound to concepts, for judgment requires concepts, and judgment is an act of the human mind. The mature Aquinas's approach to God's efficient causality and human freedom allows him to move beyond an emphasis on interior divine manifestations that threaten to become another set of veils between us and God. The same approach enables Thomas to adopt a Dionysian insistence on the primacy of confused knowledge in contemplative perfection, a knowledge that partly penetrates the veils of Scripture and material creation. The key role played by the Spirit's motion ironically reinforces the function of mediations in unitive knowledge: mystical ascent comes not by attaining new visions (formal causality) but by better grasping revelation's richness virtually contained in the Scriptures. Consequently, embodied or image-bound cognition enjoys revalorization. The mystic's noetic act still returns to phantasms. Thomas deplatonizes Dionysius, *perhaps* without knowing it.

Next, neither gift of the Spirit seems to involve a form of operative grace; the theology of the gifts thus better harmonizes with the dynamic *imago* and the doctrine of creatures' perfection by their proper acts. Moses and Hierotheus cooperate with God in darkness. I thus critiqued several scholars' emphasis on mystical passivity in Thomas's doctrine of gifted wisdom. Thomas links the grace of Hierotheus with habitual charity's connaturality or inclination to the beloved without explicitly mentioning actual charity. Thus neither gift of the Spirit seems to demand an *act* of charity for its operation: the gifts truly assist the theological virtues and remain subordinate to them. The mystical gifts that Moses and Hierotheus receive are properly noetic, in contrast to Affective Dionysianism. The beloved disciple of John's Gospel is Aquinas's model mystic, not Moses or Hierotheus. This, too, reinforces the importance of cooperating in grace, as implied in the theology of charity as friendship and friendship's mutuality. Chapter 8 offered the first sustained textual argument that a believer's existing habitual charity probably suffices for the gift of wisdom's actualization. The *Summa* carefully balances the need for revelation-derived noetic content with the Spirit's direct motion and charity's guiding inclination to describe the function of wise judgment. The focus thus turns back to the Spirit's motion in the intellect, assisted by charity's habitual inclination to the beloved. The intellect retains primacy over the will in the gift of wisdom's operation. Here the background study of the psychology of love (especially love as connaturality) bore fruit. I also distinguished between the gift of wisdom's act and a new double mission of the divine persons without excluding the possibility of their simultaneity. I noted the gift of wisdom's relation to extraordinary gifts such as charismatic speech. A sharp contrast with Bonaventure's mysticism emerged.

The study on the gift wisdom surfaced the secondary status of experience for this gift, yet without excluding experience. The distance between Aquinas's presentation of Hierotheus in the *Commentary on the Divine Names* and in the *Summa* came to light, with a shift from the will to the intellect. The intrinsic compatibility and simultaneity of connatural knowledge, Spirit-induced acts, and active rational reflection in the gift of wisdom's operation was brought out: grace elevates nature. Wisdom's fruit was more clearly shown to consist of an interplay of sources: the intelligible content of the articles of faith, charity's inclination, and a Spirit-induced judgment.

I noted that Thomas, unlike the early Cologne Albert, posits universal access to the summit of noetic union via growth in grace. This universality partly follows from the fact that the noetic ladder to union is primarily constituted by the articles of faith derived from Scripture rather than by Scripture as a whole or a complete series of technical negations. Thus even illiterate peasants can imitate Moses and Hierotheus. On a related theme, Aquinas proposes varying degrees of dwelling in the dark cloud and of suffering divine things, degrees determined by growth in grace and charity. More than the early Cologne Albert, Aquinas sees growth in the theological virtues, virtues aided by the Spirit's operation in his gifts, as the key to mystical ascent. Union thus occurs through progressive intensification, not neatly distinct stages. Also, the life of virtue elevated by grace, a grace available to all, replaces a Dionysian monastic theology focused on liturgy and study, although the latter practices are part of the life of virtue. Aquinas quietly takes perfect union beyond the confines of the episcopate, the monastery, and the *studium*.

As in Thomas's doctrine of the missions, the essential though nonexhaustive function of concept-bound cognition emerged in his theology of the Spirit's gifts. For the missions as well as the gifts of understanding and wisdom, concepts continue to have a role in cognitive union, yet the noetic fruit attained thereby may well burst the bounds of what concepts can express. This became especially clear in Thomas's focus on judgment in wisdom's act and the instinctual orientation that wisdom receives from charity. We should note the parallel with (acquired theological wisdom's) divine naming as a judgment that points toward an inadequately yet necessarily conceptualized divine perfection. Consequently, Aquinas grants kataphatism priority in his mystical theology, yet he retains an important apophatic element as well: some graced insights can hardly be put into words.

Thomas's mystical theology radically distinguishes itself from that of Bonaventure, not to mention Thomas Gallus. I showed the lack of evidence for Aquinas's (and Albert's) direct engagement with Gallus. We saw considerable evolutions in Thomas's thought on the gifts of understanding and wisdom, going well beyond Dionysius and Albert: a clearer doctrine of the Spirit's motion, more emphasis on the function of Scripture and tradition, less emphasis on experience, a stronger link with the theological virtues, and an extensive exposition on the beatitudes essentially missing in Albert. Aquinas also works out a rather sober structure for the Spirit's intellectual gifts, for he uses the merit-reward distinction to reserve some graces for pilgrim saints, but his virtual silence on hierarchies of ascent and his insistence that the seven gifts are necessary for salvation increase Thomas's distance from the Areopagite's division of material and immaterial contemplative stages. The same silence distinguishes Aquinas from Augustine's hierarchy of progress in the beatitudes.

Albert influences Thomas's way of reading Dionysius on a wide breadth of themes, from the hermeneutic of grace-nature to the insertion of the dynamic *imago* into mystical darkness and the taming of Dionysian apophatism. The two friars' work on the Areopagite touches the heart of their theologies of union. Albert's influence on Aquinas's mysticism is far from peripheral. The latter also extensively modifies Albertian doctrines and interpretive strategies. Still, it makes little sense to separate Aquinas's theology from the heart of Albertian thought (at least up to 1250), as Alain de Libera has proposed. The German friar's thought was sufficiently complex and fluid to leave deep imprints on multiple schools of theology.

FURTHER STUDIES

Chapters 4 and 8 presented the first extensive historical trialogue between Dionysius, Albert, and Thomas on union with God. The same chapters undertook the hitherto most extensive textual studies of union in Albert's *Commentary on the Mystical Theology* and of Thomas's comments on Dionysian union. I thus offer substantial material for the study of thirteenth-century Latin Dionysianism on a range of issues, from scholastic strategies for synthesizing the Areopagite with Aristotle to the question of Dionysian influence on theologies of grace.

Albert's vast theological corpus offers many avenues for future explorations of his mysticism. A closer look at his pre-1242 works might nuance our perspective of the "early Albert's" mystical doctrine, not to mention his teaching on various background themes. Also, his much-studied later philosophical work *De Intellectu et Intelligibili* has never been thoroughly compared to his commentaries on Dionysius.

The hard-to-date biblical commentaries and his late *Summa theologiae* should be compared more fully with his early Cologne mysticism. I mentioned at the end of chapter 4 that Dionysius's influence seems to recede in Albert's *Summa theologiae* discussions of union, a claim that requires confirmation and explanation.

The early (and late) Albert's mystical theology still needs to be put in relation with the emerging lay spiritualities of thirteenth-century Germany, especially the Beguine movement. Albert preached vernacular sermons in cities such as Cologne, and Beguines were certainly among his listeners. Furthermore, Albert's Dominican students provided extensive pastoral care to Beguine women.[1] The rich vein of Beguine mysticism may bear indirect traces of Albert's doctrine.

All of these comparative projects could illumine our understanding of how Rhineland mysticism emerged. Which Albert became the father of the Rhineland school: The Parisian *baccalaureus*, the Cologne commentator of Dionysius, the post-1250 Peripatetic philosopher, the elderly author of the *Summa theologiae*, or some combination thereof? And which (if any) Dionysian Albert marked Meister Eckhart: the subtly kataphatic theologian, the occasionally apophatic adventurer, or the critic of Augustinian noetics? Which disciple undertook the more extensive appropriation and modification of Albert's Dionysianism: Thomas or Eckhart?

Aquinas's mysticism understood through his Greek sources also deserves closer comparison to Maximos's Christ-centered mystical theology, for Thomas's mature Christology is firmly rooted in the ancient Ecumenical Councils. Also, Aquinas's virtue-centered doctrine, which emphasizes Spirit-empowered cooperation in union and Scripture's elevating light, provides resources for a contemporary mystical theology that looks for union with God through daily Christian practices and the liturgy more than by interior phenomena or meditative techniques.

Dionysian mysticism traversed the thirteenth century through two major streams: the affective reading of Gallus, Grosseteste, and Bo-

---

1. Anzulewicz, "Im Wirkungskreis des Albertus Magnus: Zur Geisteswelt der Christiana von Stommeln in der Stadt Köln," in *Gottesschau und Gottesliebe: Die Mystikerin Christiana von Stommeln 1242–1312*, edited by Guido von Büren, Susanne Richter, and Marcell Perse, 92–100 (Regensburg, Germany: Schnell and Steiner, 2012).

naventure, and the more intellectual reading of Albert and Thomas. Albert helped bring to birth at least two schools of mysticism: a Thomistic and a German Dominican school. He and his students developed *scholastic* forms of mystical theology. The latter became part of *sacra doctrina*, a shift facilitated by the Dionysian emphasis on intellect as the site of union. This integration partly parallels mystical theology's firm insertion in the church fathers' theological reflections on the central mysteries of faith. Albert and Thomas developed the heritage of Greek mysticism for the medieval Latin West and beyond.

Bibliography

ANCIENT AND MEDIEVAL AUTHORS

Albertus Magnus. *De Intellectu et Intelligibili*. Borgnet Edition 9. Paris: 1890.

———. *Commentarii in libros Sententiarum*. 6 vols. Borgnet Edition 25—30. Paris: 1893–94.

———. *De IV coaequaevis*. Borgnet Edition 34. Paris: 1895.

———. *De bono*. Edited by Heinrich Kühle, Carl Feckes, Bernhard Geyer, and Wilhelm Kübel. Cologne Edition 28. Münster: Aschendorff, 1951.

———. *Postilla Super Isaiam*. Edited by Ferdinand Siepmann and Heinrich Ostlender. Cologne Edition 19. Münster: Aschendorff, 1952.

———. *De incarnatione*. Edited by A. Ohlmeyer, Ignatius Backes, and Wilhelm Kübel. Cologne Edition 26. Münster: Aschendorff, 1958.

———. *De resurrectione*. Edited by A. Ohlmeyer, Ignatius Backes, and Wilhelm Kübel. Cologne Edition 26. Münster: Aschendorff, 1958.

———. *Super Dionysium De divinis nominibus*. Edited by Paul Simon. Cologne Edition. Vol. 37, part 1. Münster: Aschendorff, 1972.

———. *De natura boni*. Edited by Ephrem Filthaut. Cologne Edition. Vol. 25, part 1. Münster: Aschendorff, 1974.

———. *Summa theologiae sive de mirabili scientia Dei I.1*. Edited by Dionysius Siedler. Cologne Edition. Vol. 34, part 1. Münster: Aschendorff, 1978.

———. *Super Dionysii Mysticam theologiam et Epistulas*. Edited by Paul Simon. Cologne Edition. Vol. 37, part 2. Münster: Aschendorff, 1978.

———. *Super Ethica: Commentum et Quaestiones, Libros VI–X*. Edited by Wilhelm Kübel. Cologne Edition. Vol. 14, part 2. Münster: Aschendorff, 1987.

———. *Quaestiones*. Edited by Albert Fries, Wilhelm Kübel, and Henryk Anzulewicz. Cologne Edition. Vol. 25, part 2. Münster: Aschendorff, 1993.

———. *Super Dionysium De caelesti hierarchia*. Edited by Paul Simon and Wilhelm Kübel. Cologne Edition. Vol. 36, part 1. Münster: Aschendorff, 1993.

———. *Super Dionysium De ecclesiastica hierarchia*. Edited by Maria Burger,

Paul Simon, and Wilhelm Kübel. Cologne Edition. Vol. 36, part 2. Münster: Aschendorff, 1999.

———. *De homine*. Edited by Henryk Anzulewicz and Joachim R. Söder. Cologne Edition. Vol. 27, part 2. Münster: Aschendorff, 2008.

Albertus Magnus and Thomas Aquinas. *Albert and Thomas: Selected Writings*. Edited and translated by Simon Tugwell. Classics of Western Spirituality. New York: Paulist Press, 1988.

Alexander of Hales. *Glossa in quatuor libros Sententiarum Petri Lombardi*. Bibliotheca Franciscana Scholastica Medii Aevi 12–15. 4 vols. Quaracchi: Ex Typographia Collegii S. Bonaventurae, 1951–57.

Aquinas, Thomas. *Scriptum super libros Sententiarum*. Vols. 1–2 edited by Pierre Mandonnet. Vols. 3–4 edited by Maria Fabianus Moos. Paris: P. Lethielleux, 1927–47.

———. *In librum Beati Dionysii De divinis nominibus expositio*. Edited by Ceslaus Pera. Rome and Turin: Marietti, 1950.

———. *Super Evangelium Sancti Ioannis lectura*. Edited by Raphael Cai. Rome and Turin: Marietti, 1952.

———. *Summa theologiae*. 4 vols. Ottawa: Commissio Piana, 1953.

———. *Super Epistolas S. Pauli lectura*. 2 vols. Edited by Raphael Cai. Rome and Turin: Marietti, 1953.

———. *Summa contra Gentiles*. 3 vols. Edited by Ceslaus Pera, Petrus Marc, and Petrus Caramello. Rome and Turin: Marietti, 1961.

———. *Quaestio disputata de caritate*. In Vol. 2 of *Quaestiones disputatae*. Edited by P. Bazzi, M. Calcaterra, T. S. Centi, E. Odetto, and P. M. Pession. Rome and Turin: Marietti, 1965.

———. *Quaestiones disputatae de potentia*. In Vol. 2 of *Quaestiones disputatae*. Edited by P. Bazzi, M. Calcaterra, T. S. Centi, E. Odetto, and P. M. Pession. Rome and Turin: Marietti, 1965.

———. *Quaestiones disputatae de veritate*. Leonine Edition. Vol. 22, parts 1–3. Rome: Editori di san Tommaso, 1970–76.

———. *Expositio super Isaiam ad litteram*. Leonine Edition 28. Rome: Editori di san Tommaso, 1974.

———. *In quatuor libros Sententiarum*. Opera Omnia 1. Edited by Roberto Busa. Stuttgart: Frommann-Holzboog, 1980.

———. *Quaestiones disputatae de malo*. Edited by Pierre-Marie Gils. Leonine Edition 23. Paris: Cerf; Rome: Commissio Leonina, 1982.

———. *De memoria et reminiscencia*. Leonine Edition. Vol. 45, part 2. Paris: Vrin; Rome: Commissio Leonina, 1985.

———. *Super Boetium de Trinitate*. Edited by Pierre-Marie Gils. Leonine Edition 50. Paris: Cerf; Commissio Leonina, 1992.

———. *Quaestiones disputatae de anima*. Edited by B. Carlos Bazán. Leonine Edition. Vol. 24, part 1. Paris: Cerf; Rome: Commissio Leonina, 1996.

Bibliography

———. *Super librum de causis expositio*. Edited by Henri-Dominique Saffrey. Textes philosophiques du Moyen Âge 21. 2nd ed. Paris: Vrin, 2002.

———. *Lectura romana in primum Sententiarum Petri Lombardi*. Edited by Leonard E. Boyle and John F. Boyle. Studies and Texts 152. Toronto: Pontifical Institute of Medieval Studies, 2006.

———. *The Academic Sermons*. Translated by Mark-Robin Hoogland. Fathers of the Church, Medieval Continuation 11. Washington, D.C.: The Catholic University of America Press, 2010.

Augustine. *De Sermone domini in monte libros duos*. Edited by Almut Mutzenbecher. CCSL 35. Turnhout: Brepols, 1967.

———. *De trinitate libri XV*. Edited by W. J. Mountain and F. Glorie. CCSL. Vol. 50, part 2. Turnout: Brepols, 1968.

———. *La Genèse au sens littéral en douze livres*. 2 vols. Edited by P. Agaësse and A. Solignac. Bibliothèque augustinienne 48–49. Paris: Desclée de Brouwer, 1972.

———. *Confessionum libri XIII*. Edited by Lucas Verheijen. CCSL 27. Turnhout: Brepols, 1981.

———. *Retractationum libri II*. Edited by Almut Mutzenbecher. CCSL 57. Turnhout: Brepols, 1984.

Averroes. *Commentarium Magnum in Aristotelis De Anima Libros*. Edited by F. Stuart Crawford. Corpus Commentariorum Averrois in Aristotelem, Versionum Latinarum. Vol. 6, part 1. Cambridge, Mass.: Medieval Academy of America, 1953.

Avicenna Latinus. *Liber de Anima seu Sextus de Naturalibus IV–V*. Edited by S. Van Riet. Leiden: E. J. Brill, 1968.

Bonaventure. *Commentaria in quatuor libros Sententiarum*. 4 vols. Quaracchi: Ex Typographia Collegii S. Bonaventurae, 1882–89.

———. *Collationes in Hexaëmeron*. In *Opera Omnia*. Vol. 5. Quaracchi: Ex Typographia Collegii S. Bonaventurae, 1891.

Denifle, Heinrich, ed. *Chartularium Universitatis Parisiensis*. Vol. 1. Paris: 1889.

Dionysius Areopagita. *The Works of Dionysius the Areopagite*. Translated by John D. Parker. London: James Parker, 1897.

———. *Dionysiaca*. 2 vols. Edited by Philippe Chevallier. Paris: Desclée de Brouwer, 1937–50.

———. *The Divine Names and Mystical Theology*. Translated by John D. Jones. Medieval Philosophical Texts in Translation 21. Milwaukee: Marquette University Press, 1980.

———. *Pseudo-Dionysius: The Complete Works*. Edited and Translated by Colm Luibheid and Paul Rorem. Classics of Western Spirituality. New York: Paulist Press, 1987.

———. *Corpus Dionysiacum I: De divinis nominibus*. Edited by Beate Regina Suchla. Patristische Texte und Studien 33. Berlin: Walter de Gruyter, 1990.

———. *Corpus Dionysiacum II: De coelesti hierarchia, De ecclesiastica hierarchia, De mystica theologia, Epistulae*. Edited by Günter Heil and Adolf Martin Ritter. Patristische Texte und Studien 36. Berlin: Walter de Gruyter, 1991.

———. *Patrologia Graeca-Latina* 3. Turnhout: Brepols, 2001.

Eriugena, John Scotus. *Periphyseon*, bks. I–IV. Edited by I. P. Sheldon-Williams. Scriptores Latini Hiberniae 7, 9, 11, 13. Dublin: Dublin Institute for Advanced Studies, 1972–95.

Gallus, Thomas. *Extractio de divinis nominibus = Paraphrase sur le traité des noms divins*. In Dionysius Areopagita, *Dionysiaca*, 1:673–708. 1937.

———. *Extractio de mystica theologia = Paraphrase sur la théologie mystique*. In Dionysius Areopagita, *Dionysiaca*, 1:709–12. 1937.

———. *Explanatio de divinis nominibus*. In *Explanatio in libros Dionysii*. Edited by Declan Anthony Lawell. Corpus Christianorum Continuatio Mediaeualis 223. Turnhout: Brepols, 2011.

———. *Explanatio super mystica theologia*. In *Explanatio in libros Dionysii*, edited by Declan Anthony Lawell. 2011.

Gallus, Thomas, and Robert Grosseteste. *Mystical Theology: The Glosses by Thomas Gallus and the Commentary of Robert Grosseteste on "De Mystica Theologia."* Edited by James McEvoy. Dallas Medieval Texts in Translation 3. Leuven: Peeters, 2003.

Gregory of Nyssa. *La vie de Moïse*. Edited and translated by Jean Daniélou. 3rd ed. Sources Chrétiennes 1 bis. Paris: Cerf, 2007.

Harrington, L. Michael, editor. *A Thirteenth Century Textbook of Mystical Theology at the University of Paris: The "Mystical Theology" of Dionysius the Areopagite in Eriugena's Latin Translation with the Scholia translated by Anastasius the Librarian and Excerpts from Eriugena's "Periphyseon."* Dallas Medieval Texts and Translations 4. Leuven: Peeters, 2004.

———. *On the Ecclesiastical Hierarchy: The Thirteenth-Century Paris Textbook Edition*. Dallas Medieval Texts and Translations 12. Leuven: Peeters, 2011.

Lamoreaux, John C., and Paul P. Rorem, eds. *John of Scythopolis and the Dionysian Corpus: Annotating the Areopagite*. Oxford Early Christian Studies. Oxford: Oxford University Press, 1998.

Migne. *Patrologia graeca* (PG). 161 vols. Paris, 1857–66.

Philip the Chancellor. *Summa de Bono*. 2 vols. Edited by Nicolas Wicki. Corpus Philosophorum medii aevi. Bern: Francke, 1985.

Proclus. *The Elements of Theology*. Translated by E. R. Dodds. 2nd ed. Oxford: Clarendon Press, 1963.

De Spiritu et Anima. Patrologia Latina 40. Turnhout: Brepols, n.d.

William of Auxerre. *Summa Aurea*. 5 vols. Spicilegium Bonaventurianum 16–20. Grottaferrata: Editiones Collegii S. Bonaventurae, 1980–86.

William of Saint-Thierry. *Le Miroir de la foi*. Sources Chrétiennes 301. Paris: Cerf, 1982.

SECONDARY SOURCES

Aertsen, Jan A., and Andreas Speer, eds. *Was ist die Philosophie im Mittelalter?* Miscellanea Mediaevalia 26. Berlin: Walter de Gruyter, 1998.

Allegro, Giuseppe, and Guglielmo Russino. Introduction to *Tenebra luminosissima: Commento alla "Teologia Mistica" di Dionigi l'Areopagita*, by Albertus Magnus. Edited by Allegro and Russino, 3–42. Machina Philosophorum 15. Palermo: Officina di Studi Medievali, 2007.

Andereggen, Ignacio. "La originalidad del Comentario de Santo Tomás al *De Divinis Nominibus* de Dionisio Areopagita." In de Andia, *Denys l'Aréopagite et sa postérité*, 439–55.

Anzulewicz, Henryk. "Der Anthropologieentwurf des Albertus Magnus und die Frage nach dem Begriff und wissenschaftssystematischen Ort einer mittelalterlichen Anthropologie." In Aertsen and Speer, *Was ist die Philosophie im Mittelalter?*, 756–66. 1998.

———. *De forma resultante in speculo: Die theologische Relevanz des Bildbegriffs und des Spiegelbildmodells in den Frühwerken des Albertus Magnus.* 2 vols. Beiträge zur Geschichte der Philosophie und Theologie des Mittelalters, Neue Folge. Vol. 53, parts 1–2. Münster: Aschendorff, 1999.

———. "Neuere Forschung zu Albertus Magnus: Bestandsaufnahme und Problemstellungen." *Recherches de théologie ancienne et médiévale* 66 (1999): 163–206.

———. "Die Denkstruktur des Albertus Magnus: Ihre Dekodierung und ihre Relevanz für die Begrifflichkeit und Terminologie." In *L'élaboration du vocabulaire philosophique au Moyen Âge*, edited by Jacqueline Hamesse and Carlos Steel, 369–96. Rencontres de Philosophie Médiévale 8. Turnhout: Brepols, 2000.

———. "Pseudo-Dionysius Areopagita und das Strukturprinzip des Denkens von Albert dem Grossen." In Boiadjiev, Kapriev, and Speer, *Die Dionysius-Rezeption im Mittelalter*, 251–95. 2000.

———. "Die Rekonstruktion der Denkstruktur des Albertus Magnus: Skizze und Thesen eines Forschungsprojektes." *Theologie und Glaube* 90 (2000): 602–12.

———. "Entwicklung und Stellung der Intellekttheorie im System des Albertus Magnus." *Archives d'histoire doctrinale et littéraire du moyen âge* 70 (2003): 165–218.

———. "Albertus Magnus (1200–1280)." In *Kölner Theologen: Von Rupert von Deutz bis Wilhelm Nyssen*, edited by Sebastian Cüppers, 31–67. Cologne: Marzellen, 2004.

———. Introduction. *Über den Menschen*, by Albertus Magnus. Edited and translated by Henry Anzulewicz and Joachim R. Söder, ix–xlix. Philosophische Bibliothek 531. Hamburg: Felix Meiner, 2004.

———. "Memoria und reminiscentia bei Albertus Magnus." In *La mémoire du temps au Moyen Âge*, edited by Agostino Paravicini Bagliani, 163–200. Micrologus' Library 12. Florence: Edizioni del Galluzzo, 2005.

———. "Zur Entwicklung und Stellung der Intellekttheorie im System des Albertus Magnus." In Pacheco and Meirinhos, *Intellect et imagination*, 3:1317–34. 2006.

———. Preface to Albertus Magnus, *De homine*, v–xlii. 2008.

———. "Vermögenspsychologische Grundlagen Kognitiver Leistung des Intellektes nach Albertus Magnus." *Acta Mediaevalia* 22 (2009): 95–116.

———. "Albertus Magnus über die *ars de symbolica theologia* des Dionysius Areopagita." *Teología y Vida* 51 (2010): 307–43.

———. "Rezeption und Reinterpretation: Pseudo-Dionysius Areopagita, die Peripatetiker und die Umdeutung der augustinischen Illuminationslehre bei Albertus Magnus." In *Kulturkontakte und Rezeptionsvorgänge in der Theologie des 12. und 13. Jahrhunderts*, edited by Ulrich Köpf and Dieter R. Bauer, 103–26. Archa Verbi, Subsidia 8. Münster: Aschendorff, 2011.

———. "Im Wirkungskreis des Albertus Magnus: Zur Geisteswelt der Christina von Stommeln in der Stadt Köln." In *Gottesschau und Gottesliebe: Die Mystikerin Christina von Stommeln 1242–1312*, edited by Guido von Büren, Susanne Richter, and Marcell Perse, 91–102. Regensburg, Germany: Schnell and Steiner, 2012.

———. "Anthropology: The Concept of Man in Albert the Great." In Resnick, *Companion to Albert the Great*, 325–46. 2013.

———. "Metaphysics and Its Relation to Theology in Albert's Thought." In Resnick, *Companion to Albert the Great*, 553–61. 2013.

———. "Plato and Platonic/Neoplatonic Sources in Albert." In Resnick, *Companion to Albert the Great*, 595–601. 2013.

———. "The Systematic Theology of Albert the Great." In Resnick, *Companion to Albert the Great*, 15–67. 2013.

Anzulewicz, Henryk, and Caterina Rigo. "'Reductio ad esse divinum': Zur Vollendung des Menschen nach Albertus Magnus." In *Ende und Vollendung: Eschatologische Perspektiven im Mittelalter*, edited by Jan A. Aertsen and Martin Pickave, 388–416. Miscellanea Mediaevalia 29. Berlin: Walter de Gruyter, 2001.

Ayres, Lewis. *Nicaea and Its Legacy: An Approach to Fourth-Century Trinitarian Theology*. Oxford: Oxford University Press, 2004.

———. *Augustine and the Trinity*. Cambridge: Cambridge University Press, 2010.

Backes, Jakob. "Der Geist als höherer Teil der Seele nach Albert dem Großen." In *Studia Albertina: Festschrift für B. Geyer zum 70. Geburtstage*, edited by Heinrich Ostlender, 52–67. Beiträge zur Geschichte der Philosophie und Theologie des Mittelalters, Supplementum 4. Münster: Aschendorff, 1952.

———. "Die Glaubensanalyse Alberts des Großen." *Franziskanische Studien* 72 (1990): 272–88.

Bazán, B. Carlos. "The Human Soul: Form *and* Substance? Thomas Aquinas'

Critique of Eclectic Aristotelianism." *Archives d'histoire doctrinale et littéraire du moyen âge* 64 (1997): 95–126.
Beierwaltes, Werner. "Reflexion und Einung: Zur Mystik Plotins." In von Balthasar, Beierwaltes, and Haas, *Grundfragen der Mystik*, 7–36. 1974.
———. *Denken des Einen: Studien zur neuplatonischen Philosophie und ihrer Wirkungsgeschichte*. Frankfurt am Main: Klostermann, 1985.
———. *Platonismus im Christentum*. Philosophische Abhandlungen 73. Frankfurt am Main: Klostermann, 1998.
Berger, David. "Aspekte der Mystischen Theologie im Thomismus." In *Doctor Communis*. New Series. Vol. 3, 33–69. Vatican City: Pontificia Academia Sancti Thomae Aquinatis, 2002.
Bertolacci, Amos. "Albert's Use of Avicenna and Islamic Philosophy." In Resnick, *Companion to Albert the Great*, 601–11. 2013.
Blankenhorn, Bernhard. "The Instrumental Causality of the Sacraments: Thomas Aquinas and Louis-Marie Chauvet." *Nova et Vetera* (English ed.) 4 (2006): 255–94.
———. "The Place of Romans 6 in Aquinas's Doctrine of Sacramental Causality: A Balance of History and Metaphysics." In *Ressourcement Thomism: Sacred Doctrine, the Sacraments and the Moral Life*, edited by Reinhard Hütter and Matthew Levering, 136–49. Washington, D.C.: The Catholic University of America Press, 2010.
———. "How the Early Albertus Magnus Transformed Augustinian Interiority." *Freiburger Zeitschrift für Philosophie und Theologie* 58 (2011): 351–86.
———. "Aquinas as Interpreter of Augustinian Illumination in Light of Albertus Magnus." *Nova et Vetera* (English ed.) 10 (2012): 689–713.
Bobik, Joseph. "Aquinas on 'Communicatio': The Foundation of Friendship and 'Caritas.'" *Modern Schoolman* 64 (1986): 1–18.
Boiadjiev, Tzotcho, Georgi Kapriev, and Andreas Speer, eds. *Die Dionysius-Rezeption im Mittelalter*. Rencontres de Philosophie Médiévale 9. Turnhout: Brepols, 2000.
Boland, Vivian. "'Non solum discens sed et patiens divina': The Wanderings of an Aristotelian Fragment." In *Roma, magistra mundi: Itineraria culturae medievalis*, edited by Jacqueline Hamesse, 1:55–69. Textes et Études du Moyen Âge 10. Louvain-la-Neuve: Fédération Internationale des Instituts d'Études Médiévales, 1998.
Bonino, Serge-Thomas. "Le rôle de l'image dans la connaissance prophétique d'après saint Thomas d'Aquin." *RT* 89 (1989): 533–68.
———. "'Les voiles sacrés': À propos d'une citation de Denys." In *Atti del IX Congresso Tomistico Internazionale*, edited by Pontificia Accademia Romana di San Tommaso d'Aquino, 158–71. Studi Tomistici 45. Vatican City: Libreria Editrice Vaticana, 1992.
———. "La simplicité de Dieu." In *Studi 1996*, edited by Dietrich Lorenz, 117–52. Rome: Pontificia Università San Tommaso, 1997.

Bonnewijn, Olivier. *La béatitude et les béatitudes: Une approche thomiste de l'éthique*. Rome: Pontifica Università Lateranense. 2001.

Booth, Edward. "St. Augustine's 'notitia sui' related to Aristotle and the Early Neo-Platonists." *Augustiniana* 27 (1977): 70–132, 364–401; 28 (1978): 183–221; 29 (1979): 97–124.

———. "Saint Thomas Aquinas's Critique of Saint Augustine's Conceptions of the Image of God in the Human Soul." In *Gott und sein Bild: Augustins "De Trinitate" im Spiegel gegenwärtiger Forschung*, edited by Johannes Brachtendorf, 219–39. Munich: Ferdinand Schöningh, 2000.

Bougerol, Jacques Guy. "Saint Bonaventure et le Pseudo-Denys l'Aréopagite." Supplement, *Études Franciscaines* 18 (1968): 33–123.

Boyle, Leonard E. *Facing History: A Different Thomas Aquinas*. Textes et Études du Moyen Âge 13. Louvain-la-Neuve: Fédération Internationale des Instituts d'Études Médiévales, 2000.

Brachtendorf, Johannes. *Die Struktur des menschlichen Geistes nach Augustinus: Selbstreflexion und Erkenntnis Gottes in "De Trinitate."* Paradeigmata 19. Hamburg: Felix Meiner, 2000.

Burger, Maria. "Das Verhältnis von Philosophie und Theologie in den Dionysius-Kommentaren Alberts des Großen." In Aertsen and Speer, *Was ist die Philosophie im Mittelalter?*, 579–86. 1998.

———. "Albertus Magnus: Kritische Anfragen an das Werk des Pseudo-Dionysius Areopagita." In Boiadjiev, Kapriev, and Speer, *Die Dionysius-Rezeption im Mittelalter*, 297–316. 2000.

———. "Albertus Magnus: Möglichkeiten theologischer Gotteserkenntnis." In Pacheco and Meirinhos, *Intellect et imagination*, 3:1335–47. 2006.

———. "'Fides et ratio' als Erkenntnisprinzipien der Theologie bei Albertus Magnus." In Honnefelder, Möhle, and del Barrio, *Via Alberti: Texte—Quellen—Interpretationen*, 37–58. 2009.

———. "Thomas Aquinas's Glosses on the Dionysius Commentaries of Albert the Great in Codex 30 of the Cologne Cathedral Library." In Honnefelder, Möhle, and del Barrio, *Via Alberti: Texte—Quellen—Interpretationen*, 561–74. 2009.

Burggraf, Jutta. "Introduccíon al pensamiento trinitario de San Alberto Magno." In *Excerpta e dissertationibus in sacra theologia*, 15:9–84. Pamplona: EUNSA, 1988.

Burrell, David, and Isabelle Moulin. "Albert, Aquinas, and Dionysius." In Coakley and Stang, *Re-thinking Dionysius*, 103–19. 2009.

Caparello, Adriana. "*De Divinis Nominibus*: aspetti lessicografici e il vocabolario Albertino." *Angelicum* 77 (2000): 65–98.

Catania, Francis J. "'Knowable' and 'Nameable' in Albert the Great's *Commentary on the Divine Names*." In Kovach and Shahan, *Albert the Great*, 97–128. 1980.

Cessario, Romanus. "A Thomist Interpretation of Faith: The Gifts of Understanding and Knowledge." In *Novitas et Veritas Vitae: Aux sources du renou-*

veau de la morale chrétienne, edited by Carlos-Josaphat Pinto de Oliveira, 67–102. Fribourg, Switzerland: Éditions universitaires, 1991.

Chenu, Marie-Dominique. "Le dernier avatar de la théologie orientale en Occident au XIIIe siècle." In *Mélanges Auguste Pelzer*, 159–81. Louvain: Bibliothèque de l'Université de Louvain, 1947.

———. "L'amour dans la foi." In *Parole de Dieu*, 1:105–11. 1964.

———. "Contribution à l'histoire du traité de la foi." In *Parole de Dieu*, 1:31–50. 1964.

———. *La Parole de Dieu*. Vol. 1, *La foi dans l'intelligence*. Cogitatio Fidei 10. Paris: Cerf, 1964.

———. "La psychologie de la foi dans la théologie du XIIIe siècle." In *Parole de Dieu*, 1:77–104. 1964.

———. *Toward Understanding Saint Thomas*. Translated by A.-M. Landry and D. Hughes. Chicago: Henry Regnery, 1964.

Coakley, Sarah, and Charles M Stang, eds. *Re-Thinking Dionysius the Areopagite*. London: Wiley-Blackwell, 2009.

Colish, Marcia L. *Peter Lombard*. 2 vols. Brill's Studies in Intellectual History. Vol. 41, parts 1–2. Leiden: E. J. Brill, 1994.

Congar, Yves. "Albert le Grand théologien de la grâce sanctifiante." *La Vie Spirituelle* 34 (1933): 109–40.

———. *Tradition and Traditions*. San Diego: Basilica Press, 1966.

Conticello, Carmelo Giuseppe. "*De Contemplatione* (Angelicum, 1920): La thèse inédite de doctorat du P. M.-D. Chenu." *RSPT* 75 (1991): 363–422.

Coolman, Boyd Taylor. *Knowing God by Experience: The Spiritual Senses in the Theology of William of Auxerre*. Washington D.C.: The Catholic University of America Press, 2004.

———. "The Medieval Affective Dionysian Tradition." In Coakley and Stang, *Re-Thinking Dionyius*, 85–102. 2009.

Cottier, Georges. "Intellectus et ratio." *RT* 88 (1988): 215–28.

———. "Désir naturel de voir Dieu." *Gregorianum* 78 (1997): 679–98.

———. *Le désir de Dieu: Sur les traces de saint Thomas*. Paris: Parole et Silence, 2002.

Courth, Franz. *Handbuch der Dogmengeschichte*. Band 2, Faszikel 1b, *Trinität in der Scholastik*. Freiburg im Breisgau: Herder, 1985.

Craemer-Ruegenberg, Ingrid. "Alberts Seelen- und Intellektlehre." In *Albert der Grosse, seine Zeit, sein Werk, seine Wirkung*, edited by Albert Zimmermann, 104–15. Miscellanea Mediaevalia 14. Berlin: Walter de Gruyter, 1981.

Crouse, Robert. "Knowledge." In Fitzgerald and Cavadini, *Augustine Through the Ages*, 486–88. 1999.

Cunningham, Francis L. B. *The Indwelling of the Trinity: A Historico-Doctrinal Study of the Theory of St. Thomas Aquinas*. Dubuque, Iowa: Priory Press, 1955.

Dales, Richard C. *The Problem of the Rational Soul in the Thirteenth Century*. Brill's Studies in Intellectual History 65. Leiden: E. J. Brill, 1995.

D'Ancona Costa, Cristina. *Recherches sur le Liber de Causis*. Études de Philosophie Médiévale 72. Paris: Vrin, 1995.

Dauphinais, Michael. "Loving the Lord Your God: The 'Imago Dei' in Saint Thomas Aquinas." *Thomist* 63 (1999): 241–67.

Dauphinais, Michael, Barry David, and Matthew Levering, eds. *Aquinas the Augustinian*. Washington, D.C.: The Catholic University of America Press, 2007.

De Andia, Ysabel. *Henosis: L'union à Dieu chez Denys l'Aréopagite*. Philosophia Antiqua 71. Leiden: E. J. Brill, 1996.

———. *Denys l'Aréopagite: Tradition et Métamorphoses*. Paris: Vrin, 2006.

———. "'Pati divina' chez Denys l'Aréopagite, Thomas d'Aquin et Jacques Maritain." In *Saint Thomas d'Aquin*, edited by Thierry-Dominique Humbrecht, 549–89. Les Cahiers d'Histoire de la Philosophie. Paris: Cerf, 2010.

———. *La Voie et le Voyageur: Essai d'anthropologie de la vie spirituelle*. Paris: Cerf, 2012.

———, ed. *Denys l'Aréopagite et sa postérité en Orient et en Occident*. Paris: Institut d'Études Augustiniennes, 1997.

De Belloy, Camille. *La visite de Dieu: Essai sur les missions des personnes divines selon saint Thomas d'Aquin*. Geneva: Ad Solem, 2006.

———. "Habitation et missions des personnes divines selon Thomas d'Aquin: Principes de distinction, normes d'intégration." *RSPT* 92 (2008): 225–40.

De Blic, Jacques. "Pour l'histoire de la théologie des dons avant saint Thomas." *Revue d'Ascétique et de Mystique* 22 (1946): 117–79.

De Contenson, Pierre-Marie. "S. Thomas et l'avicennisme latin." *RSPT* 43 (1959): 3–31.

De Halleux, André. "Palamisme et Scolastique." In *Patrologie et œcuménisme: Recueil d'études*. Bibliotheca Ephemeridum Theologicarum Lovaniensium 93. Leuven: Leuven University Press, 1990, 782–815.

Delfino, Robert A. "Mystical Theology in Aquinas and Maritain." In *Jacques Maritain and the Many Ways of Knowing*, edited by Douglas A. Ollivant, 253–68. Washington, D.C.: The Catholic University of America Press, 2002.

De Libera, Alain. "Albert le Grand et Maître Eckhart: Les raisons d'une 'mystique.'" *Communio* 17 (1992): 83–98.

———. "Albert le Grand ou l'antiplatonisme sans Platon." In *Contre Platon*, vol. 1, *Le Platonisme dévoilé*, edited by Monique Dixsaut, 247–71. Paris: Vrin, 1993.

———. *La mystique rhénane d'Albert le Grand à Maître Eckhart*. Paris: Seuil, 1994.

———. Notes to *L'intelligence et la pensée: Sur le "De Anima,"* by Averroes, 175–396. 2nd ed. Paris: Flammarion, 1998.

———. *Raison et foi: Archéologie d'une crise d'Albert le Grand à Jean-Paul II*. L'ordre philosophique. Paris: Seuil, 2003.

———. *Métaphysique et noétique: Albert le Grand. Problèmes et controverses*. Paris: Vrin, 2005.

Dictionnaire de Spiritualité. 17 vols. Paris: Letouzey et Ané, 1932–95.
Dobler, Emil. *Falsche Väterzitate bei Thomas von Aquin.* Dokimion 27. Fribourg, Switzerland: Universitätsverlag, 2001.
Dohmen, Christoph. *Exodus 19–40.* Herders Theologischer Kommentar zum Alten Testament. Freiburg im Breisgau: Herder, 2004.
Doms, Herbert. *Die Gnadenlehre des seligen Albertus Magnus.* Breslauer Studien zur historischen Theologie 13. Breslau: 1929.

———. "Ewige Verklärung und ewige Verwerfung nach dem hl. Albertus Magnus." *Divus Thomas* 10 (1932): 143–61.

Dondaine, Hyacinthe F. "Saint Albert et le grec." *Recherches de théologie ancienne et médiévale* 17 (1950): 315–19.

———. "S. Thomas et Scot Érigène." *RSPT* 35 (1951): 31–33.

———. "L'objet et le 'medium' de la vision béatifique chez les théologiens du XIIIe siècle." *Recherches de théologie ancienne et médiévale* 19 (1952): 60–99.

———. "Les scolastiques citent-ils les Pères de première main?" *RSPT* 36 (1952): 231–43.

———. *Le Corpus dionysien de l'Université de Paris au XIIIe siècle.* Rome: Edizioni di Storia e letteratura, 1953.

———. "Cognoscere de Deo 'quid est.'" *Recherches de théologie ancienne et médiévale* 22 (1955): 72–78.

Ducharme, Léonard. "The Individual Human Being in Saint Albert's Earlier Writings." In Kovach and Shahan, *Albert the Great,* 131–60. 1980.
Durand, Emmanuel. "Du concours des effets de nature et de grâce en 'sacra doctrina': Une clé pour l'équilibre d'une théologie d'inspiration thomasienne." *Nova et Vetera* (French ed.) 80 (2005): 7–22.
Durantel, J. *Saint Thomas et le Pseudo-Denys.* Paris: Félix Alcan, 1919.
Du Roy, Olivier. *L'intelligence de la foi en la Trinité selon saint Augustin: Genèse de sa théologie trinitaire jusqu'en 391.* Paris: Institut d'Études Augustiniennes, 1966.
Emery, Gilles. *La Trinité créatrice: Trinité et création dans les commentaires aux "Sentences" de Thomas d'Aquin et de ses précurseurs Albert le Grand et Bonaventure.* Bibliothèque Thomiste 47. Paris: Vrin, 1995.

———. "The Treatise of St. Thomas on the Trinity in the *Summa contra Gentiles.*" In *Trinity in Aquinas.* Translated by Heather Buttery, 71–120. Ypsilanti, Mich.: Sapientia Press, 2003.

———. "Missions invisibles et missions visibles: Le Christ et son Esprit." *RT* 106 (2006): 51–99.

———. *The Trinitarian Theology of Saint Thomas Aquinas.* Translated by Francesca Aran Murphy. Oxford: Oxford University Press, 2007.

———. *Trinity, Church, and the Human Person: Thomistic Essays.* Naples, Fla.: Sapientia Press, 2007.

———. "Trinity and Truth: The Son as Truth and the Spirit of Truth in St. Thomas Aquinas." In *Trinity, Church, and the Human Person.* Translated by Mary Thomas Noble, 73–114. 2007.

———. "The Unity of Man, Body and Soul, in St. Thomas Aquinas." In *Trinity, Church, and the Human Person*. Translated by Therese Scarpelli, 209–35. 2007.

———. "'Theologia' and 'Dispensatio': The Centrality of the Divine Missions in St. Thomas's Trinitarian Theology." *Thomist* 74 (2010): 515–61.

———. "L'inhabitation de Dieu Trinité dans les justes." *Nova et Vetera* (French ed.) 88 (2013): 155–84.

Erb, Heather McAdam. "'Pati Divina': Mystical Union in Aquinas." In *Faith, Scholarship, and Culture in the 21st Century*, edited by Alice Ramos and Marie I. George, 73–96. Washington, D.C.: The Catholic University of America Press, 2002.

Fabro, Cornelio. "Platonism, Neo-Platonism and Thomism: Convergences and Divergences." *New Scholasticism* 44 (1970): 69–100.

Feder, Alfred. "Des Aquinaten Kommentar zu Pseudo-Dionysius' *De Divinis Nominibus*: Ein Beitrag zur Arbeitsmethode des hl. Thomas." *Scholastik* 1 (1926): 321–51.

Festugière, A. J. *Contemplation et vie contemplative selon Platon*. 4th ed. Paris: Vrin, 1975.

Fitzgerald, Allan D., and John C. Cavadini, eds. *Augustine Through the Ages: An Encyclopedia*. Grand Rapids, Mich.: Eerdmans, 1999.

Flasch, Kurt. *Das philosophische Denken im Mittelalter: von Augustinus zu Machiavelli*. Stuttgart: Reclam, 1986.

———. *Meister Eckhart: Die Geburt der "Deutschen Mystik" aus dem Geist der arabischen Philosophie*. Munich: C. H. Beck, 2006.

———. *Dietrich von Freiberg: Philosophie, Theologie, Naturforschung um 1300*. Frankfurt am Main: Vittorio Klostermann, 2007.

Floucat, Yves. "L'intellection et son verbe selon saint Thomas d'Aquin." *RT* 97 (1997): 443–84, 640–93.

Führer, Markus. "The Contemplative Function of the Agent Intellect in the Psychology of Albert the Great." In *Historia Philosophiae Medii Aevi: Studien zur Geschichte der Philosophie des Mittelalters*, edited by Burkhard Mojsisch and Olaf Pluta, 305–19. Philadelphia: B. R. Grüner, 1991.

———. "Albertus Magnus' Theory of Divine Illumination." In Senner, *Albertus Magnus, Zum Gedenken*, 141–55. 2001.

———. "Albert the Great and Mystical Epistemology." In Resnick, *Companion to Albert the Great*, 137–61. 2013.

Gardeil, Ambroise. "Les dons du Saint Esprit." In *Dictionnaire de théologie catholique*, edited by E. Mangenot. Vol. 4, part 2, cols. 1728–81. Paris: L. Letouzey et Âne, 1920.

———. *La structure de l'âme et l'expérience mystique*. 2 vols. Paris: J. Gabalda, 1927.

———. "L'expérience mystique pure dans le cadre des 'Missions divines' I." Supplement, *La Vie Spirituelle* 31 (June 1932): 129–46.

———. "L'expérience mystique pure dans le cadre des 'Missions divines' II: Les mission des divine personnes." Supplement, *La Vie Spirituelle* 32 (July–August 1932): 1–21.

———. "L'expérience mystique pure dans le cadre des 'Missions divines' III: La connaissance expérimentale de Dieu." Supplement, *La Vie Spirituelle* 32 (September 1932): 65–76.

Gardeil, H.-D. Notes to *Somme théologique, Les origines de l'homme: 1a, Questions 90–102*, by Thomas Aquinas, 287–452. Paris: Cerf, 1963.

Garrigou-Lagrange, Réginald. "Le mode suprahumain des dons du Saint-Esprit dans la *Somme Théologique* de S. Thomas." Supplement, *La Vie Spirituelle* 7 (March 1923): 124–36.

———. "L'habitation de la sainte Trinité et l'expérience mystique." *RT* 33 (1928): 449–74.

———. "L'union de la vie intellectuelle et de la vie intérieure chez Albert le Grand." Supplement, *La Vie Spirituelle* 34 (1933): 50–64.

———. *Christian Perfection and Contemplation According to St. Thomas Aquinas and St. John of the Cross*. Translated by M. Timothea Doyle. St. Louis: Herder, 1937.

Gauthier, René-Antoine. Introduction to *Lectura in librum de anima a quodam discipulo reportata*, by Anonymi Magistri Artium (c. 1245–50), 1*–22*. Spicilegium Bonaventurianum 24. Grottaferrata: Editiones Collegii S. Bonaventurae, 1985.

Geenen, Godefroid. "Une étude inédite sur le Ps. Denys et S. Thomas." *Divus Thomas* 31 (1953): 169–84.

Gersh, Stephen. *From Iamblichus to Eriugena: An Investigation of the Pre-history and Evolution of the Pseudo-Dionysian Tradition*. Leiden: E. J. Brill, 1978.

Gils, Pierre-Marie. "Le Ms. *Napoli, Biblioteca Nazionale I.B. 54* est-il de la main de S. Thomas?" *RSPT* 49 (1965): 37–59.

Gilson, Étienne. "L'âme raisonnable chez Albert le Grand." *Archives d'histoire doctrinale et littéraire du moyen âge* 14 (1943): 5–72.

———. "Propos sur l'être et sa notion." In *San Tommaso e il pensiero moderno*, edited by Antonio Piolanti, 7–17. Studi Tomistici 3. Rome: Città Nuova, 1974.

———. *Pourquoi saint Thomas a critiqué saint Augustin*. Paris: Vrin, 1986.

Girón-Negrón, Luis M. "Dionysian Thought in Sixteenth-Century Spanish Mystical Theology." In Coakley and Stang, *Re-Thinking Dionysius*, 163–76. 2009.

Golitzin, Alexander. "On the Other Hand: A Response to Fr. Paul Wesche's Recent Article on Dionysius." *St. Vladimir's Theological Quarterly* 34 (1990): 305–23.

———. *Et introibo ad altare Dei: The Mystagogy of Dionysius Areopagita, With Special Reference to Its Predecessors in the Eastern Christian Tradition*. Analecta Vlatadon 59. Thessaloniki: Patriarchikon Idruma Paterikon Meleton, 1994.

González Ayesta, Cruz. *El don de sabiduría según Santo Tomás: Divinización, filiación y connaturalidad*. Colección Teológica 92. Navarra: EUNSA, 1998.

Goodman, L. E. *Avicenna*. London: Routledge, 1992.
Goris, Harm. "Theology and Theory of the Word in Aquinas: Understanding Augustine by Innovating Aristotle." In Dauphinais, David, and Levering, *Aquinas the Augustinian*, 62–78. 2007.
Grabmann, Martin. "Der Einfluss Alberts der Grossen auf das mittelalterliche Geistesleben: Das deutsche Element in der mittelalterlichen Scholastik und Mystik." In *Mittelalterliches Geistesleben*, 2:325–412. Munich: Max Heuber, 1936.
Graf, Thomas. "Die Lehre des hl. Albertus Magnus über das psychologische Subjekt der Gnade und Tugenden." *Divus Thomas* 10 (1932): 162–94.
Guagliardo, Vincent A. Introduction to *Commentary on the Book of Causes*, by Thomas Aquinas. Edited and translated by Vincent A. Guagliardo, Charles R. Hess, and Richard C. Taylor, ix–xxxii. Washington, D.C.: The Catholic University of America Press, 1996.
Haberl, Ferdinand. *Die Inkarnationslehre des heiligen Albertus Magnus*. Freiburg im Breisgau: Herder, 1939.
Hamman, Adalbert-Gautier. *L'homme, image de Dieu: Essai d'une anthropologie chrétienne dans l'Église des cinq premiers siècles*. Paris: Desclée de Brouwer, 1987.
Harrington, L. Michael. Introduction to *Thirteenth Century Textbook*, edited by L. Michael Harrington, 1–42. 2004.
Hasse, Dag N. "The Early Albertus Magnus and His Arabic Sources on the Theory of the Soul." *Vivarium* 46 (2008): 232–52.
Hellmeier, Paul Dominikus. *Anima et intellectus: Albertus Magnus und Thomas von Aquin über Seele und Intellekt des Menschen*. Beiträge zur Geschichte der Philosophie und Theologie des Mittelalters, Neue Folge 75. Münster: Aschendorff, 2011.
Hergan, Jeffrey P. *St. Albert the Great's Theory of the Beatific Vision*. New York: Peter Lang, 2002.
Hiedl, Augustin. "Zur Basler Ausgabe des Sentenzenkommentars Alberts des Grossen vom Jahre 1506." In *Wege zur Buchwissenschaft*, edited by Otto Wenig, 195–233. Bonner Beiträge zur Bibliotheks- und Bücherkunde 14. Bonn: 1966.
Hipp, Stephen A. *"Person" in Christian Tradition and the Conception of Saint Albert the Great: A Systematic Study of Its Concept as Illuminated by the Mysteries of the Trinity and the Incarnation*. Beiträge zur Geschichte der Philosophie und Theologie des Mittelalters, Neue Folge 57. Münster: Aschendorff, 2001.
Hödl, Ludwig. "Die 'Entdivinisierung' des menschlichen Intellekts in der mittelalterlichen Philosophie und Theologie." In *Zusammenhänge, Einflüsse, Wirkungen*, edited by Joerg O. Fichte, Karl Heinz Gröller, and Bernhard Schimmelpfennig, 57–70. Berlin: Walter de Gruyter, 1986.
Hofer, Andrew. "Dionysian Elements in Thomas Aquinas's Christology: A Case of the Authority and Ambiguity of Pseudo-Dionysius." *Thomist* 72 (2008): 409–42.

Honnefelder, Ludger. "Albertus Magnus 1200–2000." In Senner, *Albertus Magnus, Zum Gedenken*, xvii–xxiv. 2001.

———. "Die philosophiegeschichtliche Bedeutung Alberts des Großen." In *Albertus Magnus und die Anfänge der Aristoteles-Rezeption im lateinischen Mittelalter: Von Richardus Rufus bis zu Franciscus de Mayronis*, edited by Ludger Honnefelder, Rega Wood, Mechthild Dreyer, and Marc-Aeilko Aris, 249–80. Subsidia Albertina 1. Münster: Aschendorff, 2005.

Honnefelder, Ludger, Hannes Möhle, and Susana Bullido del Barrio, eds. *Via Alberti: Texte—Quellen—Interpretationen*. Subsidia Albertina 2. Münster: Aschendorff, 2009.

Horst, Ulrich. *Die Gaben des Heiligen Geistes nach Thomas von Aquin*. Veröffentlichungen des Grabmann-Institutes 46. Berlin: Akademie Verlag, 2001.

Hoye, William J. "Die Unerkennbarkeit Gottes als die letzte Erkenntnis nach Thomas von Aquin." In *Thomas von Aquin*, edited by Albert Zimmermann, 117–39. Miscellanea Mediaevalia 19. Berlin: Walter de Gruyter, 1988.

———. "Die Vereinigung mit dem gänzlich Unerkannten nach Bonaventura, Nikolaus von Kues und Thomas von Aquin." In Boiadjiev, Kapriev, and Speer, *Dionysius-Rezeption*, 478–504. 2000.

———. "Mystische Theologie nach Albert dem Großen." In Senner, *Albertus Magnus, Zum Gedenken*, 587–603. 2001.

Humbrecht, Thierry-Dominique. "Noms divins: Les sources de saint Thomas au XIIIe siècle (II)." *RT* 105 (2005): 551–93.

———. *Théologie négative et noms divins chez saint Thomas d'Aquin*. Bibliothèque Thomiste 57. Paris: Vrin, 2005.

———. "Albert le Grand commentateur de la *Théologie mystique* de Denys." *RSPT* 90 (2006): 225–71.

———. *Trinité et création au prisme de la voie négative chez saint Thomas d'Aquin*. Bibliothèque de la Revue Thomiste. Paris: Parole et Silence, 2011.

Hyman, Arthur. "Aristotle's Theory of the Intellect and Its Interpretation by Averroes." In *Studies in Aristotle*, edited by Dominic J. O'Meara, 161–91. Studies in Philosophy and the History of Philosophy 9. Washington, D.C.: The Catholic University of America Press, 1981.

Imbach, Ruedi, and Adriano Oliva. *La philosophie de Thomas d'Aquin*. Paris: Vrin, 2009.

Javelet, Robert. "Thomas Gallus ou les écritures dans une dialectique mystique." In *L'homme devant Dieu: Mélanges offerts au père Henri de Lubac*, 2:99–110. Paris: Aubier, 1964.

Jeauneau, Édouard. "Pseudo-Dionysius, Gregory of Nyssa, and Maximus the Confessor in the Works of John Scotus Eriugena." In *Études érigéniennes*, 175–87. Paris: Institut d'Études Augustiniennes, 1987.

Jeßberger, Ludwig. *Das Abhängigkeitsverhältnis des hl. Thomas von Aquin von Albertus Magnus und Bonaventura im dritten Buche des Sentenzenkommentars*. Würzburg: Richard Mayr, 1936.

John of Saint Thomas. *Cursus Theologicus, In Iam-IIae: De donis Spiritus Sancti.* Collectioz Lavallensis. Québec: Armand Mathieu and Hervé Gagné, 1958.

Jones, John D. Introduction to *The Divine Names and Mystical Theology*, by Dionysius Areopagita, 15–106. 1980.

———. "The *Divine Names* in John Sarracen's Translation: Misconstruing Dionysius's Language About God?" *American Catholic Philosophical Quarterly* 82 (2008): 661–82.

———. "(Mis?)-Reading the *Divine Names* as a Science: Aquinas's Interpretation of the *Divine Names* of (Pseudo) Dionysius Areopagite." *St. Vladimir's Theological Quarterly* 52 (2008): 142–71.

Journet, Charles. *Connaissance et inconnaissance de Dieu.* Paris: Egloff, 1943.

Juárez, Guillermo A. *Dios Trinidad en todas las creaturas y en los santos: Estudio histórico-sistemático de la doctrina del "Comentario a las Sentencias" de Santo Tomás de Aquino sobre la omnipresencia y la inhabitación.* Córdoba, Argentina: Ediciones del Copista, 2008.

Keaty, Anthony W. "Thomas's Authority for Identifying Charity as Friendship: Aristotle or John 15?" *Thomist* 62 (1998): 581–601.

Kennedy, Leonard A. "St. Albert the Great's Doctrine of Divine Illumination." *Modern Schoolman* 40 (1962): 23–37.

Kharlamov, Vladmir. *The Beauty of the Unity and the Harmony of the Whole: The Concept of Theosis in the Theology of Pseudo-Dionysius the Areopagite.* Eugene, Ore.: Wipf and Stock, 2009.

Knepper, Timothy D. "Not Not: The Method and Logic of Dionysian Negation." *American Catholic Philosophical Quarterly* 82 (2008): 619–37.

Koch, Josef. "Augustinischer und Dionysischer Neuplatonismus und das Mittelalter." In *Platonismus in der Philosophie des Mittelalters*, edited by Werner Beierwaltes, 317–42. Wege der Forschung 197. Darmstadt: Wissenschaftliche Buchgesellschaft, 1969.

Kovach, Francis J., and Robert W. Shahan, eds. *Albert the Great: Commemorative Essays.* Norman: University of Oklahoma Press, 1980.

Krämer, Klaus. *Imago Trinitatis: Die Gottebenbildlichkeit des Menschen in der Theologie des Thomas von Aquin.* Freiburger theologische Studien 164. Freiburg im Breisgau: Herder, 2000.

Kromholtz, Bryan. *On the Last Day: The Time of the Resurrection of the Dead according to Thomas Aquinas.* Studia Friburgensia 110. Fribourg, Switzerland: Academic Press, 2010.

Kübel, Wilhelm. "Das Salerno Autographfragment des Thomas von Aquin und die Edition des Kommentars zu Ps. Dionysius, *De caelesti hierarchia* des Albertus Magnus." *Bulletin de Philosophie Médiévale* 38 (1996): 125–28.

Kwasniewski, Peter A. "St. Thomas, Exstasis, and Union with the Beloved." *Thomist* 61 (1997): 587–603.

Labourdette, Marie-Michel. "Dons du Saint-Esprit: Saint Thomas et la théologie thomiste." *DS* 3 (1957): cols. 1610–35.

Bibliography 485

———. *Cours de théologie morale*. Vol. 10, *La charité*. Toulouse: 1960.
Larchet, Jean-Claude. *La Divinisation de l'homme selon saint Maxime le Confesseur*. Cogitatio Fidei 194. Paris: Cerf, 1996.
———. *La théologie des énergies divines: Des origines à saint Jean Damascène*. Cogitatio Fidei 272. Paris: Cerf, 2010.
Lavaud, M.-H. "Les dons du Saint-Esprit d'après Albert le Grand." *RT* 36 (1931): 162–83.
Leinsle, Ulrich G. *Introduction to Scholastic Theology*. Translated by Michael J. Miller. Washington, D.C.: The Catholic University of America Press, 2010.
Lenzi, Massimiliano. "Alberto e Tommaso sullo statuto dell'anima umana." *Archives d'histoire doctrinale et littéraire du moyen âge* 74 (2007): 27–58.
Lévy, Antoine. *Le créé et l'incréé: Maxime le Confesseur et Thomas d'Aquin, Aux sources de la querelle palamienne*. Bibliothèque Thomiste 59. Paris: Vrin, 2006.
Lluch-Baixauli, Miguel. "Sobre el Comentario Albertino a la *Mystica Theologia* de Dionisio." In *Die Kölner Universität im Mittelalter: Geistige Wurzeln und soziale Wirklichkeit*, edited by Albert Zimmermann, 68–76. Miscellanea Mediaevalia 20. Berlin: Walter de Gruyter, 1989.
Lonergan, Bernard. *Grace and Freedom: Operative Grace in the Thought of St. Thomas Aquinas*. Collected Works of Bernard Lonergan 1. Toronto: University of Toronto Press, 2000.
Lossky, Vladimir. *The Mystical Theology of the Eastern Church*. Crestwood, N.Y.: St. Vladimir's Seminary Press, 1976.
Lottin, Odon. *Psychologie et morale au XIIe et XIIIe siècles*. Vol. 3, part 2, sect. 1. Louvain: Abbaye du Mont César; Gembloux: J. Duculot, 1949.
Louth, Andrew. *The Origins of the Christian Mystical Tradition: From Plato to Denys*. Oxford: Clarendon Press, 1981.
Maillard, Pierre-Yves. *La vision de Dieu chez Thomas d'Aquin*. Bibliothèque Thomiste 53. Paris: Vrin, 2001.
Maréchal, Joseph. *Études sur la psychologie des mystiques*. 2 vols. Paris: Desclée de Brouwer. 1937.
Maritain, Jacques. *Distinguish to Unite or the Degrees of Knowledge*. Translated by Gerald B. Phelan. London: Geoffrey Bles, 1959.
Mayer, Rupert Johannes. *De veritate, quid est? Vom Wesen der Wahrheit: Ein Gespräch mit Thomas von Aquin*. Studia Friburgensia 92. Fribourg, Switzerland: Universitätsverlag, 2002.
———. "Stockwerkphilosophie gegen Stockwerktheologie? Zum 'desiderium naturale' bei Henri de Lubac und Thomas von Aquin." *Freiburger Zeitschrift für Philosophie und Theologie* 56 (2009): 164–93.
McDonough, Conor. "Grounding Speech and Silence: Cataphatism and Apophatism in Denys and Aquinas." *Irish Theological Quarterly* 76 (2011): 57–76.
McEvoy, James. Introduction to Gallus and Grosseteste, *Mystical Theology*, 3–13, 55–58. 2003.
McGinn, Bernard. *The Presence of God: A History of Western Christian Mysticism*.

Vol. 1, *The Foundations of Mysticism: Origins to the 5th Century*. New York: Crossroad, 1991. Vol. 2, *The Growth of Mysticism: Gregory the Great through the 12th Century*. New York: Crossroad, 1994. Vol. 3, *The Flowering of Mysticism: Men and Women in the New Mysticism, 1200–1350*. New York: Crossroad, 1998. Vol. 4, *The Harvest of Mysticism in Medieval Germany*. New York: Crossroad, 2005.

McGuiness, Joseph Ignatius. "The Distinctive Nature of the Gift of Understanding." *Thomist* 3 (1941): 217–78.

McKay, Angela M. "The Infused and Acquired Virtues in Aquinas' Moral Philosophy." Ph.D. diss., University of Notre Dame, 2004.

Meersseman, Gilles M. "La contemplation mystique d'après le bienheureux Albert est-elle immédiate?" *RT* 36 (1931): 184–97.

Meis, Anneliese. "El misterio de la alteridad en Alberto Magno: *Super Mysticam Theologiam Dionysii*." *Teología y Vida* 47 (2006): 541–74.

———. Introduction to *Sobre la Teología Mística de Dionisio*, by Albertus Magnus. Edited by Meis, 17–35. Anales de la Facultad de Teología 59. Santiago, Chile: Pontificia Universidad Católica de Chile, 2008.

———. "La influencia de Gregorio Magno en Alberto Magno: *Super Dionysii Mysticam Theologiam et Epistulas*." *Teología y Vida* 51 (2010): 345–64.

Merriell, D. Juvenal. *To the Image of the Trinity: A Study in the Development of Aquinas' Teaching*. Studies and Texts 96. Toronto: Pontifical Institute of Medieval Studies, 1990.

Mojsisch, Burkhard. "La psychologie philosophique d'Albert la Grand et la théorie de l'intellect de Dietrich de Freiberg: Essaie de comparaison." *Archives de Philosophie* 43 (1980): 675–93.

Mongillo, Dalmazio. "Les béatitudes et la béatitude: Le dynamisme de la *Somme de théologie* de Thomas d'Aquin, une lecture de la Ia-IIae q. 69." *RSPT* 78 (1994): 373–88.

Montagnes, Bernard. "Les deux fonctions de la sagesse: Ordonner et juger." *RSPT* 53 (1969): 675–86.

Moonan, Lawrence. "What Is a Negative Theology? Albert's Answer." In Senner, *Albertus Magnus, Zum Gedenken*, 605–18. 2001.

Moraga Esquivel, José M. "El ocultamiento luminoso de Dios Alberto Magno: *Super Mysticam Theologiam Dionysii*." *Veritas: Revista de filosofía y teología* 19 (2008): 345–70.

Moreno, Antonio. "The Nature of St. Thomas' Knowledge 'Per Connaturalitatem.'" *Angelicum* 47 (1970): 43–62.

Morerod, Charles. "La mystique dans l'épistémologie de Jacques Maritain." *Nova et Vetera* (French ed.) 83 (2008): 121–50.

Moulin, Isabelle. "Albert's Doctrine of Substance." In Resnick, *Companion to Albert the Great*, 648–58. 2013.

Mulchahey, M. Michèle. "The *Studium* at Cologne and Its Role Within Early Dominican Education." *Listening* 43 (2008): 118–47.

Narváez, Mauricio. "Portée herméneutique de la notion d' 'intentio' chez Thomas d'Aquin." *Revue Philosophique de Louvain* 99 (2001): 201–19.
Nash, Ronald H. "Wisdom." In Fitzgerald and Cavadini, *Augustine Through the Ages*, 885–87. 1999.
———. *The Light of the Mind: St. Augustine's Theory of Knowledge*. Lima, Ohio: Academic Renewal Press, 2003.
Neidl, Walter M. *"Thearchia": Die Frage nach dem Sinn von Gott bei Pseudo-Dionysius Areopagita und Thomas von Aquin*. Innsbruck: J. Habbel, 1973.
Nicolas, Jean-Hervé. *Dieu connu comme inconnu*. Bibliothèque française de philosophie. Paris: Desclée de Brouwer, 1966.
Noble, H.-D. Notes to *Somme théologique, La charité*, by Thomas Aquinas. Vol. 1, 2a–2ae, Questions 23–26. Paris: Tournai, 1936, 231–360.
O'Callaghan, John P. "'Verbum Mentis': Philosophical or Theological Doctrine in Aquinas?" *Proceedings of the American Catholic Philosophical Association* 74 (2000): 103–19.
———. *Thomist Realism and the Linguistic Turn: Toward a More Perfect Form of Existence*. Notre Dame, Ind.: University of Notre Dame Press, 2002.
O'Connor, Edward D. "Appendix 4: The Evolution of St. Thomas's Thought on the Gifts." In *Summa Theologiae*, by Thomas Aquinas. Vol. 24, *The Gifts of the Holy Spirit*, edited by Edward D. O'Connor, 110–30. New York: McGraw-Hill, 1974.
Oliva, Adriano. *Les débuts de l'enseignement de Thomas d'Aquin et sa conception de la "sacra doctrina," avec l'édition du prologue de son Commentaire des "Sentences."* Bibliothèque Thomiste 58. Paris: Vrin, 2006.
O'Meara, Dominic. *Plotin: Une introduction aux "Ennéades."* 2nd ed. Vestigia 10. Fribourg, Switzerland: Academic Press, 2004.
O'Rourke, Fran. *Pseudo-Dionysius and the Metaphysics of Aquinas*. Notre Dame, Ind.: University of Notre Dame Press, 2005.
Owens, Joseph. "Aquinas: 'Darkness of Ignorance' in the Most Refined Notion of God." *Southwestern Journal of Philosophy* 5 (1974): 93–110.
Patfoort, Albert. *Thomas d'Aquin, les clefs d'une théologie*. Paris: FAC, 1983.
———. "Cognitio ista est quasi experimentalis." *Angelicum* 63 (1986): 3–13.
———. "Missions divines et expérience des Personnes divines selon s. Thomas." *Angelicum* 63 (1986): 545–59.
Pachas, José Antonio. "La alteridad a la luz del misterio de Dios en el *Super Dionysii Mysticam Theologiam* de san Alberto Magno." *Archa Verbi: Yearbook for the Study of Medieval Theology* 6 (2009): 133–57.
Pacheco, Maria Cândida, and José Francisco Meirinhos, eds. *Intellect et imagination dans la Philosophie Médiévale*. 3 vols. Rencontres de Philosophie Médiévale. Vol. 11, parts 1–3. Turnhout: Brepols, 2006.
Pagnoni-Sturlese, Maria-Rita. "A propos du néoplatonisme d'Albert le Grand." *Archives de Philosophie* 43 (1980): 635–54.
Pegis, Anton C. "Penitus Manet ignotum." *Medieval Studies* 27 (1965): 212–26.

Perczel, István. "The Earliest Syriac Reception of Dionysius." In Coakley and Stang, *Re-Thinking Dionysius*, 27–42. 2009.

Perl, Eric D. *Theophany: The Neoplatonic Philosophy of Dionysius the Areopagite*. Albany, N.Y.: SUNY Press, 2007.

Philips, Gérard. *L'union personnelle avec le Dieu vivant: Essai sur l'origine et le sens de la grâce créée*. Bibliotheca Ephemeridum Theologicarum Lovaniensium 36. Gembloux: J. Duculot, 1974.

Pieper, Josef. *Philosophia negativa: Zwei Versuche über Thomas von Aquin*. Munich: Kösel, 1953.

Pinckaers, Servais. *The Sources of Christian Ethics*. Translated by Mary Thomas Noble. Washington, D.C.: The Catholic University of America Press, 1995.

———. *La vie selon l'Esprit: Essai de théologie spirituelle selon saint Paul et saint Thomas d'Aquin*. Amateca. Vol. 17, part 2. Luxembourg: Éditions Saint-Paul, 1996.

———. "Morality and the Movement of the Holy Spirit: Aquinas's Doctrine of 'Instinctus.'" In *The Pinckaers Reader: Renewing Thomistic Moral Theology*. Edited and translated by John Berkman and Craig Steven Titus. Washington, D.C.: The Catholic University of America Press, 2005, 385–95.

———. *Plaidoyer pour la vertu*. Paris: Parole et Silence, 2007.

Pinsent, Andrew. "The Gifts and Fruits of the Holy Spirit." In *The Oxford Handbook of Aquinas*, edited by Brian Davies and Eleonore Stump, 475–88. Oxford: Oxford University Press, 2012.

Poirel, Dominique. *Hugues de Saint-Victor*. Paris: Cerf, 1998.

Prades, Javier. *"Deus specialiter est in sanctis per gratiam": El misterio de la inhabitación de la Trinidad, en los escritos de Santo Tomás*. Analecta Gregoriana 261. Rome: Editrice Pontificia Università Gregoriana, 1993.

Pritzl, Kurt. "The Place of Intellect in Aristotle." *Proceedings of the American Catholic Philosophical Association* 80 (2006): 57–75.

Prügl, Thomas, and Marianne Schlosser, eds. *Kirchenbild und Spiritualität: Dominikanische Beiträge zur Ekklesiologie und zum kirchlichen Leben im Mittelalter*. Munich: Ferdinand Schöningh, 2007.

Puech, Henri-Charles. "La ténèbre mystique chez le Pseudo-Denys et dans la tradition patristique." *Études Carmélitaines* 23 (1938): 33–53.

Putallaz, François-Xavier. *Le sens de la réflexion chez Thomas d'Aquin*. Études de Philosophie Médiévale 66. Paris: Vrin, 1991.

Quelquejeu, Bernard. "'Naturalia manent integra': Contribution à l'étude de la portée, méthodologique et doctrinale, de l'axiome théologique 'Gratia praesupponit naturam.'" *RSPT* 49 (1965): 640–55.

Rahner, Karl. "Remarks on the Dogmatic Treatise *De Trinitate*." In *Theological Investigations*. Vol. 4. Baltimore: Helicon, 1966.

Ramelow, Tilman Anselm. "Language without Reduction: Aquinas and the Linguistic Turn." *Angelicum* 85 (2008): 497–517.

Ramirez, Santiago M. *Los dones del Espíritu Santo*. Biblioteca de teólogos españoles. Vol. 30, part 7. Madrid: 1978.

Resnick, Irven M., ed. *A Companion to Albert the Great: Theology, Philosophy and the Sciences*. Brill's Companions to the Christian Tradition 38. Leiden: E. J. Brill, 2013.

Ribes Montané, Pedro. "Razón humana y conocimiento de Dios en San Alberto Magno." *Espíritu* 30 (1981): 121–44.

Riordan, William. *Divine Light: The Theology of Denys the Areopagite*. San Francisco: Ignatius Press, 2008.

Rist, John M. *Eros and Psyche: Studies in Plato, Plotinus and Origen*. Phoenix Supplementary 6. Toronto: University of Toronto Press, 1967.

———. "Pseudo-Dionysius, Neoplatonism and the Weakness of the Soul." In *From Athens to Chartres: Neoplatonism and Medieval Thought, Studies in Honour of Edouard Jeauneau*, edited by Haijo Jan Westra, 135–61. Leiden: E. J. Brill, 1992.

Ritacco-Gayoso, Graciela. "Intelligible Light and Love: A Note on Dionysius and Saint Thomas." *New Scholasticism* 63 (1989): 156–72.

Rocca, Gregory P. *Speaking the Incomprehensible God: Thomas Aquinas on the Interplay of Positive and Negative Theology*. Washington, D.C.: The Catholic University of America Press, 2004.

Roques, René. "Contemplation, extase et ténèbre chez le Pseudo-Denys." In *DS* 2.2 (1953): cols. 1885–1911.

———. *L'univers dionysien: Structure hiérarchique du monde selon le Pseudo-Denys*. Théologie 29. Paris: Aubier, 1954.

———. "Denys l'Aréopagite." In *DS* 3 (1957): cols. 244–86.

Rorem, Paul P. *Biblical and Liturgical Symbols within the Pseudo-Dionysian Synthesis*. Studies and Texts 71. Toronto: Pontifical Institute of Medieval Studies, 1984.

———. *Pseudo-Dionysius: A Commentary on the Texts and an Introduction to Their Influence*. Oxford: Oxford University Press, 1993.

———. *Eriugena's Commentary on the Dionysian "Celestial Hierarchy."* Studies and Texts 150. Toronto: Pontifical Institute of Medieval Studies, 2005.

———. "The Early Latin Dionysius: Eriugena and Hugh of St. Victor." In Coakley and Stang, *Re-Thinking Dionyius*, 71–84. 2009.

Rose, Miriam. *Fides caritate formata: Das Verhältnis von Glaube und Liebe in der Summa Theologiae des Thomas von Aquin*. Forschungen zur systematischen und ökumenischen Theologie 112. Göttingen: Vandenhoeck and Ruprecht, 2007.

Roy, Louis. "Wainwright, Maritain, and Aquinas on Transcendent Experiences." *Thomist* 54 (1990): 655–72.

Roy, Lucien. *Lumière et Sagesse: La grâce mystique dans la théologie de saint Thomas d'Aquin*. Studia Collegii Maximi Immaculatae Conceptionis 6. Montreal: L'Immaculée-Conception, 1948.

Ruello, Francis. *Les "Noms divins" et leurs "raisons" selon saint Albert le Grand commentateur du "De Divinis Nominibus."* Bibliothèque Thomiste 35. Paris: Vrin, 1963.

———. "Le commentaire du *De divinis nominibus* de Denys par Albert le Grand: Problèmes et méthode." *Archives de Philosophie* 43 (1980): 589–613.

Ruh, Kurt. "Die *Mystica Theologia* des Dionysius Pseudo-Areopagita im Lichte mittelalterlicher Kommentatoren." *Zeitschrift für deutsches Altertum und deutsche Literatur* 122 (1993): 127–45.

———. *Geschichte der abendländischen Mystik*. Vol. 3, *Die Mystik des deutschen Predigerordens und ihre Grundlegung durch die Hochscholastik*. Munich: C. H. Beck, 1996.

Runggaldier, Edmund. *Die menschliche Seele bei Albertus Magnus: Ein nicht-reduktionistischer Beitrag zum Leib-Seele-Problem*. Lectio Albertina 11. Münster: Aschendorff, 2010.

Russell, Norman. *The Doctrine of Deification in the Greek Patristic Tradition*. Oxford Early Christian Studies. Oxford: Oxford University Press, 2004.

Sabathé, Martin. *La Trinité rédemptrice dans le "Commentaire de l'évangile de saint Jean" par Thomas d'Aquin*. Bibliothèque Thomiste 62. Paris: Vrin, 2011.

Salas, Victor. "Albertus Magnus and Thomas Aquinas on the Analogy Between God and Creatures." *Medieval Studies* 72 (2010): 283–312.

Schenk, Richard. "From Providence to Grace: Thomas Aquinas and the Platonisms of the Mid-Thirteenth Century." *Nova et Vetera* (English ed.) 3 (2005): 307–20.

Schlosser, Marianne. *Cognitio et amor: Zum kognitiven und voluntativen Grund der Gotteserfahrung nach Bonaventura*. Veröffentlichungen des Grabmann-Institutes 35. Munich: Ferdinand Schöningh, 1990.

———. *Lucerna in caliginoso loco: Aspekte des Prophetie-Begriffes in der scholastischen Theologie*. Veröffentlichungen des Grabmann-Institutes 43. Munich: Ferdinand Schöningh, 2000.

———. "Sapientia per Spiritum sanctum revelata: Anmerkungen zur 'saptientia nulliformis.'" In *Gegenwart der Offenbarung: Zu den Bonaventura-Forschungen Joseph Ratzingers*, edited by Marianne Schlosser and Franz-Xaver Heibl, 283–306. Ratzinger Studien 2. Regensburg, Germany: Friedrich Pustet, 2011.

Schmaus, Michael. "Die trinitarische Gottebenbildlichkeit nach dem *Sentenzenkommentar* Alberts des Großen." In *Virtus Politica: Festgabe zum 75. Geburtstag von Alfons Hufnagel*, edited by Joseph Möller and Helmut K. Kohlenberger, 277–306. Stuttgart: Frommann, 1974.

Schneider, Johannes. *Das Gute und die Liebe nach der Lehre von Albert des Grossen*. Veröffentlichungen des Grabmann-Institutes 3. Munich: Ferdinand Schöningh, 1967.

Schillebeeckx, Edward. "L'instinct de la foi selon s. Thomas d'Aquin." *RSPT* 48 (1964): 377–408.

Senner, Walter. "Albertus Magnus als Gründungsregens des Kölner *Studium generale* der Dominikaner." In *Geistesleben im 13. Jahrhundert,* edited by Jan A. Aertsen and Andreas Speer, 149–69. Miscellanea Mediaevalia 27. Berlin: Walter de Gruyter, 2000.

———. "Thomas von Aquin und die Kirchenväter: Eine quantitative Übersicht." In Prügl and Schlosser, *Kirchenbild und Spiritualität,* 25–42. 2007.

———. *Alberts des Großen Verständnis von Theologie und Philosophie.* Lectio Albertina 9. Münster: Aschendorff, 2009.

———, ed. *Albertus Magnus, Zum Gedenken nach 800 Jahren: Neue Zugänge, Aspekte und Perspektiven.* Quellen und Forschungen zur Geschichte des Dominikanerordens 10. Berlin: Akademie Verlag, 2001.

Sherwin, Michael S. *By Knowledge and By Love: Charity and Knowledge in the Moral Theology of St. Thomas Aquinas.* Washington, D.C.: The Catholic University of America Press, 2005.

———. "Aquinas, Augustine and the Medieval Scholastic Crisis concerning Charity." In Dauphinais and Levering, *Aquinas the Augustinian,* 181–204. 2007.

Siassos, Lambross. "Des théophanies créées? Anciennes interprétations de la 1e Lettre de Denys l'Aréopagite." In de Andia, *Denys l'Aréopagite et sa postérité,* 227–35. 1997.

Sicouly, Pablo C. "Gebet als *instrumentum theologiae:* Zu einer Aussage Alberts des Großen in seinem Kommentar zu Ps.-Dionysius' *De divinis nominibus.*" In Senner, *Albertus Magnus, Zum Gedenken,* 619–31. 2001.

Simonin, H.-D. "Autour de la solution thomiste du problème de l'amour." *Archives d'histoire doctrinale et littéraire du moyen âge* 6 (1931): 174–275.

———. "Quelques aspects de la doctrine spirituelle d'Albert le Grand." *La Vie Spirituelle* 34 (1933): 141–55.

Siorvanes, Lucas. *Proclus: Neo-Platonic Philosophy and Science.* Edinburgh: Edinburgh University Press, 1996.

Söder, Joachim R. "Die Erprobung der Vernunft: Vom Umgang mit Traditionen in *De homine.*" In Senner, *Albertus Magnus, Zum Gedenken,* 1–13. 2001.

Somme, Luc-Thomas. *Fils adoptifs de Dieu par Jésus Christ: La filiation divine par adoption dans la théologie de saint Thomas d'Aquin.* Bibliothèque Thomiste 49. Paris: Vrin, 1997.

Spezzano, Daria E. "The Grace of the Holy Spirit, the Virtue of Charity and the Gift of Wisdom: Deification in Thomas Aquinas' *Summa Theologiae.*" Ph.D. diss., University of Notre Dame, 2011.

Stein, Edith. "Ways to Know God: The *Symbolic Theology* of Dionysius the Areopagite and Its Factual Presuppositions." *Thomist* 9 (1946): 379–420.

Still, Carl N. "'Gifted Knowledge': An Exception to Thomistic Epistemology?" *Thomist* 63 (1999): 173–90.

Stock, Wiebke-Marie. *Theurgisches Denken: Zur "Kirchlichen Hierarchie" des Dionysius Areopagita.* Transformation der Antike 4. Berlin: Walter de Gruyter, 2008.

Stoeckle, Bernhard. *"Gratia supponit naturam":* Geschichte und Analyse eines theologischen Axioms. Studia Anselmiana 49. Rome: Herder, 1962.

Stohr, Albert. *Die Trinitätslehre Ulrichs von Strassburg, mit besonderer Berücksichtigung ihres Verhältnisses zu Albert dem Grossen und Thomas von Aquin.* Münsterische Beiträge zur Theologie 13. Münster: Aschendorff, 1928.

Stroud, James W. "Thomas Aquinas' Exposition of the Gifts of the Holy Spirit: Development in his Thought and Rival Interpretations." Ph. D. diss., The Catholic University of America, 2012.

Studer, Basil. *Schola Christiana: Die Theologie zwischen Nizäa und Chalcedon.* Munich: Ferdinand Schöningh, 1998.

———. *Augustinus "De Trinitate": Eine Einführung.* Munich: Ferdinand Schöningh, 2005.

Sturlese, Loris. "Albert der Große und die deutsche philosophische Kultur des Mittelalters." *Freiburger Zeitschrift für Philosophie und Theologie* 28 (1981): 133–47.

———. *Die Deutsche Philosophie im Mittelalter: Von Bonifatius bis zu Albert dem Großen (748–1280).* Munich: C. H. Beck, 1993.

———. *Vernunft und Glück: Die Lehre vom "intelletus adeptus" und die mentale Glückseligkeit bei Albert dem Großen.* Lectio Albertina 7. Münster: Aschendorff, 2005.

Suchla, Beate Regina. *Die sogenannten Maximus-Scholien des Corpus Dionysiacum Areopagiticum.* Göttingen: Vandenhoeck and Ruprecht, 1980.

———. Notes to *Die Namen Gottes,* by Dionysius Areopagita. Translated by Beate Regina Suchla, 104–23. Bibliothek der Griechischen Literatur 26. Stuttgart: Anton Hiersemann, 1988.

———. *Dionysius Areopagita: Leben, Werk, Wirkung.* Freiburg im Breisgau: Herder, 2008.

Synave, Paul, and Pierre Benoit. Notes to *Somme Théologique, la prophétie: 2a–2ae, Questions 171–78,* by Thomas Aquinas. Edited by Jean-Pierre Torrell, 225–378. Paris: Cerf, 2005.

Teske, Roland. "William of Auvergne's Spiritualist Concept of the Human Being." In *Autour de Guillaume d'Auvergne (mort en 1249),* edited by Franco Morenzoni and Jean-Yves Tilliette, 35–53. Bibliothèque d'Histoire Culturelle du Moyen Âge 2. Turnhout: Brepols, 2005.

Te Velde, Rudi. *Aquinas on God: The "Divine Science" of the "Summa Theologiae."* Aldershot: Ashgate, 2005.

Théry, Gabriel. "L'autographe de S. Thomas conservé à la Biblioteca Nazionale de Naples." *Archivum Fratrum Praedicatorum* 1 (1931): 15–86.

———. "Le manuscrit Vat. grec 370 et saint Thomas d'Aquin." *Archives d'histoire doctrinale et littéraire du moyen âge* 6 (1931): 5–23.

———. "Documents concernant Jean Sarrazin, reviseur de la traduction érigénienne du *Corpus Dionysiacum.*" *Archives d'histoire doctrinale et littéraire du moyen âge* 18 (1950–51): 45–87.

Torrell, Jean-Pierre. "La pratique pastorale d'un théologien du XIIIe siècle: Thomas d'Aquin prédicateur." *RT* 82 (1982): 213–45.

———. *Recherches sur la théorie de la prophétie au Moyen Âge, XIIe–XIVe siècles: Études et textes*. Dokimion 13. Fribourg, Switzerland: Éditions universitaires, 1992.

———. "Lire saint Thomas autrement." In Boyle, *Facing History*, ix–xxxiv. 2000.

———. "La vision de Dieu 'per essentiam' selon saint Thomas d'Aquin." In *Recherches thomasiennes*, 177–97. Bibliothèque Thomiste 52. Paris: Vrin, 2000.

———. "Nature et grâce chez Thomas d'Aquin." *RT* 101 (2001): 167–202.

———. *Saint Thomas Aquinas*. Vol. 2, *Spiritual Master*. Translated by Robert Royal. Washington, D.C.: The Catholic University of America Press, 2003.

———. Introduction to *Somme Théologique, la prophétie: 2a-2ae, Questions 171–178*, by Thomas Aquinas, 11*–133*. Paris: Cerf, 2005.

———. *Saint Thomas Aquinas*. Vol. 1, *The Person and his Work*. Translated by Robert Royal. 2nd ed. Washington, D.C.: The Catholic University of America Press, 2005.

———. Notes to *Questions disputées sur la vérité, Question XII: La prophétie (De prophetia)*, by Thomas Aquinas, 191–240. Paris: Vrin, 2006.

———. Notes to *Encyclopédie Jésus le Christ chez saint Thomas d'Aquin*, by Thomas Aquinas. Paris: Cerf, 2008.

———. *Christ and Spirituality in St. Thomas Aquinas*. Translated by Bernhard Blankenhorn. Washington, D.C.: The Catholic University of America Press, 2011.

Trottmann, Christian. *La vision béatifique: Des disputes scolastiques à sa définition par Benoît XII*. Bibliothèque des Écoles françaises d'Athènes et de Rome 248. Rome: École Française de Rome, 1995.

———. "'Facies' et 'essentia' dans les conceptions médiévales de la vision de Dieu." *Micrologus* 5 (1997): 3–18.

———. *Théologie et noétique au XIIIe siècle: À la recherche d'un statut*. Études de Philosophie Médiévale 78. Paris: Vrin, 1999.

Tschipke, Theophil. *Die Menschheit Christi als Heilsorgan der Gottheit: Unter besonderer Berücksichtigung der Lehre des heiligen Thomas von Aquin*. Freiburger theologische Studien 55. Freiburg im Breisgau: Herder, 1940.

Tugwell, Simon. "Albert the Great: Introduction." In *Albert and Thomas: Selected Writings*, by Albertus Magnus and Thomas Aquinas, 3–129. 1988.

Turbessi, Joseph. "Denys l'Aréopagite: En Occident, Saint Albert le Grand et saint Thomas d'Aquin." In *DS* 3 (1957): cols. 343–56.

Turner, Denys. "Apophatism, Idolatry and the Claims of Reason." In *Silence and the Word: Negative Theology and Incarnation*, edited by Oliver Davies and Denys Turner, 11–34. Cambridge: Cambridge University Press, 2002.

Twohill, M. Dominic. "The Background and St. Thomas Aquinas' Reading of the de Divinis Nominibus of the Pseudo-Dionysius." Ph.D. diss. Fordham University, 1960.

Van den Berg, R. M. *Proclus' Hymns: Essays, Translations, Commentary*. Philosophia Antiqua 90. Leiden: E. J. Brill, 2001.
Van Fleteren, Frederick. "Mysticism in the *Confessiones*: A Controversy Revisited." In *Augustine: Mystic and Mystagogue*, edited by Frederick Van Fleteren, Joseph C. Schnaubelt, and Joseph Reino, 309–36. Collectanea Augustiniana 3. New York: Peter Lang, 1994.
———. "Nature." In Fitzgerald and Cavadini, *Augustine Through the Ages*, 585–87. 1999.
Venard, Olivier-Thomas. *Thomas d'Aquin, poète théologien*. Vol. 2, *La langue de l'ineffable: Essai sur le fondement théologique de la métaphysique*. Geneva: Ad Solem, 2004.
Von Balthasar, Hans Urs. "Das Scholienwerk des Johannes von Scythopolis." *Scholastik* 15 (1940): 16–38.
———. "Zur Ortsbestimmung christlicher Mystik." In von Balthasar, Beierwaltes, and Haas, *Grundfragen der Mystik*, 37–71. 1974.
———. *The Glory of the Lord: A Theological Aesthetics*. Vol. 2, *Studies in Theological Style: Clerical Style*. San Francisco: Ignatius Press, 1984.
Von Balthasar, Hans Urs, Werner Beierwaltes, and Alois M. Haas, eds. *Grundfragen der Mystik*. Einsiedeln: Johannes Verlag, 1974.
Waldmann, Michael. "Thomas von Aquin und die *Mystische Theologie* des Pseudo-Dionysius." *Geist und Leben* 22 (1949): 121–45.
Wawrykow, Joseph. "Christ and the Gifts of the Holy Spirit According to Thomas Aquinas." In Prügl and Schlosser, *Kirchenbild und Spiritualität*, 43–62.
Wéber, Édouard. *Dialogue et dissensions entre saint Bonaventure et saint Thomas d'Aquin à Paris (1252–1273)*. Bibliothèque Thomiste 41. Paris: Vrin, 1974.
———. "L'interprétation par Albert le Grand de la *Théologie Mystique* de Denys le ps-Aréopagite." In *Albertus Magnus: Doctor universalis, 1280/1980*, edited by Gerbert Meyer and Albert Zimmermann, 409–39. Mainz: Matthias-Grünewald, 1980.
———. "La relation de la philosophie et de la théologie selon Albert le Grand." *Archives de Philosophie* 43 (1980): 559–88.
———. "Langage et méthode négatifs chez Albert le Grand." *RSPT* 65 (1981): 75–99.
———. *La personne humaine au XIIIe siècle*. Bibliothèque Thomiste 46. Paris: Vrin, 1991.
———. Introduction to *Commentaire de la "Théologie mystique" de Denys le pseudo-aréopagite suivi de celui des épîtres I–V*, by Albertus Magnus. Edited and translated by Édouard Wéber, 7–58. Sagesses Chrétiennes. Paris: Cerf, 1993.
———. "Les emprunts majeurs à Averroès chez Albert le Grand et dans son école." In *Averroismus im Mittelalter und in der Renaissance*, edited by Friedrich Niewöhner and Loris Sturlese, 149–79. Zürich: Spur, 1994.
———. "Négativité et causalité: leur articulation dans l'apophatisme de l'école d'Albert le Grand." In *Albertus Magnus und der Albertismus: Deutsche philoso-

phische Kultur des Mittelalters, edited by Maarten J. F. M. Hoenen and Alain de Libera, 51–90. Leiden: E. J. Brill, 1995.

———. "L'apophatisme dionysien chez Albert le Grand et dans son école." In de Andia, *Denys l'Aréopagite et sa postérité*, 379–403. 1997.

Weertz, Heinrich. *Die Gotteslehre des Pseudo-Dionysius Areopagita und ihre Einwirkung auf Thomas von Aquin*. Cologne: Theissing, 1908.

Weisheipl, James A. "Albertus Magnus and Universal Hylomorphism: Avicebron, a Note on Thirteenth-Century Augustinianism." In Kovach and Shahan, *Albert the Great*, 239–60. 1980.

———. *Thomas d'Aquino and Albert His Teacher*. The Étienne Gilson Series 2. Toronto: Pontifical Institute of Medieval Studies, 1980.

———. "Albert der Große: Leben und Werke." In *Albertus Magnus: Sein Leben und seine Bedeutung*, edited by Manfred Entrich, 9–60. Cologne: Styria, 1982.

Weismantel, Tobias. *Ars nominandi Deum: Die Ontosemantik der Gottesprädikate in den Dionysiuskommentaren des Albertus Magnus*. Regensburger Studien zur Theologie 69. Frankfurt am Main: Peter Lang, 2010.

Westra, Laura. "The Soul's Noetic Ascent to the One in Plotinus and to God in Aquinas." *New Scholasticism* 58 (1984): 99–126.

Wicki, Nikolaus. *Die Lehre von der himmlischen Seligkeit in der mittelalterlichen Scholastik von Petrus Lombardus bis Thomas von Aquin*. Studia Friburgensia, Neue Folge 9. Fribourg, Switzerland: Universitätsverlag, 1954.

Wieland, Georg. *Zwischen Natur und Vernunft: Alberts des Großen Begriff vom Menschen*. Lectio Albertina 2. Münster: Aschendorff, 1999.

Wielockx, Robert. "Zur *Summa Theologiae* des Albertus Magnus." *Ephemerides Theologicae Lovanienses* 66 (1990): 78–110.

Williams, A. N. *The Ground of Union: Deification in Aquinas and Palamas*. Oxford: Oxford University Press, 1999.

Wippel, John F. *The Metaphysical Thought of Thomas Aquinas: From Finite Being to Uncreated Being*. Monographs of the Society for Medieval and Renaissance Philosophy 1. Washington, D.C.: The Catholic University of America Press, 2000.

Index of Names

Agaësse, P., 128n18
Alexander of Hales, 52n6, 75, 91, 93n139, 94n141, 96, 101, 103, 106, 120, 221
Al-Ghazali, 77
Allegro, Giuseppe, xvii, 191n195, 202n219
Anastasius the Librarian, 31–32, 105
Andrew of Crete, 31
Anzulewicz, vii, xvn8, 50n2, 51n4, 59n34, 106n170, 125n10, 130n27, 148n68, 190n192, 467n1
Aristotle, 51, 56, 58, 61, 63, 67, 75, 77–78, 86–87, 107–108, 121–22, 124–30, 133, 135–36, 163–64, 177, 190, 206, 215–17, 220–23, 225–32, 234–35, 237, 240–42, 247, 261–62, 268, 271, 273, 285–86, 293, 295, 300, 302, 304–305, 310–12, 316–17, 326, 353–55, 378, 381–82, 402, 404, 412, 418, 422–23, 431, 441, 444–45, 447, 452–56, 460, 462
Augustine, St. xxii, xxx, 43, 51, 53, 56–65, 67–70, 74, 81, 86, 88, 90, 93–94, 98–99, 104, 108, 120–21, 127–29, 131–33, 135, 141–42, 170, 190, 199n213, 206, 209, 215–17, 221, 225, 232–37, 239–44, 248, 257, 282, 285, 300, 317, 393, 396, 398–99, 430–31, 451–53, 460, 466
Averroes (Ibn-Rushd), 50–51, 60–61, 67, 102, 107–10, 130, 136, 159, 162–64, 225, 292–93
Avicenna (Ibn-Sina), 52n6, 53, 60n36, 67, 77, 86
Ayres, Lewis, 11n30, 128n18, 236n64, 240n79, 242n86, 243n91, 244n93, 300n10

Bacon, Roger, 52n6
Balaam, 337
Bartholomew, St., 19, 21, 24, 181–83, 204–5
Basil of Caesarea, St., 11n30, 199n213
Bataillon, Louis, 362n98
Bazán, B. Carlos, 52n6, 222n20, 224n27
Beierwaltes, Werner, 7n11, 9n23, 10n26, 17n58, 402n202
Benoit, Pierre, 376n133
Bernard of Clairvaux, xxiii, 45, 53n8, 72, 79, 108
Blankenhorn, Bernhard, 57n26, 125n7, 129n22, 234n61, 268n73
Bobik, Joseph, 286n136, 289n150
Bonaventure, St., xviin1, xxiii, 44, 205, 216–21, 225, 240, 247, 267, 383–84, 386–87, 413, 436–37, 440–41, 454, 463–65
Bonino, Serge-Thomas, 229n42, 229n44, 297n2, 301n13, 304n25
Bonnewijn, Olivier, 277n101
Booth, Edward, 242n86
Bougerol, Jacques Guy, xviin1, 387n160
Boyle, Leonard E., 319n2
Brachtendorf, Johannes, 56n22, 69n64, 225n31, 236n64, 241n82, 242n86, 244n93
Burger, Maria, vii, 33n8, 50n1, 51, 123n3
Busa, Roberto, xxxiii

497

Index of Names

Charles the Bald, 32
Chenu, Marie-Dominique, xi, xiin1, xviii, 37n20, 82n102, 282n119, 425n259, 445
Clement of Alexandria, St. 4
Congar, Yves, 76n87, 87n118, 157n90
Conticello, Carmelo Giuseppe, 425n259
Coolman, Boyd Taylor, vii, 44n42, 45nn46–47, 96n144, 96n147, 437n288
Cottier, Georges, 219n12, 384n149
Courth, Franz, 74n82
Crouse, Robert, 58n30, 232n54

Dauphinais, Michael, 245n95, 247n101
de Andia, Ysabel, vii, xv, xviiin18, 5n6, 8n14, 9nn19–20, 9nn22–23, 10n25, 10n29, 11, 12n34, 12n37, 13nn39–41, 14nn42–43, 14nn45–46, 15nn47–50, 16n51, 16nn53–55, 18n66, 19nn67–68, 20nn70–71, 21nn75–76, 22n79, 23n84, 24n87, 25nn90–91, 25n93, 25n95, 26n97, 26nn100–103, 27n105, 28, 29nn112–13, 38nn22–23, 42n36, 140n50, 147n67, 167n124, 169n131, 172n138, 186n180, 190, 191n194, 290n152, 321n8, 328n27, 332n35, 334n42, 336n46, 341nn56–57, 347n68, 348n74, 373n125, 376n131, 380n142, 425n256, 425n258, 429n268
de Belloy, Camille, 250n1, 252n9, 254n18
de Blic, Jacques, 91n128
de Contenson, Pierre-Marie, 292n160
de Halleux, André, 27n104
Delfino, Robert A., 259n37
de Libera, Alain, xvii, 60n36, 77n91, 159, 162nn110–11, 163n112, 164, 174n144, 181n163, 191n195, 200n214, 202n216, 212n231, 466
Delp, Mark, vii
Dohmen, Christoph, 374n127
Doms, Herbert, 63n43, 67n54, 78n94, 86n117, 110n183
Dondaine, Hyacinthe F., 31n2, 32n5, 32n7, 33n9, 102n158, 103n162, 123n2, 301n111, 319n3
Ducharme, Léonard, 53n11, 54n13, 55n16
Durand, Emmanuel, 369n115
Durantel, J., xviiin15
Du Roy, Olivier, 69n64, 128n18, 232n54

Eckhart, Meister, xvi, 212, 458, 467
Emery, Gilles, vii, 50n1, 68n59, 70nn65–66, 123n4, 221n18, 222n20, 224n27, 241n81, 241n84, 244n92, 246n98, 250nn1–2, 251n5, 252nn8–9, 253n15, 254n18, 255n20, 255nn23–24, 256n25, 256n28, 257nn29–30, 258n33, 258n35, 269n74, 284n133, 322n12, 363n101, 371n119, 424n252
Erasmus, xiv
Erb, Heather McAdam, 430n272
Eriugena, John Scotus, 31–32, 33n8, 37, 39–42, 95n142, 106n172, 110, 123, 142–43, 149, 155, 168, 169n132, 170, 176, 379–80, 387n158, 400n195, 400n197, 412

Festugière, A. J., 402n202
Flasch, Kurt, 106n172, 207nn227–28, 446
Floucat, Yves, 241n81
Führer, Markus, 57n27

Gallus, Thomas, xxiii, xxxiii, 32, 34, 42, 44–45, 95n142, 146, 204n222, 205, 211, 387n160, 413, 437nn287–88, 443, 465, 467–68
Gardeil, Ambroise, xviii, 259n36, 275n96, 394n181, 408n213, 425n258, 428n266
Garrigou-Lagrange, Réginald, xviii, 257n30, 272n87, 275n95, 276n100, 280n115, 425n257, 428n266, 430n272, 433n282
Gauthier, René, 230n48, 318n1
Germanus I, 31
Gersh, Stephen, xv
Gils, Pierre-Marie, xvin9
Gilson, Étienne, 357n88, 359
Girón-Negrón, Luis M., 44n41
Golitzin, Alexander, xvn6, 13n41, 14n43, 17n62, 23n83, 28, 29n111
González Ayesta, Cruz, 270n77, 272n87, 273n90, 276n98, 280n114, 394n180, 394n182, 423n249, 424n253, 425n256, 426n261, 428n265, 431n275, 432n278, 433n282, 455
Goodman, L. E., 60n36
Goris, Harm, 241n81
Gregory the Great, St., 43, 91, 94, 203n220, 271, 365, 413

Index of Names

Gregory Nazianzen, St., 37
Gregory of Nyssa, St., 8, 11n30, 14, 20, 22, 26, 101–2, 322n12, 376n131
Gregory of Palamas, 11, 338n52
Grosseteste, Robert, 44–45, 123n2, 467–68
Guagliardo, Vincent A., 378n137
Guéric of Saint-Quentin, 50

Hamman, A.-G., 216n4, 246n100
Harrington, L. Michael, 31n2, 32n6, 34n11, 35n12, 36n15,
Hellmeier, Paul Dominikus, 53n7
Hergan, Jeffrey P., 102n159
Hiedl, Augustin, 50n1
Hierotheus, xvi, xviii, xxiii, xxv, xxix, 13–17, 42, 94–97, 100, 117, 120, 139, 142–44, 200–202, 216, 248, 270, 296, 317, 320, 328, 387, 400n199, 411–22, 424n250, 429, 434–35, 437–39, 446, 460, 463–65
Hilduin, Abbot, 123n2,
Horst, Ulrich, 97, 270n77, 271n83, 272n87, 392n176, 424n254, 426n261, 427n262, 433n281
Hoye, William J., xvii, 159, 162n109, 191n195, 202n216, 404n207
Hugh of St. Victor, xxiii, 32, 34, 42–44, 52n6, 81, 82n102
Humbrecht, Thierry-Dominique, xviin14, xviiin16, xviiin18, 118n196, 150n73, 157n88, 189n188, 191n195, 194n200, 196n207, 297n1, 300nn6–7, 300n9, 301n13, 302n17, 304n23, 305n28, 306n32, 308n37, 311n45, 323n16, 339n53, 343n62, 357n88, 360nn93–94, 370nn117–18, 382n146, 383n147, 404n207
Hugh of Balma, 44
Hyman, Arthur, 60n36

Imbach, Ruedi, 215n1, 319n2
Irenaeus of Lyon, 216

Jeauneau, Edouard, 39n25, 41n33
Jeßberger, Ludwig, 383n148
John Damascene, St., 157, 234, 246, 300, 322n12
John of the Cross, 44

John of La Rochelle, 94–95n141
John of Saint Thomas, xviii, 276n98, 277n101, 280n114, 394–96, 425n257
Jones, John D., xxxii, 338n52
Journet, Charles, 371n120, 408n213
Juárez, Guillermo A., 68n58, 69n61, 69n63, 70n69, 71n73, 75n84, 250n3, 251n4, 252n7, 252nn10–11, 253n14, 255nn20–21, 258n32, 294n166

Keaty, Anthony W., 285n134, 286n137
Koch, Hugo, xiv
Krämer, Klaus, 63n44, 240n80, 243n89
Kromholtz, Bryan, 224n27
Kwasniewski, Peter A., 289n151

Labourdette, Marie-Michel, 256n27, 275n96, 278–80, 290n156, 425–26
Larchet, Jean-Claude, xvn6, 11n32, 24n87, 38n23
Lavaud, M.-H., 91n128
Leinsle, Ulrich G., xiiin1, 319n4
Lévy, Antoine, 37, 39nn24–25, 41n34, 102n158, 109n181, 206n226, 266n62, 446–47
Lluch-Baixauli, Miguel, 196n207
Lombard, Peter, 51, 52n6, 54, 56, 62, 76, 81, 86, 218–19, 233, 239
Lonergan, Bernard, 260n38, 261n41, 262n46, 264n55
Lossky, Vladmir, xiin2, xvn6
Lottin, Odon, 91n129, 92n131, 94n141
Louth, Andrew, 6n10, 7n12, 20n71

Maillard, Pierre-Yves, 376–77n133
Maimonides, 114, 300, 311
Mali, Franz, vii
Maritain, Jacques, xviii, 259n37, 357n88, 360n94, 394n181, 408n213, 428n266, 430n271, 433n282
Maximos the Confessor, St., 31–32, 37–42, 101–2, 104, 110, 117, 329
Mayer, Rupert J., 219n12
McEvoy, James, 44n42, 45n45, 45n48
McGinn, Bernard, xiin2, xvii, xxiiin21, 43n37, 44n40, 165n119, 191n195, 200–202, 205, 387n160, 413n225, 429n268

McGuiness, Joseph Ignatius, 395n184
McKay, Angela M., 275n96
Meersseman, Gilles M., 184n171
Meis, Anneliese, xvii, 162n109, 191n195, 202n216, 203n220
Merriell, D. Juvenal, 66n53, 232n55, 233n57, 240nn78–80, 242n87, 243n90, 244nn92–93
Mongillo, Dalmazio, 277n102, 397n188
Montagnes, Bernard, 412n222, 431n275
Moonan, Lawrence, 149n70
Moraga Esquivel, José M., 143n58
Moreno, Antonio, 419n239, 423n249
Morerod, Charles, 408n213, 430n271
Mulchahey, M. Michèle, 122n1, 319n2

Narváez, Mauricio, xiin1, 313n49
Nash, Roland H., 232n54, 431n274
Nemesius, 54
Nicolas, Jean-Hervé, 428n266
Noble, H.-D., 286n136

O'Callaghan, John P., 231n50, 231n53
Odo Rigaldus, 94n141
Oliva, Adriano, 51, 215n1, 318n1, 319n2, 357n89
O'Meara, Dominic, 7n11, 10n26
Origen, 4, 20
O'Rourke, Fran, xviiin16, 305n27, 312n46, 312n48, 322n13, 382n146

Pachas, José Antonio, 159, 176n151
Parker, John D., xxxii
Patfoort, Albert, 258n32, 258n35, 299n3, 364n102
Paul, St., xiv, 3, 14–16, 18, 25, 43, 86, 88–89, 128, 139–40, 147, 176–77, 249–50, 373, 376–77, 414, 421
Perczel, István, 3n1
Philip the Chancellor, 91, 93n139, 94–95n141, 413
Philips, Gérard, 86n117
Philo, 4, 20, 22, 376n131
Pieper, Josef, 231n50
Pinckaers, Servais, 272n87, 277n102, 278n104, 278n107, 398n190, 455
Plato, xiv, xxi, 6–7, 10, 77, 223,

Plotinus, 4, 6–7, 10, 15, 28, 34–36, 130, 186, 195, 198, 221, 232, 235, 339, 443
Poirel, Dominique, 43n39
Prades, Javier, 254n19
Pritzl, Kurt, 231n50, 231n53
Proclus, xiv, 4, 6–8, 10, 13, 18, 54, 57, 89, 222, 228, 234, 262, 332, 336, 378–79, 381, 404, 441, 443, 454
Puech, Henri-Charles, xiin3, 13n38, 17n57, 20n72, 23n86, 25n90, 26n97, 26n99, 376n131
Putallaz, François-Xavier, 226n36, 232n56, 236nn64–65

Quelquejeu, Bernard, 216n3, 217n5, 220n16

Rahner, Karl, 245n97
Ramelow, Tilman Anselm, 241n82, 302n18
Reid, Fr., 371n122
Riordan, William, xiv, 4n3, 5n8, 7nn12–13, 8n16, 9n21, 10n28, 18n65, 25nn90–91, 28n109, 129n23
Rist, John M., xvn7, 18n66
Rocca, Gregory P., 297n1, 300n10, 302n17, 303n19, 303n21, 304n23, 305n27, 306n32, 308n37, 310n44, 315nn54–55
Roques, René, xiv–xv, 4n1, 5nn6–7, 6n9, 8nn17–18, 12n34, 13nn38–39, 14n44, 18n63, 18n66, 23n83, 24n87, 25n94, 27n105, 28, 231n51, 400n196
Rorem, Paul P., 5n4, 5n6, 5n8, 8n16, 10n24, 10nn27–28, 14n43, 16n52, 16n56, 17nn59–62, 18n66, 20n70, 21n73, 21n75, 22n79–80, 23n83, 26n98, 31n3, 43nn37–38, 44nn40–42, 45n47, 104n167, 124n6, 169n131, 176n150, 321n8, 334n40, 334n42
Roy, Louis, 428n266
Roy, Lucien, 272n89, 276n100
Ruello, Francis, xviiin14, 135n41, 149n70, 150n73
Ruh, Kurt, xvii, 191n195, 212n231
Russino, Guglielmo, xvii, 191n195, 202n219

Sabathé, Martin, 256n25,
Salas, Victor, 157n88, 305n28
Sarracenus, John, 32–33, 95, 123, 143n57,

Index of Names

144n59, 166–68, 169n132, 313n50, 319, 338n52, 379–80, 387n158, 400, 411–12
Schenk, Richard, vii, 126n11, 217n6
Schlosser, Marianne, 177n152, 216n2, 220n16, 225n30, 376n133, 384n150, 387n159, 436n286, 437nn288–89
Schmaus, Michael, 64n45
Schneider, Johannes, 86n114
Senner, Walter, vii, xvin10, 50n1, 82n102
Severus of Antioch, 4
Sherwin, Michael S., 238nn69–71, 239n76, 281n116, 282n119, 283nn123–25, 283n127, 288nn141–42, 288n145, 289n149, 412n219
Sicouly, Pablo C., 141n53, 165n119, 182n167
Simonin, H.-D., 238n72
Siorvanes, Lucas, 234n61
Söder, Joachim R., 51n4
Somme, Luc-Thomas, 266n64
Spezzano, Daria E., 271n82, 278n104
Stein, Edith, St., 8n16
Stiglmayr, Josef, xiv
Still, Carl N., 402n200
Stock, Wiebke-Marie, 7n15
Stoeckle, Bernhard, 216n4, 217n6, 218n10
Stohr, Albert, 71n71
Stroud, James W., 270n77
Studer, Basil, 199n213, 431n274
Sturlese, Loris, 51n4, 129n22, 207n227
Suchla, Beate Regina, 4nn1–2, 5n5, 17n59, 31nn1–3, 328n26
Synave, Paul, 376n133

Teresa of Avila, St., 44
Teske, Roland, 222n19
Te Velde, Rudi, 301n14
Théry, Gabriel, 33n10, 319n3
Torrell, Jean-Pierre, xiiin1, xviii, 76n88, 106n170, 122n1, 216n3, 219n12, 223n22, 253n13, 257n30, 258n35, 268n71, 268n73, 269n76, 287n140, 291n157, 299n5, 318n1, 319n2, 360n95, 361nn97–98, 371n121, 372n123, 376n133, 433n279

Trottmann, Christian, 29n113, 102n158, 103nn161–62, 106n172, 165n119, 166n121, 204n223, 219n14, 230n48
Tschipke, Theophil, 79n96
Tugwell, Simon, xvii, xxxiin25, 50n1, 51n3, 85n111, 127n16, 128n21, 138n47, 149n70, 159, 163n14, 183n170, 191n195, 445

Valla, Lorenzo, xiv
van den Berg, R. M., 7n12
Van Fleteren, Frederick, 128n18, 216n4
Venard, Olivier-Thomas, 368n113
von Balthasar, Hans Urs, xiv–xv, 6n9, 7n11, 8nn15–16, 13n41, 29n114, 280n115

Wéber, Édouard, vii, xvii, 52n6, 55n18, 57n25, 63n43, 75n84, 85n111, 102n159, 103n164, 107nn173–74, 113n189, 117n195, 118n197, 133n33, 138n47, 141n52, 143n58, 147, 148n69, 152n76, 153n79, 158, 159n94, 159n97, 162nn108–9, 163n113, 175n147, 181n163, 191n195, 192n197, 197n209, 197n211, 200–201, 202n216, 203n220, 204n222, 221n18, 222n20, 223n22, 225n30, 225n33, 226nn34–35, 230n48, 245n197, 292nn159–60, 445
Weisheipl, James A., 50n1, 53n10, 53n11, 101n156
Weismantel, Tobias, xviin14, 149n70, 162n108
Westra, Laura, 360n93
Wicki, Nikolaus, 110n183
Wieland, Georg, 51n4
Wielockx, Robert, 149n71
William of Auvergne, 52n6, 101–103, 221–22
William of Auxerre, 93n137, 94n141, 95–96, 98, 386, 413
William of Saint-Thierry, xxiii, 53n8, 67n55
Williams, A. N., 247n101, 266n64
Wippel, John F., 261n42

Subject Index

action. *See* causality; cooperation; divine action; divine light; processions
Acts, Book of, 3
active life, 246–47, 289, 454
Affective Dionysianism, 32, 34, 42–45, 74, 110–11, 149–56, 165, 203–4, 211, 288, 387, 436–37, 444, 454, 461, 464–68
affirmative names, 5, 8–13, 19–21, 24–25, 29, 36–40, 111–19, 123–24, 148–56, 187–89, 193–99, 208–10, 300–303, 305–16, 320, 323–26, 332–33, 336, 342–50, 352, 367–68, 377–80, 392, 401, 405–9, 435, 439, 444–48, 450, 456, 458–61. *See also* analogy; *triplex via*
agent intellect, 55–62, 64–67, 77, 102, 107–9, 159, 162–64, 173–74, 206–7, 224–25, 229–31, 233, 235–37, 248, 292–94, 456
analogy. *See* affirmative names; negative names; *triplex via*
angels, 3, 29, 40, 43, 76, 89, 105–106, 126–27n15, 129–30, 162n108, 163, 172–75, 181, 217, 222, 229–30, 347, 349–51, 367, 373, 386, 406, 440, 446
anthropology, xiii, xxi, xxix–xxx, 6, 8, 21, 27, 41–42, 49–68, 99, 124–30, 162, 196, 206–207, 216–26, 386, 389, 402, 443–45, 447, 451–53, 462. *See also* body; intellect; knowledge; love; soul; will
aphairesis, 11–12, 25, 38, 186, 199, 308, 313, 336–37, 340, 342, 345, 349. *See also* negations.
Apocalypse, Book of, 258

apophasis, 11–12, 25, 38, 310, 313, 340–42, 345, 348–49. *See also* negations
apostles, 286–87, 328–29, 338
articles of faith, 112; as object of faith, 81, 95, 390, 415; and unitive knowledge, 84–85, 391–92, 407, 415, 427–28, 430, 439–40, 455, 460–65
asceticism. *See* purification
assimiliation to God. *See* conformity to the divine persons
Assumption of Mary. *See* Dormition
Augustinianism, xxi, 41, 44–45, 51–54, 57–58, 60–62, 64, 67–68, 102–3, 109–10, 119–21, 124–31, 206–7, 215–16, 218, 221, 230, 444–47, 453

beatific vision, 29, 38, 79–80, 89–90, 101–10, 130n25, 135–36, 181–82, 291–94
beatitudes, 91–92, 396–99, 402–3, 433–34, 460, 466
Bible. *See* Scripture
bishop: as mystic, 17, 22–23, 27, 199, 405, 439, 444
body: as means to union, 125–26, 200; as obstacle to union, 6, 61–62, 373; relation to the immaterial soul, 8, 53–54, 124–26, 221–24, 227

Canticle of Canticles. *See* Song of Songs
Causality, xiii, xxiii–xxiv, xxxi, 112–13, 150–56, 221–54, 303–5, 313–14, 343–44, 351; efficient, xxiv, 54, 69, 72, 76–79,

Subject Index

87–89, 106, 109, 134, 238, 287–88, 251–53, 263–64, 266, 269, 271–76, 294, 304, 440, 445–47, 454, 463; exemplary, 69–73, 79, 156–57, 251–53, 255, 268–69, 271–72, 294, 305, 433–34, 454; formal, xxiv, 71, 76, 87–89, 100, 106, 109, 134, 238, 264, 266, 276–78, 287–88, 294, 298, 440, 446, 463; primary and secondary, 57, 134, 260–62, 264, 266, 274; principal and instrumental, 260–61, 268–69, 274–76; *See also* divine action; divine light

charisms, 76, 431–33, 440. *See also* prophecy; wisdom

charity, xxii, xxiv, xxxi, 18, 25, 69–75, 83, 86–91, 93, 141–48, 211, 253–58, 271, 279–80, 285–91, 295, 410–11, 416, 418, 424–29, 446, 449, 455, 461–64; as created, 86–87; as measure of union, 290, 434, 440, 455. *See also* love; mission

Christology, xiii, xxiv, 3, 9, 16, 28, 38–39, 41–42, 79–80, 131–36, 207, 267–69, 286–87, 294–95, 454–55. *See also* mysteries of Christ

Colossians, Letter to the, 88–89

conformity: to Christ, xxiv, 79; to the divine persons, 5, 9, 240, 243–44, 252, 254–55, 266, 291–92

connaturality, xxv, 126–27, 235, 238, 279–80, 287, 304, 348–49, 360, 394, 416, 419, 423–29, 436, 464

consciousness: of God, 20; of union, xii, 72–73, 258, 454

contemplation: philosophical, 6–9, 148–49, 159, 163–65, 171, 174n144, 175–77, 180–81, 184, 192, 196n207, 207–8, 357–60, 363–65, 368–71, 382–83, 438, 451, 459

cooperation: in grace, xxiv, 77–78, 111, 264; in union, xi, xiii, xxii, xxiv–xxv, 14, 34–39, 41, 87–88, 100, 108, 120–21, 134–36, 139, 156, 168–71, 175–80, 185, 205–6, 208–10, 241–42, 256, 262, 266, 273–79, 287, 292–95, 333–34, 338–39, 345–46, 360, 366, 379–82, 401–2, 406–10, 424–25, 430, 435, 437, 444–45, 447–49, 452–59, 462–64

creation: of Adam and Eve, 76, 135, 218–20; *ex nihilo*, 7; as a means to contemplate God, 9, 24, 29, 113, 115–16, 125, 130, 151–52, 171–75, 178–84, 188–89, 194, 198, 208–9, 299–305, 311–12, 349, 354–55, 359, 363–64, 368, 382, 401, 435, 437–38, 448–49, 453–54, 461; as an obstacle to union, 12, 14, 61–62, 67, 126, 129, 136, 186–89, 195–96, 312, 326

Creed. *See* articles of faith

darkness, as light, 21, 23–25, 372–73, 375. *See also* Moses; silence

dialectic of naming, 12–13, 29, 36, 38, 116–18, 341–43, 346, 447

divine action: immediate, xi, xiii, xxiii–xxiv, 70, 105–7, 132, 138, 206, 208, 210–11, 250–51, 253–54, 260–65, 271–80, 295, 387, 404, 410, 412–13, 416, 420, 425–28, 432–33, 435–36, 439–41, 445–47, 449, 454–56, 459–60, 463–65. *See also* causality; divine light; missions

divine energies, 10–11, 24n87, 29n113, 38, 41

divine light, 3–5, 9, 14–15, 21, 23, 25–27, 29, 34–35, 37, 80–85, 94–95, 99, 123, 129–42, 147, 158–64, 167–68, 171–75, 178–79, 182–84, 191, 198–201, 205–6, 339. *See also* darkness

divine powers. *See* divine light; processions

divinization, 5, 9, 15, 17, 27, 29, 38, 41, 133–34, 137, 164, 200, 216–17, 248, 265–67, 294n167, 355–56, 370, 377, 411, 444, 449

Dormition, 17, 29, 420

Ecclesiastes, 123

ecstasy: of love, 18–19, 25, 90, 139–40, 144–47, 320, 434, 436; of the mind, 9, 15–17, 34–36, 41, 45, 138–40, 146–47, 156, 171, 176, 185, 289–90, 334–35, 345–46, 355, 380

eminence, 36–37, 41, 111n184, 118, 152–56, 186–89, 208, 301–303, 306, 308–10, 312–16, 324–27, 336–53, 361–68, 378–80, 404–9, 438, 456, 458. *See also* analogy; *triplex via*

Subject Index

Enjoyment, 88, 255, 285
eros, 7, 18, 290, 334–35
eschatology, xxvi, 28–29, 53–54, 89–90, 101–10, 135–36, 183n170, 223–24, 291–94, 446–47, 456. *See also* light of glory; vision of God
esse/essentia distinction, 224–26, 248, 304n23, 305
essence of God, 10–12, 14, 23, 29, 36–41, 102–108, 112–14, 118, 135, 149, 151, 154–55, 177, 292–93, 300, 347. *See also* incomprehensibility of God; quiddity; substantial divine naming
essence-power-operation triad, 75–76, 113, 133, 225–26
Eucharist, xiii, 5, 16–17, 22
exemplarity of Christ (moral and ontological), 269. *See also* causality
Exodus, Book of, xii, 17, 22, 112, 114, 179, 367, 372–77, 385, 459
experience of God, xii, 16–18, 20, 38, 42, 72–74, 93–97, 101, 142–43, 295, 357, 360, 368n113, 413, 421, 428–29, 436–37, 439–40, 451, 454, 464

faith, xii, xxxi, 72, 80–85, 91, 93, 111–12, 136–41, 158–64, 171, 193, 211, 253–58, 281–85, 322–23, 364, 392, 405, 420, 422–23, 425, 430; and intellect, xxiv, 81–82, 137–38, 158, 281–85, 445–46; limits of, xxxi, 95, 99, 146–47, 193, 271, 282, 284, 288, 385, 389–91, 415, 455; and the will, 81–82, 138, 282–84, 445; and union above mind, 138–39, 143, 159–61, 176–78, 183, 191, 198, 200–201, 208–10, 284–85, 323, 326–35, 339, 352, 355–56, 370–71, 406–8, 410–11, 447–49, 457–58, 461
Father, God the, xxii, 70–71, 83–84, 87, 95, 109, 131–34, 159, 200, 244–45, 250–52, 254–55, 294–95, 362–63
Filioque, 71, 244–45, 255–56, 259
First Letter to the Corinthians, 91, 103, 144, 177, 181, 327, 330, 399, 412, 414–15, 416n230, 421–22, 432
finality of the human being, 218–19, 247, 452

First Letter to Timothy, 88, 372–73, 375
five ways to demonstrate God's existence, 297, 299–300
flux, 55–56, 77–79, 88–90, 100, 119, 140, 156, 161, 208, 268, 291, 305, 445–46. *See also* grace
form, intelligible, 58, 128, 229–31, 292–93, 353–55, 360–61, 408, 459
friendship: and charity, 285–91. *See also* charity; love

Galatians, Letter to, 18, 143
Genesis, Book of, 219–20, 365, 371
gifts of the Holy Spirit (in general), xvi, xxiv–xxv, xxxi, 72, 85, 91–101, 131, 143–44, 147, 161–62, 171, 173, 175–77, 201, 203–4, 208–11, 257n30, 263–64, 270–80, 296, 449–50, 455
grace, xxxi, 132, 168–72, 176–80, 262–69, 283–84, 337–40, 352, 367; actual, xxiv; 119, 208–209, 211, 262–64, 283, 287–88, 295, 440–41, 449, 454; cooperating, 77–78, 176, 209–11, 262–64, 272, 295, 445, 454–56; as created, xxiv, xxxi, 9, 69–79, 84, 86n117, 97, 105–107, 132–34, 136, 174–75, 179, 204–206, 209–10, 252–56, 265–66, 445; as efficient cause, 77–78, 109, 134, 253, 265–66, 447; as flux, 76–79; as formal cause, 71, 76, 106, 109, 134, 253, 265–66; as motion to God, xxxi, 78, 133; operating, 263, 425–26, 463–64. *See also* divine light; divinization; gifts of the Holy Spirit; instrumental causality; missions; nature

habitus, 62–63, 71–74, 76, 78, 80, 83–84, 91–93, 97, 100, 119, 133, 136, 160, 168–70, 179, 193, 198, 201, 205, 208–209, 211, 233, 242–45, 252–54, 256–58, 263–67, 270–72, 276–81, 283–84, 287–89, 322, 377, 388, 393–94, 407, 410, 412–13, 419–20, 423–24, 426–28, 435–36
heaven. *See* vision of God
Hebrews, Letter to, 16
hierarchy, 5–7, 14–16. *See also* angels; bishop; liturgy

Subject Index

history, place of, 28, 67, 71, 74, 78, 230, 440–41
Holy Spirit. *See* missions; Trinity

illumination and Augustine's epistemology, 57–64, 67, 99, 128, 233–36, 452. *See also* knowledge
imagination. *See* phantasms
image of God, xxii–xxiii, xxvii, xxx, 9, 56, 62–68, 130, 134, 168–71, 176, 190, 205–10, 233–35, 239–47, 248, 254–56, 290–93, 317, 338, 409–10, 434–35, 438, 445, 448, 453, 462. *See also* memory
imitation: of Christ, 79
inclination, 238, 246, 289. *See also* connaturality
incomprehensibility of God, 26, 34–37, 40, 45, 104–106, 112–16, 149–50, 155–56, 167–69, 185, 197–98, 211, 292, 300, 307–308, 313–14, 324–26, 331, 337–38, 343–47, 351–53, 366, 368, 373, 405, 407–408, 456
indwelling of the Trinity. *See* mission
instrumental causality. *See* causality
intellect, as faculty, 55–56, 62; as site of union, xi, xiii, xvi, 34–35, 38, 46, 71–74, 81–82, 110, 119, 168–71, 189–91, 197–99, 203–204, 211, 254–58, 327–31, 333–56, 358–60, 367–70, 378–81, 410, 413, 415, 423–25, 434–37, 449, 455, 458, 461–62
Isaiah, Book of, 273, 371, 376

James, Letter of, 131, 422
John, First Letter of, 290, 414
John, Gospel of, 133, 257, 286, 317, 371, 415
John, Saint, 434, 464
judgment, 168, 198, 236, 240, 242, 298, 302–304, 307, 309, 316, 338, 349, 366, 377, 388; and faith, 282–85, 335, 394–96, 408; and the gifts of the Holy Spirit, 394–96, 407–9

knowledge, xxi, xxvi, xxx, 62–74; as acquired, xxii, xxvi, 8, 13, 21, 25, 39, 58–62; conceptual, xxi–xxii, 7, 24–26, 128, 184n171, 208, 241–42, 258–59, 282, 285, 298, 303–304, 316, 328–34, 347, 354–55, 359, 360n93, 373, 375–77, 408–10, 428–31, 433, 435, 437, 439–40, 453–54, 457–62, 465; and faith, 81–83; habitual, 62–64, 72–74; as infused/gifted, xxvi, 6, 8–9, 14–16, 26–27, 38, 41, 45, 57, 82–85, 92–100, 113, 201–203, 391–92, 397–98, 404–9, 412–17, 419–23, 427–28, 435, 440–41, 460–61, 463–64; mediated, xi, xxi–xxiii, xxx, 8, 14–15, 95–101, 113, 125–29, 139, 168–69, 178–84, 188–91, 194, 199, 204–206, 208–9, 219–20, 222–23, 228–35, 248, 258, 281–84, 300–302, 323–24, 329–31, 337–38, 343, 345–48, 354–55, 368–72, 377–78, 382, 401–402, 406–407, 448, 451–62; by presence, 62–67, 127–29, 232; of self, xxi, 55–57, 63–64, 232, 235–37, 248, 453; and union, xxi, 7, 14, 16, 26–27, 34, 37–38, 72–73, 80, 189–91, 199, 203–204, 210, 231–32, 241, 254–55, 282, 292–93, 337–60, 363–64, 366–71, 434

laity: and union, 22, 27–28, 139–41, 204–5, 248, 334, 356, 380–81, 401, 404–5, 439, 449–50, 460, 465. *See also* active life
light of glory, xxvi, 105–7, 109, 135, 183n170, 293–95, 446
liturgy, xiii, 3, 5–8, 13–17, 20–23, 27–28, 125, 137, 181–83, 321, 334
logoi, 38, 171–74, 179–80, 181n163, 348–49
love, xiii, xvi: of benevolence, 46–48; and knowledge, 43–45, 71, 74–75, 84–85, 90, 110, 141–44, 201–203, 211, 238, 245, 255–56, 286–89, 291, 293–95, 387, 412–21, 424–29, 434, 436–37, 455, 464; of neighbor, 246–47, 454; psychology of, xxv, xxx, 238–39, 246, 248, 411–12, 425; unites, xxiii, 18, 142, 203–4, 211, 238–39, 245, 254–55, 287–91, 419–20. *See also* charity
Luke, Gospel of, 391

Mass. *See* Eucharist; liturgy
memory, xxii–xxiii, 6–8, 58–59, 62–67, 128, 169, 206–7, 209, 232–34, 244–45, 248, 291, 445, 447, 451, 453, 462. *See also* image of God

merit, 79, 89, 256, 277, 290, 396–98, 402–3
metaphor, 150, 228. *See also* symbols
mind. *See* intellect; *noûs*
mirror of eternity, 163, 173
missions of the Son and the Spirit, xxiii–xxiv, xxx–xxxi, 68–75, 83–84, 93, 96–97, 100, 109, 131–34, 141–42, 159, 164, 169, 172, 200–201, 205–06, 210, 240, 243, 249–59, 266, 287, 294–95, 317, 331, 333, 369–71, 424, 428–29, 433–34, 445, 449, 464
mode of signifying, 117–18, 150–53, 193–97, 302–304, 306–10, 312, 315–16, 347–48, 351, 356, 406, 450
monastic life, 27, 334, 404–405, 439, 465
Moses, xii, xvi, xxviii–xxix, 3, 13–17, 19–27, 34–35, 44, 72, 78, 97, 99–100, 111n184, 128, 131, 139–40, 154, 165–67, 171–89, 199, 201, 203–206, 208, 210, 215–16, 259, 296, 298, 312, 317, 332, 341, 343, 348–49, 354, 357–63, 366–83, 385–89, 396, 403–6, 410, 434–38, 444, 448–49, 459–61, 464–65
motions of the soul (straight, oblique, circular), 129–30
mysteries of Christ, 268–69, 454–55
mysticism, definition of, xii

naming and union, xxvi–xxvii, xxviii, 5, 13, 24, 117, 165, 185–99, 204, 208–10, 323, 326, 336–52, 355–56, 361–63, 438, 447–50, 459, 462
nature and grace, xxii, xxx, 57–60, 64, 79, 103, 106n172, 108, 123, 135–62, 207, 216–21, 227–29, 247–48, 264, 282, 285, 402, 446, 448, 452–53, 462
negations, 5, 8–14, 19–21, 24–26, 29, 115–18, 149–56, 158, 163, 165–68, 170, 185–99, 201, 203, 208–10, 300–303, 307–16, 320–21, 323–26, 335–53, 358–63, 367–68, 377–80, 385–87, 392, 401, 405–9, 435, 438–39, 444, 448–50, 456–61; transcending negations, 11–13, 154–55, 197, 199, 306, 308, 313, 336–42, 345, 347, 382, 444, 458. *See also* aphairesis; apophasis; triplex via
Neo-Platonism. *See* Platonism

noûs, 6–7, 18, 312, 400, 402
Numbers, Book of, 337, 376

oracles, 20–21, 166–67, 321, 328, 332–33, 458
one and being as names of God, 381–82
original sin, 125, 218–20

participation, 5, 29
Paschal Mystery. *See* mysteries of Christ
Passivity in union, xiii, xxiv–xxv, 13, 15–16, 21, 25–27, 39, 41, 74, 116–19, 121, 139, 169, 174–78, 180, 210, 242, 248, 276, 291, 335–36, 350, 360n94, 407, 437, 455, 464. *See also* silence
phantasms, 61, 64, 111–12, 126, 136, 139, 220, 227–30, 247, 298, 369, 388, 401–2, 408, 430–31, 433, 439, 453, 456–57, 460–63
Platonism, xiv–xv, 6–8, 10, 17–18, 20, 28, 77–79, 221–23, 232, 234, 248
prayer, xiii, 141–42
preaching, 334, 376–77
priest as mystic, 22
processions, as divine activity in Dionysius, 11–13, 105; and divine naming, 9–13, 24, 38, 174, 187–88, 310–11; in the Trinity, 68–70, 74, 200, 244, 250–51, 255. *See also* missions
prophecy, 173–74, 177, 179, 228–29, 234, 237, 369–72, 376–78, 432–33. *See also* charisms; visions
proportion: lacking between God and creatures, 7–9, 102–5, 125–27, 136–37, 225
purification, 6, 13–14, 22, 99, 111, 141; of the appetites, 397–404; of the intellect, 111–12, 139–41, 157, 392, 397–405

quiddity of God, 105, 135, 149, 155, 194n200, 300–301, 324–26, 341, 352, 358–59, 365–71

rapture, 128, 376–78
rationes. *See* logoi
reasoning, act of, 14–15, 34–35, 231, 389–90, 413, 424–25. *See also* knowledge
remotions. *See* negations

Subject Index

res significata, 113, 116–18, 150–54, 195–97, 208, 304–10, 315–16, 351, 382, 391, 405–6, 450, 458–59

revelation, xxii, xxviii, 14, 20, 28, 43, 81–82, 99, 198, 230, 281–83, 285–87, 320–24, 328–29, 354–56, 369–71, 373–78, 383, 405–8, 435–41, 450–51, 455, 457–63

Rhineland Mysticism, xi, xiv, 212, 467

Romans, Letter to, 9, 217, 253, 274

sacra doctrina, 299, 321–24, 355, 437–38, 456–57

sacraments, xiii, 207–208. *See also* Eucharist; liturgy

scholia, 31–42, 46, 104, 110, 117–18, 123, 130, 149, 156, 162n108, 166–67, 170, 175, 182, 184, 444, 447.

Scripture as path to union, xxvi, 5, 15, 20–21, 28–29, 44, 67, 99, 137–39, 142–45, 151, 166–67, 198–99, 207, 209, 285, 327–31, 354–55, 369–71, 377–78, 391, 401, 405–9, 417, 420–21, 435, 437–41, 447–48, 450–51, 457–63, 465

Second Book of Kings, 369

Second Letter to the Corinthians, 43

silence and union, 13–15, 21, 24–27, 34–36, 38–41, 114, 118, 175–78, 195, 209, 298, 314–15, 331–38, 347–50, 353, 383, 438, 461. *See also* darkness; passivity

similitude: creatures as similitudes of God, 6–9, 14, 304–5

Song of Songs, 18, 45, 290n152

soul: ontology of the faculties, 55–56, 66, 225–26, 232–33, 235, 239, 265; as substance, 53–54, 56, 62, 221–24; impassioned and passionless parts of, 8, 12, 112, 227, 400, 402; *quo/quod* structure, 55–56

spark of the soul, xiii, xxii, 19, 45

stages of ascent to union, 5, 7–8, 14, 16, 20–26, 137, 140, 198, 276n98, 280–81, 341–46, 348–49, 398–99, 443, 465–66

substantial divine naming, 10–13, 24–25, 37–40, 112–16, 149–51, 154–56, 193, 197, 208, 299, 305–6, 308, 311–14, 327, 366, 380, 447

substantial form: unicity of, 54–56, 62, 221–25, 230, 247, 260, 293, 304, 430, 444, 462

suffering divine things, xvi, xxiii, xxv, 16–17, 42, 94–97, 142–44, 202, 320, 411–14, 417, 422–25, 428–30, 434, 463, 465

Summa Theologiae, structure of, 297, 299–301, 321–22

symbols, and contemplation, 7–8, 22, 61, 116, 137. *See also* veils

theologian: as mystic, 199, 203–204, 356, 449–50, 465

theological virtues, xxiv, xxvi, xxxi, 65–66, 76, 317. *See also* charity; faith; love

theophanies, xxvi, 29, 105–7, 109, 179, 293, 299, 446–47

tradition, 5, 14–17, 440. *See also* hierarchy

transcendence of God, 12–13, 15–16, 23–25, 38–39, 117–18, 193–95, 197–99, 313, 342–43, 456. *See also* incomprehensibility of God

transcendentals, 311–12, 316, 381–82, 453, 456

Trinity and the spiritual life, xi, xiii, xxiii, 9, 16, 28, 66, 68–75, 210, 240–47, 250–59, 294–95, 361–63, 448, 453–54. *See also* image of God; missions

triplex via, 111n184, 117–18, 150–55, 192, 196n207, 197n209, 199, 248, 299–303, 308–10, 312–16, 336–52, 361–64, 367–72, 375, 377–80, 405–9, 436, 438, 447–48, 451, 456, 458–62

understanding, gift of, xxiv–xxv, xxviii–xxix, 91–94, 97–101, 364–65, 383–411, 446, 459–66

union beyond mind, xxi, xxiii, 7, 13–14, 18, 26, 29, 42, 45, 90, 114, 119, 156, 174–77, 184–85, 327–34, 355–56, 379–80, 410, 420, 448, 454, 457–58. *See also* faith; understanding

unknowing, xviii, 9, 14, 23–26, 34–35, 127, 156, 175, 178–80, 184–85, 190, 199–200, 327, 330–31, 340–46, 354–55, 360–61, 363–64, 366–68, 374–75, 377–78, 382–83, 449, 458–60 veils, 5, 23, 29, 99, 181–83, 228, 321, 385, 452, 463. *See also* symbols.

virtue. *See* active life; charity; faith; gifts of the Holy Spirit; understanding; wisdom

visions, mystical, xii, 74, 98, 126–27n15, 163–64, 365, 371, 376–78, 433. *See also* prophecy

will, 260–61, 263–64; and intellect, 18, 43–45, 141–42, 220, 237–38, 248, 264; as site of union, 18, 45–46, 71–72, 74, 110, 147–48, 203n220, 287, 289–90, 294, 411–12, 417–18, 462; and the gift of wisdom, 412–29, 436–37, 439, 463

wisdom: and the mission of the Son, xxiii, 69–75, 200, 251–53; as a gift of the Spirit, xviii, xxiv–xxv, 91–97, 101, 200–203, 364–65, 411–37, 446, 463–66. *See also* missions

Wisdom, Book of, 9

word of the heart, 240–42, 244–45, 409–10, 434–35, 453

THOMISTIC RESSOURCEMENT SERIES

Series Editors: Matthew Levering
Thomas Joseph White, OP

The Trinity
An Introduction to Catholic Doctrine on the Triune God (2011)
Gilles Emery, OP
Translated by Matthew Levering

Christ and Spirituality in St. Thomas Aquinas (2011)
Jean-Pierre Torrell, OP

Introduction to the Mystery of the Church (2014)
Benoît-Dominique de La Soujeole, OP
Translated by Michael J. Miller

www.ingramcontent.com/pod-product-compliance
Lightning Source LLC
Chambersburg PA
CBHW051932290426
44110CB00015B/1947